CORRECTIVE READING TECHNIQUES

FOR CLASSROOM TEACHERS

—— I ——

THIRD EDITION

Joan P. Gipe
University of New Orleans

Gorsuch Scarisbrick, Publishers
Scottsdale, Arizona

To my students throughout the years,
Charlie too, and
in spite of Tillie

Pages 135–136 reprinted by permission of Lynn K. Rhodes and Curt Dudley-Marling, *Readers and Writers with a Difference: A Holistic Approach to Teaching Disabled and Remedial Students.* (Heinemann, A Division of Reed Elsevier, Inc., Portsmouth, NH, 1988).

Publisher:	John W. Gorsuch
Editor:	Nils Anderson
Developmental Editor:	Gay L. Pauley
Production Manager:	A. Colette Kelly
Sales & Marketing:	Don DeLong
Cover Design:	Jill Wood, Woodshed Productions
Typesetting:	ProType Graphics

Gorsuch Scarisbrick, Publishers
8233 Via Paseo del Norte, Suite F-400
Scottsdale, Arizona 85258

10 9 8 7 6 5 4 3

ISBN 0-89787-537-0

Copyright © 1987, 1991, 1995 by Gorsuch Scarisbrick, Publishers

Printed in the United States of America.

Library of Congress Cataloging-in-Publication Data

Gipe, Joan P.
   Corrective reading techniques for classroom teachers / Joan P.
Gipe.—3rd ed.
     p. cm.
   Rev. ed. of: Corrective reading techniques. © 1991.
   Includes bibliographical references (p.) and index.
   ISBN 0-89787-537-0
   1. Reading—Remedial teaching.   I. Gipe, Joan P.   Corrective
reading techniques.   II. Title.
LB1050.5.G545   1995
372.4'3—dc20   94-31403
                                                        CIP

ABBREVIATED CONTENTS

For a complete Table of Contents, see page v.

CONTENTS

9   READING COMPREHENSION: FOUNDATIONS   212

10   READING COMPREHENSION AND STRATEGIC READING FOR NARRATIVE TEXT   250

11   STUDY SKILLS   284

12   STRATEGIC READING FOR EXPOSITORY TEXT   322

13   DEVELOPING READING OF LINGUISTICALLY DIVERSE STUDENTS   348

ILLUSTRATIONS

PREFACE

This text, now in its third edition, has always been intended for two groups of people: (1) undergraduate students enrolled in teacher education programs that include a practicum or field experience allowing each student to work with readers experiencing difficulty and (2) classroom teachers at all levels who wish to expand their repertoire of techniques for working with readers experiencing difficulty. My continuing goal is to provide preservice and classroom teachers with both a guide and a resource for meeting the needs of readers experiencing difficulty who can be found in every classroom.

A conscious effort has been made to present techniques appropriate to, or easily modified for, any grade level from primary through secondary school. Students can experience difficulty or learning gaps at any point in their literacy development, perhaps most often when asked to read material such as expository text that requires strategic reading behaviors.

This edition continues to provide teachers with techniques for (1) recognizing readers with difficulties, (2) identifying readers' specific strengths and needs, and (3) planning instruction that takes into account the processes needed to perform a certain reading task. The philosophy underlying this analytic approach and its implications for reading instruction are presented in some detail.

Preparing this third edition presented me with an opportunity to reexamine my own beliefs about and philosophy for supporting developing readers. In recent years my work with undergraduate teacher preparation has served to accent several aspects of professional development. I have begun to view *myself* as a "teacher in progress" along with my undergraduate students; we are simply at different points on a continuum of professional development. I continue to learn much from working with these university students as well as from the young students and classroom teachers we encounter. As a result of my growing recognition that I am a member of a community of learners, I have become more aware of the negative language used to describe those learners who traditionally have been referred to as "disabled readers." My response throughout this edition has been to rework my use of language to better communicate a positive view of students' efforts to achieve literacy.

Another change in this edition is the inclusion of writing as a means of supporting reading development. The newest techniques all tend to integrate reading and writing; children's literature is also used in many cases. To explore these new techniques, a chapter focusing solely on the reading/writing connection has been added.

This new edition consists of two major sections: Part I, "Foundations," and Part II, "The Major Domains." Part I introduces the nature of corrective reading and analytic teaching, describes the analytic process, discusses reading-related factors such as physical, psychological, and environmental correlates, and discusses ways to assess and evaluate reading performance. Part II provides specific information on instructional techniques for the major literacy domains of oral and written language, word recognition, comprehension and strategic reading for narrative text, and study skills and strategic reading for expository text, as well as for the special topic of linguistically diverse students. Emphasis is given to comprehension-fostering and comprehension-monitoring instructions. The extensive coverage of instructional techniques for all the literacy domains and for all grade levels is a strength of this text.

The chapters in Part I are best studied in the order presented, while the chapters in Part II are independent of one another and can be studied in any order. This text organization corresponds especially well to a course organization that includes a practicum or clinic experience. While a theoretical basis is provided for the suggestions made throughout the text, with many research studies cited, the overall flavor of the text remains more applied than theoretical.

Certain format features aid learning from the text. Each chapter begins with a list of learning objectives, an extended study guide, and important vocabulary words. Each chapter also features an overview that can be read before the chapter and again afterward as a synthesis. An annotated list of suggested readings at the end of each chapter helps the reader gain further understanding of the concepts discussed. These features aid the reader in preparing to read each chapter and in studying the material and aid the instructor in anticipating topics that may need additional explanation or hands-on experience. (An instructor's manual is also available for support in these areas.) The appendices provide specific aids for determining readability of written material, assessing instructional environments, examining readers' attitudes toward reading and self-concept, determining spelling development, analyzing writing samples, and locating quality, culturally diverse literature.

Acknowledgments

Thanks to colleagues and students across the country, and to the staff at Gorsuch Scarisbrick, this text is now in its third edition. While its intended audience and primary focus on the analytic process have not changed, this edition contains a greater number of examples of instructional techniques appropriate for older students. Suggestions for instruction continue to focus on the use of whole text and include writing whenever possible. As mentioned earlier, the new Chapter 7, "The Reading/Writing Connection," emphasizes this new component.

The feedback from my own students and from other instructors and students who used the previous editions provided the impetus for the changes in this edition. I sincerely thank all who offered suggestions for this new edition, including Mary Jane Urbanowicz of Shippensburg University, Rhea Ashmore of The University of Montana, and Bette Heins of Stetson University. Special thanks to Dr. Peggy C. Price and her students at Stephen F. Austin State University and to Dr. Dick Watson of Emporia State University for their thorough and thoughtful readings and reviews of the revised manuscript. I hope all of you will find this third edition even more appealing and helpful than the previous ones.

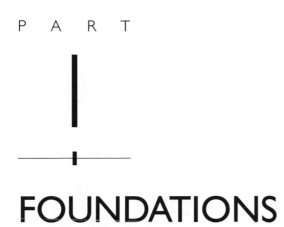

FOUNDATIONS

P A R T

FUNDAMENTAL ASPECTS OF CORRECTIVE READING

OBJECTIVES

After you have read this chapter, you should be able to

1. identify dimensions of the reading process;
2. explain the importance of teachers developing a set of beliefs about reading;
3. describe several characteristics of a whole-language philosophy and a skills-based philosophy of reading instruction;
4. explain the nature of a corrective reading program;
5. describe characteristics of corrective readers.

KEY CONCEPTS AND TERMS

academic reading
aliterates
cognition
corrective reading
emergent literacy
graphophonics
language
language comprehension

language production
morphology
phonology
pragmatic cue system
recreational reading
semantics
syntax

STUDY OUTLINE

1. Introduction
2. Dimensions of reading
   a. Reading as a language process
   b. Reading as a cognitive process
   c. Reading as a psychological or affective process
   d. Reading as a physiological process
3. Reading is an emerging process
4. Beliefs about reading
   a. Current views
   b. Personal beliefs
5. Two major goals of every reading program
   a. Academic reading
   b. Recreational reading
6. What is corrective reading?
   a. As used in this text
   b. The corrective reading program
7. Who is the corrective reader?
8. Summary
9. Suggested readings

OVERVIEW

This chapter reviews basic concepts about the reading process in general and explains the importance of developing a set of beliefs about reading in order to establish an effective reading program. The review of basic concepts of developmental reading is brief, but this does not mean that learnings from a first course in reading instruction are considered unimportant. They form the foundation for the content in this text and are essential to expanding your knowledge about teaching reading.

This chapter continues by exploring the nature of corrective reading and describing characteristics of readers who are considered "corrective." This chapter is only a beginning, however. The rest of the text, reading courses that you may take in the future, and the experiences you will have working with students will give you additional knowledge and insight regarding the reading process and ways of helping students who experience breakdowns in the reading process.

INTRODUCTION

Helping students learn to read and extend their literacy development is one of the most important tasks facing classroom teachers at all levels. Reading opens the door to learning almost anything. Reading provides a source of information and enjoyment, and children who were read to before entering school are already aware of its benefits. Upon entering school, most children look forward to learning how to read. Unfortunately, not all are successful.

The many methods and approaches used to teach reading work with most students. But what goes wrong for the others? What does or does not happen in the process of teaching reading that hinders a student in learning to read or further developing literacy abilities? To answer these questions, we need to understand the reading process.

DIMENSIONS OF READING

It is important to note at this time that while the term *reading* is being used, it has become more and more apparent that *literacy* learning involves writing, speaking, listening, and thinking as well as reading. Thus, the *process* of reading is complex. How it all actually works is not clear, but some aspects that usually interact during the process have been identified.

Reading as a Language Process

Language enables individuals to communicate, that is, give and receive information, thoughts, and ideas. As young children learn to read and write, they are already giving and receiving information by speaking and listening. We know that a strong oral language base facilitates reading and writing development.

Some components of language important to the reading process are phonology, syntax, morphology, and semantics. Briefly, **phonology** refers to the system of speech sounds, **syntax** to word order and the way words are combined into phrases and sentences, **morphology** to the internal structure of words and meaningful word parts (prefixes, suffixes, word endings and inflections, compound words), and **semantics** to word meanings or to understanding the concepts represented by the language.

While reading is basically an act of communication between an author and a reader, it is only one aspect of the communication process. Reading, writing, speaking, and listening are mutually supportive and must be seen as interrelated and developing concurrently.

Communication does not exist in a vacuum. Usually a message has both a sender and a receiver. The sender has specific intentions and produces a message that is reconstructed by the receiver. The sophisticated system through which meaning is expressed is **language.** The sender uses this system for particular functions, such as sharing a personal experience, asking a question, or complaining. The sender can also use language to persuade, inspire, comfort, or encourage others.

Sending a message is called **language production,** which can be either oral or written; receiving or decoding the message is **language comprehension.** Speaking, therefore, is the production of oral language, while listening is the comprehension of oral language. Similarly, writing and reading are the production and comprehension, respectively, of written language.

These four aspects of language can also be compared in other ways. Reading and listening share common receptive and constructive processes, while writing and speaking share common expressive processes. As Fox and Allen (1983) state:

> Writing suggests the reading of one's compositions by others and the input that reading experiences can give to written language. In addition, speaking will be drawn out with writing because it is the other expressive skill. Since oral language initially precedes written language, experiences in oral composition influence success in written composition. Listening, the remaining segment, is firmly attached to speaking and reading. . . . because the language that one hears, especially the "story language" one hears when books are read aloud or when stories are told, is another source of written expression. (p. 12)

Schallert, Kleiman, and Rubin (1977) summarize some of the differences between oral and written language. Oral and written language can differ in physical characteristics; speech transmits auditory information, while writing transmits visual information. Speech is usually temporary, while writing is more permanent. Speech has meaningful verbal clues, such as intonation, stress, and rhythm, and nonverbal clues, such as gestures or eye expressions. On the other hand, listeners do not have the luxury of previewing speech for organization of main points, while good readers usually sample a text and skim, scan, skip, and reread. Doake (1988, p. 30) cites as the most obvious distinction that oral language usually occurs in conversation, making it "situationally bound." As a result, oral language is accompanied by intonation, gestures, facial expressions, and other "body language," and can be incomplete, redundant, repetitious, and ambiguous. Written language is not "situationally bound." Readers are on their own in seeking the message of the author. The written language carries the total meaning because the author is not there to clarify the meaning. Therefore, written language is usually more complete, formal, complex, highly crafted, and without as many redundancies.

A firm language base, resulting from many hours spent experiencing written language through activities such as book sharings, is crucial to success in reading. Students generally bring to school a wealth of language and cultural experiences upon which teachers can build literacy. Goodman (1973) analyzes the oral reading behaviors of students and demonstrates that they use specific language cues to predict meaning in the reading comprehension process. These he terms the *graphophonic, syntactic,* and *semantic* cue systems. As users of language, students bring to the reading task expectations about language that are basic to their ability to make sense of printed text. For example, assume a student encounters the unknown word *sidewalk* in the sentence "The dog ran down the _____ ." The reader may rely on one or all of the following: (1) the syntactic cue system, which indicates the unknown word is a noun (2) the semantic cue system, which indicates the possible words that would make sense (e.g., street, alley, path, stairs, hill, sidewalk, and so on) in the context of the sentence (3) the **graphophonic** cue system, which provides sound and symbol clues, in this case, an initial sound of *s*, a final sound of *k*, and a possible long *i* because of the vowel-consonant-silent *e* pattern.

Additionally, language is only really meaningful "when functioning in some environment" (Halliday, 1978, p. 28). Therefore, language users also develop a **pragmatic cue system,** that is, rules related to the use of language in context. For example, the sentence "This is bad" can be interpreted several ways depending on the context of the situation. Consider the two different meanings of the sentence if it were spoken by a mother upon finding her small child pulling everything out of the kitchen cabinets or by two teenagers enjoying a rock concert. Similarly, one might say in an informal conversational setting, "The dog buried the bone"; but in a more formal context, such as writing, this statement might become "The bone was buried by the dog."

Engelmann (1969) describes another situation that reflects the importance of language to success in reading. If a student is able to read a sentence, for example, "The brown dog is not mine," but unable to understand it, this may indicate not a reading problem but the result of a language difference. For instance, for a student whose first language is Spanish, the order in which words occur in English sentences may not communicate meaning. Because language is so critical as an underlying process for success in reading, students who are linguistically diverse require special attention. This topic is discussed in more depth in Chapter 13, "Developing Reading of Linguistically Diverse Students."

Reading as a Cognitive Process

Cognition refers to the nature of knowing and to intellectual development. A child's ability to form concepts is basic to cognition. Early or prelanguage concepts are cognitive, that is, young children develop ways of organizing and understanding their experiences even before acquiring language (Bowerman, 1976). Forming concepts, then, is an attempt to classify one's experiences. When young children call all men "Daddy," they are demonstrating that they have formed a concept of "Daddy" as a man. However, they have not yet learned to distinguish that "Daddy" is a man who has the specific attribute of being *their* father.

The more experience learners have with their environment, and the richer that environment, the more concepts they develop. A limited conceptual development affects reading. Even if a reader correctly pronounces the words, understanding is hindered unless those words represent familiar concepts. Active involvement with their world provides students with the necessary background for concept development and, ultimately, for literacy development. Cognitive development is crucial to reading comprehension, and is discussed in more detail in Chapter 9, "Reading Comprehension: Foundations."

Reading comprehension also depends on the student's abilities to reason, perceive relationships among concepts, remember, and use information, that is, the student's intellectual ability. Intelligence as a reading-related factor is further discussed in Chapter 4, "Reading-Related Factors."

Reading as a Psychological or Affective Process

The student's self-concept, attitudes in general, attitudes toward reading, interests, and motivation for reading affect the reading process. Each of these factors is closely related to the student's experiential background in both home and community.

Psychological factors are crucial both in helping students learn to read and improve their reading. The desire to learn or improve reading must be present; unless success is experienced, the tendency is to avoid the reading situation. This is only human nature; all of us avoid the things we do poorly.

Developing positive self-concepts and attitudes is often the most important part of a student's reading program. This important dimension of the reading process is discussed in more detail in Chapter 2, "Analytic Teaching: Meeting All Students' Instructional Needs," in Chapter 4, "Reading-Related Factors," and in Chapter 6, "Assessing and Evaluating Reading Performance with Direct Measures."

Reading as a Physiological Process

Anticipating the reading act in turn activates the language and cognitive processes (i.e., nonvisual information). However, for reading to proceed, printed stimuli (i.e., visual information) must be received by the brain. These stimuli normally enter through a visual process. If a reader is blind, the stimuli may enter through a tactile process, as in using braille, or through auditory means, as in listening to a taped reading. Under normal circumstances the reader must be able to focus on the printed stimuli, move the eyes from left to right, make return sweeps, discriminate likenesses and differences, and discriminate figure-ground relationships. In addition to visual acuity, physiological factors include good health, auditory acuity, and neurological functioning. Physiological and other reading-related factors, such as intelligence and social-emotional and environmental factors, are discussed in Chapter 4, "Reading-Related Factors."

READING IS AN EMERGING PROCESS

Emergent literacy is a relatively new concept that provides fresh insights into young children's literacy learning (Teale & Sulzby, 1989). Viewed from the child's perspective, early literacy learning is as much a social activity as it is a cognitive one. Studies (Doake, 1988; Henderson & Beers, 1980; Kastler, Roser, & Hoffman, 1987; Taylor & Dorsey-Gaines, 1988; Teale & Sulzby, 1986) observing children in their homes and communities provide the basis for the following conclusions (modified from Teale & Sulzby, 1989, pp. 3–4):

1. Learning to read and write begins at birth as children are placed in contact with print in their environment (e.g., alphabet books, being read to, labels, signs, and logos). Experimentation with writing begins as scribbles.

2. Children view reading and writing as a functional activity. Their experiences show literacy events as ways to get things done (e.g., reading a recipe to bake cookies, writing checks to pay bills).

3. Reading and writing development occurs simultaneously in young children and in relationship to oral language development. As reading experiences influence oral language, writing experiences influence reading, and developing reading ability influences writing. Thus each of these areas provides support for the development of the others.

4. Children learn through active involvement, constructing for themselves an understanding of written language. Through a process of trial and error, of forming and testing hypotheses about the symbols used in written language and the sounds used in oral language, children learn how written language works. Their emerging knowledge is revealed by their attempts at spelling.

These insights strongly imply a need to connect reading and writing instruction more closely than has been done in the past. This important component of effective literacy instruction is discussed in Chapter 7, "The Reading/Writing Connection."

BELIEFS ABOUT READING

Reading is a complex human endeavor. Edmund Huey (1908) believed that developing a complete description of the reading process would be psychology's greatest achievement, equivalent to explaining the intricate workings of the human mind. Regardless of how complex reading is, teachers are expected to help students learn to read and, therefore, must have some insight into the reading process. To be effective facilitators of reading growth, teachers must develop their own personal philosophy about reading.

A teacher's beliefs or theoretical orientation about reading can make a significant difference in the approach (i.e., basal, intensive phonics, language experience, literature-based), materials (i.e., basal readers, skill sheets, workbooks, children's literature), and techniques or methods (i.e., directed reading-thinking activity, cloze procedure, book sharings, creative bookmaking, reading response logs) chosen to help students read (Richards, 1985). Teachers who believe that the reading process basically involves learning a sequential set of subskills will undoubtedly stress those in their instruction. Those who believe that reading is primarily the act of processing language in print will approach its teaching quite differently. Authors of reading materials reflect their own beliefs about reading, and perhaps those of the marketplace, in the materials they produce. Thus a teacher's beliefs, approach, and techniques may be in harmony with the materials available, but the opposite is also possible.

Current Views

In May of 1989, at the annual meeting of the International Reading Association, five well-respected literacy experts shared their views on "the past, present, and future of literacy education" (Aaron, Chall, Durkin, Goodman & Strickland, 1990a, 1990b). They discussed the two prevailing views of "whole language" instruction and "skills-based" instruction. Unfortunately many people, including teachers, often interpret these two stances as advocating use of children's literature versus use of the basal reader, or no direct instruction of phonics versus direct instruction of phonics. But there is certainly more to these two perspectives than the material used for instruction or whether phonics should be taught directly or not. In fact, at that same meeting Paul Crowley made this statement: "Materials in the hands of a teacher who holds a skills model are skills materials. Materials in the hands of a teacher who holds a whole language model are whole language materials."

Knowledge about the ways in which humans learn, along with increasing knowledge about the emergence and development of literacy, will influence one's beliefs about literacy instruction. For example, whole language proponents take a developmental view of literacy growth, claiming that students should be exposed to a form of reading and writing instruction more like the process of learning to talk, in which experimentation and approximation are accepted and encouraged. All learning activities are based on students' interests and needs and are placed in meaningful contexts. Students are encouraged to integrate new information with what they have already learned. Fragmenting and fractionalizing areas of literacy learning are avoided, so not only are reading, writing, listening, and speaking integrated within language arts, they are often integrated *across* the curriculum. In other words, learning is not subdivided into artificial subject area time periods. Whole language classrooms generally encourage students to take an active part in their own learning, with much cooperation and collaboration among students and teachers. Harste, Woodward, and Burke (1984, p. 43) describe these classroom environments as "littered with literacy," including professionally published as well as student-authored works. Evaluation in whole language classrooms focuses on learners' strengths, not their weaknesses. Each student's literacy behaviors become the indicators of "developing knowledge and underlying competence" (Goodman, Goodman & Hood, 1989, p. xiii).

Proponents of skills-based instruction take a more behaviorist view of literacy growth, focusing on the products of reading and writing. They believe there are important subskills related to reading and writing that students must learn before becoming adept in the area of literacy (e.g., recognizing long and short vowel sounds, stating main ideas, drawing conclusions, comparing and contrasting, identifying pronouns, writing adverbial clauses, using guide words). They emphasize that learning the code for written language is a key subskill in learning to read. Teaching subskills and then assessing student mastery of subskills are common activities found in such programs. Advocates of a skills-oriented reading program are particularly concerned with students who read poorly. They believe that a carefully controlled reading program, in which behaviors are examined one by one, will lead more students to maturity in reading, and that without specific subskills instruction, many students may not become proficient readers.

Many educators find something of value in both the whole language and skills-based approaches. Specifically they believe that "reading is a cognitive process, meaning results from the interaction between reader and text, [and] processing proceeds from whole to part and part to whole . . . [As a result] different emphases in instruction are appropriate at different times" (Lipson & Wixson, 1991, p. 12). These beliefs describe what is called the interactive model.

As we gain greater knowledge about the human learning process and the nature of the learning context, we will need to reexamine our beliefs about literacy instruction. It is through continued reading and teaching experience that belief systems about learning change; as belief systems change, instruction will change accordingly. These changes are never easy and they take time. Routman (1991, p. 27) shares the stages in her own movement toward whole language:

1. I can't do this. It's too hard, and I don't know enough.
2. Maybe if I find out about it, it's possible.
3. I'll do exactly what the experts say.
4. I'll adapt the experts' work to my own contexts.
5. I trust myself as an observer-teacher-learner-evaluator.

Personal Beliefs

The focus in this text is similar to the interactive model, falling somewhere between the whole language and skills-based perspectives. While I might personally espouse a holistic philosophy, I also recognize that many classrooms do *not*; thus there are few models for others to observe, basal readers are still widely used, and some classroom teachers discover a lack of institutional support for abandoning familiar ways. On the other hand, there has been so much positive publicity for the whole language movement that some administrators and school districts have *mandated* that their schools adopt whole language views (Weaver, 1991). Of course, one cannot mandate someone else's beliefs. Even if teachers aspire to a holistic philosophy, they may find themselves "between a rock and a hard place" as so aptly described by Mosenthal (1989, p. 628). Thus, the suggestions in this text are made in the hope that they may serve as aids in *transition* from a traditional subskills view of corrective reading to one that represents a more student-centered strategic view of reading (i.e., the majority of the instructional suggestions emphasize the development of strategies, or systematic plans, for constructing meaning using materials/topics of interest to the student), and that helps troubled readers "revalue" themselves as language learners (Goodman, 1986).

For me, reading is a transaction that takes place between a reader and a text in a particular situation. The reader constructs meaning by actively processing graphic, syntactic, and semantic cues representing language, and by actively using memories of past experiences to aid in building new thoughts and/or revising, reinforcing, or expanding current thoughts. Along with my personal definition of what reading is all about, my views about the assessment and evaluation of reading growth are changing, for I too am a "teacher in process." For example, at this point in my professional development, the lines between instruction, assessment, and evaluation are becoming blurred. It seems to me that good instruction and good assessment involve the same activities. It follows then that the key to helping readers grow is good instruction.

I encourage you to formulate your own beliefs about reading so that you can better evaluate what is suggested in this and other texts and in materials such as basal reader manuals. Your beliefs will help you make decisions about what to teach and how best to teach it. Don't be afraid to change your beliefs or your instructional practices as you read more and experience working with students.

TWO MAJOR GOALS OF EVERY READING PROGRAM

When planning a reading program, a teacher is responsible for addressing long-term goals for student literacy achievement. These goals generally fall into two categories:

1. Academic or instructional reading
2. Recreational or independent reading

Academic Reading

Good instructional programs usually have well-specified goals. Major objectives for **academic reading** include increasing proficiency in strategies for comprehending what one reads, expanding sight vocabulary, and improving ability to decode words, as well as learning to locate and organize information and understanding the special and technical vocabularies of the various content subjects. The means teachers choose to achieve these goals will reflect their individual philosophies about reading, and the way in which teachers combine theory and practice will determine the effectiveness of the reading program.

Recreational Reading

Recreational or independent reading deals primarily with fostering positive interests, attitudes, and habits concerning reading. If teachers and others fail to encourage the desire to read in children and young adults, many students will become **aliterates:** persons who can read but choose not to. Building positive attitudes toward reading is of particular concern when working with students who have difficulty reading.

Frustration, failure, and overemphasis on skills and drills may kill the desire to learn to read. When this happens, teachers' jobs become much more demanding. They must not only handle the instructional facets of reading but try to overcome the negative attitudes of the student as well.

Major objectives for recreational reading include: (1) providing students with the opportunity to practice reading in a relaxed atmosphere (2) sharing good literature with students (3) making provisions for students to share books with one another.

The two goals of the reading program should be maintained and balanced throughout the elementary school years, although emphasis may change according to the needs of the students. Both goals are equally important for student reading programs at all levels of education.

WHAT IS CORRECTIVE READING?

As Used in This Text

Corrective reading refers to a type of instruction. Good instruction requires that teachers recognize each student's individual strengths and needs. The term *corrective* is used in this text in a descriptive sense, to suggest that for a student experiencing difficulty with some aspect of literacy, the situation can be ameliorated in some way and growth in literacy can continue. Thus the term *corrective reading* maintains a positive view of the learner and looks at ways to adjust the learning environment to better meet the student's needs. All of us have been in need of corrective instruction at some time or another, when we haven't quite grasped a new concept, or after an extended illness or absence causing us to miss certain information, or even as a result of a poorly planned and/or presented learning experience.

The Corrective Reading Program

The purpose of the corrective reading program, then, is to provide instruction within the regular classroom setting for students who demonstrate learning gaps for whatever reason. These students should not need corrective instruction on a long-term, year-after-year basis. Those who seem to require long-term help should be considered candidates for remedial instruction, which examines a complex interaction of factors that may impact the student's lack of literacy growth, such as poor health, perceptual or physical disabilities, or lack of motivation.

The corrective reading program is conceptualized as fluid, dynamic, and short-term. Students work to overcome their reading difficulties on an individual or small-group basis structured around their needs. After a relatively brief period of appropriate instruction and practice, these students should achieve success.

More careful analysis may be needed for students remaining unsuccessful after many weeks of instruction. Intensive individual assistance by qualified personnel other than the classroom teacher may be necessary. If these resources are unavailable in the school system, teachers must do the best they can for these students within the corrective program.

Materials used in a corrective reading program range from typical basal readers and workbooks to games for motivation and practice, language experience stories, trade books, and children's literature. Teachers may use any instructional materials available or they may design their own, but the instruction should focus on specific areas identified through careful analysis. For this analysis, teachers may use observations, checklists, surveys, anecdotal records, and informal reading inventories, as well as standardized measures such as diagnostic tests if they are available and appropriate to the teacher's needs. These and other assessment procedures and tools are discussed at length throughout Chapters 2, 3, 4, 5, and 6.

Many factors influence the classroom instructional program, including class size, experience and expertise of the teacher, and the availability of supplemental materials and extra help for teachers, such as a reading teacher, teacher aides, parents, and other paraprofessionals. The teacher's role in implementing a corrective reading program in the classroom setting is a major topic of the next chapter, "Analytic Teaching."

WHO IS THE CORRECTIVE READER?

The classroom teacher has primary responsibility for identifying readers in need of assistance and support. Initial identification may simply be based on a low reading achievement test score. For example, the vocabulary subtest score on an achievement test may be considerably lower, or higher, than the comprehension subtest score. Or a student may demonstrate consistently poor classroom performance in reading.

As indicated earlier, readers who reveal some gap(s) in their literacy growth require corrective instruction. For the most part, then, corrective readers are making progress in their literacy development, although it may be at a slower rate than many of their classmates. Generally, corrective readers are able to recall and discuss selections read to them better than they can recall and discuss selections they read themselves. While they seem to be able to learn from nonprint media more easily than from printed material, corrective readers do demonstrate some independence in reading. They are able to engage in recreational reading without direct assistance. Additionally, corrective readers' attitudes toward improving their reading are for the most part positive, and they do not need constant and sophisticated motivational encouragement (Smith, Otto & Hansen, 1978).

Goodman (1986) provides a more socio-emotional description of the corrective reader:

> There are lots of ineffective and troubled readers and writers. You easily recognize them. They are often in conflict with themselves and usually their own worst enemies. . . . they try to read and write by busily attacking words and looking up spellings. They mistrust their own language strategies and become dependent on teachers to tell them what to do as they read and write. They are reluctant to take the necessary risks, with the result that their reading and writing looks far less competent than it actually is. They believe that everyone knows they are literacy failures, and they act the part. . . . [they] do have strengths . . . but through lack of self-confidence and overkill on isolated skills, they don't recognize their own strengths. (pp. 55–56)

It is important to remember that decisions about individual students' reading abilities should reflect the multidimensional nature of the reading process. The total reader must be considered, not just achievement test scores or other standardized measures. For example, students with defeatist attitudes may be overlooked completely if only test scores are used. The remainder of this text focuses on helping teachers identify readers who need support as literacy learners, analyze their specific strengths and needs, and provide appropriate corrective instruction. What it means to consider the total reader is addressed in a discussion of analytic teaching (Chapter 2). This overview of analytic teaching is followed by a discussion of the analytic process (Chapter 3). Topics range from the gathering and interpretation of information (Chapters 2–6) to the implementation of effective instructional techniques for the major domains of reading (Chapters 7–13). Many useful assessment and instructional procedures for language development, word recognition, comprehension, study skills, and strategic reading are provided.

SUMMARY

In order to provide effective reading instruction for the wide range of reading abilities found in the classroom, teachers must be able to recognize in readers signs of needing assistance and support in their efforts. This chapter reviews the reading process and discusses the importance of teachers developing a personal philosophy about reading. Two major goals of any reading program are identified. Individual teachers can achieve these goals in a variety of ways, depending on their individual beliefs about reading. The concept of corrective reading instruction is introduced, and characteristics of corrective readers are discussed.

SUGGESTED READINGS

Aaron, I.E., Chall, J.S., Durkin, D., Goodman, K., & Strickland, D.S. (1990a, 1990b). The past, present, and future of literacy education: Comments from a panel of distinguished educators, Part I. *The Reading Teacher, 43,* 302–311. Part II. *The Reading Teacher, 43,* 370–380.

> *Presented in a conversational form with each speaker's contributions identified, these two articles provide insight into current topics in literacy education. The panelists also provide some needed historical perspective on the current issues.*

Doake, D.B. (1988). *Reading begins at birth.* NY: Scholastic.

> *One of Scholastic's Bright Idea educational paperbacks, this highly readable book provides much of the background for understanding how we learn to read and will give the reader a clear understanding of emergent literacy and the underlying concepts of a holistic philosophy.*

Weaver, C. (1991, Winter). Whole language: What it is and isn't. *Michigan Journal of Reading, 24,* 2–9.

> *This article provides a good summary of the whole language philosophy. Included is a valuable mini-bibliography of other books and articles that define and characterize whole language.*

2

ANALYTIC TEACHING: MEETING ALL STUDENTS' INSTRUCTIONAL NEEDS

Janet C. Richards

OBJECTIVES

After you have read this chapter, you should be able to

1. discuss and appreciate how students are unique;
2. define analytic teaching;
3. explain the prerequisites for analytic teaching;
4. explain how analytic teaching encourages and builds on students' literacy success through individualization of instruction;
5. discuss the importance of honest, student-centered communication;
6. explain how to teach with thematic units of instruction;

7. understand the importance of reflective thinking;
8. discuss the role of the teacher as a reflective decision maker;
9. explain how to group for literacy instruction;
10. discuss various types of record keeping that document students' literacy progress;
11. explain the importance of teacher observation;
12. discuss why students need opportunities to self-evaluate their literacy accomplishments.

KEY CONCEPTS AND TERMS

ad hoc groups
affective domain

analytic style
analytic teaching

The author wishes to thank Dr. Janet C. Richards, The University of Southern Mississippi–Gulf Park, for contributing this chapter.

Appalachian dialect
authentic literacy tasks
basic story features
Black English Vernacular (BEV)
cognitive domain
ESL students
global style

literature genre
multiple disciplines
orientation
perspectives
reading style
reflective thinking
thematic units of instruction

STUDY OUTLINE

1. Introduction
   a. English-as-second-language (ESL) students
   b. Differing dialects
   c. Unstable home environments
   d. Mainstreaming
   e. Teacher accountability
   f. Decreases in federal and state funding
2. Analytic teaching: Meeting all students' literacy instructional needs and interests
   a. Knowledge of how human beings learn and acquire knowledge
   b. Knowledge of the processes of reading and writing
   c. Appreciation of student differences
      • Cognitive domain
      • Affective domain
   d. Belief in students as capable human beings
3. Functions of the analytic teacher
   a. Observation
      • How and what to observe
      • After observation
   b. Communication

   c. Reflective thinking
   d. Decisions
   e. Involving students in meaningful, functional literacy activities through thematic units of instruction
   f. Assisting students who need extra time and help
      • Flexible reading groups
      • Ad hoc grouping
      • Alternate group instruction
      • Student reading group designation
   g. Student–teacher conferences
   h. Documentation and record keeping
   i. Classroom management
      • Effective management gives teachers time
      • Rules and consequences
   j. Testing
   k. Assessment and evaluation
4. Summary
5. Suggested readings

OVERVIEW

In this chapter the definition and rationale for analytic teaching are presented. The prerequisites for analytic teaching are discussed and some specific functions of the analytic teacher are explained. The chapter provides an overview of how analytic teachers (1) involve their students in meaningful, functional literacy activities (2) assist students who need extra time and help (3) help students formulate plans concerning their reading and writing instruction (4) document students' literacy progress and interests (5) incorporate effective classroom management systems that encourage students to take responsibility for their actions (6) depend most upon ongoing observation, deliberate reflection, and continuous assessment to determine students' literacy achievements and instructional needs. The chapter concludes with a summary and offers suggested readings.

INTRODUCTION

Each student is unique. Teachers value the diversity of their students and appreciate their varied background experiences, talents, and interests. At the same time, teachers recognize that the personal reading and writing needs of each student must be met. More than ever before, the need is urgent for teachers to develop better ways of helping all students become successful, motivated literacy learners. A number of factors contribute to this need.

English as Second Language (ESL) Students

Many teachers work with large numbers of students whose first language is not English. Experts estimate that increased immigration will bring even more **ESL students** to U.S. classrooms (Pallas, Natriello & McDill, 1989). Teachers want to help their ESL students learn to read and write English successfully. Therefore, teachers must become knowledgeable about their ESL students' ethnic backgrounds and recognize how background experiences and first language impact ESL students' English reading and writing competence and attitudes toward literacy activities (Field & Aebersold, 1990; Heath, 1986). (See the listing at the end of this chapter for children's books especially well suited for use with the young ESL learner.)

Differing Dialects

Students may speak variations of standard English influenced by the area in which they grew up or their social or ethnic group, such as **Appalachian dialect,** which is spoken in many settlements in eastern Kentucky (see Prescourt, 1982), and **Black English Vernacular (BEV),** a variety of English spoken by some African-Americans. Their speech patterns may not exactly match the standard English that is printed in their books or spoken by their teachers. Nonetheless, teachers recognize that most dialects are as highly structured and logical as standard English. Teachers value and affirm these students' ideas, opinions, "language and culture in the same way they . . . respect the [ideas, opinions,] language and culture of students who are learning English as a second language" (Roe, Stoodt & Burns, 1991, p. 184). (See Chapter 13 for more information on linguistically diverse students.)

Unstable Home Environments

The number of students living in single-parent homes or in poverty has increased (Ellwood, 1988; Roe, Stoodt & Burns, 1991; The Associated Press, 1993). Additionally, because many parents must begin their work day long before school opens and may continue working long after school closes, a significant number of students are characterized as "latchkey" or day-care children. Students must also cope with parents who are physically or verbally abusive, parents who argue or divorce, frequent moves because of economic considerations, and siblings or parents who abuse alcohol or drugs. Each of these circumstances contributes to a student's anxieties, and can result in anger, confusion, depression, poor self-image, erratic school attendance, and inability to perform in school. Teachers are challenged to meet the special instructional and emotional needs of students in unstable home environments. (See Chapter 4 for more information on environmental factors affecting students.)

Mainstreaming

The mainstreaming of students with exceptional needs is now common. Students retained in a grade, students identified as crack-cocaine babies, and students with health impairments, learning disabilities, Fetal Alcohol Syndrome, severe speech or hearing problems, emotional disabilities, physical handicaps, or deficits in perceptual, motor, or attentional skills (Clark-Johnson, 1988) are no longer denied the joy of participating in regular class activities. (Refer to Chapter 4 for more information.) Additionally, intellectually gifted and artistically talented students must be challenged and helped to reach their full potential in regular classrooms.

Teacher Accountability

National interest in improved public education has placed added demands on classroom teachers to be as effective as possible. Pressure from parents and school administrators requires that teachers demonstrate quality teaching behaviors.

Decreases in Federal and State Funding

Decreases in funding at the federal and state levels have reduced the number of on-site reading specialists, counselors, social workers, and librarians. As a result, today's teachers must accept full responsibility for helping all students become successful readers and writers. How can a classroom teacher begin to meet the diverse literacy instructional needs of all students? One way is through analytic teaching.

ANALYTIC TEACHING: MEETING ALL STUDENTS' LITERACY INSTRUCTIONAL NEEDS AND INTERESTS

Analytic teaching refers to a humanistic way of meeting and serving all students' instructional needs and a way of observing and assessing students' literacy development that recognizes, respects, and appreciates students' abilities. Irrespective of one's beliefs about literacy instruction (e.g., whole language, skills, or interactive), analytic teaching begins with a teacher's firm convictions that (1) all students can learn and have the capabilities to become successful readers and writers, (2) diversity "has special value within the classroom community because it provides challenges that lead students and teachers to new learning" (Au, 1993a, p. 74), and (3) all students deserve equal opportunities for success. Analytic teaching comprises activities that foster student–teacher communication, student choice, and student empowerment. This type of teaching encourages students to set some goals for learning and assume some responsibility for evaluating their own achievements and instructional needs. An effective analytic teacher meets several prerequisites.

Knowledge of How Human Beings Learn and Acquire Knowledge

Analytic teachers have a good understanding of how human beings learn and acquire knowledge. Research in cognitive, educational, and developmental psychology and in reading and early childhood research (e.g., see Morrow & Smith, 1990; Wadsworth, 1989; Thibault & McKee, 1982; Vygotsky, 1986; Wong Fillmore, 1986) tells us that human beings learn best in social situations that allow them to interact, discuss, and collaborate with one another. Further, human beings learn best when they (1) are actively involved in personally meaningful activities (2) have opportunities to think, explore, discover, reason, and continuously interact with their environment in order to make sense of new information (as opposed to absorbing facts) (3) can make connections between new ideas and concepts and their previously acquired background knowledge (4) are encouraged "to develop a sense of ownership and responsibility for their own learning" (Harste, Short & Burke, 1988, p. 243) (5) can learn new, developmentally appropriate "skills" (e.g., the parts of a friendly letter) within more global **authentic literacy tasks** (i.e., genuine) such as exchanging letters with a real pen pal rather than filling in ditto sheets.

Knowledge of the Processes of Reading and Writing

Analytic teachers also have knowledge of reading and writing processes. The analytic teacher is a lifelong student of literacy. Attending reading and language arts conferences, taking university courses, reading professional journals, and discussing new literacy ideas with colleagues are professional activities that enhance analytic teachers' knowledge about current literacy theories and expand their repertories of reading and writing instructional techniques.

Analytic teachers also know what they believe about good reading and writing instruction and base their practices on those beliefs. Depending upon their **perspectives** (i.e., beliefs), analytic teachers transform basal texts, children's and adolescents' magazines, visual and performing arts materials, creative writing supplies, and quality, developmentally appropriate fiction and nonfiction into a sound, research-based literacy program. Most important, regardless of **orientation** (i.e., beliefs), analytic teachers know that the ultimate goal of reading is to achieve comprehension, and that reading and writing are mutually supportive processes.

Appreciation of Student Differences

Analytic teachers know that students naturally differ and that no two students pass through the same developmental stages of reading and writing in the same way or at the same time. Students differ in both the cognitive and affective dimensions.

Cognitive domain differences include background information, which refers to prior experiences and knowledge; linguistic competence, which refers to how well a student understands and uses oral and written language; first or home language; cognitive functioning or intellectual development; metacognitive abilities (the "ability to question . . . [one's] own thought processes, according to Coley & Hoffman, 1990, p. 497); readiness for specific reading instruction; ability to remain on task; and **reading style,** which refers in part to a reader's preference for processing written information in a **global style** (i.e., preferring to concentrate on main ideas) or in an **analytic style** (i.e., preferring to concentrate on smaller portions of text, such as facts, dates, and names) (Weaver, 1994). (See Carbo, Dunn & Dunn, 1986, for more information on reading style.)

Affective domain differences include personality dimensions (e.g., extroversion or introversion); degree of interest in literature; perceptions about the importance of reading; motivation to read; persistence in completing tasks; culturally acquired attitudes and values; expectations for reading success; feelings of self-esteem and belonging; a sense of control over one's environment (Rotter, 1966); a passive or active orientation to learning (Torgeson, 1982); and achievement needs (Willig, Harnisch, Hill & Maehr, 1983).

Belief in Students as Capable Human Beings

Analytic teachers know that all students possess ability to learn. These teachers believe that students are capable human beings who want to learn and are ready to learn at some point on the reading and writing instructional continuum. Analytic teachers also believe that students are capable of making good decisions concerning their educational needs.

If you appreciate, welcome, and celebrate each student's unique qualities and talents, and believe in students' desires to learn, you possess the prerequisite humanistic components necessary for successful analytic teaching.

FUNCTIONS OF THE ANALYTIC TEACHER

Observation

Analytic teachers are concerned with teaching all students effectively—not with covering a specified amount of reading material. Therefore, analytic teachers constantly observe their students to watch for the emergence of reading and writing patterns and achievements, and to determine what their students are ready to learn next. Teacher observation is never wasted time. Materials for literacy instruction (e.g., basal texts, developmentally appropriate literature, content-area texts, pictures, art and creative bookmaking supplies, and magazines) should *not* be assembled before students' literacy instructional needs and interests are determined.

How and What to Observe

During the first week of school, analytic teachers observe their students to discover their reading and writing strengths and needs. At the same time, analytic teachers notice peer interactions, students' interests, thinking abilities, and oral language patterns, and each student's level of self-esteem and ability to complete assignments. Suggestions for a week of student observation include the following:

1. *Free time.* Who interacts with whom? Who are the introverts or extroverts? Who reads independently? Who writes independently for personally important reasons? Who needs structure or freedom?

2. *Reading groups (randomly assigned).* Who can identify ideas or words they don't understand? Who uses background knowledge and context to determine unknown words?

3. *Playground.* Who displays leadership abilities? Who appears to be a follower? Who is helpful to others? Who is athletically gifted? Who needs to learn to take turns?

4. *Lunchroom.* Who appears overly hungry? Who needs to learn table manners? Who appears lethargic or tired?

5. *Class meetings.* Who speaks in complete sentences? Who has a sense of humor? Who listens carefully? Who understands and participates in problem solving or brainstorming activities? Who has difficulty hearing? Who is shy? Who offers helpful suggestions? (See Glasser, 1969, for a thorough discussion of class meetings.)

6. *Sustained silent reading (SSR).* Who can choose books on his independent reading level? Who "mouths" words? Who becomes easily distracted? Who points to words and sentences and might find a sentence marker useful? Who chooses books that complement her personal interests?

7. *Small groups.* Who completes learning tasks? Who cooperates? Who works to best abilities? Who has good ideas? Who assists "others in using a skill after mastering it themselves" (Biemiller, 1993, p. 14)?

8. *Visual and performing arts activities.* Who displays exceptional artistic or creative abilities? Who needs to learn how to use visual art media (e.g., tempera paints, water colors, fine and broad markers, crayons, colored pencils, glue, scissors, chalk)? Whose artistic accomplishments are not commensurate with age or grade level? (See Lowenfeld, 1970, for a discussion of the stages of children's art.) Who is interested in performing plays and puppet productions?

9. *Teacher reading aloud.* Who listens and remembers? Who needs opportunities to develop appropriate background knowledge in order to comprehend and appreciate stories? Who understands the relationships among **basic story features** and their connections (i.e., characters, setting, problems and solutions)? Who identifies with story characters? Who recognizes how authors portray story characters (Richards & Gipe, 1993; Richards, Gipe & Necaise, 1993)? Who recognizes and understands inferential language (e.g., metaphors, similes, and idioms)?

10. *Creative writing.* Who is willing to use invented spelling? Who is ready to learn about punctuation or paragraphing? Who needs to learn some prewriting strategies (e.g., semantic mapping, "speed writing," drawing, brainstorming, discussion)? (Please refer to Chapter 7 for a detailed discussion of student writing, activities, and lessons.)

After Observation

After initially observing students, the analytic teacher forms some general ideas about individual students and their overall literacy learning abilities. At this time the analytic teacher might tentatively decide which students:

1. Display similar interests
2. Appear to be similar in estimated reading or writing ability
3. Need many experiences to enhance background knowledge
4. Need to learn how to stay on task
5. Need to develop more motivation or self-esteem

6. Need to learn how to read for meaning
7. Need to learn about the different functions and styles of writing (see Chapter 7)

Communication

Analytic teachers work hard to ensure that they and their students interact, communicate, and work together as a community of learners. Analytic teachers wholeheartedly believe that students are willing partners in the instructional process. Therefore, they listen to their students' ideas and encourage them to share opinions.

Analytic teaching initially may require extra time. However, once students accept some responsibility for their own reading and writing instruction, the teacher gains valuable time needed to observe students daily, make ongoing decisions about students' literacy instruction, and provide opportunities to support students' literacy growth.

Short, daily, whole-class meetings are effective for fostering group communication and facilitating student–teacher communication (Glasser, 1969). These meetings are most effective when teacher and students face one another in a seated circle. Discussion topics vary according to what happens to be going on in the classroom (e.g., celebrating a birthday, planning a new unit of instruction, offering help and encouragement to students with an academic or behavior problem, solving group dilemmas). At this time, analytic teachers also compliment their students' efforts and accomplishments (e.g., "Liza really worked hard yesterday and completed her dinosaur book"; "Yesterday Jose learned how to edit punctuation in his story. He would like to explain how punctuation helps readers understand an author's message"; "Joe did a great job as the editor of our class newspaper").

Reflective Thinking

Analytic teachers are reflective practitioners. They consciously and seriously reflect on how to help each of their students become better readers and writers. It is well documented that **reflective thinking** (i.e., questioning and trying to solve educational problems in a thoughtful and deliberate manner) helps teachers make quality decisions about students and their instruction (Dewey, 1933; Grossman, 1992).

Decisions

Because analytic teachers are both observers of students and reflective practitioners, they feel confident of their abilities to formulate literacy instructional plans and long-range goals for individuals and groups of students. Professional decisions are made before, during, and after instruction. In the course of one school day, a teacher might consider all the following questions while reflecting on various students.

1. Is this student reading as well as he can? If not, why? What reading or writing strategy might help? Will an individual conference help? Will peer tutoring help?
2. Should this student remain in the reading group that is exploring poetry? If so, what additional instructional techniques may enable this student to grasp the ideas and concepts represented?
3. How can I motivate this student to become an avid, wide reader and/or an enthusiastic writer?

4. How can I plan literacy activities that will stimulate my passive learners?

Beginning teachers who are anxious to use the analytic approach to literacy instruction may find the reflective decision-making process difficult because of a lack of experience, time, understanding of reading and writing processes, or confidence in professional judgment. *Do not worry!* If you sincerely believe in the benefits of analytic teaching, you will become increasingly knowledgeable about these processes. You will consider students' self-esteem, interests, background knowledge, and special talents, and you will gain confidence and grow in your abilities as a reflective decision maker.

Involving Students in Meaningful, Functional Literacy Activities Through Thematic Units of Instruction

Many analytic teachers organize much of their instruction around particular **thematic units of instruction** (i.e., a specific topic, such as dinosaurs, outer space, or African-Americans of achievement). The most effective thematic units incorporate **multiple disciplines** (e.g., math, language arts, reading, science, art) and are planned by students and teachers together. Often, good ideas for themed units arise naturally within the context of the school day. For example, one afternoon a rabbit hopped through an open door into a rural first-grade classroom. The students and their teacher realized that they knew very little about rabbits. Immediately, a unit on rabbits was initiated. The class assembled a book display to show the variety of **literature genre** (e.g., fiction, nonfiction, poetry, fantasy, folklore) that contained works about rabbits; studied different types of rabbits; learned about rabbits' favorite foods and special characteristics; compared and contrasted the size and weight of various species of rabbits; and ended the unit by creating and presenting a puppet production titled "The Rabbit Who Came to School."

A fourth-grade class decided to create a unit on outer space when they heard a *Star Wars* tape. With their teacher's help, the students listed everything they wanted to learn about astronauts, space travel, black holes, and extraterrestrial beings. They assembled literature on space travel; wrote letters inviting an astronomer and a rocket scientist to visit their class; wrote to famous astronauts requesting autographed pictures; and graphed the number of space flights launched by different countries since the orbit of Sputnik and the amount of time different astronauts have logged in space shuttle flights. Culminating activities included making mobiles of the solar system and reading about outer space to first- and second-grade students.

Another unit was initiated when two kindergarten students were asked to deliver a message to the principal and could not find his office. During a class meeting the students decided that since a large part of their day was spent at school, they needed to know who worked in the cafeteria, the custodian's and secretary's names, and where to find the school nurse. They "wrote" letters inviting the school workers to visit their room to discuss their particular school-related work responsibilities; listened to stories and informative texts about school workers; and made a creative *big book* titled "Our School Nurse, Principal, Custodian, and Secretary."

When a guest speaker discussed the customs of nobility in the Middle Ages, a group of seventh graders decided to devote their next unit to medieval life. The students brainstormed what they wanted to learn about life in the Middle Ages and discussed how to find the answers to their questions. They wrote in journals, taking the part of nobles or peasants; mixed paint in medieval style by combining tempera and egg yolks;

created large murals; built castles from sugar cubes, Legos, blocks, and papier maché; and ended the unit by inviting parents and friends to a "Medieval Feast." Students and teacher dressed in medieval costumes, and Gregorian chants played softly as students read their journals, stories, and *expository voice* compositions about the Middle Ages. (See Britton, Burgess, Martin, McLeod & Rosen, 1975, and Chapter 7 in this text for a discussion of *voices* of composition.)

In each of these units, students were encouraged to accept some responsibility for their learning and multiple disciplines were incorporated.

Assisting Students Who Need Extra Time and Help

Flexible Reading Groups

Most teachers group students for reading instruction. Reading groups need to be flexible because students' instructional needs change daily. Therefore, analytic teachers do not lock students into a particular reading track.

Analytic teachers communicate to students the reasons for reading-group flexibility. Students receive direct reading instruction in the area they need at a particular time. Analytic teachers think of individual students and their reading needs. They are not bound by practices like comparing one student against another or following basal text manual suggestions.

Ad Hoc Grouping

The analytic teacher continually thinks "Who is ready to learn what now?" or "Who needs a little extra help in understanding this concept?" **Ad hoc groups** are easily formed to meet a group of students' instructional needs or interests and are disbanded when students' needs have been met. For example, analytic teachers implement teacher-guided writing lessons based upon their students' individual writing needs. Thus students can immediately apply what they learn to their own independent writing efforts (see Chapter 7).

Alternate Group Instruction

Analytic teachers alternate the order of their reading-group instruction so that the same students do not always have to wait for their turn. Three reading groups seem to be as much as teachers can manage effectively. In analytic teaching, the first reading group is not the advanced group, nor is the third reading group the less able group. Groups are formed to expedite reading instruction according to individual students' needs and interests.

Student Reading Group Designation

Some analytic teachers place a chart adjacent to their reading-group space on which students may sign up for reading-group participation according to topic (Fig. 2.1). Students may sign up for any of three reading groups, which encourages them to accept some responsibility for their own learning. Additionally, if one group is reading about a particular topic such as "African-Americans of Achievement," the analytic teacher encourages students who are particularly interested in that topic to sit in on that reading group, regardless of their reading ability. Perhaps on another day, a lesson covers a word identification strategy. The analytic teacher knows which students would benefit from a preview or review of this particular reading strategy and groups students accordingly.

Student–Teacher Conferences

Students are quite capable of helping the teacher formulate plans concerning their literacy instruction. The analytic teacher conducts daily informal conferences and also schedules weekly student conferences to discuss an individual student's literacy

---

FIGURE
2.1

Example of a student sign-up sheet.

Options for students include: 1) previewing and voting for the literature selection they particularly wish to read; 2) offering suggestions for additional literature selections to be included under a listed topic; 3) brainstorming ideas for further extensions of topics; 4) offering suggestions for future reading topics.

GROUP 1	GROUP 2	GROUP 3
Topic: *Dinosaurs*	**Topic:** *African-Americans of Achievement*	**Topic:** *All Sorts of Survivors*
Literature:	**Literature:**	**Literature:**
1. *A Dozen Dinosaurs*	1. *Sounder*	1. *The True Confessions of Charlotte Doyle*
2. *Dinosaurs, Dinosaurs*	2. *Nat Turner: Slave Revolt Leader*	2. *Dear Mr. Henshaw*
3. *100 Dinosaurs from A to Z*	3. *James Weldon Johnson: Author*	3. *Sarah, Plain and Tall*
Extensions:	**Extensions:**	**Extensions:**
1. Create papier maché dinosaurs	1. Readers theatre	1. Create a play about survivors
2. Graph sizes of different dinosaurs	2. Interview and write about a friend or relative who is a person of achievement	2. Write about a time when you "survived"
3. Visit kindergarten to give short talks on dinosaurs	3. Create a book based upon a person of achievement	3. Create a chart depicting the personal traits of the survivors portrayed in the books listed above
1._____	1._____	1._____
2._____	2._____	2._____
3._____	3._____	3._____
4._____	4._____	4._____
5._____	5._____	5._____

The author wishes to thank Kathy Babin, Millie Breun, and Rosa Porter, graduate students at The University of Southern Mississippi, for contributing suggestions for the reading topics and literature listed above.

Armour, R. (1967). *A Dozen Dinosaurs.* New York: McGraw Hill.
Armstrong, W. (1969). *Sounder.* New York: Harper and Row.
Avi [Wortis]. (1990). *The True Confessions of Charlotte Doyle.* New York: Avon.
Bison, T. (1988). *Nat Turner: Slave Revolt Leader.* Danbury, CT: Grolier.
Cleary, B. (1983). *Dear Mr. Henshaw.* New York: Dell.
Craig, M. (1968). *Dinosaurs, Dinosaurs.* New York: Four Winds Press.
MacLachlan, P. (1985). *Sarah, Plain and Tall.* New York: Harper and Row.
Tolbert-Rouchaleau, J. (1988). *James Weldon Johnson: Author.* Danbury, CT: Grolier.
Wilson, R. (1986). *100 Dinosaurs from A to Z.* New York: Grosset and Dunlap.

progress, strengths, problems, interests, and goals. At this time the teacher can also suggest some literature selections a student may enjoy reading, or perhaps teach a mini-lesson on a reading comprehension or writing strategy that may benefit the student. Students look forward to student–teacher conferences when teachers are nonjudgmental, empathic, fair, and honest and show that they are learners along with their students.

Documentation and Record Keeping

Analytic teachers understand the importance of keeping records to monitor students' literacy progress and their changing interests. Documentation includes nature and content of student–teacher conferences (Fig. 2.2), records of teacher observations, examples of students' work, comments and suggestions from students, and notes on specific reading comprehension and writing strategies employed by students. Documentation can be accomplished through a checklist (Fig. 2.3; see also Chapter 6), anecdotal records (Fig. 2.4; see also Chapters 4, 6), student self-evaluation (Fig. 2.5), examples of students' work gathered in *working* and *showcase portfolios* (see Chapter 7 for a discussion of these portfolios), tape recordings, videos, photographs, and students' comments about their achievements and instructional needs.

Classroom Management

Analytic teachers know that effective classroom management is simply a common-sense way of organizing all class activities so that both students and teacher know what is expected and accept responsibility for what happens during the school day.

Example of student–teacher conference documentation.

FIGURE
2.2

Name: **Jo Ellen**   Date: **March 12**

Topics of discussion:	Teacher's comments:
Literature read or heard	Is reading <u>Cousins</u> by Virginia Hamilton
Reading comprehension strategies	Explained that she uses prediction strategies often
Achievements	
Problems	
Behavior	
Weekly goals	1. Complete <u>Cousins</u> 2. Begin writing a play based on the main characters in <u>Cousins</u>
Long-term goals	1. Write and direct a three-act play

Hamilton, V. (1990). *Cousins.* New York: Putnam and Grosset.

FIGURE
2.3

Example of a checklist.

Name: _Scotty_   Date: _October 10_

	Yes	No	Comments
Enjoys listening to literature selections	✓		always listens closely and gives opinions on story content
Responds enthusiastically to literature heard or read by creating art projects, writing in literature response journals, creating stories, books, and drama activities	✓		• created a dinosaur diorama • writes daily in his literature response journal • actively participates in our playwriting interest group
Is developing reading independence			
Is learning to use reading comprehension strategies according to need (e.g., word identification, KWL, It reminds me of)		✓	still over-reliant on graphophonic cues to determine unknown words (review three-step word identification plan)

FIGURE
2.4

Example of an anecdotal record.

Name: _Keyotta_

12/3/93   Is learning to use her background knowledge and the context of a passage to determine unknown words in text.

1/5/94   Is becoming a motivated wide reader. She has read three books this week—topics: outer space, baby animals, African-Americans of achievement.

1/12/94   Still needs to develop confidence in her abilities to use her background knowledge and the context of a passage to determine unknown words.

1/27/94   Has become interested in wild animals and their habitats (assemble literature on this topic).

2/14/94   Created and presented a play to the kindergarten—topic: animals and Africa.

Example of a student self-evaluation checklist.

Name: **Mary Alice**   Date: **May 9**

	Yes	No	My Explanation
I completed my reading goals for this week	✓		I finished the first chapter of Sarah, Plain and Tall.
I monitored my reading comprehension		✓	I forgot to write down what I didn't understand.
I learned something new as I read	✓		Sarah was a mail-order bride. Long ago, people lived very far away from each other, so they didn't get to meet each other. When they wanted to get married, men would sometimes advertise for a bride.
I helped someone with his or her reading	✓		I gave Angela a suggestion for her creative dinosaur book.

MacLachlan, P. (1985). *Sarah, Plain and Tall.* New York: Harper and Row.

Effective Management Gives Teachers Time

Teachers need energy and time to teach. A good classroom management system encourages students to take responsibility for their actions and frees the teacher for facilitating instruction. As Spaulding (1983) notes: "A classroom management scheme that relies on strict teacher direction deprives students of opportunities to learn self-management skills" (p. 48). Analytic teachers always plan their management system in conjunction with the students in their classroom.

Rules and Consequences

Rules concerning student behavior should be joint decisions of teacher and students. Rules should always be stated concisely and in a positive manner. For example, rules for young students might include the following:

1. We speak softly.
2. We listen when others speak.
3. In large groups we raise our hand when we want to speak.
4. We care for and return supplies to their proper place.

5. We clean up our area.

6. We share.

7. We are kind.

8. We always do our best work and use our best manners.

Older students appreciate more concisely stated rules such as:

1. We respect ourselves and others.

2. We listen carefully to others' ideas and concerns.

3. We give 100% effort to our academic work and our behavior.

Consequences for inappropriate behavior should also be formulated through cooperative student–teacher efforts. For example, students and their teacher might decide that students who exhibit inappropriate behavior should be given a warning. If students continue behaving inappropriately they must return quietly to their seats or sit in a special "time out" place for a designated amount of time. When "time out" is completed, students are always warmly welcomed back to the group.

Testing

Analytic teachers depend most upon ongoing observation to determine their students' literacy strengths, achievements, and instructional needs. Occasionally, analytic teachers may decide that they need to administer a test. Although testing is a very small portion of analytic teaching, it can provide some classroom-based information about students that may be useful. The following classroom-based tests (see Chapter 6) are employed by analytic teachers: 1) informal reading inventories 2) cloze or maze passages 3) story retellings.

Remember, though, that analytic teachers never group students according to test scores alone. Testing only indicates what students accomplish on a particular test on a particular day. The analytic teacher makes professional decisions about students' literacy instruction only after considerable, careful, and deliberate observation and reflection.

Assessment and Evaluation

Analytic teachers know that continual assessment of each student's literacy progress is essential in determining future instruction. Student evaluation should be based on the following:

1. Motivation for reading and writing

2. Growth in ability to read for comprehension

3. Growth in ability to employ word identification strategies

4. Growth in ability to recognize and understand basic story features and their connections

5. Growth in ability to appreciate and judge the quality of literature read or heard

6. Growth in ability to compare and contrast the structure of poetic and expository text

7. Growth in ability to use reading comprehension strategies based upon need
8. Growth in ability to monitor reading comprehension
9. Development of wide reading interests
10. Growth in ability to write on a wide range of topics using different *voices of composition* (see Chapter 7)

Analytic teachers know that it is especially important for students to learn how to evaluate their own literacy achievements and progress. Students who can evaluate their own work in terms of strengths and needs develop responsibility for their own learning (Tierney, Carter, & DeSai, 1991). Analytic teachers know that "risk-free environments are necessary in order for this to happen" (Glazer, 1993, p. 108). A simple checklist like the one shown in Fig. 2.5 may help students evaluate their achievements.

SUMMARY

Analytic teachers recognize and appreciate the uniqueness of each of their students. Diverse groups of students may include ESL students, students who speak dialects, students from unstable home environments, and students with exceptional needs. National interest in improved education requires teachers to be as effective as possible, while decreased funding for support personnel requires teachers to accept full responsibility for their students' learning. Analytic teaching allows teachers to meet the needs of all their students.

Analytic teachers have a good sense of how human beings learn. They also possess knowledge of reading and writing processes. Along with a sound, research-based literacy instructional program, analytic teachers employ the following activities to assist students in becoming successful readers and writers:

1. Open, honest student–teacher communication
2. Ongoing observation of students
3. Reflective thinking and decision making
4. Involving students in meaningful, functional literacy activities
5. Flexible grouping and regrouping
6. Formal and informal student–teacher conferences
7. Effective classroom management
8. Helping students learn to self-evaluate their literacy achievements and needs

Analytic teaching helps students become successful, motivated readers and writers because:

1. Students are involved in planning their own instruction.
2. Students are informed about their progress.
3. Students are not locked into one instructional group.
4. Student–teacher communication is open, honest, and nonjudgmental.
5. Students learn new, developmentally appropriate skills within global, authentic literacy tasks.

CHILDREN'S LITERATURE FOR THE YOUNG ESL LEARNER[1]

Choral Reading/Predictable Plots

These stories contain repetitive lines and/or predictable patterns. Choral reading allows students to read within the safety of a group; thus they are more likely to take risks. Students who cannot read independently can participate successfully by orally "reading" the lines of repetition they recall from memory.

dePaola, Tomie. (1975). *Strega nona*. Englewood Cliffs, NJ: Prentice Hall.

Martin, Bill Jr. (1983). *Brown bear, brown bear, what do you see?* New York: Holt.

Martin, Bill Jr. (1991). *Polar bear, what do you hear?* New York: Holt.

Peek, Merle. (1985). *Mary wore her red dress (and Henry wore his green sneakers)*. New York: Ticknor and Fields.

Soule, Jean Conder. (1964). *Never tease a weasel*. New York: Parents Magazine Press.

Books in Rhyme

Stories in rhyme are usually helpful to young ESL students because the text is simple and has a rhythmic pattern for them to follow. There are many books in this category in any public library.

Hawkins, Colin and Hawkins, Jack. (1986). *Tog the dog*. New York: Putnam's Sons.

Leonard, Marcia. (1988). *Find that puppy*. (also *Catch that mouse, Follow that car, Chase that pig*) New York: Bantam Books.

Milios, Rita. (1988). *Bears, bears everywhere*. Chicago: Children's Press. (a series)

Yektai, Niki. (1987). *Bears in pairs*. New York: Bradbury Press.

Young, James. (1990). *A million chameleons*. Canada: Little Brown.

Homophones, Homographs, and Idioms

Many young ESL learners have trouble understanding common English expressions; they take many idioms literally. For example, "It's raining cats and dogs!" would bring looks of amazement at the thought of cats and dogs falling from the sky. In the Spanish language, for instance, there aren't any words that have multiple meanings and there are no homonyms. Therefore, the following books are especially helpful for the young ESL learner whose first language is Spanish.

Cox, James. (1980). *Put your foot in your mouth and other silly sayings*. New York: Random House.

Gwynne, Fred. (1970). *The king who rained*. New York: Prentice Hall (also *A chocolate moose for dinner,* 1976).

Hunt, Bernice Kohn. (1975). *Your ant is a which*. New York: Harcourt Brace Jovanovich.

---

[1]The author is grateful to Rhonda Pukof-Guttuso, a former student, for preparing this list.

Terban, Marvin. (1990). *Punching the clock: Funny action idioms.* New York: Clarion (also *Eight ate: A feast of homonym riddles,* 1982; *In a pickle and other funny idioms,* 1983; *Mad as a wet hen and other funny idioms,* 1987).

Synonyms and Antonyms

Gillham, Bill and Hulme, Susan. (1984). *Let's look for opposites.* London: Methuem Children's Books.

Hanson, Joan. (1972). *Antonyms.* Minneapolis, MN: Lerner.

Hoban, Tana. (1976). *Push pull empty full: A book of opposites.* New York: Macmillan.

Prepositions

Hoban, Tana. (1973). *Over under and through and other spatial concepts.* New York: Macmillan.

Hoban, Tana. (1991). *All about where.* New York: Greenwill Books.

SUGGESTED READINGS

Au, K. (1993). *Literacy instruction in multicultural settings.* New York: Harcourt Brace Jovanovich.

> *Explains how and why culture and first language impact students' literacy abilities, background knowledge, and perceptions and attitudes toward learning.*

Book Links: Connecting Books, Libraries, and Classrooms. Chicago: American Library Association.

> *This new magazine, published six times a year, helps teachers integrate the best in children's literature into the classroom. Each issue offers annotated bibliographies for a variety of genre and topics as well as suggestions for their use, such as in thematic units.*

Pallas, A., Natriello, G., & McDill, E. (1989). Changing nature of the disadvantaged population: Current dimensions and future trends. *Educational Researcher, 18* (5), 16–22.

> *Identifies the current state of the educationally disadvantaged population in the U.S. and discusses implications for U.S. education. Projections indicate that the number of ESL children and children of poverty will increase substantially in the next few years.*

Vygotsky, L. (1986). Problems of general psychology (N. Minick, Trans.). In R. Reiber and A. Carton (Eds.), *The collected works of L.S. Vygotsky: Vol. 1.* New York: Plenum.

> *Minick discusses Vygotsky's learning theories in an understandable manner. Human beings learn best when they can 1) interact with their environment and come to their own understandings 2) discuss and collaborate in social situations, and 3) accept some responsibility for their own learning.*

White, C. (1990). *Jevon doesn't sit at the back anymore.* New York: Scholastic.

> *This short monograph is the story of one teacher's efforts to observe and record what happened in her own classroom. She learned that a strong community of learners can be forged when teachers take the time to learn the strengths and differences of individual students.*

3

THE ANALYTIC PROCESS: ITS NATURE AND VALUE

OBJECTIVES

After you have read this chapter, you should be able to

1. define the analytic process;
2. justify the analytic process and contrast it with assumptive teaching;
3. cite the four levels of the analytic process;
4. list the major reading domains and areas within each;
5. describe the steps in the paradigm for the analytic process;

6. explain the usefulness of the two teaching models, nondirective and direct instruction;
7. describe teacher objectives and correlated student-learning objectives;
8. discuss the difference between didactic and discovery teaching;
9. contrast problem-solving questions and facilitating questions.

KEY CONCEPTS AND TERMS

analytic process
assumptive teaching
covert cognitive
deductive teaching
diagnosis
didactic teaching
direct instruction
discovery teaching
empirical evidence
evaluation activity
facilitating questions
independent practice

inductive teaching
instructional reading level
nondirective teaching
overt behaviors
paradigm
problem-solving questions
screening
structured practice
teachable units
teaching hypothesis
transfer of training

STUDY OUTLINE

1. Introduction
2. Justification for the analytic process
   a. Problems associated with assumptive teaching
   b. The analytic process paradigm
3. Analyzing components of the reading process
   a. Four levels of analysis and correlative diagnostic questions
      • Level 1: Determining lack of success in reading
      • Level 2: Determining the domain(s) in which difficulty occurs
      • Level 3: Determining the area(s) within the domain(s)
         1) Within the domain of oral and written language ability
         2) Within the domain of word recognition
         3) Within the domain of reading comprehension and strategic reading for narrative text
         4) Within the domain of study skills and strategic reading for expository text
      • Level 4: Determining the teachable units within each area
   b. Components outside the major domains: Reading-related factors
4. Basic steps in the analytic process
   a. Examination of reading behaviors
      • Gathering information
      • Evaluating the information
   b. Generation of possible teaching hypotheses
      • Determining alternatives
      • Selecting a tentative hypothesis
   c. Teaching
      • Nondirective teaching model
         1) Catharsis

2) Insight
3) Integration
   • Direct instruction model
      1) Direct instruction/modeling
      2) Structured practice
      3) Independent practice
      4) Evaluation activity
   d. Reexamination of reading behaviors
      • Gathering information
      • Evaluating the information
      • Generating possible teaching hypotheses
      • Selecting a teaching hypothesis
5. From teaching hypotheses to lesson plans
   a. Objectives
      • Teacher objectives and correlated student learning objectives
      • Writing student learning objectives
         1) The condition
         2) The observable behavior
            (a) Motoric
            (b) Verbal
            (c) Cognitive
         3) The criterion
   b. Procedures
      • Planning the steps
         1) Procedural steps
         2) Teaching steps
            (a) For didactic teaching
            (b) For discovery teaching
      • Planning the questions
         1) Problem-solving questions
         2) Facilitating questions
      • Assessment during the lesson
6. A complete lesson
7. Summary
8. Suggested readings

OVERVIEW

In this chapter the analytic process is defined and its importance to classroom teachers discussed. The analytic process is also contrasted with assumptive teaching to help teachers avoid the potential errors associated with the latter approach.

Four levels of analysis used to identify the reading strengths and needs of students are described. The effective teacher begins with an analysis of the learner's general reading perfor-

mance. If the student is not succeeding in reading, the teacher proceeds to the second level of analysis involving four major domains of reading: (1) oral and written language ability (2) word recognition (3) comprehension and strategic reading for narrative text and (4) study skills and strategic reading for expository text. If the learner demonstrates difficulty within one or more of the domains, a third level of analysis, involving areas within domains, is suggested. Finally, the teacher uses a fourth level of analysis, searching for specific strengths and difficulties in order to plan appropriate lessons. Thus, instructional decisions are primarily based upon the analyses at levels three and four, which yield teachable units.

A basic paradigm for the analytic process is then outlined: gathering data; evaluating the data; generating possible teaching hypotheses; deciding on the best possible instructional plan to use; and carrying out the instructional plan in order to gather further data and to reevaluate. The fluid, continuous, and cyclical nature of the analytic process becomes apparent.

Translating teaching hypotheses into lesson plans is then explained. This explanation includes a discussion of objectives, teaching strategies, and questioning techniques. The chapter ends with an example of a complete lesson plan.

INTRODUCTION

The analytic process can be used by any classroom teacher in any curricular area. It is not confined to reading, nor is it a reading method. Rather, the **analytic process** is defined here as a systematic way to help teachers observe and assess aspects of the reading process in their students, identify areas of strength and need for individual students, and provide instruction for specific reading domains regardless of the curricular area or the teaching methods used.

Our current understanding of the reading process recognizes the importance of the reader, the text, and the context of the reading task. As Barr suggests (cited in Berglund, 1987), teachers must "look with new eyes" at students while they are reading. Rather than depend on test instruments, even nonstandardized ones such as informal reading inventories, teachers should initially gain insights into students' reading ability by observing their individual competence in areas such as oral reading, story retellings, written summaries, answers to key questions that reveal the important understandings of material read, and background knowledge. The analytic process described in this chapter recognizes the transactive nature of reading which, in turn, requires assessment procedures that are also transactive, that is, allowing learners to "use active strategies for constructing meaning as they interact with print" (Rhodes & Dudley-Marling, 1988, p. 29). Katherine Au (1993b) has referred to this view of assessment as classroom-based assessment.

JUSTIFICATION FOR THE ANALYTIC PROCESS

Problems Associated with Assumptive Teaching

Sometimes teachers make inappropriate assumptions about the reading status of their pupils. Herber (1970) calls the resulting instruction **assumptive teaching**. While teachers make many unfortunate specific assumptions, most fall into two general categories.

First, teachers often assume their pupils need to learn something when, in fact, they already have learned it. When this assumption is made, those pupils are in a *minimal growth* instructional setting. The teacher may spend a great deal of time and energy teaching something that is of little use to those receiving instruction. This type of assumptive teaching leads to student boredom, inattentiveness, and disruptive behavior. Second, and perhaps of vital significance to all concerned with corrective reading, teachers may assume their pupils have learned something when, in fact, they have not. If this occurs with some regularity, reading deficits will accrue and students will slip into a *no growth* instructional setting. Teaching a lesson well will not guarantee that pupils learn. Figure 3.1 lists common assumptions that teachers should try to avoid.

Assuming too much about students can lead to a mismatch between the learner and the instructional program. For example, if a sixth-grade teacher gives everyone in the class a sixth-grade text at the beginning of the school year, the teacher has assumed that all the students are reading at the level of the text and will profit from instruction at this level. This is a dangerous assumption to make. Teachers must verify that each student in the class can respond appropriately to assigned reading materials.

Similarly, faulty assumptions about individual students can lead to inappropriate teaching. Consider the following example: A fifth-grade teacher accurately determines each student's **instructional reading level** (grade level of material that is challenging but not frustrating for the student to read successfully with normal classroom instruction). Two boys, according to test results, are reading at third-grade level. The teacher gives both of them appropriate reading materials, assuming that instruction can proceed in a manner similar to that of a typical basal reading program, in this case, reading and reviewing stories and workbook exercises at the third-grade level. This teacher has done well in finding each boy's proper instructional reading level but has failed to pursue the *reasons* that each boy is unsuccessful with age-appropriate material. One boy may be reading at third-grade level because he is having difficulty with the word meanings and comprehension, while the other boy may be having difficulty recognizing the printed

---

Common assumptions classroom teachers should avoid.

FIGURE

3.1

1. Assuming a child has attained readiness for a particular learning
2. Assuming that a report card grade reflects the instructional level of a child
3. Assuming that a report card grade from one teacher means the same as that from another teacher
4. Assuming that all teachers develop independent reading habits in all pupils in the primary grades
5. Assuming that all teachers use instructional material diversified in difficulty and content in each grade
6. Assuming that readers having difficulty are able to use material on a frustration level of difficulty
7. Assuming that group instruction is the best method to meet the reading needs of all pupils
8. Assuming that a basal reader series constitutes an entire reading program
9. Assuming that children can learn a new skill without direct instruction
10. Assuming that children who read well will read widely
11. Assuming that teacher–pupil relationships are unimportant to reading growth
12. Assuming that mastery of reading skills and mastery of reading are identical
13. Assuming that instruction for "different" children is identical to instruction for "normal" children
14. Assuming that all children have the same capacity for learning
15. Assuming that reading deficiencies are nonexistent when the class average on standardized reading tests reaches or exceeds the norm
16. Assuming that the child's reading abilities remained unchanged over the summer
17. Assuming that individual difficulties in word analysis in the intermediate grades will correct themselves
18. Assuming that all materials are adequate and appropriate as corrective materials
19. Assuming that teachers make only fortunate assumptions

form of the words. Each needs a corrective program designed for his particular reading needs. After the learner is given appropriate materials (see Appendix A for readability methods to determine difficulty levels of materials), deeper analyses of strengths and weaknesses within that level are essential to avoid inappropriate teaching assumptions.

Assumptions have features similar to hypotheses. Both terms connote the involvement of a hunch or a notion about something. They differ in that the word *assumption* implies that the hunch is accepted or taken for granted, while the word *hypothesis* always implies tentativeness and the need for verification, after which acceptance or rejection occurs.

The Analytic Process Paradigm

A loose and unstructured corrective reading program, based on unverified assumptions, often perpetuates reading problems in the classroom. Employing the analytic process alleviates many of the unfortunate results of faulty teacher assumptions. The reason is that the analytic process follows a **paradigm**, or pattern. The teacher (1) examines reading behaviors (2) forms teaching hypotheses (3) teaches (4) reexamines reading behaviors. This paradigm can be expanded to allow for necessary specificity in terms of individual strengths and difficulties, and also to allow for *teacher* self-assessment. The process is simple in that it parallels a natural instructional progression; as you will see later in this chapter, however, it can become quite intricate when put to use, and requires a knowledgeable teacher—one who knows what to look for and how to interpret behaviors observed.

ANALYZING COMPONENTS OF THE READING PROCESS

Reading is recognized as a total dynamic and transactive process; representing its components in isolation and in static form is a distortion of the process itself. Some distortion is acceptable, however, if it helps one to better understand the process. For corrective reading purposes, reading behaviors must be analyzed to attain the level of specificity needed for direct instruction. Additionally, the kinds of materials students read and the nature of the methods, materials, and tasks used in the classroom, as well as the social and cultural environment of the classroom, must also be analyzed (see Appendix B for an instructional environment survey). This latter analysis can lead to *changes* in the teacher's methods, materials, tasks, and approach.

Figure 3.2 represents a conceptualization of the components involved in the reading process, *not the process itself.* The components discussed in this section are those frequently referred to in the literature, but they have been chosen arbitrarily. Little or no **empirical evidence**, evidence supported by experiment, verifies that these components do, in fact, exist and can be broken down into smaller sets and subsets that suggest a hierarchy of specific reading tasks. Keep in mind that the following is one way, not necessarily the only way, to analyze the reading process.

Study the figure to see how the parts are interrelated (as indicated by the arrows). While it may appear that fractionated reading subskills are being emphasized by efforts

FIGURE 3.2 Components of the reading process.

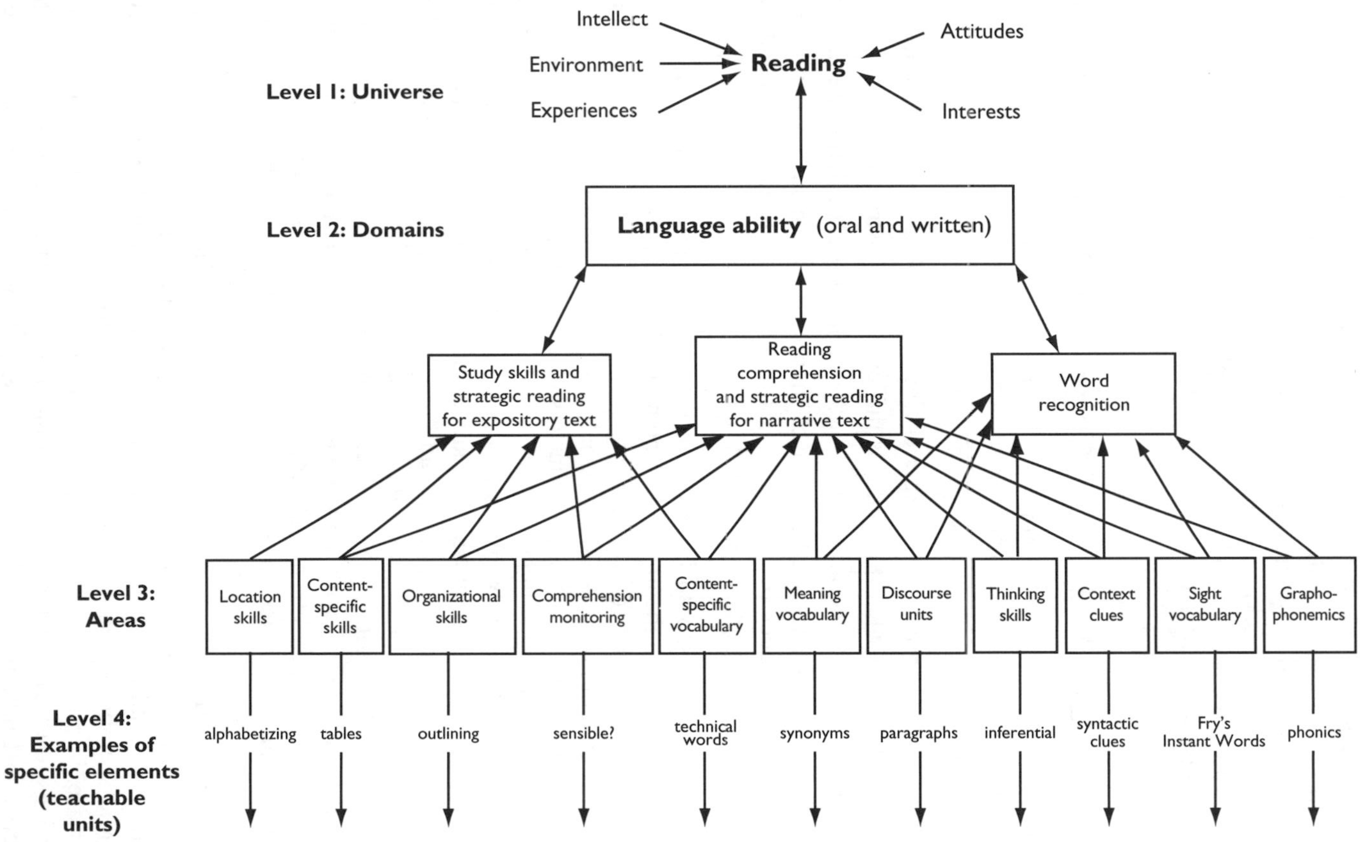

Level 1: Universe

Reading

Intellect
Environment
Experiences

Attitudes
Interests

Level 2: Domains

Language ability (oral and written)

Word recognition

Reading comprehension and strategic reading for narrative text

Study skills and strategic reading for expository text

Level 3: Areas

Location skills
Content-specific skills
Organizational skills
Comprehension monitoring
Content-specific vocabulary
Meaning vocabulary
Discourse units
Thinking skills
Context clues
Sight vocabulary
Grapho-phonemics

Level 4: Examples of specific elements (teachable units)

alphabetizing
tables
outlining
sensible?
technical words
synonyms
paragraphs
inferential
syntactic clues
Fry's Instant Words
phonics

to deal with components of the reading process, this is not the case. Analysis begins with the broadest element and, as necessary, proceeds to finer discriminations to determine specific areas for instruction. Notice that the figure also demonstrates the importance of universal influences that are part of the whole child (e.g., environment, intellectual ability, background experiences, attitudes and interests). Reading strategies that consider the whole student can be taught directly, and an attempt is made in this text to suggest appropriate ways to teach these strategies.

Four Levels of Analysis and Correlative Diagnostic Questions

Four levels of analysis are proposed. Each level has a correlative diagnostic question, and some questions have important related subquestions. The four correlative diagnostic questions are:

Level 1: Is the learner experiencing a lack of success in reading?

Level 2: In what domain(s) is difficulty demonstrated?

Level 3: In what area(s) within the domain(s) is difficulty demonstrated?

Level 4: What specific teachable unit(s) can be identified that will help the reader be more successful? Or, is the difficulty related to one of the universal influences?

The questions should be asked in sequence because the answer to each question directs the teacher to the appropriate point at which to proceed on the next level of analysis. As you read the following discussion, be aware that it describes an analysis that continues as though the learner has only one specific area of concern, which is unlikely. Corrective readers often have clusters of learning gaps; furthermore, certain fundamental difficulties preclude analysis in other domains. For example, if a student is having serious difficulty with word recognition, it is unlikely that comprehension can be adequately assessed. Some students are unable to construct the author's message (comprehension) because they cannot read the words. Therefore, the analytical process outlined here is not as precise as it may appear at first glance.

Because the reading process is complex, teachers should always approach analysis of reading difficulties with the knowledge that the resulting hypotheses may be imprecise or only partially correct. During the teaching phase, hypotheses and instructional practices can be verified, modified, and further adapted to the needs of the corrective reader. This again points out the integrated nature of instruction and assessment.

Although the emphasis appears to be on identifying areas of concern, the analytic process will also reveal strengths. Reading strengths play a crucial role in planning appropriate reading instruction and can be used to support the learner's efforts to overcome a specific difficulty. It is very important to determine those strategies the reader *does* use, in order to identify areas that can be further developed. The strengths a learner brings to reading determines the point at which instruction can begin. Thus, the attitude of instruction becomes one of "moving forward" as opposed to "catching up" (Jewell & Zintz, 1986). Specific techniques for implementing this, as well as for other aspects of the analytic process, are discussed in detail in later chapters.

Level 1: Determining Lack of Success in Reading

At this level of analysis only one diagnostic question needs to be answered:

- Is the learner experiencing a lack of success in reading?[1]

A teacher may find the answer to this question several ways. The most obvious way would be by listening to the student read. Teachers are strongly advised to collect information about each of their students' reading abilities, using the trade books, textbooks, readers, and skill development books available in the classroom. Informal reading inventories are also a common means of analyzing reading behaviors.

Another indication of reading ability may be the student's score on a standardized reading achievement test, usually readily available in the student's cumulative folder. But be careful not to let one test score identify the student's level of success. Reading achievement tests probably do a good job of identifying good readers, so by comparison teachers can identify students who have been unsuccessful. On the other hand, teachers must be careful not to assume that students who score high have the reading abilities necessary for any reading tasks not represented on the test (Farr & Carey, 1986).

The teacher may notice a discrepancy between a student's reading achievement test scores and mathematics achievement test scores. Reading difficulties *may* be indicated if the mathematics scores are higher. Or a reading achievement test score alone may suggest further analysis if, for example, the scores on the vocabulary and comprehension subtests vary significantly.

Using a student's achievement records, the teacher may expect to find one of three basic patterns (Kennedy, 1977):

1. From the beginning of formal reading instruction, the student failed to achieve as rapidly as average intellectual ability would warrant.
2. The student had a successful beginning, but progress gradually slowed.
3. The student had a successful beginning, but progress suddenly dropped.

The first pattern may reveal students whose test results are unduly influenced by some reading-related factor (see Chapter 4).

The second pattern may not be recognized until a student has already experienced difficulty. Teachers must be alert to the proportionate gains that a student makes through the years, as in the following example: Six-year-old Jody makes good progress through first grade and her end-of-the-year test shows an average level of achievement. By the end of second grade, Jody's achievement is slightly below average. At that point Jody's teacher might feel concern about her progress or decide that her score merely reflects the imprecise nature of tests. When the third-grade test reveals that Jody is further below average, however, this teacher should recognize the pattern and decide that Jody needs assistance.

The third pattern, good progress followed by a sudden drop, may have a number of causes. It may indicate an omission of instruction, an emotional factor interfering with the student's learning rate, such as a recent divorce or a death in the family, or something as simple as the student not feeling well on the day of the test. The teacher should continue with the analytic process to pinpoint possible learning gaps.

Level 2: Determining the Domain(s) in Which Difficulty Occurs

Once teachers have identified students displaying difficulty with reading, they must begin to determine where the difficulty lies. The reading process can be characterized

---

[1]It should be noted that for this question, as with *all* the diagnostic questions that follow, a follow-up question needs to be asked: "Under what conditions or in what situations?"

by certain universals, or reading-related factors, and the four major domains: *oral and written language ability, word recognition, comprehension and strategic reading for narrative text, and study skills* and *strategic reading for expository text* (this last domain is often referred to as "reading to learn," or content-area reading). Usually, a student exhibits difficulty within one or more of these domains and demonstrates strengths in others. The four primary diagnostic questions to be answered are as follows:

- Does the learner demonstrate underdeveloped oral and/or written language ability?
- Does the learner have difficulty with word recognition?
- Does the learner have difficulty with comprehension?
- Does the learner have difficulty with study skills or with strategic reading?

When the answer to a question in the second level of analysis is no, analysis in that domain ends. When the answer to a question is yes, that domain is analyzed further to define the difficulty more precisely. If the answer to *all* the questions in the second level of analysis is no, the teacher must consider reading-related factors and may require the help of a specialist to meet the needs of the student. If the answer to several of the questions is yes, the teacher should consider whether difficulty in one domain is influencing another and, if so, provide instruction in the dominant domain.

Level 3: Determining the Area(s) Within the Domain(s)

Experts disagree about dividing the domains into smaller segments. Some label the segments differently, and others resist the separation process even for the purpose of analysis. Thus, neither empirical data nor the consensus of experts directly supports the manner in which the domains will be segmented here for analytical purposes.

Despite these differences, the domains *are* divided into smaller parts for communication and instructional purposes. From a practical point of view, you should be aware that these areas are discussed at length in the literature, that the category labels can be found in many texts on developmental, corrective, and remedial reading, and that these smaller units are acknowledged and used in many reading systems today. Even for those with a holistic philosophy, the search for answers to why a student experiences a lack of success with literacy tasks must include consideration of these areas so that appropriate instructional opportunities can be developed.

Oral and written language ability. Referring again to Figure 3.2, notice that language ability spans the other three reading domains. This component of the reading process lies at its core and is of concern when a student performs very poorly on assessment instruments or when a beginning reader has trouble with simple reading tasks. A correlative diagnostic question to be asked when a student performs so poorly is:

- Does the learner demonstrate underdeveloped oral (i.e., speaking and/or listening) and/or written language ability?

Primary grade teachers are likely to ask this question often, and its frequency generally diminishes as grade level increases. However, teachers at all levels should ask themselves if their students have the oral and written language competence needed for a particular reading task. As the concept of emergent literacy implies, oral and written language competence develops only in a learning environment in which "children have frequent opportunities to use language and to hear or see language being used in meaningful, communicative contexts" (Rhodes & Dudley-Marling, 1988, p. 77). ESL (English as a Second Language) teachers are especially interested in providing such environments (see Chapters 2, 13).

Word recognition. If a student has difficulty with word recognition, more specific information must be sought by asking the following diagnostic questions:

- Does the learner have a word recognition strategy?
- Does the learner have difficulty in the area of sight vocabulary?
- Does the learner have difficulty in the area of word analysis?
- Does the learner have difficulty in the area of context clues?

Answers to these questions tell the teacher whether to terminate these particular lines of analysis or continue them to level 4. Chapter 8 details these areas of difficulty in word recognition and provides suggestions for assessment and instruction. The important point to remember here is that any area(s) associated with word recognition can be out of balance for a particular student. Many readers termed *disabled* have difficulties so severe that they are prohibited from reaching the heart of reading comprehension.

Reading comprehension and strategic reading for narrative text. Much has been learned about reading comprehension in recent years and it is clear that comprehension is deeply intertwined with memory, thinking, and language. When a student is reading with poor comprehension, the following diagnostic questions should be carefully considered:

- Does the learner have difficulty with meaning vocabulary?
- Does the learner have difficulty with thinking or problem-solving skills associated with comprehension of narrative text, such as identifying story features, predicting events, or evaluating a character's actions?
- Does the learner have difficulty recognizing his own inability to understand what was read?

Answers to these questions tell the teacher whether to terminate or continue the analysis in one or more of the areas listed.

Some students, especially those in the early elementary grades, appear to have trouble with comprehension when the difficulty actually lies in the domain of word recognition. Therefore, when students of any age are experiencing difficulty typically associated with first and second graders, teachers should ask the following question:

- Does this apparent comprehension problem result from difficulty with word recognition?

Similarly, especially in the upper grades, an apparent comprehension problem may in reality reflect difficulty with study skills and/or strategic reading of expository text. If the student is experiencing difficulty reading content-area material, the following question is suggested:

- Does the learner's apparent comprehension problem result from difficulty in study skills and/or strategic reading for expository text?

This question and the one preceding it probably should be considered transitional questions. They demonstrate how reading comprehension impacts the other domains discussed. Chapters 9 and 10 provide suggestions for assessment and instruction in the domain of reading comprehension.

Study skills and strategic reading for expository text. When students have problems in the domain of study skills and strategic reading of expository text, their abilities in this domain warrant deeper analysis. The following questions are suggested:

- Does the learner have difficulty locating information?
- Does the learner have difficulty organizing information?
- Does the learner have difficulty with content-specific vocabulary?
- Does the learner have difficulty with content-specific skills, such as reading visual displays, formulas, or other unique symbols?
- Does the learner have difficulty recognizing whether the text is meaningful to her?

The answers to these questions tell the teacher whether to continue analysis at level 4. Chapters 11 and 12 provide suggestions for assessment and instruction in the domain of study skills and strategic reading for expository text.

Level 4: Determining the Teachable Units Within Each Area

Within each of the areas identified at level 3 are specific learning segments or **teachable units** that would benefit the student. A teachable unit is defined as a bit of information small enough to be taught directly. For example, within the domain of study skills and strategic reading for expository text, one area is *location skills*. Within this area are several units that are important and teachable. Examples include learning to locate the table of contents, identify a chapter, or contrast the functions of a table of contents, an index, and a glossary. Because the number of teachable units is too great to be dealt with in this introductory chapter, they are discussed in the chapters presenting various instructional practices for the major literacy domains.

Components Outside the Major Domains: Reading-Related Factors

Almost all physical, psychological, and environmental problems may impede reading progress. For example, an inadequate background of experience, or one divergent from the majority of students in the class, can seriously affect comprehension, attitude toward reading, and perhaps the acquisition of word recognition strategies. Reading-related factors (see Chapter 4) must be considered independent entities that may adversely affect *any* area of the school curriculum, not just reading. These factors warrant considerable study and should be pursued in advanced coursework typically found at the graduate level.

Correlative diagnostic questions associated with reading-related factors include:

- Does this learner demonstrate the influence of a factor related to reading?
- Has this learner had opportunities for reading and writing related to his needs and interests? (In other words, is the learner possibly a "victim" of the curriculum or poor instruction?)

Poor attitudes toward and disinterest in reading hinder reading achievement. Teachers must ask questions about their students' attitudes and interests, their own teaching practices, and the curriculum itself, regardless of the domain in which the reading difficulty occurs:

- Does the learner have a negative attitude toward reading?
- Does the learner lack interest in reading?
- If someone asked my students, "What is reading?" what would they say?
- Is my curriculum so skills-oriented that students never have the opportunity to read for their own purposes? (See Appendix B for an instructional environment survey.)

The answers to the correlative diagnostic questions for these additional components are typically obtained not through tests but through observation, surveys, and interviews.

BASIC STEPS IN THE ANALYTIC PROCESS

In the previous section, the components of the reading process were partitioned into smaller units associated with the levels of analysis. This section provides information on the basic steps involved in the analytic process. These steps can be used to answer the questions posed for any of the domains, areas, or specific tasks mentioned earlier. The paradigm for the analytic process, mentioned earlier in this chapter, will now be expanded.

Examination of Reading Behaviors

Step 1: Gathering Information

Many sources of information about students are available to teachers. In addition to the learner, other sources of information include cumulative records (containing relevant medical information, test scores, grades); discussion with others who have had opportunities to observe the student inside the classroom (such as a previous teacher) and outside the classroom (such as parents); work samples (daily oral and written work, dated material such as that found in portfolios); and additional assessment measures (results of informal reading inventories, interest and attitude surveys, teacher-made and classroom-based measures). Assembling all available information possible about students is called **screening**, which simply means surveying a group of people in order to sort them in some way. Screening is of special interest for level 1 analysis and provides much of the information necessary to answer the question, "Is the learner experiencing a lack of success in reading?" This first step involves teacher action; the following steps represent the teacher's thought processes.

Step 2: Evaluating the Information

In this step, teachers judge the quality of the information gathered. They try to establish students' instructional reading levels, find a pattern or set of behaviors indicative of students' strengths and needs, and identify possible areas for development or assistance. If only such information as standardized test scores is available, teachers must verify these scores through other means. Most often teachers utilize classroom-based measures. Chapters 5 and 6 discuss specific assessment measures, and later chapters provide additional suggestions for classroom-based assessment of particular areas.

Steps 1 and 2 together are roughly equivalent to **diagnosis,** or identification of reading difficulties from behaviors. The outcome can range from a global diagnosis, as determined by the first and second levels of analysis, to identification of specific difficulties represented by the third and fourth levels. The teachable units eventually identified must then be translated into teaching objectives.

Generation of Possible Teaching Hypotheses

Step 1: Determining Alternatives

Once teachers have identified students needing assistance, they need to consider how best to provide that assistance. Numerous instructional procedures are available, and many of these will be detailed in the following chapters. For now, simply consider a **teaching hypothesis** to be an instructional plan based on a student's identified educational need.

Step 2: Selecting a Tentative Hypothesis

The teacher then evaluates the alternatives generated in step 1 and decides which instructional plan seems best for the particular student. This decision may be influenced by information regarding the student's interests or self-concept. Once an instructional plan is selected, the teacher develops lessons and the teaching phase begins. These plans are usually most effective when teacher and student(s) develop them together.

Teaching

Although corrective instruction may be designed for an individual's needs, it is often carried out in a small group. By providing group instruction to students having similar needs, classroom teachers are implementing effective classroom management. (Specific management ideas were introduced in Chapter 2.) Additionally, there are many alternative models of teaching, all with specific purposes and the power to help students learn (Joyce & Weil, 1986). Different purposes require different teaching models, so it is important for teachers to develop and use a large repertoire of teaching models. Two models are presented here—the Nondirective Teaching Model and the Direct Instruction Model.

Nondirective Teaching

When the instructional purpose is to help students set personal goals, the nondirective teaching model is an ideal choice. "The Nondirective Teaching Model focuses on *facilitating* learning . . . **Nondirective teaching** is student-centered in that the facilitator attempts to see the world as the student sees it . . . The primary means used is the nondirective interview strategy, a mode in which the teacher mirrors students' thoughts and feelings. By using reflective comments, the teacher raises the students' consciousness of their own perceptions and feelings, thus helping them clarify their ideas" (Joyce & Weil, 1986, p. 144).

Step 1: Catharsis

Students who have not been successful in literacy learning are likely to have some feelings about their struggles. For example, a student who is having difficulty with writing will likely feel tense or defensive when asked to write. The teacher's first step is to help the learner release those feelings so that other, more positive aspects of their writing can be explored. For example, the teacher might say, "When I'm asked to write a report for the school principal I have a hard time getting started—that makes me feel nervous and panicky. How do you feel when I ask you to write?"

Step 2: Insight

As students become aware of the reason(s) for their behaviors they can begin to more clearly see behavioral options. These new insights help the students set goals. Questions that might be asked at this step include:

- What is difficult for you as a writer (reader)?
- What is easy for you as a writer (reader)?
- What do good writers (readers) do?
- What are your goals as a writer (reader)?

Step 3: Integration

When students begin to take positive actions, these actions initially may be intermittent and/or unfocused but eventually begin to focus on a single area, giving students the direction they need.

Because the nondirective teaching model is student-centered, it is less activity-oriented and more a set of principles for interacting with students in response to a situation. Teacher questions and responses are aimed at initiating and maintaining conversation to help students clarify their own thinking. Some examples are:

- "How do you feel when that happens?"
- "Kind of like it doesn't matter what you do, it always turns out the same."
- "Maybe you feel you will be wrong."
- "It sounds to me like your reasons for your actions today are (restate student's reasons)"
- "The last idea you had was really strong. Could you explain it some more to me?"

One possible outcome of nondirective teaching is that students will begin to feel more in charge of their own learning.

Direct Instruction

Direct instruction refers to a model of teaching that is highly structured and teacher directed. This model can be particularly effective in helping readers who have difficulty understanding how to read more strategically; the teacher begins the lesson by providing "mental modeling" to share the reasoning processes involved in expert reading (Herrmann, 1988). Direct instruction, also referred to as "strategy lessons" (Slaughter, 1988), is necessary in any reading program. Such lessons are not always completed in one session with a student. More often, strategies will be learned and practiced over a series of sessions. Thus, a lesson may span several days.

Step 1: Direct Instruction/Modeling

The direct instruction model requires that the teacher be *actively* involved in the lesson by first explaining and then modeling or demonstrating the new concept or strategy.

Thus, once the particular strategy to be modeled has been identified, the teacher must plan how to introduce the lesson, what to say while modeling, and how to best show the reasoning process. Usually, a *thinking out loud* technique is used to reveal the actual reasoning process followed by the teacher while reading. For example, if the strategy to be modeled is prediction making, the teacher may decide to read a story to the class. After reading the title, the teacher stops, thinks out loud what the story might be about, *and states why.* The teacher proceeds with reading the story, stopping and thinking out loud at points that provide information confirming or rejecting earlier predictions, and always stating why the prediction was confirmed or not and how the text is helping to change the teacher's predictions.

Step 2: Structured Practice

Once the teacher has modeled a strategy, the students must be given the opportunity for **structured practice**, that is, to practice what has been demonstrated with the teacher still involved. In this way the teacher begins to determine the accuracy of the teaching hypothesis as well as the effectiveness of the lesson. The teacher is checking to see how accurately students have interpreted the modeling. Depending on students' responses, additional modeling may need to occur.

Step 3: Independent Practice

Independent practice provides an opportunity for students to apply what they have learned, without the teacher's help. This kind of practice gives further information on the accuracy of hypotheses and effectiveness of the lesson. If students seem unable or unwilling to participate in this independent practice, there are several possible reasons: the hypothesis may be inaccurate, the lesson may need to be revised, or students may not have developed the ability to work independently. In any case, providing for independent practice gives the teacher additional information.

Step 4: Evaluation Activity

The **evaluation activity** is a way of directly assessing the effectiveness of the lesson(s) and the accuracy of the hypothesis. These activities are usually teacher-made and relate directly to the kinds of tasks demonstrated in the modeling and practice. If the hypothesis was appropriate and learning occurred, opportunities for further practice should be provided; if the hypothesis was not appropriate, alternative hypotheses should be considered.

Reexamination of Reading Behaviors

Step 1: Gathering Information

This second examination of reading behaviors differs in several ways from the first. The first time the teacher gathers information about a student, it is essentially new information. This second examination of behaviors, however, follows an instructional sequence of events, making the analysis much more dependent on the teacher's insights and observations. This analysis overlaps considerably with the preceding teaching stage: as the teacher teaches, information is gathered.

Step 2: Evaluating the Information

This evaluation is based on information provided by the instructional sequence. The teacher must decide whether the lesson was effective and whether the teaching hypothesis was appropriate.

Step 3: Generating Possible Teaching Hypotheses

New hypotheses are needed if the lesson is effective and the desired behaviors are learned. New hypotheses are also needed if the original one was inappropriate because the teacher will proceed to a new lesson. In both instances, this step depends on the teacher's perceptions of the lesson and the results of the evaluation activity.

Step 4: Selecting a Teaching Hypothesis

Based on *all* the available information, a new hypothesis is selected and a lesson planned. This takes the teacher back into the teaching phase and the whole cycle begins again.

FROM TEACHING HYPOTHESES TO LESSON PLANS

Once a teaching hypothesis has been selected, the teacher designs a corresponding lesson plan or set of lesson plans. The lesson plan(s) depicts the manner in which the desired reading behavior is to be achieved. Good lesson plans for corrective reading contain three important elements: (1) specific learner objectives (2) procedures and materials designed to help the learners achieve the objectives (3) activities designed to assess whether the pupils have achieved these objectives.

Objectives

When working with corrective readers, objectives and teaching procedures emerge from the teacher's knowledge of each student. The typical steps of a directed reading lesson, such as motivation, introduction of new vocabulary, guided silent reading, oral rereading, and skill development, may or may not be the same for students receiving corrective instruction. More often, a corrective reading lesson deals with a specific reading strategy. For example, a teachable unit in using context clues may require several weeks or months of lessons. It becomes a major teaching strand with long-term goals (for more than one lesson) and specific lesson plan objectives, such as learning to identify certain words in a sentence as clues to what the unknown word might be.

If more than one reading domain is involved, as is likely, each should receive attention through instruction that integrates them as much as possible. Similarly, if several sessions on one area of concern are required, a variety of materials and procedures focusing on that area is needed. Teachers should try to provide diversity in learning activities to achieve the lesson objectives. For example, many instructional formats are available for teaching initial consonant blends through the use of children's literature, puzzles, and learning games. The effective teacher takes advantage of several of these techniques, utilizing different materials and procedures until the learner experiences several successful sessions.

Success experiences should always be interspersed within corrective instruction.

Every lesson should provide opportunities for students to do things they are able to perform well, even though the time spent this way may be minimal. This procedure helps counteract negative feelings the learner may be experiencing about the more challenging aspects of the lesson. Thus, each lesson includes learning activities that focus on areas of strength to enhance self-concept.

Teacher Objectives and Correlated Student Learning Objectives

Teachers, especially beginning teachers, are often understandably confused about objectives because they tend to think about objectives from the teacher's point of view rather than from the student-learning point of view. To avoid this confusion, teachers can state objectives from both perspectives. When writing teaching objectives you can begin with the words "To teach . . ." and specify the content you want to teach or the student wants to learn. The correlated student learning objective, which helps the teacher and student focus on student behavior, should be stated in terms of student performance because such objectives lend themselves to evaluation of the lesson's effectiveness. To use the earlier example of a teachable unit in context clues, the teacher's objective might be:

> To teach use of context clues to aid in figuring out words unknown in print.

> The correlated student learning objective might be:

> At the end of this lesson, the student will be given a portion of a language experience story having five sentences, each containing a blank followed by three word choices. The student will be able to underline words in the sentence that help in choosing the one word that correctly completes the sentence. The student should be able to complete 80%, or four of the five sentences, accurately.

Writing Student Learning Objectives

Student learning objectives should include three components: (1) the condition (2) the observable behavior (3) the criterion. The *condition* refers to the setting or context in which the behavior will occur. Following are examples:

> Using a 250-word section from a social studies text . . . Given a 10-item worksheet on sequence of events . . . Given a 100-word paragraph . . . Using a list of the 12 vocabulary words . . . During a silent reading of Taro Yashima's book *Umbrella* . . .

The *observable behavior* refers to that which the teacher expects the student to *demonstrate*. For best results, verbs that express observable behaviors should be used. While several types of observable behaviors can be prescribed, they fall into two general categories, motoric and verbal. Note that **overt behaviors** reflect the result of mental activities. Verbs that require unobservable, or **covert cognitive**, mental activity should be avoided because the activity cannot be verified easily. Covert cognitive activities can only be assumed to have happened if the resulting behaviors are observed. Examples of motoric, verbal, and covert cognitive verbs are as follows:

Motoric: point, circle, mark, write, underline
Verbal: say, read orally, tell, retell, paraphrase
Covert: know, learn, remember, decide, participate, listen

The primary strength of overt verbal behaviors is their ready accessibility to the teacher in a discussion–recitation setting. Answering the teacher's questions and reading orally are common verbal reading behaviors. Probably the greatest weakness of overt verbal behaviors is that they do not lend themselves to easy record keeping, particularly in a group or informal setting. Recording overt oral behaviors accurately requires that the teacher work with students individually. This may mean working directly with the student or listening to a taped reading by the student.

One means of recording oral behavior is the use of an informal reading inventory (discussed in Chapter 6). Even though the process of recording oral reading behaviors is time-consuming, the results are often highly beneficial to planning corrective instruction. Teachers are also strongly encouraged to jot down notes as they observe students throughout the day. These informal notes can be reviewed at the end of the day to assist in teacher decision making.

Motoric behaviors, especially marking or writing, have the advantage of being relatively permanent and readily scored. Motoric behaviors also can be recorded for more than one student at a time. Record keeping can be less time-consuming than recording and scoring oral reading behaviors for each student, although interpreting students' written products does require time and thought.

For learners who have not had many opportunities to write, writing words and sentences may be a difficult task. Those who experience reading difficulties often write and spell at a lower developmental level than that of their reading. This is all the more reason for these learners to be given opportunities to write, although the quantity of writing and spelling required to complete an activity might be limited initially until confidence increases. Multiple-choice questions that require marking and questions requiring short written answers are suggested, particularly if a written model is available for copying. If a daily writing journal is employed as an instructional practice, students' writing abilities will likely improve more rapidly. (More information about the reading/writing connection can be found in Chapter 7.)

The teacher should also try to balance the use of students' verbal and motoric behavioral responses in evaluation. Verbal behaviors can be used during the teaching phase of a lesson when the teacher judges pupil response on an informal, impressionistic basis. Motoric or writing behaviors, such as tests, workbook activities, and other independent practice activities, can be used primarily for ongoing assessment or evaluation.

The *criterion* element of a student learning objective serves as the basis for deciding whether the lesson helped the learner reach a higher performance level than earlier behaviors indicated. The criterion itself is a matter of subjective judgment, and the teacher needs to take into account the fact that certain strategies are learned over a period of time. Early in a corrective program the criterion level may be low, but as the student learns, this level is raised. For instance, the teacher and Bill agree that he needs to self-correct his miscues more often. If currently he *never* self-corrects, the initial criterion may call for Bill to self-correct "at least once." Later, after much instruction and practice, this criterion may be raised to "most miscues will be self-corrected." Examples of criteria are as follows:

. . . with 7 out of 10 correct . . . with 85 percent accuracy . . . at least 5 times

Following are two complete examples of student learning objectives:

Condition:	Following the shared reading of *Bringing the rain to Kapiti Plain,* and a mini-lesson on *long a* spelling patterns,
Behavior:	the student will make a list of words from the story that have a *long a* sound
Criterion:	with both of the two *long a* patterns in the story represented *(ai, aCE).*

Condition:	Given a 200-word paragraph from his language experience story,
Behavior:	Hue will read out loud and show evidence of self-monitoring by verbally correcting
Criterion:	at least half his miscues.

The value of student learning objectives is not in their precise writing. These objectives cannot be written at all unless the teacher has thought about the student's needs and how to go about helping the student. These objectives provide direction for the teacher as well as documentation for later reflection. Following a lesson, the teacher should review the student learning objective and ask questions such as: "Was this goal achieved? Why/why not? Is it still an important goal? Did I learn anything new about the student from this lesson? Should the goal be changed?"

Procedures

The heart of every lesson resides in the teaching procedures. Teachers' roles change rather dramatically from analyzing reading behaviors and forming teaching hypotheses to instructing. Teachers also use assessment procedures during their lessons. Wise teachers are constantly evaluating whether students are grasping the various points of the lesson. Those teachers who are able to "reflect-in-action" can modify lessons while they are ongoing (Schön, 1987).

When planning the procedures for a lesson, teachers should focus on two considerations: the steps in the lesson and the questions involved.

Planning the Steps

Procedural steps. Many steps, such as changing learning activities, reviewing the lesson, and preparing for independent practice activities, are procedural in nature. These steps are necessary but they are only peripheral to the teaching function, which is the focus here.

Teaching steps. The steps planned for teaching a student something new need to be considered quite carefully. Teachers have options, or alternative techniques, for presenting new concepts. For contrast, two are mentioned here: didactic (also called deductive) and discovery (also called inductive) teaching techniques. In **didactic**, or **deductive teaching**, new information is given to the pupil in a direct fashion. An example is "giving" the student a new word and telling him to learn it.

Teacher: Jimmy, the word is *tray, tray.* Now you say it.

The lesson may continue with the presentation of more new words and appropriate practice activities. This technique is direct, efficient, and often works well for specific purposes. It is limited, however, in that it provides little opportunity for students to be actively involved or to learn to generalize the specific word recognition process to other unknown words (**transfer of training**). To be sure, some learners are capable of making their own generalizations and transferring these learnings to other tasks. Typically, however, students having difficulty with reading also have trouble transferring what they have learned from one task to another. The discovery approach to teaching may better help these students learn the process (e.g., analyzing the word) as well as the product (the word itself, in this case).

In **discovery**, or **inductive teaching**, learners are encouraged to seek generalizations for themselves. The teacher's function is to observe the ways students carry out this process and to provide reinforcement and additional clues to aid learning when they are needed. Providing clues helps prevent undue frustration if pupils have trouble making the "discovery." The teacher also helps students learn how to discover knowledge, that is, the transfer process itself. The word *tray* can again be used as an example.

Teacher:	Jimmy, you have told me this word in your story is a new word (teacher points to the word *tray* in the sentence, *The cookie tray fell down*). How can you figure it out?
Jimmy:	(No response)
Teacher:	Look at the rest of the words in the sentence. Do they help you?
Jimmy:	(No response)
Teacher:	Do you see anything or any part of this word you might already know?
Jimmy:	It starts the same as train.
Teacher:	Good! Anything else?
Jimmy:	No.
Teacher:	How about the ending?
Jimmy:	Well, it ends like *say* and *may*.
Teacher:	Yes, go on.
Jimmy:	Tr-tr-tr-ay–tray. I think it's *tray*.
Teacher:	Very good, Jimmy. Now let's check it out in the sentence to see if it makes sense.
Jimmy:	The cookie *tray* fell down. Yes, that makes sense. The new word is *tray*.
Teacher:	That's great, Jimmy. You are becoming a good word detective. Let's make a card for your word bank . . . great! Now, on the back of the card I want you to write a new sentence using the word *tray* (or the teacher can write a dictated sentence). Then you can practice this word later so you can read it quickly. If you have trouble remembering this word, turn your card over and read your sentence for help. You might also want to add this word to your personal dictionary with a picture and your new sentence.

Notice how much more teacher time and effort are involved when the discovery approach is used. But notice also that the teacher is getting the pupil actively involved in developing a strategy for analyzing unknown words. The minimal clues given to the learner and the use of ample praise for risk taking help reduce negative feelings of failure and frustration.

Planning the Questions

The second important consideration when planning a lesson is questions that may help the students during the lesson. The teacher cannot always plan the exact questions but should be prepared to use certain types of questions during the lesson. Two types are discussed in this section, and the use of teachers' questions is addressed frequently throughout the remainder of this text.

Problem-solving questions. The use of **problem-solving questions** is to move a student from thinking "I don't know the answer" to a more dynamic frame of mind equivalent to "How can I try to solve this problem?" An example of this type of question taken from the previous dialogue is:

"How can you figure out the word, Jimmy?"

Often a question of this type signals subtly to the pupil that the teacher is accepting of lack of knowledge—that it is okay if a person does not know the word or answer. The student can then focus on the problem without feeling a sense of embarrassment or failure if a guess is wrong. The teacher thereby increases the probability that active student participation will occur without the learner feeling threatened.

Facilitating questions. Pupils frequently are not able to solve a problem on their own. A second type of question, called a **facilitating question**, encourages continued thinking. The purpose of facilitating questions is to make discovery easier for the learner. Examples are paraphrased from the previous dialogue:

"Do the rest of the words in the sentence help you?"
"Do you see any part of this word you might know?"

Some facilitating questions encourage pupils to *focus* on a point they may have overlooked:

"How about the ending of the word?"

Other facilitating questions present clues in the form of questions:

"Do you think the new word ends like these that you already know?" (The teacher writes or says appropriate examples.)

Facilitating questions demonstrate the teacher's efforts to guide students to discovery through active participation. In the example the teacher wants Jimmy to learn the word *tray*, but all that effort to teach one word is hardly justifiable. The underlying purpose of this activity is to help students learn part of the process involved in figuring out new words. The teacher and students focus on the process of analyzing a particular word so that the steps in the thought processes can be learned and so that the general thinking strategy practiced here by Jimmy with the aid of his teacher will eventually transfer to other unknown words that he encounters when the teacher is not present.

One purpose of problem-solving and facilitating questions is to help the pupil actively seek answers to the immediate question. Far more important, however, is their role in helping students develop independent thinking strategies that can be applied to many other situations.

Assessment During the Lesson

This section has briefly illustrated the teaching task and discussed significant parts of lesson planning. One important issue remains. During the lesson, while the teacher is teaching, the opportunity for direct assessment of student learning is always present. The most expeditious way to assess directly is to ask questions during the course of the lesson that elicit oral responses. The teacher asks a question or a set of questions about each point being taught. Asking for examples or illustrations also provides assessment information. If the teacher is reviewing content recently taught, the lesson should be opened with general questions that start with "Who remembers . . ." or "Can someone tell us . . ." If the students are having trouble the teacher can give clues or hints, which often can be stated as facilitating or focusing questions.

One good teaching procedure is to provide a brief, structured practice session on the topic, but with new examples for students to solve. Corrective readers often learn content more quickly if they can practice with the teacher and classmates. Misperceptions and incorrect learnings can be corrected immediately. A written worksheet, or chalkboard or transparency practice on the topics, provides a common focus for the group and helps prepare them for any evaluation activity that may follow.

Once teachers become familiar with their students, they can use the structured practice session as a guide to the students' readiness to take a quiz or to participate in some other evaluation activity. If the students do poorly during practice, the quiz should be deferred and further instruction or a second practice period given.

A COMPLETE LESSON

The outline below, representing the basic steps in the analytic process, should serve as a general guide to and summary of this process. It is generally applicable to all of the components involved in the reading process.

1. Examine reading behaviors
   a. Gather information
   b. Evaluate information
2. Generate possible teaching hypotheses
   a. Identify several alternatives
   b. Select a tentative hypothesis
3. Teach (decide upon appropriate teaching model)
   a. Use nondirective teaching
      1) Encourage student catharsis
      2) Facilitate student insight
      3) Encourage integration of thought and action
      4) Reflect on interaction with student
   b. Use direct instruction
      1) Provide modeling
      2) Provide structured practice with teacher
      3) Allow independent practice
      4) Provide evaluation activity/reflect on lesson
4. Reexamine reading behaviors
   a. Gather information
   b. Evaluate information
   c. Generate teaching hypotheses
   d. Select a teaching hypothesis

It is important to recognize the link between 3a4 and 3b4, the evaluation/reflection at the end of the lesson, and 4a, 4b, and 4c, the gathering and evaluating of information, and generating of new teaching hypotheses. Teaching and assessment often occur simultaneously. Without evaluation or reflection on the lesson, the analytic process is incomplete. Furthermore, if a teacher never examines student artifacts and chooses to use only observational evaluation procedures, judgment of student learning has not been adequately verified. Thus, the teacher *assumes* the lesson was learned, and that assumption is subject to the pitfalls of assumptive teaching. While a written evaluation activity is not needed for every student for every lesson, the risk of assuming learning has taken place is much higher for students having reading difficulties.

Figure 3.3 presents an example of a plan for one session in a series of sessions in which the K-W-L strategy (see Chapter 12) is being learned. Following a direct instruction model, the teacher has previously modeled the strategy and has provided structured and independent practice with the new strategy. This session represents a review of the student's ability to independently complete a K-W-L strategy sheet. [Note that the material in brackets in Figure 3.3 is explanatory material for you, the reader, and not part of the lesson plan.]

FIGURE 3.3

Sample lesson plan.*

Teacher's Name:	Session #14
Date:	Child's Name
School:	Age: 10, Grade: 5

Goal: *[This is the purpose and rationale for the lesson from the teacher's perspective.]*
I intend to use this session to complete the K-W-L strategy lesson on Harriet Tubman that we began last week for the purpose of enhancing J.'s comprehension, particularly with informational text. I assume that J. has taken some time over the weekend to review the passage that she read silently at our last meeting (see session #13 for reference), and has continued to record information on the K-W-L strategy sheet. I will also give J. the opportunity to expand her knowledge in particular categories, which she suggested, dealing with the subject.

Procedures: *[How will you go about achieving your goal?]*

1. J. will display the work done on her own at home and we will discuss the items she listed under the heading "What We Learned." (A copy of her chart is available.) We will go on to discuss information about Harriet Tubman that J. would like to investigate further.
2. We will take turns reading particular (i.e., favorite) sections from the Harriet Tubman book aloud. I will choose sections that deal with the topics J. chose as wanting to learn more about.
3. J. will then record suggestions of subtopics for further research in other materials (e.g., encyclopedia, social studies text).
4. I will give J. the opportunity to read, or have read to her, the book *Harriet and The Promised Land,* by Jacob Lawrence.

Evaluation: *[How will you know your goal has been achieved? What will the student be able to do to convince you that your lesson was effective; in other words, what is the student learning objective?]*
Given a brief, teacher-made cloze passage, J. will be able to identify and write in the blanks at least five pieces of information on the subject of Harriet Tubman. (Completed passage is available.)

continued

FIGURE

3.3

Reflection: *[Reflections provide an analysis of the lesson, not a blow-by-blow description of the lesson's procedures. It is important to discuss the outcome of any evaluation activity, and what those results indicate for the next lesson. It is also important to evaluate your own teaching effectiveness as well as the effectiveness of the procedures you used. Try to summarize from this specific experience to teaching in general, what did you learn that will help you in your professional growth?]*

The K-W-L strategy employed in this lesson to help J. recognize and identify significant information within informational text was apparently quite successful. J. completed the entire cloze passage with 100% accuracy! She was so proud! In addition, something I added to the lesson plan procedures during the lesson: J. was able to comprise a list of four facts that she already knew about the subject, Harriet Tubman, and give suggestions about information that might be acquired from an encyclopedia passage (we were able to begin this research project). As J. began to read the encyclopedia passage, she became very excited every time information she was to look for was "right there." Therefore, I believe the "What We Want to Find Out" portion of the K-W-L strategy was most beneficial to J. She was able to see that information that she herself suggested had substantial value, and also that this step of the strategy is an important one. The bits of information and the questions that J. posed were able to be answered immediately in the reading. Great instant feedback! From the text *Harriet and The Promised Land,* J. chose to add three new words to her vocabulary file box: fowl, chariot, and disguise.

I felt so good about this sequence of lessons using the K-W-L strategy. It works great for informational text, especially since this type of text is often difficult and seemingly boring to students. It really provides the student with direction and a purpose for reading. I think I could use this strategy too with my college texts! J. promises she will use her K-W-L charts again—I hope she will. I think the lessons went well because I took it slow. I modeled the use of the chart first with a short passage; then we worked together on the Harriet Tubman book. It is also an easy strategy to catch on to. Even though it took three sessions to complete, it was worth it. J. really understands the benefits of using the strategy. When she was able to get a perfect score on the cloze passage she realized the benefit of the strategy. That's why I think she just might continue to use it.

I learned how important it is to model new strategies, or really anything you want students to do, so students are clear about what to do. It is also important that they be able to experience some success with the new strategy so they can appreciate its value. Since J. is still interested in this topic, we will continue to search for answers to her questions.

*Special thanks to Stacy Scarpero, a university student, for agreeing to share this lesson plan.

SUMMARY

In this chapter, the analytic process has been defined and explained. The analytic process is contrasted with assumptive teaching and a justification for the process is presented.

A large portion of this chapter discusses the components of the reading process. The reading universe is partitioned into the major domains of oral and written language ability, word recognition, comprehension, study skills and strategic reading, and additional components such as linguistic diversity and reading-related factors. When necessary, each of the domains can be analyzed to identify areas for instruction, such as context clues. Continued analysis ultimately leads to specific teachable units within each area, for example, learning to use word order clues. Important correlative diagnostic questions related to each level of analysis and the additional components affecting the domains are presented.

Another major section of this chapter deals with moving from the formation of teaching hypotheses to the preparation of lessons. Examples of teacher and student learning objectives are provided. Two teaching models, nondirective and direct instruction, are explained. Procedures for lessons include determining the steps for deductive and inductive teaching. Problem-solving and facilitating questions, designed to promote active learner involvement and transfer of thought processes, are discussed. Finally, a complete lesson plan is presented.

SUGGESTED READINGS

Herrmann, B.A. (1988). Two approaches for helping poor readers become more strategic. *The Reading Teacher, 42,* 24–28.

This article provides explicit examples of teaching procedures helpful for working with students having reading difficulty. The examples include the actual dialogue between the teacher and student.

Joyce, B., & Weil, M. (1986). *Models of teaching,* (3d ed.). Englewood Cliffs, NJ: Prentice-Hall.

This text contains a wealth of examples of teaching models. Must reading for teachers who are always looking to expand their teaching repertoire.

Schön, D.A. (1987). Teaching artistry through reflection-in-action. Chapter 2 in *Educating the reflective practitioner*. San Francisco, CA: Jossey-Bass.

This chapter provides an in-depth look at the concept of reflecting-in-action. While difficult reading, it is important for beginning professionals to understand that enhanced professional practice requires continued learning throughout one's career.

Spiegel, D.L. (1992). Blending whole language and systematic direct instruction. *The Reading Teacher, 46,* 38–44.

This commentary discusses the value of systematic direct instruction and attempts to point out that such instruction is not incongruent with the whole language philosophy.

CHAPTER

4

READING-RELATED FACTORS

OBJECTIVES

After you have read this chapter, you should be able to

1. identify three basic categories of reading-related factors associated with reading difficulties;
2. explain the teacher's role with regard to each of the basic categories of reading-related factors;
3. recognize symptoms of poor general health or possible visual, auditory, or neurological problems;
4. prepare objective anecdotal records;
5. suggest ways to establish a classroom environment that might help alleviate the stress for a student with mild emotional adjustment problems.

KEY CONCEPTS AND TERMS

affect
at-risk
attentive listening
attributional retraining
auditory acuity
auditory blending
auditory comprehension
auditory discrimination
auditory memory
auditory perception
bibliotherapy
cognition
emotional maltreatment

intelligence
listening
non-reading factors
physical abuse
physical neglect
psychomotor
reading-related factors
sexual abuse
variables
visual acuity
visually impaired
visual perception

STUDY OUTLINE

OVERVIEW

For many years educators and others have been concerned because too many students fail to learn to read, or read so ineffectively that eventually the struggle leads to avoidance of reading altogether. All teachers will find such students in their classrooms and should be prepared to help them as much as they can. The list of potential causes for reading failure is long and includes such factors as lack of or inappropriate experiences, emotional blocking, lack of motivation, poor health, hunger, inability to perceive objects and sounds, dysfunction of the central nervous system, processing problems, low intelligence, and poor teaching. Only one factor in this list, poor teaching, can be directly controlled and substantially changed by educators. The remaining factors (plus many others) are not directly related to teaching reading, but are important to all learning; thus they are referred to as **reading-related factors**, or **non-reading factors**.

Other (non-teaching) professionals and concerned citizens often condemn the teaching profession for not assuming responsibility for correcting the problems presented by factors that arise and are perpetuated outside the school setting. This condemnation is unjustified without considering the sources of the problems and assigning responsibility to others as well.

Teachers are not physicians, psychologists, or sociologists; reading problems caused by non-instructional factors must be treated in concert with specialists in other disciplines. Many school systems today appropriately use interdisciplinary teams to work through these problems.

Although classroom teachers without advanced training in clinical reading are not expected to have in-depth knowledge of reading problems based outside the school and classroom, they must be aware of some important factors that may contribute to reading difficulties. One purpose of this chapter is to raise the awareness level regarding contributing causes to serious reading difficulties. With increased awareness, teachers should become more confident in observing and documenting behaviors and physical symptoms that suggest a reading-related factor. They can then describe these observations to appropriate specialists who, in turn, can help decide whether a reading-related factor is involved. Teachers thus serve as screening agents.

Teachers in the early grades have the first opportunity to observe these behaviors and symptoms. If they refer young children promptly, much can be done to alleviate contributing causes before they become the basis of severe reading problems.

HISTORICAL BACKGROUND

The interest in concomitant factors associated with reading failure originated to a great extent with clinicians from other disciplines. They observed that many of their clients and patients also had reading problems. These observations suggested further study to determine if, in fact, the concomitant factors were causing reading difficulties. Many studies conducted early in the twentieth century compared good and poor readers to determine the incidence of specific factors. In general, these early studies, referred to as "head count" studies, revealed that students labeled "reading-disabled" exhibited concomitant non-reading factors more frequently than good readers did. This finding held for several different types of reading-related factors.

More recent correlational studies tend to verify the findings of the earlier "head count" studies. These studies yield relatively high correlations between two factors, or **variables**, the factor of reading development and whatever non-reading factor is being investigated. Unfortunately, many people have misinterpreted the results of these correlational studies. The proper interpretation of high correlation coefficients is that the *relationship* between reading achievement and the other factor is high. The conclusion that the non-reading factor caused the reading difficulty (or vice versa) *cannot* be drawn from a correlational study, because an unknown factor may be influencing both the non-reading factor and level of reading achievement.

Another research approach identifies a large group of people exhibiting a particular non-reading factor and assesses their performance in reading. Such studies often reveal a wide range of reading achievement scores, indicating that some people with the factor read satisfactorily and some do not. Those who read well somehow compensate for the non-reading factor. Therefore, it is extremely important for teachers and others to know that the presence of a particular non-reading factor is no guarantee that the student will not learn to read. It *is* reasonable to conclude, however, that the presence of the non-reading factor may impede reading progress. Furthermore, when a student manifests the presence of two or more non-reading factors, the chances for success in reading are lessened and the student is considered **at-risk**. The multiple causation hypothesis (Monroe, 1932; Robinson, 1946) must be considered seriously, but in no way as an excuse for not providing the best instruction for the student.

THREE BASIC CATEGORIES

Factors associated with reading difficulties can be placed in one of three basic categories: physical (including neurophysical), psychological, and environmental, which includes instructional factors. Teachers, by the very nature of their role and their training, should be held responsible for instructional factors associated with poor reading achievement. Thus, this text focuses on helping teachers identify students making poor progress in reading and provide appropriate instruction for these students. The improvement of reading instruction through better informed teachers is a major goal of this text.

Physical Factors

General Health

Learning to read is a demanding task for many students. A student must be alert, attentive, and capable of working for a sustained period of time. Any physical condition that lowers the level of stamina or impairs vitality can have a deleterious effect on learning. Serious illnesses and prolonged absences from school obviously may result in learning gaps. Many conscientious parents and teachers work hard to alleviate such problems; homebound instruction is also provided by many school systems for students who are bedridden or otherwise incapacitated for extended periods of time.

More subtle forms of illness and physical problems sometimes elude parents and teachers. Chronic low-grade infections, glandular disturbances, allergies, and persistent minor illnesses such as mild respiratory problems can induce a general malaise and lower the vitality level. Insufficient sleep may inhibit learning, and malnutrition may lower ability to attend and learn.

Teachers, of course, are not physicians and cannot appropriately assume medical responsibilities. Yet they do function as substitute parents while school is in session and must be sensitive to the general well-being of each student in their class. When teachers are concerned about possible health problems, they should seek help from the school nurse and principal. Communication with the parents should be initiated according to local school policies.

Occasionally teachers encounter parents who resist counseling efforts regarding their child's health. Little can be done to help the student directly when this happens. If the problem is serious enough, however, legal procedures can be instigated. Usually other community agencies, such as the child welfare department, become involved in these cases.

When students are not in good health, teachers must try to accommodate their problems as much as possible. Let these students rest, put their heads on their desks, go to the nurse's office, or whatever seems reasonable for the particular problem involved.

Visual Acuity

Visual acuity is keenness of vision. Acuity problems are usually physiologically based and can be corrected by ophthalmologists or optometrists. The role of the classroom teacher is to identify students with visual acuity problems that may have gone unnoticed by parents or other teachers.

While some students learn to read in spite of visual problems, the emphasis here is not so much on the relationship to reading difficulty as it is on comfort and efficiency. When students can deal comfortably with print at normal near-point distance (about 14 to 18 inches), the chances are good that they will be able to attend to a task as long as is necessary. Discomforts such as headaches or burning or watery eyes diminish their chances considerably. Learners who see relatively clearly work more efficiently for longer periods of time without having to direct undue energy to accommodate visual deficiencies.

Assessment techniques. Some school systems hire reading (or other) specialists who are trained to help identify students with vision problems. Even with special training, however, these people are not vision specialists, and their work should be considered as screening only. Instruments typically used for screening purposes are the *Keystone School Vision Screening Test* (Keystone View) and the *Master Ortho-Rater Visual Efficiency Test* (Bausch and Lomb). Other devices often used for the screening of vision are the *Rader Visual Acuity Screening Chart* (Modern Education Corporation), the *Snellen Chart*, and the *Spache Binocular Reading Test* (Keystone View).

Probably the most important assessment function for classroom teachers is to observe the behavior of their students. The Optometric Extension Program Foundation Inc. (in Thau, 1991) has compiled an excellent checklist to help teachers make reliable observations of visual behavior that could interfere with academic progress (Figure 4.1). If several of these behaviors are observed, the teacher should refer the student to an appropriate vision specialist, whether inside or outside of the school setting.

Teachers' responsibilities. The classroom teacher does not initiate correction of visual acuity problems. These problems are often resolved through proper prescription of glasses. If the vision specialist believes a problem can be corrected through visual therapy, such activities typically are conducted by the parents under a doctor's supervision or by special teachers working with the student on a one-to-one basis outside the regular classroom.

Classroom teachers should ensure the best possible conditions to accommodate the needs of students having mild vision problems. Students with far-point problems (i.e., myopia, or nearsightedness) should be able to see the chalkboard better when their desks are closer to it. Prescription lenses will reduce this problem, as they will farsightedness (i.e., hyperopia) and astigmatism. Ample light is necessary, and students should be reminded occasionally to rest their eyes after lengthy reading assignments. Ease of reading rather than speed should be emphasized.

For students who have been classified as **visually impaired**, sightsaving books printed in large type (12 to 24 point) can be requested for use in regular classrooms (see Suggested Readings at the end of this chapter for sources of large-print materials). Visually impaired students function quite well in a regular classroom. In addition to large-print materials, methods using tactile discrimination and word tracing are useful.

Visual Perception

Visual perception skills include visual discrimination of form, visual closure, constancy, and visual memory. A student may have normal visual acuity skills but underdeveloped visual perception skills.

Visual discrimination of form, a skill commonly referred to as visual discrimination, requires recognizing similarities and differences between letters and words in reading. For example, the student must be able to distinguish between *H* and *K* or *c, e,* and *o.*

Visual closure is the ability to identify or complete, from an incomplete presentation, an object, picture, letter, or word. The student must identify the whole even though the whole is not provided. For example, the student must be able to recognize that

needs another feature or that has teeth missing or

that f__tb_ll represents the word football.

Educator's checklist: Observable clues to classroom vision problems.

Student's name _____ Date _____

1. Appearance of eyes:
One eye turns in or out at any time _____
Reddened eyes or lids _____
Eyes tear excessively _____
Encrusted eyelids _____
Frequent styes on lids _____

2. Complaints when using eyes at desk:
Headaches in forehead or temples _____
Burning or itching after reading or desk work _____
Nausea or dizziness _____
Print blurs after reading a short time _____

3. Behavioral signs of visual problems:
A. *Eye movement abilities (Ocular motility)*
Head turns as reads across page _____
Loses place often during reading _____
Needs finger or marker to keep place _____
Displays short attention span in reading or copying _____
Too frequently omits words _____
Repeatedly omits "small" words _____
Writes up or down hill on paper _____
Rereads or skips lines unknowingly _____
Orients drawings poorly on page _____

B. *Eye teaming abilities (binocularity)*
Complains of seeing double (diplopia) _____
Repeats letters within words _____
Omits letters, numbers, or phrases _____
Misaligns digits in number columns _____
Squints, closes or covers one eye _____
Tilts head extremely while working at desk _____
Consistently shows gross postural deviations at all desk activities _____

C. *Eye-hand coordination abilities*
Must feel things to assist in any interpretation required _____
Eyes not used to "steer" hand movements (extreme lack of orientation, placement of words or drawings on page) _____
Writes crookedly, poorly spaced, cannot stay on ruled lines _____
Misaligns both horizontal and vertical series of numbers _____
Uses hand or fingers to keep place on the page _____

Uses other hand as "spacer" to control spacing and alignment on page _____
Repeatedly confuses left–right directions _____

D. *Visual form perception (visual comparison, visual imagery, visualization)*
Mistakes words with same or similar beginnings _____
Fails to recognize same word in next sentence _____
Reverses letters and/or words in writing and copying _____
Confuses likenesses and minor differences _____
Confuses same word in same sentence _____
Repeatedly confuses similar beginnings and endings of words _____
Fails to visualize what is read either silently or orally _____
Whispers to self for reinforcement while reading silently _____
Returns to "drawing with fingers" to decide likes and differences _____

E. *Refractive status (nearsightedness, farsightedness, focus problems, etc.)*
Comprehension reduces as reading continues; loses interest too quickly _____
Mispronounces similar words as continues reading _____
Blinks excessively at desk tasks and/or reading; not elsewhere _____
Holds book too closely; face too close to desk surface _____
Avoids all possible near-centered tasks _____
Complains of discomfort in tasks that demand visual interpretation _____
Closes or covers one eye when reading or doing desk work _____
Makes errors in copying from chalkboard to paper on desk _____
Makes errors in copying from reference book to notebook _____
Squints to see chalkboard, or requests to move nearer _____
Rubs eyes during or after short periods of visual activity _____
Fatigues easily; blinks to make chalkboard clear up after desk task _____

The concept of *constancy* is a factor when a figure, letter, or word remains the same regardless of a change in shape, orientation, size, or color. This concept is critical for reading because many types of print are used and students must not be confused by slight changes, for example, *a* and a. Also, many letters that are the same in shape are different letters because of their orientation, or placement: for example, *b* and *d; p* and *q;* or *n, u,* and *c.* In the world of objects, orientation has never made a difference—a chair is a chair no matter which way you turn it. However, when dealing with letters and words, orientation can make a difference.

Visual memory is the ability to remember the sequence of letters in words. This ability is most obviously reflected in spelling; however, it is also important in reading when words are encountered having the same or many similar letters but a different sequence. For example, a student lacking in visual memory may have difficulty distinguishing between *ate, eat,* and *tea.* Many mature readers have to tax their visual memory skills upon encountering *through, though,* and *thorough.*

Assessment techniques. There are several standardized instruments that assess visual discrimination, visual closure, constancy, and visual memory skills. The following are examples:

- *Clymer-Barrett Prereading Battery,* Personnel Press
- *Gates-MacGinitie Readiness Skills Test,* Riverside
- *Macmillan Reading Readiness Skills Test,* Macmillan
- *Metropolitan Readiness Tests,* The Psychological Corporation
- *Murphy-Durrell Reading Readiness Analysis,* The Psychological Corporation

If teachers know the characteristics of the various visual perception skills, they can develop classroom activities to assess these visual abilities. Worksheets can be easily prepared that request students to identify the "same letter or word." (e.g., o l c o c e; cake l coke cake coke) or the "letter or word that is different" (e.g., b b o b ; bed bad bed bed).

Visual closure tasks at an early stage usually involve picture or shape completion tasks. In the following example, the student is asked to complete the second drawing so it looks like the first.

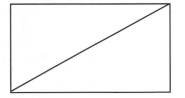 

Constancy is often assessed as a specially designed visual discrimination task. Again, finding the "alikes" or "differents" is the direction, for example: d l b b b d or p l p q p.

Visual memory is more difficult to assess. Initially, the teacher may use a modification of the party game in which several objects are presented on a tray for viewing, then covered, and participants are asked to write down as many as they can remember. For classroom use, three or four objects may be shown. The teacher then covers them, removes one, shows the remaining objects, and asks the student what was removed.

Letters and words can be assessed in a similar fashion. A word or letter is shown for about two seconds. The student is then asked to locate the word or letter from a list of words or letters. Consistently poor performance on spelling tests or in written work beyond third or fourth grade may also indicate a need for visual memory practice.

Teachers' responsibilities. Many practice activities are readily available to teachers in developmental reading texts and activity books for helping students develop visual perception skills. Some of the more representative exercises are provided here.

1. Have the student mark the letter that is like the one at the beginning of the row:
   B I E B D
2. Direct students to identify "what's missing?" in a picture.
3. Direct the students to mark the letter or letter group that looks like the first item in each row:

   ap I   pa   la   ap
   bl I   lb   bl   bi
   du I   du   bu   ud
4. Show the student a series of letters, remove the series, and have the student write from memory what was seen. Reshow the series if necessary until the student succeeds.

Auditory Acuity

Auditory acuity is keenness of hearing. Students obviously need to hear adequately in school. Students with high-tone hearing deficits have more difficulties learning to read than those with low-tone deficits. The consonants that give distinction and meaning to speech in our language are relatively high-pitched (especially *s, l* and *t*), whereas vowel sounds are lower in pitch. Most teachers of young children are female, and their voices are higher than those of males. Thus, it is understandable why high-tone deficits might be more critical than low-tone deficits when teaching young children to read. Much early reading work involves oral–aural participation. Successful performance with phonics activities also requires good auditory acuity.

Hearing loss is a medical matter best handled by a hearing specialist or otologist. The teacher can be of considerable help, however, by identifying students suspected of having hearing deficits.

Assessment techniques. Screening for auditory acuity with an audiometer is a reliable procedure. However, teachers must be specially trained in the use of this sensitive instrument, and even then, results should be considered tentative. Students who do not pass the audiometric screening should be referred to a hearing specialist in the school or to other proper personnel for professional diagnosis. Reliable audiometers for school use are manufactured by Beltone, Grason-Stadler, Maico, and Zenith. Different models are available for both group and individual assessment procedures.

Classroom teachers must be sensitive to and observant of behaviors or physical symptoms that suggest hearing loss. The list of common symptoms in Figure 4.2 (Kennedy, 1977, p. 391) will help the teacher identify students who should be seen by the school nurse, speech and hearing specialist, or reading specialist. A decision can then be made whether to suggest medical assistance.

F I G U R E

4.2

Checklist of symptoms of hearing difficulties.

	Yes	No
Inclines one ear toward speaker when listening	_____	_____
Holds mouth open while listening	_____	_____
Holds head at angle when taking part in discussion	_____	_____
Reads in unnatural tone of voice	_____	_____
Uses faulty pronunciation on common words	_____	_____
Has indistinct enunciation	_____	_____
Often asks to have instructions and directions repeated	_____	_____
Breathes through mouth	_____	_____
Has discharge from ears	_____	_____
Frequently complains of earache or sinusitis	_____	_____
Has frequent head colds	_____	_____
Complains of buzzing noise in ears	_____	_____
Seems to be inattentive or indifferent	_____	_____
Does poorly in games with oral directions	_____	_____
Has trouble following trend of thought during oral discussions	_____	_____

Reproduced by permission of the publisher, F. E. Peacock Publishers, Inc., Itasca, Ill., from Eddie C. Kennedy, *Classroom Approaches to Remedial Reading,* 1977, p. 391.

Fortunately, many school systems have speech and hearing specialists. Young children entering school are usually screened by the specialist, and many possible problems are identified early. Teachers find these services helpful, and the speech teacher is usually eager to consult with and assist the faculty with students experiencing hearing loss.

Sometimes teachers can jump to the conclusion that there is a hearing deficit when a student shows particular physical symptoms. Some symptoms may be only temporary because of congestion from colds or an ear infection. The wise teacher will observe behavior over a period of time, perhaps three to four weeks, to determine if the behaviors or symptoms persist. If they do, referral should be considered.

Teachers can structure activities to help determine hearing loss. Some examples follow.

- *Simon Says.* The teacher plays *Simon Says* with small groups. The students are told to face away and follow the directions. If a student consistently has trouble keeping up with classmates, the teacher may suspect a hearing deficit.
- *Low voice or whisper test.* The teacher stands about 20 feet away from the student (first on one side, then the other). The student is then asked to repeat the words the teacher says in a normal, clear voice. A student who cannot do this task at 15 or fewer feet may have a hearing deficit. A variation of this procedure is to talk softly (or whisper) while standing just behind a student. If the student does not respond to the same volumes as other students, a hearing deficit may exist.
- *Watch tick test.* The teacher holds a stopwatch or loudly ticking wristwatch about 12 inches from the student's ear, gradually extending the distance to about 48

inches. Students with normal hearing should hear the ticks 40 to 48 inches from the ear (Kennedy, 1977). If the distance is less than 40 inches, a deficit may exist, and the teacher should consider referral.

Results of these assessment procedures vary depending on factors such as noise level of the environment, differences in teachers' voices, and loudness of watches. A good way to judge the adequacy of these procedures is to test several students, and notice those who differ significantly from the overall group. If a student's responses consistently deviate from the peer group, more reliable and sophisticated assessment procedures performed by the appropriate specialist are probably in order.

Teachers' responsibilities. Corrective work for students with auditory acuity impairments, particularly those who are deaf or hard of hearing, is an intricate task that requires specially prepared teachers. Facilities for these learners are usually provided in special schools or special education classes. However, most students with mild hearing impairments or with deficits corrected by prosthetic devices (e.g., hearing aids) function quite well within the regular classroom. Special provisions need to be considered, such as seating the student close to where the teacher and others are talking. It is also helpful for the speaker to face these students directly so they will have the advantage of watching lips closely if needed. Clear enunciation is essential.

Students who have hearing impairments may have difficulty when oral discussion and recitation are in progress. Listening to others read may be difficult, too. Teachers should stress silent reading and a visual approach to word analysis for these students. Phonics may be difficult or, for some, impossible to learn. Emphasis during instruction in word recognition (see Chapter 8) should be placed on the uses of visual and structural analysis techniques and context clues.

Listening Skills

While most students have adequate auditory acuity for learning to read, additional auditory skills, classified as listening skills, are important to consider.

Listening, as another aspect of language ability, is an area in which much assumptive teaching occurs. Many teachers believe listening develops naturally and is simply a matter of either paying attention or not paying attention. Not true. After extensive study, Lundsteen (1979, p. 15) concluded that **listening** is "the process by which spoken language is converted to meaning in the mind."

Assessment techniques. The assessment of listening skills covers a wide range of abilities. At its basic level, listening includes auditory acuity; that is, the student must be able to hear noises and sounds. Unfortunately, many teachers equate the ability to hear with the ability to listen. Listening also requires **auditory perception**, the ability to discriminate, remember (auditory memory), and blend sounds together. Listening involves *attending* to the sounds and concentrating on getting the message. Because students with difficulty in reading may also be more easily distracted, **attentive listening** becomes a crucial area to assess. Listening requires **auditory comprehension**, or the ability to make meaning from the oral message. Auditory comprehension ranges from literal understanding of the message to critical evaluation of what was heard. All of these components must be considered to assess listening skills accurately.

As with visual perception, a number of skills are included in the area of auditory perception: discrimination, memory, and blending. **Auditory discrimination** is the ability to distinguish sounds, **auditory memory** is the ability to remember a sequence of sounds, and **auditory blending** refers to the blending of phonemes to form a word.

When their auditory discrimination skills are being assessed, students should face away from the teacher to eliminate the possibility of lip reading. Some common procedures follow.

1. Pronounce word pairs (e.g., big-pig, pat-pot, some-come, rug-run). Direct the student to answer "same" if the two words sound the same, or "not the same" or "different" if the two words sound different in any way. Several examples should be given for practice, and enough word pairs to assess all positions reliably (beginning, middle, end); probably about ten pairs are adequate for each position.

2. The same concept can be modified for use with a group of students by providing each student a sheet of paper listing the item number followed by the words *same* and *not the same,* or *yes* and *no* (Fig. 4.3). Again, word pairs are pronounced by the teacher (standing behind the group) and students are to circle "yes" or "same" if the two words sound the same and "no" or "not the same" or "different" if they sound different.

The assessment of auditory memory evaluates a student's ability to follow oral directions and remember information presented orally in class. Generally, assessment requires students to recall and reproduce a series of unrelated words. For example, the teacher may say, "Listen to these words and be ready to repeat them in the same order: cow . . . tie . . . bed. Now you say them." With young children, several practice items are needed. The number of words can also be increased if three appear to be too easy. Rae and Potter (1981) give additional formats (Fig. 4.4).

Testing the ability to pay attention is complicated; a student may be attending to the speaker without being able to understand the speaker (Norton, 1993). Therefore, Otto and Smith (1980) suggest that procedures designed to assess attention should *not* stress the student's ability to process ideas.

According to Norton (1993, p. 129), "ability to follow oral directions explicitly demands attentive listening." Because idea processing is not being evaluated, directions must be simple. For example, a young child may be told: "Take out your blue crayon,

FIGURE 4.3   Sheet used in testing auditory discrimination.

1.	yes	no
2.	yes	no
	or	
3.	same	not the same
4.	same	different
	and so on	

Assessing auditory memory.

Auditory Memory Test: Level I

Directions to the teacher:

Level I is to be given individually. The teacher will need a small box (approximately 3 by 5 inches) with a lid, a small ball, a nail, a paper clip, and a pencil with an eraser.

An index card with an X on it is also needed. Spread items on a table in front of the child and place the index card to the child's left as a starting point.

You may repeat once if the child hesitates on the first three combinations below. Do not repeat for numbers 4 to 7.

Directions to the child:

Can you tell me the names of the things I've put on the table? Good. Now I'm going to say the names of some of the things. When I do, I want you to put them in a row on the table. I'll say only some of them and you are to put them in the same order I say them. The first one goes right under this X. (Point to card.) Be sure to wait until I say "go" before you pick anything up. Let's try it.

1. Ball, nail. Go. (Have child return them each time.)
2. Box, pencil. Go.
3. Clip, box, nail. Go.
4. Ball, clip, box. Go.
5. Nail, box, clip, pencil. Go.
6. Box, nail, ball, clip. Go.
7. Pencil, ball, box, nail, clip. Go.

Auditory Memory Test: Level II

Directions to the teacher:

The various parts of this test may be given to individuals or groups. Children will have an answer sheet to mark (see p. 79). It is sometimes necessary to practice reading the material in advance to avoid mispronunciations and to avoid stressing a particular answer. You may repeat once.

Directions to the children:

Today you are going to have to be good listeners and remember what I read to you. After I read, I will ask you to put some numbers in front of pictures that tell the order in which you heard the words I said. Don't do any writing until I say "begin." Let's try sample A. Listen to the words I say: "dog, bird, cloud." Now, put a one in front of the picture of the first word I said, and a two in front of the second word. (Pause.) Listen again: dog, bird, cloud. Did you put a one in front of the picture of the dog? What did you put the two in front of? What would you put in front of the picture of the cloud? Good! (Check answers to make sure they all understand.) Let's begin now.

Sample A _____ dog, bird, cloud.

1. _____ car, house
2. _____ boy, rabbit, dog.
3. _____ The wall is by the fence.
4. _____ The girl and the cat sat in front of the tree.
5. _____ The horse and the dog ran over the hill to the house.
6. _____ The fountain by the house has birds and butterflies on it.
7. _____ The many-colored leaves are falling from the trees and the children are raking them.
8. _____ Put your comb and brush on the table and sit in the chair by the fireplace.
9. _____ The train passed two houses, a barn, and a tree as it sped along.
10. _____ The book is about a rabbit, a dog, and a boy who lived in the forest by the hills.

continued

F I G U R E   *continued*

4.4

Auditory Memory Test: Level II

Name _____   Grade _____

PART I   SECTION A   CHILD'S ANSWER SHEET

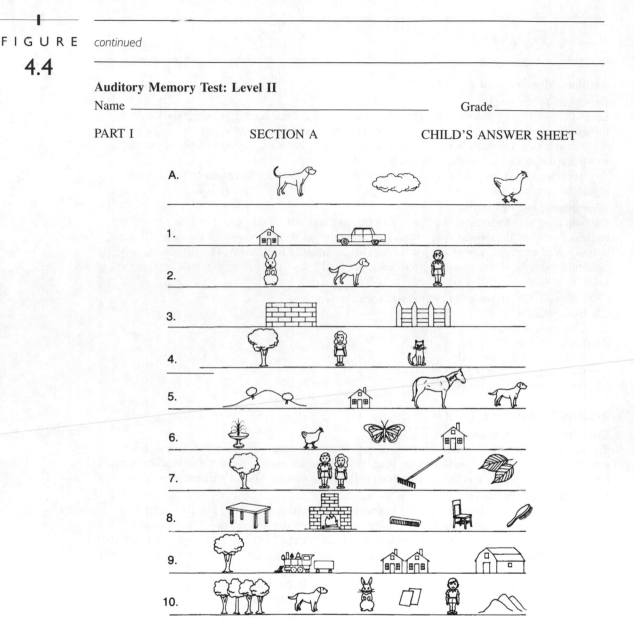

From G. Rae and T. Potter, *Informal Reading Diagnosis: A Practical Guide for the Classroom Teacher*, 2nd ed. © 1981, pp. 40, 41, 147. Reprinted by permission of Prentice-Hall, Inc., Englewood Cliffs, NJ.

your green crayon, and your red crayon. Pick up the red crayon and show it to me." Or for older students: "Take out a piece of paper and a pencil. Put the point of your pencil on the top center of the paper and draw a circle the size of a quarter. Draw a larger circle below the first circle. Draw a smaller circle inside the first circle." The older the student, the more complicated the oral directions might be.

Instructional practices described later in this section can also be used for assessment. Several group standardized tests assess listening comprehension. Three of these are *The Cooperative Primary Tests,* the *Durrell Listening–Reading Series* and the *Brown-Carlsen Listening Comprehension Test.*

The Cooperative Primary Tests, published by Educational Testing Service, Cooperative Test Division, Princeton, NJ 08540, provide two assessment forms for grades 1 through 3. In each test the teacher reads words, sentences, stories, and poems; the child marks correct pictures.

The Durrell Listening–Reading Series has three levels (primary, grades 1–2; intermediate, grades 3–6; advanced, grades 7–9) that compare reading and listening abilities for vocabulary and sentences. Optional responses are read to the students so they do not have to read to answer the questions.

The Brown-Carlsen Listening Comprehension Test is designed for grades 9 through 13 and contains five subtests: Immediate Recall, Following Directions, Recognizing Transitions, Recognizing Word Meanings, and Lecture Comprehension. Both the Durrell and Brown-Carlsen tests are available from The Psychological Corporation, 757 Third Avenue, New York, NY, 10017.

Classroom teachers are likely to rely on listening assessments they prepare themselves. One common technique uses an individually administered informal reading inventory. Instead of the student reading the graded passages, the passages are read to the student and comprehension questions asked. The listening comprehension level is the highest level at which the student can correctly answer at least 75 percent of the comprehension questions. For more specific listening skills, such as listening for main ideas, sequence, details, and so forth, activities that are used to teach these skills can also be used for assessment.

Teachers' responsibilities. Students are not naturally good or poor listeners. Listening skills can, and must, be taught. To develop auditory discrimination skill, the teacher should begin with practice in listening for known sounds within known words. This not only provides success for the student but also a better idea of the nature of the task. The teacher must understand that "poor auditory discrimination is often accompanied by inaccurate or indistinct speech. The child who pronounces *with* as *wiv* is not likely to notice any difference between final *v* and *th* in words. It is hard for many children to discriminate among short vowel sounds because those sounds do not differ greatly" (Harris & Sipay, 1990, pp. 456–457). Therefore, in such cases the teacher must decide whether instruction in auditory discrimination would be time well spent, or whether visual learning should be emphasized until articulation has improved.

Useful activities for auditory discrimination development follow. The first three activities are particularly representative of those currently found in use in classroom settings in which phonics instruction is emphasized.

1. Students are asked to locate or mark pictures that begin or end with a particular sound.
2. Students are asked to listen to pairs of words and determine if they begin or end with the same sound.
3. Pictures are provided, with a choice of two letters for each picture. Students are to choose the letter that represents the beginning or ending sound of the picture.
4. Using a familiar story or nursery rhyme, the teacher selects words to be changed to new words by altering one or two sounds. The teacher then reads the story slowly while the students listen for words that sound wrong. Students must identify the incorrect word and state what the word should sound like. The teacher

then continues reading. Brown (1982) calls this activity "fractured fables" and provides an example:

Little Bo *Beep* has lost her *shape*
And doesn't know where to find them.
Leaf them alone, and they'll come home
Wagging their *tells* behind them. (p. 248)

Auditory memory exercises are designed to develop the ability to attend to, recognize, and recall sequences of numbers, letters, and words. The following are representative activities.

1. Give students a series of numbers to dial on a telephone or type on a typewriter or microcomputer.
2. Require students to repeat clapping patterns (e.g., clap/clap-clap/clap).
3. Require students to decide if two sound patterns are alike. Claps, taps, or toy flutes can be used (e.g., -/-/-; -/-/—).
4. Pronounce two words for the students, then repeat one of them. Students are required to note if the repeated word was the first or second word of the pair.
5. Have students repeat a series of three to seven unrelated words in sequence, from memory.

Auditory blending is also discussed in Chapter 8, but a few activities are presented here for explanatory purposes.

1. Have students join beginning consonant sounds to ending phonograms (e.g., /b/ -ake, /k/ -ake, /f/ -ake, /l/ -ake, /m/-ake).
2. Combine visuals with the auditory task given above. While pronouncing /k/ -ake, show the word card cake and continue by covering the initial consonant with the various other consonants, for example, make .
3. Provide riddles, such as, "I'm thinking of a word that starts like man, /m/, and ends like lake, ake. What is the word?"

Attentive listening is indeed a prerequisite to academic success. Wilt (1958) reports that attentive listening is required by elementary school students for as much as 60 percent of their time in school. All too commonly students ask for directions to be repeated or are scolded for not following directions. Oftentimes, the teacher may have to take responsibility for this inattentiveness. Otto and Smith (1980, p. 307) suggest four factors of inattentiveness: "(1) poor motivation to hear the speaker's message, (2) too much teacher talk, (3) excessive noise and other distractions, and (4) lack of a mental set for anticipating the speaker's message. By careful attention to these four factors, a teacher can help students become more attentive listeners."

Specific activities and methods help students develop attentive listening. *Simon Says* involves careful listening to directions. A leader gives an oral command, and the group must do as told *if* the "magic" words "Simon says" precede the command. If the command is not preceded by "Simon says," those students who obey the command are eliminated from the game.

To encourage students to listen, give oral directions only once. When a student requests a repetition, ask other students to recall and restate the directions. Learning centers for listening can easily be developed. Listening center supplies may include commercial or teacher-made tapes, records, cassettes, CDs, radios, and accompanying printed materials.

Furness (1971) claims that it is especially appropriate for students with listening comprehension difficulties and learning difficulties in general to number the steps of the oral directions, repeat the number of steps involved, and relate each step to its number. Otto and Smith (1980) stress anticipation of what the speaker will say, much like a directed listening–thinking activity.

Students with listening comprehension difficulties need help in defining the purposes for their listening. For example, to help students listen to oral directions, key words such as "first," "second," and "finally" may be stressed. Have students close their eyes and visualize themselves carrying out each step of the directions as they hear it. Then ask them to describe each step. Finally, have them physically perform the activity.

Some additional activities for developing attentive listening follow.

- Using *Pin the Tail on the Donkey,* direct the blindfolded student to move to the right, to the left, and so on.
- Using a cassette tape, provide a series of numbers *once,* such as 8-5-2-6-9. Ask which number is closest to the sum of two plus two.
- Have each student prepare a two-minute talk on "How to Make a Peanut Butter Sandwich." As the directions are spoken, ask the listeners to first visualize themselves following the directions, and next, ask some volunteers to do *exactly* as the speaker directed. (This activity can be just as valuable for the speaker.)
- To help students listen attentively and for details, play simple listening games with increasingly difficult instructions given to one student and then another. For example, "Jim, take the book from the second shelf and carry it to the windowsill." "Bill, you take it from the windowsill to the library corner and then to my desk." "Janet, you take it from the desk and walk around the desk twice with it, then carry it to the library corner and then to the windowsill, and finally back to the second shelf." And so forth.

An effective listener must be able to follow a sequence of ideas, perceive their organization, recognize the main ideas and important details, predict outcomes, and critically evaluate what is heard. The same can be said for an effective comprehender. Thus, many of the comprehension activities found in Chapter 10 can be used, with only slight modifications, for instruction in auditory comprehension. In addition, the following techniques and activities are recommended.

1. *Listening for main ideas and supporting details.* The teacher selects paragraphs in which the main idea is stated (easiest) or inferred (more difficult). These paragraphs should also state several supporting details. The difficulty level of the paragraphs conforms to the students' ability level. One easy example follows.

I have a new puppy. It is little. It can run and jump. My puppy can do tricks.
The puppy is funny.

The teacher reads the paragraph and asks the students to listen carefully for the main idea. After they have suggested a main idea, they should tell why. A request for a good title might be substituted for the term *main idea* in case students are unfamiliar with this term. In either circumstance, the students are told that the main idea, or title, can be turned into a question in order to find the supporting details. For example:

What is a new puppy like?
Why is the puppy funny?

After students hear the paragraph read once more, they are asked to identify supporting details. The main idea question will be answered by the supporting details. In other words, of the two questions suggested, one will be answered by the supporting details. For example:

It is little.
It can run and jump.
It can do tricks.
It is funny.

These details best answer the first question, so the first sentence, "I have a new puppy," represents the main idea. If working with titles, "A New Puppy" or "My Puppy" is an appropriate suggestion. Descriptive paragraphs are especially helpful for this activity.

2. *Listening for details that do and do not support the main idea.* Further development of listening skills includes a weighing of information for its importance to the topic. The teacher may read a paragraph in which one detail does not relate to the rest of the paragraph or to the main idea. The students are then asked to state the main idea, the supporting details, and the non-supporting detail. For example:

Bob and Mary do not know what to do. They don't want to watch TV. They looked for a game to play, but could not find one they liked. Mother went to visit her friend.

3. *Listening for sequence.* Activities to develop this skill first stress listening for key words that signify sequences, such as "first," "second," and "finally." Once the students have been alerted to these key words, they listen to an oral presentation that emphasizes the usefulness of such words. For example:

I have a picture of three monkeys. The first monkey is covering his eyes. The next one is covering his ears. The third one is covering his mouth with his hands. On the bottom a sign says, "See no evil, hear no evil, speak no evil."

Point out to students how the key words signal a certain sequence. This can be demonstrated by rearranging the order of the paragraph to make less sense. Also help students discover the usefulness of the introductory statement, "I have a picture of three monkeys," and show how each of the monkeys is then identified by a signal word: "first," "next," "third." This type of activity can be easily adapted to develop understanding of paragraph structure in preparation for writing paragraphs.

Other activities include cutting up comic strips into their individual frames, whiting out the words, mixing up the frames, and then reading the original comic strip aloud while the students put the strip back in order. A flannel board provides the opportunity for students to listen to a story, hear its sequential organization, then retell it via pictures or main idea statements in proper sequence.

4. *Listening to predict outcomes.* The procedure is much like that of a directed reading–thinking activity (Stauffer, 1981). The title of a story is read to the students and they are asked to write a prediction, or suggest to the teacher, what they think they will hear about in the story. The teacher discusses the reasons for these predictions with the students and then reads the story. Some stories lend themselves to breaks where repredicting can occur. This activity motivates students to listen carefully to see if their individual predictions are correct. Films can also be used in this manner, or a talk or lecture can be stopped at certain points to have students predict what the speaker will say next. The level can be very easy (predicting the next word in a sentence) or more difficult (predicting the possible content or conclusion).

5. *Listening to evaluate.* Students are aided in this area by learning to develop questions to be answered by listening and to listen for cause and effect relationships,

propaganda, or persuasive statements. As for any lesson, students must be prepared, in this case by being given something to anticipate. For example, after the topic of the talk or lecture is previewed, the students are asked to list three questions they would like to hear answered. A planned study guide helps students use what they already know and alerts them to information particularly important to understanding what they will hear. Devine (1981, pp. 24–25) suggests that an effective listening guide should include:

a. A preview of the talk, including a statement of its purpose and perhaps even an outline

b. A list of new words and concepts

c. Questions for students to think about as they listen

d. Space for students to write questions *they* want answered as they listen

e. Provision for *anticipation* (that is, some problem, question, or student concern that students can look forward to learning about as they listen)

f. Questions to help the student–listener personalize what is being said, for example, "Have you ever had an experience like this?" or "In what way does this affect your own life?"

g. Space for students to write such things as main ideas and supporting details

h. Appropriate visuals that can be duplicated in the guide (e.g., graphs, tables)

i. Follow-up activities (e.g., possible test questions, related readings)

Activities for evaluative listening may include (1) identifying cause and effect and (2) discriminating information from propaganda.

For *identifying cause and effect,* a cause is stated, followed by the reading of a series of consequences, some of which are results of the cause and others that are not. Students are to identify any matching cause–effect relationships. For example:

Cause

It was the hottest summer that had ever been recorded.

Effects

• The greatest danger was the possibility of frostbite. *(No match)*

• The hospital reported large numbers of cases of heatstroke. *(Match)*

• After a while, a bad water shortage developed. *(Match)*

• Most people dressed carefully, wearing many layers of clothes. *(No match)*

• It was uncomfortable to leave your home to go outdoors. *(Match)*

For *discriminating information from propaganda,* television commercials provide a never-ending source of material. Tapes are prepared to be analyzed and later placed in listening centers to give practice in listening for persuasive statements. A speaker whose purpose is to persuade also provides information while trying to convince the listener of something. Listeners are constantly exposed to such situations. Examples other than the TV commercial include the campaigning politician at all levels of government, the salesperson (e.g., cars, magazines, appliances), and very often our friends. The listener must be able to distinguish statements that inform from those that are intended to persuade. The listener then examines and evaluates only the information before deciding what to do. Students are first instructed in the differences between informative and persuasive statements. For example:

Information tells you about the item being sold.

1. This bicycle comes with a headlight and a rear light.

2. This bicycle is lightweight (twenty pounds) and has hand brakes.

Persuasion tries to make you think you want to buy what is being sold.

1. This bicycle is only for people who want the best.
2. Famous stars prefer this bicycle.

A list of statements is then read to students and they determine which inform and which persuade. For example:

- These knives are made of stainless steel. *(Information)*
- Our gum contains no sugar. *(Information)*
- Why not use what the pros use? *(Persuasion)*
- The jackets come in three sizes. *(Information)*
- Just what you've been waiting for! *(Persuasion)*
- The rubber sole will keep you from slipping. *(Information)*
- This is a nonalkaline pH shampoo. *(Information)*
- This is a special gift for that special person. *(Persuasion)*
- This dish will not chip or crack. *(Information)*
- Everyone thinks _____ is the best. *(Persuasion)*

In conclusion, listening must be considered a vital aspect of language ability although it is often overlooked. It may be mistakenly assumed that a student who hears well also listens well. Instruction in listening skills must begin in the early grades to help students prepare and develop independence for such tasks as notetaking and class discussions.

The lack of listening materials places even greater responsibility for the development of instructional practices on the classroom teacher. The following questions (Burns, 1980, p. 113) alert teachers to their responsibilities.

1. Do I provide a classroom environment (emotional and physical) that encourages good listening?
2. Am I a good listener and do I really listen to the pupils?
3. Do I use appropriate tone, pitch, volume, and speed in my speaking?
4. Do I vary the classroom program to provide listening experiences (films, discussions, debates, reports) that are of interest to the students?
5. Am I aware of opportunities for teaching listening throughout the day?
6. Do I help pupils see the purpose of listening in each activity?
7. Do I help students see the importance and value of being good listeners?
8. Do I build a program in which listening skills are consistently taught and practiced?

Other listening strategies may be found in the professional literature. One of the most complete collections is still *Listening Aids Through the Grades* (Russell & Russell, 1979), which includes almost 200 teaching ideas ranging from general to specific and from simple to complex.

Neurological Factors

Reading, which is basically thinking, requires a brain that is functioning adequately. Fortunately, most people have central nervous systems that work well enough to allow them to learn to read. The exceptions are rare: perhaps 20 to 30 percent of children with *severe* reading problems show signs of neurological deficits (Denckla, 1972). Among these are a few children who have neurological disorders that interfere with learning to read and with achievement in other curriculum areas.

Considerable confusion exists concerning students who have learning problems due to neurological involvement. These children have been labeled "learning disabled," "dyslexic," exhibiting "undifferentiated attention deficit disorder," "attention-deficit hyperactivity disorder" and a host of other exotic terms. Terms of that nature are avoided in this text because they are counterproductive to helping teachers teach students to read.

Harris and Sipay (1990) recommend that students who demonstrate a number of the symptoms listed in Figure 4.5 be referred to a pediatric neurologist.

Assessment techniques. If a neurological factor is suspected, family physicians usually refer children to a pediatric neurologist for a complete workup. In addition to standard medical procedures, such as electroencephalograms, doctors examine children for so-called soft signs. Sometimes results are obtained from observing and recording psychological rather than physical symptoms. A diagnosis based on soft signs is considered to have doubtful validity (Kavale & Forness, 1985). When psychological data are used as a basis for a physiological diagnosis, that diagnosis should be considered as suggestive rather than conclusive.

Teachers' responsibilities. Accurately assessing neurological involvement is difficult even for medical and psychological specialists. Therefore, teachers must be extremely cautious and conservative regarding assessment.

Two types of data can generally be used, a child's medical history and observed symptoms. Teachers should be aware that the symptoms listed in the checklist in Figure 4.5 are tentative and, at best, suggestive. Additionally, Copeland and Love (1990) provide several checklists related to attention deficit disorders along with guidelines for teachers. When neurological impairment is suspected, teachers should refer the child to a specialist, using established channels provided by the school system.

Checklist for possible neurological factors.

FIGURE 4.5

	Yes	No
History		
Family history suggesting hereditary factors	_____	_____
Serious problems during pregnancy	_____	_____
Serious problems during birth	_____	_____
Serious problems immediately after birth	_____	_____
Serious medical history (e.g., high fever)	_____	_____
Serious blow to head	_____	_____
Seizures or convulsions	_____	_____
Behavioral symptoms		
Poor balance, awkwardness	_____	_____
Delayed speech development	_____	_____
Extreme distractibility	_____	_____
Wide mood swings	_____	_____
Disorganization in time and space	_____	_____

Psychological Factors

Psychological factors refer to processes of the mind or psyche. Because of the delicate nature of the brain, many psychological studies are necessarily indirect, abstract, and theoretical; thus, their findings are more tentative than those of investigations in the physical sciences. Information from psychological investigations is subject to different interpretations, frequently dependent on the theoretical positions of the researcher.

Three psychological areas of concern to teachers are the cognitive, the affective, and the psychomotor domains. **Cognition** can be considered roughly as thinking, while **affect** refers to feelings. The **psychomotor** domain refers to the psychological field of physical activity. What people think and what they feel often are not the same, although the two processes are frequently so interrelated that it is difficult to separate them. Teachers of reading are primarily concerned with students' thinking, but to be truly effective they also need to be concerned with feelings. Two important psychological factors are considered in the following section: intelligence, which is a cognitive factor, and social and emotional adjustment, which are in the affective domain.

Cognition—Intelligence

Intelligence can be broadly conceptualized as reflecting a person's general ability to think, to act purposefully, and to solve problems. Intelligence is an abstract, elusive concept that has been a source of debate for years by psychologists and educators alike. Because no one has ever seen or experienced intelligence, it can only be talked about.

A more operational definition is that intelligence is what tests measure. Such a definition reminds us that a student's intelligence is often judged on the basis of a test score. This score may or may not accurately reflect true mental capacity; an intelligence test score is only an estimate of mental capacity and reflects the rate of mental development based on a relatively small sample of specific test items.

Reading is an intellectual process, and intelligence, however it may be defined, unquestionably influences the successful acquisition of reading skills and, in later years, the rate and comprehension of what one reads. Low intelligence is probably not a direct cause of reading difficulties but indirectly can interfere with learning to read. Teachers must adjust the curriculum to meet the needs of students thought to have lower intelligence. Generally, these learners require a more structured reading program, more practice and repetition, and individual assistance. An analytic approach to teaching enhances their chances of learning to read to the best of their ability.

Assessment techniques. Because the assessment of intelligence infers the use of intelligence test scores, several relevant issues must be considered. Schools using intelligence tests depend, for the most part, on group intelligence tests. Generally, tests used for young children in primary grades are constructed so that they do not require reading, for example, the *Pintner-Cunningham* and the *Kuhlman-Anderson Measure of Academic Potential*. However, there is concern that intelligence tests that are non-language based may not be tapping the verbal abilities needed in learning to read, because the correlation between reading and non-language intelligence tests is quite low. Group intelligence tests for upper elementary and secondary students usually require reading, and readers with difficulties usually score poorly on these tests. When this occurs, it is difficult to separate low reading ability from low mental ability, and teacher judgment becomes extremely important. When teachers are concerned about a student's intellectual ability, particularly if that student is having serious difficulty reading, referral to the school psychologist for further assessment is recommended.

Teachers' responsibilities. The use of intelligence test scores has become a sensitive political issue in recent years. Increasingly, schools are discontinuing the use of intelligence tests except under specific conditions that usually involve a trained specialist (such as a school psychologist) using either the appropriate Wechsler (e.g., WISC-R) or Stanford-Binet scale, both of which require special training for administering and interpreting. Many classroom teachers, then, must use their own judgment regarding a student's cognitive ability.

One method often used by classroom teachers is to determine a student's ability to understand and control oral language (i.e., listening comprehension and speaking). The assumption is that, with instruction, students should be able to read and understand written language as well as they hear, understand, and can use oral language (refer to Chapter 6).

Affective—Emotional and Social Adjustment Factors

How people perceive themselves and the world around them gauges their emotional and social adjustment. People who do not feel good about themselves often have problems resolving inner conflicts and relating effectively with others in their environment. This generalization holds true for students who have trouble reading.

Studies of the incidence of emotional maladjustment among effective and ineffective readers in general show no clear differences, although they suggest that serious reading problems are likely to be accompanied by adjustment problems. It would be very dangerous to conclude, however, that emotional instability causes reading problems. A more appropriate conclusion is that adjustment problems are likely to contribute to reading problems. Behavior problems probably interact with other causes of reading failure to make learning to read even more difficult for ineffective readers.

Another issue to consider is the degree of maladjustment. Severe emotional dysfunction hinders progress in learning more than do moderate problems. Deep-seated problems are more difficult to remedy and tend to interfere longer than milder, more transitory problems.

Whether psychological adjustment problems are a cause or a result of reading difficulties is not clear, but the presence of these factors can be safely assumed to inhibit reading progress. Quite often, students who improve in reading also improve in terms of self-concept. Thus, the classroom teacher should make every effort to help students feel good about themselves, *especially* if they have difficulty with academic subjects such as reading.

Assessment techniques. Discussion of assessment techniques will be brief because most require formal training in the areas of projective techniques, interviews, and other specialized psychological procedures. One fairly reliable source for assessing self-concept is the *Piers-Harris Children's Self Concept Scale* (Piers & Harris, 1969). This instrument consists of 80 yes–no items and can be administered to groups as well as individuals. Kuder-Richardson Formula 21 reliability estimates range from .78 to .93 for the instrument.

Self-concept, as measured in the Piers-Harris instrument, is assumed to refer to a set of relatively stable self-attitudes (Wylie, 1974). The items on the instrument are evaluative as well as descriptive. For example, consider item 2 (I am a happy person), item 5 (I am smart), and item 20 (I give up easily). Responses to these and all other items reflect the ways in which the person responding both describes and evaluates himself or herself.

The *Eighth Mental Measurements Yearbook* (Buros, 1978) contains a detailed and generally favorable review of the *Piers-Harris Children's Self Concept Scale,* and the interested reader is referred to that source.

Teachers' responsibilities. Responsible classroom teachers are concerned with the well-being of their students, including their social and emotional well-being. Occasionally teachers observe students who seem to exhibit unusually severe maladjustment in these areas. Teachers may have an advantage over parents in identifying contributing social and emotional factors because they are not as close emotionally to the students and also because they can compare one student's behavior with that of many others. After teachers have taught for a few years, they have a fairly good idea of what constitutes bizarre or aberrant behavior. While teachers should not dabble in amateur psychology, they should note unusual behaviors in students, particularly when those behaviors are frequent and persistent.

When teachers become aware of possible maladjustment, they should reflect on precisely what the student is doing to cause concern. Figure 4.6 provides a checklist of some of the symptoms associated with psychosocial problems.

FIGURE 4.6

Checklist of symptoms associated with emotional maladjustment.

	Yes	No
General Traits or Behavior		
1. Displays signs of excessive shyness	____	____
2. Displays signs of introversion	____	____
3. Displays signs of lack of confidence	____	____
4. Gives up easily on school tasks	____	____
5. Plays alone	____	____
6. Daydreams	____	____
7. Displays signs of overdependence	____	____
8. Seeks approval excessively	____	____
9. Has numerous unexplained absences	____	____
10. Displays signs of nervousness	____	____
11. Does not work cooperatively with classmates	____	____
12. Argues and fights with classmates	____	____
13. Constantly disrupts class	____	____
Reading-Related Traits or Behavior		
14. Shows fear of the reading task	____	____
15. Refuses to read orally	____	____
16. Displays antagonism toward reading	____	____
17. Does not get along with others in reading group	____	____
18. Does not attend during reading lesson	____	____
19. Does not complete reading assignments	____	____
20. Displays fear or nervousness during recitation	____	____

Many other behaviors are also possible symptoms. A checklist helps teachers organize their thoughts and prepare a case for referral to the school psychologist, guidance counselor, or school social worker. In many school systems these specialists have a heavy workload and the waiting period after referral can be many months. A well-prepared and documented referral by a thoughtful teacher may expedite response.

Carefully prepared anecdotal records comprise a teacher's best tool in presenting a case for referral. Remember that behaviors should be described objectively rather than presented as tentative conclusions. Valuable information is lost when conclusions are the only thing noted. The objective details will be helpful in revealing patterns of behavior when anecdotal records are reviewed over time. Consider the following examples:

Date	Conclusions	vs.	Objective Description
11/18	Jennifer had a temper tantrum.		Today, when Jennifer discovered she did not have her paper posted on the "my best effort" bulletin board, she ran up to the board, ripped off several papers belonging to classmates, then began to cry.
11/20	Jennifer fought with Susan in the cafeteria line.		Susan accidentally pushed Jennifer while they were in the cafeteria line. Jennifer then began to hit and kick Susan. Her facial expression frightened both Susan and me.
12/5	Jennifer refused to participate in the reading group and at other times today.		Jennifer was unusually quiet today. When I asked her comprehension questions, she dropped her head and eyes. I let someone else answer. Later when I tried to reengage her in the group activity, she still would not respond. I tried several other times to communicate with her today and had no luck. She did not talk with me all day.

The incomplete sentence technique is often used to gain insights into the student's feelings about reading and self in general. Typically, a student will be asked to complete 20 to 50 sentence starters either orally or in writing. Some examples follow.

My reading group _____.

The teacher thinks I _____.

My books _____.

Information from such an instrument should be considered tentative and must be verified because students often respond as they think the teacher wants them to. This is a limitation of any self-reporting technique. A frequently used incomplete sentence test was developed by Boning and Boning (1957) and can be found in Appendix C.

Fortunately, most students exhibiting severe social or emotional maladjustment have already been identified and placed in special therapeutic programs before they enter school. Most school systems today also have special classes for students displaying social or emotional maladjustment. Some students with relatively mild adjustment problems function quite well within the regular classroom. But sometimes these students do *not* learn well, and their response to failure and frustration from not learning academic subjects interact negatively with their already negative self-concept, leading to further maladjustment. This can create a negative spiral that worsens with time.

Failure can also have a devastating effect on well-adjusted people. Johnston and Winograd (1985) believe that many of the problems exhibited by readers in difficulty are related to their passive involvement in reading. This indicates that the teacher can make a positive impact by providing a program that insures active participation, strategy instruction, and **attributional retraining** (teaching pupils to accept responsibility for their successes and failures and that effort and persistence may help to overcome failure) (Borkowski, Wehing & Turner, 1986). Following are suggestions for helping students displaying evidence of lowered self-esteem whether from lack of accomplishment in reading or from other sources. They can also be appropriately used with most students.

1. *Create a facilitative learning environment.* The teacher must make special efforts to establish a warm, trusting working relationship with readers in difficulty. Teachers should listen carefully. Often students feel the need to discuss what is bothering them with a trusted adult, but teachers may be so preoccupied that they fail to hear the clues given. Dialogue journals can provide students and teachers a vehicle for "talking" to each other (Staton, 1988). Teachers also must be careful not to use their own values to judge non-reading behaviors, lest they contribute negatively to any maladjustments. On the other hand, learners often need reassurance and suggestions, particularly regarding their troubles, whether they are academic or of a different nature. The teacher must establish a free and open atmosphere but at the same time set certain limits. The teacher should maintain those limits, being pleasant but firm when necessary. The purpose of establishing rapport is to create an environment in which a learner's self-confidence and self-esteem are nurtured.

2. *Create opportunities for success.* The axiom "nothing succeeds like success" is particularly appropriate for students having trouble reading. Teachers help structure success experiences by ensuring that students work at a difficulty level that is easy enough for them. Find something they can read easily, even if it is their own name. Increasing the difficulty level if it is too easy is healthier than decreasing it after failure.

More difficult tasks can be spaced among easier ones. Students often can work with new and difficult tasks for only a few minutes before becoming too frustrated to continue. Interspersing success experiences among such tasks often relieves undue pressure.

Older students often respond negatively to "baby stuff." This problem can be avoided if teachers use materials that appear more mature than they really are. High interest –low vocabulary books and stories without pictures of younger children are recommended. Some excellent picture books are available that lend themselves to sophisticated uses that will appeal to the older students' sensibilities (see Danielson, 1992; Neal & Moore, 1991-1992; Polette, 1989). Cross-age tutoring programs can also be effective ways to help older students gain much needed practice with easier materials (Juel, 1991; Labbo & Teale, 1990; Morrice & Simmons, 1991).

A process called **bibliotherapy** can provide opportunities for troubled students to identify with a character or situation in a book and experience a catharsis or perhaps gain insight into their own problems (Dreyer, 1987). Bibliotherapy, then, can help a student come to grips with personal problems and realize that reading can be a useful activity for personal growth (D'Alessandro, 1990). For example, *Golden Daffodils* (Gould, 1982) is a book about Janis, a fifth-grade student who has cerebral palsy, being mainstreamed into a regular classroom. Students with and without physical handicaps can better understand themselves and others when reading about the obstacles Janis must overcome.

3. *Provide ample reward and reinforcement.* Because many ineffective readers have less than adequate confidence in their ability to learn to read, they often need more encouragement than other students. Praise students when they succeed or when they attempt a task that is difficult and threatening. Social reinforcement can be given verbally ("very good," "nice try") or nonverbally (a reassuring smile, a pat on the back).

A more structured approach, using behavior modification techniques adapted to individual needs, often helps students having more serious problems. Extrinsic reinforcers applied by the teacher should in time be integrated into the learner's own personality structure. When this occurs, and the student personally feels the reward of accomplishment, the reinforcement becomes intrinsic. When students enjoy reading or when they are pleased about accomplishing a particular reading task, the reinforcement becomes the satisfaction gained from doing the activity. One consideration often overlooked by teachers is that some students need considerable practice before they can attain a sense of satisfaction. Sometimes teachers try to push too fast for growth, changing learning tasks before the learner reaches the satisfaction of mastery.

4. *Encourage student participation.* Generally speaking, students who are involved in analyzing, planning, and evaluating their own reading are those who profit most from corrective instruction. Teachers should support students in understanding what they need to learn to improve their reading. With teacher help, many students can verify, even if intuitively, the reality of their identified learning gaps. They can also demonstrate to the teacher their ability to be successful at certain tasks that an original analysis may have suggested were too difficult. Timely, meaningful interaction between pupil and teacher leads to efficient and enjoyable learning.

When students recognize their need and realize their desire to know a variety of reading strategies, their goals become much clearer and attainment of those goals is consequently facilitated. Students like to keep track of their progress in attaining goals, and teachers should encourage them to make progress charts or otherwise keep their own record of their growth. These charts and graphs become concrete evidence of success that helps the learner maintain goal-directed behaviors. They also become an important evaluation tool for both student and teacher. Maintaining a portfolio is a natural way for students to keep track of their own progress and development over time (DeFina, 1992; Glazer & Brown, 1993; Tierney, Carter, & Desai, 1991). For best results, at least four one-to-one teacher–student conferences are required each semester, with student self-analysis occurring more frequently (Farr, 1992).

Common psychological factors that negatively influence reading achievement have been discussed in this section, while other psychological factors that occur less frequently have not. More detailed information can be obtained from books directed toward those training to become reading specialists.

Environmental Factors

Much of what occurs in the environment, or surrounding world, directly and indirectly influences the people who live in that environment. Environmental factors that have a strong negative influence on school achievement and reading progress include debilitating poverty, unfortunate conditions within the home, schools that are physically inadequate for or unresponsive to students' instructional needs, and societal ills. These environmental factors put students at-risk and make them academically vulnerable.

Poverty

In recent years considerable evidence has demonstrated that economic differences have a strong relationship with school achievement. Low income and poverty have a positive correlation with low achievement (Dyer, 1968). Schools in economically distressed areas, such as ghettos, barrios, among urban housing developments, and in certain rural areas, generally do not offer the same benefits to students as the more affluent systems characteristic of suburban school districts. Poor students from minority groups, in particular, have been denied the benefits of a good education (Kozol, 1991).

Students from impoverished circumstances, some perhaps homeless, come to school with experiences and backgrounds that vary considerably from their upper- and middle-class peers. Thus, the content of the school's reading program may be inappropriate for these students. While academically vulnerable due to their economic circumstances, these students can learn. They need enhanced conceptual, experiential, and language opportunities in school to ensure their literacy development. These students must also be made to see themselves as competent readers and writers, and they will do so as teachers help them master literacy tasks. Careful selection of literature to be used in the classroom can help affirm the identities of students of diverse backgrounds (see Appendix F for a listing of books appropriate for this purpose).

Negative Home Environment

The family and home have a significant role in providing the proper setting to promote school achievement. For instance, within groups labeled poor or culturally different from the majority in a geographic area, family values vary. Many students from economically poor homes are successful in school, and much of their success probably emanates from within their homes.

On the other hand, unfortunate home environments are found in every social, cultural, and economic group. When a home is unstable and the family setting does not nurture feelings of security, learning problems may arise. Factors frequently mentioned are broken homes, family conflicts, sibling rivalry, and quarreling, overprotective, dominating, neglecting, or abusive parents. No one can deny that these factors have negative effects on a child. However, many children exposed to these conditions successfully learn to read. Hence the response to problems at home is a highly individual, idiosyncratic matter.

Negative School Environment

Schools and instructional programs are often blamed for causing reading failures. Common responses from schools have been to increase the amount of testing, demand national standards, or to mandate a particular curriculum (Alexander, 1993; Farr, 1992; Frazee, 1993; Newmann & Wehlage, 1993). Such responses have led to mixed results, sometimes benefiting and sometimes hindering student learning.

Poor teaching is frequently cited as a reason for students not learning to read well (Shannon, 1989). Among the many complaints, the more common are: using unsuitable teaching methods; using overly difficult reading materials; using dull or otherwise inappropriate reading methods and materials; overemphasizing skills in isolation, especially phonics; giving too much or too little emphasis to reading skills; and teaching reading without integrating it into other curricular areas (see Shannon, 1990, for an historical treatment of the philosophies and practices of alternative literacy programs).

Improved instruction can best be facilitated by administrators and teachers working collaboratively. Administrators can work to alleviate certain rigid school policies that lead to imbalanced curricula and other inappropriate outcomes. Examples of such policies are (1) requiring teachers to emphasize reading subskills to the detriment of reading as a transactive process (2) overemphasis on the affective domain to the detriment of cognitive learnings (3) requiring teachers to instruct students in a specific sequence at a specific time, to the detriment of students needing supplementary or corrective instruction (4) requiring students to attain a specified level of achievement before they are promoted, to the detriment of students who are doing their best and achieving, but below some arbitrary level. Teachers become frustrated and their efforts are hindered by such unfortunate administrative policies. On the other hand, teachers can work to remain as informed as possible about their students' needs and current pedagogical knowledge.

Societal Ills

It is a major challenge of schools today to educate students who are at risk for their personal safety and survival. The National Clearinghouse on Child Abuse and Neglect Information (1-800-FYI-3366) reports that in 1991 approximately 2.7 million children were physically abused or neglected or sexually abused in the United States, a number that has doubled since 1980. Of these numbers, approximately 44 percent were cases of neglect, 24 percent physical abuse, 15 percent sexual abuse, and 17 percent other forms of maltreatment. Sexual abuse is all too common and drugs threaten children while still in the womb. Many abuse victims are young children; in 1988, 35 percent of all reported child sex abuse cases involved girls under 6 (Blume, 1990). Besides **sexual abuse** (sexual exploitation, molestation, child prostitution), there is **physical abuse** (nonaccidental injury to a child resulting in bruises, burns, broken bones, and/or internal injuries), **emotional maltreatment** (constant belittling, verbal abuse, inappropriate parenting, and neglect), and **physical neglect** (abandonment or inadequate provision of food, clothing, shelter, supervision) (Bear, Schenk, & Buckner, 1992/1993). Child abuse is far too common for teachers not to be knowledgeable about its physical and behavioral indicators (see Fig. 4.7). Teachers have the best opportunity to identify these students and having done so, are required by law to report such cases. But a teacher's help doesn't stop there. All the suggestions made earlier with regard to emotional and social adjustment apply here as well (see Bear, Schenk, & Buckner, 1992/1993).

Crack-cocaine has also had a serious effect on today's classrooms. "Approximately 400,000 children are born annually to mothers who used crack or cocaine during pregnancy" (Waller, 1992/1993, p. 57). While the child's intelligence is not affected, its affective and social skills are damaged. According to Waller (1992/1993):

> Crack-affected infants are often averse to being touched and to being looked at, as these strong stimuli threaten to overload them . . . and often fail to bond with a caregiver. This failure to bond is an important indicator that the child may have great difficulty forming relationships in the future . . . As toddlers, crack-affected children are often hyperactive, late in developing language, and late in walking. They are self-absorbed, impulsive, unaware of others, and unable to focus attention for any length of time. By age 3, they are often isolated because other children do not trust their unpredictable mood swings and sometimes violent outbursts . . . . Crack-affected toddlers can do what they are told and when, but they cannot plan their own time or activities . . . Teachers report that cocaine-affected school-age children are still impulsive and sometimes violent. Also, they are distractible,

FIGURE Indicators of child abuse.

4.7

	Physical Indicators	Behavioral Indicators	
Physical Abuse	• unexplained bruises (in various stages of healing), welts, human bite marks, bald spots • unexplained burns, especially cigarette burns or immersion-burns (glove-like) • unexplained fractures, lacerations, or abrasions	• self-destructive • withdrawn and aggressive—behavioral extremes • uncomfortable with physical contact • arrives at school early or stays late as if afraid	• chronic runaway (adolescents) • complains of soreness or moves uncomfortably • wears clothing inappropriate to weather, possibly to cover body
Physical Neglect	• abandonment • unattended medical needs • consistent lack of supervision • consistent hunger, inappropriate dress, poor hygiene • lice, distended stomach, emaciated	• regularly displays fatigue or listlessness, falls asleep in class • steals food, begs from classmates • reports that no caretaker is at home	• frequently absent or tardy • self-destructive • school dropout (adolescents)
Sexual Abuse	• torn, stained, or bloodied underclothing • pain or itching in genital area • difficulty walking or sitting • bruises or bleeding in external genitalia • venereal disease • frequent urinary or yeast infections	• withdrawn, chronic depression • excessive seductiveness • role reversal, overly concerned for siblings • poor self-esteem, self-devaluation, lack of confidence • peer problems, lack of involvement • massive weight change	• suicide attempts (especially adolescents) • hysteria, lack of emotional control • sudden school difficulties • inappropriate sex play or premature understanding of sex • threatened by physical contact, closeness • promiscuity
Emotional Maltreatment	• speech disorders • delayed physical development • substance abuse • ulcers, asthma, severe allergies	• habit disorders (sucking, rocking) • antisocial, destructive • neurotic traits (sleep disorders, inhibition of play)	• passive and aggressive—behavioral extremes • delinquent behavior (especially adolescents) • developmentally delayed

hyperactive, and disruptive . . . show memory problems . . . are slow to develop friendships . . . remain isolated, even into high school . . . (p. 58).

The special needs of cocaine-affected children are most effectively met in an "intervention environment where special techniques will be used" (see Waller, 1992/1993, p. 59). Placement in such programs generally continues one to three years, after which these students return to regular classes.

Teachers' Responsibilities

Naturally, classroom teachers should be aware of environmental factors that may be interfering with a student's reading accomplishments. It is very difficult, on an individual basis, to designate a specific environmental factor as *the* cause of a student's reading difficulties. Rather, this factor should be considered as a possible contributor to reading difficulties. Teachers are not sociologists or social workers, and few have been trained in techniques that pinpoint contributing factors. The role of the teacher is one of identifying *possible* contributing factors and referring the student to appropriate specialists or agencies in accordance with school policies. School districts often have social workers, counselors, and nurses to help teachers in the decision-making process.

Many schools have special programs for students from conditions of poverty, such as government-subsidized breakfast and lunch programs. Many communities today have mental health clinics that deal with family adjustment problems on a sliding fee basis that can be afforded by those of modest circumstances. Community welfare agencies often have child welfare departments concerned with children caught in untenable living conditions, including homeless or abusive situations. Thus, a major responsibility of teachers is to be knowledgeable regarding community services available to the students they teach and to their families.

To assist any possible referral that might be made in the future, anecdotal records should be used to document teacher observations with a high level of objectivity. This means the teacher must be careful to describe behaviors rather than simply assign labels, such as "this child's father is abusive." Teachers must remember not to overlook the privacy rights of students and their families. *Anecdotal records must never read like gossip.*

Instructional factors should be within the control of school personnel, specifically the classroom teacher and the principal. School-based personnel should assume responsibility for providing instructional factors that promote rather than inhibit learning to read. To maximize instruction in the classroom, teachers must first consider their students—their needs and interests, how they learn best, and how they might learn the joy of reading. These considerations are of major concern throughout the instructional chapters that follow.

SUMMARY

The intent of this chapter is not to study causes and correlates of reading failure but to help make teachers aware of the variety of factors that affect the reading process. Many of the factors mentioned, such as overall health, intelligence, and emotional maladjustment, affect learning in general. Other factors, including visual and auditory acuity, visual perception, and listening skills, are more directly related to reading.

In many cases the teacher can only refer students with such problems to other resources. Physicians, including neurologists, and psychologists may be needed if one of the related factors is severe. In some cases, teachers can give specific help, for example, with visual perception skills or auditory comprehension. In all cases, teachers should be understanding and caring and attempt to make the educational environment comfortable and risk-free for learners experiencing difficulty.

SUGGESTED READINGS

Themed issue: Students at risk. (December 1992/January 1993). *Educational Leadership,* 50 (4).

> *This entire issue is worthwhile reading on today's students. After reading the articles in this issue the reader will have a firm understanding of what it means when the term "at-risk" is used.*

Thau, A.P. (1991). Vision and literacy. *Journal of Reading, 35* (3), 196–199.

> *This article, written by a doctor of optometry, provides a glossary of terms related to vision and discusses vision's connection with reading. An educator's checklist is reproduced in the article.*

The following list shows U.S. publishers of large print editions of adult general interest or young adult books, as listed in the 1989 edition of *Literary Market Place.*

American Printing House for the Blind
Box 6085
Louisville, KY 40206
502-895-2405
1,400 titles in print

John Curley & Assoc.
Box 37
South Yarmouth, MA 02664
617-394-1280
800-621-0182
1,700 titles in print

G.K. Hall & Co.
70 Lincoln St.
Boston, MA 02111
617-423-3990
800-343-2806
3,500 titles in print

Jewish Braille Institute of America
110 E. 30th St.
New York, NY 10016
212-889-2525
10,000 titles in print

Walker & Co.
720 Fifth Avenue
New York, NY 10019
212-265-3632
800-AT-WALKER
1,400 titles in print

5

ASSESSING AND EVALUATING READING PERFORMANCE WITH INDIRECT MEASURES

OBJECTIVES

After you have read this chapter, you should be able to

1. define and describe briefly the following measurement terms: validity, reliability, and standard error of measurement;

2. list four purposes of reading tests and measures;

3. interpret these scores: grade equivalent, percentile, NCE, and stanine;

4. describe the differences among the following tests: reading survey tests, diagnostic reading tests, and text-related tests;

5. describe the differences between norm-referenced and criterion-referenced tests.

KEY CONCEPTS AND TERMS

assessment

at-level testing

construct validity

content validity

correlation coefficients

criterion-referenced tests

direct assessment

end-of-unit tests

evaluation

formal tests

grade equivalent scores

indirect assessment

mastery tests

NCE scores

norm-referenced tests

norms

out-of-level testing

percentile scores

performance assessments

reliability

standard deviation

standard error of measurement

standardized tests

standard scores

stanine scores

text-related tests

validity

STUDY OUTLINE

1. Introduction
2. Assessment and evaluation: basic concepts
   a. Definitions
      - Percentile scores
      - Standard scores
      - Stanine scores
      - NCE scores
      - Grade-equivalent scores
   b. Basic measurement concepts
      - Validity
        1) Content validity
        2) Construct validity
      - Reliability
      - Standard error of measurement
3. Types of tests
   a. Standardized test
   b. Classroom-based test
   c. Oral reading test
   d. Silent reading test

   e. Survey test
   f. Diagnostic test
   g. Criterion-referenced test
   h. Text-related test
   i. Individual test
   j. Group test
4. Purposes of testing in reading
5. Choosing and administering published reading tests
   a. Standardized reading survey tests
      - The *Gates-MacGinitie Reading Tests*
      - The *Nelson Reading Skills Test*
   b. Standardized diagnostic reading tests
      - Individually administered diagnostic tests
      - Group-administered diagnostic tests
   c. Criterion-referenced tests
6. Summary
7. Suggested readings

OVERVIEW

Knowledge of the analytic process alone is not sufficient for effective corrective reading instruction. Along with many other relevant facts, teachers must know (1) the variety of tools used to assess reading performance (2) when, where, and with whom the tools can be used (3) what the strengths and weaknesses of the tools are. Chapters 5 and 6 are designed to help teachers understand the purposes, instruments, and procedures useful in assessment.

In the first section of Chapter 5, concepts relevant to assessment, tests and measurement,

and analysis of reading achievement are discussed. Explanations are given of the different types of scores used in tests and their strengths and weaknesses. The purposes of testing are included as well as a brief discussion of different kinds of tests.

The second major section of this chapter contains a discussion of several commonly known reading tests. Standardized reading survey tests and standardized diagnostic reading tests are discussed in some detail, and examples are provided for consideration.

INTRODUCTION

At the time of this writing, educational assessment is in the midst of fundamental change due in large part to changes in instructional practices toward more constructive, integrated, and holistic approaches (Jongsma & Farr, 1993). While our knowledge of the reading process has become more clearly defined as a constructive and transactive process between the reader, the text, and the context of the reading, and "our pedagogy has expanded to reflect current research about learning literacy skills," our tests and testing environments are just beginning to change (Glazer, Searfoss, & Gentile, 1988, p. 7).

More and more states, school districts, and schools are moving away from assessing the kinds of isolated pieces of knowledge evaluated in standardized tests and toward

performance assessments in which students read, write, and solve problems in genuine ways such as taking and supporting a point of view on a specific issue. Two states in particular, Illinois and Michigan, are attempting to develop tests that reflect an interactive view of reading (Illinois State Board of Education, 1988; Michigan Educational Assessment Program, 1987). But this is not an easy period for administrators, teachers, and all those struggling to create new forms of assessment that reflect emerging curricula and standards. For example, we teachers even need to reexamine the language we use when we talk about assessment. As Peter Johnston (1992) points out,

> we refer to our own observations as "subjective," "informal," and "anecdotal," whereas we refer to tests as "objective" and "formal." Our own language devalues the close knowledge we have and values distance. It would be more helpful if we referred to our own assessments as "direct documentation" and test-based assessments as "indirect" and "invasive." These uses of language are far from trivial. They show that we do not value our own assessment knowledge. Our unfortunate cultural concern for control, distance, objectification, and quantification . . . does not favor teachers, whose knowledge is often intuitive, usually nonnumerical, more inclined to the narrative, and gained through personal involvement . . . Detailed knowledge comes from proximity and involvement, not distance. (p. 61)

As I reflect upon Peter Johnston's words and the work of others (Wolf, 1993), I, too, find it more accurate to use the term **indirect assessment** to refer to the standardized, norm-referenced types of tests discussed in this chapter, and the term **direct assessment** to refer to the classroom-based, or teacher-based, assessment techniques discussed in Chapter 6.

Currently, the indirect measures, while perhaps less meaningful to the teacher in terms of instructional planning because of their distance from what happens in the classroom, *are* administered in schools and are likely to be around for some time to come, as there continues to be a need for large-scale testing within school districts. At this point the reader is advised to review the resolution passed by the 1991 Delegates Assembly of the International Reading Association, the major professional organization of reading educators, in its entirety (Fig. 5.1).

This chapter is informative of the basic concepts related to indirect measures, enabling teachers to better decide for themselves how valuable a particular test score may or may not be. Also, the information found here should help teachers better discuss standardized test results with the parents of their students.

A review of the basic concepts of assessment and evaluation includes definitions, measurement concepts, a brief discussion of different kinds of tests, and, more specific to the goal of this text, purposes of testing in reading. After this review, the chapter proceeds with a discussion of particular reading tests.

ASSESSMENT AND EVALUATION: BASIC CONCEPTS

Definitions

Both assessment and evaluation are critical to the analytic process. Many educators use the terms interchangeably; however, **assessment** usually refers to the process of gathering data about a learner's strengths and difficulties, while **evaluation** refers to the pro-

Text of an International Reading Association resolution on literacy assessment (one of four adopted by the 1991 Delegates Assembly).

THE IMPORTANCE OF APPROPRIATE INTERPRETATION AND USE OF ASSESSMENT RESULTS

Whereas . . . the International Reading Association recognizes that one valid purpose for assessment is monitoring the outcomes of instruction at the level of the school, the community, the state or province, or the nation, and that a second valid, and distinct, purpose for assessment is to provide input information to the teacher and the pupil for the guidance and improvement of instruction and learning, and

Whereas . . . large scale assessments for the purpose of monitoring outcomes and classroom assessments for the guidance and improvement of instruction and learning, presently require different approaches and techniques appropriate to the needs of those who use assessment results, and

Whereas . . . large scale assessments do not address the question of how to improve teaching and learning and because such data are subject to misinterpretation and error when applied to small groups or individuals. Be it therefore

Resolved that users of assessment results recognize the importance of considering a variety of observation, procedures, and instruments; be it further

Resolved that users of assessment results take into account the specific purposes for which assessments are made and the settings in which assessments are conducted; be it further

Resolved that where large scale assessments are conducted for the purpose of monitoring outcomes results should not be reported for individual pupils, classes, or schools.

From *Journal of Reading, 35,* 5: 407, Feb. 1991 by the 1991 Delegates Assembly. Reprinted with permission of the International Reading Association.

cess of judging achievement or growth, or of decision making. Thus, evaluation implies the need to use assessment techniques to obtain information for making judgments or decisions.

In schools, reading achievement is frequently evaluated through the use of standardized achievement tests. **Standardized tests** are so called because they have been administered in the same way to a large group of students (who represent students for whom the test was designed) in order to establish a reference or norm group. The scores of these students then become the **norms** and can be used for comparison with the scores of other students taking the test. Thus, the term **norm-referenced** is also used to describe a standardized test. Part of the standardization procedure involves preparing a standard set of directions for administration that includes directions to students and time allotment for completing subtests. This standard set of directions is another reason these tests are called standardized, and because the directions for administration must be strictly adhered to, the tests have also become known as **formal tests**.

Several other terms associated with standardized testing will be used throughout the remainder of this chapter. Those related to interpreting standardized test scores will be defined here. Other important terms are defined in the next section. Because a standardized test is norm-referenced, norm tables are included in the test manual to tell you how the raw scores are converted into normed scores. These normed scores include percentile scores, standard scores such as stanines and normal curve equivalent scores, and grade equivalent scores. Each will be defined here. For help in seeing how some of these scores and others relate to the normal curve, refer to Figure 5.2.

Percentile Scores

Percentile scores, converted from raw scores, compare students only with others of the same grade or age. Students who receive a percentile score of 63 have done as well as or better than 63 percent of students in the norm group. The percentile scores *do not* represent the percentage of items answered correctly. Percentile scores can range from 1 to 99 (Fig. 5.2) and can be compared directly with other subtests or tests taken previously. Interpretation of percentile scores is limited, however, to comparing students with those in the norm groups or those in the same classroom or school. For example, if fourth-grader Georgia's raw score of 17 converts to the twelfth percentile on the reading comprehension subtest, the proper interpretation is that Georgia has done as well as or better than 12 percent of a large sample of children who took this test. If her score on the vocabulary subtest converted to the sixth percentile, the teacher can say that Georgia performed slightly better in reading comprehension than in vocabulary. The teacher *cannot*, however, average the two percentiles and say that, overall, Georgia scored at the ninth percentile. That is an inaccurate statement because of the way percentiles bunch up in the middle of a normal distribution; distances between scores are not equal. The teacher may also compare Georgia's score with those of her classmates who took the same test or with her previous scores on this test. That information can help the teacher place Georgia into an appropriate group for instructional reading purposes, but is not at all helpful for deeper-level analytic purposes. Therefore, the teacher must still rely on other means of assessing reading behaviors to help identify Georgia's specific areas of reading strength and difficulty.

Standard Scores

Standard scores are derived from raw scores in such a way as to obtain uniformly spaced scores. Standard scores indicate an individual score's distance from the average, or mean, score in terms of the variability of the distribution of all scores. Variability is indicated by a number called the **standard deviation**. (The higher the standard deviation, the more variability in the scores.) Standard scores allow comparisons to be made among scores on different tests and subtests. Some standardized achievement tests convert raw scores according to an average standard score of 50 with a standard deviation of 10 (see T-scores, Fig. 5.2). For example, if Jerry earned a raw score of 52 on a math test and 42 on a reading test, the scores cannot be directly compared because they do not reflect anything about the total distribution of scores for all the students taking the tests. By converting the raw scores to standard scores, each of Jerry's scores can be considered in relation to an average score of 50 and a standard deviation of 10. Jerry's scores con-

The normal distribution, percentiles, and selected standard scores.

F I G U R E

5.2

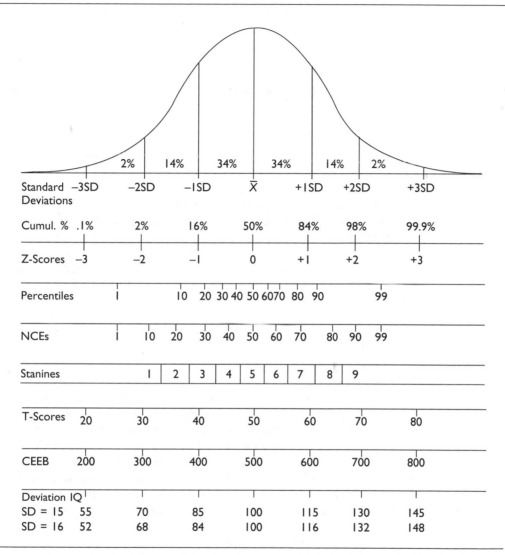

Reproduced by permission from *Test Service Bulletin No. 148*, 1986. The Psychological Corporation, San Antonio, Texas.

vert to a standard score of 80 on the math test and 48 on the reading test. Jerry therefore did much better on the math test than on the reading test, but the raw scores did not indicate such a large difference. Jerry also scored well above average on the math test. The average is 50; thus 80 is 30 points or 3 (30 divided by 10) standard deviations above the mean. On the other hand, Jerry did just about average on the reading test.

Stanine Scores

Stanine scores are standard scores for which the raw scores have been converted into nine equally spaced parts, with a stanine of 1 being low and 9 being high. A stanine of

5 is considered average, and the standard deviation is approximately 2 (Fig. 5.2). Stanine scores are interpreted similarly to percentiles, with the major difference being the number and size of units involved; there are 99 percentile units and only 9 stanines. For interpretation purposes, stanines 1, 2, and 3 reflect poor performance, stanines 4, 5, and 6 reflect average performance, and stanines 7, 8, and 9 reflect good performance on a test.

NCE Scores

Another kind of standard score based on a normal curve, the **normal curve equivalent (NCE)**, is a norm that has recently come into use. NCE scores range from 1 to 99 with a mean of 50, and in these ways they are similar to percentile scores. The points in between are different from percentiles, however. Percentile scores tend to pile up around the mean and spread farther apart upon approaching the extremes; NCE scores are in equal units.

Other standard scores that are seen in Figure 5.2 are Z-scores, CEEBs, and Deviation IQs. Z-scores simply specify standard deviation units with a mean of 0 and a standard deviation of 1. Thus Z-scores may be positive or negative. CEEBs are college board scores reported for such tests as the Scholastic Aptitude Test (SAT) or the Graduate Record Exam (GRE). Their mean is 500 with a standard deviation of 100. The Deviation IQs are intelligence test scores for such tests as the Wechsler or Stanford-Binet intelligence tests. The mean is 100 with a standard deviation of 15 (Wechsler) or 16 (Stanford-Binet).

Grade Equivalent Scores

Grade equivalent scores are usually stated in terms of years and tenths of years. For example, if the average raw score of beginning fourth-grade children in the norm group is 33, then 33 is assigned the grade equivalent of 4.1 (fourth grade, first month). Any child who scores 33 raw score points receives a grade equivalent score of 4.1.

Grade equivalent scores *appear* easy for teachers to interpret because the reference point is a grade in school, but interpretation actually has some serious limitations. The farther away a pupil's score is from the average, the greater the chances are that the grade equivalent will be misinterpreted. Grade equivalent scores for average children are probably accurate, but low or high scores are susceptible to error of interpretation. It is particularly important for teachers of students who are reading poorly to remember this. To continue with the example of the fourth grader, if Georgia scores 17 raw score points (a fairly low score), which converts to a grade equivalent score of 2.1 according to the norm table found in the test manual, the teacher should *not* conclude that Georgia is reading in a manner similar to a beginning second-grade child. All that can be said is that Georgia is reading poorly compared to her fourth-grade classmates and that she earned the same raw score as the average of second graders in the first month of second grade.

Grade equivalent scores do *not* indicate grade placement for a student. For example, Tommy, a third grader, takes the test containing second-, third-, and fourth-grade material and receives a grade equivalent score of 5.3. This does *not* mean that Tommy is able to handle fifth-grade, third-month material because he was never tested on fifth-grade material. It only means that Tommy can perform second-, third-, and fourth-grade tasks in the test as well as average students in the third month of fifth grade can perform these (below grade level) tasks.

Grade equivalent scores have been so seriously misinterpreted that the International Reading Association passed a resolution calling upon publishers to eliminate grade equivalents from their tests. This resolution can be read in its entirety in Figure 5.3. Percentile scores, stanines, or NCEs are recommended for comparing a student's performance to that of the norm group.

Basic Measurement Concepts

Successful assessment and evaluation in reading depend considerably on the tools teachers use. These tools can be called tests in the broadest sense of that term, but tests can range from informal reading inventories, to teacher-made spelling tests, to the highly structured standardized achievement tests. Some concepts are basic to all measurement

---

International Reading Association resolution regarding the misuse of grade equivalent scores.

FIGURE
5.3

MISUSE OF GRADE EQUIVALENTS

Whereas, standardized, norm-referenced tests can provide information useful to teachers, students, and parents, if the results of such tests are used properly, and

Whereas, proper use of any standardized test depends on a thorough understanding of the test's purpose, the way it was developed, and any limitations it has, and

Whereas, failure to fully understand these factors can lead to serious misuse of test results, and

Whereas, one of the most serious misuses of tests is the reliance on a grade equivalent as an indicator of absolute performance, when a grade equivalent should be interpreted as an indicator of a test-taker's performance in relation to the performance of other test-takers used to norm the test, and

Whereas, in reading education, the misuse of grade equivalents has led to such mistaken assumptions as: (1) a grade equivalent of 5.0, on a reading test means that the test-taker will be able to read fifth grade material, and (2) a grade equivalent of 10.0 by a fourth grade student means that student reads like a tenth grader even though the test may include only sixth grade material as its top level of difficulty, and

Whereas, the misuse of grade equivalents promotes misunderstanding of a student's reading ability and leads to underreliance on other norm-referenced scores which are much less susceptible to misinterpretation and misunderstanding, be it

Resolved, that the International Reading Association strongly advocates that those who administer standardized reading tests abandon the practice of using grade equivalents to report performance of either individuals or groups of test-takers and be it further

Resolved, that the president or executive director of the Association write to test publishers urging them to eliminate grade equivalents from their tests.

Resolution passed by the Delegates Assembly of the International Reading Association, April 1981. Reprinted with permission of the International Reading Association.

systems, regardless of how they are constructed or used. Among the more important concepts are validity, reliability, and standard error of measurement.

Validity

The most important of all measurement characteristics is **validity**. A test is valid if, in fact, *it measures what it claims to measure and does the task for which it is intended.* The critical question for the teacher to ask is: Does this test measure what I have been teaching? Sternberg (1991, p. 540) reminds us that "we need to be considerably more cautious in our use of test scores and that we need at least to think about creating tests that are more realistic simulations of people's behavior in the kinds of situations in which they use the aptitudes and achievements that we measure . . . Reading tests [are] considerably less valid as measures of real-world reading behavior than most people have wanted to believe." (see Table 5.1).

Test content that matches a teacher's instructional objectives is said to have **content validity**. If the match is poor, the test is an invalid measure of those particular instructional objectives. For example, a teacher has been concentrating on teaching reading comprehension for the past three months and now wants to test the pupils. A test measuring reading comprehension would be valid; one measuring phonics knowledge would be invalid because the test would not measure what had been taught. The phonics test is not a bad test in and of itself; rather, it is inappropriate for the purpose intended. Kavale (1979) suggests that teachers can best determine content validity by actually taking the test.

TABLE 5.1

Differences between reading as it occurs in tests and outside them.

STANDARD TESTS	SCHOOL/EVERYDAY LIFE
1. Passages are short.	Passages are moderate to long.
2. Learning from reading is massed.	Learning from reading is distributed.
3. Recall is immediate.	Recall is delayed.
4. Recall is entirely intentional.	Recall is largely incidental.
5. Comprehension is based on a single type of question, usually multiple choice.	Comprehension is based on multiple types of assessments.
6. The reasoning in the passage is very tight.	The reasoning in the passages is variable and often loose.
7. Assessments measure evaluation of arguments.	Assessments measure construction as well as evaluation of arguments.
8. Reading passages tend to be emotionally neutral.	Reading passages tend to be emotionally charged.
9. Reading passages are often unmotivating and boring.	Reading passages are often motivating and interesting.
10. Reading situations minimize distractions.	Reading situations contain distractions.
11. Evaluations are for a single purpose.	Evaluations are for multiple purposes.
12. Students do the reading because they have to.	Students often (but not always) do the reading because they want to.

From Robert J. Sternberg, "Are We Reading Too Much into Reading Comprehension Tests?," *Journal of Reading*, April 1991. Reprinted with permission of Robert J. Sternberg and the International Reading Association.

Teachers are unlikely to make an error in situations in which the validity issue is so clearly apparent as in the example above, but occasionally the matter is more subtle. Consider, for instance, the use of a test called "Vocabulary Knowledge" when the match between the test and the lessons taught is a matter of approach. If the teacher has used a modified cloze procedure approach, and the test measures vocabulary from a synonym-matching approach, the test would not be highly valid because it does not assess vocabulary as it was taught. Teachers and school administrators must be jointly responsible for choosing appropriate tests.

Another type of validity is called **construct validity**. This refers to the degree to which a test measures a certain ability or trait. For example, an intelligence test is said to have construct validity to the extent that it actually measures intelligence. Because most traits cannot be measured directly, tests having construct validity measure behaviors believed to reflect the trait. The titles of some tests imply construct validity without providing empirical information in the test manual to support the existence of the validity (Sax, 1980). Such a practice is misleading to teachers and to others who may not be knowledgeable about measurement concepts. A test on reading comprehension, for example, should provide evidence that the test, in fact, measures reading comprehension.

Many tests designed to measure word recognition skills have been questioned on the basis of their construct validity. If a syllabication subtest asks students to identify the number of syllables in various words, and the words are spoken by the examiner, the construct validity of the test can be questioned. In the real reading situation, the students *see* and do not *hear* the words that they must syllabicate. Thus the question is whether the behaviors measured by oral presentation measure the same trait required during the process of silent reading.

Construct validity is typically supported by **correlation coefficients** that indicate how strongly two variables are related. To be of most value for assessment, the subtests involved must be relatively independent, as reflected by low correlation coefficients ranging from 0.00 to 0.70. A high correlation (0.70 to 1.00) indicates a strong relationship between the subtests; in that case, the subtests are too interrelated to measure the different aptitudes they purport to measure.

Statistical procedures are available to determine test validity, but they are not directly related to the major purposes of this book. They are vital, however, for teachers who are asked to evaluate and select standardized tests for their school or school district. Both George Spache (1976b) and Kenneth Kavale (1979) add important issues relevant to selecting standardized tests in reading. These readings are highly recommended for those who select and use such instruments.

Reliability

The consistency or dependability of a test and its measurements denotes its **reliability**. If a teacher were to give the same test to a group of students more than once (test–retest) within a short time frame (so that growth isn't being measured), and the scores on the tests are nearly the same for each student, the test is considered reliable because it yields essentially the same score each time it is given.

Reliability is also expressed through a correlation coefficient. The higher the correlation coefficient, the more dependable are the scores obtained from the test. A coefficient of .90 or above is considered very reliable; if it is below .80, the teacher should be cautious in making decisions about the individual students. Reliability can be estimated in a number of statistical ways, and each has a different name. Test manuals indicate the type of reliability by using terms such as *split-half reliability, parallel forms reliability,* and *Kuder-Richardson reliability.* In any case, a high correlation coefficient is desirable.

No test of reading is perfectly consistent. Some common conditions affecting reliability are: (1) objectivity in scoring (2) needed variability among scores of students being tested (3) number of items on the test (4) difficulty level (5) standardization of test administration and interpretation (Sax, 1980).

Objectivity in scoring is critical. If different teachers independently score the same test but arrive at different scores, reliability cannot be very high. Multiple-choice tests are relatively free from problems of this type compared to more subjective measures, such as essay tests.

Reliability also depends on the variability of the students taking the tests. If everyone taking the test functions at the same level and gets the same score, reliability of that test is zero, because student variability is lacking.

The easiest and most efficient way to improve reliability is to increase the number of items on the test, provided that the added items consistently measure what the original items measure. This explains, in part, why some tests are so long. In instances of behavioral observation, the teacher must increase the number of times the student is observed performing a specific task.

Difficulty level also affects reliability. A very easy or very hard test does not measure individual differences because all student responses tend to be the same (Sax, 1980). Clearly such a test cannot be used for analytic purposes.

Standardization of test administration and interpretation, or criteria for scoring and interpreting, provides more reliable information. Tests and assessment measures that lack such clear guidelines result in interpretations that are highly dependent on the person making the assessment.

Standard Error of Measurement

When a score is obtained for a student, the teacher should ask how much confidence can be placed in it as the student's *true* score. Many test manuals describe a statistic known as the **standard error of measurement** (SEmeas or SEM). This statistic indicates the extent to which an individual's score can be expected to vary each time the test is taken. Edward Fry (1980), in a review of the Metropolitan Achievement Tests, clearly explains the SEM:

> Now we all know that every test has a certain amount of slop in it. Statisticians call this slop the Standard Error of Measurement. It means how much an individual's score is likely to jump around on repeated testings. You see the problem is, "if a student scores high one day, and lower the next day, on the same test, which score is correct?" Well, theoretically if you retook the test many times and there was no practice effect, you could average the scores and get a "true score," which is the score you really want. But you can't give the test a lot of times in the real world; so you give it just once and estimate how far away you could be from the true score. This distance is called the Standard Error of Measurement (SEM), and good statisticians that they are, the authors of the Metropolitan have given us the SEM for this test. Let's apply it to Janie Guesser's score. The SEM is 17 Standard Score points. This means that two-thirds of the time, Janie, or anyone else who got a raw score of 40, would have a true standard score between 733 and 697 [699]. You add

and subtract the SEM from the obtained score to get the band of probability [confidence interval].

That might sound a little technical, but you can read it slowly in any measurement textbook. However, let's make it a little more meaningful. An upper level Standard Score of 733 gives her a grade equivalent score of 6.7 and a percentile of 69. The lower level Standard Score of 697 [699] will give a grade equivalent score of 4.8 and a percentile of 48. This means that Janie, or any student getting 40 items right, has a true grade score between 4.8 and 6.7 for two out of three testings. In one out of three testings the true score would fall either above or below that band.

Hence when we test a student who is in the middle of the range for the intermediate level of the Metropolitan Reading Test, we know only that the true score lies in a band almost two years wide. Test scores aren't quite as accurate as some people think.[1] (pp. 199–200)

Ideally, we would like to use a test with high validity, high reliability, and a small SEM. The concept of the SEM is not restricted to standardized tests, however. Teacher observations, surveys and checklists, informal reading inventories, criterion-referenced tests, and text-related tests, which will be defined a little later, also have a potentially large SEM because they have not been given to large groups of students with the intention of revising to lower the SEM. Thus there is considerable potential for error with direct measures as well as with indirect measures. Before making a decision about a student's ability, the teacher must consider a variety of information (e.g., test score plus informal observation plus workbook page). The nature of assessment is multidimensional, much as literacy is a multidimensional process.

TYPES OF TESTS

Reading tests can be categorized in several ways:

1. Standardized (indirect, norm-referenced) or classroom-based (direct, nonstandardized)
2. Oral or silent
3. Survey, diagnostic, criterion-referenced, or text-related
4. Administered to individuals or administered to a group

Standardized Test

A standardized or norm-referenced test has been tried out on a large number of people to establish a norm group. Individual performances can then be compared to that of the norm group.

---

[1]From Edward Fry, "Test Review: Metropolitan Achievement Tests," *The Reading Teacher,* November 1980, pp. 196–201. Reprinted with permission of the author and the International Reading Association.

Classroom-Based Test

Classroom-based tests are generally not standardized and norm groups have not been established. Most classroom-based assessments are considered direct because they are designed with particular students and instructional focuses in mind. Any time a teacher designs an activity to collect information about some aspect of a student's ability, or uses an instrument that requires personal and immediate interpretation, a direct assessment is being made. Direct measures, however, are only as good as the person who devises or uses them. Chapter 6 deals more specifically with the topic of classroom-based assessment and includes such instruments as informal reading inventories, cloze passages, and interest/attitude surveys.

Oral Reading Test

An oral reading test requires the student to read aloud, which is the overt behavior being assessed. Oral reading provides a rich source of behavioral responses that are most often used to analyze two types of reading behaviors: fluency and word identification skills. Recently, oral reading responses have also been analyzed for evidence of the thought processes involved in mature reading (more on this in Chapter 6).

Silent Reading Test

A silent reading test requires the students to read to themselves and give responses to questions on the material. These responses can be given orally or in writing, depending on whether the test is an individual or a group test. The major advantage of silent reading tests is that they lend themselves to group assessment procedures, which are much less time-consuming than working with individual students.

Survey Test

A survey test, also called an achievement test, is designed to sample broad knowledge or proficiency in a given area. Scores reflect overall reading achievement. Because these tests are generally standardized, the group that takes the test can be compared with the norm group and general areas of strength and difficulty can be identified. Most reading achievement tests provide scores for the two subtests of vocabulary and comprehension plus a total reading score. Unfortunately, there are no standardized reading achievement tests that assess the strategies a reader uses.

Diagnostic Test

The diagnostic test attempts to measure discrete reading subskills. These subtest scores are then examined to determine areas of strength and difficulty. Some typical subtests are auditory discrimination, auditory vocabulary, phonetic analysis, structural analysis, and reading comprehension.

Criterion-Referenced Test

A **criterion-referenced test** measures how well an individual performs a specific task. Usually a desired level of performance is specified, thus the term *criterion*. For example, the content of a criterion-referenced test may be final consonant sounds. In order to say that Jimmy knows final consonant sounds, he may have to respond correctly to 90 percent or more of the test items. Jimmy's performance is not compared with group performance. Teachers set the criterion level to coincide with their expectations for a particular individual.

Text-Related Test

In addition to core materials found in most classrooms (e.g., basal readers, workbooks, and teacher's manuals), most publishers provide ancillary materials, including tests, to help assess student learning. These **text-related tests** measure acquisition of strategies and subskills emphasized in a reader or text at a particular level. Such tests have the advantage of content validity, because they are intended to measure the content learned from the reading materials just completed. While carefully constructed, they usually have not been as carefully normed as previously mentioned standardized tests. They also measure a smaller number of subskills and objectives. Good students may not have a chance to show what they can do; they often *top the test* (i.e., obtain very high scores). The tests can, however, indicate students who need assistance. Thus they can have considerable analytic value for the classroom teacher.

Many basal systems contain **end-of-unit tests** in the teacher's manual or in the student workbooks. These tests should not be overlooked by teachers; they provide useful information regarding student accomplishment of relatively small learning segments. Extension procedures are often recommended for students who do not perform well on these tests.

Individual Test

An individual test is designed to be given to one person at a time. The efficiency is low because fewer students can be tested in a given amount of time. However, some reading strategies can only be assessed through an individual test. The ability to monitor and self-correct oral reading miscues is one example. Other advantages of individual tests include the flexibility to modify or clarify directions for some students and the opportunity to observe other behaviors, in addition to reading, during the testing situation.

Group Test

A group test is given to several students at the same time. These tests solve the problem of inefficiency that characterizes the use of individual tests. Group tests come with specific directions (both oral and written in some cases) and written materials (usually an answer sheet or test booklet).

In summary then, many kinds of tests are available. However, each of the classifications just defined does not necessarily indicate a distinct type of test. One test may fall into more than one classification. For example, standardized achievement tests are not only survey tests but can also be group tests and silent tests as well. Likewise, a diagnostic test may be an individual or a group test or oral reading test. The most important thing in testing is to know *why* a particular test needs to be administered.

PURPOSES OF TESTING IN READING

Testing has many different purposes and many tests are available, so care must be taken to choose a test appropriate for a specific purpose. As Kavale (1979) says, "If the uses for the test results are not known in advance, the best test to use is none at all" (p. 9).

Test selection should be based on answers to the questions *what, who, by whom, for what* (Merwin, 1973). Kavale (1979) provides some examples of how these questions might be answered. For instance, a test is needed to:

1. assess reading achievement *(what)* of [an eighth-] grade student *(who)* by the teacher *(by whom)* to help determine the student's instructional reading level *(for what)*.
2. assess word attack skills *(what)* of a [second-] grade child *(who)* by the teacher *(by whom)* to determine if particular phonics knowledge is needed *(for what)*.
3. assess gain in reading achievement *(what)* of a group of fourth graders *(who)* by a curriculum supervisor *(by whom)* to determine the effectiveness of a new set of instructional materials *(for what)*. (p. 10)

Using Merwin's guidelines, the answer to the *for what* question represents the specific purpose for testing, but the other questions are equally important to the selection of a test.

Because of the great number of purposes for testing in reading, all cannot be listed; however, some examples are particularly relevant for classroom teachers:

1. Organizing the class into reading, skill, or interest groups
2. Assessing reading levels of individual students
3. Identifying specific reading difficulties in areas such as word identification, inferential comprehension, or vocabulary development
4. Evaluating individuals or small groups

CHOOSING AND ADMINISTERING PUBLISHED READING TESTS

Once the purpose for testing has been established, a test can be selected. Just because a test is published or its title indicates it may be appropriate does not mean you have found a quality test. The best procedure for determining the quality of a particular test is to examine the instrument itself (include the test's technical manual) and consult a professional review of the test. The most thorough resource for such reviews is the *Mental Measurements Yearbook,* now in its eleventh edition (Kramer & Conoley, 1992). This resource contains detailed information about many tests such as what they purport to measure, basic statistical data, costs of purchasing, and reviews of the tests by scholars. The International Reading Association (IRA) occasionally publishes test reviews in *The Reading Teacher* and *Journal of Reading,* two of its popular professional journals. IRA also published L. M. Schell's *Diagnostic and Criterion-Referenced Reading Tests: Review and Evaluation* (1981), which reviews twelve tests considered important by reading professionals.

Along with the tests themselves, publishers provide examiner manuals and several additional aids, such as scoring keys and record sheets. A test's technical manual or examiner manual contains vital information that must be studied before giving the test. A good test manual contains directions for test administration and scoring and information to aid effective interpretation of the scores. Additional information of a statistical and technical nature, such as validity and reliability coefficients and the SEM, are usually found in the technical manual.

Teachers must carefully follow directions when administering standardized tests. Tests are designed to give every pupil, as nearly as possible, the same chance when taking the test. If teachers do not follow standardized directions, scores cannot be used reliably and validly. Directions should never be rushed or examples omitted. On the other hand, teachers should never give more information to pupils than is specified in the test manual. Deviations from the directions or test time will put the pupils in a context different from the norm group, and norms for the test will not be appropriate. It is imperative, therefore, that teachers follow instructions precisely or note any deviations from the standardized procedures.

The testing environment is an important consideration because classroom conditions affect the reliability of test results. The classroom should be well lighted, ventilated, and free from undue noise or interruptions. A sufficient number of tests, answer sheets, and marking pencils should be readily available. Pupils unaccustomed to taking tests should be briefed beforehand regarding such test-taking behaviors as no talking, no helping, and no drinks of water. In classrooms in which cooperative learning groups and conversation are the norm, these testing requirements can certainly affect results (McAuliffe, 1993). Most students would benefit from a practice session using practice booklets, which are often available with standardized tests. At times teachers have difficulty maintaining the neutral role needed during the testing period, but the temptation to help students must be resisted. The roles of teacher and tester are *not* the same.

Standardized Reading Survey Tests

Standardized tests most widely used in schools today are achievement test batteries such as the *California Achievement Tests, Iowa Tests of Basic Skills, Metropolitan Achievement Tests,* and *Stanford Achievement Tests.* These batteries typically yield two or three reading scores plus scores for other subject areas, such as arithmetic and social studies. Common areas assessed in reading are vocabulary, comprehension, total reading (often a combination of the vocabulary and comprehension scores), and less frequently, measures of study skills and rate of reading.

These tests can be helpful to classroom teachers in two important ways. First, they allow teachers to compare students within their classroom to determine their relative standing (rank order), which should aid in grouping for instruction. Second, they give teachers an opportunity to identify areas of strength and difficulty for individual students relative to the norm group, in the curricular areas being tested. For example, a student may demonstrate strength in arithmetic computation and difficulty with the subtests of a reading survey test. This can be a clue that the student has the potential to read better.

Survey reading tests are similar to the reading subtests on achievement test batteries. When reading is the focus of testing, a survey test saves time and money because other content areas are not included. These tests help in placement and are often used in pre- and post-intervention assessments to determine whether students have benefited from that particular intervention. Survey tests can be helpful for inexperienced teachers who may not yet know what to expect from learners at a particular developmental age or grade level. Teachers should be aware, however, that scores from these tests probably reflect either maximum or minimum performance on the part of many students. They usually either try hard to do their best on tests of this type, or give up altogether and answer questions randomly. In either case, their scores tend to reflect a level of concentration and performance not typical in their day-to-day reading activities.

While survey reading tests help teachers with level 1 analysis, identifying those students who may need assistance in their reading development, and perhaps with level 2 analysis, identifying the major domain in which reading difficulties are occurring, they are not designed to do more than this. Other tests and assessment procedures are more helpful for analyzing reading behaviors at levels 2, 3 (areas of difficulty), and 4 (teachable units), and they can supplement data obtained from survey tests. Also consider that there are students who are effective readers but never do well on standardized tests.

Most recently developed survey reading tests, including the two discussed in this section, are designed to be administered in one of two ways. The first, called **at-level testing**, uses a single level of the test for a specified grade level. For example, level A of the test is to be used for first and second grades, level B for third and fourth grades, and level C for fifth and sixth grades. A third-grade teacher would administer the level B test to all students in the class.

The second option, called **out-of-level testing**, allows the teacher to select the level of the test that best reflects the average achievement of the class. For example, a teacher of students whose average achievement is atypically low or high could select a level better suited to the students, thus increasing reliability. If out-of-level testing is desired, be sure to check the teacher's manual of the test being used for further information.

The *Gates-MacGinitie Reading Tests, Level A* (1989) is used here as an example for children in first grade. Other levels of the *Gates-MacGinitie Reading Tests* are available for grade levels through high school (level R = readiness, level B = grade 2, C = 3, D = 4–6, E = 7–9, and F = 10–12). The *Nelson Reading Skills Tests, Level A* (1977) has been chosen as an example for children in third or fourth grade. Other levels are also available (level B = grade 5–6; level C = 7–9).

The Gates-MacGinitie Reading Tests

Level A of the *Gates-MacGinitie Reading Tests* is designed to assess reading progress for students in first grade. It consists of two subtests, vocabulary and comprehension, with an optional decoding subtest for levels A and B. On the vocabulary subtest, the child is asked to choose the word from four choices that best represents a picture. Items are arranged in order of increasing difficulty. The score is the number correct.

The comprehension subtest also contains items arranged in order of increasing difficulty. The students are asked to read one to four sentences per item and then to mark, from among four pictures, the one that best represents ("goes with") the story. The score is the number correct. Raw scores can be converted to standard scores, percentiles, and grade equivalent scores for interpretation purposes.

The Nelson Reading Skills Test

The *Nelson Reading Skills Test, Level A,* is designed to be used with pupils in grades 3 and 4. As with the *Gates-MacGinitie*, two subtests assess vocabulary and comprehension. However, level A only has three optional subtests: sound-symbol correspondence, root words, and syllabication.

To test knowledge of vocabulary, students are asked to select a synonym for a given word from among four possible choices. In contrast to level A of the Gates-MacGinitie test, level A of the Nelson test expects children to read stimulus words to complete the sentence; the test for first graders uses pictures. This change, observed in many reading tests, represents the shift away from the use of pictures in tests as children mature in reading development.

The vocabulary subtest contains items arranged in order of increasing difficulty. Because the test is designed to survey more than one grade level, a spread of items in terms of difficulty is needed. Younger children are not expected to complete the more difficult items, and the teacher needs to prepare them for this outcome. A brief discussion before testing will help avoid possible frustration.

The comprehension subtest also contains paragraphs of increasing difficulty. Students are asked to read each paragraph and answer questions cast in a multiple-choice format. The score is the number of items correct.

Raw scores for both subtests are totaled, converted to stanines and percentiles, and entered into the test booklet. The teacher has available at least three scores for the student: vocabulary, paragraph reading, and total reading. Each optional subtest will provide an additional score.

Both the Gates-MacGinitie and Nelson reading tests survey students' knowledge of vocabulary and their general understanding of sentences and paragraphs. Clearly these tests are designed to assess the domain of reading comprehension. As is typical of many survey tests, they do not reveal performance in other reading domains, except through inference or administration of the optional decoding subtests.

Standardized Diagnostic Reading Tests

The major purpose of standardized diagnostic reading tests is to help teachers identify students' specific areas of strength and difficulty. A graphic profile is used to compare subtest scores for individuals and to determine level of ability in the reading areas. Because diagnostic assessment is directed at identifying specific strengths and areas of difficulty, the total test score is much less meaningful than the profile because it represents a composite performance. Reviewing the profile for an entire class can aid appropriate grouping for instruction. In the class summary profile for a fourth-grade urban classroom seen in Figure 5.4, the teacher circled stanines that are in the low range (1, 2, and 3). Such a procedure helps a teacher readily identify students who may need assistance in one reading domain (e.g., Marcus T., reading comprehension), or several (e.g., Irwin J., all domains). The teacher can also begin to form tentative hypotheses for instruction and groupings (see comments in Fig. 5.4).

FIGURE
5.4

Graphic profile for comparing subtest scores.

Teacher __Ms. B.__ Grade __4__ Date __October__

Pupil's Name	Auditory discrimination	Phonic analysis	Structural analysis	Auditory vocabulary	Literal comprehension	Inferential comprehension	Total comprehension	Comments
Duane B.	③	4	5	4	4	4	4	VERIFY AUDITORY DISCRIMINATION
Elizabeth B.	6	4	6	5	5	4	5	COULD PEER TUTOR?
Isaiah D.	5	5	③	③	4	③	③	VOCABULARY AND INFERENTIAL COMP.
Rebeka D.	8	6	7	8	7	7	7	COULD PEER TUTOR?
Irwin J.	①	②	③	③	②	②	②	COMPREHENSION STRATEGIES 1ST
Austin J.	4	4	4	4	②	①	②	COMP. STRATEGIES – FOCUS INFERENTIAL
Brandon M.	5	5	②	②	4	4	4	COMBINE VOCAB. AND AFFIXES
Latasha M.	5	5	4	4	①	①	①	COMPREHENSION. DOES LATASHA RELY
Natasha M.	5	③	6	5	5	5	5	TOO MUCH ON HER TWIN, NATASHA?
Kalisha M.	③	4	6	③	③	①	②	FOCUS ON INFERENTIAL COMP.
Paul M.	5	4	5	③	③	③	③	SOME COMP. ASSISTANCE
Bichhuy N.	②	②	4	5	5	5	5	LANGUAGE INTERFERENCE?
Julius P.	7	9	9	9	9	8	8	COULD PEER TUTOR?
David P.	4	①	4	①	①	①	①	COMP. STRATEGIES LEA? VERIFY STRUCT.
Eric T.	①	②	5	②	②	②	②	COMPREHENSION - 1ST/ VERIFY STRUCTURAL
Marcus T.	5	4	4	4	②	②	②	COMPREHENSION STRATEGIES
Brian T.	4	①	5	4	③	③	③	VERIFY PHONIC SCORE
								10/17 NEED
								COMPREHENSION ASSISTANCE

Individually Administered Diagnostic Tests

Several diagnostic reading tests are designed for individual testing. For best results, teachers need special training in administering, scoring, and interpreting these tests. This is not a realistic expectation for many classroom teachers. The tests are also time-consuming to administer, score, and interpret, so they cannot usually be justified for classroom purposes. Individual diagnostic tests should be used only by teachers and other specialists who have the necessary training, experience, and time to justify their use. They are mentioned here for those who wish to pursue this topic independently. Following are four widely used, individually administered, standardized, diagnostic tests:

1. *Gates-McKillop Reading Diagnostic Tests* recently revised to *Gates-McKillop-Horowitz Reading Diagnostic Tests*
2. *Durrell Analysis of Reading Difficulty*
3. *Spache Diagnostic Reading Scales*
4. *Woodcock Reading Mastery Tests*

All four of these tests are reviewed by Schell (1981).

Group-Administered Diagnostic Tests

The most common diagnostic reading test used by classroom teachers is the *Stanford Diagnostic Reading Test* (Karlsen & Gardner, 1986). The four levels of the Stanford Diagnostic Reading Test (SDRT) cover grades 1 through 12 and community colleges, with two parallel forms at each level (Schell, 1981). The levels are designated by color: (1) red level for grades 1 and 2, (2) green level for grades 3 and 4, (3) brown level for grades 5 through 8, (4) blue level for grades 9 through 12. All forms have out-of-level norms.

Four components of reading are assessed: decoding, vocabulary, comprehension, and rate. The red level is used in grades 1 and 2 and also for older students reading at these lower levels. The red level measures auditory discrimination, phonic analysis, auditory vocabulary, word recognition, and comprehension of short sentences and paragraphs. The green level is used in grades 3 and 4 and with low achievers in grade 5. The green level measures auditory discrimination, phonic and structural analysis, auditory vocabulary, and literal and inferential comprehension. The brown level is used in grades 5 through 8 and with low-achieving high school students. The brown level measures phonic and structural analysis; auditory vocabulary; literal and inferential comprehension of textual, functional, and recreational reading material; and reading rate. The blue level is used from the end of eighth grade through high school and at the community college level with students considered relatively poor readers. The blue level measures phonic and structural analysis; knowledge of the meanings of words and parts of words, such as affixes and roots; reading rate to include skimming and scanning; and literal and inferential comprehension of textual, functional, and recreational reading material.

While several of these skills subtests are administered for all four levels, the specific skills are measured differently. For example, the phonic analysis subtest for the red level measures the reader's ability to discriminate among consonant sounds represented by single consonant letters, consonant clusters, and digraphs in the initial and final positions, while the same subtest for the brown level measures whether the reader can recognize the same consonant sounds represented by the same spelling or two different spellings (e.g., *f*ace and *r*ain; *f*oam and gra*ph*; *p*ie and re*p*ly; *s*ugar and na*ti*on). The changes in what is measured from level to level are intended to reflect the developmental characteristics of the reading process. Teachers will have to decide if these subtests provide valid (content validity) assessments for their students.

The test materials for the SDRT include test booklets, answer folders, and the following manuals and aids: *Directions for Administering, Norms Booklet, Manual for Interpreting, Handbook of Instructional Techniques and Materials,* and *Multilevel Norms Booklet.* Both hand- and machine-scorable answer folders are provided. If a teacher administers all the subtests of the SDRT, class summary and instructional group placement information can be generated by using The Psychological Corporation's scoring service. Of course, such information is most useful if the SDRT is administered as early as possible in the fall of the school year.

The last two sections of this chapter have presented information on standardized survey reading tests and standardized diagnostic reading tests. These tests are widely used for assessing reading achievement and reading difficulties, and the results can be helpful in that they give teachers working hypotheses to verify in the context of "real" reading during classroom instruction.

Criterion-Referenced Tests

Criterion-referenced tests, or skills management systems, are assessment/instructional materials that focus on reading subskills. They are also referred to as **mastery tests** because students are said to have mastered a subskill when they attain the specified criterion. Teachers have actually been using the concept of a criterion-referenced test for years. Anytime they develop a test to measure some specific objective and designate a specific grade as passing, they are using the concept of criterion-referenced testing.

The assumption underlying criterion-referenced tests and the manner in which they are constructed is different from norm-referenced tests. Criterion-referenced tests focus on whether a student (or group of students) has learned a particular set of reading subskills. This is different from the norm-referenced test that compares learners with a norm group on general ability in the major reading domains. Table 5.2 compares and contrasts norm-referenced and criterion-referenced tests.

For criterion-referenced or mastery tests, interpretation of the results appears quite simple and straightforward in that 80 percent indicates passing or mastery of a subskill and less than 80 percent indicates failure or nonmastery. The decision-making process is simplified for teachers. Using the score as a basis, they decide whether a student has learned the subskill; if mastery is attained, the next decision is whether to move on to another subskill or to a higher level of difficulty for the subskill under consideration. If the student has not mastered the subskill, the teacher decides either to reteach or to review the particular subskill involved.

Several problems arise with criterion-referenced tests. Of great concern to some reading educators is the lack of empirical data or research evidence to substantiate the existence of specific reading subskills (Farr & Carey, 1986). They claim that even if the subskills exist, the order in which they should be learned is unknown and arbitrary (Duffy, 1978).

Teachers also should be aware that some students learn their reading subskills well but still cannot read adequately, if at all. Likewise, some students read adequately but still fail reading subskills tests (Jackson, 1981; McNeil, 1974). A pure subskills approach to teaching reading can lead to troubled readers just as a no-skills approach

Comparison of norm- and criterion-referenced tests.

TABLE

5.2

NORM-REFERENCED	CRITERION-REFERENCED
1. Norm-referenced tests assess the student's knowledge about the particular subject or content being tested.	1. Criterion-referenced tests assess the student's ability to perform a specific task.
2. Norm-referenced tests compare a student's performance with that of the norm group. (During the last phase of test construction, a final draft form is given to a large number of students who are representative of the students for whom the test was designed. This is the *norm group*.)	2. Criterion-referenced tests determine whether students possess the skills needed to move to the next level of learning.
3. Norm-referenced tests can be used annually as pretests and post-tests to determine student gain while comparing these gains to those of the norm group.	3. Criterion-referenced tests can be used as pretests and post-tests to determine which skills need to be taught and which skills have been mastered.
4. Norm-referenced tests contain items that are considered to be precise, valid, and reliable in order to discriminate among the weakest and best students.	4. Criterion-referenced tests contain items that determine whether the student is able to use the learned skill in particular situations.
5. Norm-referenced tests have a high degree of validity.	5. Criterion-referenced tests have only content validity; the items assess the ability needed to perform a given behavior.
6. Norm-referenced tests have a high degree of reliability. They consistently measure the same behavior with each administration of the test. This factor is *essential* for norm-referenced tests.	6. Criterion-referenced tests are not concerned with statistical calculations of reliability. If students are retested, they should not make the same score.
7. Interpretation of the student's score on norm-referenced tests depends on the scores obtained by the norm group.	7. Interpretation of the student's score on criterion-referenced tests depends upon whether the student is able to perform a specific task.
8. Norm-referenced test scores yield global measurements of general abilities.	8. Criterion-referenced test scores yield exact measures of ability to achieve specific objectives.
9. Norm-referenced test scores are interpreted in terms of norms that have been statistically listed in the test manual by the author or the publisher.	9. Criterion-referenced test scores are interpreted in terms of a score that is considered acceptable by the teacher, and by examining specific items that were correct or incorrect.
10. Norm-referenced test items are written to create variability among the individual scores in a particular group.	10. Criterion-referenced test items are designed to assess ability to perform a specific task as stated by a behavioral objective.

From Eddie Kennedy, *Classroom Approaches to Remedial Reading*, 1977, pp. 82–83. Adapted by permission of the publisher, F. E. Peacock, Publishers, Inc., Itasca, IL.

can. This probably reflects inappropriate *use* of tests for planning instruction rather than inappropriate tests themselves. As with norm-referenced tests, teachers must interpret results of criterion-referenced tests as working hypotheses that need to be verified in the context of "real" reading.

Two of the more widely used criterion-referenced systems available are:

- *The Prescriptive Reading Inventory (PRI)* (1980)
- *The Wisconsin Design for Reading Skill Development* (Otto & Askov, 1972)

The number of objectives covered, the number of items per objective, and the criteria for mastery vary greatly from system to system. Careful scrutiny of commercial criterion-referenced materials is thus extremely important to insure that the objectives covered are those desired for the reading program. Edward Robbins (1981), in a review of the *Prescriptive Reading Inventory,* discusses a number of factors to consider in deciding if the objectives of a criterion-referenced system match the objectives of the reading program. These factors include checking to see (1) if the testing context is consistent with the instructional context (2) how closely the distribution of subskills in the test matches that in the school's reading program (3) if the specific subskill activity is assessed in such a way that performance is attributable to knowing the subskill (4) how well the placement of subskills in the various levels of the test correspond to the school's reading program. Anyone anticipating using a criterion-referenced test would be wise to consult Robbins's review.

SUMMARY

The early part of this chapter reviews the state of fundamental change that assessment is undergoing. New ways of thinking about assessment and evaluation are introduced. Several important measurement concepts, such as content and construct validity, reliability, and standard error of measurement, are discussed.

The second part of the chapter discusses selection, administration, scoring, and interpretation of standardized tests. Particular attention is given to published diagnostic reading tests that are easily administered and currently used by classroom teachers. Criterion-referenced tests are also explained and contrasted with norm-referenced tests.

SUGGESTED READINGS

Baumann, J.F. (1988). *Reading assessment: An instructional decision-making perspective.* Columbus, OH: Merrill.

Chapter 5 is recommended reading for those teachers who rely on standardized tests for decision making. Entitled "Using standardized reading tests to make screening and diagnostic decisions," this chapter presents a thoughtful treatment of the information made available to teachers using these instruments.

Farr, R. (1992). Putting it all together: Solving the reading assessment puzzle. *The Reading Teacher, 46,* 26–37.

> *This distinguished educator, Roger Farr, has written extensively on reading assessment. In this article, Dr. Farr discusses conflicting views on reading assessment and proposes linkages among various approaches as a solution.*

Johnston, P. (1992). Nontechnical assessment. *The Reading Teacher, 46,* 60–62.

> *An informative summary of assessment issues and content of Johnston's larger work,* Constructive Evaluation of Literate Activity *(1992), Longman. He stresses the need to know reading and writing better, to know our students better, and to become more reflective.*

CHAPTER

ASSESSING AND EVALUATING READING PERFORMANCE WITH DIRECT MEASURES

OBJECTIVES

After you have read this chapter, you should be able to

1. compare and contrast the following direct measures: informal reading inventories, cloze procedure, checklists and rating scales, observations and interviews, and work samples;

2. administer and interpret an informal reading inventory, cloze passages, retellings, interest and attitude surveys;

3. discuss the value of the information obtained through direct measures for use at analytical levels 3 and 4.

KEY CONCEPTS AND TERMS

anecdotal records
cloze procedure
emergent literacy
frustration reading level
independent reading level
informal reading inventory
instructional reading level
interactive assessment
listening capacity

maze technique
miscue
miscue analysis
passage dependent
protocol
qualitative analysis
quantitative analysis
running records

STUDY OUTLINE

1. Introduction
2. Commonly used direct measures
   a. Informal reading inventories (IRIs)
      - Three reading levels
        1) Independent reading level
        2) Instructional reading level
        3) Frustration reading level
      - Constructing and administering IRIs
      - Scoring IRIs
      - Interpreting IRIs
        1) Establishing reading levels
        2) Analyzing results of the IRI
      - Listening capacity

   b. Cloze procedure (maze procedure)
   c. Assessment by observation and conferences
      - Observation
      - Conferences
   d. Checklists and rating scales
   e. Interest and attitude surveys
   f. Work samples
   g. Oral and written language samples
3. Putting it all together: A vignette
4. Summary
5. Suggested readings

OVERVIEW

While the indirect measures discussed in the preceding chapter can be helpful tools for a global analysis of reading achievement, their main function for classroom teachers is to supplement or support information obtained by direct, classroom-based measures. The deeper the level of analysis required, the more the need for direct, individual, and frequent observation of behaviors. This chapter discusses some of the procedures you may use in the analytic process, such as informal reading inventories, cloze and maze techniques, retellings, and the use of checklists and surveys.

Teachers must often rely on their own assessment measures and classroom-based procedures to help them identify, particularly at the level 4 analysis, specific learning segments or units that are *teachable*. Observations, conferences, checklists, rating scales, interviews, and work samples are examples of the direct assessment tools used. Suggestions for constructing, administering, and interpreting each of these tools are discussed in this chapter.

INTRODUCTION

For many years teachers have felt that standardized measures in reading do not give sufficient information for instructional decision making. The main justification for using classroom-based tests and measures is that they supply useful information for direct teaching applications. Because these measures often involve the actual materials and tasks used in the classroom, the teacher obtains a more realistic view of how the reader functions within the instructional setting.

Direct assessments occur frequently; thus the reliability of such assessments is increased. If standardized reading tests were given as often the process would be extremely time-consuming, subtracting substantially from available teaching time, already at a premium in the classroom. Furthermore, the cost would be prohibitive. Also, the information yielded by many standardized tests is not the type that teachers want most; that is, information that tells whether specific strategies have been learned or what strategies or skills might be taught next.

A number of direct measures that help teachers assess and evaluate students' reading behaviors will be explained in this chapter. No one technique is sufficient, nor should the results of standardized, diagnostic, or criterion-referenced tests be overlooked. Both types of tests and measures provide information for analyzing students' reading behaviors and for planning instruction.

COMMONLY USED DIRECT MEASURES

Informal Reading Inventories

The **informal reading inventory** is probably the most widely known nonstandardized, direct measure. Major purposes for using this measure include: (1) to help the teacher observe a student's strategic reading behaviors with material of various grade levels (2) to aid the teacher in choosing appropriate texts, readers, or other reading materials for each student in the class (3) to aid the teacher in identifying three different reading levels—the independent reading level, the instructional reading level, and the frustration reading level (4) to aid the teacher in learning more about each pupil's reading strengths and needs.

An informal reading inventory (IRI) consists of a series of graded passages that students read and answer questions about. Inventories can be (1) published instruments, in which passages and questions are carefully constructed to reflect reading grade levels accurately (2) teacher-made, with passages selected from the reading materials used in the school (3) constructed by a publisher to accompany a particular basal reader series. Lists of words graded by difficulty often are used as quick screening devices to determine a starting point for reading passages. Passages are then read orally, silently, or both, depending on the teacher's purpose. Word recognition errors are recorded for the oral selections, while comprehension is checked for passages read orally or silently. Rate of reading can also be obtained by recording the time spent reading the passages.

An advantage of a well-constructed teacher-made IRI is that its content is generally quite valid, that is, it tests pupils on reading materials used in their school. Some educators (e.g., Harris & Sipay, 1990) indicate that results from IRIs are more accurate than results of standardized tests for placement purposes. It is claimed that results from standardized tests tend to overestimate students' reading levels. Typically, studies suggest that children are able to read materials one-half to one year above the suggested placement from results of IRIs (Farr & Carey, 1986), although differences of opinion exist on this issue.

Probably the greatest disadvantage of many IRIs is that they assess reading comprehension—the heart of reading—using as few as five test items per level. The reliability of test results can be seriously questioned when so few items are used. The questions are not always well written, nor do they necessarily discriminate between good and poor readers (Davis, 1978). Most inventories also claim to provide information on comprehension subskills (e.g., determining main ideas, recalling details, identifying cause and effect, inferring word meanings from context); however, research shows they do not, so IRIs should not be used for this purpose (Duffelmeyer & Duffelmeyer, 1989; Duffelmeyer, Robinson, & Squier, 1989; Schell & Hanna, 1981). Furthermore, comprehension is frequently assessed on *oral* reading of the passages. This is of particular concern with ineffective readers and readers in the early elementary grades, who may expend their cognitive abilities trying to do well reading aloud, thereby diverting some attention from understanding the author's message.

IRIs are time-consuming to administer and interpret, especially if administered to an individual to record oral reading behaviors. Average administration time per student is thirty minutes. Interpretation time can be at least as much and probably more. However, as will be discussed later, every student does not need to be assessed with an IRI.

Many publishers of basal reading series include IRIs in their supplementary materials. These IRIs are constructed specifically to be used with their reading series. Using publisher-constructed IRIs seems to be a good alternative to developing your own, particularly in view of the trend to include stories in basal readers with readability levels that are not controlled as carefully as in the past. One potential problem with using basal reader IRIs is that a student can test out of a basal reader level, not because of ability to read and comprehend the material, but because the particular basal story was read the preceding year or term when the student may have been inappropriately placed.

Today, many teachers are choosing to use published IRIs because of the time required to construct an IRI. Examples of some published inventories are the *Analytical Reading Inventory* (Woods & Moe, 1989), the *Basic Reading Inventory* (Johns, 1991), the *Ekwall/Shanker Reading Inventory* (Ekwall & Shanker, 1993), the *Flynt-Cooter Reading Inventory for the Classroom* (Flynt & Cooter, 1993), the *Qualitative Reading Inventory* (Leslie & Caldwell, 1990), and the *Secondary and College Reading Inventory* (Johns, 1990). These published IRIs may or may not be better than teacher-made IRIs. The important measurement concepts of reliability and validity must be considered. For individual assessment purposes a desirable reliability coefficient is .90. Authors of published IRIs should provide this information in their administration manuals.

The question of validity is also critical. Does the IRI measure what it is intended to measure? To answer this question, you must recall the four major purposes for administering an IRI and remember that the issue of validity differs somewhat for each one. For example, if the purpose is to aid the teacher in placing a pupil in an appropriate reader, then a basal series publisher-constructed or teacher-made IRI based on the reading series being used may be more valid because the passages are taken from the materials being used.

Another validity issue is related to the purpose of identifying the three reading levels. For some time, writers and users of informal reading inventories have chosen to use the arbitrary criteria set up by Betts (1946) to distinguish the independent (99% word recognition, 90% comprehension), instructional (95% word recognition, 75% comprehension), and frustration (90% or less word recognition, 50% or less comprehension) reading levels discussed in the next section. These criteria were based on data obtained from 41 fourth-grade students who read the passages silently before reading them aloud. Not until 1970, when William Powell adjusted these criteria to be dependent on the grade level of the child being tested, were the Betts criteria challenged. Powell (1970) found that children who could comprehend material reasonably well (70–75%) achieved average word recognition scores ranging from 83% to 94% across grades 1 through 6. Older readers were even more accurate in word recognition. Unfortunately, too little research evidence is available either to support the Betts criteria (Roberts, 1976) or to define appropriate criteria for establishing the three reading levels. Published IRIs are generally consistent in using the Betts criteria, with only a few exceptions. Regardless, the scoring criteria are clearly noted in each inventory's administration manual.

It is important to remember that IRIs are nonstandardized measures and thus can be used flexibly. Published IRIs provide what sound like rigid procedures for administration; however, teachers using published IRIs understand their own purpose(s) for using the IRI, employ good judgment, and rely on their knowledge of the reading process. For example, a study by Cardarelli (1988) points out that by allowing students to look back at a passage to answer the comprehension questions, over half these students increased their scores sufficiently to change frustration reading levels to instructional reading levels. This procedure makes good sense if a teacher normally allows students to look back in their textbooks for answers to questions rather than insisting that the students answer the questions from memory as directed in most IRI manuals.

In any event, teachers must use other direct assessment procedures to supplement results of IRIs on comprehension. For instance, the student being assessed should be encouraged to recall as much about the passage or story as possible *before* questions are asked. This procedure is called "retelling the story," and is adapted from a published instrument called the *Reading Miscue Inventory* (Goodman & Burke, 1972). General comprehension questions can be asked if the student does not respond freely. For example:

Tell me about . . .

Who was in the story?

What happened?

Where did this happen?

How did it happen?

Why do you think the story was written?

Teachers may choose to record a student's free retelling by making check marks on a previously prepared outline of the story that identifies major points from the passage related to characters, events, plot, and theme (Fig. 6.1). If these items are not mentioned, the teacher asks questions, also prepared in advance, to help elicit desired information. Nevertheless, questions about retellings should not supply information or insights the reader did not provide in the retelling. Most questions should be of the WH– variety and refer to information already given by the reader. These questions, when asked following a story, should be keyed toward the elements of a story. For example, as modified from Weaver, (1994, pp. 247–249):

Characters:

What else can you tell me about (name of character(s) provided in the retelling)?

Who else was in the story besides (the characters mentioned)?

Events:

What else happened?

What happened after (event provided in the retelling)?

Where (or when) did (event mentioned in the retelling) happen?

How did (event mentioned in the retelling) happen?

Plot:

Why do you think (action(s) mentioned in the retelling) happened?

What was the main problem for (character mentioned in retelling)?

Theme:

How did you feel when (event mentioned in the retelling) happened?

What do you think the author might have been trying to tell us in the story?

List of major points to be used to record a student's free recall of the Aesop fable "The Lion and the Mouse."

FIGURE

6.1

Main Points for Retelling

_____ sleeping lion

_____ lion awakened by mouse who ran across his paw and up his nose

_____ lion wanted to kill mouse

_____ mouse promised that someday he could help the lion if he would let him go

_____ lion let mouse go

_____ later, lion was caught in a hunter's net made of rope

_____ lion roared loudly

_____ mouse recognized the lion's roar

_____ mouse helped the lion by chewing through the rope of the net

_____ lion was freed by the mouse

_____ Moral: Even small acts of kindness are important

Setting:

Where/when did the story take place?

How was (character or event mentioned in the retelling) important to the story?

These questions can easily be modified for retellings of expository material. For example:

- What else can you tell me about (topic of passage mentioned in retelling)?
- What else was this passage/section about besides (the topic mentioned)?
- What other information did the author provide about (topic, or important concept briefly mentioned in the retelling)?
- What happened after (event mentioned in retelling)?
- What do you think the authors are trying to tell us in this section?
- How was (event or fact mentioned in the retelling) important to this passage?
- How do you think you might use this information?
- How is this information like anything you have read about before?

For both narrative and expository passages, teachers also should ask questions related to the reading event. As found in Weaver (1994, pp. 248–249), these questions are modified from the _Reading Miscue Inventory: Alternative Procedures_ (Goodman, Watson, & Burke, 1987):

Is there anything you'd like to ask me about this story [passage]?

Were there any (concepts, ideas, sentences, words) that gave you trouble? What were they?

Why did you leave this word out?

Do you know what this word means, now?

Were there times when you weren't understanding the story? Show me where. Tell me about those times.

Remember when you said the kid was a "typeical baby"? What is a "typeical baby"? (Ask about key words that were mispronounced or otherwise miscued, to see if the reader got the concept despite the miscue.)

In addition to demonstrating an understanding of story structure, story retellings reveal the reader's ability to remember facts, make inferences, and recall sequence (Morrow, 1985a, 1985b). To evaluate retellings a holistic scoring system is recommended. Irwin (1991) provides such a system, which is reproduced in Figure 6.2. To assess silent reading for groups or for students in the upper grades, a written retelling is possible (Smith & Jackson, 1985). The use of a story frame or a paragraph frame (see Chapter 10) lends itself well to this purpose.

The "think-aloud" procedure (Brown, 1985; Kavale & Schreiner, 1979; Olshavsky, 1976/1977) addresses the criticism that comprehension questions do not assess the process of comprehension. This procedure requires readers to verbalize their thoughts while reading. These verbalizations provide insights into the ways individual readers derive meaning from text.

Three Reading Levels

Three reading levels relevant to classroom teaching can be estimated from administering and interpreting IRIs. The first level is called the **independent reading level**, which

---

FIGURE 6.2 Free recall processing checklist.

Answer each of these questions according to the following scale:

5 Yes, very well
4 Yes, more than adequately
3 Yes, adequately
2 No, not too well
1 No, poorly
NA Not applicable or can't tell

1. ___ Did the student recall a sufficient number of ideas?
2. ___ Did the student recall the ideas accurately?
3. ___ Did the student select the most important details to recall?
4. ___ Did the student understand explicit pronouns and connectives?
5. ___ Did the student infer important implicitly stated information?
6. ___ Did the student include the explicitly stated main points?
7. ___ Did the student create any new summarizing statements?
8. ___ Did the student use the organizational pattern used by the author?
9. ___ Did the student elaborate appropriately?
10. ___ Did the student know how to adjust strategies to the purpose given?

What effective comprehension processes were evident in the student's recall?

What comprehension processes were not evident, or seemed to be causing problems?

To what extent was the student's performance as just described affected by each of the following?

1. Limited prior knowledge or vocabulary
2. Limited motivation or interest
3. Cultural differences
4. Decoding problems
5. Difficulties in the text
6. Social context
7. Discomfort with the task
8. Other environmental influences

From Irwin, J., *Teaching Reading Comprehension Processes,* © 1991 by Allyn and Bacon. Reprinted by permission.

refers to the difficulty level at which a learner reads comfortably without teacher help. Students should be reading library books and other materials for pleasure at this level, with little or no difficulty recognizing words or comprehending. School reading to be done at home should be at students' independent reading levels. Students learn to read for fun and enjoyment when they read easy materials. At this level they develop favorable attitudes toward and positive interests in reading.

At the **instructional reading level**, students read with some direction and supervision. Students are usually placed in basal readers written at their instructional reading levels, but most other materials pupils read *should not* be this difficult unless a teacher or someone else is available to help them. Without help, tension and other unfortunate outcomes may result (Arnold & Sherry, 1975). Too often, a single content area textbook is used for instructional purposes. This practice assumes that all students in a class have the same instructional reading level.

The **frustration reading level** is one at which reading deteriorates and students cannot continue reading because the material is too hard even with instruction and guidance. Physical behaviors frequently associated with frustration include frowning, crying, squirming, whispering, or rebelliousness. Teachers should guide students away from reading materials at this level.

Constructing and Administering IRIs

The informal reading inventory is ideally based on reading materials regularly used in the school, including content area textbooks. The selections, chosen from as many books as possible in the series, might range from 50 words at the primer level to 100–150 words in grades 1 through 3, to 200–250 words or so beyond grade 3. Stories should be well formed and cohesive enough to allow development of comprehension questions. These questions should be **passage dependent**, that is, answerable upon reading the passage, and balanced between literal and inferential comprehension. For help in writing questions, Johnson and Kress (1965), Pearson and Johnson (1978), and Valmont (1972) are recommended readings. Also, longer selections and more comprehension questions increase the reliability of the results.

In order to assess free recall, a list of the main points of each selection will need to be prepared (refer to Fig. 6.1). The selections, list of free recall main points, and questions are typed on separate sheets of paper and duplicated. These pages become the **protocol**, or record sheet, that the teacher uses for testing purposes. If the entire set of graded readers or textbooks is difficult to obtain, the teacher may, with permission from the publisher, reproduce the pages from the texts and bind them together in a notebook. A sample of about twenty words introduced in each text can be placed in list format to be used for "quick" screening purposes.

Once the protocols and the student's notebook are prepared, the IRI is given. With a published inventory, begin by asking the learner to read the word lists, starting with the lowest level list available. If the first list is read with at least 80 percent accuracy, the next level can be tried. If reading with less than 80 percent accuracy, the pupil begins with the easiest passage. The student continues to read the word lists until the 80 percent criterion is *not* met. At this point the student is asked to read the selection corresponding to the highest level word list on which he scored 100 percent. Beginning at an easier level helps to insure that the first selection will be read successfully. When using a published inventory, the criteria for determining starting points may vary. You should carefully read the directions for administration found at the beginning of the inventory being used.

The student reads selections of increasing difficulty while the teacher codes behaviors in oral reading and comprehension. There are two popular ways to code passages read orally: by using traditional miscue codes, which are similar to an editor's proofreading symbols, or by using **running records**, a combination of proofreading symbols and check marks. (Clay, 1985). Figure 6.3 provides an example of a coded IRI passage using traditional miscue codes. Figure 6.4 shows the same passage recorded as a running record. A tape recording allows the performance to be reviewed to verify the scoring estimated during the testing session. Reading continues until the student reaches the criteria associated with the frustration level. At this point, in addition to *not* achieving a minimum level of word recognition and comprehension, the student usually exhibits other symptoms, such as squirming in the chair or facial contortions.

For novice users of informal reading inventories, all these directions for administration may seem quite formal and intimidating. Keep in mind, however, that the essential point in all assessment is to learn more about the student as a reader—not merely to identify reading levels. Brozo (1990) makes a case for **interactive assessment** in which the teacher tries "to discover the conditions under which a student will succeed in reading" (p. 523). Using an informal reading inventory as an example Brozo illuminates the much less testlike procedures of interactive assessment, which, briefly, include beginning with a diagnostic interview to learn about interests, attitudes, and students' goals and perceptions about reading, and moving through the steps of IRI administration in an instructional manner rather than a test-taking manner. Kletzien and Bednar (1990) support this approach to assessment when they describe the value of what they term *dynamic assessment.*

> When the at-risk reader is made an active participant in the assessment, the reader gains greater confidence and a sense of control over reading strategies. The social interaction between the examiner and the reader is particularly important for these learners. Too often, they simply give up on a standardized test and receive a very low score, further depressing an already low self-concept. [Dynamic assessment/ interactive assessment] acknowledges what the reader actually can do, and thus provides a positive experience. (p. 532)

As teachers gain experience in IRI administration and begin to appreciate the flexible uses of IRIs and other assessment tools, interactive assessment procedures may have more appeal. Remember the important goals of assessment, to learn students' capabilities and to guide instructional planning, as you proceed through the rest of this chapter.

Scoring IRIs

IRIs are rather easy to score for placement purposes. One scoring system for oral reading accuracy is suggested by Harris and Sipay (1990, pp. 227–228).[1]

The following should be counted as one error each:

1. Any word used that deviates from the text and disrupts the meaning
2. Any word pronounced by the teacher after the child has hesitated about five seconds

---

[1]Adapted from *How to Increase Reading Ability* by Albert J. Harris and Edward R. Sipay. 9th ed. Copyright 1940, 1949, 1956, 1961, 1968, 1970, 1975, 1980, and 1990 by Longman, Inc. Reprinted by permission of Longman, Inc., New York.

Example of a coded IRI passage.

Primer (50 words 8 sent.)

**Examiner's Introduction
(Student Booklet page 117):**

Please read this story about a child who imagines some unusual things.

Look! It is me!

I can run as fast as a train!

UP
I can jump over a (big) tall tree!

train
I can ride my bike as fast as a running goat!

the   *A*
I can see very little things far away.

I can put on a good show!

Yes, I am something!

**Comprehension Questions
and Possible Answers**

(mi)   1.   What is this story about?   *I can do things*
            (The special kid, Super kid, etc.)

(f)   2.   What does the child mean by saying, "I can run
            as fast as a train"? (can run very fast)
                                   he rides his bike fast

(f)   3.   How high can this child jump?
            (over a big tall tree)   *up a lot*

(f)   4.   How fast can the child ride the bike?
            (as fast as a running goat) *as fast as a train*

(t)   5.   What is meant by the word over?
            (above)   *like on top of something*

(f)   6.   What kind of things can the child see far away?
            (very little things)   *little things*

Symbol Key
   ∧ insertion
   O omission
   A teacher pronounced
   ∿ reversal
   ᴍᴍᴍ repetition
   UP substitution
   over

Miscue Count:

O _|||_ _|_ S _//_ A _|_ REP _|_ REV _|_

Scoring Guide	
Word Rec.	Comp.
IND 0–1	IND 0
INST 2–3	INST 1–2
FRUST 5+	FRUST 3+

FIGURE
6.4

Using running records to score oral passages.

Primer (50 words   8 sent.)

Examiner's Introduction
(Student Booklet page 117):   Please read this story about a child who imagines some unusual things.

2 errors *   ✓ is it ✓
    Look! It is me!

0 errors   ✓✓ ✓✓ ✓✓✓ ✓
    I can run as fast as a train!

2 errors   ✓✓ ✓ up ✓— ✓✓ ✓
    I can jump over a big tall tree!

2 errors   ✓✓ ✓ ✓ ✓ ✓ ✓✓ train —
    I can ride my bike as fast as a running goat!

2 errors   ✓✓ ✓ the ✓ T ✓
    I can see very little things far away.

0 errors   ✓✓ ✓✓✓ ———— R
    I can put on a good show!

0 errors   ✓ ✓✓ ✓
    Yes, I am something!

Comprehension Questions
and Possible Answers

(mi) 1. What is this story about?   *I can do things*
    (The special kid, Super kid, etc.)

(f) 2. What does the child mean by saying, "I can run as fast as a train"?
    (can run very fast)   *he rides his bike fast*

(f) 3. How high can this child jump?   *up a lot*
    (over a big tall tree)

(t) 4. How fast can the child ride the bike?
    (as fast as a running goat)   *as fast as a train*

(t) 5. What is meant by the word over?
    (above)   *like on top of something*

(f) 6. What kind of things can the child see far away?
    (very little things)   *little things*

* Based on criteria and directions for scoring as outlined in Clay (1985, pp. 19–21, 115).

$$\frac{\text{Running Words}}{\text{Errors}} = \frac{50}{8}$$

Error Rate = 1:6.25

$$\text{Accuracy} = 100 - \frac{8}{50} \times \frac{100}{1}$$

= 84% = Hard text
(< 90% = too difficult)

8 errors
Miscue Count:

0 2 | | s 4 A | REP | REV —

Scoring Guide	
Word Rec.	Comp.
IND 0–1	IND 0
INST 2–3	INST 1–2
* FRUST 5+	FRUST 3+

The following should be counted as only one error, regardless of the number of times the error is made:

1. Repeated substitutions (one word substituted for another such as *when for then*). Flynt and Cooter (1993) follow Clay's (1985) guidelines, which are to count this substitution as an error each time it is made. Repeated substitution errors of proper names are counted only once (e.g., *Bobby* for *Billy*).

2. Repetitions (individual words or groups of words that are said more than once). There is disagreement on counting repetitions as errors. For example: Spache (1976) counts two or more words repeated as a repetition error; Ekwall and Shanker (1993) think *all* repetitions should be counted as errors; Taylor, Harris, and Pearson (1988) do *not* count repetitions as errors at all; Flynt and Cooter (1993) do not even record repetitions. Generally I favor noting repetitions but *not* counting them as errors. Repetitions usually occur for a reason and demonstrate that the reader is concerned with maintaining understanding of material read. However, if there are a great number of repetitions this may indicate the material is too difficult.

3. Repeated errors on the same word, even though the errors themselves may be different. Again, variation among authors of published inventories exists. For example, Leslie and Caldwell (1990) count once as an error a repeated miscue that maintains meaning (e.g., *phone* for *telephone*), but count as errors each miscue on the same word when the pronunciation changes the meaning (e.g., *expect* and *export* for *expert* would count as two errors).

The following should *not* be counted as errors:

1. Pronunciations or miscues that reflect cultural or regional dialects
2. Spontaneous self-corrections
3. Hesitations
4. Ignoring or misinterpreting punctuation marks

The total errors are counted and converted to a percentage score based on the number of words pronounced correctly and the total number of words in the selection.

In addition to recording oral reading behaviors, retellings and responses to comprehension questions asked after each selection are also recorded. Sometimes these responses can be scored as the student answers the questions. More often, however, judgment about performance can only be made in relation to what the student read and how the student has responded. Therefore, it is best to analyze these responses carefully at a later time.

Interpreting IRIs

Establishing reading levels. Once the teacher has obtained scores on (1) oral reading behaviors and (2) comprehension of silent or oral reading or both for the selections read, the scores are assembled in a table such as that in Figure 6.5 to aid interpretation of results. All published inventories provide a similar table, usually called a summary sheet. When interpreting results of an IRI, remember that these inventories are subject to error of measurement. Thus, the criteria for establishing the independent, instructional, and frustration reading levels must be interpreted judiciously. The teacher surveys the assembled scores and makes judgments about the estimated reading levels based on the pro-

F I G U R E

6.5

Sample table to aid interpretation of scores for reading accuracy and comprehension.

Summary of Results of Informal Reading Inventory

Name: _____Sandra_____   Grade: _____Beginning 4th_____

Level of Text	Oral Reading		Silent Reading	Reading Level
	Percent Accuracy	Percent Comprehension	Percent Comprehension	
2^1	99	100	100	Independent
2^2	97	80	90	Instructional
3^1	98	100	100	Independent
3^2	94	80	100	Instructional
4	93	80	90	Instructional
5	88	50	70	Frustration

Estimated independent reading level: 3^1

Estimated instructional reading level: 4*

Estimated frustration reading level: 5

* or 3^2–4, if a range is desired.

gression of scores as well as the scores themselves. Results of research by Powell and Dunkeld (1971) and Cooper (1952) would indicate that the student's grade level should also be a consideration (see Table 6.1). As indicated earlier, there is not absolute agreement on the criteria to be used to determine reading levels.

Almost always, interpretation requires some estimating and interpolating. In interpreting Sandra's scores (Fig. 6.5), chances are good that Sandra's independent reading level is third grade and that the 80 percent comprehension score obtained at the 2^2 reader level for oral reading reflects error of measurement. The instructional reading level is probably fourth grade, the higher of the two sets of scores yielding that outcome, especially in light of the silent reading comprehension score. Notice also that the 94 and 93 percent accuracy scores are slightly below the Betts criterion of 95 percent, but are acceptable for the instructional level according to both the Powell and Dunkeld and the Cooper criteria.

Once reading levels have been estimated, the teacher verifies these tentative working hypotheses (i.e., independent reading level equals beginning third grade; instructional reading level, fourth grade; frustration reading level, fifth grade). This is accomplished by placing Sandra in fourth grade level materials to see if she can deal effectively with the texts and accompanying lessons. Verification of placement in materials is critical to effective analysis and instructional planning. Without verification, all the analytic effort may be for naught.

Work by Beck (1981), Berliner (1981), Gambrell, Wilson, and Gantt (1981), and Jorgenson (1977) suggests that student achievement in reading, especially for developing readers, is positively affected if a large portion of instructional time is spent with

Powell and Dunkeld and Cooper criteria for determining informal reading inventory instructional reading levels.	T A B L E 6.1

Powell and Dunkeld Criteria for Instructional Level

Grades 1–2   88–97.9% word recognition
             70–89% comprehension

Grades 3–5   92–97.9% word recognition
             70–89% comprehension

Grades 6+   94.4–97.9% word recognition
             70–89% comprehension

Cooper Criteria for Instructional Level

Grades 2–3   95–98% word recognition
             70% minimum comprehension

Intermediate   91–96% word recognition
grades   60% minimum comprehension

---

relatively easy material (error rates of 2 to 5 percent), with regular exposure to more difficult material. Beck (1981) explains that in this way the reader is allowed "to develop fluent and automatic responses in less difficult text while encountering a challenge to develop new knowledge and strategies in more difficult text" (p. 89).

The best advice might be to be conservative. If reading levels are unclear or other characteristics about a student deserve consideration (e.g., immature personality, general academic difficulty, poor work habits, or disruptive home background), the student should be placed in the easier material under consideration (Haller & Waterman, 1985).

Analyzing results of the IRI. Analysis of IRI results beyond establishing the three reading levels provides a wealth of information. Oral reading behaviors and comprehension performance can be examined further to find patterns in a student's reading behaviors and shed light on that student's reading strategies. Borrowing heavily from the *Reading Miscue Inventory* developed by Goodman and Burke (1972), coded oral reading behaviors can be thought of as miscues. A **miscue** is defined as an observed response that differs from the expected response, that is, the reader does not say exactly what is written. With this inventory, Goodman and Burke introduced the notion of **qualitative analysis**; rather than simply count errors (**quantitative analysis**), the examiner attempts to analyze the reader's strategies. Miscue analysis will be discussed in more detail below.

The rationale for analyzing miscues is that not all unexpected responses are equally serious. For example, if the reader inserts *very* before the word *happy* in the sentence "Tom was not happy," the meaning of the sentence has not been seriously altered. The teacher may overlook miscues if meaning is not changed. This kind of qualitative analysis often reveals that students are extracting meaning from what they read despite apparent word recognition errors. This is especially important for learners from dialectically different cultures than that of most of the students. If nothing else, the qualitative analysis makes the teacher aware of the language functioning of the student who speaks a different dialect. At its best, the qualitative analysis makes the teacher aware of the student's reading strategies.

A detailed **miscue analysis** is not necessary for every reader, not even for every reader experiencing difficulty. A thorough miscue analysis might only be done for readers who demonstrate especially perplexing reading miscues. For such cases the teacher is referred to Goodman and Burke's *Reading Miscue Inventory* (1972).

To determine the instructional needs of most students, a simple form of miscue analysis is extremely useful. A partial analysis that looks at the use of graphophonic, syntactic, and semantic cues and asks whether the reader views reading as a meaning-making process provides valuable information about areas of strength and need. This underlying philosophy of determining whether the reader is reading for meaning and what strategies the reader is using is essential in miscue analysis.

A brief set of questions can be asked about miscues to provide insight into the reader's use of language cues and reading strategies. These questions should (1) emphasize that reading for meaning is more important than exact reproduction of the surface structure (2) aid the teacher in identifying both a reader's strengths and needs (3) acknowledge the importance of self-corrections of miscues that do not fit the context. Figure 6.6 shows the results of such an analysis.

In a much abbreviated version of miscue analysis, a teacher might simply ask whether the miscue changed meaning (unacceptable), whether it was acceptable in context, or whether it was corrected. A simple form also might be used for periodic assessments of oral reading behaviors (Fig. 6.7). With this form, the teacher can compare the responses to these questions. If "Yes" is checked for question 3 and "No" or "Sometimes" for question 1, the student may be relying too heavily on graphophonic cues. Instruction in the use of syntactic and semantic context clues would be in order. On the other hand, if "Yes" is checked for question 1 and "No" or "Sometimes" is checked for question 3, the student may be relying too heavily on context clues. Instruction in phonics or structural analysis would be advisable. This instruction might include such facilitating questions as "Do you see any part of the word that you know?" (e.g., *run* in *running*), or "What word do you know that starts with _____ , and would make sense?"

As discussed earlier, free recalls could precede asking the comprehension questions provided in published IRIs. As the miscue analysis and evaluation of comprehension performance are being conducted, factual summary statements for observed reading behaviors and strategies can be made. Instructional goals will become more evident from examination of these summary statements. Examples of summary statements can be found in Figure 6.8. Summary statements can be written for each level of material, the type of material (i.e., narrative or expository), listening comprehension, and for any other relevant observations such as written language samples and oral language samples (discussed later in this chapter).

Listening Capacity

Another piece of information that can sometimes be estimated by an IRI is **listening capacity**, also called the listening comprehension level. This is the highest level at which the student can understand 75 percent of the material read aloud by the teacher. The teacher reads and asks questions about a selection beginning at the next level above the frustration reading level. This score is sometimes used as an indication of a learner's ability to understand oral language.

continued

FIGURE 6.6

Example of miscue and comprehension qualitative analyses based on a fifth grader's oral reading of passages from the Woods and Moe *Analytical Reading Inventory*.

Miscue Analysis Chart

Student: Jason

Level of Passage	Miscue in Context	Acceptable — Syntax	Acceptable — Semantics	Unacceptable	Self-Correction of Unacceptable Miscues	Graphic Similarity — Initial	Graphic Similarity — Medial	Graphic Similarity — Final	Unknown Words
3	Suddenly he dashed home and soon returned with a bucket of yellow (paint) one of black, and several brushes.			✓					
3	I thought you might want to paint your and ⊕ clubhouse yellow with black stripes.			✓	✓				
4	con-di-tion The pony's condition was growing worse as his breathing grew harder and harder.	✓	✓			✓		✓	
4	bucket At nightfall Jody brought a blanket from the house so he could sleep near Gabilan.	✓		✓		✓	✓	✓	
4	blizzards Looking up he saw buzzards, the birds of death, flying overhead.	✓		✓		✓		✓	
4	blizzard perching A buzzard was perched on his dying pony's head.	✓	✓	✓		✓✓	✓	✓	
	Column Total	5	2	5	1/5	5	2	4	0
	Total No. of Miscues Analyzed	7	7	7		7	7	7	7
	Percentage	71%	29%	71%	20%	71%	29%	57%	0%

F I G U R E *continued*

6.6

Comprehension Analysis Chart

Lower Level				Higher Level			
Level of Passage		Oral	Silent	Level of Passage		Oral	Silent
2	No. Correct	3		2	No. Correct	3	
	Total Possible	3			Total Possible	3	
	Percentage	100%			Percentage	100%	
3	No. Correct	4		3	No. Correct	3	
	Total Possible	4			Total Possible	4	
	Percentage	100%			Percentage	75%	
4	No. Correct	3		4	No. Correct	3	
	Total Possible	4			Total Possible	4	
	Percentage	75%			Percentage	75%	
5	No. Correct	2		5	No. Correct	2	
	Total Possible	4			Total Possible	4	
	Percentage	50%			Percentage	50%	
	No. Correct				No. Correct		
	Total Possible				Total Possible		
	Percentage	LISTENING			Percentage	LISTENING	
6	No. Correct		1	6	No. Correct		2
	Total Possible		4		Total Possible		4
	Percentage		25%		Percentage		50%
5	No. Correct		4	5	No. Correct		3
	Total Possible		4		Total Possible		4
	Percentage		100%		Percentage		75%
	No. Correct				No. Correct		
	Total Possible				Total Possible		
	Percentage				Percentage		
Total No. Correct		12		Total No. Correct		11	
Total No. Questions		15		Total No. Questions		15	
Total Percentage		80%		Total Percentage		73%	

Listening comprehension is sometimes considered an estimate of reading expectancy; that is, if the student were able to read the material, the listening comprehension level, or listening capacity, represents the level at which it could be understood. Rubin (1982) says, "a child may have excellent comprehension ability, but it may be masked because of word recognition problems" (p. 49). As Spache (1976a) states, "there is a definite relationship between listening comprehension and verbal intelligence" (p. 63). He reports a correlation of .75 between listening comprehension as tested by the Spache

---

Form for assessing oral reading behavior.

F I G U R E

6.7

	Yes	No	Sometimes
1. Do the reader's miscues make sense in context?			
2. Does the reader correct unacceptable miscues?			
3. Does the reader pay too much attention to graphophonic cues and not enough to syntactic or semantic cues?*			

*A miscue may be graphically similar in the initial, medial, or final position (or some combination) and be unacceptable in terms of meaning. For example, a reader paying more attention to graphophonic cues than semantic or syntactic cues might substitute *his* for *this* in the sentence "This time it was ready."

Summary statements based on the miscue and comprehension analysis charts for Jason.

F I G U R E

6.8

SUMMARY STATEMENTS

Name:	Jason	**Date:**	December
Age:	10	**Level of Material:**	3–6
Grade:	5	**Type of Material:**	Narrative

1. The majority of Jason's miscues (71%) are unacceptable; that is, they change meaning.

2. Jason only self-corrected 20% (1 out of 5) of his miscues.

3. The majority of Jason's miscues (71%) are acceptable syntactically; that is, they maintain the same part of speech as the original text.

4. Jason is aware of context clues, but does not use these clues consistently.

5. Jason's substitutions are usually graphophonically similar to the initial and final position of the word in text.

6. Jason's substitutions involve words of more than one syllable (4 out of 5).

7. Jason's substitutions involve words that may not be in his meaning vocabulary.

8. Jason's oral reading comprehension is consistent for both lower and higher levels of questions.

9. Jason's oral reading comprehension level is consistent with his word recognition abilities.

10. Jason's listening comprehension is approximately one year higher than his oral reading comprehension.

Diagnostic Reading Scales and the Wechsler Intelligence Scale for Children (WISC) verbal IQ test. However, listening comprehension is probably not a valid indicator of reading potential for primary-grade children. For other learners, if the listening comprehension level is higher than the instructional reading level, the student may be reading below what can be expected, or the student may need to further develop listening skills.

Similar results were found in research by Sticht and Beck (1976); that is, listening comprehension surpasses reading comprehension until about grade seven. First graders are struggling with word recognition. Likewise, second and third graders may sometimes be unfairly labeled as underachievers if listening comprehension is found to be higher than reading comprehension. As students learn to read, which appears to take longer (grades 6–8) than the traditionally designated primary grades (1–3), their reading comprehension skills overtake their listening comprehension skills. As stated by Sticht and James (1984), "precisely what is happening that makes this additional time necessary is not certain, though it may be that in the first three or four years of school, children learn the rudiments of reading–decoding . . . while an additional two to three years of practice is required for the automaticity of reading to equal that of auding [listening comprehension]" (p. 307).

In addition, training in listening comprehension skills often produces similar gains in reading comprehension (Kelty, 1955; Hoffman, 1978). To know when a listening comprehension test reflects the reading potential of a student, therefore, is difficult to say. If the teacher can reasonably expect students to have better reading skills than they do (grade 4 and up), then the listening comprehension ability apparently is a fairly accurate indication of potential. Also, if a student's reading skills build upon earlier acquired listening skills, listening comprehension can be used as an indication of early potential for the beginning reader (Sticht & James, 1984).

Teachers can look to other types of observations for supporting evidence:

1. Success on a nonverbal task can show that a learner has academic potential. If a student has been in school at least two years, a test of arithmetic computation, a nonverbal task, can be used to estimate academic potential (Wilson & Cleland, 1989). Arithmetic computation scores that are noticeably better than reading achievement scores can indicate reading difficulty. Caution is necessary, however, because arithmetic computation scores do not accurately indicate potential in readers with serious difficulties. Nonreading factors, such as lack of motivation or other psychological reactions to previous failures, are usually involved (see Chapter 4).

2. Careful observation of a student's general responsiveness both on the playground and in the classroom gives the teacher some idea of intellectual potential. Wilson and Cleland (1989) suggest the following noticeable characteristics of reading potential:

   • Ability to listen and speak effectively in class discussions
   • Ability to achieve more successfully in arithmetic than in subjects that require reading
   • Ability to interact effectively in peer group activities
   • Ability to demonstrate alert attitudes toward the world
   • Ability to perform satisfactorily on spelling tests
   • Ability to think in abstract terms and mentally perform complex functions
   • Ability to understand scientific concepts (p. 67)

While effective teachers are generally quite accurate in their judgments of academic achievement (Hoge & Coladarci, 1989), all teachers need to remain keenly aware that bias is a frequent component in forming judgments about achievement. Too often these judgments are based on physical attractiveness, gender, race, past performance of a sibling, some prior impression such as a test score, or even a student's name. While achievement potentials of aggressive, talkative, popular, well-behaved, or over-age students are likely to be overestimated, the potentials of the shy, unattractive, or unpopular students are likely to be underestimated. Ritts, Patterson, and Tubbs (1992), in a review of research investigating teachers' expectations, impressions, and judgments, conclude "that highly physically attractive students, compared to their unattractive counterparts, are the beneficiaries of more favorable judgments by teachers. This attractiveness effect is reflected in teachers' more positive expectancies of physically attractive students in terms of their intelligence, academic potential, grades, and other attributes" (p. 422). This conclusion would support the recommendations made by Hoge and Coladarci (1989) that "greater efforts should be made to sensitize teachers to the extent and importance of the assessment role in the teaching process [through familiarization] with the interpretation of different types of assessment devices, including norm-referenced tests, observational procedures, and judgmental measures" (p. 310).

Cloze Procedure

Another measure that is used for initially determining or verifying the instructional reading level is the **cloze procedure**. This requires a reader to fill in blanks for words that have been systematically deleted from the written selection. In the most common form of cloze test, every fifth word is deleted. These tests are more typically administered to groups of students in the upper elementary and secondary levels to assess suitability of textbook material (see Appendix A).

Cloze tests are relatively easy and inexpensive to construct, administer, and interpret. The following steps are suggested in preparing a cloze test passage.

1. Select a passage containing 250 to 300 words (Bormuth, 1975). Be sure the passage does not depend on information presented earlier in the text (i.e., a passage with many pronouns). The passage should be representative of the content of the book.
2. Keep the first sentence intact.
3. Beginning with the second sentence, delete words at a consistent interval (e.g., every fifth, seventh, or tenth word) for a total of fifty deletions (Bormuth, 1975). Replace the deleted words with blanks of equal length. Duplicate the desired number of copies.
4. If the blanks are numbered, prepare an answer sheet with corresponding numbers for students to use in recording their responses.
5. If desired, students can write their responses directly on the blanks.

Administration of the cloze test is fairly straightforward. Students who have never experienced a cloze test should be given some practice with the procedure first. This practice test should use material easy for the students to read and should contain at least ten deletions (Pikulski & Tobin, 1982).

Instructions for the cloze test *must* direct the students to read through the entire passage before trying to fill in the blanks. Students should also be told that only one word goes in each blank and that misspellings are not counted as errors. Although the test is untimed, the teacher may want to set a reasonable time limit.

Scoring a cloze test is an often misunderstood procedure. Only exact words should be considered acceptable as correct responses. This decision is not arbitrary; it is based on considerable research (Gallant, 1964; Henk & Selders, 1984; McKenna, 1976; Miller & Coleman, 1967; Ruddell, 1964; Taylor, 1953) in which exact word replacement scores were compared to synonym replacement scores. The synonym scores were higher than the exact word scores but the two scores were highly correlated (.95 and above). Because students essentially ranked the same using either technique, giving credit for synonyms has no advantage when the purpose of the test is to estimate students' instructional levels. Preparing a list of acceptable synonyms as part of cloze test preparation would simply not be worth the time or effort (Pikulski & Tobin, 1982).

In addition to yielding slightly higher scores, synonym replacements would invalidate the scoring guidelines. Criterion scores have been established for determining independent, instructional, and frustration reading levels using exact word replacement scores. Thus, to allow synonyms would yield an inflated score and the available criteria could not be used appropriately. Pikulski and Tobin (1982) have synthesized the research on criterion scores and suggest the following guidelines:

> **Independent level:** Students who obtain cloze scores of at least 50 percent should be able to read the material with relative ease. No teacher guidance should be necessary. Consequently, this material should be appropriate for homework assignments and other types of independent projects.
>
> **Instructional level:** Students scoring between 30 and 50 percent should be able to use the material for instructional purposes. However, some guidance will be necessary to help them master the demands of the material.
>
> **Frustration level:** Students scoring lower than 30 percent will usually find the material much too challenging. Since there is almost no potential for success, the material should be definitely avoided. (pp. 53, 54)

The disadvantage of the cloze procedure is that its effectiveness as an assessment tool is not clearly established. Carefully constructed cloze tests could potentially provide helpful information regarding a reader's use of syntactic and semantic cues during silent reading. But teachers still need to observe other dimensions of the reading process. In addition to textbook selections, cloze passages can also be constructed from students' own written stories or other familiar materials and used instructionally to show readers how to use the syntactic, semantic, and graphophonic cue systems. When used for instructional purposes, cloze passage construction can be modified in many ways to suit specific purposes. Cloze as an instructional tool is discussed in more detail in Chapter 8.

A popular variation of the cloze procedure is the **maze technique**. Instead of deleting words from a passage, the maze procedure gives the reader a number of words from which to choose. While this format may have more appeal for the test taker, construction of the test is more time-consuming and more prone to error than the cloze procedure. Guthrie, Siefert, Burnham, and Caplan (1974) suggest the following guidelines for constructing a maze test.

1. Select a representative passage of about 120 words.
2. Beginning with the second sentence, replace words at constant intervals (e.g., every fifth or tenth word) with three word choices. These should include the correct word itself, a word that is the same part of speech as the correct word, and a word that is a different part of speech.

3. Vary the position of the correct word.

4. Duplicate copies.

As of yet, little research has been done on the maze technique, and criterion scores should be considered tentative. Guthrie et al. (1974) suggest that 85 percent or higher accuracy reflects an independent level, 60 to 75 percent, an instructional level, and below 50 percent, the frustration level. More research is needed on the maze technique before its use as a placement tool is recommended.

Assessment by Observation and Conferences

Observation

A large amount of information about a student's ability to read can be obtained through observation of reading behavior. A decision should never be made on the basis of one observation, however. Teachers who try to organize the instructional setting specifically to improve and enhance behavioral observation increase the reliability of those observations. For example, the more opportunities students have to show the teacher that they know the initial consonant blend *st* or that they can use word order clues to predict the next word in a sentence, the more reliable is the information. *More opportunities* is analogous to *more items* on a test, an important way that test makers achieve reliability.

Observing students is a skill that teachers develop over time through practice. Rhodes and Dudley-Marling (1988, pp. 37–38) provide some excellent guidelines for observing children's literacy development.[2] They are as follows:

1. Reading and writing should be observed over a period of time in a number of different contexts. For example, contexts for silent reading might include teacher-initiated versus student-initiated reading, reading different types of material (content-area reading, novels, comics, etc.), and reading for different purposes.

2. The setting, as well as students' reading and writing behaviors, must be thoroughly considered. By setting we mean information about the physical setting, who initiated the activity, the teacher's instructions (if any), and the teacher's approach to teaching reading and writing.

    Students' previous instruction is also an important part of the setting. For example, students' oral sharing of what they've read may be limited to rote recall because this was what previous teachers expected. In some cases even the principal's behavior (perhaps following the dictum that only "basic skills" be taught) may be relevant. Any information that can contribute to an understanding of students' reading and writing development should be considered.

3. Teachers should also consider their own behavior as part of students' instructional setting. Teachers may find that their feedback to students' miscues may encourage the belief that reading is a matter of getting the words right. Or teachers may find that students' discussion of their reading and writing is more thoughtful when teachers increase their "wait time" (the amount of time teachers give students to respond to their prompts or questions).

4. Observations should be regularly summarized and recorded. If someone not acquainted with the child or the setting read the record of the observations,

---

[2]Reproduced with permission from Lynn K. Rhodes and Curt Dudley-Marling: *Readers and Writers with a Difference*. Portsmouth, N.H., Heinemann Educational Books, 1988.

would they have a clear picture of what went on? Even if the observations aren't going to be shared with anyone else, they can still be confusing to the teacher who wrote them several weeks or months later if the record of the observation is not sufficiently explicit. Teachers will learn how explicit to make observational records by rereading past records and finding out what is confusing and what they would like to have remembered more about.

5. In many cases it's helpful if observations are supplemented with pictures, audio-tapes, or videotapes. Teachers may, for example, tape their students' oral reading and listen to the tape in the car on the way home. Audio- and videotapes and pictures will also be especially helpful for sharing information about students' reading and writing with parents.

6. Observations of students don't have to be unobtrusive. It's fine if students are aware that they are being observed, especially if observation is a routine practice in the classroom. It's helpful to let students know that they are being observed and why ("I just want to see what you do while you're writing"). Observation will affect students' performance only if students are rarely observed in their classrooms.

7. There are times when it's useful to ask students questions to clarify what has been observed. While observing a student's restlessness during silent reading, for example, a teacher might ask, "What's the problem? You seem restless about something."

8. Observation need not be excessively time-consuming. In some cases it may be necessary to sit back and watch students as they read and write, but these observations needn't take more than several minutes. In general, the richest source of information will be close attention to students as they respond to instruction and as they read and write.

As with miscue analysis, through observation teachers are looking for the strategies a reader uses that are both appropriate and inappropriate. Those that are inappropriate become areas of instructional focus, while appropriate strategies are encouraged and built upon.

Obtaining feedback, or an overt response, from each student is critical and can be accomplished in several ways. Careful planning includes every-pupil response techniques (Cunningham, 1982; Hopkins, 1979), written work, and perhaps some taped readings. When reviewing these overt responses teachers must keep in mind the reason they initiated the behavior and what it is they are looking for. This is a good reason for developing checklists or rating scales as a way of organizing information (see Figure 6.9).

Conferences

Even teachers who carefully plan opportunities for observation will have unanswered questions about the progress of some students. Thus the teacher must structure short periods of time to focus more directly on behavioral responses of individual students. These periods are usually called teacher–student conferences.

The teacher arranges a conference any time during the day when 5 to 20 minutes can be spared for an individual student. A variety of assessment procedures (IRIs, a written lesson, teacher-made exercises) can be used to gather information, but usually the teacher is interested in finding answers to the specific questions that motivated the conference. For instance, if the student has made inconsistent responses (e.g., sometimes observing

Checklist for appraising early reading development.

Student _____ Teacher _____ Date _____

Age _____ Grade _____ School _____

CHARACTERISTICS	Yes	No
Cognition		
1. Understands grade-level material read aloud	____	____
2. Remembers new words used in class	____	____
3. Remembers content of stories discussed in class	____	____
Language		
1. Speaks in complete sentences	____	____
2. Speaking vocabulary is adequate	____	____
3. Speaking vocabulary is advanced	____	____
4. Speech is normal	____	____
5. Hearing is normal	____	____
General Reading		
1. When being read to, the child:		
a. sometimes finishes the sentence (anticipates what is next)	____	____
b. sometimes follows along with finger	____	____
c. pays attention	____	____
2. Recognizes signs (e.g., stop signs), labels (e.g., "Wheaties"), or logos (e.g., "McDonald's")	____	____
3. Recognizes his/her name	____	____
4. Recognizes letters in (*state what context*)	____	____
5. Recognizes words in (*state what context*)	____	____
6. Remembers words taught as whole words	____	____
7. Attempts to blend sound units	____	____
8. Can guess new words from context	____	____
9. Skips words when reading in order to use context	____	____
10. Skips unknown words totally in order to maintain comprehension	____	____
11. Reads fluently	____	____
12. Reads with little or no transposing of letters/words	____	____
13. Observes punctuation in oral reading	____	____
14. Reads silently with little or no finger pointing to text	____	____
15. Reads silently with little or no subvocalizing	____	____
16. Recalls facts of material read	____	____
17. Can summarize main points of material read	____	____
18. Can locate answers to questions	____	____
19. Comprehends narrative material	____	____
20. Comprehends expository material	____	____
21. Adjusts reading speed according to reading purpose or difficulty of material	____	____
Motivation		
1. Enjoys being read to	____	____
2. Knows that books have a top and bottom, and turns pages front to back	____	____
3. Talks about books he/she listened to or read	____	____
4. Looks at books on his/her own	____	____
5. Has favorite book(s)	____	____

Additional Comments and Observations:

punctuation and sometimes not) during the instructional period or on written work, the teacher will want to know whether meaning is being affected for the student.

Conferences between the student and the teacher may reveal potential areas of instructional need. If these are identified early, the effectiveness of a corrective reading program will be enhanced. Most learners, including high achievers, falter from time to time in their learning. Brief timely conferences pay great dividends because they identify areas of difficulty before they become serious reading problems.

Checklists and Rating Scales

While observation provides much information about reading behavior, teachers cannot possibly remember all the behaviors of 25 to 30 pupils in a class, even if notebooks and **anecdotal records** (informal notes to aid recall of observed behaviors; see also Chapter 4) are used. A system must be organized to aid interpretation of what has been observed. Such record-keeping systems are available in the form of checklists and rating scales.

Checklists and rating scales evolve around the important sets of behaviors being considered. Common areas in reading are language development, word recognition, comprehension, and oral and silent reading. Other relevant nonreading factors are intelligence, health, emotional stability, vision, hearing, and listening (see Chapter 4). Teachers may make their own checklists, but many good checklists and rating scales are already available. You may be wise to choose one or more of these designed by specialists and scholars in reading and add to or modify your collection as needed.

Checklists and rating scales are scored differently. A checklist asks the teacher to judge on a yes–no basis whether the behavior is exhibited. A rating scale, on the other hand, asks the teacher to judge the *degree* to which or *frequency* with which the behavior is exhibited. A five-point scale is common, with ratings similar to the following:

1 = not exhibited
2 = rarely exhibited
3 = sometimes exhibited
4 = often exhibited
5 = always exhibited

Checklists and rating scales provide a structured approach to observation. Most published informal reading inventories have behavioral checklists, which are helpful and can influence teacher judgment in determining reading levels.

A checklist can also be used to summarize the performance of several students instead of one child. This procedure is useful because teachers are usually working with groups of students functioning at different levels. The checklist in Figure 6.10 can be used to record the progress of a group of students using a particular set of reading materials or receiving instruction at a level different from other classmates.

Checklists and rating scales are a good source of information for planning instruction. Successful use of such procedures, however, largely depends on the experience and expertise of the user (Shertzer & Linden, 1979). Inexperienced teachers often feel insecure making judgments about reading behavior. The wise teacher, when in doubt, will verify the information on a checklist by comparison with a variety of text materials and activities. Verification in real reading situations is highly recommended.

Checklist of oral reading characteristics for a group of students.

Date: Names:	Harry	Susie	Leroy	Mark	Daisy	Kenya
Comprehension						
Recalls facts						
Makes inferences						
Word Recognition/Decoding						
Has adequate sight vocabulary						
Needs few or no words pronounced						
Mispronounces few words						
Omits few or no words						
Inserts few or no words						
Uses context adequately						
Uses strategies in addition to context						
Knows high-utility words						
Analyzes words visually						
Knows symbol–sound associations						
Can blend sounds						
Fluency						
Has few or no hesitations						
Has few or no repetitions						
Phrases appropriately						
Reads phrases or groups of words						
Pays attention to punctuation						
Reads at an appropriate rate						
Usually or always keeps place						
Demonstrates proper use of voice						
Demonstrates proper enunciation						
Demonstrates proper expression						
Uses proper volume						
Observations						
Seldom shows signs of tension						
Reads with little or no finger pointing						
Holds book at appropriate distance						
Concentrates on task at hand						

Comments:

Interest and Attitude Surveys

Interests and attitudes are important student characteristics that are neither easily nor quickly determined by observation. Asking requires the least time and effort. Teachers can gather the information in casual conversations with students, or more efficiently, through the use of interest and attitude surveys. These surveys can be conducted as interviews, in written format, or some combination of each.

Interest and attitude surveys suggest instructional techniques that may be useful in working with the student. If interests are known, the teacher uses materials that deal with those interests. If the student has a negative attitude, expected in students having serious reading difficulties, the teacher makes special efforts to motivate the learner and improve attitudes toward reading.

Obtaining information on interests consists of asking a series of questions regarding students' favorite activities, whether they have pets or hobbies, what television programs they watch, and so forth. An example of an interest inventory is presented in Figure 6.11.

FIGURE 6.11   Sample interest inventory.

Inventory of Pupil Interests and Activities

Name _____ Age _____ Grade _____
School _____ Date _____ Interviewer _____

1. What is your favorite TV show?
2. Who is your favorite TV character?
3. If you could make up a TV show, what would it be about?
4. Do you have a favorite movie?
5. Do you have any pets?
6. What is your favorite animal?
7. If you could be any living thing, what would you be?
8. Where have you traveled? Name three places.
9. Name all the different types of transportation you have experienced (train, bus, auto, boat, wagon, airplane, jet, truck, buggy, subway, bicycle, ship).
10. If you received two airplane tickets for anywhere in the world, where would you go?
11. If you had a time machine for any time and place in the past or future, where would you go and when?
12. What is your favorite subject?
13. What is the latest book you've read? Did you enjoy it? Why or why not?
14. What kind of books do you read at home?
15. If it were a rainy day at home, what would you do?
    If it were a sunny day at home, what would you do?
16. What is your favorite sport?
17. What is your favorite hobby?
18. If I gave you $100 to buy whatever you wanted, what would you do with the money?

Attitude surveys also ask questions, but of a different nature. Usually students respond yes or no, or indicate some degree of feeling (e.g., strongly agree, agree, don't know, disagree, strongly disagree). Figure 6.12 contains representative items from an attitude survey appropriate for primary grades.

Attitude surveys should also address students' perceptions of reading as a process and perceptions of themselves as readers. For example, an interview format can be used to provide teachers relevant information about students' perceptions of themselves as readers and writers. The interview might include some of the following key questions:

- Do you like to read (write)?
- What is your favorite book (or who is your favorite author)?
- When do you read (write)?
- Do you think you are a good reader (writer)? Why or why not?
- Who is the best reader (writer) you know? Why?
- When you get to a word you do not know, what do you do?
- If someone asked you for help figuring out a word, how would you help?
- When you do not understand what you read, what do you do?
- Would you rather read (write) or ride a bike?
- Would you rather read (write) or watch TV?
- Would you rather read a story or write a story?
- Would you rather read (write) or sleep?
- Would you rather read (write) or draw?
- Would you rather read (write) or do arithmetic homework?
- Would you rather read (write) or help do the dishes?
- When you write, what kinds of problems do you have? What do you do about them?
- Do you ever make changes in what you write? What kind of changes?

Open-ended statements are also used to assess attitudes. For example, the student might be asked to complete the following sentences:

Reading is————————————————————————.

I think reading————————————————————————.

Most books————————————————————————.

My parents————————————————————————.

Teachers————————————————————————.

The entire *Incomplete Sentence Projective Test* (Boning & Boning, 1957) can be found in Appendix C.

Many interest and attitude surveys are available for use or modification by teachers. Some of these are listed below.

Harris, L. A., & Smith, C. B. (1980). *Reading instruction* (3rd ed., p. 428). New York: Holt, Rinehart and Winston.

Lapp, D., & Flood, J. (1983). *Teaching reading to every child* (2nd ed., pp. 363–365). New York: Macmillan.

FIGURE
6.12

Primary grades attitude survey.

(Teacher: Before administering this survey, be sure children can distinguish the three faces as feeling happy, don't care, and feeling sad, respectively. You might want to ask a few practice questions, such as "How do you feel about Christmas?" or "How do you feel about going to bed early?" Feel free to add items to the survey. For group administration, students can either color in or mark the face that represents the way they feel about each question. Individuals can either point to or hold up individual face cards to indicate their feelings.)

1. How do you feel when your teacher reads a story to you?

2. How do you feel about reading out loud in class?

3. How do you feel about going to the library?

4. How do you feel when you come to a new word in your book?

5. How do you feel about your reading group?

6. How do you feel about getting a book for a present?

7. How do you feel when you read at home?

8. How do you feel when you read to your mom, dad, or a friend?

9. How do you feel about reading a story before bedtime?

10. How do you feel when you don't understand what you read?

McKenna, M. C., & Kear, D. J. (1990). Measuring attitude toward reading: A new tool for teachers. *The Reading Teacher, 43,* 626–639.

Strickler, D., & Eller, W. (1980). Attitudes and interests. In P. Lamb and R. Arnold (Eds.), *Teaching reading* (p. 386). Belmont, CA: Wadsworth.

Tullock-Rhody, R., & Alexander, J. E. (1980). A scale for assessing attitudes toward reading in secondary schools. *Journal of Reading, 23,* 609–614.

In addition, a standardized instrument, the *Estes Attitude Scales* (Estes, Estes, Richards & Roettger, 1981) is available in both elementary and secondary forms. As reviewed in the *Ninth Mental Measurements Yearbook* (Mitchell, 1985), the *Estes Attitude Scales* measure attitudes toward school subjects. The elementary form for grades 2–6 includes items for math, reading, and science; the secondary form for grades 6–12 includes items for English, math, reading, science, and social studies. The scales take 20–30 minutes to administer. Reliability is reported as .76–.88 for the elementary scale and .76–.93 for the secondary scale, which are quite respectable for measures of this sort. The *Estes Attitude Scales* would be useful for obtaining affective data for comparisons at local levels.

This instrument is especially valuable in light of the research that shows the importance of considering attitudes toward content areas at the middle and secondary levels (Alexander & Cobb, 1992). A positive attitude toward reading in a content area undeniably has an impact on achievement in that subject.

Work Samples

Teachers have many options for assessing reading and writing development regularly as students complete written assignments, worksheets, workbook pages, or any other tangible product (e.g., art, journal writing, videotapes, dramatic productions). By carefully selecting and analyzing work samples, the teacher has the means to assess students' needs on a continuing basis. Additionally, students have the opportunity to see their own development if they are keeping portfolios (refer to suggested readings in this chapter and also see Chapter 7 for types of portfolios). Because instruction and assessment overlap to a great extent, the instructional suggestions presented in the following chapters can also serve as assessment measures.

Oral and Written Language Samples

Analysis of reading behaviors cannot ignore the student's other language skills, because reading is a language process. The mental processes involved in the production skills of speaking and writing are probably similar to those involved in the receptive skills of listening and reading (Loban, 1976; Pickert & Chase, 1978; Shanahan, 1980), and develop in parallel, interactive ways (Teale & Sulzby, 1986). Marie Clay (1967), an educator interested in better descriptions of young children's reading and writing behaviors for the purpose of early detection of reading difficulties, researched five-year-old children entering school in New Zealand. She found that these young children showed visual sensitivity to letters and words, knew to move from left to right, from top to bottom, and from front to back when looking at books, and were able to match spoken word and written word units. Such competence makes it apparent that children's literacy development does not begin when they enter school; rather, these competencies have been *emerging* since birth outside of school situations (Doake, 1988). Thus, the term **emergent literacy** (see Chapter 1) is used to describe the transformation that occurs when children, having been exposed to printed material, actively attempt to discover how oral and written language are related.

One good way to sample young children's oral and written language is to ask them to draw, talk, and then write about what they have produced. After the drawing and writing are complete, ask the child to read what was written. If a child seems reluctant, the teacher might invite the child to draw a picture of her family and write something about each member.

Wordless picture books are a good source of oral language samples as well as written samples for any age student, including older students (for suggested titles see Danielson, 1992; Johnson-Weber, 1989; Neal & Moore, 1991/92; Polette, 1989; Rutland, 1987). Oral language samples can be tape recorded for later transcription, and written samples, with teacher notations, collected and dated to document growth.

Sulzby (1985) has developed a 7-point scale for assessing various levels of sophistication in students' attempts at rereading their own written language. For example, a score of 2 is given to the behavior of the learner producing random marks on paper but refusing to reread them; a score of 4 is given for a learner attempting to reread what was written, but not keeping eyes on the print; and a score of 7 is given when the learner's eyes are following the print and there is a match between voice and print. This type of assessment not only can inform the teacher about a student's understanding of literacy concepts, but can also promote students' literacy development by drawing their attention to the distinctions between oral and written language.

Writing also plays an important role in learning our alphabetic system, that is, graphic symbols representing oral language. Writing forces learners to attend to the visual features of print, which in turn helps them become aware of letter–sound patterns and their relation to words. As young children hear and see stories read over and over, learn letter names, print or spell words, and try to read and write new words, they will learn, naturally, the written English alphabetic system. Of course, progress can be enhanced with encouragement, modeling, and instruction geared toward the student's current level of understanding about print. An analysis of students' invented spellings reveals development of such phonic skills as segmentation (breaking words into parts), blending (putting sounds together to form words), and letter–sound correspondences. (See Appendix D for stages of spelling development and a spelling test that can be used to sample students' spelling.)

In addition to analyzing spelling, a more focused analysis of written language samples can reveal students' knowledge of writing. Examination of writing samples should be made with the intention of providing feedback to students that will help them become more skillful writers. A system that looks at the qualities of good writing as well as the process of writing might serve a teacher's needs best. Appendix E provides guidelines for evaluating and scoring writing and an example for two different approaches to analyzing a writing sample. Chapter 7 also provides suggestions for instructional practices that support a reading–writing connection.

Students build their own rules for oral grammar and written language based on their observations and explorations with print (Noyce & Christie, 1989). By listening to students speak and by examining their writing samples, we gain insight into what they have already learned about oral and written language.

PUTTING IT ALL TOGETHER: A VIGNETTE

The vignette that follows will demonstrate the analytic process as it was implemented by one classroom teacher at the beginning of a school year.[3]

THE SCHOOL CONTEXT

An urban, public elementary school with a diverse, at-risk, lower socioeconomic student population has 32 students in the third grade.

THE TEACHER

Ms. Johnson, a dedicated teacher who has helped make the classroom an inviting, exciting place, has been teaching for four years.

Ms. Johnson has collected a wide variety of literature at different grade levels and has created an attractive area for individual silent reading. She displays students' work, including art projects, language experience stories, and students' creative books. Learning centers are interesting, appealing, and orderly. Ms. Johnson believes that reading quality fiction and nonfiction to her students enhances their love of reading, reading comprehension, oral language, and writing abilities. She also supplies multiple copies of literature selections for her students so that she can teach reading using quality fiction and nonfiction. Occasionally she uses basal text stories with her reading group if they are pertinent to a thematic unit being studied.

Ms. Johnson also observes her students carefully and notes their particular literacy instructional needs. She then forms ad hoc groups according to student needs (e.g., helping students understand paragraphing or learn the importance of predicting and hypothesizing about text ideas and events). Ms. Johnson sincerely likes her students and her job. She is energetic, empathic, open to new ideas, and is confident in her abilities to influence her students in positive ways and in her abilities to make sound educational decisions.

Ms. Johnson conducts daily whole class meetings and encourages her students to discuss problems, pleasures, and reading goals.

During the first week of school, Ms. Johnson carefully observed each of the students in her classroom during free time, reading groups, lunch, whole group instruction, art, music, independent reading, and morning class meetings. She placed each student's name on an individual page of a large notebook. She noted peer interactions, language ability, ability to complete assignments, and apparent feelings of self-esteem for each student. She also made tentative notes concerning each student's apparent listening abilities and reading and writing strengths.

Also during the first week of school, Ms. Johnson asked for her students' help. She explained that she would meet individually with each student to discuss personal reading goals and interests. She also told her students that she wanted them to experience as much success as possible. Ms. Johnson discussed the reasons for flexible reading groups and student conferences as well.

---

[3]The author wishes to thank Dr. Janet C. Richards for this hypothetical example.

JAMIKA

One of Ms. Johnson's students was Jamika. During the first week of school, when Ms. Johnson wrote her initial ideas about students in her notebook, she made the following notes on Jamika.

Jamika (Birthdate: 3/13/86)

1. Quiet
2. Cooperative
3. Polite
4. Appears to have adequate oral language abilities
5. Appears interested in class activities
6. Appears healthy

Ms. Johnson observed Jamika further and added notebook comments.

7. Does not volunteer to share ideas and opinions about literature heard or read
8. Follows along carefully as teacher reads
9. Understands basic story features and their connections (see Chapter 7)
10. Appears anxious

Ms. Johnson began to formulate some questions about Jamika. She asked:

- Why does Jamika exhibit apparent passive behavior?
- Does Jamika lack self-confidence and self-esteem?
- Is the reading material too difficult for Jamika?
- What reading comprehension strategies might help Jamika?

Ms. Johnson decided to look at Jamika's cumulative folder and then make additional notebook comments.

11. Youngest of three siblings
12. Above average grades in first and second grades
13. Average and slightly below average standardized test scores
14. Many absences in first and second grade because of illness

Ms. Johnson decided to have a conference with Jamika. Because the teacher was an active, empathic listener and communicated with Jamika in a nonjudgmental manner, Jamika felt comfortable in sharing her thoughts. After the conference Ms. Johnson wrote:

15. Brother and sister both high achievers
16. Believes that she is not as "smart" as her siblings

Ms. Johnson decided to gather some definite information about Jamika's literacy abilities. She wanted some answers to these questions:

- Is Jamika reading to her fullest potential?
- What is Jamika's instructional reading level? Independent reading level? Listening comprehension level?
- Is Jamika a corrective reader, possibly because of missing reading instruction due to illness?

- What are Jamika's general writing abilities?
- What writing behaviors does Jamika exhibit? (see Chapter 7)
- What perceptions does Jamika have about reading and writing?
- What perceptions does Jamika have about herself as a reader and writer?
- What are Jamika's interests?

Ms. Johnson decided to get some ideas about Jamika's interests and reading ability using an interest inventory and an informal reading inventory. She worked with Jamika while the class was actively involved in learning center activities. Afterwards she recorded the results in her notebook.

17. Interested in dinosaurs and baby animals
18. Adequate sight vocabulary commensurate with third grade
19. Reading independently at second grade
20. Reading instructionally at third grade
21. Listening comprehension level is fifth grade

Ms. Johnson then invited Jamika to write an informal letter or story of her choice. As Jamika wrote, Ms. Johnson observed her and made notes about her writing behaviors.

22. Jamika wrote in the expressive voice (see Chapter 7). She wrote about a trip to Disneyworld.
23. Jamika used standard and transitional spelling commensurate with her age and grade (e.g., "Dizneewrld").
24. Jamika wrote legibly and was overly concerned with forming graphemes correctly.
25. Jamika used appropriate capitalization and punctuation at the end of sentences.
26. Jamika did not use a plan for writing nor did she reread her work or revise.
27. Jamika appeared to be very anxious as she wrote.

Next, Ms. Johnson interviewed Jamika to determine her perceptions about reading and writing. She asked Jamika questions such as: Do you like to read? Why or why not? What do you do when you come to a word that you don't know? How do you figure it out? Do you think that you are a good reader? Why or why not? Why do people write? How do you decide what to write? What part of writing do you like the most? The least? Why? Are you a good writer? Why? Why not? (See earlier section in this chapter for additional questions.)

After examining Jamika's responses to these questions, Ms. Johnson wrote the following tentative hypotheses in her notebook:

- Needs to develop motivation to read
- Needs to develop confidence in herself as a reader and writer
- Needs to learn word identification plans (see Chapter 8)
- Needs to learn to read for comprehension and actively seek meaning (see Chapter 10)
- Needs to learn some prewriting strategies (see Chapter 7)
- Needs to learn editing techniques

After analyzing and reflecting upon Jamika's IRI results, writing behaviors, perceptions about writing, oral language abilities, and affective dimensional behaviors, Ms. Johnson decided that Jamika probably had far greater reading and writing potential than she demonstrated. Ms. Johnson added the following to her tentative hypotheses:

- Lack of motivation, possibly due to poor self-esteem; lack of confidence; lack of reading and writing success in first and second grades.
- Possible feelings of inadequacy because of high-achieving older siblings
- Insufficient knowledge about the processes of reading and writing

Ms. Johnson decided to plan a program of reading/writing instruction together with Jamika. After the planning conference, she wrote the following instructional alternatives for Jamika.

LITERACY INSTRUCTIONAL PLAN

1. Place in ad hoc groups focusing on word identification plans and reading comprehension techniques
2. Assign creative bookmaking
3. Assemble literature that meets Jamika's interests (i.e., dinosaurs and baby animals)
4. Teach reading comprehension techniques that help Jamika learn to read for meaning
5. Provide opportunities for Jamika to engage in collaborative writing activities
6. Help Jamika engage in numerous nonstructured writing activities
7. Establish dialogue journal with Jamika to foster a reading/writing connection and provide a risk-free opportunity for Jamika to write
8. Provide teacher-guided writing lessons such as "Writing Cohesive Paragraphs" (see Chapter 7)
9. Arrange physical examination, including visual and auditory acuity
10. Schedule student–parent–teacher conference

Ms. Johnson will continue to observe Jamika's literacy progress throughout the school year. She plans to continue student–teacher conferences and informal communication, teacher support, and providing for Jamika's success as a reader and writer.

SUMMARY

A variety of direct measures have been presented. These classroom-based assessment procedures are valuable to the teacher for gathering information and verifying tentative teaching hypotheses in the analytic process. Appropriate use of both classroom-based and standardized measures is most effective in learning students' reading needs. The chapter ends with an example of one teacher's implementation of the analytic process.

SUGGESTED READINGS

Afflerbach, P. (1993). Report cards and reading. *The Reading Teacher, 46,* 458–465.

It is one thing to gather information through direct assessments and another to report the results of such information to parents. This article discusses key issues in developing report cards that are more consistent with use of direct assessments.

DeFina, A.A. (1992). *Portfolio assessment: Getting started.* New York: Scholastic.

This most readable book, written by a classroom teacher/teacher educator, provides detailed information about portfolios for beginners or those wishing to refine or expand their use of portfolios. Numerous charts and examples give the specifics needed for assessing reading and writing abilities.

Nolan, E.A., and Berry, M. (1993). Learning to listen. *The Reading Teacher, 46,* 606–608.

This brief article shares the very real concerns associated with one teacher's movement to reliance on more direct measures of assessment. The importance of communicating with parents is made clear.

Rhodes, L.K., and Nathenson-Mejia, S. (1992). Anecdotal records: A powerful tool for ongoing literacy assessment. *The Reading Teacher, 45,* 502–509.

This article provides detailed discussion of anecdotal records for process assessment. Samples with corresponding analyses show how anecdotal records support the analytic process of gathering information to advise instructional planning and in turn generate new teaching hypotheses.

PART

II

THE MAJOR DOMAINS

THE READING/WRITING CONNECTION

Janet C. Richards

OBJECTIVES

After you have read this chapter, you should be able to

1. explain how reading and writing are mutually supportive processes;
2. discuss how writers gain valuable knowledge about reading;
3. discuss the importance of a writing program for corrective reading students;
4. define the role of an effective writing teacher;
5. explain how to implement writing lessons and activities in a corrective reading program;
6. define and explain the differences and benefits of nonstructured, collaborative, teacher-guided, and creative writing;
7. explain the relationship between writing instruction and writing assessment;
8. discuss the value of helping students learn to assess their own writing.

KEY CONCEPTS AND TERMS

collaborative writing activities
creative writing
dialogue journaling
emergent writers
language conventions
language functions
nonstructured writing activities

personal dictionaries
semantics
showcase portfolios
syntax
teacher-guided writing lessons
voices of composing
working portfolios

The author wishes to thank Dr. Janet C. Richards, The University of Southern Mississippi—Gulf Park, for contributing this chapter.

STUDY OUTLINE

1. Introduction
2. The importance of a writing program for corrective readers
3. The role of the writing teacher in a corrective reading program
4. Implementing the writing program
   a. Observations, initial assessments, and instructional decisions
   b. Nonstructured writing activities
   c. Structured lessons and activities
      • Collaborative writing activities
         1) "Write a Sentence/Make a Story"
         2) "Add a Word/Stretch the Sentence"
         3) "Add a Paragraph/Write a Book"
         4) Dialogue journals
      • Teacher-guided writing lessons
         1) Personal dictionary sharing
         2) Teacher dictation

3) Rephrasing
4) Writing cohesive paragraphs
   • Creative writing: The starting point
      1) Prewriting strategies
         a) "Speed writing"
         b) "Story features and their connections"
      2) Composing
      3) Editing
      4) Sharing
5. Writing instruction and assessment: A continuous process
   a. Shared observations
   b. Postwriting questionnaires
   c. Portfolios
6. Summary
7. Suggested readings

Author's Note: This invited chapter by Dr. Richards presents the concepts and practices of the reading/writing connection by sharing the workings of an actual program in progress. Those readers who are also currently working with students may therefore find this chapter especially helpful for getting started. In the learning context described in this chapter, elementary education majors enrolled in a corrective reading methods course each work with a group of three to five students for one hour twice weekly throughout a semester. As teacher educators, we are firmly committed to the idea that all students learn best when they have opportunities to read, write, and share ideas as part of a supportive community of language learners and users. "Learning is a social process that is made more powerful when learners are encouraged to interact and think with others" (Short, 1993, p. 156).

Also, we have found that with some slight modifications, the techniques described in this chapter are as applicable to secondary students as they are to elementary and middle school students. Secondary teachers can easily adapt the ideas discussed to suit their students' literacy instructional needs and interests.

The students' writing samples that you will see throughout this chapter were contributed by them and we sincerely thank them. Also, the brief explanations of "Add a Paragraph/Write a Book" and "Writing Cohesive Paragraphs" were previously discussed in *READ: Exploration and Discovery,* a journal of the Louisiana Reading Association. The editors of *READ* have graciously given their permission to include these lessons in this chapter. We also wish to thank all of the wonderful university students whose professional development is displayed in this chapter.

OVERVIEW

This chapter explains how reading and writing are mutually supportive processes. The chapter discusses the importance of a writing program for corrective readers and the role of the writing teacher in a corrective reading program. The chapter explains how to implement a writing program that includes observations, initial assessments, and instructional decisions, and discusses nonstructured writing activities and structured

writing lessons (i.e., collaborative, teacher-guided, and creative writing).

Also included in this chapter is a discussion of the importance of continual assessment of students' writing progress and the link between writing instruction and assessment. The chapter concludes with suggestions that help students learn to assess their own writing progress, and a summary. Suggested readings are offered.

INTRODUCTION

Students in our corrective reading program write as much as they read. Connecting reading and writing instruction makes sense. Both are thinking, meaning-making processes. Each supports, complements, and contributes to the other's development (Ross & Roe, 1990).

Children's awareness and understanding of reading and writing develop concurrently. Experts in children's emergent (i.e., early) literacy behaviors note that young children spontaneously engage in pretend reading and writing in their individual and group play. For example, my three-year-old granddaughter enjoys role-playing the part of a McDonald's waitress. She "writes" her family's orders for Big Macs and Happy Meals, "reads" the orders, and "serves" the food.

Knowledge of reading does not precede knowledge of writing (Bromley, 1989). Writing promotes reading. Writers read extensively to gain information about present or future writing topics and to revise their writing. They also read when they write collaboratively with a partner and when they share their work with others (Atwell, 1980).

Writers become familiar with different **language functions** (i.e., purposes), styles, and **voices of composing** such as poetry, grocery lists, news articles, personal diaries, letters of invitation, stories, and reports. Further, as they write and observe others write, they construct knowledge about **language conventions** such as spelling, punctuation, capitalization, and paragraphing. For example, as one six-year-old in our program journaled with her university tutor, she commented, "I'm making dots at the end of sentences just like you do."

Writers are "less likely to be intimidated by written language" (Newkirk, 1982, p. 457). By becoming authors themselves, young students learn that written language can be changed, deleted, or expanded. It is not something that is rigid and beyond criticism. Studies show that in classrooms where students write extensively, reading scores go up (Graves & Murray, 1980). "Daily writing promotes and enhances reading" (Dionisio, 1989, p. 747).

THE IMPORTANCE OF A WRITING PROGRAM FOR CORRECTIVE READERS

It is especially important to connect reading and writing instruction for corrective readers. Many of these learners have had few positive writing experiences. Therefore, they write as little as possible. Since reading and writing develop simultaneously, and strengthen and build upon each other, it is imperative that students with reading difficulties have opportunities to write and observe others as they write (Wiseman, 1992). For these (and all) learners, "reading and writing instruction shouldn't be separated, nor should writing instruction be postponed until students are able readers" (Rhodes & Dudley-Marling, 1988, p. 14).

THE ROLE OF THE WRITING TEACHER IN A CORRECTIVE READING PROGRAM

The role of the writing teacher in a corrective reading program is no different from the role of good writing teachers in any program. Good writing teachers are good writers themselves (Graves, 1988). They are enthusiastic about writing and wholeheartedly "believe that their children can write" (Daniels, 1991, p. 169). These teachers know that writing creatively is a complex, problem-solving process in which writers move back and forth between planning, composing, and revising their work. They recognize and support the developmental nature of children's spelling (please refer to Appendix D), and encourage students to concentrate first on the messages they are trying to convey rather than limit themselves to writing only words they can spell correctly. They know where their "students fall along the [spelling] developmental continuum" (O'Flahavan & Blassberg, 1992, p. 409). These teachers understand that students learn how to spell in conventional ways by engaging in meaningful reading and writing activities (Bartch, 1992). Good writing teachers understand that the "stage of writing is set by what the teacher does, not by what the teacher says" (Graves, 1988, p. 12). Therefore, teachers are learners about writing along with their students. They demonstrate and model the various functions of writing and freely share their writing experiences (Juliebö & Edwards, 1989).

Good writing teachers also understand that students learn about writing by writing for their own purposes and audiences as part of a larger community of language users. Consequently, they never require their students to complete meaningless, isolated writing tasks, such as copying sentences from the board or writing weekly spelling words five times each. Instead, they create a learning context in which students feel free to take risks, experiment with writing, and use writing to communicate meaning (Anderson, Raphael, Englert, & Stevens, 1992). Most important, good writing teachers know that "the key to helping readers [and writers] in trouble is to help them revalue themselves as language learners and users" (Goodman, 1982, p. 88).

IMPLEMENTING THE WRITING PROGRAM

Students in our corrective reading program begin writing, and thinking and talking about writing, at their first tutoring session. In order to get an idea about each new group of students' general writing abilities, their university tutors invite them to write an informal letter or story on a subject of their choice (Fig. 7.1). The tutors encourage **emergent writers** (i.e., beginning writers) to write any words, alphabet letters, numbers, or symbols they know, or to convey a message by scribbling or drawing a picture (Fig. 7.2). As the students write, their tutors continually reassure them that their writing samples will not be graded but will be used to help plan future writing lessons and activities. If students request help in spelling, their tutors encourage them to use invented spelling (refer to Appendix D) by saying, "Just spell it the best way you can."

Antonia's story for assessing general writing abilities.

If a dinosaur came to lunch
I would screm I would feed
him frinck fisee and I would
feed him auntil he snuwsd
and I would snike out and
win he wock up he would
eat and eat he would
eat donunuts a cake and
Milk and cuokise and popsikls
and pop tort and it would
eat eveyting in the word
he defuntle eat he.

Emergent writer's initial writing sample.

Theis dig da Y   My name
1234567891011121314516171819
20Cat.dog9i95up.
The

Observations, Initial Assessments, and Instructional Decisions

As the students write, their university tutors carefully observe and make notes about each student's writing behaviors (e.g., "John re-read and revised his story"; "Melissa spoke aloud to herself as she wrote"; "Matt erased extensively and used body language indicating that he was anxious and frustrated about writing"). Later, the tutors analyze the writing samples (Fig. 7.3), guided by a developmental writing checklist (Fig. 7.4).

Tutor's analysis of Antonia's first writing sample.

F I G U R E

7.3

ANTONIA

Antonia is eight years old. Her completed composition follows a logical progression and is interesting/enjoyable for the reader. Antonia wrote in both the expressive and imaginative *voices*. She wrote about herself (i.e., "I"), and created an imaginary story about a dinosaur. Antonia used standard and transitional spelling (e.g., "screm" (scream), "hem" (him), "frinck fisee" (french fries), "auntil" (until), "snuwsd" (snoozed), "snike" (sneak), "wock" (woke), "donunts" (doughnuts), "cuokise" (cookies), "pop tort" (poptarts), "eveyting" (everything), "word" (world), "defuntle" (definitely). Antonia wrote legibly and formed graphemes correctly. She capitalized the first word of the composition and *I* appropriately.

Antonia did not use a plan for writing. She completed her first draft and did not reread or revise. Antonia did not write for a specific audience. She did not title her composition nor include any punctuation until the end of the composition. The entire piece consists of one long sentence with "and" used as a connector throughout.

INITIAL INSTRUCTIONAL DECISIONS

1. Encourage Antonia to participate in many nonstructured writing activities. She expresses herself well and combines *voices* effectively. We need to encourage her creativity and help her write for her own purposes and for her own audiences.

2. Develop Antonia's awareness of *audience* (i.e., to whom is she writing?).

3. One of Antonia's immediate writing needs is using appropriate punctuation. In structured writing activities, point out the use of punctuation. Explain to Antonia how punctuation helps readers understand an author's writing.

4. Consider initiating a small unit on dinosaurs. Antonia is very interested in this topic.

5. Antonia is a good storyteller. She would probably enjoy participating in "Add a Paragraph/Write a Book."

6. Model use of punctuation in dialogue journal activities.

7. Use teacher dictation to help draw Antonia's attention to punctuation.

8. Antonia would probably enjoy reading about dinosaurs. Assemble a literature collection composed of dinosaur books (fiction, nonfiction, poetry, jokes).

9. Antonia's story could contain two paragraphs (e.g., first paragraph: "If a dinosaur came to lunch I would scream. I would feed him french fries and I would feed him until he snoozed"). Use teacher-guided activities, and introduce *Cohesive Paragraphs* to demonstrate the concept of paragraphing.

10. Antonia uses interesting, descriptive vocabulary (e.g., snoozed; definitely). Compliment Antonia on use of interesting words. Consider *Rephrasing* activities.

11. When reading, draw Antonia's attention to titles of stories and books. Discuss how authors choose titles for their work. Discuss why authors title their compositions, stories, and books.

12. Perhaps Antonia would like to learn the standard spelling of some of the descriptive words she used in her composition.

13. Continue to observe Antonia daily in order to revise/extend instructional decisions.

At this first session, the university tutors also attempt to determine their students' perceptions about writing by recording students' responses to questions on a writing perception survey (Fig. 7.5). The tutors then carefully reflect upon these three pieces of information (observation notes, writing sample analysis, and student's responses to questions on the writing perception survey), to get a sense of what each student knows and thinks about written language. This information, coupled with data gathered from an informal reading inventory and an interest survey (refer to Chapter 6), gives us insight into each student's literacy development, interests, and experiences.

At the same time, however, we recognize that students' writing abilities and understanding about writing grow daily. Therefore, ongoing observation is a necessity. In order to ascertain each student's ever changing writing (and reading) instructional needs, "the richest source of information . . . [is] close attention to students as they respond to instruction" (Rhodes & Dudley-Marling, 1988, p. 38).

FIGURE 7.4 Developmental writing checklist.

Name: _____   Date: _____

UNDERSTANDS THE WRITING PROCESS

1. Developed and used a plan for writing (e.g., semantic map, lists, outline, drawings, notes) (circle which apply)   YES NO
2. Referred to a plan when writing   YES NO
3. Re-read first draft and revised writing   YES NO
4. Rearranged words, sentences and paragraphs   YES NO
5. Revised vocabulary to include descriptive words and a variety of verbs   YES NO
6. Wrote for a specific audience (e.g., teacher, family, friend)   YES NO
7. Completed composition follows a logical progression   YES NO
8. Completed composition is interesting/enjoyable for the reader   YES NO
9. Used expressive *voice*; imaginative *voice*; expository *voice* (Give examples) (Circle which *voices* apply)   YES NO
10. Combined *voices* appropriately (Give examples)   YES NO

DEVELOPMENTAL STAGE OF SPELLING
(Circle which stage most applies and give examples)

1. prephonemic
2. early phonemic
3. letter name
4. transitional
5. standard

KNOWLEDGE OF MECHANICS

1. Titled the composition   YES NO
2. Used periods appropriately   YES NO
3. Used question marks appropriately   YES NO
4. Used commas appropriately   YES NO
5. Used exclamation marks appropriately   YES NO
6. Used quotation marks appropriately   YES NO
7. Used appropriate capitalization   YES NO
8. Indented paragraphs   YES NO
9. Wrote in complete sentences   YES NO
10. Wrote legibly   YES NO
11. Formed graphemes correctly   YES NO

(Items suggested by Tompkins & Hoskisson, 1991; Rhodes & Dudley-Marling, 1988)

FIGURE

7.5

Writing perception survey.

Name: _____ Date: _____

1. Why do people write?
2. How can you learn to write stories?
3. What stories would you like to write? Why?
4. Why do people write?
5. What is the difference between writing a story and writing a composition that explains or describes or tells somebody how to do something?
6. If you were teaching someone to write well, what would you tell them to do?
7. When you write, what do you do first?
8. How do you decide what to write?
9. What part of writing do you like the most? Why?
10. What part of writing do you like the least? Why?
11. When you are writing and get stuck, what do you do?
12. How do you know if your writing is any good?
13. If you were writing your own books, what would you write about?
14. Are you a good writer? Why? Why not?

Questions suggested by Hanson, 1987, pp. 32–33; Tompkins & Hoskisson, 1991, p. 261; Rhodes & Dudley-Marling, 1988, p. 62.

Nonstructured Writing Activities

There are always personally important reasons to write during our tutoring sessions. When writing is a natural and purposeful activity, everyone wants to write. For instance, a student may decide to take stock of all the books he has written (Fig. 7.6); a group may create a mural illustrating and telling a favorite story; two friends may spontaneously exchange informal notes concerning their feelings (Fig. 7.7). These types of **nonstructured writing activities** are "primarily student-centered with pupils writing about what is of most interest and concern to them" (Templeton, 1991, p. 218). By participating in nonstructured writing activities, students gain knowledge about written language without direct instruction (Rhodes & Dudley-Marling, 1988). Nonstructured writing activities also help foster a supportive, risk-free environment. In turn, a risk-free environment encourages students to write.

Structured Writing Lessons and Activities

Throughout the semester our students also engage in more structured writing lessons and activities that we categorize as 1) collaborative writing 2) teacher-guided writing 3) creative writing. In these more focused writing endeavors, "the [student's] purposes come first but the teacher deliberately creates a setting in which writing in different forms can be perceived as useful" (Nathan, Temple, Juntunen, & Temple, 1989, p. 93).

Collaborative Writing Activities

Language is facilitated in social contexts (Bloome & Egan-Robertson, 1993). **Collaborative writing activities** give our students opportunities to enjoy writing with a

FIGURE
7.6

Student's writing record.

Here is all my books I
wrotin.

Beauty and the Beast.

The Lizrd.

Michelle and The Casle.

The rabbit who had
no friends.

The cat who ate all the fish.

Once I was taking a nap.

My bedroom and bed.

All my dogs.

FIGURE
7.7

Informal notes between two students.

Aplie 7, 1993

Dear Ria,

I was going to let you
have my egg But you can
Just say I am tired.

No you are not. You'r friend
Be mine too O.K. I like
you now. you are my two
Best friend!

partner, or a group of friends, and a university tutor who serves as a role model. When writers plan, discuss, respond to one another, and write together, they spark one another's creativity and become less anxious about individual performance (Newman, 1985). Four collaborative writing activities our students particularly enjoy are (1) "Write a Sentence/Make a Story," (2) "Add a Word/Stretch the Sentence," (3) "Add a Paragraph/ Write a Book," (4) dialogue journaling. The tutors model each of these activities for their students before having their students participate.

"Write a Sentence/Make a Story." This activity links reading and writing and helps develop students' understanding of basic story features and their connections (i.e., characters, setting, problems, and solutions). To begin this activity, three to five students and their university tutor sit in a circle around a table. On a large sheet of paper each participant writes his/her idea for the first sentence of an imaginative story. If there are six participants there are six different sentences (e.g., "Joanne got a rabbit for her birthday" or "Shane loved to play baseball"). Participants then pass their papers to the person on their right, who reads the sentence and adds a second sentence to the story (e.g., "One day Joanne took her rabbit to the playground" or "Shane played baseball everyday with his friends").

Participants continue passing their papers, adding one additional sentence to each of the stories until they receive their original papers. Group members may pass their papers around the circle a second or third time if they decide that their stories need further development. Emergent writers, those just beginning their writing development, participate in "Write a Sentence/Make a Story" by drawing sentence pictures or dictating their sentence ideas to their tutors.

At the end of the activity, participants read their collaboratively created stories aloud for everyone's enjoyment. Tutors also lead a discussion about the characters, setting, problems, and solutions in each story, and how these basic story elements connect to one another (see Chapter 12). Figure 7.8 shows an example of a collaborative story for a tutor and two students.

"Add a Word/Stretch the Sentence." This activity promotes a reading/writing connection, helps students construct knowledge about the subtle interplay and interconnectedness of **syntax** and **semantics** (i.e., word order in sentences and meaning, respectively), improves students' control of written syntax (Nutter & Safran, 1984), and helps students construct more elaborate written sentences.

To start the activity, students and their tutor sit in a circle around a table. On a large sheet of paper each participant creates a beginning sentence of a composition in any *voice*. For example, "I love tutoring class" is written in the *expressive voice;* "The zoo has a dinosaur exhibit" is written in the *expository voice;* "Once there lived three little puppies" is written in the *imaginative* or *poetic voice* (see Britton, Burgess, Martin, McLeod & Rosen, 1975, for a thorough discussion of voices of composition). Next, participants pass their papers to the person on their right, who reads the last sentence and rewrites it, adding one additional word in any appropriate place in the sentence (e.g., "I really love tutoring class" or "The zoo has opened a dinosaur exhibit"). Emergent writers participate in this activity by dictating their original sentence and each of their "stretched" sentence ideas to their university tutors.

At the end of the activity, students and tutors take turns reading aloud their original sentence and each of the "stretched" sentences for the group's enjoyment. They also discuss how the meaning of each original sentence was expanded or changed (Fig. 7.9).

"Add a Paragraph/Write a Book." This activity promotes a reading/writing connection, alleviates writers' anxieties, and helps students construct knowledge about basic story features and their relationships. To initiate this activity, tutors place the first paragraph of an imaginative story at the beginning of a book made from blank pages stapled together. When time permits, individual students and their tutors add either an anonymous or an author-signed paragraph to the story. As the story progresses, students and tutors take turns reading the partially completed story aloud for the group's enjoyment. They also discuss their ideas for further story development. Once the book is completed, participants

---

FIGURE 7.8

Example of a collaborative story.

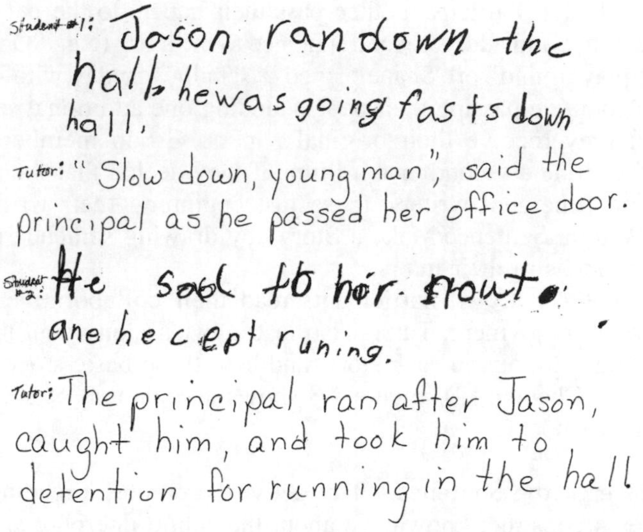

FIGURE 7.9

Example of "stretched" sentence.

share their collaborative authorship efforts with peers in the tutoring program and in their regular classrooms.

Dialogue journals. Tutors in our program journal with each of their students at every tutoring session. The journal entries are private and are read only by the two journal partners. **Dialogue journaling** provides a way for tutors and individual students to "carry on a conversation over time, sharing ideas, feelings and concerns in writing" (Staton, 1987, p. 47). Journaling also fosters a reading/writing connection and motivates students to write. Writing collaboratively with an equal partner enhances students' informal writing abilities and writing confidence as well. For instance, because of insecurity or lack of writing experience, some of our students initially choose to convey a journal message by drawing a picture or dictating a message. However, as the semester progresses, these students begin to feel more comfortable about writing and have learned a great deal about written language. Many of our students model and imitate the language functions (e.g., reporting facts or opinions, asking questions) and language conventions (e.g., using exclamation marks or closing entries by writing "love") their tutors use in their own journal entries.

As shown in the series of three nonconsecutive days of journaling seen in Figure 7.10, when Tonya entered our program she wrote just a few words and drew hearts to show her feelings. The following week she answered her tutor's question, attempted to write complete sentences, and modeled her tutor's use of question marks. Six days later Tonya wrote a long journal entry in which she shared a considerable amount of information and feelings.

Journal writing is never considered a writing assignment. Therefore, the university tutors never correct their students' spelling, punctuation, or capitalization. Instead they try to be particularly responsive to what their students write. They never ask their students too many questions or write only about their own interests and concerns. Rather, they compliment their students' work (e.g., "I liked your story about wolves"), support and affirm their students' efforts (e.g., "You really are trying hard and it shows!"), and write honest, interesting, personal messages that encourage and entice their students to respond (Young & Crow, 1992).

Teacher-Guided Writing Lessons

Many teachers recognize that, in order to become proficient writers, students experiencing serious difficulty usually need to engage in activities that draw their attention to certain aspects of language they may otherwise disregard or overlook (Hillocks, 1986). Short, **teacher-guided writing lessons** provide a way to help students focus upon and practice "new writing skills without being overwhelmed" (Bryson & Scardamalia, 1991, p. 164). These types of lessons concentrate on discrete aspects of written language such as spelling, punctuation, and capitalization, and also include more global aspects of composing such as prewriting strategies, paragraphing, and editing (Templeton, 1991).

The university tutors design teacher-guided writing lessons based upon their students' immediate writing needs. Therefore, the students view these types of mini-lessons as personally useful and meaningful because they immediately are able to apply the concepts they learn in their own independent writing and revision efforts. Four teacher-guided writing lessons particularly effective for our students are "Personal Dictionary Sharing," "Teacher Dictation," "Rephrasing," and "Writing Cohesive Paragraphs." Features of these four lessons can easily be modified or adapted to suit the writing needs of diverse groups of learners in any educational setting. Spelling can also be addressed within the context of these lessons.

F I G U R E   Dialogue journal entries.

7.10

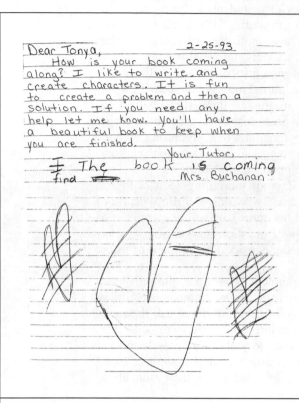

Dear Tonya,   2-25-93
    How is your book coming
along? I like to write and
create characters. It is fun
to create a problem and then a
solution. If you need any
help let me know. You'll have
a beautiful book to keep when
you are finished.
                    Your Tutor,
    I The book is coming
find   Mrs. Buchanan

3-16-93
Dear Tonya,
    I'm really looking forward to
my spring break. What do you have
planned?
                    Mrs. Buchanan
    yes I have planned for
springbreak

    I have a good good

    I hop you have good
spring break and I
hop I have a good
springbreak to.
    My baby brother
His to go to the
hospital today
be caues he
bart His hand is
working good
but he have iny
hard time
what it. My big
brother is going
to the race
out I dot what
to go beccaues
I think that
races or
broing to go.

Dear Tonya,   3-4-93
    Did you get to play with
your friends? My daughters have
the Pretty Princess game too. They
love to play it. Did you like
how your book turned out? I
think you did an excellent job.
I think you are a very good writer.
You should not be afraid to
write because you are very good at
creating story ideas. Tell me about
some of your favorite books.
                    Your Tutor,
    Yes I get to play
    with my friends. Mrs. Buchanan

    I do to?

    I Love to play it to?

    Go sole EB for
    the "Oak Bark

"Personal Dictionary Sharing." This teacher-guided lesson provides opportunities for students to share and talk about interesting spelling words they have used while writing, or unusual words they have discovered during tutoring sessions (e.g., while reading or listening to children's literature, or interacting with guest speakers, peers, and tutors). Participating in "Personal Dictionary Sharing" also facilitates students' gradual transition from invented spelling to standard spelling by developing their awareness of spelling conventions and focusing their attention on specific features of individual words (e.g., number of syllables, beginning or ending with a consonant blend, affixes, vowel/consonant patterns, etc.).

Prior to introducing this lesson we make each student's **personal dictionary** by stapling together twenty-six blank sheets of paper and placing one alphabet letter (A to Z) on each blank page. Older students usually prefer using hard-cover notebooks for their dictionaries. If necessary, tutors help students turn to the appropriate page of their dictionary and enter their new words in a meaningful sentence with the new word underlined (e.g., "*Marsupials* use their pouches to keep their babies warm and safe"). During the lesson, tutors invite individual students to write their newly entered words in sentences on the board or on a chart for the group's enjoyment and enlightenment. Students share the ways they discovered their new words, and the group discusses the spelling features of each word and the various ways each word might be used in diverse contexts. Tutors use many of these newly discovered words in the "Teacher Dictation" lesson described next.

"Teacher Dictation." This teacher-guided lesson connects the processes of listening, writing, and reading, and enhances students' understanding of language conventions at the sentence level (i.e., spelling, punctuation, and capitalization). Studies show that language conventions such as punctuation are a particular problem for students having serious difficulty (Norton, 1993). To begin this teacher-guided lesson, students listen carefully as their tutor dictates a sentence that contains particular aspects of language that students are ready to address in their independent writing. For example, if some students are ready to learn about capitalizing the first word of a sentence, a tutor might dictate the sentence "Wild animals live in the zoo." Students then write the dictated sentence. Their tutors also write the sentences on a large chart or chalkboard while modeling their thinking aloud (e.g., "I need to begin a sentence with a capital letter"). Tutors then read aloud the dictated sentence as students follow along.

The next step is a discussion of the particular language conventions pertinent to the sentence (e.g., "The word *wild* begins with a capital letter because it is the first word of the sentence"). To complete the lesson, tutors help their students edit or "fix" any problems in their sentences such as adding a period or editing spelling. As the semester progresses students take over the tutor's role and dictate sentences to the group.

"Rephrasing." This teacher-guided writing lesson connects listening, writing, and reading, enhances and expands students' vocabulary, and helps students generate language and "discover how it works" (Kean & Personke, 1976, p. 313). The procedure for this lesson is similar to the "Teacher Dictation" activity described in the previous section: 1) tutors dictate a sentence, 2) students and tutors write the sentence, 3) tutors read the dictated sentence aloud as students follow along, 4) if necessary, students edit their writing with their tutor's help.

In the next step, students take turns rephrasing the sentence orally or in writing by creating variations in vocabulary and attempting to keep the original meaning of the sentence intact. For example, participants might rephrase the sentence, "Today is Tuesday" as "This is the third day of the week"; "This is the day before Wednesday"; "This is the day after Monday"; or "This is the day before the fourth day of the week." Participants then share all their rephrased sentence ideas and discuss any possible meaning changes that may have occurred. Groups often write and display all their sentence variations on sentence strips or charts in order to share their work with others (Fig. 7.11).

"Writing Cohesive Paragraphs." This lesson provides a strategic plan students can follow independently to improve their abilities to write paragraphs that focus on a central theme. To begin the lesson, tutors help their students develop a prewriting semantic map on a topic of the student's choice, such as the map about dogs in Figure 7.12.

Next, tutors help their students categorize and label the concepts in the map. Most students usually require considerable help in this step. Students then rank the categories according to the order in which they might place the information in a composition (Fig. 7.13). (See also K-W-L Plus in Chapter 12.)

Tutors then help their students think about how to organize the composition into an opening paragraph, subsequent paragraphs, and a closing paragraph. For example, in an expository voice composition about dogs, the student may decide that the opening paragraph might present a short history of dogs. Subsequent paragraphs may equal the number of categories included in the conceptual map (e.g., a paragraph about the breeds of dogs, dogs' physical attributes, dogs' activities, and preferred foods of dogs). A closing paragraph might present a summary of ideas in the composition.

Since writers usually discover new or "just thought of" ideas as they write, the university tutors encourage their students to incorporate these new ideas into the appropriate categories of their semantic maps. If necessary, students may decide to create an additional category for a new idea. In this way, they consciously choose to use the new information by inserting these ideas into the appropriate paragraphs in the composition.

Creative Writing: The Starting Point

Creative writing includes fiction, drama, and poetry (Norton, 1993). All good creative writing starts with experiences. Therefore, the starting point in our creative writing pro-

---

FIGURE
7.11

Example of oral rephrasing.

Tutor:	The boys and girls cooked a meal.
Barbie:	The children fixed cocoa.
Tonya:	The kids made a cake.
Brad:	The children made a pie.
Chris:	The kids made sweet potatoes for dinner.
Jessica:	The friends made dinner.
Marian:	The kids made biscuits.

A prewriting semantic map.

F I G U R E
7.12

Categorizing from semantic map on dogs.

F I G U R E
7.13

dog's activities
run
jump
play   4th
growl   paragraph
bark
sleep

dog's attributes
paws
eyes   3rd
four legs   paragraph
hair/fur
tails

breeds of dogs
poodles   2nd
              paragraph
retrievers
mixed breeds
? need more
  information

dogs eat
dog food   5th
bones   paragraph
? need
  more
  information

history of dogs
? need information

1st paragraph

gram is to provide diverse experiences for our students that give them a "natural thing to write about next" (Allen, Brown, & Yatvin, 1986, p. 463). Some of the experiences we provide for our students include: (1) reading, listening to, and discussing quality fiction and nonfiction (2) inviting and listening to guest speakers talk on wide-ranging topics such as dinosaurs, Great Britain, and rabbits (3) designing, creating, and flying kites (4) making and eating cakes and banana splits (5) preparing and serving a tea party for others (6) presenting plays and Readers Theatre productions for others to enjoy (7) making a substance similar to Play-Doh™ to use as sculpture materials (8) creating and playing literacy board games (9) walking outside to view clouds, toads, flowers, rain, or shadows (10) planning and participating in a Literacy Celebration Day at which food is served, students' work is displayed, and students, tutors, parents, grandparents, and classroom teachers have an opportunity to celebrate our students' literacy successes.

Prewriting strategies. Prewriting strategies help students generate ideas for writing and determine what they know or need to know about a creative writing topic. Two prewriting strategies our students especially enjoy are "Speed Writing" and "Story Features and their Connections."

"Speed Writing," also known as "Free Writing" or "Timed Focused Writing" (Norton, 1993; Rhodes & Dudley-Marling, 1988), alleviates writers' anxieties about composing, helps writers generate ideas for writing, and frees writers from worrying about language conventions.

Participants in "Speed Writing" write non-stop for a certain amount of time (e.g., two to five minutes) without erasing, crossing out, or requesting help with spelling. The idea is to relax and let ideas emerge.

At the end of the designated writing time authors share their efforts with the group. Listeners ask questions and offer one another comments and suggestions that may help authors clarify or further develop their work.

"Story Features and Their Connections" is a prewriting strategy that helps writers plan their imaginative stories in a thoughtful, organized, and interesting way by considering the four basic story features of characters, settings, problems, and solutions. To implement this strategy tutors help their students fill in semantic maps based upon their ideas about the specific feature they might include in a story. The story features map pictured in Figure 7.14 was created by a group of sixth graders. The group decided to portray three characters named Lisa, Chad, and Sam; include three settings (i.e., a school, a Florida beach, and a bungee jumping park); create two problems (i.e., a group of students needs money for a trip and Chad hurts his leg); and offer a solution for each problem.

When the story features map was filled in, the sixth graders brainstormed how their story features might connect to one another. The map shows that the three characters connect to the Florida beach (i.e., a setting) because the characters travel to Florida. The map also illustrates how the problem of "needing money" is solved when the three characters earn money by cutting grass.

After completing the map and determining the connections among the story features, the sixth graders wrote a first draft of their story and titled it "Bungee Jumping." Once our students have a sound understanding of the four basic story features and their interconnections, their university tutors help them focus on other important parts and connections of well-formed stories such as episodes (i.e., a series of actions and happenings), and a resolution (i.e., the final outcome of a story).

Composing. As our students compose their imaginative stories, books, plays, and poems, and write letters to favorite authors, and create recipes (Fig. 7.15), we encourage them to concentrate first on their messages and to "spell and punctuate as they think best" (Allen,

Story features map.

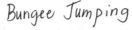

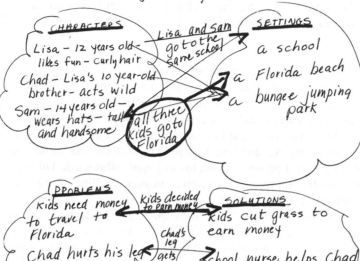

Student letter to a favorite author and student recipe for cooking turkey.

thurs 1-21-93
dear tomie depapla i hope you write
more stre ga nona Books. I like fin'mcool
and watch out for the chicken feet in
your soup. love sam yeur intresdid reader

_____

to cook a turkey you need a turkey

important

Sam's resahpeay

step 1. freze it!
step 2. thade it!
step 3. put sauce on it!
step 4. put it in the oven!
step 5. cook it for a Hour!
step 6. eat it!

Brown, & Yatvin, 1986, p. 463). Good writers never worry about correct language conventions (i.e, spelling, punctuation, capitalization, and paragraphing) until they are ready to edit their work. During these composing sessions the university tutors circulate and interact among their students, offering encouragement, and providing guidance if asked. The tutors also ask their students questions designed to encourage them to experiment with writing and further develop their work (e.g., "Tell me more about this new character in your story. I want to know what he looks like so that I'll recognize him if I meet him") (Graves, 1993).

Editing. "Overemphasis on the mechanics of writing and neatness in the early stages of writing development often overshadows the ideas students are trying to express" (Searfoss, 1993, p. 12). Therefore, when our students' first drafts are completed, editing decisions are guided by each student's evolving literacy development and corresponding ability to complete revision tasks. It makes no sense to require a student to conduct extensive, personally meaningless revisions if she (1) is anxious and hesitant about writing (2) has just begun to commit personal thoughts to paper (Rhodes & Dudley-Marling, 1988) (3) is developmentally not ready to use conventional spelling or punctuation or (4) has just begun to believe in herself as a writer (Daniels, 1991).

Spelling problems especially "tend to inhibit many [older] students who would otherwise be imaginative, intelligent writers" (Silva & Yarborough, 1990, p. 48). Therefore, some spelling guidance is appropriate for our older students. For example, privately and informally we draw students' attention to misspelled words during editing (Templeton, 1991). We also help our students enter difficult spelling words in complete sentences in their personal dictionaries.

Students also find that it is useful to record interesting words, words that do not follow a typical spelling pattern, past tense words, and words and their synonyms and antonyms in a word study notebook (Henderson, 1990). Thinking and talking about spelling, and focusing attention on words help our students become more proficient spellers and enhance their oral language and vocabulary as well.

Sharing. After our students complete any developmentally appropriate revision tasks and are satisfied with their work, the university tutors invite them to share their writing efforts with peers. In these sharing sessions students and tutors offer positive feedback to each writer (e.g., "I really liked the part in your story where the giant meets the wicked prince"), and each writer's efforts are applauded and celebrated as a literacy accomplishment.

WRITING INSTRUCTION AND ASSESSMENT: A CONTINUOUS PROCESS

We agree with literacy experts who state that "writing is a developmental process that evolves much like oral language" (Glazer & Brown, 1993, p. 47). Daily assessment, conducted as our students write and respond to literacy lessons and activities, allows us to observe and understand the writing behaviors and processes our students employ. This ongoing approach to assessment also helps us concentrate on individual students' progress over time rather than measure one student against another.

Assessment that takes place within the context of authentic teaching and learning requires the university tutors to (1) observe their students carefully as they write and interact with one another (2) concentrate on determining students' writing strengths rather than deficiencies (3) "note what a student is developmentally ready to learn" (Glazer & Brown, 1993, p. 52) (4) document students' writing progress and the writing processes they employ guided by observation notes and writing checklists (such as the developmental writing checklist) (5) reflect upon and consider what each student knows about written language. Studying this information provides the university tutors with directions for future writing lessons. Thus, writing instruction and assessment merge and become a mutually supportive, continuous process (Glazer & Brown, 1993; Snider, Lima, & DeVito, 1994).

We also agree on the importance of helping students learn how to assess their own writing progress. "By engaging students in self-assessments students learn they are ultimately responsible for their own learning" (Tierney, Carter, & Desai, 1991, p. 59). We use three different formats to increase our students' involvement in self-assessing their writing (1) shared observations (2) postwriting questionnaires (3) portfolios.

Shared Observations

Students cannot begin to monitor or assess their own writing behaviors and progress until they know something about the processes good writers use and recognize their own composing behaviors. Therefore, the university tutors share their observation notes with each of their students in short, informal conferences (e.g., "Today I noticed that you re-read your story and edited your punctuation. All good writers edit punctuation when they are satisfied with the message they have written. Good for you").

Postwriting Questionnaires

Our students also find it helpful to respond to a postwriting questionnaire when they have completed a piece of writing. Postwriting checklists (see also Glazer & Brown, 1993) and questionnaires serve as self-monitoring tools that help emerging writers of any age develop an awareness about their writing behaviors (Fig. 7.16).

Portfolios

Our students keep all of the writing they do throughout the semester in two different folders labeled "working portfolios" and "showcase portfolios" (Tierney, Carter & Desai, 1991). **Working portfolios** house (1) the student's writing in progress (2) work that may never be completed (3) first drafts (4) revision pages (5) work generated during writing lessons and activities (e.g., "Speed Writing" efforts) (6) ideas for possible future writing (e.g., drawings, notes, concept maps, and pictures) and (7) copies of completed postwriting questionnaires. This type of portfolio documents all of the student's writing during nonstructured, collaborative, teacher-guided, and creative writing activities.

Showcase portfolios contain examples of writing chosen by students because the work is special to them in some way. For example, each writing artifact included in the showcase portfolio is accompanied by a short statement or caption that explains why the writer chose that particular piece for inclusion (e.g., "This is the first story I ever wrote"; "I worked very hard on the ending of this story"; or "I want to be a ballerina when I grow up so I wrote a story about a dancer"). With our students' permission both types of portfolios, working and showcase, are displayed during Literacy Celebration Day.

The writing included in the working and showcase portfolios helps provide us with concrete evidence concerning individual students' improvements, efforts, personal writing interests, and perceptions about themselves as writers (Tierney, Carter, & DeSai, 1991). More important, portfolios provide a way for our students to take some responsibility for organizing their work and help them self-evaluate their achievements and writing instructional needs.

FIGURE 7.16   A self-assessment postwriting questionnaire.

Name: _____   Date: _____

This Piece of Writing

1. What part of the writing process was most successful for you (e.g., brainstorming ideas, composing, editing)?
2. What writing strategies did you use (e.g., "Story Features and their Connections," Semantic Mapping, "Speed Writing")?
3. What part of the writing process was least successful for you (e.g., brainstorming ideas, first draft, editing)?
4. What pleases you most about this piece of writing?
5. In which *voice* did you write?
6. Are you comfortable with this *voice* of composing? Did you choose to write in this *voice*?
7. What is the topic of this piece? Have you written before on this topic? Why did you choose to write on this topic?
8. How did you organize your writing?
9. What type of mechanical errors caused you the most trouble in this piece (e.g., capitalization, paragraphing, punctuation, spelling)?

Your Next Piece of Writing*

1. What topic interests you for your next piece of writing? Why?
2. For which audience will you write this next piece? Why?
3. How do you plan on gathering information for this topic?
4. How do you plan on organizing this piece of writing?

Or consider the following set of questions for younger writers.**

1. What's good about this writing?
2. What problems did you have as you wrote?
3. What prewriting strategies did you use?
4. What postwriting strategies did you use?
5. What would you like to try in your next piece of writing?

*Adapted from Norton, 1992, p. 246.
**Adapted from Graves, 1993.

SUMMARY

It makes sense to connect reading and writing instruction. Each process supports and contributes to the other's development. It is especially important to connect reading and writing instruction for corrective readers, regardless of age. Many of these learners write very little because they have had few positive writing experiences. Because reading and writing develop concurrently, strengthening each other, it is crucial that students with reading difficulties have opportunities to write.

The role of the writing teacher in a corrective reading program is no different from that of all good writing teachers. Good writing teachers recognize that writing is a social process. They understand that their students learn about writing by writing for their own purposes and audiences. Above all, they wholeheartedly "believe that their students can write" (Daniels, 1991, p. 169).

Implementing a writing program for corrective readers entails collecting information about each student's knowledge and preconceptions of written language. Ongoing observation is also a necessity in order to assess students' ever changing progress and the processes they employ as they write.

Transferring the principles and practices described in this one particular tutorial program to a classroom setting is not difficult. The teacher need only set a goal to create a learning community that provides students "with lots of invitations to write, to read, and to learn" (Revel-Wood, 1988, p. 169). In addition to the many kinds of activities already described in this chapter, a suggestion easily incorporated into any classroom is to consider a *message board* as a way of providing students opportunities to "talk" to each other, as well as for teachers and students to share problems, make requests or suggestions, ask a favor or give a reminder, make announcements and assignments, share a joke or riddle as well as current events, and hang various sign-up sheets. Only one restriction should be made: messages can be hung publicly or in a sealed envelope or folded paper but all messages *must be signed* (Harste, Short, & Burke, 1988).

Corrective reading students enjoy participating in nonstructured writing activities that allow them to write about subjects that interest and concern them. They also benefit from more structured writing lessons and activities categorized as collaborative, teacher-guided, and creative. Portfolios provide a way for students to keep a record of their writing efforts.

More important, selecting work to include in portfolios and making decisions about the reasons the work is important give students opportunities to self-evaluate their writing progress.

SUGGESTED READINGS

Daniels, H. (1991). Commentary on Chapter 5 (Teaching writing to students at-risk for academic failure). In B. Means, C. Chalmers, and M. Knapp (Eds.), *Teaching advanced skills to at-risk students: Views from research and practice* (pp. 168–175). San Francisco, CA: Jossey-Bass.

> *At-risk students become better writers when they spend less time on skill/drill activities and more time composing for their own purposes and audiences. These (and*

all) writers benefit from social interaction, peer collaboration, and time given to sharing drafts and completed work with peers.

Graves, D. (1992). Help students learn to read their portfolios. In D. Graves and B. Sunstein (Eds.), *Portfolio Portraits* (pp. 85–95). Portsmouth, NH: Heinemann.

Before students can evaluate their own writing, they need to understand the characteristics of good writing. Graves offers four approaches designed to help students learn to self-assess their writing.

Manning, G., Manning, M., & Long, R. (1990). *Reading and writing in the middle grades: A whole-language view.* Washington, DC: National Education Association.

This publication is for teachers of grades four through seven (middle school) who want to know more about how to put whole language theory into practice. The reader will visit the classrooms of eight model teachers in the middle grades. Chapter 3, "Developing Writers," is particularly relevant in that it discusses an approach called Writing Workshop *in detail, as well as other writing strategies appropriate for middle graders.*

8

WORD RECOGNITION

OBJECTIVES

After you have read this chapter, you should be able to

1. explain the difference between products of word analysis instruction and the process of word recognition;

2. list the major areas of skill development for word recognition;

3. develop a sequence for instruction of a word unknown in print;

4. choose and develop materials and exercises appropriate for instruction in the process of word recognition;

5. devise an instructional program in word recognition for a corrective student.

KEY CONCEPTS AND TERMS

analytical vocabulary

auditory blending

automaticity

context

expectancy clues

listening vocabulary

meaning clues

meaning vocabulary

onsets

perceptual unit

phonemic awareness

phonics

picture clues

productive language

psychological set

reading vocabulary

recoding

rimes

scriptal information

sight vocabulary

sight words

structural analysis

syndrome

visual synthesizing

STUDY OUTLINE

OVERVIEW

The heart of the reading process is comprehension, understanding what is read. Students with word recognition difficulties generally fall into one of two categories. Either they do not use meaning, or what they already know about the text, to process print effectively, or they lack phonemic awareness and thus do not understand what letters and their combinations are supposed to represent. As a result, reading is not an interesting or pleasant experience but a frustrating, laborious task.

Instruction in word recognition is important to comprehension. However, the major goal of understanding what is read can sometimes get lost in programs that emphasize word recognition. When this happens the teacher is responsible for putting word recognition in proper perspective, for the students must never lose sight of the major purpose of their efforts—comprehension. Reading is a meaning-making process.

The causes of word recognition difficulties are myriad, but three common types related to reading instruction are: (1) too little instruction in word recognition (2) too much instruction in word recognition (3) instruction that is *imbalanced* (e.g., too much phonics and no contextual analysis) in terms of the major areas of this important domain.

The traditional skill strands for word recognition are sight vocabulary, phonic analysis, structural analysis, contextual analysis, and dictionary skills. In this chapter aspects of all these skill strands are addressed, but from the perspective of particular cognitive processes necessary for success in applying these skills. For example, the importance of developing listening vocabulary as a foundation for subsequent sight vocabulary development is discussed. The concept of **automaticity** is emphasized at both the word and word element levels, because the efficient reader must learn these units so thoroughly that little effort is needed to recognize a new word or word part. Of course, automaticity is best achieved by practice in reading whole, meaningful text, not by isolated word drills.

Likewise, context clues, including expectancy, picture, and meaning clues, are strongly oriented to meaning and thinking, specifically the semantic and syntactic cue systems. Visual analysis itself is less of a thinking skill, yet a learner uses considerable thought in its application. Segmenting unknown words visually, or in any other fashion, is not an easy task for the new reader or for the corrective reader. The section entitled "Inadequate Knowledge of Word Parts" centers on graphophonemic aspects: (1) structural analysis, which involves meaning-bearing units, and (2) phonics, which is less meaningful in orientation. Correction of blending and synthesizing deficiencies is also stressed and related to the word recognition process.

Each section begins with a general discussion followed by an explanation of behaviors to look for and assessment techniques to use. Each section ends with detailed suggestions for instruction. These are only samples of the many types of activities and procedures possible.

INTRODUCTION

The reading process begins by using nonvisual information (e.g., expectations about the text) to perceive such visual stimuli as letters, words, and sentences; it is completed when the message of the author is understood. Between these two points, readers encounter words they do not recognize. When this happens, they must have a strategy for recognizing or analyzing these words. No one knows precisely how word analysis works, but reading experts generally agree that when context fails to trigger word recognition, readers need to identify the word parts, say the parts, and then reassemble them so that they cue a meaningful response.

Figuring out words unknown in print is only one of many processes used in constructing meaning from print. These processes are dynamic and interactive, changing as a student's knowledge and skills increase. For example, word analysis and word identification influence a reader's ability to understand what is read. What a reader understands in a passage or sentence influences the ability to decode other unknown words. These processes are symbiotic, reciprocal, and interactive. Thus, in this chapter, word recognition is conceptualized as an interaction among the skills learned (the *product* of word analysis instruction) with the way the student analyzes the unknown words (the *process* of word recognition). The more knowledge and skills readers have, the easier and more efficient word recognition will be. Further, the more background and understanding readers bring to the reading passage, the better will be their use of contextual analysis to decode unknown words.

The size of visual stimuli used for analysis is often referred to as the **perceptual unit** or unit of analysis. Reading instruction has a long methodological history, with method being closely related to the unit of analysis. Different methods have emphasized teaching symbol–sound correspondence using letters of the alphabet, syllables, words, sentences, or whole stories. Historically, students have learned to read successfully with each method.

Likewise, some students have trouble learning to read with each method, and different methods tend to yield different types of reading difficulties. You will find exercise examples in this chapter that focus on small units of analysis, such as word parts, but you will also find suggestions for teaching that use larger analytical units typically associated with a holistic or psycholinguistic view of teaching reading. Invariably, the goal of all decoding instruction is to develop independent readers who not only comprehend what they read but who also choose to read. We do not want to make decoding instruction so boring or laborious as to "turn kids off" to reading.

I believe that students with word recognition difficulties profit from learning a variety of analytic units, depending largely on the individual's specific strategy needs. I also believe that many, if not all, beginning readers must learn to analyze words, but that this analysis is only effective when they already know the words' meanings. If the word meaning does not exist in the student's *listening* (or understanding) *vocabulary,* all the effort to analyze the word is wasted because it does not trigger a meaningful response. Unfortunately, beginning readers and many corrective readers do not know if the word exists in their understanding vocabularies until *after* they have worked to analyze the word. Only when they are sure their efforts have identified the correct word do they feel the possibility of success.

Sadly, these students have no sure way of determining whether they have misanalyzed a word or the word is new to them in terms of meaning. This dilemma facing the young or corrective reader disappears or lessens only with maturity in reading. The best defense against this dilemma is to *develop in the student, from the very beginning, the need to demand meaning from what is read*. If meaning does not result from analytic effort, the student must seek help. Further, students should have a balanced set of word analysis skills and varied techniques to allow them to approach problem-solving of unknown words with flexibility.

Teachers of corrective readers need to focus instruction on three long-term goals involving word study: (1) building a listening vocabulary (2) building a sight vocabulary (3) building a balanced set of word recognition skills. The following poem[1] sums up word recognition well.

> When I get stuck on a word in a book,
> There are lots of things to do.
> I can do them all, please, by myself;
> I don't need help from you.
>
> I can look at the pictures to get a hint,
> Or think what the story's about.
> I can "get my mouth ready" to say the first letter,
> A kind of "sounding out."
> I can chop the word into smaller parts,
> Like *on* and *ing* and *ly,*
> Or find smaller words in compound words
> Like *raincoat* and *bumblebee.*
> I can think of a word that makes sense in that place,
> Guess or say "blank" and read on
> Until the sentence has reached its end,
> Then go back and try these on:
>> "Does it make sense?"
>> "Can we say it that way?"
>> "Does it *look* right to me?"
> Chances are the right word will pop out like the sun
> In my *own* mind, can't you see?
>
> If I've thought of and tried out most of these things
> And I *still* do not know what to do,
> *Then* I may turn around and ask
> For some help to get me through.

INADEQUATE LISTENING VOCABULARY

All teachers wish to support students in gaining knowledge. Frequently this means teaching new concepts and elaborating on more basic ones. Words reflect these concepts. When students have opportunities to experience new areas of knowledge, they learn new words and their meanings, thereby expanding their **meaning vocabulary**.

---

[1]From Jill Marie Warner, "Independent Strategies," *The Reading Teacher*, May 1993, p. 710. Reprinted with permission of Jill Marie Warner and the International Reading Association.

This is referred to as **listening vocabulary** when the word is heard and understood in speech and as **reading vocabulary** when the word is read and understood in print.

Many students come to school with good listening vocabularies; they continue to add to their store of concepts and word meanings as they proceed through the curriculum. Some students, however, have limited knowledge of the world or nontraditional knowledge that is at odds with traditional expectations. World knowledge affects a student's attempts to analyze words unknown in print. No matter how hard students try to analyze a word, and no matter how accurate their analytical skills may be, they cannot trigger a meaningful response if the word is not in their listening vocabulary. Goodman (1968) refers to this incomplete process as **recoding**. To illustrate the point, try to pronounce the following words: miscreant, putative, egregious. If you have previously heard these words, chances are good that you will feel secure with their pronunciation. If not, chances are equally good that your pronunciation will be incorrect. Make several guesses (hypotheses) about the pronunciation of the words. For fun, if you don't know the meanings of these words, try to guess the meanings from the words provided.

miscreant	*putative*	*egregious*
mistake	reputed	helpful
hero	punishable	dreadful
degenerate	ugly	powerful
relapse	childlike	tolerable

If you still feel a bit insecure with their meanings, read the following sentences, which may help clarify them.

The *miscreant* defaced Michelangelo's *Pieta*.

Charles's terrier is the *putative* sire of the litter of pups.

Crashing into the train was an *egregious* mistake.

If you knew all the other words in the sentences, you may have used the context to identify the *meaning* of each word and thus you were able to understand the sentence. In all cases, however, the context may not be sufficient. Regardless, you *still* do not know how the word "sounds" because it is not yet in your listening vocabulary. Therefore, it is not in your meaning vocabulary; you would not be able to associate a meaning with the word until you heard it used in a context from which you could derive its meaning. In reality, upon encountering such words while reading, mature readers attempt to use context and apply their graphophonic knowledge and do whatever is necessary to maintain the meaning of the passage. Sometimes the word is not important to the overall understanding of the passage and so mature readers skip it. If it turns out the word *is* important, mature readers consult a dictionary or ask someone. This kind of thoughtful behavior, a strategy, is something we need to teach students.

Assessment

Limitations in listening vocabulary are often detectable during oral reading and present a typical **syndrome**, or set of observable behaviors or signs. These readers seem quite successful in analyzing words except for a notable exception. When asked to figure out a word, they demonstrate knowledge of word analysis, blending skills, and use of context clues, coming close to an acceptable pronunciation, but still cannot come up with the word. This suggests that they do not know the meaning of the word being analyzed. Frequent occurrence of this behavior suggests that these students are meeting too many words with meanings they should but do not know.

If using standardized test results, a comparison can be made of vocabulary subtest scores and subtest scores that assess word recognition skills. When vocabulary knowledge is considerably weaker than other word analysis skills, a limitation has been identified. The *Stanford Diagnostic Reading Tests* (Karlsen & Gardner, 1986) comprise one of the few group standardized tests available that can be used for this purpose. Finally, another assessment procedure is to ask students directly if they know what a word means.

Instruction

Following are examples of activities recommended to expand listening vocabularies. These activities encompass many areas of the curriculum, so they are appropriate for any age/grade level.

1. Provide many and varied first-hand experiences.
   a. Arrange field trips, preceded and followed by discussions that are deliberately planned to use and review relevant vocabulary. As Durkin (1978) states, "Experience and vocabulary do not grow together automatically. . . . Teachers should have made some decisions beforehand about the concepts and words that ought to come alive as a result of the experience" (p. 380).
   b. Develop interest centers in the classroom, arranged and maintained by both teacher and students, utilizing appropriate charts and labels. Such interest centers also provide discussion topics.
2. Provide vicarious experiences.
   a. Invite speakers to talk about relevant areas of study. Before the speaker comes and after the presentation, the teacher should initiate discussion and elaborate on important concepts and vocabulary.
   b. Make full use of carefully selected appropriate media, for example, films, filmstrips, transparencies, tapes, models, and computer simulations.
3. Provide increased opportunities for silent reading of relatively easy materials and for reading aloud to students. Explanations and elaborations by authors frequently add dimensions of meaning. This activity is particularly important for more mature readers who lack experience in a particular area; such an activity could be conceptualized as learning about the world through books. Authors often help by giving context clues that define words or terms and elaborate meanings.
4. Guide the development and use of dictionaries that relate either to a topic of special interest to the student or to a group project or thematic unit.
   a. Have young children construct personal picture dictionaries.
   b. Have students construct personal spelling dictionaries (see Chapter 7).
   c. Have students construct personal vocabulary notebooks.
   d. Have students prepare alphabet books for a particular topic (e.g., see *Animalia,* Base, 1986).
5. Guide the direct study of words through such activities as listing synonyms, antonyms, or affixes and searching for word derivations.

6. Use exercises such as the following with follow-up directions to use these words in written stories:

a. Exercises emphasizing sensory impressions (selected children's literature can provide the stimulus for such exercises, e.g., *Click, Rumble, Roar: Poems about Machines,* Hopkins, 1987, and scores of books about animals)

1) Put an *X* by the words that describe something you hear:

_____ sour _____ swish _____ clap

_____ sunny _____ bang _____ cold

Add other words you know that describe something you hear.

2) Underline the words that tell how an animal moves:

slither   bright   paddle

gallop   hair   waddle

Add other words you know that tell how animals move.

b. Exercises to develop differentiated meanings

1) Circle the words that mean almost the same as *fat:*

pudgy   chubby   overweight

skinny   clean   rotund

2) Draw a line connecting a word from list A to a word in list B that is opposite:

A	B
cheerful	rested
anxious	glum
tired	interested
bored	calm

Johnson and Pearson's *Teaching Reading Vocabulary* (1984) contains a wealth of suggestions for vocabulary instruction.

INADEQUATE SIGHT VOCABULARY

Sight vocabulary refers to words in print that are recognized instantly and effortlessly. Mature readers perceive most words they encounter in this fashion. Most children entering school, on the other hand, begin with few or no words that they can read quickly with ease.

Students seem to learn words in three phases. At first encounter they do not recognize the word in print, although it may exist in their listening vocabularies. Then, with repeated exposure, they recognize it partially but still need to analyze its representation in graphic form. (These words make up the **analytical vocabulary**; the student says the word correctly but *not* quickly.) Finally, after several encounters, the word is recognized instantly. Every word that students read should be considered a candidate for their sight vocabularies, with the possible exception of rare, unusual, or foreign words. As a student reads more and more, words accumulate in the student's sight vocabulary and need no further study because they are recognized automatically (LaBerge & Samuels, 1976).

The concept of sight vocabulary should not be confused with that of **sight words**. The latter term refers to a relatively small set of words in our language that do not conform to rules of pronunciation or analytical techniques learned by children beginning to read. Examples are *to, of, are, come,* and *you.* Also included are words that appear so frequently that they must be thoroughly learned as soon as possible. The Dolch (1953) list of 220 words and the Moe (1972a, 1972b) lists of 210 high-frequency words account for over 50 percent of the words found in reading materials for children (and adults). Other lists of high frequency words include the *Harris-Jacobson Core Words* (1972), the *ESA (Educational Service Associates) Word List* (1977), the *Great Atlantic and Pacific Word List* (1972), and the Fry list of *Instant Words* (Fry, Kress, & Fountoukidis, 1993). Fry's first three hundred *Instant Words* are provided in Appendix G. These three hundred words account for about 65 percent of all written materials.

Sight words should be given high priority for every young child's sight vocabulary, but they should not be considered the only words to be learned to the point of instant recognition. Since sight words are usually words whose function is to connect other words, they often have no concrete referent. For this reason, use of phrases rather than isolated words provides a more meaningful presentation (e.g., be good; here is a(n) . . . ; there are . . .). For a list of phrases based on the Dolch word list, see Rinsky's (1993) *Teaching Word Recognition Skills* (p. 73). Rinsky also makes a point of including words associated with the computer age as an essential part of sight vocabulary. She provides a list of about 130 such words (Rinsky, 1993, p. 75).

Assessment

Students who have not committed words to their sight vocabularies are relatively easy to spot. They do not recognize many words on a page. They frequently are word-by-word readers. When reading orally they analyze nearly every word, sounding out words or word parts with painful slowness. By the time they reach the end of the sentence they often have forgotten much, if not all, of what they read.

A sight vocabulary word can be recognized in about one-half second or less. The classroom teacher can assess this speed in several ways. A good source for words is the glossary found in the student's present texts, one of the high-frequency word lists, or words the student has been working on recently, such as words used in a language experience story or in a new thematic unit.

The following is a good group procedure for screening purposes. Construct a test using words from the texts available for student use, from graded word lists such as the *ESA Word List* (1977) or the *Basic Elementary Reading Vocabularies* (Harris & Jacobson, 1972), or from the word lists from a published informal reading inventory. On each line, type three or four (depending on the maturity level of the group) words of approximately the same difficulty level. Test item difficulty is increased by using words that are visually similar (e.g., *though, through, thought*) and decreased by using visually dissimilar words (e.g., *though, paper, statue*). Duplicate copies for each member of the group and one for yourself to use as a key. A practice test is always a good idea, especially with young children, to help them know what to do when the test is given.

To prepare students for a speed test, the teacher should tell them the following:

1. This is a speed test, and not like real reading when you can look back and forth as much as you want.

2. You will have to hurry your looks (fixations). You may only have time to glance once at each word, then mark the one I say.

3. Some of you may have trouble with this test, but don't worry. If you do, we'll schedule some time to practice these and other words. It's okay if you don't do too well.

4. If you miss a word, be ready to go on to the next line.

In administering the test the teacher says the stimulus word twice, then allows about five seconds for pupils to respond before proceeding to the next item.

Scoring procedures are straightforward, with the number of items correct indicating the performance level. More important for screening purposes, however, is locating the stragglers in the group. Those who have done poorly on the group test should be further observed individually.

To assess individual students, make two typewritten copies of the words in list format (one word per line) and give one copy to the student. Ask the student to read the words to you as quickly as possible, while you check accuracy and rapidity from your copy (this reading might be tape recorded for later analysis). Remember, accurate but slow is *wrong* for sight vocabulary. Words must be read accurately and quickly. For differentiation, words read correctly but slowly are referred to as being in a student's analytical vocabulary.

A second procedure is to make small typewritten or neatly printed flash cards from the word list and show them for about one-half second, allowing the student a moment to respond. If necessary, record the response on your copy of the word list from which the flash cards were made. These words can be used in sentences on the back of each card to test for recognition in context. Additionally, this procedure can be structured a bit differently by using a commercial or teacher-made tachistoscope or a microcomputer. DLM's *Word Radar* (Chaffin, Maxwell, & Thompson, 1983) is a software program that presents words from basic sight word lists in a motivating arcade fashion.

Standardized assessment is possible by using timed flash words from the *Gates-McKillop-Horowitz Reading Diagnostic Tests* (1982) or the flash words of the *Durrell Analysis of Reading Difficulty* (1980).

Instruction

Repetition and practice are key concepts for the improvement of sight vocabulary. Many students attain speed and accuracy simply by reading often and meeting the words in their books. Probably the most natural way of meeting common words repeatedly is through extensive recreational reading of relatively easy materials or materials chosen by the students, as in a literature-based program. This type of reading exposes the student to many known words that will assist recognition of those that are unknown. Predictable books (such as Eric Carle's *The Very Hungry Caterpillar,* 1987, or Bill Martin's *Brown Bear, Brown Bear*, 1982) contain a lot of repetition and provide an excellent source of easy reading, as do language experience stories. The value of predictable language to reading fluency is a topic further discussed in Chapter 9.

A more direct approach may be needed for students with more serious sight vocabulary deficiencies. These students often have had an unfortunate experience with a program or teacher overemphasizing analytical techniques or synthetic phonics. These students acquire the bad habit of looking for parts in all words rather than just unknown words. They try to sound out everything. Exercises that ask them to analyze words into smaller units *should be avoided*. Techniques that promote fluent reading, such as neurological impress, echo reading, and repeated readings (discussed in detail in Chapter 9) are recommended.

Direct teaching of sight vocabulary words might proceed as follows (McNinch, 1981). The teacher recites a sentence containing the word to be learned and then writes the word, followed by several more sentences using the word, on the chalkboard, overhead transparency, or on sentence strips.

Teacher: "I *heard* you were sick."

   (teacher writes)

     heard

Mary *heard* a new joke.

Have you *heard* anything else?

John said he *heard* what you said.

Next, the teacher draws attention to the word in isolation by asking questions about it and providing practice in writing it, such as:

What letter does the word begin with?

What's the last letter in the word?

How many letters are in this word?

Spell the word.

Trace the word in the air.

Spell, say, spell, write the word.

Following this focus on the word's graphic form, students must read the word in a phrase or sentence or use it in a phrase or sentence created by the student. Students should also practice reading the word in whole text. The text might be one developed by the teacher or a book, poem, or language experience story.

Finally, independent practice must be provided. The word might become part of a game or the student could be asked to find the word used in other printed material such as books, magazines, or newspapers.

Three effective programs for increasing sight vocabulary are the language experience approach (LEA), Fernald's (1943) VAKT (visual, auditory, kinesthetic, tactile) approach, and intensive word practice (Moe & Manning, 1984). While the LEA can also be used to teach a word recognition strategy, the VAKT approach and intensive word practice are used specifically to help students learn *troublesome* sight words.

Many ineffective readers are motivated to increase their knowledge of the word recognition process when material that they have dictated is written down or typed for them. With the LEA, the teacher is also assured that the words used in follow-up activities are part of the student's listening vocabulary.

Any language experience material should be the result of a direct experience of the learner (or learners, in the case of a group production). In addition to developing stories and accounts about field trips, an unusual classroom event, or the actions of a classroom pet, teachers plan many interesting *experiences* for students to write about. Some examples might include reading an exciting book to the students, working with clay or Play-Doh™ making no-bake cookies, painting pumpkins for Halloween, performing a science experiment, or sharing family pictures. In the example that follows, the teacher gave each student a marshmallow and directed them to think about how it looks, feels, smells, and lastly, tastes. Then a group account was dictated.

The Marshmallow

A marshmallow is soft, white, and fluffy. It is shaped like a drum. It looks like a pillow. It's too small for a pillow. It can roll. The marshmallow smells sweet, airy, and delicious. It's squeezable. It's sticky. There is powder on the outside of it. It tastes like a sponge. It makes you want another one.

Following dictation, the teacher reads the entire account back to the students as they follow along. Any changes students wish to make to the account should be made at this time. (Note that this step also provides the teacher many teaching opportunities. For example, students may notice many uses of *it* and *it's*. If not, the teacher should point them out. The teacher can then ask about the referent for *it* and discuss the nature of pronouns in a real and meaningful context, since the students themselves created the account. In this particular example, a discussion of adjectives would also be appropriate. Additionally, features of words might be important to point out. In this example, features such as compound words, syllabication between two consonants, vowel–consonant–silent e pattern, as well as the vowel–consonant pattern are among the possibilities. The teacher can also take this opportunity to expand conceptual knowledge by introducing material that discusses the marshmallow plant (see "The Marshmallow" in *Childcraft: The how and why library,* Vol. 6, 1971, p. 177).

Once material has been dictated and read by the teacher, the student reads it. Even if the material is just a caption for a picture drawn by the student, the words from the material are used in many ways to ensure repeated exposures. First, the student should write each word in a personal dictionary with a self-generated sentence or picture or both. In this way, if the student comes across one of the words again and cannot remember it, the teacher can direct the student to his personal dictionary to find the word. The sentence and/or picture will provide the needed help. Not only are new words learned through this approach, but alphabet knowledge and dictionary skills begin to develop, as does a strategy for becoming an independent reader.

Additional activities, such as matching words from students' stories put on cards to words found in other printed material (e.g., basal readers, story books), and playing sight vocabulary games such as a vocabulary version of bingo, are appropriate. The teacher should insist that the word be pronounced each time it is matched, or encountered in the game. Arranging word cards to form sentences also reinforces recognition of the words in other contexts. Any teacher concerned that the words students use in their language experience stories will not help them in other reading tasks need only compare those words to a word list such as Fry's (Appendix G).

As soon as possible, students should do their own writing of stories. As discussed in Chapter 7, students' efforts at writing will help them learn the nature of written language. (For an excellent article on how to use LEA to encourage process writing see Karnowski, 1989.) "Writing also focuses [students'] attention on the visual features of print, aiding letter and word recognition" (Noyce & Christie, 1989). At this point, you might be thinking that students having difficulty with reading often say that they do not want to write. These students are generally not very confident of their writing abilities. This is all the more reason that they be given opportunities to write in a safe, pressure-free environment. Dialogue journals provide an excellent vehicle for risk-free writing. These journals are *never* graded, and since the teacher responds in writing, a model for spelling and handwriting, as well as grammar and sentence structure, is always available to the student. The function is clear—to communicate with another person. Students write in a bound notebook to their teacher about anything they want (early or limited writers may even draw pictures to get across a message). The teacher writes back in the same notebook, responding naturally, as in conversation. The following exchanges provide an idea of what dialogue journal writing with a teacher is like (see also Chapter 7, Figure 7.10).

Mark	*Teacher*
it wa relley hot today. I got to go see a moove on Saterday.	I know what you mean about being hot! It really did feel hot in our classroom. Is it hard for you to concentrate when you feel uncomfortable? It's hard for me. What movie did you see? Did you like it? Tell me more about it.
I see the movee big it wuz funne My dad tak me we lafd hard.	I'm glad you enjoyed the movie, *BIG*. I like funny movies the best. Maybe I can get my husband to take me. Do you think I would like the movie?

Students with very limited sight vocabularies can be provided sentence starters to get them going. Initially, high-frequency words can be used to create *pattern books*. These are merely sheets of paper stapled together. For instance, the teacher might provide several sheets of paper with "I like to eat _____ ." written on each. The student then draws a picture of the food and the teacher writes the word for the food item on the blank line. This is done for each page. When completed, a cover with a title such as "*Things I Like to Eat* by Kalisha" can be created and attached to the stapled sheets. Of course, Kalisha then reads the book. Many words can be taught this way. Other examples of sentence starters are:

"I like to play _____ ."
"I like to go _____ ."
"_____ are big."
"_____ are little."
"My favorite _____ is _____ ."

The VAKT approach begins with the teacher eliciting a word from the student that the student wants to learn. This word is written or printed in crayon on a strip of paper, in letters large enough for the learner to trace by direct finger contact. The student is then shown how to trace the word and told how to pronounce it at the same time. Following the teacher's example, the student traces and pronounces the word. This continues until the student feels ready to write the word from memory. If the student is successful, the session is terminated. If not, tracing continues. Words successfully written from memory should be checked for recognition later in the day or the next day.

After a period of time that varies from learner to learner, the student reaches a point at which tracing can be eliminated. Instead, someone pronounces the word and the student looks at it and repeats it as often as necessary, until she can write it from memory. If the written word is incorrect, the student looks at the word more carefully while pronouncing it and tries once more to write it from memory. Strict use of the VAKT approach, which includes charting the number of times a word needs to be traced before it is learned, is probably not necessary for most students. Usually the tracing technique itself is sufficient.

Intensive word practice (Moe & Manning, 1984) also uses a multisensory approach. Usually, three to six new or troublesome words are randomly placed among other words in each of four sections on a word practice sheet (Fig. 8.1). Sentences using the new

FIGURE

8.1

Example of an intensive word practice sheet for three new sight words: this, was, in.

1		2	
boy	was	this	on
on	in	was	the
the	this	in	boy
3		**4**	
on	in	boy	on
the	was	in	was
this	boy	the	this

1. My milk is in this cup.
2. Mother was in the house.
3. This is the dog I like.

words in a meaningful context are placed beneath the four sections. The procedure emphasizes listening skills and following directions as well as practicing troublesome words, and can be used with a group.

First, the students are directed to fold the paper on the bottom line to separate the sentences from the word boxes. They should see only the numbered boxes. Next, the students are instructed to fold the paper again on the line that separates boxes 1 and 2 from boxes 3 and 4. Finally, the students are directed to fold the paper on the vertical line so they can only see box 1.

The teacher has previously prepared large word cards, each containing one of the new words to be learned; for this example, cards are needed for *this, was,* and *in.* The teacher gives the directions for box 1, instructing the students to mark in some way each of the new words while the teacher pronounces the word and shows the word card. Two repetitions of the word should be sufficient. For example, while showing the word card for *this,* the teacher might say, "I want you to draw a circle around *this.* Draw a circle around *this.*" While showing the word card for *was,* the teacher might say, "Put a line under *was.* Put a line under *was.*" Likewise, for the word card *in,* the teacher might say, "Draw a box around *in.* Draw a box around *in.* Now turn your paper over so you just see box 2."

The directions for box 2 also instruct the students to mark the new words. This time, however, the teacher shows but does not pronounce the word. It is hoped that the students are mentally pronouncing the words as they look back and forth from word card to paper. The directions proceed as follows: "Put a line under _____" (while showing *was*). "Draw a box around _____" (while showing *this*). "Draw two lines under _____" (while showing *in*). Students are then directed to refold their papers so only boxes 3 and 4 can be seen.

For box 3 the teacher pronounces the word but does not show it. All directions are oral. "Put a line under *this.*" "Draw a circle around *in.*" "Draw a box around *was.*"

For box 4 the students are simply told to circle the three words practiced in the lesson. Success with box 4 indicates that the student has at least visual memory for the words taught. Not until the sentences are read at the bottom of the page can the teacher judge whether the students have learned to pronounce the words as well. Students are asked to underline the new words in the sentences and to read the sentences.

The following exercises, and many like them found in developmental texts, activity books, and microcomputer software, are used to develop the habit of looking at words rapidly.

1. Exercises with flash cards. This activity can be done alone, with another student, or with the teacher. Flash cards should be used in conjunction with sentences or other meaningful contexts. Examples can be seen in 2a and 2b below.

2. Exercises emphasizing expectancy or context clues.

   a. A snowman melts in the _____ .

      sun   cold   man

   b. The bird is in the _____ .

      boy   tree   table

   c. Random House's *Word Blaster* (1981). Sentences are displayed on the screen with one word missing, and the student chooses the appropriate word from a line of five to complete each sentence. Letter–sound, sentence–structure, and contextual vocabulary clues must be used to select the correct word. The student first reads the sentence and then "blasts" a word to fill the blank from a line traveling across the screen above the sentence. When hit, the correct word falls into the blank. After two incorrect tries, the correct word automatically drops into the sentence.

3. Exercises requiring quick scanning of a group of words.

   a. See how fast you can find the word that does not belong in each list. Put a line through it.

1	*2*	*3*
boy	dog	pie
girl	look	cake
pipe	bird	much

   b. Put an X by the things you can find in the food store.

meat	soup	dogs
house	candy	cans
eggs	truck	milk

4. Activities and games using individual words.

   a. *Fish pond.* Make word cards with a new (or review) vocabulary word on one side and an easy sentence on the other side with the word underlined. Affix a paper clip to each. Put in fish pond. Attach a small magnet to the end of a fishing pole. If a player fishes out a word and reads it correctly and quickly, two points are scored; if the sentence helps the player say the word, 1 point is scored.

   b. *Rocket ship.* Make a large poster board with slots to hold cards placed at appropriate intervals representing the route of the trip to the moon (or wherever). Make a stack of cards writing a sentence on each one containing the word being practiced. The word should be underlined and in isolation above the sentence. Students take turns drawing from the stack of cards. If they read the word correctly, they put the card in the appropriate slot marking the next step in the trip to the moon.

c. *Bang.* Make a "bang" card for every five word cards. The word cards have the word of interest on one side and a sentence using the word on the other. (This 5 to 1 ratio can be changed depending on how long you want the game to last: the more "bang" cards, the longer the game will last.) Cards are placed in a bag or box and students take turns drawing them out one at a time. If a word card is drawn and the word pronounced correctly, the card is kept. If the sentence needs to be read to pronounce the word, that one card is returned to the bag. If a "bang" card is drawn, *all* word cards collected up to that point are placed back in the bag. This element of chance enables learners of different abilities to play together and also provides the necessary repetition of new words. The first player to collect five (or three or ten) words is the winner.

d. *DLM's Word Radar* (Chaffin, Maxwell, & Thompson, 1983). Presented in an arcade game format, *Word Radar* provides practice in matching *isolated* words that appear frequently on sight word lists. Words are practiced at 8 word length levels (24 words in each of 8 lists increasing in word length), at 9 different speeds, (1 is slowest, 9 is fastest), and at 3 difficulty levels (level 1 has 4 words on the screen at a time; level 2 has 8 words; and level 3 has 12 words). Student progress sheets and worksheets are included, as well as a manual that explains a variety of uses. This software provides a motivating way to practice basic sight words.

5. Activities for adolescent readers. While the Bang game described above may be suitable for any age, students in upper elementary and middle school generally require more age-appropriate activities for practicing words, even though their abilities may be closer to those of much younger students. Curtis and McCart (1992) present several gamelike activities using words that are more challenging both linguistically and cognitively (e.g., flammable, combustible, rayon, crayon, mayonnaise). Their suggestions often have students working in pairs, which further encourages the students to want to work hard. One of their examples is *Beat the Clock,* a speeded word recognition activity. Student pairs record the time it takes them to read through the words. Timings at the beginning and end of the week give a gauge of progress. Points can be awarded. (p. 398)

WORD RECOGNITION PROCESSES

Knowledge of and ability to use the following word recognition processes give students the needed flexibility to identify and analyze unknown words. Sometimes students need to use only one of these processes. At other times, two or more are needed and are used either separately or together as parallel processes. The five word recognition processes to be discussed are listed below.

1. Context clues
   a. Expectancy clues
   b. Picture clues
   c. Meaning clues
2. Visual analysis

3. Knowledge of word parts
   a. Structural analysis
   b. Phonic analysis
4. Blending and synthesizing
5. Dictionary skills

Parallels can readily be seen between these word recognition processes and the major skill strands recognized by many reading instructional systems today: namely, sight vocabulary, contextual analysis, phonic analysis, structural analysis, and dictionary skills. These strands are usually organized so that a skill is introduced in a series of lessons, then reviewed from time to time. In a basal series, early lessons often review previously taught skills before introducing new skills. This gives teachers an opportunity to assess whether students have retained the skills. Some series also provide end-of-reader tests for assessing skill development.

The skills are usually sequenced from easy to difficult, according to the author's logic and experience. Thus, skill sequences vary from one reading series to another, with differences ranging from slight to considerable. When a student changes from one reading program to another that is quite different, the teacher must monitor progress carefully to insure that the student does not experience learning gaps during the transition.

Each reading series has its own scope and sequence of word recognition skills (Fig. 8.2). Teachers must know the scope and sequence of any program used in their school, particularly the skills taught in immediately preceding and subsequent materials. When teachers are aware of the skills sequence they can facilitate transition from level to level by using appropriate assessment and instructional techniques. If a school system is not using an instructional program with scope and sequence information, teachers must do their own analyses and assume that, in general, the students have received skills instruction randomly or on a basis other than that represented here. In whole language classrooms these skills are generally learned when opportunities present themselves, and always in the context of whole text (see Mills, O'Keefe, & Stephens, 1992).

As Figure 8.2 indicates, teachable units are much smaller than the major strand labels identified earlier. The concept of major skill strands is roughly equated to that of level 3 analysis, that is, areas within the domain of word recognition. The subskills listed in the scope and sequence chart are more specific than the strands, representing elements at level 4 analysis. Our attention will now be directed to difficulties typically associated with processes involved in using the major skill strands.

INADEQUATE USE OF CONTEXT CLUES

Expectancy and Picture Clues

Two important context clues, **expectancy clues** and **picture clues**, relate directly to understanding what is about to be read. Expectancy clues are related to **psychological set**; that is, when people are introduced to a topic, certain related concepts rise to the thresholds of their minds. These ideas, especially the words associated with them, become more readily available from memory storage. In essence, the nonvisual information, or schemata, that the reader has for a topic is activated. When teachers intro-

One reading program's scope and sequence for word recognition behaviors.

Emerging Abilities

1. Learning letter names
2. Developing awareness of letter–sound relationships
3. Hearing similarities and differences in beginning and ending phonemes
4. Recognizing rhyming sounds
5. Demonstrating left-to-right orientation
6. Tracing, matching, and copying letters and words
7. Demonstrating awareness of word boundaries in writing
8. Pointing to known words while being read to

First Grade

1. Begin alphabetizing skill (picture dictionary)
2. Begin using initial consonants in a modified cloze (use of context)
3. Begin consonant digraphs with context
4. Begin consonant blends with context
5. Begin short vowels with context
6. Begin spelling patterns
7. Begin final consonants with context
8. Begin initial and final consonant substitution with context
9. Begin common inflectional endings with context
10. Begin long vowels with context
11. Begin common suffixes with context
12. Begin compound words with context

Second Grade

1. Review previous letter–sound correspondences
2. Begin unusual consonants and consonant digraphs (c, g, silent t) with context
3. Begin unusual vowels (y) with context
4. Begin vowel digraphs and diphthongs with context
5. Introduce schwa with context
6. Begin r-controlled and l-controlled vowels with context
7. Introduce concept of syllabication (# of vowel sounds = # of syllables)
8. Continue compound words
9. Continue suffixes
10. Begin prefixes with context
11. Begin spelling changes involved in suffixes and inflected endings

Third Grade

1. Review previous letter–sound correspondences
2. Begin difficult consonant blends (triple letters)
3. Begin unusual and difficult vowels and vowel clusters
4. Introduce structural analysis (concept of roots and affixes, compounds)
5. Introduce more complex spelling patterns
6. Introduce two- and three-syllable words (syllable patterns)
7. Begin inductive teaching of consistent phonics rules and their application
8. Begin dictionary skills using diacritical markings and pronunciation spellings

duce new material to develop background and experiences, they promote the use of expectancy clues. For example, when students know they will be hearing a selection about how birds build their nests, the words they expect to hear are quite different from those expected in a story about a fire in the basement. Teachers might begin by asking students what they already know about birds building nests, and then writing these ideas down so the students can see the words they have used.

Pictures also function as clues to readers, suggesting certain sets of words that might occur in the story. A picture of two youngsters playing on a raft in a pond elicits many words in the mind that are different from a picture of the same children working to build a raft for the pond. Thus, both expectancy and picture clues help the reader anticipate words that might occur in a selection or segment of a story. These concepts are closely related to ideas regarding a reader's ability to organize mentally the material about to be read. Obviously, this ability is also related to background and experience, or **scriptal information** (Pearson & Johnson, 1978), as will be discussed in Chapter 9. Some students who have difficulty using context clues often do not have the conceptual development for dealing with the ideas found in many classroom reading materials. Understanding is thus unlikely, and decoding such content has little value. More familiar material must be used in these cases. Students' own language experience stories are an appropriate beginning.

Assessment

Students will have problems with expectancy and picture clues if they cannot anticipate what may happen (what words may be present) in a story about a given topic, a given set of illustrations, or both. A good way to directly assess a student's ability to use these clues is to ask questions before reading.

> "The selection we are going to read today is about Neil Armstrong, the first man on the moon. What special words do you think we will meet in this selection?"
>
> "This paragraph will tell us how the pioneers kept warm in the winter. Before we read, let's guess how they might have done it."
>
> "You're right, Shayne. This is a picture of the wolf in bed waiting for Little Red Riding Hood. What words do you think we will need to know in this part of the story?"

Notice that these questions are to be answered orally; while the teachers have no objective measures of expectancy, still they can identify those who are having considerable trouble anticipating forthcoming events and the words possibly associated with them. Difficulty may be the result of not being able to use expectancy clues adequately, or inadequate experiential, conceptual, or language background. The best way to differentiate among these is to sample behavior across a wide variety of content.

Instruction

Techniques to improve the use of expectancy clues generally give the stimulus (the subject or topic of concern or a picture portraying it) and call for **productive language** from the student, that is, to respond by generating or identifying possible words that may appear. This process differs from reading, which is a receptive language process. The following activities are suggested.

1. Activities to develop use of expectancy clues
   a. Have small groups or individuals prepare to write a story about a given topic of interest. Before students begin writing, the teacher should promote a discussion of words to be used in the story, writing some on the chalkboard as the discussion proceeds.
      1) For beginning readers, use techniques involved in the LEA, in which the teacher does the writing.
      2) The Fernald (1943) technique or modifications thereof should be used as soon as possible.
   b. Use exercises requiring knowledge of a particular topic.
      1) These words are about cars, airplanes, or both. Mark the words about cars with a *C*; mark the ones about airplanes with an *A*; and mark those about both with a *B*.

         _____ hood   _____ landing   _____ engine
         _____ wings   _____ wheels   _____ garage
         _____ body   _____ bumper   _____ tail

2. Activities to develop expectancy through use of picture clues
   a. Display a picture with several different items on it, such as the produce in a market, candies in a store window, or a barnyard scene. Ask the students to name the items; write them down for further reference.
   b. Show a set of two to four pictures (comic strips are a good source). Tell the students the pictures can be arranged to tell a story. Ask them to arrange the pictures. They may then choose partners and tell each other (or the teacher) their stories.
   c. Call attention to a picture and talk about what may be expected to come next in the story. Verify predictions after the story is read.

Meaning Clues

Meaning clues are more specific to the content being read than expectancy and picture clues. **Context**, as related to meaning clues, is defined as the words surrounding a target word. The target word represents the unknown word to be decoded. Meaning clues often exist within the sentence being read, but they can also exist within phrases or other sentences. Context usually restricts alternative words that fit meaningfully into the slot represented by the target word. Consider the following examples:

As the vaulter began to rise into the air, his pole _____ .
She put the cake mix in the bowl, then _____ one-half cup of water.

Meaning clues can be used effectively for analyzing unknown words only if the surrounding words are easily read. When the reading matter is too difficult, the reader becomes discouraged and may guess more and demand less meaning from the passage.

Assessment

Students who do not use meaning clues might lack scriptal data or have poorly developed language skills, but more likely they have not been shown how to use such clues.

These students can be identified by comparing their analysis of unknown words in isolation to their analysis of unknown words in context. Analysis of a word in context should be easier than analysis of the same word in isolation because language and context limit the word choices that fit meaningfully. If students have learned to *demand meaning* from every sentence they read, they are more likely to be aware of their difficulty and of the unknown word. If not, a major teaching task has been identified (see also Chapter 9 for strategies to teach use of context clues to infer word meanings).

Teachers should suspect inadequate use of context when a student makes wild attempts at an unknown word. Wild guessing indicates misuse of context and lack of word analysis skills. Also, many substitutions that graphically resemble the actual word but are semantically incorrect (e.g., horse and house) and substitutions that are not self-corrected indicate inadequate use of meaning clues.

Teachers can structure a set of tasks to evaluate the student's ability. Select a few words the student does not know, using one of the methods discussed earlier in this chapter. Present the words first in isolation, then in context. If trouble with the words occurs consistently *in both settings,* the student is probably not using context as an aid to word recognition. The following illustrates the two settings, words in isolation and words in context.

Words in Isolation	*Words in Context*
train	We heard the whistle as we walked along the _____ tracks.
night	It was very dark that _____.
stone	Tim felt a sharp _____ under his foot.
wrong	The car was going the _____ way down the one-way street.

The use of meaning clues may be assessed with standardized instruments that contain subtests on words in isolation and words in context. Two such instruments are the group-administered *Silent Reading Diagnostic Test* (Bond, Balow, & Hoyt, 1976) and the individually administered *Gates-McKillop-Horowitz Reading Diagnostic Tests* (1982).

Instruction

Techniques for developing the use of meaning clues should be presented in larger discourse units in order to take advantage of all available language clues. It is advisable to begin with easy materials. If the student has to guess too many words, language clues will be obscured. I recommend beginning with a ratio of about 1 target word for every 15 to 20 words. Once students understand how the process works and what they are supposed to do, the ratio can be decreased.

The standard deletion ratio of one deletion every fifth word suggested for *assessing comprehension* (Bormuth, 1967, 1968; Rankin & Culhane, 1969) is *inappropriate for teaching* the use of context clues as an aid for analyzing unknown words because it distracts from the analytical task at hand and asks the student to guess too frequently. The task can be discouraging for readers who are already frustrated with the reading task. Alternatives to reduce this frustration include using a sentence or two with one word deleted, using a multiple-choice format (maze), and adding letters or other word parts to the slot. The following are representative activities.

1. Exercises utilizing thought units of a paragraph

    One day when the lion was looking for food, he walked into a trap. The trap was made of strong _____ , and the lion couldn't get out. The lion jumped this way and that way. He tried and tried. All day _____ , the lion worked to get out of the trap. But he couldn't get _____ .

2. Riddles with meaning clues that give the answer

   It has four legs.

   It has a back.

   You sit on it.

   It is a _____ .

   dog   cat   chair

3. Exercises using the meaning of a sentence

   a. He climbed it to paint the ceiling.

      lake   looking   ladder

   b. The car is in the _____ .

      house   church   garage

4. Exercises using context and word parts of the target word

   a. The car is in the g _____ .

   b. He is cl _____ ing the ladder.

For all of these exercises, the most important aspect is incorporation of a teacher-led discussion (Valmont, 1983). This discussion points out the clues that lead to a certain word being suggested. For example, in the riddle exercise, the first two clues (four legs, a back) also describe a dog, cat, or other animal. You must have the third clue (something to sit on) before dog and cat are eliminated and chair becomes the answer. Any unknown word can be approached the same way. The context provides certain clues, and several words are suggested. The teacher is responsible for leading a discussion of what the clues are, why some words fit better than others, and which words are equally acceptable.

In summary, meaning clues are important aids in analyzing unknown words. These clues help the reader anticipate words that might occur in the selection. In addition to the anticipation factor, context serves as a language clue to the unknown word and is a means to verify the accuracy of the thought unit containing the unknown word. Probably the single most important word recognition skill is the effective use of context clues (Heilman, 1976).

Using context and other meaning clues alone is not enough for effective, efficient word recognition, however. Both younger readers and readers having difficulty may rely too heavily on context (Gough, 1984; Nicholson, Lillas, & Rzoska, 1988; Stanovich, 1980). Overemphasizing these and neglecting other decoding skills can lead to unfortunate learning outcomes. When this happens, students guess too often when they encounter words unknown in print, resulting in a distorted or misunderstood message. This outcome must be addressed immediately; if it is allowed to continue, the student may develop the bad habit of *not* expecting meaning from the passage.

INADEQUATE VISUAL ANALYSIS

During the course of reading, students may become aware that they do not know a word after they have looked at it. The symbol (word) has not cued a meaningful response, and the context has not been a sufficient aid; therefore, they must figure out the word some other way. First, they must visually inspect the word and try to break it into smaller parts or spelling patterns that can then be pronounced. Thus, visual analysis precedes phonic or structural analysis, although it is possible that the "smaller parts" might also be structural elements. Phonic exercises that emphasize "sounding it out" as a first step fail to communicate to students that they have to segment visually before they sound.

Visual segmentation of an unknown word embedded in a sentence providing no helpful context clues presents especially difficult analytic problems. Durkin (1978) claims that decoding in such circumstances occurs at the syllable level, where only visual clues can be used. She identifies eight syllabication generalizations that help decode syllables. A problem with this procedure is that the students must memorize and be able to apply all of the rules before precision can be attained—an unrealistic expectation for students already in reading difficulty. The following might be a simpler, although less precise, set of *content rules* to help students begin visual segmentation of words into syllables.

1. Every syllable has one vowel sound.
2. Syllables contain *about* three letters (plus or minus two letters).
3. Syllables are often divided between two consonants (plan-ter, pic-ture).
4. In a syllable with more than one vowel letter, the final *e* or the second vowel is often silent.

These four content rules, plus basic knowledge of letter–sound correspondences, are needed before students can begin to analyze unknown words independently. (For a listing of the more consistent phonic and syllabication content rules, see Appendix H.) Note, however, that these rules are useful in that they capture patterns of spelling. Productive use of these rules lies in relevant experiences, not in rote memorization.

It must be noted here that use of this visual analysis process and those that follow assumes **phonemic awareness**, that is, an ability to manipulate letters, sounds, and spellings to read words never seen before. Griffith and Olson (1992, p. 518) define phonemic awareness as "an understanding of the structure of *spoken* language." It includes such abilities as recognizing and producing rhyming words, blending and segmenting phonemes, and splitting syllables (e.g., *m* + *ake* = *make* and *cow* + *boy* = *cowboy*). It is *not* the same as phonics (learning letter-sound correspondences), but can be considered a prerequisite to success in phonics instruction. Experimenting with the sounds of our language as well as with writing can adequately serve to make students phonemically aware. Literature assists students in alliteration, rhyming, blending and segmenting, and manipulation of phonemes (see Griffith & Olson, 1992, for further information). Some examples are: *Animalia* (Base, 1986), with its "Lazy lions lounging in the local library"; *Sheep on a Ship* (Shaw, 1989), with "It rains and hails and shakes the sails. Sheep wake up and grab the rails"; the *Jamberry* poem (Degen, 1983), containing "Hatberry/Shoeberry/In my Canoeberry"; and *Don't Forget the Bacon!* (Hutchins, 1976), in which "a cake for tea" becomes "a cape for me" becomes "a rake for leaves."

Monosyllabic Words

Students must also be able to apply at least three basic phonic process rules. The following process rules are adapted from Durkin's (1978) discussion on blending syllables. They are included in this section on visual analysis because they may be of help to students who have unsuccessfully tried to use the *initial consonant plus context clues* strategy and are unaware of how to continue. The next step in an analytical strategy must begin with visual segmentation of unknown words and then proceed to sounding and blending. The three basic phonic process rules are as follows:

1. Find and say the sound for the vowel or vowel cluster as determined by the spelling pattern.
2. Find, add, and say the sound for the consonant(s) that come(s) before the vowel(s).
3. Find, add, and say the sound for the consonant(s) that come(s) after the vowel(s).

This strategy is illustrated in Figure 8.3 using monosyllabic words initially. The first syllabication content rule is all that is needed for beginners to decode little words. The words are ordered from easy to hard, suggesting a developmental sequence implied in content rules: going from simple consonants and short vowels to the more complex letter combinations. Thus, for students beginning to learn this strategy the three-step process remains constant, but the difficulty level is increased when specific words involve more complex phonic rules.

Polysyllabic Words

Once students become facile at analyzing unknown monosyllabic words, the focus of the strategy changes to polysyllabic words. The remaining three syllabication rules must then be learned. This process is quite difficult for some students, and they simply give up when asked to analyze big words. They must be encouraged to use the following process rules:

1. Find the vowels.
2. Try to make syllables using the consonants before and after the vowels.
3. Say the trial syllables.
4. Blend the trial syllables.
5. Verify with the meaning of the sentence.

This strategy, while helpful, is not precise, and students must be cautioned that if the word they come up with does not fit, they must try to resegment the syllables or try different possible vowel sounds. In the advanced syllabication process in Figure 8.3, notice that no effort has been made to ask students to figure out syllables as they are technically defined in the dictionary (Arnold & Miller, 1980).

Once a student begins using the steps, another word or word part may be recognized, and the steps may be short-circuited somewhat. The identification of vowels and addition of consonants frequently triggers this recognition. For example, a student may easily recognize *ment* in *apartment* once analysis begins. Such short circuiting should be encouraged. Notice, also, that the division of *apartment* in step 2 is incorrect, but the student comes up with the word anyway.

As students develop a word recognition strategy, they are constantly adding to their skills repertoire. Consider the following possible strategies for figuring out a new word as a student adds analytical units (the products of instruction) to the memory store. In the example, replacing an *X* with letters implies that the student can visually identify and say that word part.

Target sentence:

I want something to eat.

When a child can read a few words but does not yet have any word analysis skills:

I want xxxxxxxxx to eat.

(Child skips word or stops at unknown word.)

Applying the process rules in analyzing unknown words.

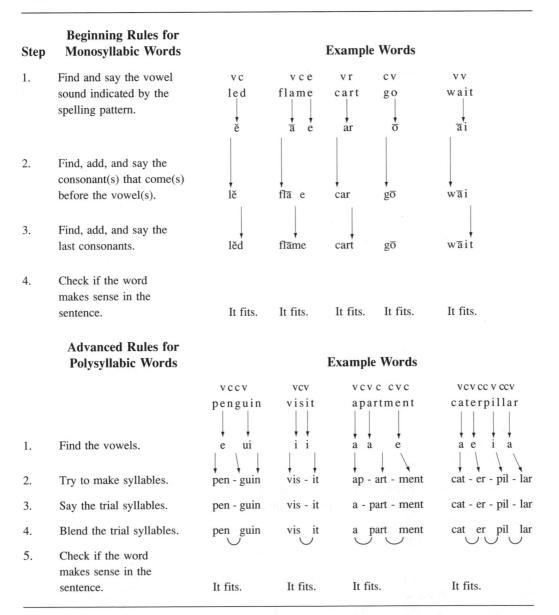

Step	Beginning Rules for Monosyllabic Words	Example Words				
1.	Find and say the vowel sound indicated by the spelling pattern.	v c l e d ↓ ĕ	v c e f l a m e ↓ ā e	v r c a r t ↓ ar	c v g o ↓ ō	v v w a i t ↓ ā i
2.	Find, add, and say the consonant(s) that come(s) before the vowel(s).	lĕ	flā e	car	gō	wā i
3.	Find, add, and say the last consonants.	lĕd	flāme	cart	gō	wā i t
4.	Check if the word makes sense in the sentence.	It fits.	It fits.	It fits.	It fits.	It fits.

Step	Advanced Rules for Polysyllabic Words	Example Words			
		v c c v p e n g u i n	v c v v i s i t	v c v c c v c a p a r t m e n t	v c v c c v c c v c a t e r p i l l a r
1.	Find the vowels.	e ui	i i	a a e	a e i a
2.	Try to make syllables.	pen - guin	vis - it	ap - art - ment	cat - er - pil - lar
3.	Say the trial syllables.	pen - guin	vis - it	a - part - ment	cat - er - pil - lar
4.	Blend the trial syllables.	pen guin	vis it	a part ment	cat er pil lar
5.	Check if the word makes sense in the sentence.	It fits.	It fits.	It fits.	It fits.

Add visual segmentation and ability to sound beginning consonants:
> I want sxxxxxxxx to eat. "I want spaghetti to eat."
>
> (Child fails, but the guess is sensible.)

Add knowledge of common word endings:
> I want sxxxxxxing to eat. "I want s-s-s-ing to eat."
>
> (Child fails.)

Add knowledge of one common word:
> I want somexxing to eat. "I want some-ing—something—to eat."
>
> (Child succeeds by approximation.)

Add knowledge of two common words:
> I want something to eat. "I want some-thing to eat."
>
> (Child succeeds.)

Another form instruction might take is for the teacher to demonstrate and model the most appropriate word analysis process to use. For example, the teacher might model for students by beginning with one of the following statements:

1. This word is best decoded by its syllables.
2. This word is best decoded by using phonics.
3. This word is best decoded by looking for a prefix and/or suffix.

For details of this ECRI method see Rinsky, 1993, p. 116.

Two important abilities develop when visual analysis skills are learned: discrimination and memory. Visual discrimination training helps the learner see differences among letters, word parts, and words, while memory helps the learner recall these differences quickly without having to resort to a slower, more analytical approach. (For more information on these abilities, see Chapter 4.)

Assessment

Students having problems with visual analysis often have been taught letter–sound correspondences but cannot visually identify them when they are embedded in new words or in other materials. Sometimes this is inappropriately considered a lack of ability to apply phonics skills when, in fact, it reflects inability to visually segment word parts. For example, Damien has learned several consonant sounds as well as some words. He has just successfully completed an exercise in consonant substitution with the following phonograms: *an, et,* and *ill.* His efforts to read orally proceed as follows for the sentence, *Will you let Dan go with me?*

Damien:	No response. Then, "I don't know the first word."
Teacher:	"Think about our lesson this morning."
Damien:	No response.
Teacher:	"What is the first letter?"
Damien:	"W."
Teacher:	"What sound does it make?"
Damien:	"Wah, as in want."
Teacher:	"Good! Now what does the rest of the word say?"

Damien:	"Ill."
Teacher:	"Now sound them together."
Damien:	"Wah-ill—will. Will you . . ." Student does not continue.

Teacher returns to original strategy, making note that Damien had done his earlier lesson satisfactorily, but cannot independently segment the initial consonant or phonogram from the whole word. Practice in this ability is considered advisable as it may represent a lack of phonemic awareness (see earlier discussion).

Another indication of a need for visual analysis practice is continued use of inappropriate word parts even when they do not work. Trying a word element is acceptable, but if it does not work, it should be rejected and another tried. Inflexibility may suggest rigid instructional procedures. The following is an example of flexibility in efforts to analyze a word, trying different word parts.

Target sentence:	Yes, you may go with father.
Student's first trial:	"Yes, you may go with fat-her." (Student rejects this trial because sentence does not make sense.)
Student's second trial:	"Yes, you may go with fa-ther, no, father." (Student accepts this trial because the sentence makes sense.)

Few standardized tests assess visual analysis skills. Two that do are the "Word Synthesis" subtest and the "Phonics" subtest of the *Silent Reading Diagnostic Test* (Bond et al., 1976). The *Gates-McKillop-Horowitz Reading Diagnostic Tests* (1982) also have one subtest that requires the student to segment visually and then pronounce "nonsense" words.

Instruction

Instruction in visual analysis encourages students to look for known parts embedded in unknown words and then try to segment other *reasonable* word parts, that is, elements that may represent a word part. (Recall the content and process rules described earlier and begin instruction by helping learners discover these rules if needed.)

It should be noted that daily events in most classrooms provide ample opportunity for visual analysis practice within a meaningful context. In Tim O'Keefe's classroom (Mills, O'Keefe, & Stephens, 1992, p. 5), students made the following "discoveries" simply from examining their student attendance sign-in sheets.

Chiquita and Charles both have the letters *ch* at the beginning of their names.

Justin noticed that *O'Keefe* has two *e*'s together, like in Kareem's name. Then he looked around the room and saw the color words collage. He added *green* to his list of words that have two *e*'s together.

Amanda noticed that she, Justin, and Vania all have *r*'s in their last names.

The following activities can also aid instruction in visual analysis.

1. Give students sets of unknown words that contain word parts they already know.
    a. After a lesson on variants (discussed later), provide exercises such as the following:

    Draw a circle around the word endings you see. Then use each word to complete the sentences.

> look   looks   looking
>
> Johnny _____ very tired today.
>
> "_____ out!" shouted Susan, as the car came speeding toward them.
>
> "What are you _____ for?" asked Mother.

   b. After lessons on initial consonant blends, provide exercises such as this:

Here are some words. If they start with a consonant, mark a *C* and circle the consonant. If they begin with a consonant blend, mark a *B* and circle the blend.

_____cat   _____slip

_____bring   _____sing

_____try   _____wall

   c. After lessons in various structural analysis (also called morphemic analysis) elements, ask students to look for the relevant unit in the unknown words.

     1) Put a line between the two words in each of these compound words.

       sweetheart   playground   nighttime

       Then write a sentence for each of these compound words in your notebook.

     2) Draw a circle around each affix. Then complete each sentence using the base (or root) word.

       rewrite   careful   happiness

       The little boy touched his new baby sister with _____ .

       I will _____ a letter to grandmother.

       Dad told me I did a good job and that made me _____.

Students soon learn that if they segment the word in the wrong place, they may not be able to sound the "odd" word parts. They should be encouraged to try again and break the word apart in a different place, always keeping the context in mind.

"Here are some words that have been divided for you. Which one helps you most to sound it out? Put an *X* on that word."

t/hi/nk	th/in/k	th/ink	Be sure you *think* before you speak.
spr/ing	s/pri/ng	sp/ri/ng	Today is sunny and warm and feels like *spring*.

This exercise has no right or wrong answer, especially if the student arrives at the correct pronunciation. This type of practice is probably best done in an individual setting, where the teacher can encourage the learner to resegment the word if it was inappropriate on the first trial.

INADEQUATE KNOWLEDGE OF WORD PARTS

When students cannot figure out an unknown word from meaning clues alone, they must resort to analysis. Essentially, this means they must break the word down into smaller elements, as just discussed. Then they must look for a part that they already know. Common word parts are presented in Figure 8.4. Two major instructional units concerned with this knowledge are phonics and structural analysis. **Structural analysis** deals with such meaningful word parts as derivatives (affixes), variants (word endings), and compounds. **Phonics**, on the other hand, deals with letter–sound relationships or word parts that do not necessarily have meaning. Examples include consonants, vowels, digraphs, and many syllables. With phonics, students focus on learning what various word parts say, whereas with structural analysis the focus can be twofold: what the word part says and what it means.

The goal of instruction in phonics and structural analysis is for common word parts to become so well known that students can recognize them instantly and automatically (LaBerge & Samuels, 1976). When this level is attained, students do not have to spend an unusually long time analyzing unknown words. With practice, students in primary grades continually add word parts to their *instant recognition* repertoires. Notice the similarity of the concept to that of sight vocabulary, words that have become so familiar they can be recognized instantly and automatically.

Practice is the key to automaticity. Some students quickly attain the level of instant recognition, but others need much practice with reading written language before these word parts become second nature. Teachers must be diligent in providing ample practice that does not become deadly dull drill. The best solution may be to provide many opportunities to write for authentic purposes (e.g., pen pal letters, journals, lists, and messages; refer to Chapter 7) and to read easy and interesting material.

Assessment

Teachers must answer three questions about students learning word parts:

1. Does the learner know the word part?
2. Can the learner recognize the word part quickly?
3. Can the learner identify the element embedded in an unknown word?

Knowledge of word parts (Fig. 8.4) is assessed directly through observation of workbook activities and writing samples, and through oral reading during conferences.

Automaticity requires accuracy as well as alacrity. To assess knowledge of word parts with a group of young students, an exercise similar to the one below, which provides three or four word elements per line, is recommended. The teacher gives the stimulus, silently counts to three, and goes on to the next element without giving students time to be analytical.

Teacher says	*Student marks element*		
1. mm—man—mm	h	m	b
2. ing—laughing—ing	ed	s	ing
3. tion—motion—tion	tion	ilk	ton

With practice in this type of exercise, students soon learn to work as quickly as they can. Those who have difficulty with this activity should be further observed. The stimulus in this exercise is the sound and not the symbol and, therefore, it is not exactly like real reading. Measurement specialists are critical of assessment techniques of this nature, citing lack of construct validity; however, if the student can match the written version to the oral version, the teacher can be more certain that the student can also produce the oral equivalent for the written word.

The easiest and most accurate way to determine speed is to give the student a list of words containing elements recently explored and ask for the list to be read as quickly as possible. If the elements on the list can be pronounced quickly, one after another (about

F I G U R E
8.4

Common word elements.

1. Consonants

a. *one sound (usually)*
b, d, f, h, j, k, l, m,
n, p, q, r, t, v, y, z

b. *more than one sound*
c: cat, city
g: get, gem
s: sit, his, sure
x: box, exam, xylophone

2. Consonant blends

bl, br
cl, cr
dr, dw
fl, fr
gl, gr
pl, pr
sc, sch, scr, shr, sk,
sm, sn, sp, spl, spr,
st, str, sw
thr, tr, tw

3. Consonant Digraphs

a. *one sound (usually)*
ck, gh, ng, nk, sh

b. *more than one sound*
th: thing, they
wh: when, who
ch: chair, chorus, choir

4. Vowels (long, short, or controlled)

a, e, i, o, u, (y)

5. Vowel clusters

ai: mail, said
ay: say
ea: heat, head
ee: sheep
ei: receive, weigh
ie: believe, tie
ew: few
ey: key, they
oa: road, broad
oe: hoe
oi: boil
ou: though, bough, bought
ow: mow, now
oy: toy
ue: blue

6. Prefixes

ab, ad, ante, anti, auto,
be, bi, com, con, co,
de, dis, en, ex,
in, im, inter, ir,
mis, non, op, out,
per, post, pre, pro,
re, sub, super,
trans, un

7. Suffixes

able, age, al, ance, ate, ble, ence,
er, est, ful, ible, ise, ize, ish,
ist, ite, ity, ly, less,
ment, ness, ous, ship, some,
tion, ure, ward

8. Phonograms

a	e	i	o	u
	ear			
ab	eat*	ib	ob	ub
ack*		ick*	ock*	uck*
		ice*		
		icle		
ad	ed	id	od	ud
		ide*	ode	
		if		
ag	eg	ig	og	ug*
ain*		ight		
ake*		ike	oke	
all*	ell*	ill*		
ale*				
am	em	im	om	um
ame*			ome	ump*
an*	en*	in*	op*	un
		ine*	or*	ung
		ing*		
ank*		ink*		unk*
ap*		ip*	op*	up
are		ir*	ore*	
ash*	est*	is		us
at*	et	it		ush
ate*		iz		ut
awe			ow	
aw*				
ay*	ez			

9. Variants

ed, es, ing, s, 's

*Especially useful phonograms.

one-half second per unit of analysis), the student has attained the desired level of instant recognition. Flash cards may also be used instead of lists of elements and are easy to incorporate into a game format.

The teacher must observe a student reading orally to assess the use or application of knowledge of word parts embedded in unknown words. This is best done in situations enabling the teacher to note when a student comes to a word that should be easy to analyze but is not. This may occur during a reading lesson or any other time when oral reading is done. Similar behavior occurs when the student comes to the teacher to ask for a word that is not known but should be. If frequent, this behavior may suggest ineffective knowledge of word parts, inability to use meaning clues, or both.

Many tests or subtests assessing knowledge of word parts are available, such as the *Silent Reading Diagnostic Test* (Bond et al., 1976), the *Stanford Diagnostic Reading Test* (Karlsen & Gardner, 1986), and the text-related tests discussed in Chapter 5. These tests assess accuracy but not speed. Teachers use their own judgment regarding this ability, or they can directly assess this knowledge as discussed above.

Instruction

A natural way to support students in their developing knowledge of the graphophonic system is through the use of children's literature. Trachtenburg (1990) proposes a three-step whole–part–whole strategy in which the first step is the reading of a literature selection that contains many examples of a particular graphophonic element, such as *Bringing the Rain to Kapiti Plain* (Aardema, 1981). In the second step, the teacher draws attention to the particular phonic or structural analysis element for which the selection was chosen. (In *Bringing the Rain to Kapiti Plain* this might be the long sound of *a* as represented by the *ai* and *aCe* spelling patterns.) The third step involves reading another literature selection that contains examples of the element introduced in step two (e.g., *The Lace Snail,* Byars, 1975), so students make the connection that these graphophonic patterns occur throughout all reading material. (See Trachtenburg, 1990, for a list of trade books that repeat long and short vowel sounds.) There are many good follow-up activities that are useful in providing practice with word parts.

The instructional examples that follow are organized around the scope and sequence chart in Figure 8.2. Teachers designing lessons for word parts should present them within the context of familiar, meaningful language. Initial instruction in specific phonic or structural analysis elements should follow inductive, or inquiry, procedures (see Chapter 3).

1. Activities to support learning of initial consonants
   a. *Personal dictionaries.* As young children use and select new or interesting words from their language experience stories or journals, or come across them in reading their storybooks, place these words on alphabetically ordered pages to create a dictionary. A sentence and a picture should accompany each word.

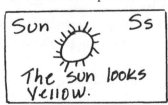

Even older students can create personal dictionaries for specialized topics. For example, seventh graders studying the Middle Ages could create a medieval dictionary based on a literature selection such as *Illuminations* (Hunt, 1989) with words like *Normans, portcullis, troubadour,* and *zither.*

b. *Choosing the beginning letter.* Instruct students to read the sentence in order to write in the missing letter. The source material has previously been read to the students and they are familiar with it.

1) The cow jumped over the _____ oon.

   r   n   m

2) Humpty Dumpty sat on a _____ all.

   w   t   c

c. *Choosing the best word.* Instruct students to read the sentence in order to write in the missing word. Again, the material is familiar.

1) Sam ate the _____ .

   ram   ham   slam

2) Jack and Jill went up the _____ .

   bill   will   hill

2. Activities to support learning initial blends and digraphs

   a. Use these letters to make a word for each of the sentences.

   <u>br sl cl</u>   <u>ch wh sh</u>

   The _____ ock struck one.   _____ icken Little said, "The sky is falling!"

   He _____ oke his crown.   Mary's lamb was _____ ite as snow.

   Don't _____ am the door.   Cinderella lost her _____ oe.

   b. Make a word for the one missing in each sentence that starts like the word that has a line under it.

   1) We have a good <u>place</u> to _____ .

   2) Let's <u>try</u> to _____ the squirrel.

   3) I <u>think</u> he is in _____ grade.

   4) <u>When</u> did the bicycle _____ break?

3. Activities to support learning vowel sounds

   a. Choose the best word to complete each sentence. The word must have a long vowel sound.

   1) She ate the candy _____ .   can   cane   mane

   2) Grass is _____ .   seen   mean   green

   b. Choose the best word to complete each sentence. The word must have a short vowel sound.

   1) Niga saw the big _____ run.   hat   rat   cape

   2) Playing games is _____ .   fun   cute   sun

4. Activities to support learning phonograms or spelling patterns

   a. Write in the best word to complete the sentence.

   1) Jack climbed the _____ .   wild   hall   hill

   2) Mark the words that end like <u>night</u>.

   _____fight   _____bright   _____light

   _____ bite   _____fright   _____recite

   c. Should the vowel sound in these words be long or short? Write *L* for long and *S* for short.

had _____   up _____   meat _____   stay _____

goat _____   pig _____   nose _____   side _____

5. Activities to support learning of variant endings

   a. Write in the blank the one word from the list of three that makes sense.

      1) Three _____ are on the desk.   book   books   booked

      2) The baby is _____ .   cry   cries   crying

6. Activities to support learning of derivatives or affixes

   a. Make a word that means the same as the key word.

sad   =   _____   +   happy

come back   =   _____   +   turn

trouble   =   _____   +   fortune

   b. Draw a circle around the root word. Pick three of the words with affixes and use each in a sentence.

timeless   recharge   unbreakable

disagree   kindness   enjoyment

7. Activities to support learning of compounds

   a. Combine these words to make three compound words. In the sentences that follow, fill in the blank by writing one of the compound words on each line.

note   ball

foot   book

card   board

      1) I left my science _____ at home.

      2) The _____ box was too big to carry.

      3) I watched the _____ game Sunday.

   b. Make a new word by drawing a line from the word on the left to the correct word on the right. Then write a sentence using the compound word.

every   some

             thing

             can

All of these activities can easily be created by students for placement in learning games or for other students.

INEFFECTIVE BLENDING AND SYNTHESIZING

As students learn to successfully segment words visually and say the word parts, they also learn to reassemble the parts to form a recognizable word. This reassembly process is referred to as blending and synthesizing. **Auditory blending** refers to a sounding process: the student says the word parts and blends them together to cue a meaningful response. This process is generally used by emerging readers when they are first learning to read, and it is a very important skill at that level of learning. **Visual synthesizing** is a more mature process and is used by readers who can analyze words mentally, without having to resort to overt sounding and blending of word parts. For typical learners, a gradual shift from auditory blending to visual synthesizing occurs as the analytical techniques and word parts become automatic. Visual synthesizing is faster than auditory blending and should be the ultimate goal.

Some students have trouble with blending and synthesizing because their reading program has overemphasized learning word parts in isolation; a few students may not be able to blend sounds orally and must learn to rely solely on visual synthesizing.

Assessment

A learner who cannot yet pronounce the various word parts obviously cannot put them back together. Assuming that the word parts are known, students who are having difficulty with auditory blending can be identified relatively easily. The teacher says the word parts slowly, with a one-second interval between parts, and asks the student to respond by saying the whole word. Following is an example of auditory blending:

Objective	Teacher	Student
letters	s – a – m	sam
letters and phonogram	s – am	sam
syllables	sam – ple	sample
combination	s – am – pling	sampling

Both the stimulus and response are at the oral level; a student who does this task successfully still may not be able to do it effectively while reading. Therefore, a stimulus must also be provided in printed form, separating the letters or word parts with dashes and spaces. Following is an example of auditory blending when the stimulus is in print:

Student reads and says	Student says
tr – ack	track
d – an – cing	dancing

When the student says the parts out loud and blends them together, the process is auditory blending. When the student simply looks at the word parts and rather quickly says the whole word aloud without sounding out the parts, the process is visual synthesizing.

Several standardized tests and subtests are available for the assessment of blending and synthesizing, including the *Roswell-Chall Auditory Blending Test* (1963) and the blending subtest of the *Diagnostic Decoding Tests* (Sipay, 1990). Teachers must choose subtests carefully, as titles are sometimes misleading.

Instruction

One of the conclusions in *Beginning to Read: Thinking and Learning about Print* (Adams, 1990) states, "because children have special difficulty analyzing the phonemic structure of words, reading programs should include explicit instruction in blending" (p. 126). The use of **onsets** (single consonants, consonant blends, and consonant digraphs occurring at the beginning of words) and **rimes** (phonograms) may be most helpful in this regard (Goswami & Mead, 1992). The biggest advantage in using rimes lies in the relatively high stability of vowel sounds within most end rimes (i.e., -ean as opposed to bea-). Rimes are far more generalizable than isolated vowels or even vowel teams. Of 286 phonograms appearing in primary grade texts, 95 percent were pronounced the same each time they were met (Durrell, 1963). In fact, nearly 500 early elementary words can be derived from the phonograms marked by an asterisk in Figure 8.4 (Wylie & Durrell, 1970).

Use of phonograms will mediate the following obstacles to blending:

1. Analyzing rimes into component parts
2. Unawareness that different onsets can be placed before the same rime to make many different words
3. Analyzing complex onsets (e.g., tw, cl, wh, squ, sch, thr) into individual phonemes.

With initial instruction, the following procedures are modeled for students. Separated word parts containing rimes are presented to the student to reassemble. Begin with known word parts in known words so that the learner understands the task.

m – eat   meat
sh – ell   shell

If the word parts are pronounced by the teacher and the student responds by saying the whole word, this is auditory blending, with the stimulus and the response both at the oral level.

Perceptual unit	*Teacher says*	*Student says*
syllables	bask – et	basket
structural elements	some – thing	something
phonic elements	p – ain – ter	painter

It is best to begin with natural word divisions represented by syllabic utterances as found in rimes and then proceed to more artificial phonic elements. Students need practice with these elements, because they are likely to segment words into elements other than syllables (e.g., mo–ney); therefore, they must be able to blend them to cue an appropriate response.

When the stimulus is changed from word parts spoken by the teacher to written word parts read by the students, the task is considered either auditory blending or visual synthesizing, depending on whether the response is primarily auditory or visual. The following exercises develop both skills.

1. When the words are in isolation

Print	*Student reads*
gra vel	gravel
gr avel	gravel
gr av el	gravel

2. When the words are in context
   a. The men walked toward the <u>gra</u> <u>vel</u> pit.
   b. Add the right word part. The men walk _____ toward the gravel pit.
   c. End of line segmentation
      The men walked <u>to-</u>
      <u>ward</u> the gravel pit.

Use of children's books, such as the Dr. Seuss series, that contain many examples of phonograms can provide much needed practice with blending in a meaningful context. (See also the earlier discussion on phonemic awareness.)

SUMMARY

Word recognition is presented as an interaction between the *process* of figuring out words unknown in print and the *products* of instruction, or knowledge of word parts. Several factors influence this interaction. One of the most important is that the word exist in the reader's listening vocabulary. The text also must be sufficiently easy to permit the reader to use context clues. Readers are not able to use their understanding of language when material is too difficult, and they are forced to resort to more artificial analytical techniques.

Another factor influencing this interaction is the size of the student's sight vocabulary. As sight vocabulary increases, the number of unrecognized words decreases. Eventually, the student encounters few unknown words; when they are encountered, they are probably not in the student's meaning vocabulary. Analytical techniques seldom help mature readers who encounter unknown words because the problem is probably lack of meaning rather than lack of appropriate word recognition facility.

Context clues such as expectancy, or anticipation of words likely to occur in the selection, play an indirect but vital part in the word analysis process. Meaning clues, or knowledge of the language surrounding an unknown word, also contribute immeasurably to an analytical strategy.

For the beginning reader, however, knowledge of word parts is an important way of relating visual symbols to words that are already in the meaning vocabulary. Disregarding context clues for the moment, the process of word recognition probably includes the following steps or stages:

1. The reader knows by looking that the word is not recognized.
2. The word is segmented visually into parts.
3. Some of the parts may be recognized.
4. The reader attempts to analyze the remaining unknown parts. The more techniques the reader has for doing this, the more successful is the outcome.
5. The word is reconstructed by auditory or visual means, or both, to approximate the word and cue a meaningful response.
6. The word is confirmed or rejected based on the meaning of the sentence when the word choice is made.

Students *without* reading difficulties probably use bits and pieces of this process intuitively. However, students *with* reading difficulties probably need direct instruction to clarify the process at points where their strategy breaks down. The teacher must use the analytic process to help identify areas of strength and need. Ultimately, students assume responsibility for analyzing words independently, always checking for sentence sense and understanding of the passage being read.

SUGGESTED READINGS

Freppon, P.A., & Dahl, K.L. (1991). Learning about phonics in a whole language class-room. Language Arts, 68, 190–197.

> *This article reflects on the Adams (1990) phonics summary and provides an exam-ple of an urban kindergarten student who learns phonics in the context of a whole language classroom. Principles for phonics instruction in whole language class-rooms are provided.*

Mills, H., O'Keefe, T., & Stephens, D. (1992). *Looking closely: Exploring the role of phonics in one whole language classroom* (Chapter 2). Urbana, IL: National Council of Teachers of English.

> *Chapter 2 in this interesting monograph takes the reader through a day in Tim O'Keefe's classroom, highlighting the role of graphophonemics. This monograph is meant to reassure those teachers who think whole language classrooms ignore phonics instruction by showing how phonics is addressed within the context of authentic reading, writing, and learning experiences.*

Routman, R. (1992). Teach skills with a strategy. *Instructor,* May/June, 34–37.

> *This article focuses on the difference between skills and strategies and presents ideas for teaching phonics strategically. A self-evaluation for teachers is also included to help those who want to move toward teaching for strategies in reading.*

Trachtenburg, P. (1990). Using children's literature to enhance phonics instruction. *The Reading Teacher, 43,* 648–654.

> *A most helpful article for teachers who want to include more children's literature in their reading programs but are worried about addressing phonics instruction. The author provides an instructional scenario for doing just this, as well as a list of trade books to support teachers' efforts at linking children's literature and phonics instruction.*

9

READING COMPREHENSION: FOUNDATIONS

OBJECTIVES

After you have read this chapter, you should be able to

1. list and describe the major factors affecting the comprehension process;

2. tell what behaviors a less skilled comprehender is likely to exhibit;

3. explain the various theories and models of the comprehension process;

4. develop assessment activities for word meanings;

5. devise an instructional program in vocabulary development for a corrective student.

KEY CONCEPTS AND TERMS

abstract referent
associative words
concrete referent
homophones
integrative processing
linguistic competence
macroprocessing
microprocessing
phonological system

process of comprehension
products of comprehension
rauding theory
schema
semantic system
specialized vocabulary
structured overview
syntactic system
transactional

STUDY OUTLINE

1. Background
2. Factors affecting the comprehension process
   a. Factors within the reader
      - Linguistic competence
      - Decoding ability
      - Prior knowledge or experience
      - Interests and attitudes
   b. Factors within the written message
      - Words
      - Sentences, paragraphs, and longer units of discourse
   c. Environmental factors
3. Theories and models of the comprehension process
   a. Schema theory
   b. Reading comprehension as cognitive-based processing
   c. Reading comprehension as sociocognitive processing
   d. Reading comprehension as transactional
   e. Reading comprehension as transactional-sociopsycholinguistic

   f. Reading comprehension as influenced by attitude
4. Skilled versus less skilled comprehenders
5. Assessment and instruction for comprehension
   a. Assessing decoding skills
   b. Instruction for increased reading fluency
      - Predictable language
      - Neurological impress method (NIM)
      - Repeated readings
      - Echo reading
      - Readers theater
   c. Assessing knowledge of word meanings
   d. Instruction for word meanings
      - General instructional procedures
      - Synonyms
      - Antonyms
      - Homophones
      - Associative words
      - Classifying or categorizing activities
   e. Instruction for specialized vocabulary
6. Summary
7. Suggested readings

OVERVIEW

Despite the great emphasis that has been placed on enhancing literacy development in recent years, something still seems to go wrong for too many students. While many programs are successful, the lament continues that "Johnny still doesn't understand what he reads!"

In dealing with the **products of comprehension**, such as finding the main idea, drawing conclusions, and predicting outcomes, the processes involved in achieving those products are frequently ignored. In other words, if Johnny has trouble predicting outcomes, he usually is confronted with skill sheets on predicting outcomes without being taught *how* to predict an outcome, that is, the process of predicting outcomes. The difference between the two is considerable.

In this and the following chapter, you will be introduced to thinking about comprehension as a process. More specifically, you will learn what to look for in the less skilled comprehender to determine why comprehension is breaking down. This will enable you to do a better job of assessing comprehension. Recommendations for instruction in various comprehension processes are then provided.

Word meanings and the ability to interact with and organize text will be discussed at length. For study purposes, the discussion is divided into two chapters. The first deals briefly with recent theory about the comprehension process and the crucial element of word meanings, while the second examines comprehension of whole text and strategic reading of narrative text.

These two chapters will help you think of comprehension as a process and not simply as a list of products or skills. A basic understanding of comprehension terminology and a working knowledge of questioning skills are assumed. Any terms considered new are defined or explained.

BACKGROUND

Concern for understanding reading comprehension is not new, and many attempts have been made to define it. Early scholars such as Edmund Burke Huey (1908) stated that to understand reading would be to understand the most intricate workings of the mind; Thorndike (1917) defined reading as thinking.

Historically, reading experts have tried to explain reading comprehension by identifying what successful comprehenders do. A frequently cited study by Davis (1944) lists nine skills considered basic to successful comprehension:[1]

1. Knowledge of word meanings
2. Ability to select appropriate meaning for a word or phrase in the light of its particular contextual setting
3. Ability to follow the organization of a passage and to identify antecedents and references in it
4. Ability to identify the main thought of a passage
5. Ability to answer questions that are specifically answered in a passage
6. Ability to answer questions that are answered in a passage, but not in the words in which the question is asked
7. Ability to draw inferences from a passage about its contents
8. Ability to recognize the literary devices used in a passage and to determine its tone and mood
9. Ability to determine a writer's purpose, intent, and point of view, i.e., to draw inferences about a writer. (p. 186)

These skills, and similar listings, are considered products of comprehension. Traditional skills-centered approaches to reading comprehension deal predominantly with the products of comprehension. Following is a representative scope and sequence listing for such an approach (Rosenshine, 1980, p. 537).

1. Literal
   Locating details
2. Simple inferential
   Understanding words in context
   Recognizing the sequence of events
   Recognizing cause and effect
   Comparing and contrasting
3. Complex inferential
   Recognizing the main idea, title, topic
   Drawing conclusions
   Predicting outcomes

Consider the following example. Through an assessment technique Banetta is found to have difficulty drawing conclusions from a passage, a *product* of comprehension. The usual procedure is to give Banetta additional practice in drawing conclusions. Unfor-

---

[1]From F. B. Davis, "Fundamental Factors of Comprehension in Reading." *Psychometrika* 9 (1944): 186. Used with permission.

tunately, whether such practice affects the *process* of drawing conclusions is not certain. On the other hand, if the underlying tasks involved in drawing conclusions were known, the procedure would be to determine the stage at which the process broke down and proceed with appropriate instruction from that point. What is really needed, then, is a better understanding of comprehension processes.

FACTORS AFFECTING THE COMPREHENSION PROCESS

Before discussing specific characteristics of the less skilled comprehender, the **process of comprehension** must be examined to learn what strategies are used by the skilled comprehender. With this in mind, areas of difference between skilled and less skilled comprehenders will be easier to recognize. The ultimate goal is to design appropriate reading comprehension instruction for the less skilled comprehender.

Key factors of the comprehension process are best grouped into three categories: (1) factors within the reader (2) factors within the written message and (3) factors within the reading environment (Pearson & Johnson, 1978).

Factors Within the Reader

Some factors within the reader that affect reading comprehension are linguistic competence, decoding ability, prior knowledge or background experience, and interests and attitudes.

Linguistic Competence

Linguistic competence refers to what the reader knows about language. Three systems are involved in learning language: phonological, syntactic, and semantic. The **phonological system** refers to knowledge of individual sounds in the language, knowledge of how these sounds are blended together to make words, and knowledge of stress, pitch, and juncture. Briefly, stress refers to such differences as:

The DOG broke the cup. (not the cat)
The dog BROKE the cup. (as opposed to just knocking it over)

Pitch refers to intonation differences, as in:

We'll leave in an hour.
We'll leave in an hour!
We'll leave in an hour?

Juncture refers to the differences between *nitrate* and *night rate* or between *icing* and *I sing*.

Goodman (1985) terms this first important system the graphophonic system and says that it includes the orthographic and phonic systems as well as the phonological. Because the cues in reading are also visual, the reader must have knowledge of the particular orthography of the language being read. In English this is an alphabetic system, as compared to Japanese, for instance, which uses a combination of Chinese characters and syllabic orthography. The reader must have knowledge of the relationships between oral and written language using an alphabetic system, better known as phonics.

The **syntactic system** refers to word order in sentences, punctuation, and the use of capital letters. Syntactic knowledge helps the reader determine whether a string of words makes a grammatically acceptable English sentence. For example:

> The dog chased the cat
>
> vs.
>
> Chased dog the cat the.

Syntactic knowledge, sometimes called *sentence sense,* also helps the reader know that two different word orders have the same meaning:

> The dog chased the cat.
>
> or
>
> The cat was chased by the dog.

Or again:

> His friend said, "The doctor is ill."
>
> or
>
> "The doctor," said his friend, "is ill."

Knowledge of syntax even enables the reader to utilize context clues to read and answer questions on material that has no real meaning:

> The ill zoo was a bab. That forn, the sossy ill zoo larped and was mitry.
> What was the ill zoo? When did the sossy ill zoo larp? Who was sossy?

In short, syntax is the primary means by which the reader determines relationships among words.

Simply being able to pronounce words and answer certain questions correctly does not insure that understanding has occurred. Because the sentences about the ill zoo had no real meaning (readers are not able to relate the nonsense words to anything already available in their minds), the importance of the semantic system becomes obvious. The **semantic system** refers to knowledge of word meanings, the underlying concepts of words, and the interrelationships among concepts. Semantic knowledge enables the reader to organize the text into a coherent structure and determine the relative importance of the various concepts found in text (e.g., main ideas versus supporting details).

Pragmatic knowledge can also be considered a part of this system. Pragmatic meaning is always partly found in the text and partly found in the context of the literacy event. The reader's schemata must be called upon to achieve pragmatic comprehension (e.g., understanding the humor in a comic strip) (Goodman, 1985, p. 832).

In summary, if the phonological, syntactic, and semantic information provided for the reader on a page of print closely matches the phonological, syntactic, and semantic abilities available in the reader's mind, understanding is likely.

Decoding Ability

When a reader approaches text in order to construct meaning, decoding will occur naturally. However, the construction of meaning will be difficult if the reader cannot readily pronounce many of the words in the passage, or is overly concerned with accurate word pronunciation. The reader who has to devote too much attention to decoding or to correct pronunciation, as in the case of oral, round-robin reading, cannot also attend to processing the meaning of the material (LaBerge & Samuels, 1974; Stanovich, 1980). Readers who identify words quickly and automatically, on the other hand, do not have to focus on decoding and can give their full attention to comprehension, especially when reading silently.

Difficulty with decoding does *not* imply, however, that comprehension cannot occur. In fact, comprehension *must* be the goal for decoding to occur more readily. Consider the following argument presented by Pearson and Johnson (1978).

> Comprehension helps word identification as much as word identification helps comprehension. That is, having understood part of the message helps you to decode another part. In short, context can help to short circuit the amount of attention you have to pay to print. (p. 15)

Decoding ability has been discussed in detail in Chapter 8, but you may conclude from this brief discussion that decoding is made easier if the reader is reading for meaning. Concern with comprehension instruction is important at every stage of reading development. The reader must *expect* and *demand* that material read *makes sense*.

Prior Knowledge or Experience

What readers bring to the reading task is critical to their understanding of what is read. A reader's background gives personal meaning to the printed page; thus not all readers comprehend material in exactly the same way. For example, if a young reader who has never been out of the city tries to read a book about life on a farm, so many words and events will be unfamiliar that the reading will probably become more of a word-calling situation. Even if this reader uses all of his linguistic competence to make predictions about what will occur in print, words such as *silo, harvester,* and *trough* and events such as birthing a calf or hauling hay will have little or no meaning. Adult readers experience the same frustrations if they try to understand material in an area they are unfamiliar with, such as a physics text, a medical journal, or legal documents. This does not imply that the reader cannot understand material concerning something not experienced, but rather that a reader must have a repertoire of relevant concepts to interpret the printed page. Consider another young reader who has always lived in the Deep South and has never experienced heavy snows. This reader is asked to read a story about a blizzard. Even though the reader has never experienced a blizzard, some relevant concepts available to the reader might be ice, the wind of a hurricane, and the possible tragedy of its aftermath.

In summary, for maximum comprehension to occur, the reader must be able to relate the printed material to personal experiences. Direct, firsthand experiences are usually best. At the very least, vicarious or secondhand experiences, such as listening to stories on a variety of concepts, seeing relevant pictures, and watching films and filmstrips, must be provided.

Interests and Attitudes

Closely related to prior knowledge and experience are interests and attitudes. Shnayer (1969) reports that interest in a topic enables readers with reading ability from two years below grade level to one year above grade level to read beyond their measured ability. Thus, a reader will better understand a book about explorers if she has an interest in history and the concept of exploration. Readers' attitudes are closely related to their interests. Attitudes are learned and probably reflect previous experiences. A reader with a poor attitude toward reading on any subject has little motivation to pick up a book and read, much less comprehend (Alexander & Cobb, 1992). Because attitude is influenced as much by factors within the reading environment as by factors within the reader, interests and attitudes are discussed further in Chapters 4 and 6.

Factors Within the Written Message

As Smith and Johnson (1980, p. 133) state, "Reading comprehension is not entirely dependent on the reader." Elements in the written message must be considered, including the words themselves, sentences, paragraphs, and longer units of discourse, such as stories.

Words

What makes some words easier to learn than others? The most researched characteristics of words are frequency and imagery. Frequency refers to how often a word occurs in the language. Several studies (Ekwall & Shanker, 1988; Jorm, 1977) have demonstrated that passages containing words that occur frequently in the language are more easily comprehended than passages containing words that do not occur frequently.

Imagery refers to how easily a word is visualized. A word with a **concrete referent**, such as *dog,* is probably easier to learn than a word with an **abstract referent**, such as *way.* Passages containing a heavy concentration of words with low imagery (abstract words) will probably be more difficult to understand than passages containing a large number of words with high imagery (Thorndyke, 1977).

The results of a study by Jorm (1977) are particularly relevant. Jorm analyzed the effects of word imagery, length, and frequency on the reading ability of good and poor readers aged eight to eleven. While word length had little effect on either type of reader, Jorm found that high-frequency words were easier to read for both good and poor readers. He also found that imagery was a facilitating factor in word recognition only for poor readers. Jorm explains that ineffective readers are more likely than good readers to use a whole word method for word recognition, and visual imagery is an aid for this type of learning. On the basis of this information, teachers are advised to carefully examine materials to be used with readers having difficulty for the occurrence of high-imagery words.

Teachers working with corrective readers must be concerned with the difficulty of material. The ratio of known words to unknown words is of greatest importance. In fact, the ratio of difficult words in a text is the most powerful predictor of text difficulty (Anderson & Freebody, 1981), and a reader's knowledge of key vocabulary predicts comprehension of text better than reading ability or achievement (Johnston, 1984). When students are provided material at their instructional reading level, the number of known words approximates 95 out of 100. Students are often taught the *five-finger method* to determine if a library book is easy enough for them to read. This idea is analogous to the instructional reading level criterion; if the student counts more than five unknown words on a page, the book is probably too difficult. (See Appendix A for help in determining readability of text material.)

Sentences, Paragraphs, and Longer Units of Written Discourse

Comprehension of written material demands much more than understanding each word in the selection. Words must be understood in relation to other words. For example, the action of a sentence (verb) works together with the actor or agent (who or what is doing the action) and with the object (who or what received the action) (Fillmore, 1968). In the sentence, "Charles is reading a magazine," the action is *reading,* the agent is *Charles,* and the object is the *magazine.* In the sentence, "The water is boiling," the action is *boiling,* the agent is not stated, and the object is the *water.* In the sentence, "Sue ran," the agent is *Sue,* the action is *ran,* and there is no object. The types of relationships that might exist among actors, agents, actions, and objects include those of cause, purpose, condition, and time (Pearson & Johnson, 1978, p. 40). For example, who or what caused the event and the outcome of the event represent causal relations. The descriptions and identifications given about the event may represent relationships of time or condition.

Readers seldom read isolated sentences, but they must comprehend relationships within sentences if they are to comprehend a paragraph (called **microprocessing**, see Irwin, 1991, p. 2). Just as sentence comprehension is more than understanding each word, paragraph comprehension (called **integrative processing**, Irwin, 1991, p. 3) is more than understanding individual sentences. Paragraphs are structured to function in longer units of written discourse. To understand a paragraph, the reader must recognize the actor or agent of the paragraph, that is, who or what the paragraph is about. The reader must also recognize the relations existing within and between paragraphs, such as cause and effect, question and answer (or problem and solution), sequence, enumeration, description, or comparison and contrast (Meyer, 1984; Sinatra, 1991). Englert and Thomas (1987) report that for instructional purposes, sequence is easiest, followed by, in order of difficulty, enumeration, description, and compare/contrast.

As with sentences, a reader does not often read isolated paragraphs. Paragraphs exist in the context of longer selections. According to Robinson (1983, p. 92), paragraphs serve specific functions: introductory, expository, narrative, descriptive, definitional, persuasive, transitional, or summary and concluding. The skilled reader recognizes how paragraphs function within the total context of the selection.

Specific relationships also exist within stories. Stemming from the work of Bartlett (1932), several studies have attempted to specify the logical relations existing within stories (Mandler & Johnson, 1977; Rumelhart, 1975; Stein & Glenn, 1979; and Thorndyke, 1977). Stories are usually organized in consistent, predictable patterns. The reader expects relations that specify themes, setting, characters, goals, and resolutions. Thorndyke (1977) states that some story structures (e.g., fairy tales and fables) become more familiar with experience and that stories with several cause–effect relations are easier to comprehend than those without causal relations.

In summary, recognizing organization is key to understanding written material. The reader must identify who or what the material is about, discover the relationship between actors or agents and actions, and determine the function or purpose of the material. This "process of synthesizing and organizing individual idea units into a summary or organized series of related general ideas is called **macroprocessing**" (Irwin, 1991, p. 4).

Environmental Factors

Essentially two environments affect reading comprehension—the home and the school. The preceding emphasis on prior knowledge and experience explains the important role of the home environment in providing the language base necessary for reading comprehension. The student with an extensive language base comes to school better equipped for the comprehension process than a student who has not been spoken to frequently, read to, taken on trips, or involved in other concept-developing activities.

The school environment refers, for the most part, to the student's classroom, teacher, and peers. However, the atmosphere of the entire school and the attitude of administrators and other teachers also affect reading comprehension, even if only in a general, indirect sense.

While the classroom teacher has the most direct influence on reading comprehension, classmates provide a source of competition or approval or a standard for comparison. Unfortunately, classmates may also have an emotionally negative influence as sources of ridicule or harassment.

Teachers can do much to affect comprehension both instructionally and emotionally. Teachers influence comprehension in a positive way through the following practices:

1. Establishing a comfortable, risk-free atmosphere in which students do not fear ridicule or penalty for failure. Teachers should provide the kind of feedback that encourages curiosity, risk-taking, and creativity.

2. Providing a model for their students. Reading is perceived as a valuable, enjoyable, and relevant activity when students see their teachers reading and are read to by their teachers.

3. Providing direct instruction. This includes preparing students for reading by discussing backgrounds and essential vocabulary of text, and by helping students establish purposes for reading with appropriate follow-up activities.

4. Choosing appropriate materials for instruction. Teachers must know their students' strengths, needs, and reading levels. Frustrating material does nothing to help comprehension.

5. Planning the type of questions they will ask. Teachers' questions are often poorly planned with respect to the objectives of the lesson (Bartolome, 1969) and do not demand much thinking beyond a literal level (Bartolome, 1969; Durkin, 1981; Guszak, 1967). Instructional techniques in this chapter and the next emphasize this important aspect of comprehension instruction.

THEORIES AND MODELS OF THE COMPREHENSION PROCESS

Schema Theory

Linguists, cognitive psychologists, and psycholinguists have used the concept of schema (plural: schemata) to understand the interaction of key factors affecting the comprehension process. The term itself is not new (Kant, 1787/1963; Bartlett, 1932), but the recognition of its importance to reading is more recent (Rumelhart, 1975, 1980, 1994). Simply put, schema theory states that all knowledge is organized into units. Within these units of knowledge, or schemata, is stored information. A **schema**, then, is a generalized description or a conceptual system for understanding knowledge—how knowledge is represented and how it is used.

According to this theory, schemata represent knowledge about concepts: objects and the relationships they have with other objects, situations, events, sequences of events, actions, and sequences of actions. A simple example is to think of your schema for *dog*. Within that schema you most likely have knowledge about dogs in general (bark, four legs, teeth, hair, tails) and probably information about specific dogs, such as collies (long hair, large, Lassie) or springer spaniels (English, docked tails, liver and white or black and white, Millie). You may also think of dogs within the greater context of animals and other living things, that is, dogs breathe, need food, and reproduce. Your knowledge of dogs might also include the fact that they are mammals and thus are warm-blooded and bear their young as opposed to laying eggs. Depending upon your personal experience, the knowledge of a dog as a pet (domesticated and loyal) or as an animal to fear (likely to bite or attack) may be a part of your schema. And so it goes with the development of a schema. Each new experience incorporates more information into one's schema.

What does all this have to do with reading comprehension? Individuals have schemata for everything. Long before students come to school, they develop schemata (units of knowledge) about everything they experience. Schemata become theories about reality. These theories not only affect the way information is interpreted, thus affecting comprehension, but also continue to change as new information is received. As stated by Rumelhart (1980),

> schemata can represent knowledge at all levels—from ideologies and cultural truths to knowledge about the meaning of a particular word, to knowledge about what patterns of excitations are associated with what letters of the alphabet. We have schemata to represent all levels of our experience, at all levels of abstraction. Finally, our schemata *are* our knowledge. All of our generic knowledge is embedded in schemata. (p. 41)

Schema theory has great importance to a discussion of corrective reading. According to Carver (1992), "ideas from schema theory are likely to have direct relevance to reading situations involving relatively hard materials that require studying" (p. 173). Carver bases this statement on his **rauding theory** (1977, 1990), which purports five basic reading processes: skimming, scanning, rauding, learning, and memorizing. Rauding, simply stated, means normal, typical, ordinary reading. In short, rauding theory holds that when individuals are using the reading process they operate with for ordinary narrative-type reading, schema theory is not directly relevant. Schema theory *is* relevant for the other processes, however, especially learning and memorizing. It can be concluded that whenever readers have to shift out of their normal reading process (rauding), schema theory and its derived variables of predicting, prior knowledge, and text type (i.e., narrative vs. expository) become quite important. Such may often be the case for corrective readers, because they may not have developed a "normal reading process." In other words, for corrective readers rauding may not exist at all or may be more likely when reading narrative-type text (e.g., stories). However, these same readers will likely need much assistance in building or activating schemata before reading expository (e.g., informational) text (see Chapter 12), or text they find difficult.

The importance of schema theory to reading comprehension also lies in how the reader uses schemata. This issue has not yet been resolved by research, although investigators agree that some mechanism activates just those schemata most relevant to the reader's task. While theories try to explain the comprehension process, related models have been developed that "serve as metaphors to explain and represent the theory" (Ruddell & Ruddell, 1994, p. 812). At the current time, five categories of models have been derived to explain literacy processes. These five classifications are termed cognitive-based, sociocognitive, transactional, transactional-sociopsycholinguistic, and attitude-influence.

Reading Comprehension as Cognitive-Based Processing

There are several models based on cognitive processing (see Ruddell, Ruddell, & Singer, 1994, p. 813). For example, the LaBerge–Samuels Model of Automatic Information Processing (Samuels, 1994) emphasizes internal aspects of attention as crucial to comprehension. Samuels (1994, p. 818-819) defines three characteristics of internal attention. The first, *alertness,* is the reader's active attempt to access relevant schemata involving letter-sound relationships, syntactic knowledge, and word meanings. *Selectivity*, the second characteristic, refers to the reader's ability to attend selectively to only that information requiring processing. The third characteristic, *limited capacity*, refers to the fact that our human brain has a limited amount of cognitive energy available for use in processing information. In other words, if a reader's cognitive energy is focused on decoding and attention cannot be directed at integrating, relating, and combining the meanings of the words decoded, then comprehension will suffer. "Automaticity in information processing, then, simply means that information is processed with little attention" (Samuels, 1994, p. 823). Comprehension difficulties occur when the reader cannot rapidly and automatically access the concepts and knowledge stored in the schemata.

One other example of a cognitive-based model is Rumelhart's (1994) Interactive Model. Information from several knowledge sources (schemata for letter–sound relationships, word meanings, syntactic relationships, event sequences, and so forth) are considered *simultaneously.* The implication is that when information from one source, such as word recognition, is deficient, the reader will rely on information from another source, for example, contextual clues or previous experience. Stanovich (1980) terms the latter kind of processing *interactive-compensatory* because the reader *(any reader)* compensates for deficiencies in one or more of the knowledge sources by using information from remaining knowledge sources. Those sources that are more concerned with concepts and semantic relationships are termed *higher-level stimuli;* sources dealing with the print itself, that is phonics, sight words, and other word attack skills, are termed *lower-level stimuli.* The interactive-compensatory model implies that the reader will rely on higher-level processes when lower-level processes are inadequate, and vice versa. Stanovich (1980) extensively reviews research demonstrating such compensation in both good and poor readers.

Reading Comprehension as Sociocognitive Processing

A sociocognitive processing model takes a constructivist view of reading comprehension; that is, the reader, the text, the teacher, and the classroom community are all involved in the construction of meaning. Ruddell and Ruddell (1994, p. 813) state, "The role of the classroom's social context and the influence of the teacher on the reader's meaning negotiation and construction are central to this model [developed by R. B. Ruddell and N. J. Unrau] as it explores the notion that participants in literacy events form and reform meanings in a hermeneutic [interpretation] circle." In other words, this model views comprehension as a process that involves meaning negotiation among text, readers, teachers, and other members of the classroom community. Schema for text meanings, academic tasks, sources of authority (i.e., residing within the text, the reader, the teacher, the classroom community, or some interaction of these), and sociocultural settings are all brought to the negotiation task. The teacher's role is one of orchestration of the instructional setting, and being knowledgeable about teaching/learning strategies and about the world.

Reading Comprehension as Transactional

The transactional model takes into account the dynamic nature of language and both aesthetic and cognitive aspects of reading. According to Rosenblatt (1994, p. 1063), "Every reading act is an event, or a transaction involving a particular reader and a particular pattern of signs, a text, and occurring at a particular time in a particular context. Instead of two fixed entities acting on one another, the reader and the text are two aspects of a total dynamic situation. The 'meaning' does not reside ready-made 'in' the text or 'in' the reader but happens or comes into being during the transaction between reader and text." Thus, text without a reader is merely a set of marks capable of being interpreted as written language. However, when a reader transacts with the text, meaning happens.

Schemata are not viewed as static but rather as active, developing, and ever changing. As readers transact with text they are changed or transformed, as is the text. Similarly, "the same text takes on different meanings in transactions with different readers or even with the same reader in different contexts or times" (Rosenblatt, 1994, p. 1078).

Reading Comprehension as Transactional-Sociopsycholinguistic

Building on Rosenblatt's transactional model, Goodman (1994) conceptualizes literacy processing as including reading, writing, and written texts. He states,

> Texts are constructed by authors to be comprehended by readers. The meaning is in the author and the reader. The text has a potential to evoke meaning but has no meaning in itself; meaning is not a characteristic of texts. This does not mean the characteristics of the text are unimportant or that either writer or reader are independent of them. How well the writer constructs the text and how well the reader reconstructs it and constructs meaning will influence comprehension. But meaning does not pass between writer and reader. It is represented by a writer in a text and constructed from a text by a reader. Characteristics of writer, text, and reader will all influence the resultant meaning. (p. 1103)

In a transactional-sociopsycholinguistic view, the reader has a highly active role. It is the individual transactions between a reader and the text characteristics that result in meaning. These characteristics include physical characteristics such as orthography—the alphabetic system, spelling, punctuation; format characteristics such as paragraphing, lists, schedules, bibliographies; macrostructure or text grammar such as that found in telephone books, recipe books, newspapers, and letters; and wording of texts such as the differences found in narrative and expository text.

Understanding is limited, however, by the reader's schemata, making what the reader brings to the text as important as the text itself. The writer also plays an important role in comprehension. Additionally, readers' and writers' schemata are changed through transactions with the text as meaning is constructed. Readers' schemata are changed as new knowledge is assimilated and accommodated. Writers' schemata are changed as new ways of organizing text to express meaning are developed. According to Goodman (1994):

How well the writer knows the audience and has built the text to suit that audience makes a major difference in text predictability and comprehension. However, since comprehension results from reader–text transactions, what the reader knows, who the reader is, what values guide the reader, and what purposes or interests the reader has will play vital roles in the reading process. It follows that what is comprehended from a given text varies among readers. Meaning is ultimately created by each reader. (p. 1127)

Reading Comprehension as Influenced by Attitude

Mathewson's (1994) Model of Attitude Influence upon Reading and Learning to Read is derived from the area of social psychology. This model attempts to explain the roles of affect and cognition in reading comprehension. The core of the attitude–influence model explains that a reader's whole attitude toward reading (i.e., prevailing feelings and evaluative beliefs about reading and action readiness for reading) will influence the intention to read, in turn influencing reading behavior. *Intention to read* is proposed as the primary mediator between attitude and reading. *Intention* is defined as "commitment to a plan for achieving one or more reading purposes at a more or less specified time in the future" (Mathewson, 1994, p. 1135). All other moderator variables (e.g., extrinsic motivation, involvement, prior knowledge, and purpose) are viewed as affecting the attitude–reading relationship by influencing the intention to read. Therefore, classroom environments that include well-stocked libraries, magazines, reading tables, and areas with comfortable chairs will enhance students' intentions to read. Mathewson (1994, p. 1148) states, "Favorable attitudes toward reading thus sustain intention to read and reading as long as readers continue to be satisfied with reading outcomes."

SKILLED VERSUS LESS SKILLED COMPREHENDERS

This is an appropriate time to consider the reader having difficulty with comprehension. The characteristics of less skilled comprehenders must be known in order to help them become more skilled.

An early review of the literature on good and poor comprehenders by Golinkoff (1975/1976) reveals that good comprehenders are adaptable and flexible. They seem to be aware that reading is a process for gaining information or expanding one's knowledge about the world. More specifically, in terms of three comprehension subskills that Golinkoff uses to compare good and poor comprehenders, the skilled comprehender is a master at decoding, accessing single word meanings, and extracting relations between words in sentences and larger units of text.

Poor comprehenders, on the other hand, are less adaptive and flexible in their reading style. They make more decoding errors and take more time to decode. They tend to read word-by-word, which implies one of three things: they are unfamiliar with the printed words (decoding), they are unaware of the clues to proper phrasing (syntactic aspects), or they are unaware that reading involves using what they already know about the concepts and contextual constraints found in the text to construct meaning. This last characteristic is also supported by McKeown's (1985) research on the acquisition of word meanings from context (semantic aspects).

While such characterizations have led to the conclusion that poor comprehenders are more concerned with pronouncing words correctly than with getting meaning from the printed page, this is not necessarily the case. Stanovich (1980) gives evidence that in some situations poor readers rely *more* on contextual information than good readers. To cope with a large number of visually unfamiliar words, some poor readers depend too much on the syntactic and semantic clues available.

Kolers (1975) presents evidence that such dependence on syntactic and semantic clues to avoid decoding may be a common source of reading difficulty. Kolers' subjects, good and poor readers between ten and fourteen years of age, read sentences in normal and reversed type. The poor readers made ten times as many substitution errors as the good readers. Also, the reading speed of the poor readers was less affected by the reversed type than that of the good readers. The poor readers guessed frequently and paid relatively little attention to the typographical (graphemic) aspects of the print. These results were interpreted as indicating an overreliance on syntactic and semantic clues.

Stanovich (1980) distinguishes between two types of contextual processing when discussing differences between good and poor comprehenders. The first type involves relating new information to known information and imposing structure on the text (text organization). The second type is the contextual hypothesis-testing strategy that allows previously understood material to help with ongoing word recognition. Good readers use both types of contextual processing, whereas poor readers are more adept at the second type. In itself this is not a problem; however, if processing is being used to aid word recognition, the reader is depleting valuable cognitive resources—resources that could otherwise be employed for making inferences or relating new information to old. Stanovich views the comprehension problem as a direct result of slow and nonautomatic word recognition skills that require the poor reader to draw on the wrong kinds of knowledge sources. As stated by Stanovich (1980):

> Given that the ability to use prior context to facilitate word recognition is not a skill that differentiates good from poor readers, there appear to be two general types of processes that good readers perform more efficiently than poor readers. Good readers appear to have superior strategies for comprehending and remembering large units of text. In addition, good readers are superior at context-free word recognition. There is some evidence indicating that good readers have automatized the recognition of word and subword units to a greater extent than poor readers. However, good readers recognize even fully automated words faster than poor readers. . . . In short, the good reader identifies words automatically and rapidly. . . . The existence of this rapid context-free recognition ability means that the word recognition of good readers is less reliant on conscious expectancies generated from the prior sentence context. The result is that more attentional capacity is left over for integrative comprehension processes. (p. 64)

A more recent study by Kletzien (1991) looked at the comprehension strategies used by good and poor comprehenders with expository material at the secondary level. Results support earlier findings (see Golinkoff, 1975/1976) that good comprehenders are more flexible in their use of strategies. By means of student self-reports Kletzien found that both good and poor comprehenders are aware of a variety of strategies, but attention to vocabulary, rereading, making inferences, and using prior knowledge were the most frequently used strategies for both groups. More strategies were used with easier material. Poor comprehenders used fewer strategies as the difficulty of the material increased. Kletzien concluded that poor comprehenders need to know when, how, and why to use a particular strategy.

Poor comprehenders apparently do not effectively use the strategies that good comprehenders do. Research by Olshavsky (1976/1977) reveals that poor readers are not proficient in using context to aid reading fluency, or in using their knowledge of the language to add information that is not in the text but would help in understanding of the material (making inferences). Olshavsky concluded that, in general, poor readers use fewer strategies than good readers, but Kletzien's research indicates that this may be due to uncertainty as to when to use a strategy rather than a lack of awareness of the strategies themselves.

Rumelhart (1980, p. 48) offers additional explanations of failure to comprehend a selection, assuming that the words are automatically recognized.

1. The reader does not have the appropriate schemata necessary (lack of conceptual background).
2. The reader has the appropriate schemata, but clues provided by the author are insufficient to suggest them.
3. The reader interprets the text but not in the way intended by the author.

These breakdowns are likely when reading something in a new field of study, something abstract, vague, technical, or too difficult.

In conclusion, comprehension demands that the reader be active, attentive, and selective while reading. As Tierney and Pearson (1994, p. 497) advocate, "teaching procedures that encourage students to monitor their own processing strategies—how they allocate attention to text versus prior knowledge, how they can tell *what* and *that* they know (i.e., metacognition), and how to apply fix-up strategies when comprehension is difficult" should be adopted.

ASSESSMENT AND INSTRUCTION FOR COMPREHENSION

The remainder of this chapter examines assessment of comprehension difficulties at the word level and suggests instructional techniques. Assessment and instruction techniques for longer text can be found in Chapter 10.

Assessing Decoding Skills

The importance of quick and automatic word recognition to comprehension is made clear in the numerous studies reviewed by Stanovich (1980). For assessment procedures related to decoding refer to Chapter 8.

Instruction for Increased Reading Fluency

The instructional methods provided here are intended to increase reading fluency which, in turn, should enable the ineffective decoder of any age or grade level to focus more on meaning than on individual words (Samuels, 1988). The increased amount of practice in reading whole text should also increase the automatic recognition of words.

Predictable Language

This method takes advantage of the rhythmic, repetitive, and redundant language structures in children's storybooks and nursery rhymes (Walker, 1992). Its assumption is that word identification is facilitated by the predictive nature of the material. Choose a book that contains a predictable pattern such as Bill Martin's (1970) *The Haunted House* ("One dark and stormy night I came upon a haunted house. I tiptoed into the yard. No one was there. I tiptoed onto the porch. No one was there. . . ."). The material should first be read aloud to the students completely through so they can hear the whole story. During this reading, emphasize the predictable parts using an enthusiastic voice. Now the students are ready for a second reading. During the second reading, ask the students to join in whenever they feel they know what to say. During subsequent readings, an oral cloze procedure can be used to give students practice in predicting upcoming words in text. Finally, students are ready to read the book on their own, using the predictable language pattern and picture clues to aid them. Students can also be asked to write their own story, using the same predictable pattern found in the book but changing the characters and/or setting. For example, the haunted house might become *The Haunted School* with a whole new set of spaces and rooms to tiptoe through.

Neurological Impress Method (NIM)

In this method the student and teacher read orally in unison (Heckelman, 1969). Sitting side by side, with the teacher slightly behind on the right side in order to read into the student's right ear, the student reads out loud with the teacher. The teacher's voice will actually be a bit ahead of the student's, especially if the student has a limited sight vocabulary. The teacher thus models fluent and expressive reading and allows the student to experience the way that feels. The teacher does not stop when the student falters. The student is directed to continue to read with the teacher as much as possible. The teacher should move a finger along the line of print being read so the student can follow more easily. This method does take some getting used to; initially using short, rhythmic, and repetitive materials, such as poems or song lyrics, might prove helpful.

Bedsworth (1991) reports impressive gains for middle school students who used NIM only 10 minutes each day for nine weeks. All three students made significant gains, 3½ years in nine weeks for silent reading. In addition, students' attitudes and perceptions about their reading became more positive. Bedsworth speculates that NIM works because it provides a nonthreatening reading experience; it is a novel approach; the attention of the learner is focused through visual, auditory, and kinesthetic–tactile modalities; and students read in units rather than word by word.

Repeated Readings

This procedure consists of doing exactly what its title says: a self-selected passage is reread orally until it is read accurately and fluently (Samuels, 1979). Repeated readings encourage the use of contextual meaning and sentence structure to predict upcoming words and to correct miscues. The student chooses the material to be read. The teacher should make a copy of the passages that will be used for repeated reading so that notations can be made as the student reads. The student reads and the teacher records errors and speed. These numbers are charted on a graph. The student then practices rereading the material silently. (During this time the teacher can work with another student.) The student then rereads the passage aloud for the second time while the teacher records errors and speed using a different color ink. Again these numbers are charted and any progress noted. This procedure is followed until a speed of 85 words per minute is achieved. A substantial amount of research shows that the process of repeated readings "helps students remember and understand more, increases their oral reading speed and accuracy, and seems to improve students' oral reading expression" (Dowhower, 1989). Additionally, a modification that supports a cooperative learning approach through the use of partners, called *paired repeated reading* (Koskinen & Blum, 1986), also seems to be effective and easy to manage in regular classrooms.

Echo Reading

Echo reading is similar to both the *neurological impress method* and *repeated readings* procedure in that the student is following a teacher's model and may need to repeat the reading that is being imitated. In echo reading (Walker, 1992), the teacher reads one sentence of text aloud with appropriate intonation and phrasing. The student then tries to imitate this oral reading model. The text reading continues in this fashion until the teacher feels the student can imitate more than one sentence at a time. This technique allows students to read text fluently that they otherwise may not have been able to handle. This technique can also be used in conjunction with repeated readings or neurological impress to model particularly troublesome sentences. Echo reading is quite helpful for the student who needs a model of fluent reading, for instance, students who focus too much on the words in a passage rather than the meaning, or those who show no concern for whether their oral reading sounds like fluent language.

Readers Theater

This technique provides a realistic opportunity for students to read orally and practice their use of intonation, inflection, and fluency. In readers theater (Sloyer, 1982), students present a dramatic interpretation of a narrative passage through an oral interpretive reading. Character parts are assigned or selected by participating students, and appropriate parts for oral reading are identified and then practiced silently. Following practice, the students read their scripts orally for an audience. (Props and costumes are not necessary.) The mood of the story is conveyed through proper intonation and phrasing. This technique is especially helpful not only for fluency, but for comprehension. When deciding what should be included in the script, the students must decide what is important in terms of dialogue and narration to the understanding of the story. Once again, the opportunity for repeated readings is present.

Assessing Knowledge of Word Meanings

In assessing knowledge of word meanings, the degree of word knowledge should be considered. According to Dale, O'Rourke, and Bamman (1971), levels of familiarity with a word proceed from total ignorance ("I never saw it before"), to an awareness ("I've heard of it, but I don't know what it means"), to a general knowledge ("I recognize it in context—it has something to do with . . ."), and finally to accurate knowledge ("I know it"). Dale et al. (1971) state that in a vocabulary program, concentration on levels 2 and 3 is probably best to move these *almost known* words into the category of *known* words. Therefore, in testing students' vocabulary knowledge for the purpose of discovering students' vocabulary needs, identifying words that are at least at an awareness level is recommended.

Dale et al. (1971, p. 20) suggest four methods of testing awareness vocabulary that are easily adaptable by classroom teachers for direct assessment.

1. *Identification.* In this simple, most direct method, the student is asked to reply orally or in writing whether the meaning of a word is known as it is used in specific text. The meaning is identified according to its definition or use, or by an associated word.

2. *Multiple choice.* The student selects the correct meaning of the tested word from three or four definitions or examples.

3. *Matching.* The tested words are presented in one column and the matching definitions are presented, out of order, in another column.

4. *Checking.* The student checks the words that are known or not known.

Within these four methods is a variety of techniques teachers can use to test vocabulary. Some examples follow.

Identification

A list of words, preferably related to material the student will be asked to read, is constructed in an easy-to-read sequence. The students are later asked to define (orally or in written form) only checked words. In preparation for a selection on skydiving, the following list might be used:

_____ sport	_____ hover
_____ speed	_____ harness
_____ target	_____ daredevil
_____ parachute	_____ coordination
_____ ripcord	_____ plummet

Multiple Choice

Words are presented in context, and several answers are provided. The student selects the best response. For example:

A. Mary was <u>hungry</u>. She wanted her _____ .
                              (flower, coat, snack)

B. He bought an <u>expensive</u> gift.
   1. very beautiful
   2. did not cost too much
   3. cost a lot

Matching

Several types of matching exercises evaluate vocabulary development. Examples of three useful types follow.

A. Matching words with definitions

1. _____ census   a. A town near a large city
2. _____ suburb   b. Areas where people live close together in towns
3. _____ urban   and cities
                       c. Where people live on the surface of the earth
                       d. A count of people
                       e. The study of where people live and carry on their
                          activities

B. Matching affixes with definitions

1. _____ pre   a. three
2. _____ es   b. someone who
3. _____ er   c. not
4. _____ bi   d. against
5. _____ un   e. two
                 f. more than one
                 g. before

C. Matching words with related words or phrases. These are matches of associations and not definitions. Lines are drawn to the matches. (The first match is done for you.)

1. owl   flies high
   eagle   called wise

2. canine   puppy
   feline   kitten

3. lions   pride
   geese   gaggle

4. carat   diamond
   caret   editing

Checking

The fourth method involves checking by the student. This alerts both the student and the teacher to vocabulary strengths and needs. Two types of self-checking tests follow.

A. If the underlined word in the sentence is used correctly, the student puts a check beside it. If both sentences in the unit are incorrect, the student checks "neither" (Gipe, 1977).

1. a. _____ The gooey <u>bramble</u> stuck to the roof of his mouth.
   b. _____ The <u>bramble</u> caught on Mary's coat.
   c. _____ Neither

2. a. _____ <u>Graphite</u> will erase the mark Jim made with his pencil.
   b. _____ <u>Graphite</u> will leave a mark on the paper.
   c. _____ Neither

3. a. _____ The cat's cries were <u>luminous</u> in the night.

   b. _____ The cat's eyes were <u>luminous</u> in the night.

   c. _____ Neither

4. a. _____ Our friend brought good <u>tidings</u>.

   b. _____ We bought some <u>tidings</u> from our friend.

   c. _____ Neither

2. The student indicates on a chosen list of words how well each word is known. The code to use might be:

   + means "I know it well."

   ✓ means "I know it somewhat."

   O means "I've seen it or heard of it."

   – means "I don't know it at all."

   For example, the following type of list, drawn from a science book, is best used analytically before new material or a unit of study is introduced.

   _____ hypothesis

   _____ experiment

   _____ interact

   _____ substance

   _____ element

These assessment methods are primarily intended to help the teacher determine strengths and gaps in students' vocabularies. They should also serve as a source of motivation for students. Once students are sensitized to words and recognize that they can expand their vocabularies, they develop a sense of excitement about words. A teacher who is enthusiastic about developing vocabulary will, in turn, enhance the students' enthusiasm. Many exercises on word meanings are found in workbooks and teachers' manuals accompanying basal readers. These exercises also serve as informal tests for vocabulary at an awareness level.

For assessment of full conceptual knowledge of vocabulary, the tasks required must be more sensitive to the specific dimensions of the vocabulary items than those used for assessing an awareness level. Simpson (1987) suggests a hierarchy of four processes that, in turn, suggest formats for assessing full conceptual knowledge. The four processes are:

1. Students should be able to recognize and generate the critical attributes, examples, and nonexamples of a concept. . . .

2. Students should be able to sense and infer relationships between concepts and their own background information. . . .

3. Students should be able to recognize and apply the concept to a variety of contexts. . . .

4. Students should be able to generate novel contexts for the targeted concept. (p. 22)

Simpson also provides examples of alternative formats for these four processes.

The vocabulary subtests in most standardized reading achievement tests probably are not valid measures of knowledge of word meanings for readers having difficulty

(Bond & Tinker, 1967, p. 281), because these students often are not able to identify or pronounce the words in the test. This does not necessarily mean that they do not know the meanings. Oral administration of the test, on the other hand, invalidates the norms for the test.

Examples of standardized tests that contain vocabulary subtests more appropriate for use with readers having difficulty are the *Gates-McKillop-Horowitz Reading Diagnostic Tests* (1982) and the *Stanford Diagnostic Reading Test* (Karlsen & Gardner, 1986).

Instruction for Word Meanings

General Instructional Procedures

While meaning vocabulary is certainly learned incidentally through experience and reading (Nagy, Anderson, & Herman, 1987), this way of learning vocabulary is slow and not at all predictable (Dale, O'Rourke, & Barbe, 1986), especially for students who do not read well or often. Readers with limited meaning vocabularies must receive direct and intense instruction focused on vocabulary expansion. Planned lessons for vocabulary development might include first-hand experience, such as field trips, in-class demonstrations, or laboratory experiences in math or science. Related discussions before, during, and after the experience use the key vocabulary words.

Vocabulary is usually taught by other than first-hand experiences, however. Words should be taught that help corrective readers comprehend material at their instructional reading levels and understand content area class discussions. These words are found in the books and content area materials being used in the classroom.

Most effective methods of teaching new vocabulary involve the use of context (Gipe, 1977; Nagy, 1988; Wixson, 1984). Typically, teachers present new vocabulary words by writing sentences on the board. Meanings are discussed and the material is then read. For corrective readers this kind of vocabulary instruction may not be appropriate. According to Goodman (1994),

> it is a mistake to think that vocabulary-building exercises [alone] can produce improved comprehension. Language is learned in the context of its use. Word meanings are built in relationship to concepts; language facilitates learning, but it is the conceptual development that creates the need for the language. Without that, words are empty forms. So vocabulary is built in the course of language use including reading. It is probably more accurate to say that people have big vocabularies because they read a lot than that they read well because they have big vocabularies. (p. 1127)

It makes more sense, then, to discuss new vocabulary *after* material is read so the reader has access to the word's appropriate use.

As noted earlier in the discussion of schema theory and comprehension, schemata relevant to the reader's task (in this case, learning the meaning of a new word) must be activated. Vocabulary instruction that encourages this activation is most effective. Students learn and retain many new vocabulary words when the words are introduced in familiar, meaningful sentences and stories. Therefore, vocabulary instruction is desirable that helps students (1) relate new vocabulary to what they already know (2) develop broader understanding of word knowledge in a variety of contexts (3) become actively involved in learning new words and (4) develop strategies for independent vocabulary acquisition (Carr & Wixson, 1986). Marzano and Marzano (1988) provide four clear principles for vocabulary instruction:

1. Wide reading and language-rich activities should be the primary vehicles for vocabulary learning. Given the large number of words students encounter in written and oral language, general language development must be encouraged as one of the most important vocabulary development strategies.

2. Direct vocabulary instruction should focus on words considered important to a given content area or to general background knowledge. Since effective direct vocabulary instruction requires a fair amount of time and complexity, teachers should select words for instruction that promise a high yield in student learning of general knowledge or of knowledge of a particular topic of instructional importance.

3. Direct vocabulary instruction should include many ways of knowing a word and provide for the development of a complex level of word knowledge. Since word knowledge is stored in many forms (mental pictures, kinesthetic associations, smells, tastes, semantic distinctions, linguistic references), direct vocabulary instruction should take advantage of many of these forms and not emphasize one to the exclusion of others.

4. Direct vocabulary instruction should include a structure by which new words not taught directly can be learned readily. Again, given the large number of words students encounter and the limited utility of direct instruction, some structure must be developed to allow the benefits of direct vocabulary instruction to go beyond the words actually taught. (pp. 11–12)

Research by Gipe (1978/1979, 1980) indicates that new word meanings are effectively taught by providing appropriate and familiar context. A four-step procedure is recommended. Students are given a passage in which the first sentence uses the new word appropriately, thereby providing valuable syntactic and semantic information. The context is composed of familiar words and situations. The second sentence of the passage describes some of the attributes of the new word. As with the first sentence, terms are already familiar to the students. The third sentence defines the new word, with care being taken to use familiar concepts. The last sentence gives the students an opportunity to relate the new word to their own lives by asking them to write an answer to a question about the word's meaning or to complete an open-ended statement that requires application of the word's meaning. An example of a complete passage follows:

The boys who wanted to sing together formed a *quintet*. There were five boys singing in the *quintet*. *Quintet* means a group of five, and this group usually sings or plays music. If you were in a *quintet,* what instrument would you want to play?

Talk Through (Piercey, 1982) is another technique that recognizes the importance of helping students relate what they already know to a word that is unfamiliar or has multiple meanings. In *Talk Through,* the teacher identifies key concept words, perhaps prior to a content area reading selection, that students are likely to find difficult. These words may be totally new, introduced previously, or possessing a different meaning from the common meaning.

The teacher begins by using the word in a sentence on the chalkboard.

The frog has gone through a complete *metamorphosis* from its days as a tadpole.[2]

At this point the teacher helps relate the meaning of the new word to students' own lives and personal experiences. The teacher *asks* students for input, as opposed to telling them what the word means. For example,

> "James, remember when you brought in a tree branch that had a cocoon attached to it? What made that cocoon?"
>
> James answers, "The caterpillars in the trees in my backyard made that cocoon."
>
> "Class, does anyone remember what happened to the cocoon? Lisa?"
>
> Lisa responds, "One day a butterfly came out of it."
>
> "Yes, and right after that happened, remember I read you the story of *The Very Hungry Caterpillar* by Eric Carle. What happened to *that* caterpillar? Tony?"
>
> Tony relates, "The caterpillar ate one bite out of lots of different things, leaves, apples, tomatoes, and then it went to sleep inside a cocoon. Then one day it became a butterfly."

The next step the teacher takes is to write the word of interest in isolation,

> metamorphosis

then writes

> meta + morphe
>
> (over)   (shape or form)

and says, "Metamorphosis comes from two Greek words—over or beyond and shape or form—combined to mean the shape or form of something changes over to a different shape or form. Our experience with the cocoon and the story of *The Very Hungry Caterpillar* showed us that the *shape* or *form* of a caterpillar changed *over* to the shape or form of a butterfly. That is what metamorphosis means."

At this point the teacher seeks to further relate the new word to students' lives.

> "What else goes through a metamorphosis that you are familiar with?"
>
> Responses: "We had some mealworms once to feed our pet chameleon. They changed into beetles."
>
> "I think some caterpillars change into moths."
>
> "My mom told me that flies lay eggs that hatch out little white worms. And then later on those worms turn back into flies."
>
> "I saw a movie once where a man turned into a wolf."
>
> "Frogs must change—it's in the sentence on the board."

And so it goes! The concept of metamorphosis is more meaningful now than if the students were simply told what it meant and then told to read the text containing the subject matter.

Corrective readers also must be taught how to use context clues as well as structural analysis (see Chapter 8) clues to help them determine the meanings of unknown words. But first, as Blachowicz and Zabroske (1990) point out, students need to be aware of the

---

[2]The author wishes to thank Mr. Herbert Ellis, Jr., a former student, for the ideas behind this example.

kinds of clues provided by context. "Context can clue you to – what a word is (what it's like); what a word isn't (what it's different from); what it looks like; something about its location or setting; something about what it's used for; what kind of thing or action it is; how something is done; a general topic or idea related to the work; other words related to the word; and so forth" (p. 506).

Buikema and Graves (1993) field-tested a vocabulary instructional unit with seventh- and eighth-grade students for the purpose of helping them learn to use descriptive context cues to infer word meanings. After beginning instruction using "What am I?" word riddles to introduce the idea of *descriptive* context cues, students were introduced to this same notion in text passages. Students could refer to a posted definition of descriptive context cues that read, "Descriptive cues give us clues as to the *sensual* aspects of an unknown word (its appearance, smell, taste, feel, or sound) or the *action* the word indicates or the *purpose* the word has" (p. 452). Following modeling and group work with sample passages for several days (instruction lasted for 5 consecutive 50-minute periods), students learned the strategy.

Students were then provided many opportunities to use the strategy with their reading materials. A sample practice worksheet to accompany this strategy is presented in Figure 9.1. The worksheet was modified to show this strategy as an adaptation of Gipe's (1978/1979) strategy discussed earlier.

Any vocabulary instruction can include the hypothesis/test strategy steps used by Blachowicz and Zabroske (1990). The steps should be modeled in stages for students. They are:

Look—before, at, after the word

Reason—to connect what you know with what the author tells you

Predict—a possible meaning

Resolve or re-do—decide if you know enough, should try again,

or consult an expert or reference (p. 506)

The easiest vocabulary exercises employ simple associations. Students use knowledge already in their schemata to work with synonyms, antonyms, homophones, **associative words** that often occur together (e.g., green–grass, bacon–eggs), and to classify (e.g., animal: dog, cat, horse). The following activities can be used as the core of lessons, as practice activities, or as learning games designed to promote vocabulary development. For these activities to be considered instructional, student and teacher must interact. If they are done independently, they become practice activities.

Synonyms

Students are often taught that synonyms are words that have the same meaning. This is not exactly true, however. Synonyms have *similar* meaning, which allows us to express the same idea in a variety of ways.

The study of synonyms is probably the easiest and most efficient place to start expanding students' vocabularies because it starts with a familiar word. The student already has a schema for the known word; by comparing synonyms the student sees the relationships between words and is able to further generalize and classify words, thus enhancing the current schema. Some characteristic synonym activities follow.[3]

---

[3]From Dale, O'Rourke, & Barbe, *Vocabulary Building: A Process Approach.* Columbus, OH: Zaner–Bloser, 1986, p. 85.

1. Underline the word that means about the same as the word underlined in the sentence. (Note that this activity encourages the use of context clues.)

   We almost missed Sue's name because she wrote so *tiny*.

   large   small   big   hot

2. Match the words with about the same meaning. (Note how the structural clue, the prefix *un*, can help with this task.)

   a. _____ large   1) unhappy

   b. _____ tiny   2) big

   c. _____ hen   3) chicken

   d. _____ sad   4) small

F I G U R E

9.1

Inferring word meanings from context.

PRACTICE WORKSHEET

Name: _____ Date: _____

Strategy Practice: Using the descriptive cues strategy, do all the following for the short paragraph below.

1. Underline the unknown word(s).
2. List in the space the descriptive cues that give hints for the word's meaning.
3. List any thoughts, experiences, or statements that helped you decide on the word's meaning.
4. Using your cue list, write a possible definition for the word.

The boys who wanted to sing together formed a <u>quintet</u>. There were five boys singing in the <u>quintet</u>. This group of five boys often sings and plays music together. If you were in a <u>quintet</u> would you want to sing or play a musical instrument?

1.   quintet

2.   to sing together
   five boys
   sings and plays music together

3.   I heard my dad talk about a barbershop quintet being at the mall on Saturday.

4.   I think a quintet is five people singing or playing musical instruments together.

3. Circle the two words that could complete each sentence.
   a. The clown did a _____ right in front of us.

   treat   stunt   trick

   b. The neighborhood kids play baseball in the _____ lot.

   empty   vacant   full

   c. A large tree _____ blew down in the storm.

   branch   leaf   limb

4. Use the words in the box to complete the paragraph. Each word will be used twice, and it will have a different meaning each time. A synonym has been provided in parentheses for each space.

keen   slim   serious

   The hikers were (eager) _____ to reach the cabin. The approaching storm could be (dangerous) _____ . Already, a (sharp) _____ wind was blowing, and the possibility of finding a cave to shelter in was (unlikely) _____. "Come on," said the guide, a tall, (thin) _____ woman. Her expression was (solemn) _____ .

These formats are easily adapted to language experience stories or other creative writings with the use of a thesaurus (see Chapter 7 for additional ideas).

Comparing synonyms helps students see the relationships between words of similar meaning and also recognize that fine distinctions often should be made. Before these fine discriminations are possible, however, gross discriminations, as in the first three exercises, must be mastered. For example, the word *tiny* from the first set of exercises has many synonyms (little, small, minute, diminutive, miniature, microscopic, and so on), but not all of these terms are interchangeable. The use of contextual clues, a dictionary, and discussion will help the student determine the most appropriate shade of meaning for the following sentences.

1. We all agreed that Mary's feet were _____ but smaller yet were Sue's

   small   tiny

   _____ feet.

   small   tiny

2. The doll was an exact _____ of a real British soldier.

   miniature   diminutive

The meanings of synonyms, while similar, are not exactly the same. Choosing a synonym depends on how the word is used. Dale, O'Rourke, and Barbe (1986) provide an excellent example for synonyms of the word *get*. The student is directed to write the best word to use in place of *get*. *Buy, catch,* and *win* are the synonyms.

1. I will *get* the ball you throw.
2. The fastest runner will *get* a prize.
3. Will you *get* a new sweater at the store? (p. 85)

This type of activity is especially valuable during editing of students' written compositions.

A group cloze activity (Jacobson, 1990) can be used to help students fine-tune their knowledge of synonyms and language use in general. The cooperative completion of a cloze passage can enhance each student's understanding and retention of the material read in addition to providing practice with the vocabulary and language patterns used by skilled writers. Basically the steps are as follows:

1. Each student individually completes the cloze passage (see Chapter 6 for construction of cloze passages).
2. In groups of three (triads), students discuss the reasons for each other's supplied words. Each student tries to convince the others that his choice is best, but if the others are convinced of another word there is no problem (or penalty) for changing words.
3. One triad then meets with a second triad to discuss word choices. Changes can again be made if reasons are clear.
4. Results are shared with the whole class. The teacher might have the original passage on an overhead transparency to allow for whole class discussion.

Certain authors of children's literature are very aware of the opportunity they have to increase vocabulary through use of synonyms (e.g., Franklyn Branley, Vicki Cobb, Joanna Cole, Ron and Nancy Goor, Kathryn Lasky, Patricia Lauber, Bianca Lavies, Molly McLaughlin, Hershell and Joan Nixon, Dorothy Patent, Laurence Pringle, Helen Roney Sattler, Jack Denton Scott, Millicent Selsam, and Seymour Simon). A good example is Molly McLaughlin's *Dragonflies* (1989). Numerous synonyms are used to help readers understand vocabulary related to dragonflies:

"This larva, or nymph, is quite different from its colorful flying parents." (p. 16)

"This remarkable lip, or labium, is one of the tools that make the 'pond monster' such a fearsome hunter." (p. 19)

"As the time for the big change, or metamorphosis, comes closer, the nymph's behavior changes, too." (p. 22)

Antonyms

Just as no two synonyms are exactly alike in meaning, no two antonyms are exact opposites. To develop the concept of opposites, however, antonyms can be grouped according to their general meaning. Most activities suggested for synonyms can be modified for antonyms:

1. The student is instructed to change the underlined word so the sentence will have almost the opposite meaning.

   Jack <u>hates</u> to read.

   Spot is a <u>fat</u> dog.

   It is a <u>hot</u> morning.

   The study of antonyms is readily adapted to the use of structural analysis clues. The teacher can purposely present pairs of words to illustrate how opposites result from the addition of certain prefixes and suffixes (e.g., happy–unhappy; fear–fearless).
2. Antonym trees are useful to help study the formation of antonyms (Fig. 9.2). Given a root word at the base of the tree, students prepare "leaves" for the tree by writing words that mean the opposite of the root word. Students soon discover the use of prefixes and suffixes in forming antonyms. Some antonyms formed from prefixes and suffixes are listed below (Dale et al., 1971, p. 57).

Prefixes Forming Antonyms

*in*doors	vs.	*out*doors	*in*hale	vs.	*ex*hale
*pre*paid	vs.	*post*paid	*sub*ordinate	vs.	*super*ordinate
*in*flate	vs.	*de*flate	*under*fed	vs.	*over*fed
*post*test	vs.	*pre*test	*pro*gress	vs.	*re*gress

Suffixes Forming Antonyms

worth*y*	vs.	worth*less*	widow	vs.	widow*er*
lion	vs.	lion*ess*	use*less*	vs.	use*ful*
beard*less*	vs.	beard*ed*	hero	vs.	hero*ine*

3. The student is told to read the sentence and choose the word that best completes the sentence.

   <u>Cowardly</u> means the opposite of a person who is _____ .

   timid   courageous   fearful

   Was the bread <u>fresh</u>, or had it become _____ ?

   burned   stale   delicious

Homophones

Words that sound alike but are different in spelling and meaning are called **homophones**. Homophones may confuse encoding and decoding tasks (e.g., distinguishing between *reed* and *read*) but may help the comprehension task (e.g., the reader knows

Antonym tree. Students make "leaves" with words opposite in meaning to the "root" word at the base of the tree.

FIGURE

9.2

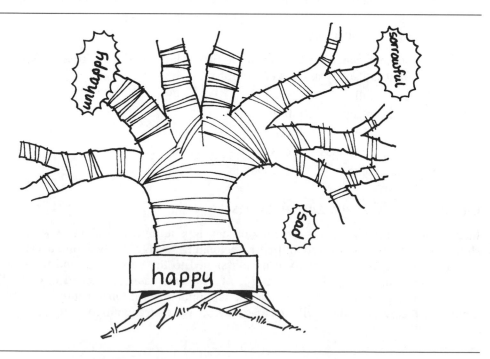

reed refers to a tall grass). As with synonyms and antonyms, the student needs much practice discriminating between one homophone and another. In the activities that follow, several approaches are presented.

1. Students practice exercises in which they are given a word and asked to supply its homophone. This task begins simply by giving letter-space clues.

   bear, <u>b</u> a r e   stare, <u>s</u> t a i r

   cite, <u>s</u> i g h t   hour, <u>o</u> u r

2. The student is directed to choose the correct homophone using context clues.

   a. They met on the *(stairs, stares)*.

   b. They spent a *(weak, week)* at the beach.

   c. We stayed for the *(hole, whole)* game.

   d. *(Meet, Meat)* me at six o'clock.

3. The student is directed to supply the correct homophone utilizing definition clues.

   a. It stops a bike. It sounds like *break* ____ ____ ____ ____ ____

   b. It's an animal skin. It sounds like *fir.* ____ ____ ____

   c. Boats stop here. It sounds like *peer.* ____ ____ ____ ____

   d. It's taking what doesn't belong to you. It sounds like *steel.*

   ____ ____ ____ ____ ____

Associative Words

Unexpected responses for associative activities are not uncommon. The teacher must be flexible regarding acceptable responses for association activities.

A. The student is directed to underline the word that best fits the sentence. Responses should be discussed as to why one choice is better than another.

   The sky is so _____ it looks like the ocean.

             blue   orange   red

B. The student matches the word in the first column with one from the second column that is usually associated with it.

   1. _____ tall   a. tiger

   2. _____ electric   b. buildings

   3. _____ green   c. energy

   4. _____ ferocious d. sky

   5. _____ blue   e. fields

Classifying or Categorizing Activities

Instruction in classifying and categorizing develops an understanding of word relationships. Once a new word is identified as belonging to an already familiar category, all attributes of the known category can be assigned to the new word, and the new word becomes known. This is also an example of how schemata are expanded. Consider the familiar category, colors, and *azure* as the unfamiliar word. Once azure is identified as a color, it receives all the attributes that may be associated with color (e.g., hue, shade, brilliance). Further, once azure is identified as the color of the blue sky, it will take on the additional attributes of the already familiar word *blue*.

A teacher can present classification or categorization activities in many ways. The following general formats can be modified to accommodate many categorizing needs. The same formats provide the basis for classification games.

1. *Direct categorization.* The student is given a worksheet with category titles and a set of words to be categorized. The student lists the words under the appropriate category title.

Word sorting (Gillet & Temple, 1994, pp. 213–217) is also used to involve students in categorizing. For example, a group (or individual) may be given a set of words that represent several different common elements:

ray	tangent	rhombus
triangle	octagon	dodecagon
hexagon	pentagon	trapezoid

The group sorts the words (e.g., rhombus, trapezoid; ray, tangent; rhombus, trapezoid, triangle, pentagon, octagon, hexagon, dodecagon) and reads out the words in one group to the rest of the class. Those listening must determine the category title (e.g., quadrilaterals; lines; polygons). Discussion follows that focuses on essential characteristics of the categories.

2. *Categorizing by omission.* The student is given a set of words (e.g., four, too, six, eight) and asked to indicate the word that does *not* fit the category represented by the majority of the words. Subsequent discussion reveals the category title.

3. *Structured vocabulary overview.* In preparation for, or in review of, a unit of study it is helpful to fit words into categories. For example, a unit on algae might call for the categories of *microscopic* and *nonmicroscopic*. The specialized vocabulary items to be classified might be desmids, Irish moss, brown kelp, and diatoms. *Fresh water* and *sea water* are two additional categories for classifying these same words.

4. *Looking for common elements.* The student is given a group of words that all have something in common. The student decides what the words have in common. For example, given the words buffalo, prairie dog, and eagle, the student may conclude that all these make their habitat in the Great Plains.

5. *Word maps.* The Frayer model of concept attainment (Frayer, Frederick, & Klausmeier, 1969) provides a basis for word map activities. This model offers a structure that encourages the independent learning of new word meanings. Briefly, concepts are presented in relation to relevant and irrelevant attributes, examples and nonexamples, and supraordinate, coordinate, and subordinate aspects of the concept. Using the Frayer model leads readily to thinking about new words in relation to known, related words. Following discussion, a new concept can be *mapped* using the structures illustrated in Figure 9.3.

Similarly, Schwartz (1988) presents a concept definition word map that describes four types of relationships: (1) the general class to which the concept belongs (what is it?) (2) the primary properties of the concept and those that distinguish it from other members of the class (what is it like?) (3) examples of the concept (what are some examples?) and (4) comparison of the new concept with an additional concept that belongs to the same *general* class but differs from the target concept (comparisons). An example of a concept definition word map is displayed in Figure 9.4.

The Frayer model of concept attainment encourages thinking about new concepts in relation to known related concepts.

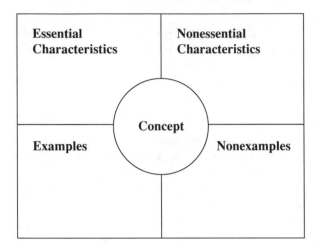

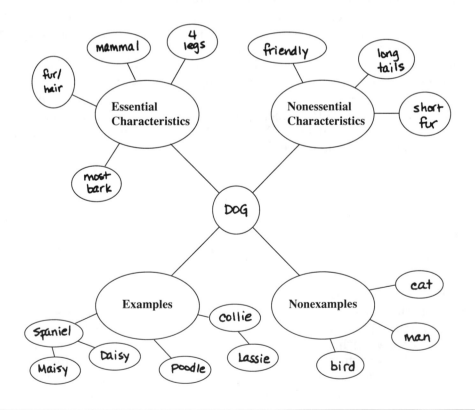

Concept definition word map.

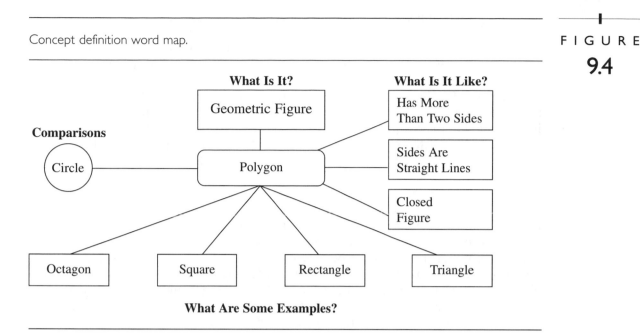

What Are Some Examples?

Instruction for Specialized Vocabulary

The **specialized vocabulary** of content areas must also be addressed directly. Content area materials may introduce ten or more technical (a meaning of a common word form specific to a content field) or unfamiliar words on a page. These words are not usually repeated often, nor are they unimportant words to the understanding of the subject matter. They are usually labels for important concepts being discussed. For example, in the area of social studies, abstract words such as *culture, technology,* and *adaptation* may be unfamiliar but extremely important to understanding the material. Not all words in content area materials are new in terms of pronunciation, however. Common words such as *mouth, matter, suit,* or *recess,* may be confusing if a specialized meaning is attached to them. While most students associate the word *recess* with time out to play, a different meaning is presented in the following sentence: "When it was time to do his homework, Bob hid in the *recess* hoping that his mother would not find him." *Mouth* may refer to the facial cavity, to a part of a musical instrument, or to the place where a stream enters a larger body of water. Content area materials abound with words that have multiple meanings.

Under most circumstances assessment of specialized vocabulary for a content area is not necessary. Instead the teacher may safely assume that the specialized words are unknown and proceed with teaching procedures.

Most teachers at all levels agree that specialized vocabulary representing a *crucial* concept is best introduced before the lesson, although research by Memory (1990) indicates no superior time of presentation (before, during, or after) for technical vocabulary. Before reading, the teacher may (1) give the students a sentence using the new word and show how the context implies the meaning or (2) provide students a brief list of words (perhaps as part of a study guide or simply to copy from the board) and direct them to look up each word's meaning in the book's glossary and copy it down for later reference while they are reading. After reading, the teacher can discuss new word meanings using the context of the material read, along with glossary definitions.

Vocabulary techniques are essentially useless without discussion. New words can be discussed in many ways that greatly enhance understanding of their meaning and, in turn, understanding of the material read. The new concept should be related to something already familiar to the students (Gipe, 1980). For example, the students may be studying history and about to confront the word *tariff,* which is unfamiliar. While tariff is new, the word *tax* is probably not. Thus, any discussion about the new word should include mention of taxes and experiences students have had with them, such as having a dollar but not being able to buy a 99¢ item unless they have more money for the tax.

New terms are probably best taught as new concepts. In addition to relating the new word to familiar concepts, the specific characteristics of the new concept must become part of the students' understanding as well. Eventually the students must be able to distinguish examples and nonexamples of the particular concept.

It is also important to provide students opportunities to identify and discuss words new to them that may not have been selected by the teacher for discussion. Haggard (1986) suggests the *Vocabulary Self-Collection Strategy* (VSS) to help students learn to identify important words and concepts, and to use passage context to determine meaning. Following the reading of a content area selection, student teams (2–5 students) select a word they feel is important to understanding that content. A spokesperson then nominates the word before the entire class and states where the word occurred in the text, the team's definition for the word, and why the team feels it is important for the class to learn. Classmates discuss the word's value and definition. Finally, with teacher guidance, words are narrowed to only those that the class wishes to learn. These words and their final agreed-upon definitions are written in learning logs or vocabulary notebooks and used in follow-up activities. This strategy can be readily adapted to any content area. Chase and Duffelmeyer (1990) developed a modification for use in English literature called *VOCAB-LIT,* and found it to be an effective tool for helping students recognize that knowledge of literary elements is essential to understanding and appreciating novels.

A specific technique developed not only for introducing new vocabulary but also for introducing overall organization of a selection, including important concepts, is the **structured overview**. This particular technique, developed by Richard Barron (1969), uses a graphic representation of terms that are indispensable to the essence of the selection to be read. The graphic representation makes this technique doubly attractive for the corrective reader. The steps for developing and using a structured overview are as follows:

1. List the vocabulary words that are important to understanding the selection. (This analysis could include both familiar and new words.)
2. Arrange these words so they show the interrelationships among the concepts represented.
3. Add to the diagram vocabulary that the students understand and that further helps to show relationships.
4. Evaluate the diagram. Does it clearly depict the major relationships? Can it be simplified and still communicate the important ideas?
5. Introduce the lesson by displaying the diagram (perhaps as a transparency for an overhead projector). Explain why you arranged the terms the way you did. Encourage the students to contribute any information they have. Give each student

familiar vocabulary terms on slips of paper. As you discuss the overview, the students then help construct it by placing their vocabulary terms in logical positions.

6. As the selection is read, continue to relate the new information to the structured overview.

An example of a structured overview was developed for a section of a social studies text dealing with explorers coming to the New World (Fig. 9.5). Students had previously studied the Incan, Aztec, and Mayan cultures.

Other examples of content area structured overviews can be found in *Improving reading in science* (Thelan, 1976), *Reading in the mathematics classroom* (Smith & Kepner, 1981), *Reading in the science classroom* (Bechtel & Franzblau, 1980), *Reading in the social studies classroom* (Bullock & Hesse, 1980), and *Teaching reading and*

Example of a structured overview for social studies.

FIGURE
9.5

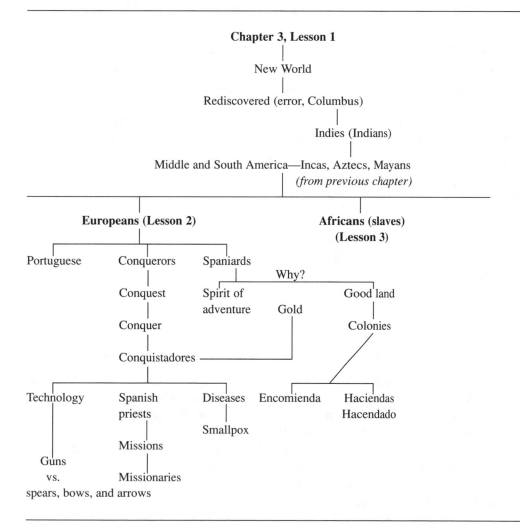

mathematics (Earle, 1976), as well as in journal articles ("Structured overviews for teaching science concepts and terms," Wolfe & Lopez, 1992/93).

Burmeister (1978) presents teaching techniques for words that have both common and specialized meanings. She suggests a two-part activity: part 1 demonstrates the common meanings and part 2 uses sentences with blanks for the unique meanings. The students must fill in the blanks in part 2. Burmeister provides examples for several content areas; a few items follow for clarification.

Mathematics

Part 1

	Term	Common Use
1.	difference	You know the *difference* between right and wrong.
2.	root	The tree *root* was growing through the sidewalk.
3.	base	Jim made it to first *base*.

Part 2

1. The subtraction operation finds the <u>(difference)</u> between two numbers.
2. Find the square <u>(root)</u> of 9.
3. The <u>(base)</u> of the triangle is 10 cm. long.

Activities that reinforce the idea that words may have several meanings are worthwhile and easily developed for any lesson; simply use a dictionary and put together a list of sentences directly from the material of interest.

Some excellent general formats for specialized vocabulary instruction and practice follow. Each activity is easily modified to fit the needs of the teacher in any content area.

Word Pairs (Stevenson & Baumann, 1979)

Use a table that allows students to show the relationship of various word pairs. Students may add word pairs to the list. The word relationships should be discussed.

Example:

Word Pair	Almost the Same	Opposite	Go Together	Not Related
land–sea		X		
ship–galleon	X			
merchant–commerce			X	
pirate–bread				X

Semantic Mapping (Johnson & Pearson, 1984; Stevenson & Baumann, 1979)

1. Select a word central to the material to be read (e.g., transportation), or from any other source of classroom interest. Write it on the chalkboard.
2. Ask the class to think of as many words as they can that are related in some way to the word you have written. Jot them on paper.
3. Have individuals share the words they have written. As they do, write the words on the board and attempt to put them into categories.
4. Number the categories and have the students name them:
   a. Kinds of transportation
   b. Places we can travel to
   c. Reasons for transportation

5. Discuss the words. This is crucial to the success of semantic mapping. Students then learn meanings of new words, new meanings for known words, and see relationships between words.

6. If time permits, select one word from the existing semantic map and begin to develop a new one (e.g., start a new map with the word *exploration*).

Constrained Categorization (Stevenson & Baumann, 1979)

Give students a chart with relevant category titles listed across the top and various letters listed along the side. Have students fill in the chart using a word that fits the category and also begins with a certain letter. Some of the words should be available in the material read. Others can be researched by groups or individuals.

Example:

	Solids	*Liquids*	*Gases*
S	salt		
C		coffee	carbon dioxide
I	ice		
E		ether	ethylene
N			neon
C		cleaning fluid	
E	earth		

Semantic Feature Analysis

1. Select a category *(shelters)*.
2. List, in a column, some words within the category *(tent, hut)*.
3. List, in a row, some features shared by some of the words *(small, exquisite)*.
4. Put pluses or minuses beside each word, beneath each feature.
5. Add additional words.
6. Add additional features.
7. Complete the expanded matrix with pluses and minuses.
8. Discover and discuss the uniqueness of each word.
9. Repeat the process with another category.

	large	small	exquisite	lovely	rustic
villa	+	−	+	+	−
cabin	−	+	−	−	+
shed	−	+	−	−	+
barn	+	−	−	−	+
tent	−	+	−	−	−

From *Teaching Reading Vocabulary,* 2nd ed., by Dale D. Johnson and P. David Pearson. Copyright © 1984 by Holt, Rinehart & Winston. Reprinted by permission of CBS College Publishing, New York.

Other beginning categories:

games	vegetables	pets
occupations	food	clothing

tools   buildings   animals
plants   transportation
Later categories:
moods   sizes   entertainment
feelings   shapes   modes of communication
commands   musical instruments

Do You Know Your Sports? (Chant & Pelow, 1979)

Note to the teacher: Many words may be categorized under two headings. For instance, *center* refers to a position played in football or basketball. *Yards* relates to the number of yards on a golf drive or the number gained or lost on a particular play in football. Simply color code the answer key to include more than one answer. In addition, many compound words are found among sports terms (Fig. 9.6). Why not use these terms to study compound words?

FIGURE

9.6

Sport terms include compound words and can be used to study the latter.

SUMMARY

A student who is successful with these basic vocabulary activities will be ready for instruction in some of the more difficult aspects of vocabulary development (e.g., analogies, connotative and denotative meanings, figures of speech, and word origins). Because these aspects of vocabulary are not easily learned, a firm vocabulary base is essential for effective reading comprehension.

SUGGESTED READINGS

Dale, E., O'Rourke, J., and Bamman, H.A. (1971). *Techniques of Teaching Vocabulary.* Palo Alto, CA: Field Educational Publication.

> *This classic work contains myriad examples of vocabulary activities. The authors support a systematic approach to vocabulary development and one that occurs within the context of communication. It is truly a work that was ahead of its time.*

Johnson, D.D. (1986). Journal of Reading: A themed issue on vocabulary instruction. *Journal of Reading, 29,* 580.

> *For a view of the issues surrounding vocabulary instruction, this themed issue is must reading. Johnson's piece in particular provides a succinct overview of the status of vocabulary instruction.*

Klein, M.L. (1988). *Teaching reading comprehension and vocabulary.* Englewood Cliffs, NJ: Prentice Hall.

> *This monograph devotes Chapter 3 to the topic of teaching reading vocabulary. Support for three models for vocabulary instruction is presented and representative activities for each are provided.*

Pittelman, S.D., Heimlich, J.E., Berglund, R.L., & French, M.P. (1991). *Semantic feature analysis classroom applications.* Newark, DE: International Reading Association.

> *This monograph is devoted solely to the instructional technique of semantic feature analysis. Examples for a variety of content areas are provided as well as applications that support integrated reading and writing.*

10

READING COMPREHENSION AND STRATEGIC READING FOR NARRATIVE TEXT

OBJECTIVES

After you have read this chapter, you should be able to

1. develop assessment activities for understanding sentences, paragraphs, and longer units of discourse;

2. devise an instructional program for a student having difficulty at any of the above levels;

3. think about reading comprehension as a process rather than a set of skill products.

KEY CONCEPTS AND TERMS

causal patterns
integrative processing
macroprocessing
mapping
microprocessing
paraphrasing
phase-out/phase-in strategy
QARs
reciprocal teaching
repeated words
replaced words

ReQAR
ReQuest Procedure
scriptally implicit
semantic webbing
story frames
story grammar
structured comprehension
text organization
textually explicit
textually implicit

OVERVIEW

This chapter continues the discussion of reading comprehension begun in Chapter 9 and views reading comprehension as a task of making connections between the text organization and the reader's prior knowledge. Three levels of text organization are considered: the sentence, the paragraph, and longer units of written discourse. Assessment and instructional techniques are related to each of these levels.

INTRODUCTION

As noted at the beginning of Chapter 9, reading comprehension is a complex skill affected by many factors. It was also pointed out that knowledge of word meanings is a critical subskill of reading comprehension. In addition to vocabulary knowledge, reading comprehension requires a number of thinking and reasoning skills. Gaining insights into relevant "subprocesses like attention, perception, encoding, comprehension, memory, information storage, and retrieval" (Pearson, 1985, p. 725) is a task that researchers, especially cognitive scientists, pursue relentlessly (see Bruer, 1993).

No longer is it acceptable to consider material "comprehended" if the reader can recall elements of the text. As Pearson (1985) has stated, "no longer do we regard text as a fixed object that the reader is supposed to 'approximate' as closely as possible as s/he reads. Instead we now view text as a sort of blueprint for meaning, a set of tracks or clues that the reader uses as s/he builds a model of what the text means" (p. 726). It is only when readers actively construct logical connections among their own prior knowledge, ideas in the text, the specific task at hand, and the situation they are in, and can express these ideas in their own words, that the text is considered comprehended.

Teachers also need to recognize the importance of prior knowledge and writing to reading comprehension. "Writing is one of the most powerful tools for developing comprehension because it can actively involve the reader in constructing a set of meanings that are useful to the individual reader" (Irwin, 1991, p. 24). Because writing activities help develop reading comprehension, many of the assessment and instruction techniques discussed in Chapter 7 are also relevant here.

ASSESSMENT AND INSTRUCTION FOR DISCOURSE UNITS

Assessing the Ability to Organize Text

Text organization refers to establishing the relationships among words, sentences, paragraphs, and longer units. As such, it is key to reading comprehension. In constructing relations between words, the reader must be able to operate at (1) a sentence level (2) a paragraph level and (3) a level involving longer passages or series of paragraphs (Irwin, 1991; Pennock, 1979). Language provides signals, some of which were discussed early in Chapter 9, that cue the reader to the relationship at hand. To evaluate a reader's ability to understand at each of the levels, the teacher can use, with some modifications, the same types of activities employed to teach sentence reading strategies, paragraph reading strategies, and longer selection reading strategies.[1]

Assessing Sentence Level Strategies

According to Irwin (1991), in the comprehension process the reader must first construct meaning "from the individual idea units in each sentence" and "decide which of these ideas to remember" (p. 2). This initial task of chunking and selectively recalling individual idea units is termed **microprocessing**. The following assessment procedures can be used to find out if the reader is able to operate at this microprocessing level.

1. Can the student recognize *who* or *what* a sentence is about? In other words, can the student identify the subject of the sentence? Give the student sentences that state the subject directly. These sentences, and any of the suggested types of sentences and paragraphs in the following sections, may be taken directly from the material being used in the classroom. For example:

Joe went into the house.

The books on the table are Adamo's.

2. Can the student recognize the predicate, or *what is being done,* in the sentence? Provide the student sentences. For example:

Shawna *kissed her mom and dad goodnight.*

They *became interested in the story right away.*

3. Can the student recognize *where* someone is or something is done? Some key signal words are *under, over, in, at, to, between, among, behind, in front of,* and *through.* Give the student sentences containing these words. For example:

Our class saw a film *in the gym.*

There was one girl *among the group of boys.*

4. Can the student recognize *when* something happens? Some key signal words are *before, after, while, later, as, now,* and *then.* Provide the student sentences containing these words. For example:

We can watch TV *after we do our homework.*

While it was raining, I read a good book.

---

[1]Discussion of these three assessment categories is based on Daniel R. Hittleman, *Developmental Reading, K–8,* 2nd ed., pp. 208–216. Copyright © 1983 Houghton Mifflin Company. Used with permission.

5. Can the student understand and use language signals that indicate information has been replaced? Some key signal words are *I, you, he, she, it, they, we, us, them, their, his, her, your, our, him, this,* and *these.* Give the student sentences that contain these key signal words and their referents. For example:

After *Mary* finished dinner, *she* started to read.

Bill wrote a story about *his* vacation.

6. Can the student recognize that words or information are sometimes left out of sentences, but the author wants the reader to mentally put the words in? The key signal is if the reader can ask *"what?"* or ask *"did what?"* where the words seem to be omitted. Provide the student sentences that make sense but seem incomplete. For example:

The rest of the family ate popcorn while Nedra made more. *(More what?)*

The teacher told the class to start writing so they began. *(Began doing what?)*

7. Can the student understand how some information in a sentence can be moved without changing the meaning of the sentence, and how punctuation can affect meaning? Give the student pairs of sentences that do and do not mean the same. The student should be able to recognize the sentence pairs that mean the same. For example:

The airplane picked up speed as it came down the runway.

As it came down the runway, the airplane picked up speed.

Before Alexander worked on his car model, he ate lunch.

Before he ate lunch, Alexander worked on his car model.

Or, given three sentences, can the student indicate which one does not mean the same? For example:

Father said, "Carol, come and play."

"Father," said Carol, "come and play."

"Carol, come and play," said Father.

8. Can the student understand that different sentences can have the same meaning? Provide the student pairs of sentences that do and do not mean the same. The student should be able to recognize the sentence pairs that mean the same. For example:

In the fall of the year the trees are painted with many colors.

Leaves on the trees have many colors in the fall.

The old horse nibbled at the grass.

The old horse was thin and feeble.

In addition to items 7 and 8, the student should be given one sentence and then asked to give another sentence that means the same, or says the same thing in another way.

Assessing Paragraph Level Strategies

Individual idea units must also be connected into a coherent whole. Making these connections requires recognizing pronoun referents, inferring causes, and identifying main ideas. "The process of understanding and inferring the relationships between individual clauses and/or sentences can be called **integrative processing**" (Irwin, 1991, p. 3). The following procedures can be used to assess integrative processing.

1. Can the student recognize *who* or *what* a paragraph is about? Key signals for determining the subject of a paragraph are repeated and replaced words. **Repeated words** are those found in almost every sentence of the paragraph. Given the following paragraph, the student should be able to recognize the repeated word and tell what (or who) the paragraph is about.

> The city of Bern, Switzerland, starts its holiday season each year with *onions*. The fourth Monday in November is *Onion* Market Day. On this day farmers display *onions* in the public square. Red, yellow, and white *onions* are piled in colorful mounds. Wreaths and garlands of *onions* are on view. Visitors can sample free *onion* cake and hot *onion* soup.

Replaced words are substitutes for words that would normally be repeated. The pronoun is the most common substitute. Given the following paragraph, the student should be able to mentally substitute each replaced word with its referent and thus recognize who (or what) the paragraph is about.

> Two *scientists* "camped" for a week at the bottom of the sea. *Their* underwater home was a cabin shaped like a barrel. *The men* did not spend all *their* time in *their* underwater bubble. *They* went out to explore the sea bottom.

2. Can the student determine the *main idea* of the paragraph? This task is very much analogous to determining a category title for a set of words. Pearson and Johnson (1978) discuss several types of main idea organizations that are useful for both assessing and teaching. Knowledge of each of these organizations can be observed by asking the student to locate the sentence that best expresses the main idea of the paragraph. The material should correspond to the student's instructional level.

  a. Explicit main idea is stated at the beginning of a paragraph.

  > Polar bears are well adapted to life in the Arctic. Their color makes them hard to see against a snowy background. A jacket of fat keeps them warm and helps them float in the water. Hair on the soles of their paws gives them good footing on ice.

  b. Explicit main idea is stated at the end of the paragraph.

  > The color of polar bears makes them hard to see against a snowy background. A jacket of fat keeps them warm and helps them float in the water. Hair on the soles of their paws gives them good footing on ice. Polar bears are well adapted to life in the Arctic.

  c. Main idea is implicit, that is, not stated.

  > The color of polar bears makes them hard to see against a snowy background. A jacket of fat keeps them warm and helps them float in the water. Hair on the soles of their paws gives them good footing on ice.

Recognizing explicit main ideas is easier than determining implicit main ideas. Both tasks are simplified by providing multiple-choice responses. Example choices should include the four types of distractors shown in the following example:

1. Polar bears are fat, hairy, and white. *(too specific)*
2. Polar bears are good swimmers. *(not mentioned)*
3. Life in the Arctic. *(too general)*
4. Polar bears are well adapted to life in the Arctic. *(right level of generality)*

Assessing Strategies for Longer Units of Written Discourse

Authors organize their ideas in such a way that an isolated paragraph may not have a main idea and can only be understood in relation to other paragraphs. Karlin (1975) emphasizes that comprehension is aided when the reader sees the relationships among ideas in a passage or story and recognizes the structure, overall function, or purpose of the material.

According to Irwin (1991), "Ideas are connected and retained in memory more effectively if they are organized around an overall organizational pattern. The main topics in an organized text make up a kind of summary. The process of synthesizing and organizing individual idea units into a summary or organized series of related general ideas can be called **macroprocessing**" (p. 4). Obviously, these relationships are more realistically studied in the context of several paragraphs or whole selections. Assessment of macroprocessing abilities may proceed as follows.

Does the student recognize **causal patterns** within a paragraph or paragraphs? Sometimes causality is cued by key words such as *because, since, for, hence, so, therefore,* and *as a result.* Many times, however, causal relations are not signaled at all, forcing the reader to provide the signal mentally. With corrective readers, both assessment and instruction should begin with the use of key words. Initially, the teacher must find out if the student recognizes cause-and-effect relationships. This is most appropriately done through direct questioning. Some examples follow. These paragraphs are read silently or orally, and students may look back at the passage after the key question is asked.

Single paragraph

The boy was being very selfish. He did not want to share his toys. *Because* of this, he played alone.

Ask: Why did the boy play alone? (Key word is in italics.)

Series of paragraphs

In the early years of our country the Mississippi River was important for both trading and travel. First it was used by the Indians, then by the Spanish explorers. Finally French fur traders used the river.

Later, the river helped many settlements get started. But *as* the railroads came, river traffic almost disappeared. Then came World War I.

As a result the United States was shipping so many goods to help fight the war, river traffic once again became important. The railroads could not carry all the goods. Today the river remains busy.

Ask: What caused Mississippi River traffic to almost disappear? Why did river traffic once again become important? (Important key words are in italics.)

Other paragraph relationships are assessed in similar fashion. Common key words (Hittleman, 1983) for the major relationships found in passages are:

- Enumeration: one, two, three, another, more, also
- Generalization: for example
- Comparison or contrast: but, however, although, yet, even though
- Sequence: first, second, third, last, before, after, while, then, later, finally
- Question and answer: why, how, when, where, what

The reader is *not* required to label the function or purpose of a paragraph or a series of paragraphs, but should be able to recognize the characteristics, or key words, for each type.

Paragraph frames (Cudd & Roberts, 1989) can also be used to assess awareness of text organizational patterns. Similar to **story frames** (Cudd & Roberts, 1987; Fowler,

1982), paragraph frames use a cloze format and provide the key words representing the organizational pattern of the text. If the material were sequentially organized, the paragraph frame would provide key words such as *first, next, then, later,* and *last* or *finally.* For example, after reading about the life cycle of a butterfly, the student would be asked to complete the following paragraph frame.

The beautiful butterfly we see in the garden has gone through four stages. First, an adult butterfly_____

_____ .

Then, _____ .

Next, _____ .

Finally, _____ .

Paragraph and story frames are not only useful for assessing awareness of text organization, but also provide a useful instructional tool for focusing on the structure of text material whether it be narrative or expository. Using story and paragraph frames for instruction is suggested later in this chapter and also in Chapter 12.

Instruction for Text Organization

No easy way has been found to improve comprehension skills. Because of the complex interrelationship among the many factors operating during comprehension, better understanding cannot be assured by having a student experience a certain activity. However, if the teacher is aware of the factors within the reader, the text, and the learning environment and tries to account for these factors in instruction, the chances for improvement appear greater.

Instructional techniques especially relevant for the poor comprehender follow and are organized according to the three major assessment categories: sentence level, paragraph level, and longer units. Underlying all comprehension instruction is the assumption that the teacher is aware of and utilizes good questioning techniques. Facilitating questions must be asked at the right times to help both the teacher and the student further understand the comprehension process. A good questioning technique models appropriate strategies and teaches students to ask themselves questions while reading; this ensures active participation and helps students realize that the material being read should and must make sense.

In summary, corrective reading students are most likely to improve in comprehension if their special needs are considered. The results of a study by Taylor (1979), especially relevant here, suggest that ineffective readers' comprehension, more so than good readers, suffers when their use of prior knowledge is restricted. Also, when provided with easy, familiar material, ineffective readers comprehend adequately. Thus the best way to begin instruction in comprehension for the corrective student is to use short, easy, familiar (in terms of background) material. For example, when students read their own writing to others, those listening might indicate they don't understand who the piece is about or how one section leads to another. Writing-group discussions help to clarify these points. The modeling that such discussions provide can effectively transfer to similar situations in reading.

Instructional Techniques for Sentences

The main purpose of instruction at the sentence level is to teach students how to note the important details of a sentence, how to use word order and punctuation to indicate the meaning of the sentence, and to realize that the same thing can be said more than one way. According to Kamm (1979), focusing on the details of a sentence is an analysis task that should begin with simple sentences such as: *The dog ran.* (Language experience and students' creative stories provide an excellent source for such sentences.) This sentence is read aloud, and the student is asked to identify the action. If the response is "running" or "ran," the sentence is shown to the student and the specific word representing the action underlined. The next question asks who or what is running, and if the student responds "the dog," the word dog is underlined twice. The student then sees "The dog ran."

Through sentence expansion (see also *add a word, stretch a sentence* in Chapter 7), the student is shown that the action and agent do not change even if words are added. For example, the sentence may be expanded to *The brown dog ran down the street.* The following sequence then applies:

- What is the action? *(ran)* Underline once.
- Who or what ran? *(dog)* Underline twice.
- What color is the dog? *(brown)*
- Where did the dog run? *(down the street)*
- How else could you describe the dog? *(black, spotted, lost, frightened)*
- Where else could the dog have run? *(away, in the house, across the street)*

A follow-up activity for this type of instruction is to transform sentences into telegrams, teaching the reader that recognition of just the important words still gives the meaning of the sentence.

Sentence expansion also allows instruction in word order. Using just the form *The brown dog ran down the street,* the student is asked, "Why might the dog run down the street?" In most responses a prepositional phrase will be added. All forms of open-ended sentences or sentence fragments aid teaching word order. For example:

The brown dog ——————— .

The brown dog ran ——————— .

Down the street ——————— .

Weaver (1979) developed a procedure for training students in sentence organization skills that was shown to transfer to reading comprehension performance. The major purpose of the technique is to teach students how to group words into organizational units. Briefly, the first step is to form word groups by identifying the action word, or verb. Then a series of questions are asked to help students group the remaining words and determine how these groups are related to the verb. Application of this technique proceeds as follows.

At first, sentences containing the words to be grouped are developed. The sentences should be short (5 to 15 words), easy for the student (i.e., containing familiar words), declarative, and in the active voice. As the student progresses, sentences increase in difficulty. Each word of the sentence is written on a separate card. No word is capitalized (except proper names and I), and no punctuation cards are included. The words are then presented to the student in scrambled order. A list of the steps of the strategy in the order to be followed is also given to the student. The teacher then demonstrates and explains how to follow the steps to unscramble the sentence. For example:

| car | to | ran |
| the | the | boy |

WH questions
1. WHo
2. WHat
3. WHere
4. WHen
5. WHy
6. HoW

Steps

1. Find the action word. (Expected response: *ran*)
2. Ask WH question, for example, "Who did this action?" (Expected response: *boy*)
3. Put the words together. (Expected response: *boy ran*)
4. Does the order make sense? (*boy ran* versus *ran boy*)
   If no, have all orders been tried?
5. Is the thought complete? If yes, go to step 7.
   If no, find helping words (auxiliary verbs, function words).
6. Go back to step 3.
7. Can the sentence be completed by adding the remaining words?
   If yes, go to step 2. If no, have all the WH questions been asked?
8. Have all the words been used? If yes, STOP. If no, go to step 2.

In this example it was possible for the student to respond that "the car ran," and this combination of words alone does make sense. However, after adding the rest of the words, "the car ran to the boy," the order is no longer sensible, and the words are reordered as directed in step 4.

This technique assumes that the student understands the concepts of verb and action word, WH questions, sensibility, and complete sentences. Eventually, a time element is introduced, and students are encouraged to keep track of their progress by trying to decrease the time required to solve the sentence anagram (i.e., as soon as the student can solve a six-word sentence within a set time limit 80 percent of the time, seven-word sentences are given). Weaver points out, however, that accuracy will probably precede speed. A student may need many opportunities for practicing and refining sentence organizational skills before becoming concerned with time.

The writing technique of sentence combining and collecting (Speaker & Speaker, 1991) can help students gain knowledge of more complicated syntactic structures—an ability that transfers to reading. For example, the sentences *The dog ran down the street* and *The dog is brown* can be combined as *The brown dog ran down the street*. (See

Chapter 7 for additional ideas.) Hughes (1975) observed that training in sentence combining was most effective for lower and middle ability students. Similarly, Neville and Searls (1991) report sentence combining has more impact on reading comprehension for elementary students.

Another aspect of sentence comprehension is synthesis (Kamm, 1979). At this stage the learner is involved in paraphrasing sentences (see *rephrasing* in Chapter 7). This **paraphrasing** takes two forms: rearrangement of the words in the sentence or substitution of words with appropriate synonyms.

One way to begin teaching paraphrasing is to provide students a set of four to seven sight words. These words are taken from students' personal word banks. The students are then shown how to form as many different sentences as possible. Each word is used only once. For example, *Bob-what-Mary-does-says* can become:

1. Bob does what Mary says.
2. Mary does what Bob says.
3. What Mary says Bob does.
4. Mary says what Bob does.
5. Bob says what Mary does.
6. What Bob says Mary does.

Once the sentences are developed, the teacher instructs the student to find those that mean the same thing and asks questions as follows. "What action goes with Bob in sentence 1?" Response: *does*. "What action goes with Mary in sentence 1?" Response: *says*. "Find any other sentences where 'Bob does' and 'Mary says' are together." Response: *sentences 3 and 4*. The conclusion to be drawn is that sentences 1, 3, and 4 mean the same thing even though the word order is different. "What about sentences 2, 5, and 6?" Response: *They have the same meaning because in all three Mary does and Bob says*.

After this kind of explicit instruction, students practice with a new set of sentences or sentence pairs. Sentences similar to those used for assessing sentence level strategies are appropriate. Instruction in comprehension should provide the student a strategy for unlocking meaning. Therefore, the teacher must ask questions that the students should ask of themselves when the time comes to work independently. Incorrect responses must be discussed as well as correct responses so that the students understand which features are important.

Comprehension instruction that focuses on deriving meaning from single sentences or pairs of sentences is also discussed by Durkin (1978/1979). She suggests providing a sentence and asking students to name everything it tells. Her example, *The little kindergarten boy was crying,* elicits the responses that tell about the boy. All the facts of the sentence are written on the board. If a student speculates on why the boy was crying, this response leads into a list of what the sentence does not tell. This latter step is an application of "negative type questions" (Willford, 1968). Such questions represent an attempt to move away from the "right answer syndrome" (Caskey, 1970) to more speculation and predicting. As an example, Willford (1968) relates:

> Watch a five or six year old. You put a picture up and say, "Okay, what can you do with a horse?" Out of a group of 10, five of them have had an experience. The others don't know what you can do with a horse. We turn it completely around and say, "What can't you do with a horse?" You ought to see the different responses we

get. Every child can tell you what you can't do with a horse. "What can't you do?" "Well you can't take a horse to bed with you." Someone else might say, "You can too if you live in a barn." This kid never thought about this. So now we find, what can you do with a horse? You can take a horse to bed with you if you live in a barn. You can flip the thing over by using a negative question as a stimulus to get a variety of answers. Kids love to do this. You may get more conversation from a single picture than any single thing you can do. (p. 103)

Sentence level instruction should move from a literal level of understanding to an implied or inferred level. Heilman and Holmes (1978), in S*muggling Language into the Teaching of Reading,* give two excellent activities for this level of instruction. To help students understand the reasoning involved, the directions and questions here have been modified.

1. Choose the best meaning for the following sentence:
   The moving van stopped in front of the empty house.
   a. The truck was probably empty.
   b. The truck was there to pick up furniture.
   c. The truck contained furniture for the people moving into the house. (p. 68)

   Questions: Why did you make the choice you made?
   What clues were in the sentence?

2. Fill in the blank. Only one word makes sense. Put two lines under any words that helped you decide what the *one* word had to be.
   a. The score was <u>tied</u> <u>seven</u> to (seven).
   b. The <u>right</u>-hand <u>glove</u> will <u>not fit</u> on your (left) hand.
   c. The <u>umpire</u> said, "(Strike) <u>three</u>, you're <u>out!</u>"

(Note how important background knowledge is at the implied or inferred level.)

At all levels of comprehension instruction, students should be directed to form mental pictures of what they are reading, and to attend to text illustrations if they are present (Gambrell & Jawitz, 1993). While an imagery strategy may not benefit all readers having comprehension difficulty, imagery instruction may facilitate the reading comprehension of readers whose reading vocabulary is adequate but whose comprehension is poor (Gambrell & Bales, 1986).

Imagery instruction begins by having students "make a picture in their heads" for specific things, such as a favorite animal or a place they have visited. These pictures are then shared so that each student can respond and listen to others' descriptions. The students are now ready to form mental pictures about the reading material. For example, if the reading contained the phrase, *As I was walking alone on that cold winter afternoon,* appropriate questions would be: "Where are you walking?" "What does the sky look like?" "How do you feel?" "How are you dressed?" Selections used for imagery instruction should not have overly elaborate descriptions. Material already rich in imagery leaves nothing for the student to visualize.

Instructional Techniques for Paragraphs

Instruction in comprehension must include teaching the reader to see the relationships among ideas in a paragraph. As with sentences, however, the corrective student must be taught literal meanings of paragraphs before implicit meanings. A technique that moves quite well from the sentence level to the paragraph level, **structured comprehension**, was developed by Marvin Cohn (1969). Cohn suggests that material selected for this technique be somewhat difficult for the students to read in their usual fashion. Passages from content area materials are recommended. Only a selection of two or three sentences is needed for this technique, as instruction proceeds sentence by sentence and can become tedious if the selection is overly long.

Once the sentences are selected, the background is given to the students to put the sentences into their appropriate context. The next step is for the students (or the teacher) to read just the first sentence aloud. Any decoding errors are simply corrected. The students are then directed to ask themselves, "Do I know what this sentence means?" They may ask the teacher as many questions as necessary to understand the sentence. Once the students' questions have been answered, the teacher asks several questions about each sentence. These questions must be prepared in advance, because Cohn recommends that certain questions always be asked if the opportunity presents itself (see below). The students may look back to the text for answers, but the answers must be written. The questions asked should require only two or three words to answer; questions requiring longer answers are put in a multiple-choice format.

Questions always to be asked seek the following information:

1. Clarification of the referent for a pronoun
2. Clarification of meaning when a word has multiple or unusual meanings
3. The meaning of figurative expressions
4. Definition of causal or other relationships left implicit

Answers for each question are discussed. For incorrect answers, the teacher demonstrates why they are incorrect and explains the reasoning behind the correct answer. Correct answers, when put back into the text, make sense; incorrect answers do not. This procedure also helps students *demand* that material read be meaningful.

Initially Cohn recommends that literal meanings be stressed more than relationships or implied information. Beginning with emphasis on the literal meaning provides more success for students and also allows them the opportunity to develop appropriate questioning techniques. The passive reader may become more actively involved through this process. Possible teacher questions for an example structured comprehension lesson can be examined in Figure 10.1.

Another technique, similar to structured comprehension, is called the **ReQuest Procedure** (*Re*ciprocal *Quest*ioning Procedure) developed by Anthony Manzo (1969, 1985). This procedure, which is used with individuals or small groups, aids students in setting their own purposes for reading. The teacher guides the students through the silent reading of as many sentences of a selection as are necessary to enable them to complete the passage independently. Once again, as in structured comprehension, questions are exchanged by student and teacher, sentence by sentence. Every question asked by a student or teacher must be answered from recall, or an explanation must be given for why it cannot be answered. The teacher's questions serve as models for the kinds of questions students should ask of themselves while reading. Also, when responding to students' questions, the teacher gives reinforcement such as "That was an excellent question" or "You might want to reword the question in this way . . ." or "I think your questions are really improving." When the teacher thinks students are ready to proceed independently (no more than three paragraphs should be handled reciprocally), a general purpose-setting question is asked: "Did we raise the best question or purpose for which to read this selection?" (Manzo, 1985). At this point, the rest of the selection is read silently.

Both of these techniques help move the student from literal understanding of sentences to understanding the relationship between sentences, and eventually to understanding entire selections. The techniques also actively involve the students in the comprehension process by having them ask questions about meaning and by emphasizing the importance of expecting material to make sense.

A technique born of Manzo's original ReQuest Procedure, which proceeds in a paragraph-by-paragraph manner, is called **reciprocal teaching** (Palincsar & Brown, 1984, 1986). Reciprocal teaching is an interactive procedure in which students are taught

---

FIGURE

10.1

Structured comprehension lesson.

Background: The student is told that the Constitution is a list of the rights that the American people have. Soon after the Constitution was written, the people wanted to add more rights. These additional rights are called the Bill of Rights.

Passage: "The Bill of Rights says that every person can speak freely. A person can criticize the government or its officials if he believes that they are not doing a good job. We call this freedom of speech."
—Herbert H. Gross, et al., *Exploring Regions of the Western Hemisphere*

Questions

Sentence 1

1. Does "speak freely" mean you won't have to pay before speaking?
2. Is the Bill of Rights a person?
3. How can the Bill of Rights "say" anything?
4. This sentence means:
   a. that the Bill of Rights thinks no one should have to pay to speak
   b. an important right of all people is to be able to say whatever they think is important to say
   c. a new law was passed that has cured people who couldn't speak, so that now they can speak

Sentence 2

1. What does "criticize" mean?
2. What does "its" refer to?
3. Who does "he" refer to?
4. Who does "they" refer to?
5. This sentence means:
   a. if the government or the people who are leaders in the government are not doing a good job, anybody can say that they aren't
   b. when the government does not do a good job, the people must believe that they are doing a good job anyway
   c. it is impossible for the government to do a bad job

Sentence 3

1. Who does "we" refer to?
2. What does "this" refer to?
3. "Freedom of speech" means no one can charge to hear a speech. True or false?
4. This sentence means:
   a. all people have the right to speak out if the government does not do what it's supposed to do
   b. the Bill of Rights is also called freedom of speech
   c. the government can say anything it wants to for free

to summarize sections of text, anticipate questions that a teacher may ask, make predictions about upcoming text, and clarify unclear sections of text. Initially, the teacher plays a major instructional role by modeling these behaviors and helping students in a collaborative effort with the wording of summaries and questions. Working specifically with seventh graders who were described as adequate decoders but poor comprehenders,[2] Palincsar and Brown were able to train the students to use the comprehension-monitoring behaviors listed above after only 15 to 20 sessions. They also trained classroom teachers to use the technique with similar success.

Reciprocal teaching can be used with either individuals or small groups. (For best results with poor comprehenders, use small groups of 2–3 students.) In any case, the adult teacher takes turns with each student participant role-playing "teacher" and leads a dialogue on a section of text read, usually a paragraph. After each section, the "teacher" asks a main idea question. If this is difficult, a summary is attempted. A clarification of some aspect of the text may be asked for, or a prediction about upcoming text may be given. Feedback and praise are given by the adult teacher whenever appropriate. In group sessions, feedback also comes from other students.

Early training sessions require much guidance from the teacher. As students become better able to summarize and ask main idea questions, the teacher's level of participation decreases. Sessions should last about 30 minutes. Although Palincsar and Brown worked with expository passages of about 1,500 words, any type or length of reading material can be used.

Sometimes the problem of not understanding material can be attributed to inappropriate phrasing. Even material used in a structured comprehension lesson can be rewritten into phrase units to aid the reader. This technique, referred to as *chunking* (Walker, 1992), "facilitates comprehension and fluency by using thought units rather than word-by-word reading" (p. 146). An example from Heilman and Holmes (1978, p. 127) follows.

This material
is written
in short phrases
so that you
can practice
seeing words
in thought units.
This helps you
read faster.
However,
remember also
that reading
in phrases
or thought units
helps the reader
get the meaning.

Echo reading (see earlier discussion in Chapter 9) can also be used to model appropriate phrasing.

---

[2]The students decoded at least 80 words per minute with a maximum of 2 words per minute incorrect and were two grades or more behind on a standardized reading comprehension test.

Before readers can determine the main idea of a paragraph or see relationships between ideas, they must be able to identify significant details. Newspaper articles are a ready source of material that lends itself to the kind of questioning involved in teaching students to look for details. The following questions may be asked regarding the article in Figure 10.2.

1. Who was involved in this event? *(residents of the nursing home, policemen, firemen)*
2. What took place? *(a fire)*
3. Where did it take place? *(Bryn Mawr Nursing Home in Minneapolis, Minnesota)*
4. When did it take place? *(Saturday, September 22)*
5. How or why did it take place? *(Police believe the fire was caused by arson.)*

Menus, recipes, and directions are additional sources of written materials rich in details for one main idea.

FIGURE
10.2

Example of newspaper article that helps students look for details.

The Times-Picayune	Sunday, September 23

Nursing Home Hit in Arson?

By JOHN LUNDQUIST

MINNEAPOLIS (AP) - Police said they believe the nursing home fire which claimed the life of one elderly resident and injured three others Saturday was the work of an arsonist.

A 38-year-old female resident of the Bryn Mawr Nursing Home, who was not identified, was taken into custody about 3½ hours after the blaze broke out, police said.

Charges were not filed immediately, police said.

Teams of firemen who responded to the three-alarm blaze helped many of the elderly at the home to safety from second floor windows. The residents were carried down ladders in rescue baskets or down stairways in their wheelchairs.

One fireman, Jeff Bartholomew, about 30, suffered smoke inhalation when he took off his mask and put it over the face of a woman he helped out of the two-story building, said Capt. Cecil Klingbile, one of the station fire chiefs on the scene.

"He took a lot of smoke when he did that," said Klingbile, who aided in the rescue.

Bartholomew was treated and released.

The Hennepin County medical examiner identified the dead woman as Fanny Anttila, 85.

Two elderly women in serious condition suffering from smoke inhalation were identified as Rose Seiger, 80, and Esther Cotter, 79.

A 75-year-old man, whose identification was being withheld until relatives had been notified, was in critical condition with second-degree burns.

Twenty-five other people were taken to hospitals but they were not admitted. David Lesperance, associate administrator, said they were "disposition cases," meaning the hospital was arranging accommodations for them.

One of the displaced residents was Richard Fobes, 71, who sat in a waiting room with his two sons.

"I was sitting in the recreation room on the first floor when the fire broke out," he said. "They (nursing home workers) told us to get in our rooms, and pretty soon they came and got us outside."

Fire Capt. Ronald Knoke said 44 firefighters from nine engine and four hook-and-ladder companies answered the alarm.

He said the fire was discovered at 9:54 a.m. (CDT) in the closet of a resident room, then spread down the hall to other parts of the second floor. Firefighters had the blaze under control at 10:28 a.m.

Knoke said most of the danger was from smoke, because of the age of the residents.

From *New Orleans Times-Picayune*. Used with permission of the Associated Press, New York.

Instruction in main ideas begins by using material with a topic sentence that explicitly states the main idea. Using the paragraph about polar bears discussed earlier, the student is first directed to find the key words or significant details, words that occur more than once, and a sentence that summarizes these details. The following questions might be asked:

What do most of the key words seem to point out?

What key words occur more than once?

What do these words relate to?

Is there a sentence that summarizes these ideas?

Polar bears are well adapted to life in the Arctic. Their color makes them hard to see against a snowy background. A jacket of fat keeps them warm and helps them float in the water. Hair on the soles of their paws gives them good footing on ice.

The first step is to underline key words, as shown in the paragraph. These key words aid in determining the significant details. In searching for recurring words, students are first led to discover the pronoun referents. Ask: "Who or what is the first sentence about?" Response: *polar bears*. Ask: "Who or what does the word *their* refer to in the second sentence?" Response: *polar bears*. "In the same sentence you see the word *them*. What does *them* refer to?" Response: *polar bears*. In actuality then, the term *polar bears* occurs quite frequently in this paragraph, which is a clue to the main topic of the paragraph. Significant details about polar bears should then be discussed by asking, "What does this paragraph tell us about polar bears?" A diagram may be used, such as that shown in Figure 10.3, and compared to students' maps used for prewriting to demonstrate how reading and writing are connected.

Going back to the paragraph, ask, "Can you choose one sentence that includes all of the supporting details or summarizes those details?" Elicit the response that the first sentence does this. Explain why this sentence summarizes the others if students have difficulty (1) recognizing that the first sentence describes the main idea of the paragraph or (2) determining why polar bears are well adapted to life in the Arctic.

Diagram for denoting main ideas and supporting details in the polar bear paragraph.

FIGURE

10.3

The usefulness of activities such as the structured comprehension lesson for teaching paragraph understanding should now be apparent. Instruction in this area helps the student know what to look for in a paragraph to determine its meaning. After instruction, the following activities should be easier for students:

1. Find the sentence that does not belong in this paragraph.

> Tommy was baking a cake for Mother's birthday. He sifted flour, added two eggs, and put it in the oven to bake. It seemed to take forever to be done. At last the potatoes were ready. The frosting was chocolate with marshmallows. (Heilman & Holmes, 1978, p. 65)

Possible questions to ask regarding this paragraph are:

- What is this paragraph about?
- Which sentence doesn't seem to belong? Why?

2. In this activity, the student attempts to determine implied information.

> Tomorrow is the big day. John has been practicing ever since school started. Now is his chance to show all his friends his special tricks. This is the time of year when spooky things are really popular. He doesn't even need to wear a costume to scare people. After the parade the older kids get to put on a show for the little ones. Gee! It will be great fun to see their faces turn white. It's a good thing it will be on the last day of the school week. They will have the weekend to recover from their fright. (Heilman & Holmes, 1978, p. 70)

- What day of the week will something important take place?

    a. Saturday   b. Sunday   c. Friday

To help students answer this question, the teacher directs their attention to the appropriate sentences. "What sentences in the paragraph mention the word *day*?" Response: *first and eighth sentences.* "Does the first sentence help us to know what day it is?" Response: *no, only tomorrow.* "What about the eighth sentence?" Response: *yes, the last day of the school week is Friday.*

- What holiday do you think it is?

    a. Halloween   b. Fourth of July   c. Easter

Once again the relevant sentences are discussed. First, the teacher elicits key words associated with Halloween, Fourth of July, and Easter. Next, the students look for key words in the paragraph. Once the words *spooky, costume, trick, scare,* and *fright,* elicited for Halloween, are also found in the paragraph, the holiday becomes apparent.

- How long has John been practicing?

    a. about two weeks   b. about two months   c. about two hours

Ask: "What sentence mentions practicing?" Response: *the second sentence.* "When does school start?" Response: *late August or early September.* "When is Halloween?" Response: *late October.* "How much time is between late August or early September and late October?" Response: *about two months.*

As noted before, prior knowledge and experience are important for success in implied information activities. Most of the guiding questions require the readers to think about something they already know or have experienced. Additional activities and discussion of implicit main ideas can be found in Pearson and Johnson's (1978) *Teaching Reading Comprehension* (Chapter 5).

The questions in the foregoing examples represent the direction that instruction in paragraph comprehension should take. Students must be shown explicitly how to deal with paragraph information. Teachers instruct best by modeling or thinking out loud with their students to reveal the strategies they themselves use. Once shown the strategy, students can practice and apply this type of thinking to material read independently. They can write their own paragraphs and plan a lesson for transmitting the main idea to other students. This gives students the opportunity to practice the question-asking strategies involved.

Instructional Techniques for Longer Units

One major difference between good and poor comprehenders is that good comprehenders apparently organize material as they read, but poor comprehenders do not. While the poor comprehender must learn organizational techniques, in the interim the reader should receive as much help as possible in organizing the material. Most of this instruction will guide students in asking the right questions about the textual material they read. Instruction is geared toward helping students think about what they already know in relation to what they are reading, and organize what is being read while reading.

Teachers should not overlook the value of group discussion. Goldenberg (1992/1993) discusses "instructional conversations" as discussion-based lessons intended to support and enhance students' conceptual and linguistic development. Figure 10.4 shows the elements of instructional conversations (ICs) with brief descriptions for each. The teacher's responsibility becomes one of weaving students' prior knowledge, experiences, and discussion comments and contributions into the ten elements. Interested readers are referred to the original source for an example exchange in an instructional conversation.

Standard instructional techniques, such as Stauffer's (1981) *directed reading–thinking activity (DRTA)* (see Figure 10.5), can be modified to suit the particular needs of students having difficulty in comprehension. Other recommended comprehension instructional techniques are Hennings' (1991) essential reading in which students survey text to predict the main idea of the selection before reading; Gillespie's (1990), Helfeldt and Henk's (1990), Manzo's (1969), and Singer's (1978) emphasis on student involvement in questioning for comprehension; and Manzo's (1975, 1985) *guided reading procedure (GRP)*. Semantic webbing (or mapping), a visual technique that specifically aids readers in organizing what they read, can be used to improve comprehension (Freedman & Reynolds, 1980; Reutzel, 1985; Sinatra, Stahl-Gemake, & Berg, 1984). Some types of cloze training (Aulls, 1978; Carr, Dewitz, & Patberg, 1989) also aid comprehension of longer selections.

The goal of all of these instructional techniques is to help students become more actively involved with text. Instruction focuses on encouraging flexibility, risk taking, and depth of thinking. Questions mold the student's thinking, rather than test for right and wrong answers. As Schwartz and Sheff (1975, pp. 151–152) state, "Instruction should provide a type of questioning that consciously directs the reader to become involved in understanding what he reads."

Examples cannot be given for all of the techniques mentioned, so you are strongly encouraged to consult the original sources. Cooper's (1986) *Improving Reading Comprehension*, Goodman and Burke's (1980) *Reading Strategies: Focus on Comprehension*, Irwin's (1992) *Teaching Reading Comprehension Processes*, Irwin and Baker's (1989) *Promoting Active Reading Comprehension Strategies*, and McNeil's (1992) *Reading Comprehension*, provide examples for some of these techniques and others as well.

Detailed examples for several comprehension instructional techniques are provided here. Some aid students in organizing the material they read, others encourage self-questioning while reading. All initially require teacher modeling.

Semantic webbing, also called **mapping**, constructs a visual display representing relationships in the content of a story or expository selection (Freedman & Reynolds, 1980; Davidson, 1982). The technique is especially helpful for readers with difficulties, because it visually demonstrates how main ideas are logically related to subordinate ideas (Sinatra, Stahl-Gemake, & Berg, 1984).

Four steps are basic in constructing a web, or map.

1. Answer the *core question.*
2. Use the answers to the core question as *web strands.*
3. Provide *strand supports,* facts, events, inferences, and generalizations taken from the story that distinguish one web strand from another.

FIGURE

10.4

Elements of instructional conversation.

Instructional Elements

1. *Thematic focus.* The teacher selects a theme or ideas to serve as a starting point for focusing the discussion and has a general plan for how the theme will unfold, including how to "chunk" the text to permit optimal exploration of the theme.

2. *Activation and use of background and relevant schemata.* The teacher either "hooks into" or provides students with pertinent background knowledge and relevant schemata necessary for understanding a text. Background knowledge and schemata are then woven into the discussion that follows.

3. *Direct teaching.* When necessary, the teacher provides direct teaching of a skill or concept.

4. *Promotion of more complex language and expression.* The teacher elicits more extended student contributions by using a variety of elicitation techniques—invitations to expand (e.g., "Tell me more about that"), questions (e.g., "What do you mean?"), restatements (e.g., "In other words,—"), and pauses.

5. *Elicitation of bases for statements or positions.* The teacher promotes students' use of text, pictures, and reasoning to support an argument or position. Without overwhelming students, the teacher probes for the bases of students' statements—e.g., "How do you know?" "What makes you think that?" "Show us where it says _____ ."

Conversational Elements

6. *Fewer "known-answer" questions.* Much of the discussion centers on questions and answers for which there might be more than one correct answer.

7. *Responsivity to student contributions.* While having an initial plan and maintaining the focus and coherence of the discussion, the teacher is also responsive to students' statements and the opportunities they provide.

8. *Connected discourse.* The discussion is characterized by multiple, interactive, connected turns; succeeding utterances build upon and extend previous ones.

9. *A challenging, but nonthreatening, atmosphere.* The teacher creates a "zone of proximal development," where a challenging atmosphere is balanced by a positive affective climate. The teacher is more collaborator than evaluator and creates an atmosphere that challenges students and allows them to negotiate and construct the meaning of the text.

10. *General participation, including self-selected turns.* The teacher encourages general participation among students. The teacher does not hold exclusive right to determine who talks, and students are encouraged to volunteer or otherwise influence the selection of speaking turns.

Example lesson using directed reading–thinking activity (DRTA).

A DRTA lesson usually contains the following components which will be highlighted in the example presented.

   I. Building Background for the Reading Selection

  II. The DRTA Cycle

      a. Students set purposes, make predictions

      b. Silent reading

      c. Students verify predictions, satisfy purposes

 III. Comprehension Check

 IV. Rereading Parts of the Selection for Specific Purposes

  V. Enrichment, or Follow-Up, Activities

DRTA Lesson

Teacher Goals:

1. To help students discover how to use the clues in text to anticipate upcoming text using both prior knowledge and context clues

2. To expose students to a more expository (informational) writing style

Student Objectives:

1. Each student will participate in the lesson by:

      a. offering answers to the opening riddle

      b. making predictions about what (who) the text will be about

      c. verifying their predictions by citing evidence in the text

      d. answering comprehension questions following the silent reading and verification of predictions

      e. writing their own "first person" riddle

Materials:

Text: *A Not So Ugly Friend* by Stan Applebaum and Victoria Cox. This text is from The Satellite Books published by Holt, Rinehart and Winston and is a Level 10 book, meaning it is intended for use with second-semester second grade readers. The text begins by using a riddle format, each page providing clues for the reader about what is being described—in other words, who is the "not so ugly friend." For example, from the first page: "I can't see you. I have no eyes, but I can feel you walking. I have no nose, but I have a mouth and I can taste. Do you know what I am?" Midway through the book the answer to the riddle is revealed, and then the book becomes informational about the earthworm and how valuable earthworms are to us—why we should consider them friends.

Procedures:

To develop *background* for this lesson, introduce the idea of "first person" riddles, as the text is written in this format. It may be an unusual format for the students. These "practice" riddles will relate to people and things very familiar in the students' lives. In teaching new concepts it is much better to relate the unfamiliar to the familiar. For example, one practice

continued

FIGURE

10.5 *continued*

riddle is: "I am something you drink. I come from a cow, and I'm white. Babies really like me a lot. Do you know what I am?" The riddles will be on individual index cards so that students can take turns reading them. After each riddle is solved, students must tell what the important clues were in the riddle that helped them solve it. At this point, students should be anxious to solve yet one more riddle, the one in the text.

The *DRTA Cycle* will begin by introducing the title of the selection. Students will be told that this text is written like the riddles they just solved. The cover of the text may also be used if desired. Predictions will be made based on the key question, "What or who do you think is the not so ugly friend?" Students' predictions will be written on the chalkboard. Once all predictions are made, each student is asked to choose one they think is correct. Their purpose for reading then is to verify whether or not their prediction is accurate. With this text, proceed one page at a time, reading silently. After each page, students will reevaluate their predictions, and make changes, although they must be able to use the clues to justify their changes or new predictions. Once the answer is revealed in the text, discuss the clues as a group. At this point a new key question is introduced, "What does the earthworm do for us?" Again, write their ideas on the board. Students again read the rest of the selection silently to verify their predictions. Discuss their predictions and which ones were supported and what new information they discovered.

The questions for the *comprehension check* include vocabulary items that may be new or are important to the understanding of the text. Sample questions are:

1. Who is this book about? (earthworm) *textually explicit*
2. Who is telling the story? (earthworm) *textually implicit*
3. Can earthworms *really* talk? (no) *scriptally implicit*
4. What is soil? (dirt, earth) *scriptally implicit; possibly textually implicit*
5. What does it mean to make the soil richer? (better for plants, helps plants grow better, provides nutrients) *scriptally implicit*
6. Why does the earthworm come out of the ground when it rains? (because the water fills the earthworm's underground hole) *textually implicit*
7. Why doesn't the earthworm like to be out in the sun? (because the sun dries out its skin) *textually implicit*
8. Where do earthworms come from (or how are they born)? (eggs) *textually explicit*
9. What did you learn about earthworms that you did not know before? (answers will vary) *textually explicit, textually implicit*
10. Can we think of earthworms as our friends? (yes, no, give reasons) *scriptally implicit, textually implicit, textually explicit*

Following the questions, students will be asked to *reread for the specific purpose* of completing a semantic map of the selection to help them organize what they have read. The core question of the map is, "What does an earthworm do?" The students are allowed to look back to the text since this is a rereading activity. Each idea can then be read aloud if desired.

The *enrichment* activity for this lesson should be done individually. The students are to write three "first person" riddles that ask "Who Am I?" or "What Am I?" as their last line. These can then be posted later for other students to solve.

4. Decide what *strand ties* exist, that is, how strands are related to each other. (Dotted lines may be used to indicate strand ties, or locations on the map itself, such as grouping.)

Before using a semantic web with students, the teacher must organize the content of the selection conceptually. For instance, in step 1, the core question, the focus of the web for *The Three Little Pigs,* is chosen by the teacher (Fig. 10.6) and placed in a central position. Answers to the core question elicited through discussion (i.e., the eight characters) become the web strands. The strand supports are facts, events, inferences, and generalizations that distinguish the characters from one another. Strand ties in this example are represented by placing the man with straw beside Pig #1, the man with twigs beside Pig #2, and so forth. Placement in sequential order also indicates the repetitive pattern in this story. The relationship between Pig #3 and the wolf is actually more complex than the strand supports in the figure indicate, however. The story contains a series of episodes in which the wolf tries to trick the pig and the pig outsmarts the wolf. If the teacher thinks further exploration of a part of the web would be beneficial, a section such as the relationship between the wolf and Pig #3 may be enlarged to examine the more complex relationships.

Questions and activities based on **story grammar** (a structure that describes the elements essential to a well-formed story; see also Chapter 7) may improve students' comprehension by enhancing their schemata for narrative material (Fitzgerald & Spiegel, 1983) and their level of involvement during reading (Dimino, Gersten, Carnine, & Blake, 1990). In Mandler and Johnson's (1977) story grammar, the story elements are described as: a setting (who, where, and when); a beginning or initiating event (the problem for the hero); a reaction (what the hero says or does in response to the problem); a goal (what the hero decides to do about the problem); an attempt (the effort or efforts to solve the problem); an outcome (the consequence or result of what the hero does); and an ending (a brief wrap-up of the whole story).

Dimino, Gersten, Carnine, and Blake (1990) investigated the use of story grammar as a framework for improving at-risk high school students' comprehension and recall of short stories. Four categories of story grammar components were modeled, explained, and practiced: conflict/problem, character information, attempts/resolution/twist, and reaction/theme. Student engagement in lessons approached in this way was high. As a result these researchers conclude that "it is unfair to deprive low-track students of the potentially rich and stimulating experiences of analyzing and discussing works by authors such as Nathaniel Hawthorne, Dorothy Parker, Toni Morrison, or Guy de Maupassant simply because their reading ability is not as high as their peers" (p. 19).

Sadow (1982, p. 520) suggests five generic questions to be asked about stories:

1. Where and when did the events in the story take place and who was involved in them? *(setting)*
2. What started the chain of events in the story? *(initiating event)*
3. What was the main character's reaction to this event? *(reaction)*
4. What did the main character do about it? *(action: goals and attempts)*
5. What happened as a result of what the main character did? *(consequence, outcome)*

A format such as that in Figure 10.7 can help students see the structure of stories. Or, a story frame (Cudd & Roberts, 1987; Fowler, 1982) can be provided, as shown in Figure 10.8.

F I G U R E   Semantic web for *The Three Little Pigs.*

10.6

Story map for *Goldilocks and the Three Bears*.

Character(s) and Setting	Goldilocks, Papa Bear, Mama Bear, Baby Bear Bear's house in the woods

Problem	Goldilocks goes into bears' house while they are out.

Goal	Goldilocks decided to make herself right at home.

P
L
O
T

Event	She tasted the bears' porridge and ate Baby Bear's.

Event	She sat in the bears' chairs and broke Baby Bear's.

Event	She lay down on the bears' beds and fell asleep on Baby Bear's.

Resolution	The 3 bears came home, found their porridge tasted, their chairs sat in, and Goldilocks in bed. She woke up and ran away.

A story frame.

Title: *Goldilocks and the Three Bears*

In this story, the problems start when _____

_____

After that, _____

_____

Next, _____

_____

Then, _____

_____

This was a problem because _____

_____

After that, _____

_____

Next, _____

_____

Then, _____

_____

The problem was solved when _____

_____

In the end, _____

_____

Questions based on story grammar and asked in conjunction with developing story maps help students see the underlying organization of ideas and relationships in a story (Beck & McKeown, 1981). For instance, in *The Three Little Pigs,* once the web strands (characters) are identified, the initiating event is asked about in order to begin eliciting information about each strand: "What caused the three pigs to go out on their own?" The responses provide strand supports for the old sow. Likewise, the reaction (in this example, three separate reactions for each pig) is elicited by asking: "What does each pig decide to do?" The goals, attempts, and outcomes follow by asking: "What does Pig #1 (Pig #2, Pig #3) decide to build?" "What is the first problem for the pigs?" "What happens to Pig #1?" "What is the next problem for the pigs?" "What happens to Pig #2?" "What is the problem for Pig #3?" "What happens to Pig #3?" "How is Pig #3 different from Pig #1 and Pig #2?" The ending is addressed by a question regarding a theme or a moral, such as, "Which pig is the hero, and why?" These questions develop the story map; however, questioning in the form of extension or enrichment can continue once the map (web) is completed.

Another strategy that shows students how story features relate to each other is *find the features and connect them* (Richards, Gipe & Necaise, 1993). The teacher first familiarizes students with the basic story feature terms of character, setting, problem, and solution. Then the connection strategy is introduced by using a familiar story and discussing the way two elements are connected. Figure 10.9 shows one way in which this discussion might be recorded for students to examine. Students can also use such a chart for prewriting, to plan their creative stories.

Semantic webs may also be introduced in incomplete form as organizers in advance of reading or writing. In an example suggested by Cleland (1981) and seen in Figure 10.10, three distinct responses are indicated; students reading the selection will know to look for three major reasons for Joel's decision. A similar approach but one that provides more detail from the story is the cloze story map (Reutzel, 1986).

The real benefit from using semantic webs and charts comes from the discussion that the teacher directs. The teacher guides the students in constructing the web or chart by pointing out relationships between ideas and characters and events in the material read. Such techniques are *not* reserved for stories, but like DRTAs, work as well with expository material. In using content area material, Davidson (1982) observed that "as students interact with one another by sharing maps and asking questions about various elements in each others' maps, they gain insights about the various reasoning processes

Example of story feature chart.

FIGURE

10.9

Student's Name David Story Title Goldilocks and the Three Bears		
FIND THE FEATURES AND CONNECT THEM		
Story Feature: Characters	Story Feature: Setting	The Connection
Mama Bear Papa Bear Baby Bear Goldilocks	the Woods	The bears lived in the woods. Goldilocks lived near the woods. Goldilocks walked in the woods.
Story Feature: Problem	Story Feature: Solution	The Connection
The porridge was too hot to eat.	The bears went a walk.	Some of the porridge got cool while the bears were gone.

FIGURE

10.10

Using semantic webs as advance organizers.

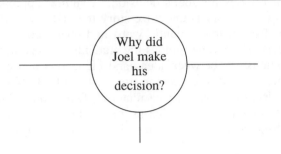

used by others" (p. 56). For detailed examples of a wide variety of mapping ideas, refer to Heimlich and Pittelman's (1986) *Semantic Mapping: Classroom Applications.*

Reutzel[3] summarizes the ways story maps, webs, and charts help teachers and students to

- plan and execute more purposeful, focused reading lessons;
- organize readers' efforts toward specific comprehension objectives;
- focus questions and discussion on the important aspects of the text;
- create a workable structure for storage and retrieval of important information learned from the text;
- provide a visually coherent summary of the text;
- furnish a structure for guiding prereading experiences;
- supply students with a model for organizing and integrating text information in the content areas;
- present events and concepts in divergent visual patterns designed to emphasize specific types of relationships;
- experience a visual representation of text arrangements to encourage sensitivity to varying text patterns;
- summon the correct collection of background experiences and knowledge to facilitate comprehension of the text;
- encourage students to think about and monitor their reading. (See Chapter 12.)

Unfortunately, many young readers and readers with difficulties have trouble relating to the human element in stories. While they may be able to name the characters in a story, these students cannot identify with the characters or understand their feelings, goals, or motives. Comprehension is certainly affected in these cases. Developing a *getting to know my character* map (Richards & Gipe, 1993; Tompkins & Hoskisson, 1991) may help students better understand stories they read, as well as develop broader social understanding in general. Through modeling and explanation of the teacher's own think-

[3]From "Story Maps Improve Comprehension," by D. Ray Reutzel, *Reading Teacher,* January 1985, page 403. Reprinted with permission of the author and the International Reading Association, Newark, Delaware.

ing, both descriptive and inferred information about a main character is discussed and placed on a map (see Figure 10.11).

Dramatizing material read can also enhance comprehension. In addition to the reading and rereading required to prepare a drama production, activities that accompany these productions, such as preparing backdrops, deciding on props, and conducting library research to verify content, help comprehension. Bidwell (1990) lists several ideas and ways to use drama in the classroom for the purposes of increasing motivation, comprehension, and fluency. Cooter and Chilcoat (1990) focus on the use of melodramas to build understanding of expository text. "Melodrama, as applied to historical

Example of a character map.

GETTING TO KNOW MY CHARACTER

Story **The Balancing Girl** My Character **Margaret**

FACTS ABOUT MY CHARACTER
1. Margaret was good at balancing.
2. She could balance books on her head.
3. She used a wheelchair.
4. She used crutches.

WHAT I KNOW ABOUT MY CHARACTER'S ACTIONS
1. Margaret made a private corner.
2. She worked all morning and made a domino castle.
3. She was careful.
4. She liked to work alone.
5. She could be quiet.
6. She could concentrate.

WHAT I KNOW ABOUT MY CHARACTER'S CONVERSATION
1. Margaret spoke up to Tommy.
2. She could tell that Tommy had knocked down her castle.
3. She was brave to speak up to Tommy.

WHAT I KNOW ABOUT MY CHARACTER'S THOUGHTS
Margaret thought, "oh no" when some dominoes fell down. She was very worried. Margaret said to herself, "Thank goodness", when the dominoes stopped falling. She was happy and relieved.

From Janet C. Richards and Joan P. Gipe, "Recognizing Information About Story Characters: A Strategy for Young and At-Risk Readers," *The Reading Teacher, 47,* Copyright © 1993 by the International Reading Association. Reprinted with permission of Janet C. Richards and Joan P. Gipe and the International Reading Association.

instruction, is an expository text response activity that uses sensational action, exuberant emotions, and somewhat stereotyped characterization to present a message about history" (p. 274). A similar response can be made to narrative material. The reading/writing connection is made most clear in preparing these productions as writing a plot, developing characters, and final script writing are revised and edited.

The ultimate goal of all reading instruction is to develop independent readers. Comprehension instruction must bring the corrective reader to the point of active communication with the text. While this kind of involvement is encouraged with the student–teacher interaction found in the structured comprehension lesson, for example, the teacher must also teach students to *ask themselves* questions about what they are reading. The teacher-posed questions of a structured comprehension lesson or a DRTA provide models for students. However, a gradual transfer from teacher-posed to student-posed questions is desirable in developing independent readers (Gillespie, 1990). This transfer, referred to by Singer (1978) as the **phase-out/phase-in strategy,** promotes active comprehension.

A most important procedure for teaching active comprehension is to ask a question that requires another question as the response. Using "The Hare and the Fox" seen in Figure 10.12, a lesson may proceed as follows with the teacher asking questions to elicit initial student questions.

Teacher: "Look at the title. What questions could you ask about this story after reading just the title?"

F I G U R E

10.12

Teaching active comprehension.

The Hare and the Fox

A small, brown hare was sitting near a creek sunning himself, when he saw a fox. The fox was getting a drink in the small stream.

The hare ran from his nest, but the fox saw him hopping in the grass. Quick as a wink, the fox was running to catch the hare.

The brown hare ran into a hole in an old log. The hole was too small for a fox.

As the hare ran from the hole, he saw the fox digging to get into it.

When the fox got inside the old log, he did not find a hare. All he saw was a hole as long as the log.

"The Hare and the Fox." From *Basic Reading*, Book C. © J. B. Lippincott Company, 1975, p. 37. Used by permission.

Possible student questions:

    "What will the hare and the fox be doing?"

    "What is a hare?"

    "What will happen to the hare?"

    "What will happen to the fox?"

    "Will the fox chase the hare?"

    "Will the fox catch and eat the hare?"

    "Will the hare get away?"

The teacher then asks questions paragraph by paragraph.

Teacher, paragraph 1: "What else would you like to know about the hare? What else about the fox?"

Possible student questions:

    "Is it a baby hare?"

    "Is the hare a fast runner?"

    "Is the fox a fast runner?"

    "Is the fox hungry?"

Teacher, paragraph 2: "What would you like to know more about when the fox starts running to catch the hare?"

Possible student questions:

    "Will the fox catch the hare?"

    "Will the hare get away?"

Teacher, paragraph 3: "Is there anything you'd like to know when the hare runs into the log?"

Possible student questions:

    "Will the hare be safe?"

    "Will the fox get in the log?"

    "Will the fox wait for the hare to come out of the log?"

Teacher, paragraph 4: "What would you like to ask when the hare runs from the log?"

Possible student questions:

    "Why did the hare run from the log?"

    "Is the fox waiting outside to catch the hare?"

    "Where will the hare run to next?"

    "Will the fox be able to catch the hare?"

Teacher, paragraph 5: "After you read the last paragraph, what questions about the hare and the fox do you still have?"

Possible student questions:

    "Did the fox run out of the log to chase the hare some more?"

    "Where did the hare go?"

    "Did the hare get away from the fox?"

    "What happened to the fox and the hare next?"

This lesson sequence supplies example questions for each paragraph in order to provide more explicit practice for the corrective reader. This procedure is not necessary for every lesson, however. The teacher may receive such a variety of questions at the initial stage that the students will be motivated enough to read the rest of the story. When students are able to find answers to their own questions, they become active comprehenders. In this particular example, the reader is not told in the text what happens to the characters. Answers to the last set of questions could be used as the basis for creative writing or a language experience story. In any case, the students become involved in reading; situations or problems are identified, and further understandings are sought while reading. Comprehension is the result.

Corrective readers also benefit from direct instruction in how to answer questions. They need to know about the different sources of information available for answering questions (Raphael & Pearson, 1985). As Raphael (1982) has pointed out, many poor comprehenders do not realize that it is both acceptable and necessary to use one's prior knowledge about the world to answer some types of comprehension questions. Thus instruction in **question–answer relationships (QARs)** is especially helpful.

Raphael's classification scheme for QARs is based on Pearson and Johnson's (1978) question taxonomy of **textually explicit** (the answer to the question is directly stated in one sentence in the text), **textually implicit** (the answer to the question is in the text but requires some integration of text material, as the answer might span several sentences or paragraphs), and **scriptally implicit** (the answer must come from the reader's prior knowledge).

In Raphael's original scheme, the first question–answer relationship (QAR) was termed *right there* because the answer is directly stated in a single sentence. The second QAR was termed *think and search* because the answer requires information that spans several sentences or paragraphs. The third QAR was termed *on my own* because readers must rely totally on their own background knowledge for the answer.

After conducting several research studies, Raphael (1986) revised her classifications to include a fourth QAR, *author and me,* which recognizes that for some questions the answer comes from the reader's background knowledge, but only in connection with information provided by the author. The revised classification scheme now consists of two main categories, *in the book* and *in my head; right there* and *putting it together* (formerly *think and search*) falling under *in the book;* and *author and me* and *on my own* falling under *in my head.*

An introductory lesson in QARs must first define all the question types. Using the nursery rhyme *Little Miss Muffet,* consider the following questions as examples of each type.

> Little Miss Muffet sat on a tuffet,
> Eating her curds and whey.
> Along came a spider that sat down beside her,
> And frightened Miss Muffet away.

1. What did Miss Muffet sit on?
   Response: A tuffet
   QAR: *Right there*
2. Why did Miss Muffet get up from the tuffet?
   Response: A spider sat beside her and scared her away
   QAR: *Putting it together*

3. What are curds and whey?

Response 1: Something to eat

QAR: *Right there*

Response 2: In making cheese, the milk is allowed to sour. The curds are the thick part that separates from the watery part, the whey (something like cottage cheese).

QAR: *On my own*

4. What do you think Miss Muffet did when she first saw the spider?

Response: She probably threw her curds and whey up in the air, screamed, and jumped up as fast as she could to get away.

QAR: *Author and me*

Depending on the age and ability of the students, follow-up lessons will be needed for practice in recognizing the category types and using this knowledge in answering

---

ReQAR procedural outline.

FIGURE

10.13

PHASE OF TEACHING REQAR	DESCRIPTION	TECHNIQUES EMPLOYED

1. Strategy information	Teacher succinctly explains
	  WHAT strategy will be learned [self-questioning].
	  WHY the strategy is important [to increase reading comprehension].
	  WHEN the strategy will be used [during reading].	

2. ReQUEST	Teacher and student take turns asking one another questions about a segment of text.	Modeling Reciprocal teaching Guided practice Independent practice
3. QAR	Teacher introduces In the Book and In My Head major categories. Teacher differentiates Right There and Putting It Together sources. Teacher differentiates Author and Me and On My Own sources.	Modeling Reciprocal teaching Guided practice Independent practice
4. ReQAR	ReQuest format serves as procedural backdrop for reinforcing QAR strategy. Student asks question. Teacher answers question and identifies QAR category. Teacher asks question. Student answers question and identifies QAR category.	
Gradual release of responsibility	Student asks question and identifies QAR category. Teacher answers question and specifies QAR source. Teacher asks question and identifies QAR category. Student answers question and specifies QAR source. Student asks question and specifies QAR source. Teacher responds, then asks next question. Student answers question and specifies QAR source.	

comprehension questions. Raphael (1986) suggests beginning QAR instruction with first- and second-grade students by introducing only the two-category distinction: *in the book* and *in my head*. Middle-grade students can learn all four QARs in one lesson although the types can still be distinguished by the two headings *in the book (right there* and *putting it together)*, and *in my head (author and me* and *on my own)*. Sample text is presented with the questions, responses, and QAR provided, and the *reasons for each classification are discussed.* Once students understand category differences, other samples of text, questions, and responses can be provided so they can identify the QAR. Finally, students, when provided text and questions only, will have learned to recognize the key words in questions that cue them as to whether the answer lies in the text or in their heads. At this point, students are well on their way in using text organization as an aid to comprehension.

Helfeldt and Henk (1990) suggest a combination of ReQuest Procedure (Manzo, 1969, 1985) and QAR instruction in a technique they term **Reciprocal Question– Answer Relationships (ReQAR)**. Intended for middle- and upper-grade students, particularly those with word recognition difficulties, the technique helps these readers anticipate the nature of teachers' questions, focus on informative parts of text, and learn how to construct appropriate responses to questions. Essentially, the goal of ReQAR is to assist students in viewing comprehension as the goal of reading. The instructional sequence can be seen in Figure 10.13.

SUMMARY

Poor comprehenders generally do not approach reading as a meaning-making task; therefore, comprehension instruction for the corrective reader must emphasize understanding as the paramount purpose of reading. Direct instruction includes use of short selections, concrete words and examples, and appropriate questions. It must be explicit, that is, involve teacher–student interaction. Teachers should verbalize for their students the strategies they themselves use while trying to comprehend text. These strategies might include finding the main idea or predicting an outcome. Comprehension instruction is not limited to intermediate grades and beyond; it *must* be taught from the first grade. Many techniques presented in this chapter can be adapted as listening activities. To be good comprehenders, students must first realize that written materials should make sense. Until this realization has been internalized by the student, no instruction in comprehension is likely to help.

SUGGESTED READINGS

Glazer, S.M. (1992). *Reading comprehension: Self-monitoring strategies to develop independent readers.* New York: Scholastic.
> *A most readable monograph presenting an explanation of the comprehension process and strategies that help children monitor and make decisions about their own reading. Ways to create classroom environments conducive to supporting independence in reading and writing are also discussed.*

McNeil, J.D. (1992). *Reading comprehension: New directions for classroom practice* (3rd ed.). New York: HarperCollins.

This book attempts to address what *should be taught as an aid to comprehension and* how *comprehension instruction should be delivered. Chapter 10 provides excellent ideas for enhancing comprehension through writing.*

Palincsar, A. S., & Brown, A.L. (1984). Reciprocal teaching of comprehension-fostering and comprehension-monitoring activities. *Cognition and Instruction, 1* (2), 117–175.

One of the most successful techniques for helping students develop a self-questioning attitude while reading is reciprocal teaching. This original source provides actual discussion scenarios so the process can be more readily understood by teachers.

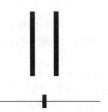

STUDY SKILLS

OBJECTIVES

After you have read this chapter, you should be able to

1. list and describe the major study skills;
2. identify prerequisite skills for a given study skill;
3. identify sources of material other than stories

for teaching study skills;

4. develop assessment activities for any study skill;
5. develop instructional activities for any study skill.

KEY CONCEPTS AND TERMS

arrays

content words

equal status relationships

expository material

GRASP

herringbone technique

locational skills

main ideas

mapping

NOTES

paraphrase

semantic webbing

study skills

subordinate relationships

summarizing

superordinate relationships

synthesizing

thought units

topic

STUDY OUTLINE

1. Introduction
2. Study skills and the corrective reader
3. Assessment for locational skills
   a. Alphabetizing
   b. Book parts
   c. Reference materials
      • Dictionary
      • Encyclopedia
   d. Reference skills
4. Instruction for developing locational skills
   a. General teaching procedures for direct instruction
   b. Specific activities
      • Alphabetical order
      • Parts of books
      • Using an index
      • Choosing resources
5. Assessment for organizing information
   a. Classifying words, phrases, and sentences
   b. Main ideas and supporting details
   c. Sequencing
   d. Summarizing and synthesizing
6. Instruction for organizing information
   a. Classifying
   b. Main ideas and supporting details
   c. Sequencing
   d. Summarizing and synthesizing
   e. Notetaking
   f. Outlining
7. Assessment for interpreting graphic and pictorial materials
8. Instruction for interpreting graphic and pictorial materials
   a. General teaching procedure
   b. Real-world usage
9. Summary
10. Suggested readings

OVERVIEW

It is not enough to help students learn how to recognize new words and how to improve their understanding of what they read. If a major goal of reading instruction is to develop truly independent readers, closer attention must be paid to the area of study skills and strategic reading for expository (nonstory) text. When a student cannot transfer knowledge of reading skills to materials other than basal readers or stories, the difficulty may lie in the area of study skills or strategic reading of expository text.

Study skills will be introduced in this chapter in a kind of hierarchy, that is, skills seen as prerequisites for other study skills will be discussed before more complex skills. This presentation will help you do a better job of assessing and teaching study skills.

More specifically, the study skills of (1) locating and organizing information and (2) interpreting graphic and pictorial material will be discussed at length. You will soon see that the techniques discussed previously to aid reading comprehension are also used to develop the study skill of organizing information. One major difference in teaching the study skills discussed here is the type of material used. The instructional examples given throughout this chapter deal with expository, or content area, material. Many examples of specific instructional techniques are provided; although teachers know that study skills should be taught, they are often at a loss regarding how to proceed. As a result, many readers become corrective readers in the area of study skills.

This chapter will help you to understand what study skills are, to recognize the importance of teaching them, and to teach them effectively. New terms will be defined or explained.

INTRODUCTION

Study skills refer to the tool aspects of reading that allow a reader to extend and expand knowledge as well as literacy abilities. Any discussion of study skills assumes that the reader has some basic knowledge of word recognition and comprehension skills—one cannot "extend and expand" something that is not present. Only minimum reading skill is necessary, however, as word recognition, comprehension, and study skills are all interrelated. Growth in one area aids growth in another. Instruction in study skills and strategic reading therefore should *not* be delayed until a reader has well-developed word recognition and comprehension skills.

The material used to teach study skills is distinctly different from that used to teach word recognition and comprehension strategies. The narrative material of the basal reader, fiction book, or language experience story does not provide an opportunity to learn and apply study skills. For example, the various uses of book parts to locate information cannot be taught when a book's table of contents lists only titles of stories. Being able to use a table of contents is an important study skill, although other book parts typically found in content area textbooks (e.g., title page, index, glossary) more readily help students realize that specific parts of books can help them locate specific kinds of information. Other study skills, such as using the card catalog or computer system in the library, or interpreting a bar graph, simply cannot be learned most effectively by relying on narrative material.

An increasing number of secondary teachers complain that "students can't read the textbook" or that "students don't know how to find information for their term project." A student who may otherwise be a good reader, or one who was thought *not* to have reading difficulties in elementary school, often cannot deal independently with secondary level textbooks and assignments. At present, direct teaching of study skills seems to be overlooked or ignored during the elementary school years. Part of the problem may be that the elementary level teacher judges a reader's progress only in the areas of comprehension and word recognition skills, and only with narrative material. The teacher then assumes that the reader can apply this ability with narrative material to the more factual material found in content area textbooks. Thus, an otherwise good reader suddenly has difficulties upon entering the intermediate grades, in which content area reading increases.

In summary, study skills are tools that enhance the reader's understanding of content area textbooks and other informative materials. Basic or prerequisite skills are found in Figure 11.1. The rest of this chapter presents specific assessment and instructional techniques for the first three of the four major categories listed previously. Strategic reading for expository text will be discussed in Chapter 12.

STUDY SKILLS AND THE CORRECTIVE READER

Study skills differ from other areas of reading in that there are identifiable prerequisite skills, or underlying abilities, that will assist the learner in the effective use of a particular study skill. For example, Rosa must have certain prerequisite abilities to use an index. The study skills checklist in Figure 11.1 arranges the subskills within each category according to an underlying hierarchy so that these prerequisite abilities can be easily identified. Thus, for Rosa to use an index effectively, she must be able to alphabetize by first, second, and third letters.

Study skills checklist.*

Student's Name:

Study Skill	Knows	In Progress	Does Not Know	Not Assessed
I. Locating information				
A. Alphabetizes by first letter				
B. Alphabetizes by second letter				
C. Alphabetizes by third letter				
D. Knows and uses book parts (e.g., table of contents, index, glossary)				
E. Knows and uses reference materials (e.g., dictionary, thesaurus, encyclopedia, directories)				
F. Uses the library (card catalog or computer system, Dewey Decimal System)				
II. Organizing information				
A. Knows and uses specialized vocabulary				
B. Categorizes information				
C. Recognizes main ideas/supporting details				
D. Sequences events				
E. Summarizes/synthesizes information				
F. Takes effective notes				
G. Outlines effectively				
III. Interpreting graphic and pictorial materials				
A. Uses pictures				
B. Uses graphs				
C. Uses tables				
D. Uses maps				
IV. Has and uses a study strategy (Chapter 12)				

*Note to teacher: Place dates in boxes rather than checkmarks to provide a chronology of skill development.

To provide appropriate help then, not only must the major area of difficulty be identified but also any gaps in prerequisite abilities. If Jackie cannot use the encyclopedia and other reference materials, she may not be able to alphabetize properly or know how to use the various book parts. Being asked to use reference materials without first learning these prerequisite abilities will likely be frustrating.

In summary, this chapter stresses the need to consider underlying abilities. This emphasis is especially relevant for the corrective reader, who characteristically has learning gaps.

ASSESSING LOCATIONAL SKILLS

Most standardized achievement tests include subtests on a limited range of **locational skills,** usually termed *work-study* skills. The most common skills tested are interpretation of tables and graphs and use of reference materials (e.g., *Iowa Test of Basic Skills; Comprehensive Test of Basic Skills).* Because the range of skills tested is small and the yield is simply a percentile, stanine, or other standard score reflecting a general level of achievement only, information obtained by the teacher for instructional purposes is minimal. The standardized test may indicate low achievement, but direct assessment will be needed to pinpoint specific teachable units.

Teacher-made tests, if constructed with some thought, are a valuable source of information for instructional decision making. In the checklist (Fig. 11.1), the ability to locate information has the prerequisite knowledge of being able to alphabetize by first, second, third, and beyond letters. Most teachers will have no difficulty devising an instrument to determine whether students have these prerequisite abilities, or subskills.

Alphabetizing

Some sample exercises for assessing the ability to alphabetize follow. They are presented in an order of increasing difficulty.

1. Present letters and have students provide the letter that comes immediately before and after.

    __(q)__ r __(s)__   _____ f _____

    _____ c _____   _____ v _____

2. Present a random listing of letters to students and have them arrange the list in alphabetical order.

    x, c, r, j, d, s, u, t, a, m

3. Provide students a random listing of familiar words that begin with different letters. Ask the students to arrange the list alphabetically, or place words alphabetically in their word banks or personal dictionaries.

    the, dog, cat, me, house, baby

4. Provide students a random listing of words that begin with the same letter but have different second letters. Ask the students to arrange the list alphabetically.

    cat, come, cup, city, cent

5. Provide students a random listing of words that are sometimes different in the first or second letter. Ask the students to arrange the list alphabetically.

   give, bed, foot, jump, gave, bad

6. Provide students a random listing of words that are alike in the first and second letters, but differ in the third. Ask them to arrange the list alphabetically.

   bowl, boat, boy, bottle

7. Provide the students a list of words that vary to any extent. Ask the students to arrange the list alphabetically.

   such, as, to, try, come, camp, look, like, boy, road, read

Book Parts

Knowledge of book parts can be checked simply by asking the student to locate a particular part and then describe its purpose or how it might be used. Figure 11.2 shows an example of a skills test for assessing knowledge of book parts in a written format. Book parts that students should be tested on are the title page; date of publication page; table of contents; lists of tables, graphs, maps, illustrations, and so on; preface or foreword; glossary; index; appendix; and bibliography or references.

Reference Materials

The ability to recognize and use a variety of reference materials needs to be assessed. Activities for assessing the more common information sources should come first. For example, use of the dictionary and encyclopedia can be assessed by the following activities.

Dictionary

1. Students must be able to alphabetize and interpret diacritical marks to use a dictionary or glossary. An exercise similar to the following, containing words that the students already know how to pronounce, is recommended.

   Directions to students: Use the pronunciation key at the top of the page and circle the correct dictionary respelling of the numbered words. The first one has been done for you.

   Pronunciation key

fat	āpe	cär	ten	ēven
hit	bīte	gō	yü as in few	to͞ol
book	up	für	ə = a in ago	

   ---

   a. dad

          dād   (dad)   däd   dəd

   b. look

          lo͞ok   look   lōk   lŏk

   c. main

          man   män   mān   mān̄

   d. cute

          cute   kute   kut   kyüt

   About ten items should be given.

FIGURE

11.2

Skills test for parts of a book.

Name: _____

KNOW YOUR BOOK

Directions:

Use your _____ book to answer these questions.

1. What is the title of this book?

2. Who are the authors?

3. When was the book copyrighted?

4. What is a copyright?

5. What company published the book?

6. What edition is this book?

7. What kind of information is in the preface?

8. Why do some books have more than one edition?

9. Give an example of how the table of contents can help you.

10. Is there a list of tables, maps, or diagrams?

11. How can this help you?

12. How are new words shown?

13. Is there a glossary?

14. How can the glossary help you?

15. Where is the index located?

16. When will you use the index?

17. Is there an appendix?

18. What information is presented in the appendix?

From *The Reading Corner*, by Harry W. Forgan, Jr. Reproduced by permission of Scott, Foresman and Company. © 1977.

2. Provide students sets of guide words from the dictionary (e.g., *mill/mind*). Ask questions about the sets: Which word will be found at the bottom of the page? Why is *mill* written before *mind?* Where will you find *mill* on this page?

3. Provide students guide words from two pages of the dictionary. Then give them other words and ask them to identify the page on which the word will be found, or whether it can be found on either page. For example:

domain/door   *downcast/drain*

dragon	double
doze	doorway
donkey	downstairs
dog	dome

4. Have students write in the guide words for the pages in their personal dictionaries.

5. Provide students a list of words and have them write the guide words of the page on which they found each word.

6. Provide the students several dictionary entries. The students should study each entry and be able to answer the questions below. Try to include a variety of parts of speech, accents, syllables, and diacritical marks. Note that dictionary activities assume knowledge that is typically taught as a decoding skill. For example, students must be able to recognize syllables, accents, and diacritical markings before a task like the following can be assigned.

Example:

freight (frāt), *n* 1. a load of goods shipped by train, ship, truck, airplane, etc. 2. the cost of shipping such goods. *v.* 1. to load with freight. 2. to send by freight.

a. What is the vowel sound heard in this word? (long a)

b. How many syllables does this word have? (one) If more than one, on what syllable is the accent?_____

c. The letter *n* means (noun).

d. The letter *v* means (verb).

e. If the guide words on a page of the dictionary were *framework* and *free,* would *freight* be on that page, on a page before, or on a page after? (after)

f. Which definition and part of speech for *freight* is being used in the following sentence? The *freight* for the package was $2.75. (second; noun)

Encyclopedia

According to Hittleman (1983, p. 297), in order to use information from an encyclopedia effectively, a reader must be able to use the encyclopedia index, information on the spine of each volume, guide words, cross references, and bibliographies at the end of articles. Each of these items needs assessing. An example skills test for assessing encyclopedia knowledge might proceed as follows:

Students are provided a set of encyclopedias. Questions are then asked about the set.

1. How many volumes are in this set of encyclopedias? _____

2. To find out more about the climate in Alaska, which volume would you use?_____

     a. How would you proceed? _____

     b. What would you look for in the index? _____

     c. On what page is the information you need? _____

3. What number and letter(s) are on the volume you would use to find information about each topic in the following list? Which pages give you information about each topic?

Topic	Number	Letter(s)	Pages
climate			
polar			
bees			
Eskimos			
whales			
zebras			

    In addition to the dictionary and encyclopedia, students should be able to use the thesaurus, directories (e.g., *The Yellow Pages*), almanacs, and periodicals. Assessment tasks are just as easily constructed for these materials as for the dictionary and encyclopedia.

Reference Skills

This major area dealing with locational skills includes use of the library, helping students go beyond the dictionary and encyclopedia as reference materials and recognize that information can be found in many other resources. To use the library effectively the student must be able to use its card catalog or computer reference system, its particular classification scheme (most likely the Dewey Decimal System or Library of Congress classification), and its special collections (e.g., periodicals; records, tapes and CDs; filmstrips and videos; trade books).

    An effective way to help students learn reference skills and, in turn, identify those needing assistance, is to create an authentic need for information to be found in the library. Providing students opportunities to research topics of their own choice is recommended by Greenlaw (1992). She suggests the use of a "curiosity" sheet at the beginning of a new unit of study (see thematic units in Chapter 2). On this sheet students list topics they are curious about, related to the subject of the unit. Once topics are identified and shared with the whole class, there are sure to be several students interested in the same topic. These students can work together on a collaborative research report—although the following steps work for individual students as well (Tompkins, 1994). At this point, students working together can brainstorm questions they would like to have answered and identify possible sources of information for answers to those questions (see Figure 11.3). A map or a data chart (see Figure 11.4) can then be developed to aid in the gathering and organizing of information. Such a chart lends itself to the paraphrasing of information since space is limited. By using several sources students also learn to synthesize information.

    When students have their questions ready, a need to visit the library has been created. If the school library is not well equipped, a field trip to the local public library should be arranged. The librarian, advised earlier of the nature of the trip, will give a thorough tour to include use of the card catalog or computer system, location of the various materials that will be helpful, and assistance when students are attempting to locate the infor-

Possible sources of information for research project.

Student Name(s): _____

Project Title: _____

Information sources we might be able to use for this research project are indicated with a check.

_____ almanac	_____ interviews	_____ posters
_____ art	_____ magazines	_____ records, tapes, or CDs
_____ atlas	_____ maps	_____ slides
_____ biographies	_____ microscopic slides	_____ television programs
_____ dictionary	_____ museum exhibits	_____ thesaurus
_____ encyclopedia	_____ newspapers	_____ video, video disks
_____ filmstrips	_____ nonfiction books	
_____ history books	_____ photographs	

Others: _____

mation for their data charts. Once the information is obtained, a report is written. In this way students also learn about and practice expository writing.

As the teacher observes all stages of this process, those students having difficulty will become apparent. Once again, the study skills checklist (Figure 11.1) serves as a record of observations for the teacher. As checklists are marked, the teacher can consider ad hoc groupings of students needing explicit instruction in related locational skills.

INSTRUCTION FOR DEVELOPING LOCATIONAL SKILLS

An attempt should be made to provide corrective readers lessons that are motivating and relevant to their experiences. Rather than using the students' textbooks and workbooks, more unusual materials are employed. Following are some items that are atypical, yet make good sources for work in the entire area of study skills.

catalogs	newspapers
TV program guides	globes
diaries	*Guinness Book of World Records*
job applications	how-to-make-it books
maps	ingredient labels
menus	advertisements
travel brochures	driver's manual
thesauruses	insurance forms
encyclopedias	weather maps and reports
magazines	police reports

FIGURE

11.4

Research map and data chart for organizing research information.

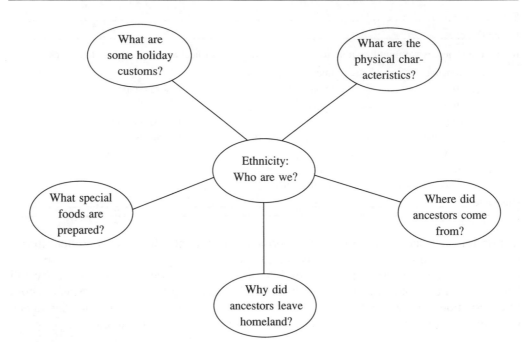

General Teaching Procedures for Direct Instruction

With some modifications, the exercises used for assessment can also serve as the basis for a lesson. The student is first made aware of the purpose for learning locational skills. For alphabetizing, students are shown that being able to alphabetize allows them to use such valuable resources as the dictionary, telephone directory, and encyclopedia. Once the purpose of the lesson is established, some motivation for pursuing the lesson may be necessary. For example, in order to play a new game, such as an alphabetizing relay, participants must know how to alphabetize.

The teacher is now ready to teach a mini-lesson to the students directly. Usually this means demonstrating how a random list of words can be arranged alphabetically. The teacher should explain the actual process used to alphabetize, showing how words are compared by first letters (or by second or third letters, depending on the specific purpose of the lesson). After the explanation, the teacher invites student feedback to see if the explanation was clear. This may mean simply asking a student to reexplain the procedure just described.

Once the students demonstrate that they understand the explanation, the teacher gives them a chance to practice the new skill with no penalties for errors. This practice stage also allows the teacher to clarify any misunderstandings. When the teacher is satisfied that the students understand the process, they are redirected to the immediate purpose, in this case the alphabetizing relay. After the relay, the teacher may evaluate each student with a worksheet exercise on the same material.

An important part of direct instruction is to give the students many opportunities to apply the newly learned skill in appropriate situations. For example, soon after the alphabetizing mini-lesson, perhaps later in the day or week, a new science term may be introduced. The teacher asks the students how they can find out what the word means and also check on its pronunciation. If no one says the dictionary, the teacher simply suggests using the dictionary and reemphasizes the skill taught in the alphabetizing mini-lesson (in this case, how the word would be found in the dictionary using the first letter as a guide).

Another planned application is development of a classroom directory. The students first list their names, last names first, on the chalkboard one at a time. Then, using the skills taught in the initial alphabetizing mini-lesson, they alphabetize the list. The directory is completed by looking up the names in the telephone directory and copying the address and telephone information. Periodic checks with similar activities should be planned to ensure that the skill is being maintained.

Thus, the steps of the mini-lesson are as follows:

1. Establish the purpose of the lesson.
2. Provide motivation for the lesson.
3. Teach the skill directly.
   a. Demonstrate and explain process.
   b. Check students' understanding of explanation.
   c. Allow opportunities for students to practice new skill.
   d. Review purpose and complete the original task (motivation).
4. Allow independent practice (e.g., a follow-up worksheet).
5. Provide application opportunities.
6. Plan for distributed practice (periodic checks).

Specific Activities

This general format can be used in planning lessons to develop the locational skills and many other study skills. Following are some especially worthwhile activities for readers having difficulty with locational skills.

Alphabetical Order

As students place new words in personal dictionaries or vocabulary notebooks (see Chapter 7), they will need to decide where to write each new word in relation to the words already written. This need provides an opportunity for activities such as the following.

1. *Directions:* Fill in the blanks using the words *before* and *after*. The first one has been done as an example.

   g is _(after)_ **e** and _(before)_ **h**   **re** is_____ **ra** and _____ **ro**

   t is _____ **u** and _____ **s**   **se** is_____ **sc** and _____ **sl**

   p is _____ **o** and _____ **q**   **br** is_____ **bu** and _____ **bl**

2. *Directions:* Circle "Yes" or "No" to answer the following questions.

   Would **margin** come before **marker?**   Yes   No

   Would **alligator** come after **allow?**   Yes   No

   Would **picnic** come before **pickles?**   Yes   No

3. *Directions:* Circle the word on the right that would come between the two words on the left.

   beam–beauty   beaver   bean   beak

   disk–display   disappear   distance   dislike

   drift–drip   drink   driveway   dried

4. *Directions:* Look at each row of words. For each row, circle the word that would come first in the dictionary. Underline the word that comes last in the dictionary.

   Example: <u>grew</u>   grade   go   (gasp)

   1. boy   down   city   over

   2. little   lot   lake   letter

   3. dance   date   days   dark

Parts of Books

Have the students locate the table of contents in any content area textbook.[1] Ask questions such as the following:

1. On what pages do you find the chapter called "The Founding of our Nation?" _(173–202)_

2. On what page does the chapter called "The Civil War Divides the Nation" begin? _(263)_

---

[1]Used for this example was the Table of Contents from H. H. Gross et al., *Exploring Regions of the Western Hemisphere*. Chicago: Follett, 1966.

3. Does this book include a chapter on what the United States is like today? *(yes, chapter 13)*

4. If you wanted to read about the settlers moving westward across the Appalachian Mountains, which chapter would you go to? *(chapter 8, "Exploring the North Central States")*

5. How many pages are in the chapter called "Exploring the New World?" *(24)*

6. Does this book have an index? *(yes, begins on page 463)*

Using an Index

Have the students locate the index in any content area textbook and use the index to find answers to questions. Students write the answer, the page on which they found it, and any heading from the index that helped them.

Choosing Resources

Give the students a variety of resource books. Ask them to decide which resource would be most appropriate for locating information to answer questions the teacher either asks or has written for them to answer independently. For example, ask whether a dictionary, telephone book, thesaurus, almanac, atlas, or encyclopedia would be used to find the following:

1. Address of a friend
2. Words that mean the same
3. Information about a certain animal
4. Population of the United States
5. Winner of the World Series in 1980

ASSESSING ORGANIZING INFORMATION

The study skill area of organizing information is the most closely related to comprehension ability, as discussed in Chapter 10. However, while such skills as finding main ideas, sequencing, summarizing, and synthesizing are end products in the reading of story material, they are prerequisite to the more commonly recognized study skills of notetaking and outlining. Thus, to be able to take effective notes and develop good outlines, the student must be able to apply the notions of main ideas, sequence, and supporting details to content-related material.

The best and most direct way to assess the ability to organize information is simply to ask students to make an outline (or map) or to take notes from a short selection. The selection should be easy for the students with regard to word identification and comprehension skills to ensure that the study skill itself is actually being assessed.

If a student has difficulty in outlining or notetaking, additional practice may not necessarily be the solution. The student may be having difficulty with prerequisite knowledge: classifying words, phrases, or sentences; main ideas; sequencing; summarizing or synthesizing; or knowledge of specialized vocabulary. This prerequisite knowledge should therefore be assessed before providing instruction that the student may not be ready for.

Classifying Words, Phrases, and Sentences

Being able to distinguish main ideas from supporting details is a prerequisite to summarizing, outlining, or drawing inferences from **expository** (explanatory, content area type) **material.** However, before students can identify main ideas in paragraphs, they must be able to distinguish **superordinate** (general or main idea), **subordinate** (specific or supporting details), and **equal status** (equally general or equally specific) **relationships** among words, phrases, and sentences. For instance, if Othell has trouble categorizing *hammer, axe,* and *lathe* as specific examples of tools, he will have difficulty identifying the main idea and supporting details in paragraphs discussing the role of tools within a social studies technology unit.

Some assessment techniques for classifying words, phrases, and sentences follow.

1. Give students a list of category titles such as *birds, mammals, planets,* and *reptiles.* Test items group the members (specific, subordinate relationships) of each category title (general, superordinate relationships), and the student must identify the correct category for the series of items. For example:
   a. deer, whale, dog (mammals)
   b. Mars, Saturn, Venus _____
   c. robin, oriole, blue jay _____
   d. alligator, chameleon, salamander _____

2. Another format combines the specific examples with the general topic. Students are directed to circle the word that represents the general topic. For example:
   a. deer (mammal) whale dog
   b. Mars Saturn planets Venus
   c. birds robin oriole blue jay
   d. alligator chameleon salamander reptiles

3. This format provides the specific items at the top of the page, followed by the skeleton of an outline format. Students must place the specific items under appropriate general headings to complete the outline. For example:

butterfly	dog	beetle	sandpiper	sparrow
Mrs. Jones	firefly	iguana	mouse	haddock
trout	frog	terrapin	swallow	herring

   I. Insects   II. Reptiles
      A. butterfly   A.
      B.   B.
      C.   C.
   III. Mammals   IV. Fish   V. Birds
      A.   A.   A.
      B.   B.   B.
      C.   C.   C.

Phrases and sentences are assessed in much the same way. Some examples follow.

4. Students are instructed to circle the phrase or sentence that describes all the other items in the list.

   a. cows and pigs   farm animals

      ducks and chickens   sheep and goats

   b. Streets fell apart.   Cars were lost.

      Windows rattled.   An earthquake occurred.

   c. Scientists dig up fossils.

      Scientists learn about dinosaurs.

      Scientists look at the size and shape of bones.

      Scientists study where the bones were found.

   d. They wanted to have their own church.

      They were separatists.

      They were Englishmen.

      They had secret church meetings.

Main Ideas and Supporting Details

When the student is able to classify words, phrases, and sentences, the next area to be assessed is that of locating the main idea (superordinate topic) and supporting details (subordinate topics) in a single expository paragraph (Aulls, 1978). As discussed in Chapter 10, **main ideas** may be explicit or implicit, and some paragraphs have no main idea at all. For assessment, paragraphs with stated main ideas should be used, as students must be able to recognize stated main ideas before being asked to determine an implicit main idea. Recall from Chapter 10 that main ideas may be stated in the first or last sentences of a paragraph or somewhere in between. Students should be given paragraphs with the main idea stated in each of the three positions and asked to underline the appropriate sentence. The *Barnell Loft Specific Skill Series* (Boning, 1985) provides placement tests, as do its booklets, "Getting the Main Idea," at levels 1 through 12, which are a ready source for assessment paragraphs. Teachers may also employ the content area materials being used in their schools; however, the students should be assessed with material at their instructional or independent reading level.

Sequencing

Sequencing is important prerequisite knowledge for outlining because outlines reflect a chronological, forward-moving summary of material read. Sequencing is especially important in studying history and conducting science experiments, because time order (first, second, third, and so on) may be critical to understanding the material. The easiest way to assess this ability is to give the student pictures, phrases, or sentences that relate a sequence of events. The items are out of order, and the student must sequence the items. For example:

Directions: Put a 1 in front of the event that would come first, a 2 for second, a 3 for third.

a. _____ The air becomes warm.

   _____ Ice and snow cover the ground.

   _____ Green leaves appear on the plants.

b. _____ Put the pan on the burner.

_____ The water boils.

_____ Pour the water into the pan.

Paragraph frames can be readily adapted for use in sequencing (see earlier discussion in Chapter 10 and see Chapter 12 for examples).

Summarizing and Synthesizing

The primary difference between **summarizing** and **synthesizing** is that a summary usually contains the essential ideas of *one* selection, while synthesizing summarizes information from *several* sources. Thus, students must be able to summarize before they can synthesize. The most obvious application of these skills is in writing a report or term paper. Summarizing and synthesizing relate to the ability to paraphrase material read. Specifically, readers must be able to locate the main idea and supporting details, apply literal and inferential thinking skills, and interpret the information in their own words.

Methods that involve *retelling* of material read (not to be confused with recall) are appropriate for assessment. In a retelling, the reader's ability to interact with, interpret, and draw conclusions from the text are assessed. Other assessment procedures are likely to include questions that ask about main ideas and inferred information. These questions may take the following general form.

What is this section about?

What was learned from this experiment?

What was the purpose of the article?

How would you describe this period of history?

Could this poem mean something else?

Explain that in your own words.

Most teacher's manuals contain questions that ask students to summarize or synthesize information at the end of chapters or units. When some students consistently have difficulty with these questions, an analysis should be made in the areas of main ideas, supporting details, and paraphrasing (Chapter 10).

INSTRUCTION FOR ORGANIZING INFORMATION

The techniques suggested here demonstrate how teachers can provide both instruction and practice in using materials that require students to apply these study skills independently. Many of the instructional techniques presented in Chapter 10 can be adapted for use in content areas. I attempt to suggest techniques for the most commonly taught content areas, in which reading difficulty may be the prime cause of poor achievement. The most valuable instructional methods employ the concepts and specialized vocabulary found in the content area material the students are or will be using.

Classifying

Aulls (1978) suggests that teaching the classification skills of superordinate, subordinate, and equality relationships, which are so important to main ideas and supporting details, involves:

> (1) an introductory teacher directed lesson; (2) a teacher directed reinforcement lesson which reviews the introductory lesson but uses different examples; (3) a pupil directed review activity where pupils work individually, in pairs or in small groups using worksheets, games or learning centers; (4) an application to one of the weekly content area reading assignments; and, (5) a posttest of ten to twenty test items. . . . Approximately 80 percent accuracy is suggested as a criterion. (p. 95)

The introductory lesson concentrates on the meaning of general (superordinate), specific (subordinate), and equal word, phrase, and sentence relationships. The discussion involves the students in making decisions first about pairs of items. For example, the teacher might ask:

"Is *beetle* the general or specific word in the pair 'beetle—insect'?" *(response)*

"How can you tell? Use the rule: Is the *(specific)* a type of *(general)*? If beetle fits the first blank it is the specific word. The word that fits the second blank is the general word."

Responses should compare "beetle, a type of insect" and "insect, a type of beetle" to conclude that beetle is the specific word.

Many examples should follow. For phrases or sentences the rule may vary:

Does (specific) describe (general)?

For example, the teacher might ask:

"Does *Englishmen* describe *Separatists* or does *Separatists* describe *Englishmen?*"

Gradually introduce the equal relationship concept by comparing three items instead of pairs. For example:

"Wanted to have their own church" *(specific)* describes "Separatists" *(general)*.

"Secret church meetings" *(specific)* describes "Separatists" *(general)*.

These two sentences demonstrate that "wanted to have their own church" and "secret church meetings" both describe "Separatists," so they are *equally specific*. Continue these lessons until students achieve 80 percent accuracy with four items.

Categorization activities similar to those found in Chapter 10 and the activities included in the assessment section in this chapter for classifying words, phrases, and sentences can also be used as bases for lessons. In addition, with corrective readers especially, some "real life" application is needed to show these students how skills that help them read better can also help them *outside* the classroom in their daily lives. An example of one such activity follows.

The Yellow Pages lists, alphabetically, categories of services available in the area. The companies providing those services are in turn listed alphabetically under their particular heading; for example, Ed's Moving Company would be found under "Movers," along with a telephone number and possibly additional information. As in a dictionary, guide words give the first and last service listed on a page. Students are given hypothetical situations and asked to determine what service is needed; this is a classification task.

Similar activities can be devised using mail order catalogs, tables of contents, indexes, almanacs, and newspapers (Cheyney, 1992; Olivares, 1993; Short & Dickerson, 1980).

Main Ideas and Supporting Details

Students who can distinguish general, specific, and equal word, phrase, and sentence relationships are ready to learn how to identify main ideas and supporting details. Aulls (1978) suggests moving from lessons in classifying to identifying the general topic of a picture. A **topic** differs from a main idea in that it is usually a word or phrase that represents the major subject of a picture, paragraph, or article. **Main ideas** are statements that give the most important ideas regarding the topic. Thus, the topic must be identified before an important idea about it can be identified.

Direct teaching is essential before students are asked to practice a new skill. The teaching sequence suggested for classifying skills also applies here. Initial lessons involve pictures and paragraphs with one topic and several details supporting that topic. For example:

> There are many kinds of seeds. There are small seeds and large seeds. There are seeds with wings that can fly through the air. There are seeds with stickers that catch on your clothes. There are seeds that can float on the water.

After reading the paragraph, students are asked to identify the topic of the paragraph from some listed words.

_____ wind   _____ wings

_____ seeds   _____ stickers

Based on the previous discussion about classifying words, phrases, and sentences as general, specific, and equal, the students are often helped with the rule, "Does _____ describe _____ ?" Specific to the example are the questions: "Are (small seeds) specific kinds of seeds?" "Are (seeds with wings) specific kinds of seeds?" Practice should follow with more paragraphs of the same simple structure.

Finally, students who can identify the topic of a paragraph are ready for instruction in main ideas. Students learn that the main idea is the most important thing that the author wants the reader to understand about the topic (Aulls, 1978).

Instruction proceeds from the writer's point of view. The teacher may suggest a topic and one important piece of information about it. For example, the teacher writes _Water is moving all the time_ on the board and states that this statement is the main idea the writer wishes to make in a paragraph. Students are then invited to supply some specific statements that describe the main idea. Some possible responses might include:

> Water moves in the ocean.
>
> It runs over rocks in streams.
>
> It falls over waterfalls.
>
> It ripples on the lake.

If students can understand main ideas from the writer's point of view, they may better understand main ideas from the reader's point of view.

Instruction proceeds to paragraphs with the main idea stated in the first sentence, followed by paragraphs with the main idea stated last, and finally to paragraphs with the main idea stated somewhere in between.

Content area textbooks can be used to help students apply what they have learned. The teacher may use an illustration that summarizes one of the written sections particularly well. Science and social studies textbooks lend themselves best to this type of activity. For example, a section may discuss the concept of the water cycle, while an accompanying illustration clearly shows the whole process. Students are asked to think of a sentence that explains the main idea of the picture and thus the concept of the water cycle. Supporting, or specific, details are then found in the text and listed as brief items below the sentence (Fig. 11.5).

Sequencing

Many activities are suitable as bases for sequencing lessons other than the more common exercises that ask the student to put comic strip frames in the proper sequence. The teacher wants to encourage students to think logically. By first relating sequencing to events in their daily lives, the teacher helps students realize that events usually occur in a sensible step-by-step fashion. Initially, activities take a very simple form.

Example: What would you do first?
1. Put the cake in the oven to bake, or combine eggs and water with the mix?
2. Put on your shoes or put on your socks?
3. Get dressed or get out of bed?

Having students follow simple written directions to make or cook something also reinforces the idea that certain steps precede others. Remind students to look for key words (e.g., *first, second, third, next, then, finally, last*) and other hints of sequence (refer to Chapter 10). For example, if a science selection deals with the growth stages of insects, the word *stages* is a hint that a sequence of events is going to be related. Students must be made aware of these hints. Many times the stages are listed, giving a numerical hint of what comes first, second, and so forth. (Be careful though; not all listings are sequential.) Having students write directions for making something so that other students can follow them also reinforces the importance of proper sequencing.

Summarizing and Synthesizing

Often techniques used to teach summarizing skills do not differ very much on the surface from activities requesting identification of main ideas. However, in summarizing, instead of the main idea being explicitly stated, the reader is asked to infer a main idea or draw a conclusion about what has been read.

One method to help students learn to summarize is teaching them to **paraphrase**, or restate text in their own words. Instruction in paraphrasing begins at a sentence level. Initially, two sentences are compared for meaning. For example:

"Do the following sentence pairs have the same meaning?"
The harbor was safe for small boats.
Small boats were protected in the harbor.

FIGURE
11.5

Example of illustration that helps students identify main idea and supporting details.

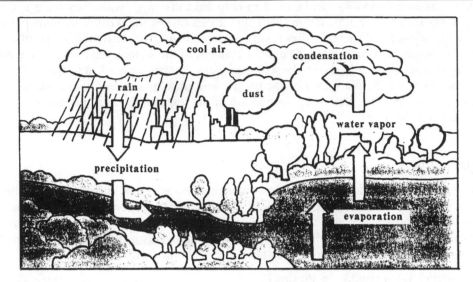

Main Idea: The evaporation and condensation of water over and over again is called the water cycle. *Supporting Details:* When water evaporates, it changes into a gas called water vapor. Water vapor is cooled as it is carried up by warm, rising air. The cooling changes it back into a liquid. The vapor condenses into a cloud. Clouds bring precipitation.

From Joseph Abruscato et al., *Holt Elementary Science*, p. 126. Copyright © 1980 by Holt, Rinehart and Winston, Publishers. Used with permission.

In order to get to the New World, the Pilgrims needed a ship.
The Pilgrims needed a ship to take them to the New World.
Most of the Pilgrims were farmers, weavers, or shopkeepers.
The Pilgrims were farmers.

At this initial level of instruction, the student must simply recognize one sentence as a paraphrase of another sentence.

The next stage in the instructional sequence moves from recognition of paraphrased sentences to production of paraphrased sentences. One method is to have students give synonyms for the **content words** (nouns, verbs, adjectives, adverbs) in a sentence, as in the following examples.

Automobiles, airplanes, and dirigibles are operated by gasoline engines.
Cars, planes, and blimps are run by gasoline engines.

When students can paraphrase sentences with ease, instruction proceeds to short paragraphs. Synonyms again are used. However, instead of trying to substitute one word for another, with paragraphs one thought unit is substituted for another. The following word problem demonstrates this procedure.

"Oranges are priced at 3 for 90¢. How much would you pay for 4 oranges?"

The first step is to divide the paragraph into **thought units**, or short phrases that contain only one idea. The thought units for this example might be listed as:

oranges are priced
3 for 90¢
how much (would you pay)
for 4 oranges

The next step is to paraphrase each thought unit. One student might suggest:

oranges cost
30¢ each
How much will 4 oranges cost?

The paraphrases may vary; the concern is that all the thought units in the original paragraph are represented in the paraphrase.

The last step is to compare various paraphrases for meaning changes. If the meaning is the same, the paraphrase is acceptable. No personal translation is incorrect as long as the meaning is the same. For example:

"Oranges cost 90¢ for 3. How much will I have to pay for 4?"
"3 oranges cost 90¢. 4 oranges will cost how much?"

In paraphrasing, other skills, such as sentence combining (Chapter 7, 10), can be applied. In fact, many comprehension skills are involved in paraphrasing: vocabulary knowledge (synonyms), literal understanding of words and sentences, sentence combining, and sentence expansion. The following example demonstrates the use of sentence combining to paraphrase.

Original: There is a plant that helps people tell the time. The plant has flowers that may be white, red, yellow, or pink. These flowers open in the late afternoon. The flowers close in the morning. The plant is named the "four-o'clock." [From *Specific Skill Series, Primary Overview, Drawing Conclusions—Booklet C* (level 3), by Richard Boning, 1985, Baldwin, NY: Barnell Loft.]

Paraphrase: There is a plant, called the "four-o'clock," that helps people tell time. Its flowers, which can be white, yellow, red, or pink, open at about four o'clock in the afternoon, and close in the morning.

As noted previously, synthesizing paraphrases and combines information from more than one source. To teach synthesizing, at least two different sources must be used. The easiest way to introduce the concept of synthesizing is to give the students two different versions of the same story and have them look for similarities and differences. Children's stories, such as *The Three Bears, Jack and the Beanstalk,* and *Cinderella,* are usually available in different versions. Summaries that make use of topics and specific details for each version can be listed on the board and then compared.

The next step is to apply this idea to content area material. Choose a topic that is presented in different ways (usually different texts or different levels of the same textbook series). As an example, here are two versions of difficulties the Pilgrims faced.

Version 1
Sickness. There was terrible sickness in Plymouth that first winter. There were some days in February when only six or seven people were well enough to take care of the ones who were sick.

By spring, about half of the Pilgrims and sailors were dead. Three whole families died during this terrible time. [From . . . *if you sailed on the Mayflower* (p. 48) by Ann McGovern, 1969, New York: Scholastic Book Services.]

Version 2

Hard times. New England winters are long and cold. Icy winds blow across the land. The Pilgrims were not used to such cold weather, nor did they have proper clothing. They got wet going to and from the *Mayflower.* So many became sick that at one time only six or seven settlers were well enough to look after the others. They moved the sick to the Common House and used it as a hospital. By the end of the winter, half the Pilgrims had died. [From *Exploring Regions of the Western Hemisphere* (pp. 120–121) by H. H. Gross, et al., 1966, Chicago: Follett.]

Guide the students to summarize each version, using topics and specific details. Paraphrasing should be encouraged. Example summaries follow for each version.

Version 1
Sickness in Plymouth *(topic)*
terrible sickness *(detail)*
first winter *(detail)*
February—only six or seven people well enough to care for others *(detail)*
by end of winter, half the Pilgrims and sailors died *(detail)*
3 whole families died *(detail)*

Version 2
Hard times for Pilgrims *(topic)*
long, cold New England winters *(detail)*
icy winds *(detail)*
Pilgrims not used to such winters *(detail)*
Pilgrims didn't have the right clothes *(detail)*
they got wet *(detail)*
so many became sick *(detail)*
at one time only six or seven settlers well enough to care for others *(detail)*
moved sick to Common House *(detail)*
Common House used as hospital *(detail)*
by end of winter, half the Pilgrims died *(detail)*

Students then compare the summaries and put a check mark by the details that occur in both versions. The teacher may wish to point out that details found in both versions are probably important and should be included in any written synthesis of the information.

Depending on the teacher's purpose and the needs of the students, the teaching sequence may proceed to a written synthesis of the two versions. Sentence-combining strategies (Chapter 7, 10) are useful at this stage. For example, the Pilgrim's "first winter" from version 1 can be described with details from version 2 such as "long, cold, New England, icy winds" and result in the following sentence:

The Pilgrims' first New England winter was long and cold with icy winds.

Instruction in summarizing and synthesizing also helps prepare students for writing reports that reflect more understanding of a subject than copying information from an encyclopedia. Hayes (1989) developed an extension of the Guided Reading Procedure (Manzo, 1975) to show students how to group details into a prose summary. His strategy is referred to as **GRASP**, the Guided Reading and Summarizing Procedure. Briefly, students read for information and are directed to remember all they can. After reading, students tell all they remember and the teacher lists *all* recollections, no matter how trivial or inaccurate. Following this listing students reread the material to add to, delete, or correct information on the list. At this point the teacher shows students how to organize the information by grouping details that belong together. Discussion about how information in each group relates to other information leads to an outline or map (see also Hill, 1991, for use of concept maps in summarizing). Once the relatedness of the information is displayed, a prose summary is developed, revised, and refined into a final summary.

Jeanne Day (1980) suggests the following basic rules of summarizing.

1. Delete trivial or unnecessary details. (For instance, a detail found in only one version in the previous example, that is, the Pilgrims got wet, could be omitted.)
2. Delete redundant material.
3. Use a category heading for items mentioned within a single category. (For example, if the text mentions *roses, lilies,* and *petunias,* substitute the word *flowers.*)
4. Combine component actions into one encompassing action. (For example, instead of noting that James ate five doughnuts on Monday, ten doughnuts on Tuesday, ten more doughnuts on Wednesday, and so on, say James ate fifty doughnuts in one week.)
5. Identify a topic sentence, or what seems to be the author's summary.
6. If a topic sentence is not apparent, make up your own.

Any summarization strategy involves teacher modeling and discussion of students' ideas and responses. In teaching the strategy, material that students find easy (independent level) should be used initially.

Notetaking

Instruction in the previous skills of summarizing and synthesizing leads directly to instruction in notetaking. In essence, when taking notes on printed material, the student is summarizing the material. If notes are being taken on material presented orally, the process assumes the additional skill of auditory comprehension (Chapter 4). In either case, the ability to summarize and translate information into one's own language is imperative.

Notetaking is a most complex skill, as evidenced by the prerequisite skills already discussed. Research by Dunkeld (1978) on taking notes while reading offers some helpful suggestions. First, students are introduced to notetaking while reading or listening to a familiar story (e.g., *The Three Bears*). Second, in the early stages of notetaking, a textbook with subheadings is used. Third, the teacher demonstrates the format of good notes on the chalkboard or overhead using students' own examples. Fourth, students are encouraged to use their notes during class discussions.

Simpson and Nist (1990) suggest a textbook annotation strategy as a way to study and take notes from texts. They conclude from their research that it is the special elements of the strategy—that actively involve students in constructing ideas and monitoring their own learning—that makes this strategy effective. Additional support for an annotation strategy is provided by Strode (1993) in her adaptation of the REAP strategy (see Chapter 12). She notes the following major benefits:

- There is more active involvement in reading since writing will occur afterwards.
- Information is processed more thoroughly and has more meaning as a result of the writing component.
- Students write more succinct summaries as a result of learning to write annotations.
- Students attend to often overlooked aspects of text.

This adaptation of REAP is an effective strategy for notetaking as well as for enhancing comprehension, specifically for main ideas, and for clearer writing.

Stahl, King, and Henk (1991) present "a four-stage instructional sequence of modeling, practicing, evaluating, and reinforcing activities for developing student-directed notetaking strategies" (p. 614). Teachers first model and provide opportunity to practice any one of a number of suggested notetaking procedures, some of which follow:

- Draw a margin and keep all running lecture notes to one side; use the other side for organization, summarizing, and labeling
- Skip lines to show change of ideas
- Use numbers, letters, and marks to indicate details
- Paraphrase
- Use underlining, circling, and different colors of ink to show importance

The unique aspect of the four-stage sequence lies in the last two stages, evaluating and reinforcing. These two stages occur simultaneously when **NOTES** (Notetaking Observation, Training and Evaluation Scales) is applied. "With NOTES, students receive both instructor feedback and peer review of the quality of their notes. They also receive reinforcement as they measure their progress with a record chart in the NOTES packet" (p. 616). NOTES evaluation criteria can be seen in Figure 11.6. The accompanying record sheets, progress charts, and evaluation directions can be found in Stahl, King, and Henk (1991).

Effective notetaking instruction provides students many short practice sessions with the clear purpose of improving their skills. At the end of each session students share their notes, so that the variety of notetaking styles (use of key words, phrases, full sentences) can be discussed.

Outlining

The underlying abilities needed for notetaking and outlining are similar. As with notetaking, outlining involves identification of main ideas and specific details. With outlining, however, these elements must be properly related. Outlines utilize any of the following formats: phrases or topics; sentences; paragraphs; or graphic representations. Instruction in outlining begins with easy material and much teacher guidance, discussion, and practice.

The first sessions in outlining should provide a completed outline of the material for the students on a worksheet, chalkboard, or overhead transparency. The assumption here is that the students will better understand the function of outlining if they can see how the writer organized the selection. After students have read the material, the reasons for selecting certain topics as main ideas and others as supporting details for the outline are discussed. For example, if the selection being read is about bees and how they communicate, the outline may appear as follows:

I. Bees communicate with each other.
    A. One bee discovers honey.
    B. Other bees soon appear.
II. Bee gives message.
    A. Scout bee returns to hive.
    B. Scout bee begins to dance.
    C. Dance tells story.

The discussion emphasizes that the major headings represent the main ideas in the selection. The subheadings provide more specific details that explain the major headings. The outline could be used before the actual reading to help students anticipate the selection's content. Through these activities, students eventually recognize the ways in which written material follows an outline. The teacher is responsible for choosing material that is simple and well-organized.

A later stage may provide students with the supporting details and instruction for filling in the main headings. Then a complete skeleton outline can be provided with a few

---

NOTES evaluation criteria.

FIGURE 11.6

VALUE POINTS AND DESCRIPTORS OF NOTETAKING HABITS

Format	4	3	2	1	0
Use of ink	I use pen consistently.		I use pen and pencil.	I use pencil.	
Handwriting	Others can read my notes.		Only I can read my notes.	I can't read my notes.	
Notebook	I use a looseleaf binder.		I use a spiral notebook.	I don't use a notebook.	
Use of page	I leave enough space for editing.		I leave some space for editing.	My notes cover the page.	

Organization	4	3	2	1	0
Headings	I use new headings for each main idea.		I use headings inconsistently.	I don't use headings for changes in main ideas.	
Subtopics	I group subtopics under headings.		I don't indent subtopics under headings.	My subtopics are not grouped.	
Recall column	I use cue words and symbols to make practice questions.		I use cue words in a recall column.	I do not use a recall column.	
Abbreviation	I abbreviate whenever possible.		I use some abbreviation.	I don't abbreviate.	
Summaries	I summarize lectures in writing.		I write a list of summary lecture topics.	I don't summarize.	

Meaning	4	3	2	1	0
Main points	I identify main points with symbols and underlining.		I list main points.	I don't list main points.	
Supporting details	I show the relationships between main ideas and details.		My notes list details.	I don't list details.	
Examples	I list examples under main points.		I list some examples.	I don't record examples.	
Restatement	I use my own words.		I use some of my own words.	I use none of my own words.	

Reprinted with permission of Norman A. Stahl and the International Reading Association.

random topics filled in and instruction for completing the outline. Eventually only the structure of the outline is given. Finally, after much practice at each stage, students will be able to formulate outlines without assistance. Examples of outlines for early instruction can be found in Figures 11.7 and 11.8.

In addition to the above techniques, the strategies of mapping (Hanf, 1971), semantic webbing (Freedman & Reynolds, 1980), and the herringbone technique (Tierney, Readence, & Dishner, 1990) are useful for developing outlining skill. **Mapping, semantic webbing**, and herringbone are graphic representations of the relationships of ideas in a

---

FIGURE

11.7

Selecting main headings for an outline.

Paris

Many people think of Paris as one of the most beautiful cities in the world. It has been called the City of Light because of the beauty of its lights at night. Colorful flower beds and famous statues line paths through lovely public gardens throughout the city. Children in Paris go to the parks to enjoy puppet shows and to sail their toy boats in the ponds.

Over the years Paris fashions have been famous throughout the world. When women want to know the latest in fashion, they look to the fashion shows in Paris. Many well-known designers of women's clothes live and work in Paris.

The city of Paris is also famous for its art. Priceless art treasures are on display in several museums. Paintings and statues are among the most popular kinds of art seen in Paris. Many people from all over the world come to Paris each year to study in the outstanding schools of art.

Put the main headings where they belong.

City of fashion
City of art
City of beauty

I. City of beauty
   A. Lights
   B. Gardens
   C. Parks

II. City of fashion
   A. Worldwide fame
   B. Fashion shows
   C. Fashion designers

III. City of art
   A. Museums of art
   B. Kinds of art
   C. Schools of art

Plan 17, Pages 127-130

Comprehension: Selecting main headings for an outline

Directions: Have pupils read the selection and complete the outline.

Exploration: On the board write cleaning a cut, treating with medicine, and bandaging. Have pupils list the materials needed under each heading.

From *Mysterious Wisteria* Activity Book, p. 56. Copyright © 1972 by The Economy Company, Oklahoma City. Reprinted with permission.

selection. The visual result clearly reveals the major topic, main idea, and supporting details. Such graphic representations have also been called **arrays** (Hansell, 1978). Hansell provides a definition: "An array is essentially a free form outline which requires that students decide how to arrange key words and phrases to show how the author fit them together" (p. 248). Therefore, in maps, webs, and arrays the student constructs an organizational design of ideas by selecting relevant information, sorting this into its proper place, and relating all facts to the whole and to the other facts. Figure 11.9 shows an example of an array for the African folktale, *Anansi the Spider* (McDermott, 1972). In this folktale, Anansi buys all the stories in the world from the Sky God. To pay for the stories, Anansi captures and gives to the Sky God a hive of hornets, a jaguar, and a great python. The diagram shows how these events fit together by the arrangement of key words and arrows designating direct relationships.

Outlining by relating subheading to main heading.

FIGURE
11.8

Make an Outline

If you wanted to use the following ideas in a report about the ocean, how would you set up an outline?

Use these words for the main headings in the outline.

Bottom of the ocean
Movement of the ocean
Life in the ocean

Put these words under the main headings in the outline.

Seaweeds
Tides
Shelves
Waves
Slopes
Fish
Floor
Shellfish
Whales
Currents

The Ocean

I. Bottom of the ocean
   A. Shelves
   B. Slopes
   C. Floor

II. Movement of the ocean
   A. Tides
   B. Waves
   C. Currents

III. Life in the ocean
   A. Seaweeds
   B. Fish
   C. Shellfish
   D. Whales

(Arrangements under each heading may vary.)

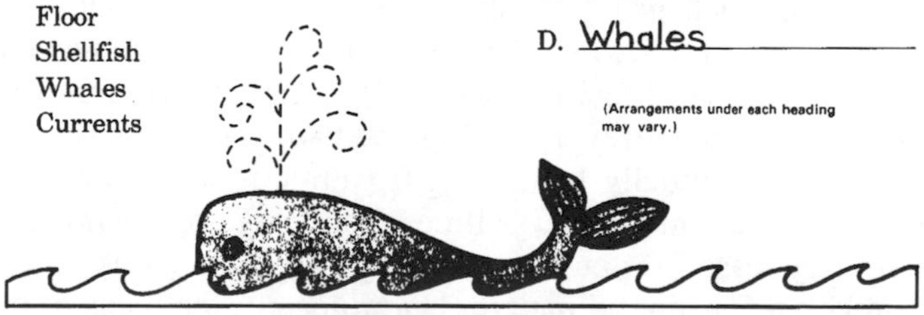

Plan 31, Pages 230-234

Study Skills: Outlining by relating subheadings to main headings

Directions: Have pupils read the instructions and complete the page independently.

Exploration: Have pupils write an article with content based on these headings and subheadings.

FIGURE
11.9

Example array showing interrelationship of character and events.

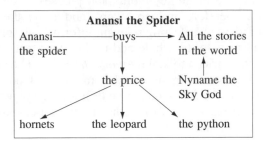

From Hansell, T. Stevenson. 1978. Stepping up to outlining. *Journal of Reading, 22:* 248–252.

Hansell's research suggests certain steps in teaching students how to prepare arrays. First, the teacher selects ten to twenty key words or phrases (assuming passages of 400 to 800 words) from the material. Next, the teacher develops questions that require students to organize what they already know about the passage, for example, "How would you capture a jaguar?"

Once this teacher preparation has been accomplished, the students are assigned to small groups. Each group receives several strips of paper that contain the key words and phrases from the passage. This step allows the teacher to pronounce and explain any of the key words or phrases if necessary. After the paper strips have been distributed, the teacher asks the organizing questions. At this point the students actually read the passage, but they are now reading for two very definite purposes: (1) to check their answers to the organizing questions against what is stated in the passage and (2) to find out how the key words and phrases are related.

The students, still in groups, compare the strips of paper to select the most important idea. This strip is placed at the top or the center to stress its importance. The other strips are positioned around it in a way that reflects the relationships in the material. This positioning must be done with teacher guidance; the teacher asks appropriate questions, encourages, and makes suggestions while moving from group to group. When the group is satisfied with the position of all the paper strips, one member copies the array onto a piece of paper, drawing arrows to show connected ideas and the direction of relationships.

The last step is for each group to share their arrays and discuss reasons for the arrangement and placement of arrows. The teacher asks extending questions at this time.

Hansell recommends at least four teacher-guided arrays be constructed before expecting students to do an unguided array. In an unguided array, students select the key words and phrases themselves. Eventually, by moving from free-form arrays to skeletal outlines, students are ready to prepare individual outlines. The array approach is useful because it focuses on the primary reason for outlining in the first place, that is, to identify relevant ideas and fit them into a meaningful pattern. Unfortunately, the focus of most instruction in outlining is on the format, which assumes students understand the relationships presented in the material—a "cart before the horse" approach. Instruction in array formation puts the horse back in front of the cart.

The **herringbone technique** (Tierney, Readence, & Dishner, 1990, pp. 312–316) is a structured outlining procedure useful for helping students organize information from text.

This strategy utilizes six basic comprehension questions to obtain the important information: who, what, where, when, how, and why.

As with arrays, the teacher must make some specific preparations for teaching the herringbone technique. Important preparation questions for the teacher to ask include:

1. What are the major concepts my students should understand from this material?
2. What are the important vocabulary items?
3. How will my students learn this information?
4. Which concepts do I expect *all* my students to master and which do I expect only my better students to achieve?

The teacher introduces the lesson as usual, with concern for developing motivation and conceptual background. Then the herringbone technique is introduced. The herringbone form (Fig. 11.10) can be easily provided to students as a photocopied handout. Students are told they will be seeking answers to the questions that appear on the form. The answers themselves can also be written right on the form. The first few lessons that involve the herringbone technique are walked through with teacher guidance, using an overhead transparency.

As students read the assigned material they will be noting answers to the following questions.

1. Who (person or group) was involved?
2. What did this person or group do?
3. When was it (the event from question 2) done?
4. Where was it done?
5. How was it done?
6. Why did it happen?

The answers to these questions help the student recognize the important relationships in the material. An example appears on the following page.

The herringbone form.

FIGURE

11.10

For a chapter in a social studies textbook entitled "Europeans Rediscover the Western Lands," the students were instructed to read the topic, "Columbus Tries to Get Help from Portugal," and to answer the six key questions. The answers to be recorded on the herringbone form were as follows:

Who?	Columbus, king of Portugal, king's experts
What?	Columbus went to the king to ask for ships and supplies to sail west to reach the Indies. King's experts thought Columbus was wrong.
When?	_____
Where?	Portugal
How?	_____
Why?	Columbus wanted to prove (1) that it was possible to sail straight west to reach the Indies because the earth is round and (2) that this route was shorter than going around Africa. King's experts knew the earth was round but thought the distance was much greater than Columbus thought.

As seen in this example, texts do not always contain all the information needed to answer the six key questions. The teacher must decide whether the missing information is important enough to look for elsewhere. The herringbone technique readily reveals these information gaps. The teacher can also use the textual answers as springboards for further discussion and research. Figure 11.11 shows the information recorded on the herringbone form.

It can be seen that mapping, webbing, array tasks and the herringbone technique use processes employed in both notetaking and outlining. More important, they give students a structure for observing relationships in text that further enhance comprehension and retention of information. When these techniques are used as prewriting strategies as well, students will quickly begin to understand text organization.

ASSESSING THE INTERPRETATION OF GRAPHIC AND PICTORIAL MATERIALS

The skills to be discussed in this section differ considerably from those discussed in the previous sections. While the previous skills overlapped with the comprehension skills discussed in Chapter 10, the reading of graphic and pictorial materials requires a unique set of skills.

As stated early in this chapter, the interpretation of tables and graphs is a subtest commonly found on standardized achievement tests. However, if the information from such a test is not readily available to the teacher (i.e., tests are machine scored), the instructional benefits are minimal. Informal measurements developed by the teacher *will* provide a readily available source of information.

Graphic and pictorial materials help readers understand text by explaining, clarifying, or providing additional information. A reader must have skill with the following materials.

1. Pictures. Students must be able to utilize pictures that present or clarify concepts, afford new experiences vicariously, or stimulate discussion. Political cartoons are included in this category.

FIGURE
11.11

Herringbone outline showing gaps in information.

2. Time lines. Students should be able to recognize time lines as graphic presentations of events in chronological order. Both the time and the event are presented on a time line.

3. Tables and charts. Students must be able to read the variety of facts presented in a table or chart. These may be in single column or multicolumn formats.

4. Graphs. Many types of graphs clarify and illustrate comparisons. Students should be able to read and interpret circle graphs, line graphs, bar graphs, and picture graphs.

5. Map and globes. Students must be able to interpret a legend and its symbols, the scale indicated, the directions of north, south, east, and west, and the lines of latitude and longitude to read maps and globes effectively.

To assess whether students can use the five types of materials listed above, the teacher simply has to develop a set of questions that can be answered only if the picture, time line, table, chart, graph, map, or globe has been read properly. These measures are quite easily constructed. The *Wisconsin Design for Reading Skill Development* has many examples in the study skills component. Scholastic Book Services' *Real Life Reading Skills* and *Map and Graph Skills* also provide teachers with such examples.

INSTRUCTION FOR INTERPRETING GRAPHIC AND PICTORIAL MATERIALS

General Teaching Procedure

Interpretation of pictorial and graphic material is best taught according to a five-step procedure (Cooper, Warncke, Ramstad, & Shipman, 1979).

1. Explanation of the use or purpose of the material being taught.
2. An understanding of the meanings of the words used to describe the material being learned.
3. The teaching of the specific skills needed for use of the tool or material.
4. A demonstration of the use of the material or tool.
5. The guidance of the students through the initial usage of the material. (p. 259)

The activities described in the remainder of this section point out how the teacher can follow each of the five steps. Because a large amount of visual information is available, teachers soon discover that readers who master interpretation of pictorial and graphic materials greatly enhance their understanding of content area materials.

When explaining the use and purpose of pictures, examples must be available for students to view during the lesson. The explanation may begin by giving students a sentence describing a scene that can be easily sketched. For example, the students may be asked to draw a picture to correspond to the following sentence:

The ball rolled down the street and hit a big tree.

The resulting drawings are shared, with a discussion of the techniques used to indicate "rolled" and "hit" (refer to step 3). Students should experience a need to indicate the passage of time in their drawings. Some may resolve this problem by showing several pictures that indicate the ball getting closer to the tree; others may use dotted lines to show the ball moving toward the tree (Fig. 11.12). Both solutions are found in content area material.

At this point, an example from a textbook is appropriate. The following sentence was taken from a science text:

The paramecium pinched in the middle and split in two.

First, this sentence may be difficult to visualize if the important words are unfamiliar (e.g., *paramecium, pinched, split*). Therefore, step 2, understanding or at least recognition of the key words, is important. The picture itself attempts to clarify concepts in the text that would otherwise be difficult to understand, as the picture associated with the example sentence clearly demonstrates (Fig. 11.13). In this case, the picture provides the reader with a better understanding of the sentence than the words themselves. The whole illustration shows how a paramecium reproduces itself. This kind of concept is best illustrat-

Pictures drawn by seven-year-old boy *(left)* and eight-year-old girl *(right)* showing rolling ball hitting a tree.

Illustration clarifying concept of paramecium splitting in two.

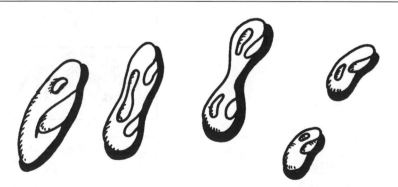

ed by a series of pictures (recall the rolling ball sentence). Other concepts are better described using arrows, or dotted lines if direction or distance is involved (Fig. 11.14).

Some illustrations have legends (a step 2 term) that the reader must use to understand the concepts involved. Students must be taught how to use these legends for pictures, maps, and titles and column headings in tables, and how to relate the pictorial or graphic information back to the text. Guidance is essential initially and can be given only by direct instruction. A variety of pictorial and graphic materials with questions relevant to interpretation is the basis of such instruction. Figure 11.15 is a familiar example. The following questions would be appropriate to use with this graph.

1. What kind of graph is this? Circle one.

   bar graph   circle graph   picture graph

2. This graph shows that <u>(50)</u> children like horses best.

3. Two animals are liked the same. What are these two animals? <u>(cats)</u> <u>(hamsters)</u>

4. How many children like dogs best? <u>(100)</u>

5. How many children were asked what their favorite pet was? <u>(200)</u>

To maintain their competence in this area, students must have many opportunities to use and apply these skills.

FIGURE

11.14

Use of arrows (left) and legend (right) to aid reader in understanding concepts involved.

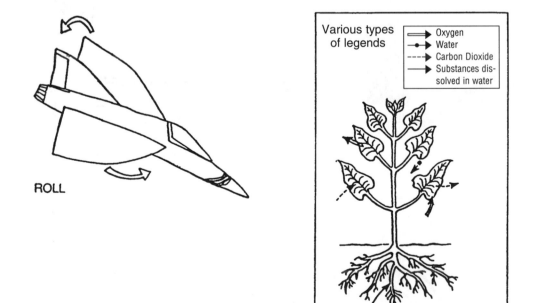

ROLL

Various types of legends
- Oxygen
- Water
- Carbon Dioxide
- Substances dissolved in water

Right-hand illustration adapted from *Science for You* by Gerald S. Craig and others. © Copyright 1965 by Ginn and Company. Used by permission of Silver Burdett Ginn Inc.

Students can be instructed in interpreting graphic materials by being asked a series of relevant questions that relate the graphic information to the question responses.

FIGURE

11.15

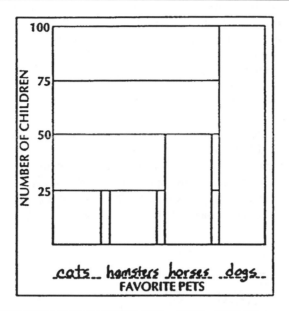

Real-World Usage

The best reinforcement activity for developing graphic and pictorial skills is real-world usage. For instance, after the lesson on the bar graph, the class could collect its own data and construct its own graph. Not only will the teacher be instructing on graph skills but on math skills as well.

Teachers must be alert to the many opportunities in daily life that help students appreciate the need for learning graphic and pictorial skills. Bus schedules, newspaper weather maps, TV guides, and city street maps are obvious items that can be brought into the classroom. Students who have been taught to graph their own progress on spelling tests could also use this skill to graph progress in a weight-loss program. Who hasn't been asked to draw a map giving directions from "my house" to "your house"? Students can help make maps "from classroom to cafeteria" or "from school to the ice-skating rink." Most large shopping malls have maps that locate the stores. In the Southeast and on the East Coast, hurricane tracking maps are free to teachers in large quantities during the hurricane season.

Knowing the students and the community in which they live broadens the opportunity to practice graphic and pictorial skills. The least that can be done for corrective readers is to give them skills needed for daily life.

SUMMARY

Students considered to be successful readers are often at a loss when given an assignment to "report on one of the following topics" or to "take notes on Chapter 6 in your history book for homework." Such assignments assume the student can locate and organize information and interpret graphic or pictorial information. In short, the student must be an independent reader *and learner*—not just a reader who can recognize words in print and understand the message.

Knowing *how* to learn is what study skill instruction is all about. Study skills must be taught directly. Teachers must "extend and expand" reading to include a variety of material. Also, study skills must be taught from the beginning. If students are to be independent learners and readers they must know how to find information they need, how to organize information, and how to interpret the visual aids accompanying information ("reading to learn"). Teachers therefore must provide reading instruction within content area classes in which students can see the application of the study skills.

Another vital aspect of study skill instruction is teaching students the value of strategic reading. This particular aspect of study skill instruction is the content of Chapter 12.

SUGGESTED READINGS

Cheyney, A.B. (1992). *Teaching reading skills through the newspaper* (3rd ed.). Newark, DE: International Reading Association.

> *This brief (59-page) monograph is a valuable resource for using the newspaper across-the-curriculum. With the newspaper a readily available resource for teachers and a motivation source for students, it can help students gain control over their own learning. Informational reading can be readily practiced within an authentic context.*

Peresich, M.L., Meadows, J.D., & Sinatra, R. (1990). Content area cognitive mapping for reading and writing proficiency. *Journal of Reading, 33,* 424–432.

> *This article shows mapping to be a practical, visual way to apply schema theory in the classroom while teaching students about text structure. Several examples of content applications are presented in the article.*

Vacca, R.T., & Vacca, J.L. (1993). *Content area reading* (4th ed.). New York: Harper-Collins.

> *Chapter 9, "Studying Texts," is particularly relevant to a discussion of study skills. Teachers working with upper elementary, middle school, or secondary students will find the suggestions in this text chapter clearly explained, with examples for many of the ideas presented.*

12

STRATEGIC READING FOR EXPOSITORY TEXT

OBJECTIVES

After you have read this chapter, you should be able to

1. identify ways to determine whether students know about and are able to use reading strategies;
2. describe the three stages of studying;
3. give examples of skimming versus scanning;
4. explain what happens in comprehension monitoring;
5. describe techniques for teaching self-questioning skills and postreading organizational skills.

KEY CONCEPTS AND TERMS

Assignment Mastery
comprehension monitoring
during reading
GRS
K–W–L
mapping
metacognition
PORPE

postreading
prereading
scanning
skimming
SQ3R Strategy
studying
think-links
understanding questions

STUDY OUTLINE

1. Introduction
2. Assessing awareness of strategic reading and study habits
3. Instructional techniques for developing strategic reading habits
   a. Stages of studying
      • Prereading
         1) Skimming
         2) Scanning
         3) Accessing prior knowledge
      • During reading
         1) Comprehension monitoring
         2) Self-questioning

   • Postreading
      1) Mapping
      2) Think-links
      3) Paragraph frames
   b. General study strategies
      • SQ3R (survey, question, read, recite, review)
      • GRS (guided reading strategy)
      • PORPE
      • Other study strategies and their acronyms
4. Summary
5. Suggested readings

OVERVIEW

How do you intend to read this chapter? The steps you follow make up your plan, or strategy. If you are a good strategic reader you might proceed in the following manner.

1. Look through the entire chapter and ask questions. How long is this chapter? How much time will I need to read it? Do the headings refer to familiar ideas, or does this material seem difficult? Do the figures (tables or graphs) appear helpful?
2. Decide upon purposes for reading. I want to know more about some of the terms used. The figures appear interesting. I want to know more about the techniques they represent.
3. Read the material. At the same time try to paraphrase sections (notetaking) and continue asking questions. Do I know what this means? Do I see how I can apply this with students? Also decide

what needs further clarification from the instructor.
4. Question yourself after the material has been read. Can you go to the objectives listed at the beginning of the chapter and honestly say you have met them? Can you outline, from memory mostly, the important points? (Your outline should resemble the study outline already provided.) Can you explain the meaning of the terms listed at the beginning of the chapter?

If you have never tried to study text chapters systematically, why not try it now, using the list above if you like. See whether employing a strategy helps you remember more. If you are convinced that using some kind of strategy helps you remember more of what you read, you will be more likely to teach good reading strategies to your students.

INTRODUCTION

Strategic readers understand that for the purpose of learning or remembering specific information, a different set of strategies is needed from that which they might use when reading for enjoyment. When the purpose of reading is studying, readers process text material with the expectation of learning or remembering something specific. Good strategic readers: (1) think about what they already know about the topic (2) clarify their purpose for reading (3) focus their attention on the content (4) monitor whether or not thcy arc understanding what they read (5) use fix-up strategies (e.g., look back, reread, read ahead, consult a dictionary) when they do not understand (6) fit new material into what they already know (7) take notes (8) think aloud to be sure of their understanding (9) create mental images to aid understanding of difficult concepts (10) summarize what they have read by mapping or using some other form of graphic organizer (11) evaluate their understanding of what they read, whether or not their purpose was achieved and, if necessary, (12) seek outside sources for additional information (Orange County Public Schools, 1985, 1986). Thus, an important characteristic of **studying** is that it is student-directed instruction. In other words, a teacher is *not* available to ask guiding questions, point out or clarify important concepts, or help with decisions about what to do next when material is not understood.

Nevertheless, teachers need to demonstrate, or model, the variety of strategies available for the purpose of studying so that students can become independent learners. Garner (1987) proposes six guidelines for effective strategy instruction.

1. Teachers must care about the processes involved in reading and studying, and must be willing to devote instructional time to them.

2. Teachers must do task analyses of strategies to be taught.

3. Teachers must present strategies as applicable to texts and tasks in more than one content domain.

4. Teachers must teach strategies over an entire year, not in just a single lesson or unit.

5. Teachers must provide students opportunities to practice strategies they have been taught.

6. Teachers must be prepared to let students teach each other about reading and studying processes. (pp. 131–138)

ASSESSING AWARENESS OF STRATEGIC READING AND STUDY HABITS

One quick way to determine whether students are aware of and use study strategies is to administer a questionnaire similar to the one found in Figure 12.1. If you worry about students answering honestly, you can give the questionnaire on an anonymous basis to the entire group. A tally of the responses to each item indicates areas in which students need instruction.

Another way to assess students' strategic reading abilities is through observation. After directing a group of students to study some reading materials for a test, observe their behavior. Some type of survey of the material should be apparent, such as a quick perusal of the title and headings or looking at pictures, charts, or graphs. Often in a survey of the material, a reader quickly reads the first and last paragraph in the various sections of the material or the introductory and summary passages.

After a survey of the material, most students start reading from the beginning. Observable behaviors, such as notetaking, underlining, looking back at previously read text, or rereading, indicate that the reader is actively studying the material.

A number of behaviors are possible when readers complete their reading. Some readers go back and try to outline the material. Others choose to go back and take notes or underline certain information.

Both the questionnaire and the observable behaviors indicate three phases in the process of studying. A student may consistently exhibit behavior for one of the phases but not for all three. These phases will be discussed in detail in the next section.

Questionnaire to determine study strategies and habits.

FIGURE

12.1

Name _____

Appendix Item **69**
Skill Test for Study Skills and Habits

Directions:
Put a check mark ( ) in the column that describes how often you do the following. Be honest. I shall help you learn to study if needed.

	Never	Sometimes	Usually
1. Do you look over what you are going to read before you read it?			
2. Do you form questions about the selection before you read it?			
3. Do you use a slower rate when you are reading your textbooks?			
4. Do you try to pronounce and define words that are in bold print or italics?			
5. Do you read the tables, graphs, and diagrams in your textbooks?			
6. Do you answer questions as you go along?			
7. Do you outline the important ideas and facts as you read?			
8. Do you reread the materials you do not understand?			
9. Do you review what you have read when you have finished?			
10. Do you set a time for study?			
11. Do you have a place to study at home or near your home? Are your supplies ready?			
12. Are you able to concentrate when studying?			
13. If you are doing math problems, do you read them carefully and then reread them to see if your answer is correct?			
14. If you must turn work in to your teacher, are you proud of it? Is it neat and well organized?			

From *The Reading Corner* by Harry W. Forgan, Jr. Reproduced by permission of Scott, Foresman and Company. © 1977.

INSTRUCTION FOR DEVELOPING STRATEGIC READING HABITS

Stages of Studying

Behaviors observed in skilled readers' studying reveal three stages. These stages are prereading, during reading, and postreading.

Briefly, the **prereading** stage is characterized by attention to the overall theme of a selection. The student prepares to read the selection by considering what is already known about the topic. Headings, subheadings, graphs, tables, and new vocabulary words are typical items of concern at this stage. The student also clarifies a specific purpose for reading that helps in focusing attention on the content to be read.

The **during reading** stage is more difficult to describe because of the wide variety of possible behaviors. Ideally, this stage is characterized by active involvement with the print. Recently, the term *comprehension monitoring* has been used to describe what should be happening at this stage (this will be discussed in a later section). Readers who monitor their comprehension continually ask themselves, "Do I understand this material?" (Baker, 1979). If material is not understood, fix-up strategies must be used. The reader also tries to relate any new information to what is already known.

In the **postreading** stage, students engage in activities that help them retain information. The most commonly used activities are organizational (outlines, maps); translational (paraphrases, annotations, formulating of questions); and repetitional (recitations, rehearsals). Instructional techniques for each stage will now be presented.

Prereading

Throughout this text I have emphasized trying to understand the processes involved in the various reading domains. Even for the domain of strategic reading for expository text, task requirements, or underlying processes, are important considerations. When the purpose is to learn and remember information, students must look over the material: titles, headings, illustrations, tables, introductions, summaries, and topic sentences. The prereading stage thus demands that students be proficient in **skimming** and **scanning**. "*Skimming* and *scanning* both refer to rapid reading during which the reader does not direct attention to all of the information on the page. *Scanning* is fast reading to obtain answers to specific questions. . . . while *skimming* is rapid reading to find out what something is about or a general idea" (Schachter, 1978, p. 149).

Flexibility in rate of reading is a skill that every student can and should practice. Even young children can be asked to skim or scan pictures for particular objects or colors. They can scan magazines or newspaper articles for a specific letter of the alphabet, or catalogs for objects beginning with a specific sound. Just about any type of printed material can be used to teach skimming and scanning, including telephone books (both yellow and white pages), menus, catalogs, newspapers, or textbooks.

Direct instruction for skimming and scanning. Corrective readers often demonstrate a tendency to read every word. As students progress through the grades, teaching them when and how to vary their reading rate takes on increasing importance. An introduction to skimming and scanning uses a technique that shows the student what is meant by flexible reading rate, or skimming and scanning. For example, ask a student to look up a classmate's phone number in the telephone book (father's name: William Jenkins). Point out that the student would not start at the beginning and read the whole book or even start at the beginning of the *J*s and read through all of the names beginning with *J*. Instead, using alphabetizing skills, the student finds the general location and then scans to locate Jenkins, William. If asked, students are usually able to identify other situations from real life in which they skim or scan material, for example, scanning the TV schedule to decide what channel to watch or a recipe to see if the needed ingredients are available.

In direct instruction, students are taught to skim and scan for a variety of purposes. Initially, directions are simple, with activities chosen specifically to teach the concepts of skimming and scanning. Eventually, activities are more directly related to what students will be expected to do on their own as strategic readers of expository material. Some specific activities follow.

1. Direct the students to scan a passage that is easy to read and underline ten verbs. The teacher might set time limits on this task and gradually decrease the time allowed.

2. Direct the students to locate five items on a menu that sell for less than three dollars.

3. With the librarian's help, give students copies of brand new book arrivals. Have each student skim a book (consider a time limit) and briefly share the general idea of the book.

4. Give students a list of questions to answer from the classified ads. Examples are: How much does the 1991 Mustang cost? What breed of cat was lost? Where can you call to buy a used dishwasher? How much does a thirty-foot sailboat cost?

5. Questions similar to those in activity 4 can be used with content area material. Tables of contents and indexes are ready sources for similar questions. Question starters are: Find the place at which . . . Locate the page on which . . . List the chapters that . . .

6. More directly related to studying is an activity that uses a content area textbook and question guide. Students are told to look specifically for the answers to the questions and *not* to read every word. Sample directions include the following:

   • Look at the paragraph headings for pages 17 through 24. After reading *just the headings,* write a sentence or two that tells what this section is about.

   • List the steps that tell how a bill is passed.

   • Read the section "The President Wears Many Hats" to find out how many different jobs the President has.

Accessing prior knowledge. Ineffective readers often start reading without first thinking about the subject of what they are reading. They fail to realize that they may already know something about the material, and that this knowledge can help them during their reading. There are several useful strategies teachers can demonstrate that will help these readers focus on what they already know about a subject.

An uncomplicated procedure discussed by Ogle (1986) that can be used with any content or grade level, individually or with groups, is the **K–W–L** strategy. The **K** step requires that the student identify what is already **k**nown about the subject. If a group is applying the strategy this step involves a brainstorming of all the information the group already knows about the subject. The **W** step requires that the student reflect on what is already known and determine what they still **w**ant to learn. Thus, the **W** becomes a question, "What do I **w**ant to find out?" The **L** step actually occurs *after* the material is read. The student writes down what was **l**earned. Students should make sure that any questions they had identified at the W stage have been answered. A chart similar to that found in Figure 12.2 can be used to provide a graphic structure for the reader.

Modifications of the K–W–L strategy have also been developed. The *What Do You . . .* chart (International Reading Association, 1988, p. 15) seen in Figure 12.3 combines aspects of K–W–L and DRTA (see Chapter 10) formats. Such a chart encourages the student to focus on the subject, the title, or the cover of a book, and distinguish between what is known for certain and what is predicted to be covered.

Depending on the age and ability of the students, a simplified version of such organizational charts might focus only on accessing prior knowledge and making predictions. Such a version is *What do you know/What do you think* (Richards, 1988, personal communication). Given a topic, title, or book cover, the student states what is known ("just the facts") before stating what is predicted. For example, given the title and cover of the story *Goldilocks and the Three Bears,* the stated facts might include:

> This is a story about a girl, Goldilocks, and three bears.
> The bears have a house in the woods (based on cover illustration).
> The girl has yellow hair (based on cover illustration).
> There are two big bears and one small bear (based on cover illustration).

Predictions are then based on the known facts, and also on the reader's familiarity with other stories of a similar nature. Responses to the question "What do you think?" might include:

> I think this story will tell about what happens to Goldilocks and the bears.
> I think the bears will scare the girl.
> I think Goldilocks visits the bears in their house in the woods.
> I think that Goldilocks will make friends with the little bear.
> I think that the bears will help Goldilocks.

FIGURE 12.2   Chart for the K–W–L strategy.

K——————— What Do I **KNOW?**	W——————— What Do I **WANT** to Learn?	L——————— What Did I **LEARN?**

What do you . . .

Know You Know	Think You Know	Think You Will Learn	Know You Learned

When a book cover or illustration is used, the first question can be changed to "What do you see?" and a three-column map can be prepared for written responses as seen in Figure 12.4. Thus, even very young students can learn to be strategic readers, beginning with familiar narrative material and moving into more difficult, expository material.

A variation of the DRTA that focuses on accessing prior knowledge is discussed by Richek (1987). The variation DRTA SOURCE helps students recognize that readers use both the text and their prior knowledge when making DRTA predictions. In DRTA SOURCE, students stop after making predictions and identify which part of each prediction was based on something in the text and which part on prior knowledge. The value of this strategy is that it helps students become aware of how important their own prior knowledge is to reading.

During Reading

A wide variety of behavior is seen in the second stage of studying. After previewing the material, good strategic readers generally start at the beginning and read through the material, engaging in what is termed **comprehension monitoring**. Through this process, students constantly evaluate their level of understanding of what is being read. The ability to monitor one's own comprehension is so critical to studying that this topic deserves further elaboration.

Comprehension monitoring. Research in the area of comprehension monitoring is fairly recent and is part of a larger area of study called **metacognition**. Instruction in metacognitive strategies can be very effective for readers having difficulty (Nolan, 1991).

FIGURE

12.4

Three-column map for *Goldilocks and the Three Bears*.

What Do You See?	What Do You Know?	What Do You Think?
a girl with yellow hair	Goldilocks is a girl	The bears will scare Goldilocks
two big bears, one little bear	There are three bears	Goldilocks will hide from the bears
house in the woods	This is a fairy tale	The story will begin "Once upon a time . . ."

Metacognition refers to one's knowledge concerning one's own cognitive processes and products or anything related to them, e.g., the learning-relevant properties of information or data. For example, I am engaging in metacognition (metamemory, metalearning, metaattention, metalanguage, or whatever) if I notice that I am having more trouble learning A than B; if it strikes me that I should double-check C before accepting it as a fact; if it occurs to me that I had better scrutinize each and every alternative in any multiple-choice type task situation before deciding which is the best one; if I sense that I had better make a note of D because I may forget. (Flavell, 1976, p. 232)

Metacognitive activities of interest for the during reading stage include keeping track of the success with which one's comprehension is proceeding and, if comprehension breaks down, taking action to remedy the failure (Baker, 1979; Baker & Brown, 1984; Brown, 1980; Garner, 1987; Markman, 1979, 1981; Wagoner, 1983). Research in this area yields ample evidence that poor comprehension-monitoring ability is characteristic of ineffective readers. Additionally, comprehension-monitoring ability is not likely to develop simply with maturity; it depends on knowledge, experience, and instruction (Brown & DeLoache, 1978).

Beginning readers and less able readers are generally deficient in evaluating their understanding of text (Baker & Brown, 1984; Garner, 1980; Markman, 1979; Paris & Myers, 1981; Winograd & Johnston, 1980). If the reader does not know whether the text has been understood, the teaching of techniques for correcting comprehension breakdowns could be premature. Thus, the first step is to help students develop their own comprehension awareness.

For readers to be able to monitor their own comprehension they need to be actively involved with what they are reading. Very young readers and those having difficulty demonstrating monitoring behaviors would benefit from the *Yes/No . . . Why?* and *It Reminds Me Of . . .* strategies (Richards & Gipe, 1992). These two strategies easily involve students by encouraging them to use their background knowledge to make decisions about their understanding of the material read. In the *Yes/No . . . Why?* strategy, the teacher and student both read silently (or orally if desired) an agreed upon portion of the text. This might be a page or a paragraph. Following the silent reading, the teacher models a *yes* and a *no*. A *yes* is something that the reader liked or understood about the passage. A *no* is something not liked or not understood about the passage. A reason for the *yes* or *no* is also provided. Then the student shares a *yes* and a *no* with reasons. For example, after reading the nursery rhyme *Jack and Jill,* the teacher might say, "My *yes* is that I like the way Jack and Jill were doing their chores because it tells me they are helpful to their mother. My *no* is that I didn't like that they fell because they got hurt." Then the student might respond with, "My *yes* is that I like the name Jill because my cousin's named Jill. My *no* is that I don't know what Jack broke. I never heard that word before." After a period of sharing *Yes/Nos*, with the teacher modeling a variety of responses to text, the student will become more involved with the material and will become better able to summarize, clarify, predict, and identify main ideas about the material.

To be able to say what a passage "reminds them of," students have to make a connection between the material and their own background, especially when the material being read needs to be learned or remembered, as with informational text (Carver, 1992). Again with teacher modeling, students can tell or write their responses about what they are reminded of following the reading of a brief portion of text. For example, after reading a paragraph in a newspaper article that talks about flooding along the Mississippi River, the teacher might say, "This reminds me of the story of Noah's ark." The teacher may choose to further elaborate, depending on the needs of the students. Then students are given the opportunity to respond to the same paragraph. As students become more comfortable with these techniques they will be better able to identify points at which they are not understanding what they read, and will then be receptive to learning what to do to improve that situation (i.e., strategic reading behaviors).

Teaching strategic reading behaviors to corrective readers is especially important because it puts them in control of their own learning. Instruction in strategic reading behaviors for expository text requires that students learn and use comprehension monitoring skills. Because one of the first steps in comprehension monitoring is recognizing whether or not the text has been understood (Baker, 1979), that seems a logical place to begin instruction. Therefore, when students are comfortable with strategies such as *Yes/No . . . Why?* and *It Reminds Me Of . . .*, they are ready to develop strategies to use during reading.

Glazer (1992) presents a *Thinkalong* strategy accompanied by a self-monitoring checklist (see Figure 12.5) for use during reading. The types of strategic behaviors that are individually modeled for students are listed here.

1. Making a picture in one's mind about the text;
2. Predicting from pictures, subtitles, and words during reading;
3. Asking oneself questions about the text;
4. Going back and rereading when the text doesn't make sense;
5. Personalizing the text based on one's own experiences;
6. Guessing the meanings of words during reading. (p. 64)

Self-questioning. Research examining self-interrogation ability reveals that this is a promising area of instruction for improving comprehension monitoring skills (Andre & Anderson, 1978/1979; Frase & Schwartz, 1975; Schmelzer, 1975). Results from these studies indicate that students remember more when they formulate questions during studying either by writing them down or verbalizing them to a friend. Nolan (1991) found that a "self-questioning with prediction-making" strategy was more effective than self-questioning alone since readers then must monitor not only whether questions are answered but also whether predictions are correct. The steps learned in this strategy are:

1. Identify the main idea.
2. Write down the main idea.
3. Think of a question based on the main idea and write it down.
4. Answer your question.
5. Predict what will happen next. (p. 135)

Anderson (1980) recommends the use of **understanding questions** to help students monitor their comprehension. Because obstacles to comprehension may occur at the word, sentence, or paragraph level, understanding questions check all three. Some exam-

FIGURE 12.5

Thinkalong self-monitoring checklist of strategic reading behaviors.

SELF-MONITORING SHEET—THINKALONGS			
Thinkalong	**Always**	**Some-times**	**Never**
I know when I don't understand something.			
I ask myself questions to understand the text.			
I make a picture in my mind to help me understand the text.			
I reread to help myself understand.			
I personalize the ideas and relate them to my own experiences. I think about something I know that fits into the new information.			
I reread when I don't know what a word means.			
Sometimes I predict what I will read about next in the text.			

Name:_____

Date:_____

ples are: Does this sentence have any new words? Is a word I know being used in a new way? Did this sentence make sense? Does this sentence fit with what I already know about the topic? What was this section about? Can I explain this in my own words? What were the important facts? Have I read something similar to this before?

Self-generation of questions may be an effective strategy because the student is forced to pause frequently, deal with the effort to understand, determine whether comprehension exists, and finally, become concerned about what to do if comprehension has not been achieved.

Instructional techniques for explicitly teaching students how to use understanding questions are not readily available. Nevertheless, it is clear that "helping poor readers become strategic readers demands modeling of mental processes" (Duffy, Roehler, & Herrmann, 1988, p. 766). A few promising techniques for training self-questioning behaviors can be found in the literature. Collins and Smith (1980) recommend a modeling technique in which the teacher demonstrates the various types of understanding questions the students could ask themselves. The teacher tries to think aloud for the students, showing them where and when they would appropriately ask questions. The actual instructional method suggested by Collins and Smith (1980) proceeds in three stages similar to Singer's (1978) active comprehension lesson and Palincsar and Brown's (1984) reciprocal teaching discussed in Chapter 10. Initially, the teacher models by reading a passage aloud, pausing, and asking relevant understanding questions along the way. The second stage includes the students by asking them to pose the understanding questions, gradually lessening the teacher's involvement. The third stage is silent reading by the students with teacher input only if difficulties are encountered.

Davey (1983, p. 45) provides important guidelines for the teacher modeling stage for "think-alouds" (see Figure 12.6). Duffy, Roehler, and Herrmann (1988) emphasize the importance of the teacher modeling the mental processes (as opposed to procedural steps) that would otherwise be invisible to the students. In this way, the students will have heard examples of appropriate reasoning they can then use to read strategically for themselves.

Paris and Lipson (1982) describe a program of instruction that relies on bulletin boards and related worksheets to teach students to use what they term *focal questions,* which are similar to the understanding questions already discussed. Their research indicates that metacognitive skills can be taught.

Once students have reached a level of awareness regarding comprehension, they can deal with the question of "what to do next" (Anderson, 1980). Anderson provides the following guidelines:

1. If a reader reads something that he or she does not understand, the reader may decide to take some strategic action immediately or may store the information in memory as a pending question.

2. If the reader stores it as a pending question, he or she may formulate a possible meaning (usually one) that is stored as a tentative hypothesis.

3. If the reader forms a pending question, he or she usually continues to read.

4. If a triggering event occurs after the reader forms the pending question (i.e., too many pending questions or repetitions of the same pending question), the reader may take some strategic action.

5. If the reader takes some strategic action, he or she may:
   a. *reread* some portion of the text in order to collect more information that will either answer a pending question or form a tentative hypothesis that is related to a pending question;

b. *jump ahead* in the text to see if there are headings or paragraphs that refer to the pending question and that might answer the pending question;

c. *consult* an outside source (e.g., dictionary, glossary, encyclopedia, expert) for an answer to some pending question;

d. make a *written record* of a pending question;

e. *think/reflect* about the pending question and related information that the reader has in memory;

f. *quit* reading the text.

6. If the strategic action is successful, the reader usually continues to read from the point at which the comprehension failure was last encountered.

7. If the strategic action is not successful, the reader usually continues to read by taking some other strategic action. (pp. 498–499)

An instructional technique described by Babbs (1984) is appropriate for this area. Using a reading plan sheet and comprehension monitoring cards, readers are first taught

---

FIGURE

12.6

Guidelines for teacher modeling of "think-alouds."

Think aloud

To help poor readers clarify their views of reading and their use of strategies, teachers can verbalize their own thoughts while reading orally. We call these activities "think-alouds."

First, select a passage to read aloud that contains points of difficulty, contradictions, ambiguities, or unknown words. (You may want to develop your own materials for this step—short, with obvious problems.) As you read the passage aloud, students follow along silently listening to how you think through these trouble spots. Here are some examples of points to make during think-alouds.

1. *Make predictions.* (Show how to develop hypotheses.)

"From the title, I predict that this section will tell how fishermen used to catch whales."

"In this next part, I think we'll find out why the men flew into the hurricane."

"I think this is a description of a computer game."

2. *Describe the picture you're forming in your head from the information.* (Show how to develop images during reading.)

"I have a picture of this scene in my mind. The car is on a dark, probably narrow, road; there are no other cars around."

3. *Share an analogy.* (Show how to link prior knowledge with new information in text.) We call this the "like-a" step.

"This is like a time we drove to Boston and had a flat tire. We were worried and we had to walk three miles for help."

4. *Verbalize a confusing point.* (Show how you monitor your ongoing comprehension.)

"This just doesn't make sense."

"This is different from what I had expected."

5. *Demonstrate fix-up strategies.* (Show how you correct your lagging comprehension.)

"I'd better reread."

"Maybe I'll read ahead to see if it gets clearer."

"I'd better change my picture of the story."

"This is a new word to me—I'd better check context to figure it out."

---

to be aware that they may have a comprehension problem while reading (the plan sheet) and then are taught strategies for dealing with comprehension failure (the cards).

The reading plan sheet asks five questions: "(1) What is reading? (2) What is my goal? (3) How difficult is the text? (4) How can I accomplish my goal? (5) How can I check on whether or not I accomplished my goal?" (Babbs, 1984, p. 201). The questions presented on this plan sheet represent a study strategy, and you may see similarities between these questions and the strategy presented in the overview to this chapter. Students should receive practice using the plan sheet so that these questions are automatically asked before beginning to read expository material.

The comprehension monitoring cards encourage readers, in a step-by-step fashion, to evaluate their own understanding of the text read and also aid readers in knowing what to do when a comprehension problem occurs. The nine cards and their identifying numbers, are as follows: (1) Click—l understand. (2) Clunk—l don't understand. (3) Read on. (4) Reread the sentence. (5) Go back and reread the paragraph. (6) Look in the glossary. (7) Ask someone. (8) What did it say? (to check comprehension at the paragraph level). (9) What do I remember? (to check comprehension at the page level) (Babbs, 1984, pp. 201–202).

A modeling procedure is recommended to teach students to use the cards. The teacher reads a sentence of text, then asks, "Did I understand that?" If the answer is yes, the Click card is raised and the teacher goes on to the next sentence. If the answer is no, the Clunk card is raised and cards 3 through 7 are selected. If the problem is with a word, the order of the strategy cards is 4–3–6–7. If the problem is with the whole sentence or with a pronoun referent, the order of the strategy cards is 4–5–3–7. The teacher models all of these possibilities, using a variety of several sentences.

After a complete paragraph has been modeled, the teacher should look away from the page and hold up card 8 and answer that question. If the question cannot be answered, the paragraph is reread without further use of the strategy cards. Likewise, after a complete page has been modeled, the teacher again looks away from the text, holds up card 9, and answers the question. If the question cannot be answered, the page is reread using card 8 after each paragraph.

Once the teacher has modeled the process, Babbs (1984) recommends that each student have a turn modeling before going on to individual practice. She also states that 15 sessions of 22 minutes each were allowed for learning both the reading plan sheet questions and the use of the comprehension monitoring cards. At that point the students could describe details of both of these elements from memory.

Another way to help students develop their self-questioning ability is to provide study guides that ask students the kinds of questions they should ask themselves. The Revised Extended Anticipation Guide (Duffelmeyer & Baum, 1992) is a good example (see Figure 12.7). Part 1 is a prereading activity in which students activate their schema for the topic by reflecting on their beliefs and/or perceptions and agreeing or disagreeing with teacher-developed statements made about the topic. Class discussion following Part 1 will reveal student differences and provide further motivation for reading the selection, in addition to reading to verify choices made in Part 1. Part 2 is completed *during* reading. Here students are constantly being asked to question their choices in Part 1. If a choice is supported by the reading the *yes* is checked and evidence or justification is written in the space provided. Likewise, if a choice is *not* supported, the *no* column is checked and a paraphrasing of what was stated in the material to refute the choice is written.

Such activities will help students form habits of 1) thinking about what they know and believe about a topic *before* reading, and 2) questioning their understanding of material

F I G U R E

12.7

Revised Extended Anticipation Guide.

PART 1:

Directions: Before you read your class assignment, read each statement in Part 1. If you believe that a statement is true, place a check in the Agree column. If you believe that a statement is false, place a check in the Disagree column. Be ready to explain your choices.

Agree	Disagree	
☑	☐	1. You can get AIDS by being near someone who has it, just as you can with a cold or the flu.
☐	☑	2. AIDS kills people by attacking a single organ, like the heart or the lungs.
☐	☑	3. Because of AIDS, donating blood is no longer safe.
☑	☐	4. An unborn baby is safe from AIDS as long as the mother doesn't inject drugs.
☑	☐	5. AIDS can be controlled with extreme rest and care.
☑	☐	6. Many people with AIDS in this country have died.

PART 2:

Directions: Now you will read information related to each of the statements in Part 1. If the information supports your choices above, place a check in the Yes column in Part 2. Then write what the text says in your own words in column (A), under "Why is my choice correct?" If the information does not support your choices, place a check in the No column. Then write what the text says in your own words in column B, under "Why is my choice incorrect?"

Support in text for my choice		(A)	(B)
Yes	No	**Why is my choice correct?**	**Why is my choice incorrect?**
1.☐	☑	_____ _____	AIDS is spread through sex and contaminated blood.
2.☑	☐	AIDS kills people by attacking their immune system.	_____ _____
3.☑	☐	Giving blood is safe because a clean needle is always used.	_____ _____
4.☐	☑	_____ _____	A pregnant woman can get AIDS in other ways.
5.☐	☑	_____ _____	There is no known cure for AIDS.
6.☑	☐	Half of the people with AIDS in this country have died.	_____ _____

during reading. (See Wood, Lapp, & Flood, 1992, *Guiding readers through text: A review of study guides,* for other examples of study guides that could be used to focus on self-questioning during reading.)

Postreading

In the final stage of studying, activities that help the student organize and remember important information are appropriate. Outlining, paraphrasing, and reciting or rehearsal of information are common activities for this last stage. These activities are usually difficult for students to master, however.

Mapping. **Mapping** aids the learner in linking ideas together (see also Chapters 9 and 10). As discussed here, mapping is intended as a substitute for the organizational activity of outlining. Hanf (1971) discusses three basic steps for designing a map: (1) identify the main idea (2) identify principal parts that support the main idea (called secondary categories) (3) identify supporting details. The skeleton of a map may be completed during the prereading stage (i.e., the title of the selection becoming the main idea or central theme and the headings becoming secondary categories that support the main idea). However, the map itself should be completed during the postreading stage from memory. The student must add the supporting details. If the map cannot be completed, the student knows to go back and reread the material. Thus there is a built-in feedback device. If the student can complete some parts of the map but not others, the map has provided feedback on categories needing further study. An example of a map for the study of a science chapter entitled "Power for Work"[1] is found in Figure 12.8.

When the K–W–L strategy discussed earlier is combined with mapping and summarization, the technique helps students construct meaning from the text in an independent fashion. This modification of K–W–L is called *K–W–L Plus* (Carr & Ogle, 1987), and has been used successfully with secondary readers having reading and writing difficulty. Basically, students must think critically about what they have read in order to organize, restructure, and apply what they have learned to the formation of a map and a written summary. Figure 12.9 shows how one ninth grader went from the K–W–L listings to a concept map. The map can then be used as an aid for preparing a written summary and also preparing for exams.

Think-links. Wilson (1981) refers to another organizational strategy called **think-links**. Upon completion of the during reading stage of study, the teacher directs the students to think about what they have read. The following steps are then taken (Fig. 12.10).

1. Write the name of the person the chapter is about (Lincoln) and some words that describe his early life.
2. Ask students for examples that show Lincoln's early life was hard, and record them.
3. Step 2 is repeated using other descriptive words.

After all of the words have been used, the students have actually reconstructed, graphically, the important parts of the material read.

---

[1]From *In Your Neighborhood* (pp. 91–96) by A. O. Baker, G. C. Maddox, and H. B. Warrin, 1955, New York: Rand McNally.

Once the teacher has helped students develop several think-links, they can start to develop them on their own. Think-links are used to summarize any type of reading material; during the instructional process, different types are constructed with the students so they can see a variety of types.

Paragraph frames. As discussed in Chapter 10, paragraph frames provide a useful instructional tool for helping students write about what they learn in content areas (Cudd & Roberts, 1989). A cloze format is used that provides sentence starters focusing on the organizational pattern of the text. Intended for students of all grade levels, the introduction of paragraph frames is easiest with sequentially ordered material. The teacher might write a brief paragraph based on a content area topic just read, using such key words as

---

F I G U R E

12.8

Example of a map for a science chapter, "Power for Work."

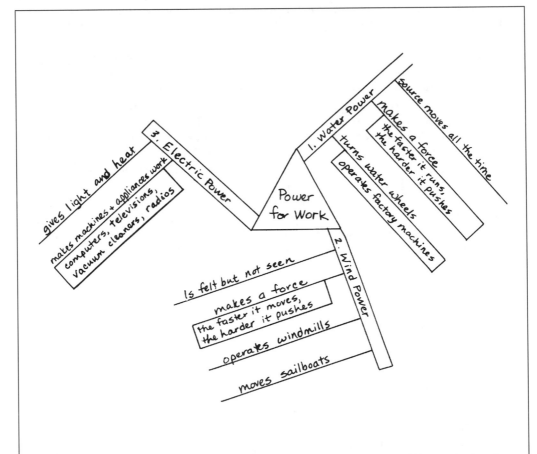

Mapping is thinking: constructing and creating the organizational design of ideas, selecting the information that is relevant, and sorting this into its proper place, relating all facts to the whole and relating facts to other facts, and finally responding with personal reaction to the material. (Hanf, 1971, p. 229)

Example of ninth grader's K–W–L worksheet and resulting concept map.

A 9th-grade disabled reader's K–W–L worksheet on killer whales

K (Know)	W (Want to know)	L (Learned)
They live in oceans. They are vicious. They eat each other. They are mammals.	Why do they attack people? How fast can they swim? What kind of fish do they eat? What is their description? How long do they live? How do they breathe?	D — They are the biggest member of the dolphin family. D — They weigh 10,000 pounds and get 30 feet long. F — They eat squids, seals, and other dolphins. A — They have good vision underwater. F — They are carnivorous (meat eaters). A — They are the second smartest animal on earth. D — They breathe through blow holes. A — They do not attack unless they are hungry.
Description Food Location		D — Warm-blooded. A — They have echo-location (sonar). L — They are found in the oceans.

Final category designations developed for column L, information learned about killer whales:
A = abilities, D = description. F = food, L = location

The 9th-grader's concept map

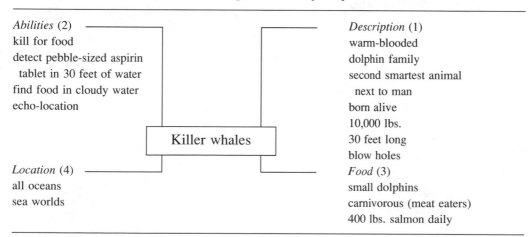

Abilities (2)
kill for food
detect pebble-sized aspirin
   tablet in 30 feet of water
find food in cloudy water
echo-location

Description (1)
warm-blooded
dolphin family
second smartest animal
   next to man
born alive
10,000 lbs.
30 feet long
blow holes

Killer whales

Location (4)
all oceans
sea worlds

Food (3)
small dolphins
carnivorous (meat eaters)
400 lbs. salmon daily

(1) through (4) indicate the order of categories the student chose later for writing a summary.

FIGURE
12.10

Think-links are used to summarize graphically the important parts of any type of reading matter.

Think-links

Step 1

Abraham Lincoln

poor   simple   hard   old-fashioned

Step 2

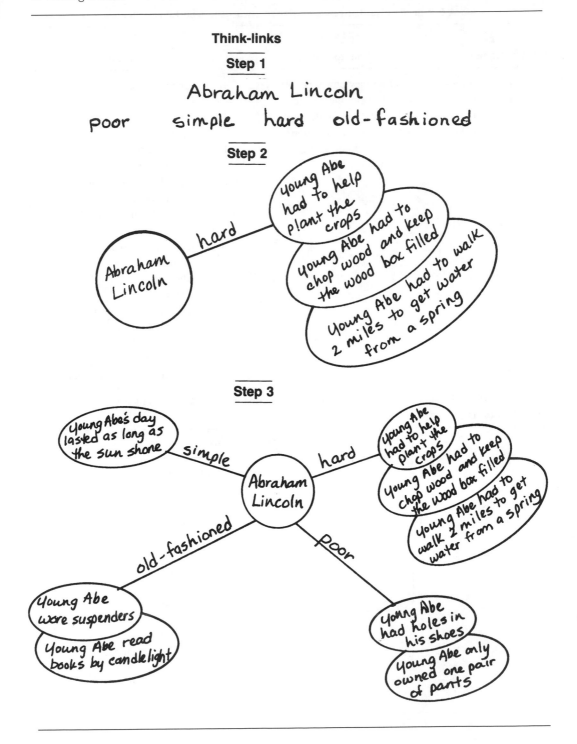

Step 3

first, next, then, now, finally, and *after this.* The individual sentences are put on sentence strips and as a group students are asked to first review the topic read and then to arrange the sentence strips in the logical sequence of events. The resulting paragraph is read for "correctness." Following the group work, individual students are to reorder the sentences on their own, write the paragraph, and illustrate the important parts. Figure 12.11 provides an example of a completed paragraph frame.

General Study Strategies

SQ3R

The most well known study strategy recommended for helping students make optimum use of study time is Robinson's (1961) **SQ3R** (survey, question, read, recite, review)

Example of a completed paragraph frame, including illustrations.

F I G U R E

12.11

Example 3 (Rob, grade 1)

Mother box turtles prepare for their babies in a very interesting way. First, she looks for a safe place to burry her eggs. Next, she digs a hole so it will be moist for her eggs. Finally, she lays her eggs, burrys the hole, and then tamps it down. After this, the mother turtle leaves her babies on their own.

Strategy. This strategy is designed to (1) provide specific purposes for reading (2) provide self-comprehension checks (3) fix information in memory (Tadlock, 1978). Briefly, in the *survey* step, the student reads the title, introductory statement, and main headings, surveys the illustrations, reads the chapter summary, and tries to construct mentally an outline of the chapter. In the *question* phase, the student again looks at the main headings. These headings are used to formulate questions to be answered in the next step. The *read* step then has the main purpose of finding answers to the questions formed in the question phase. The *recite* step has the student literally reciting the answers aloud to the questions. At this point the student should also be concerned about the quality of the answers; for example, does the author provide answers that satisfy the question? The last step, *review,* is done from memory, with the entire chapter or selection being reviewed in survey fashion. The mental outline is reconstructed. The author's main ideas are recalled, and new ways to use these ideas are considered. A second and even a third review should take place over as many days.

However, several investigations of SQ3R have shown it not to be as effective for students with reading difficulties as expected (McCormick & Cooper, 1991). Instructional adaptations to SQ3R suggested by these studies are:

- Providing shorter selections (300 words), as students did better when reading passages of this length. This presents students with an easier task
- Having frequent discussion sessions to allow for direct teacher input if reading longer selections
- Integrating discussion questions at short intervals throughout the selection, rather than asking all questions at the end of a reading

Perhaps SQ3R modifications will be more effective for students with learning difficulties. For example, Call (1991) uses SQ3R in combination with *What I Know* sheets to help students monitor their own learning (see Figure 12.12). She has field tested this combination with college students and concluded that it helps students read faster and with a purpose, helps them locate major ideas, and provides them a ready reference for test preparation.

A technique developed by Edward Strickland (1975) is called **Assignment Mastery**. The steps themselves closely parallel those in SQ3R. They are: scanning, preparation for reading, reading, recitation and review, and reading review. The biggest difference from SQ3R is that specific questions are developed for students to ask themselves during the scanning, preparation, and reading stages. These follow:

Scanning
- How difficult does the work appear to be?
- Is it a relatively large amount of work?
- Will I have to alter my schedule to get it done?
- Are the terms generally familiar?
- What is the main theme of the assignment?
- What main headings and subheadings are there?
- What words are stressed (in italics or bold print)?

Preparation for reading (with the help of a dictionary or glossary)
- Are there related terms that I use?

- Have I learned something that changes the meaning of the term from what I thought it was?
- Does the theme of the material appear to challenge or support my ideas?

Reading
- What is the meaning of what I am reading?
- What illustrations of that meaning are given?
- Can I recall any examples from my own experience that would clarify the meaning of the material?

Example of an undergraduate's *What I Know* sheet.

FIGURE

12.12

Student:___Jane Johnson_____ Date: _____

Chapter Title:___Concept teaching in content instruction_____

Purpose Question: _____

COLUMN A **What I already know:**	COLUMN B **What I now know:**	COLUMN C **What I don't know:**
Concepts are abstract ideas gathered from interrelated areas.	Concept teaching is the idea of what we are actually doing.	1. A good definition for concept teaching.
New concepts build on the old & give direction to the new concept.	Emphasis is placed on the need for concept teaching.	2. How the teacher identifies concepts.
Concepts are the ideas learned in a given subject.	Before having a content lesson look at what students need to learn & what they know. (Will help them understand the info.)	3. How concepts are organized for instruction.
	Concepts identified and teaching strategies determined before teaching begins.	4. Gagne's component of concept learning.
	The identification of concept to be taught is the 1st step in teaching.	
	Preschoolers have no set plan of learning & no organization (concrete); a *lot* of new info is *abstract*.	

Summary of learning
1. Parents are first ones to teach concepts (no certain steps).
2. Identification of concepts to be taught is first thing (organized method of teaching).
3. Teachers' responsibility to teach how to learn concepts and build upon what they already know.
4. Teachers' responsibility.

Reprinted with permission of Patricia E. Call and the International Reading Association.

- What questions should I ask my instructor that will help clarify the meaning of this material?

Strickland also stresses the underlining or outlining of main themes and illustrative examples while reading. (For a detailed description of how to teach the SQ3R Strategy, the interested reader is referred to Forgan and Mangrum's (1985) *Teaching Content Area Reading Skills,* pages 180–182.)

GRS

The guided reading strategy (Bean & Pardi, 1979) was developed specifically for corrective readers. The **guided reading strategy (GRS)** is a modification of the guided reading procedure (Manzo, 1975). Briefly, the steps of a GRS are as follows:

1. Survey the chapter or chapter sections, reading only the chapter title, subtitles, vocabulary lists, graphs, maps, and chapter questions.
2. Close the book and orally state everything remembered from the survey. The teacher records what is remembered on the board.
3. Students recheck the chapter for any missing information; this is added to the board.
4. A crucial step, the teacher and students discuss the results of the chapter survey and organize this information into a topical outline on the board. This organizing highlights the structure of the information and enhances the ability to remember it later.
5. Students read the chapter or selection silently.
6. Students complete a ten-item true–false quiz.
7. About a week later, students take a ten-item pop quiz.

Of these three strategies, the teacher may find that using the GRS as an introduction to the other strategies is most helpful.

PORPE

A strategy developed by Simpson (1986) for secondary and college level students as a less teacher-directed strategy uses writing as the main learning strategy for planning, monitoring, and evaluating the reading of any content area material. PORPE (*P*redict, *O*rganize, *R*ehearse, *P*ractice, *E*valuate) is especially useful for students preparing to take essay examinations. Once the five steps of PORPE are modeled and mastered, it becomes a learning strategy that gives the student complete independence and control. The 5 steps are briefly presented here, but interested readers are urged to refer to Simpson's (1986) detailed description of the steps, and how to teach them to students. The steps are:

1. *Predict.* Students are asked to generate possible essay questions on the material read.
2. *Organize.* Students summarize and synthesize the important ideas in the material. Charts, maps, or outlines are all possible ways for organizing the material.
3. *Rehearse.* Students recite the overall organizational structure of the chart, map, or outline, eventually adding important ideas and examples to this recitation. The purpose is to place these important ideas and organizational structure into long-term memory.

4. *Practice.* Students actually practice writing answers to the predicted essay questions from recall.

5. *Evaluate.* Students judge the quality of their responses from the perspective of the instructor. An evaluative checklist might be developed to aid in this process.

Two validation studies (Simpson, Stahl, & Hayes (1989) show PORPE to be a practical and robust strategy for long-lasting learning and student independence.

Additional Acronyms for Study Strategies

There are many other valuable study strategies but space constraints do not allow for their thorough explanation. The following listing is intended to alert you to several of these other possibilities, some of which are content-area specific. Interested readers are referred to the sources cited for more information.

AIM (Author's Intended Message)—a metacognitive strategy for constructing the main idea of text (Jacobowitz, 1990).

FLIP (Friendliness, Language, Interest, Prior Knowledge)—a framework for helping middle school and secondary students estimate the difficulty of their content area reading assignments (Schumm & Mangrum II, 1991).

PLAE (Preplan, List, Activate and Evaluate)—emphasizes the self-regulatory processes involved in planning, monitoring, and evaluating, field-tested with college developmental reading students (Simpson & Nist, 1984; Nist & Simpson, 1989). Three validation studies conclude that (1) planning is significantly related to performance on tests (Nist, Simpson, Olejnik, & Mealey, 1989), (2) PLAE positively affects both test performance and metacognitive abilities (Nist & Simpson, 1989), (3) students using PLAE outperformed those using traditional time management on four content-area examinations (Nist & Simpson, 1990).

PQRST (Preview, Question, Read, Summarize, Test)—developed to help students read physical science texts (Spache, 1963).

REAP (Read, Encode, Annotate, and Ponder)—intended to help readers synthesize an author's ideas and use writing as an aid for future recall and study of ideas (Eanet & Manzo, 1976).

SCAIT (Select key words; Complete sentences; Accept final statements; Infer; Think)—intended for high school students and utilizes cooperative learning to help students learn how to select important information from text and develop higher-level thinking skills (Wiesendanger & Bader, 1992).

SQRQCQ (Survey, Question, Read, Question, Compute, Question)—developed to help students solve mathematical reading/reasoning problems (Fay, 1965).

SUMMARY

The techniques presented here have been chosen because they stress student involvement with text and appear in the literature as promising techniques.

Teachers must be concerned with developing study strategies even for the young reader. At the early stages this may simply involve scanning printed material for a specific word or being taught to question material while reading it; that is, asking "Do I understand this?" Teacher modeling of the types of questions to ask while reading is one direct way of providing instruction in the area of self-questioning. Also, students at all levels, when given appropriate materials, can be taught to organize what they have read to aid them in remembering that material. Mapping and think-links are promising techniques because of their graphic nature.

The general study strategies discussed are most easily learned if the students have previously received instruction in the three stages of studying, because these strategies include all three phases. Study strategies do not simply develop—they must be modeled, explained, and practiced.

SUGGESTED READINGS

Freeman, E.B., and Person, D.G. (1992). *Using nonfiction trade books in the elementary classroom: From ants to zeppelins.* Urbana, IL: National Council of Teachers of English.

> *This resource will help teachers provide interesting content area material for their students. Students may be more willing to try the strategies presented in this chapter with the materials discussed in this text. Teachers who wish to use thematic units will find this book especially valuable.*

Glazer, S.M. (1992). *Reading comprehension: Self-monitoring strategies to develop independent readers.* New York: Scholastic.

> *This easily understood monograph provides a wealth of examples and checklists for helping students learn to monitor their comprehension. Guidelines for setting up a classroom environment conducive to students taking more responsibility for their own learning are also provided.*

13

DEVELOPING READING OF LINGUISTICALLY DIVERSE STUDENTS

John G. Barnitz

OBJECTIVES

After you have read this chapter, you should be able to

1. explain the relationship between communicative competence and reading development;
2. describe some of the basic characteristics of linguistic competence and sociolinguistic competence;
3. describe how language characteristics vary across cultural groups;
4. list some specific characteristics of Black English Vernacular and other varieties of English;
5. explain implications of language or dialect diversity for assessing students' language and reading abilities;
6. summarize basic principles for teaching standard English;
7. describe various approaches for supporting the reading development of linguistically diverse students;
8. appreciate and respect the language varieties of students as a first step toward developing standard English literacy.

KEY CONCEPTS AND TERMS

Black English Vernacular
communicative competence
deficit hypothesis
dialects
dialogue journals

discourse
experience–text–relationship method
language experience approach
language functions
linguistic competence

The author wishes to thank Dr. John G. Barnitz, University of New Orleans, for contributing this chapter.

morphemes
morphology
narrative ability
oral interaction
phonemes
phonology
regional dialects

social dialects
sociolinguistic competence
standard dialects
style shifting
syntax
vernacular dialects

STUDY OUTLINE

1. Communicative competence, language, and reading
2. Characteristics of linguistic variation
   a. Black English Vernacular
   b. Other language varieties
3. Principles for reading and language development
   a. Language-reading assessment

b. Standard English language arts instruction
c. Reading instruction
   • Literature-based instruction
   • Language experience approach
   • Experience–text–relationship method
4. Summary
5. Suggested readings

OVERVIEW

Teachers frequently find that many students in a corrective reading program are learners whose native tongue is either a vernacular dialect of English or another language totally. Some of these students have become poor readers because of true correlates to reading disability, while many have become poor readers as a result of teachers' unawareness of how language and dialect variation influences the reading process. Teachers' attitudes toward language varieties can either facilitate or hinder minority students' growth in literacy (Goodman & Buck, 1973). For example, as a result of the federal court case of *Martin Luther King Junior Elementary School Children* v. *Ann Arbor School District Board,* teachers are expected to understand and respect the language varieties minority children bring to the task of learning to read standard English (Labov, 1983; Smitherman, 1985.) A major implication of the

Ann Arbor case is that it established a legal precedent for parents of students in any ethnic group to expect teachers to know linguistic facts about the language varieties learners bring to school (Labov, 1983). Moreover, teachers in the 1990s recognize the need to use whole-language strategies for developing the literacy of students whose native language or dialect is not standard English. Regardless of linguistic backgrounds, *all* people bring their native varieties to the task of learning to read and write English.

The primary purposes for reading this chapter, then, are threefold: (1) to understand the nature of communicative competence as it relates to reading (2) to understand basic information about dialect and language diversity (3) to acquire some guidelines and techniques for teaching reading of standard English texts in linguistically diverse schools.

COMMUNICATIVE COMPETENCE, LANGUAGE, AND READING

A general understanding of **communicative competence** and the relationship between language development and reading development is essential. Language competence is both a prerequisite to learning to read and an intimate part of the fluent reading process. As language is basic to reading, linguistic information is an integral part of the professional knowledge of teachers of reading. In this section, I will define some basic concepts associated with communicative competence.

Communicative competence is defined by DeStefano (1978, p. 2) as "competence in language use or as the language abilities of the speaker and listener." Hymes (1974) clearly asserts that communicative abilities not only involve the basic mastery of the language system but also the use of language in social situations. Shuy (1981a) labeled these two capabilities as **linguistic competence** and **sociolinguistic competence**. Linguistic competence generally refers to mastery of the formal system of language (sounds, sentences, vocabulary), while sociolinguistic competence is the use of language "to get things done." Sociolinguistic competence is the most important aspect of communication and of language learning. Functional use of language is basic to language production and comprehension and usually precedes the formal perfection of structure. Functional use of language is also crucial to school success (Shafer, Staab, & Smith, 1983), although many traditional curricula are limited only to linguistic competence. Verbal interaction (active use of speaking, listening, writing, and reading) is critical for language and literacy acquisition, especially as learners use their culturally appropriate conversation abilities as they construct meaning for the texts they are reading (Au, 1993; Enright & McCloskey, 1988; Freeman & Freeman, 1992; Hiebert, 1991; Rigg & Allen, 1989; Tharp & Gallimore, 1988).

Shuy (1981a) described sociolinguistic competence as including, among other things, oral interaction, language functions, narrative abilities, and style shifting. **Oral interaction** is a basic human social skill that encompasses such abilities as beginning a conversation, switching topics, taking turns, or using tact in sharing bad news. It also includes basic pragmatic abilities, such as knowing what and what not to say, stating things directly and indirectly, being relevant, and so forth. These important social skills may transfer to reading because reading is a social activity (Cook-Gumperz, 1986; Vygotsky, 1978). Such skills also help one to infer the social motives of an author and better comprehend the oral interactions of characters in a story.

Language functions, as mentioned earlier, are crucial to the social use of language. Language exists because it is useful, and children learn language when they perceive the need. For instance, sixth-grade students in their **dialogue journals** (daily journals written back and forth by the child and teacher) demonstrated a wide range of **language functions:** reporting opinions and personal and general facts, responding to questions, predicting future events, complaining, giving directives, apologizing, thanking, evaluating, offering, promising, and asking various types of questions (Shuy, 1988; Staton, Shuy, Peyton, & Reed, 1988). Zulu speakers (ages 12–16) learning English also used a variety of language functions in their dialogue journals (Lindfors, 1989): teaching, inquiring, joking, informing, scolding, offering, seeking clarification, apologizing, explaining, expressing opinions, conversing, thanking, comforting, reflecting. Functional language development is essential to literacy development in that the writer must use language to bring out a certain response in the reader. Conversely, an effective reader is aware of what the author is trying to *do* with language. Therefore, functional language ability is a basic reading and writing skill.

Narrative ability encompasses another set of sociolinguistic competencies, which includes not only the above two categories, but also the fluency of expression and sequencing of ideas. Many speakers are "gifted" at composing oral stories, telling lengthy jokes, and describing traffic accidents in logical and sequential manners. Future research may prove that this ability transfers to reading narratives. If students have an intuitive awareness of how narrative discourse is ordered, they can make meaningful predictions in the reading comprehension process. Students may demonstrate strong narrative abilities, regardless of the dialect or language spoken.

Style shifting is an important language skill that refers to the ability of speakers and writers to adapt their language styles to various social contexts (i.e., different settings, participants, and topics). Just as we vary our dress depending on the social situation (formal, semiformal, casual, "grubby"), so do we shift our language. Language *variety* is a necessary part of language competence. The more variety in our language "wardrobe," the better we can survive in diverse social contexts.

What is crucial to remember is that sociolinguistic competence is a foundation for developing linguistic competence or the actual structures of the language: phonology, morphology, syntax, discourse structure, and vocabulary. Recall that **phonology** refers to the sounds **(phonemes)** and sound processes of a language. **Morphology** refers to the study of meaningful word structures **(morphemes)**. **Syntax** is the system of patterns and processes in sentence formation. **Discourse** refers to a unit of communication that relates ideas to a unified theme for a particular purpose. Vocabulary, of course, is made up of the words of the language. These surface features comprise only the tip of the iceberg of language competence; sociolinguistic competence is the essence of language communication or the rest of the iceberg below the surface (Shuy, 1981a). Focusing only on language skills or the tip of the iceberg, while ignoring the fuller iceberg, is a sure way to sink students' literacy development like the Titanic.

Language competence is intimately related to reading development. Linguists and linguistically informed reading educators understand that students bring to school a wealth of language and cultural experiences upon which teachers can guide them for building literacy. This is even true of linguistically diverse students, who have been shown to follow stages of language acquisition similar to those of middle-class learners (Steffensen, 1974, 1978) and also to acquire English literacy naturally, while they were learning the language. In other words, learners do not need to be fully proficient in standard English before learning the reading and writing process; students learn language "skills" while *doing* writing-reading in authentic contexts (Edelsky, 1986; Freeman & Freeman, 1992; Goodman & Goodman, 1978; Hudelson, 1989; Rigg & Allen, 1989). Both first and second language English speaking students' literacy is continually emerging within natural, authentic, communicative contexts. Reading and writing emerge together (Sulzby & Teale, 1991).

Reading and language development are interdependent. Earlier studies (Strickland, 1962; Ruddell, 1965; Tatham, 1970) illustrate that students with more variety and complexity of syntax in their oral language tend to be better readers. Chomsky (1972) found that children with more exposure to books were more advanced in oral language development. Eckhoff (1983) found that students learned sentence patterns through their reading and transferred them to their writing. Purcell-Gates (1988) and Purcell-Gates and Dahl (1991) found that children with literature experience in their early childhood grow in their sociolinguistic competence related to literacy. Reading instruction, therefore, cannot be isolated from the development of learners' communicative competence, regardless of the variety of language students bring to school. In the next section, some of the characteristics of dialect and language variation commonly found in classrooms are presented.

CHARACTERISTICS OF LINGUISTIC VARIATION

In this section is a brief sketch of how language varies with geographical areas and social classes. Teachers must be linguistically informed of language varieties among students in their reading programs in order to distinguish between errors and dialect or language variations.

Most of you have enjoyed traveling to different parts of the country and meeting a wide variety of people in gas stations, restaurants, hotels, resorts, or roadside fruit stands, and you have certainly noticed how pronunciation and usage patterns differ from your own. Similarly, you will notice how students in your classroom vary in their speech performance depending on their home background or place of birth. These surface variations are part of what are called **dialects**; they are fully developed linguistic systems identifiable to particular speech communities and vary in the specific combination of pronunciation, vocabulary, and usage. Dialects identifiable to a particular geographical area are called **regional dialects**. For example, Labov (1988) studied the complexity of the regional distributions of the submarine sandwich lexicon: submarine, hoagie, po'boy, grinder, hero, wedge, torpedo, and zep. Compare these and other dialect features among your classmates. How do the syntax, phonology, and lexicon of various English speakers differ regionally and socially? (See Shuy, 1967; and Wolfram & Christian, 1989).

Dialects also vary across social classes or cultural groups. These are called **social dialects**. Our speech often reflects our social status (Labov, 1975). The language varieties spoken and preferred by the more favored (usually more educated and higher-income) members of our community for conducting formal affairs are **standard dialects** (Wolfram, 1991), while the varieties used in informal settings and also pervasive among groups of lower social status are called **vernacular dialects**. Teachers must respect the language and culture of students from all social classes, while providing opportunities for all to acquire standard English.

Language also varies, as noted earlier, in terms of the social situation. One aspect of communicative competence is the ability to use language appropriate to the situation, whether formal or informal. These styles are additional complex aspects of language variation, common to all social classes (Labov, 1975). Thus, one's speech at a given instance is usually influenced by regional, social, and situational factors.

Black English Vernacular

Black English Vernacular (BEV) is a variety of English found in African-American communities and used in the most informal settings throughout the United States. BEV differs from the standard speech found in mixed communities (Labov, 1983). As is any ethnic variety of English, BEV is rule-governed, containing a systematic set of phonological and syntactic features, some of which are listed below (Burling, 1973; Labov, 1975; and Smitherman, 1985). Some of the phonological patterns/processes include:

Consonant cluster simplification	des' (desk)
Deletion /l/	hep (help)
Voiced th	den (then)
Voiceless th	tin (thin)
Vowel neutralization before nasal consonants	pin (pen)

Some of the morphological and syntactic patterns include:

Plural deletion	ten cent
Deletion of 3rd person singular	The girl walk fast.
Past tense deletion	The man call yesterday.
Existential it (there)	It was three apples in the basket.
Invariant be	He be hollin at us.
Be deleted	My momma name Annie.

Several additional facts about BEV should be understood.

1. Much communicative competence of BEV speakers is illustrated by the rich lexical and discourse styles found in African-American communities (Kochman 1972, 1981).

2. Because Black English Vernacular is a rule-governed system, the claim that it is an illegitimate or linguistically inferior language system has been disproved in studies (Labov, 1975; Burling, 1973; Steffensen, 1978) and has been disproved in federal court (Labov, 1982; Smitherman, 1985).

3. Many surface features of Black English Vernacular are shared by vernacular English speakers in lower socioeconomic groups, but the distribution or frequency of specific features varies (Labov, 1975). Language varieties develop along with social, cultural, economic, or racial boundaries in a society.

4. Part of communicative competence involves knowing when to adapt language to the appropriate settings, topics, and participants in a discourse. Therefore, many speakers shift between standard and vernacular features as appropriate to the formality of the social situation: standard English for formal situations (e.g., commerce, education, law) and vernacular for informal settings. Moreover, speakers of any dialect vary their language according to the social setting.

Other Language Varieties

A detailed discussion of other varieties of English found in the repertoire of culturally diverse students will not be undertaken here. Teachers should be aware, however, that language diversity, not just dialect diversity, can influence students' learning to read standard English, and should become familiar with other language varieties found in the United States.

Nonnative varieties of English are found throughout the United States, and learners of English as their second language will probably need assistance in learning to read English. Learners whose native language is, for example, Spanish or Vietnamese, bring a certain degree of linguistic and sociolinguistic competence in their native languages to learning to read English. Moreover, many, but certainly not all, second language learners already have some literacy exposure to and abilities in English. Some native language and literacy abilities transfer to English, although the extent of transfer may depend on the specific languages and writing systems involved (Cowan, 1976). Learners often use the rules from their native language schema in reading English as a second language. Many so-called errors are the result of the influence of the native language rather than linguistic or cognitive deficits (Flores, 1984). Therefore, it is important for teachers to learn about contrasts among languages. Although languages are too complex to be thoroughly discussed here, a few phonological and syntactic differences between English and Spanish and between English and Vietnamese are listed below.

Because the phoneme systems of Spanish and English differ, various pairs of English words that normally are pronounced differently are pronounced or heard as similar, like homonyms, by the native Spanish speaker. Geissal and Knafle (1977) explained that this is not the result of a speech or hearing problem, but rather the result of the second language learners using their native linguistic schemata in processing English. The native language, then, influences the speaking, listening, writing, and reading of the second language.

The following consonant contrasts are often not made by native Spanish speakers learning English because these contrasts are not made in Spanish (Troike, 1972, p. 312):

ch/sh	chair / share	watch / wash
s/z	sip / zip	racer / razor
n/ng	sin / sing	
b/v	bat / vat	rabble / ravel
t/th	tin / thin	
s/th	sin / thin	
d/th	den / then	ladder / lather

Spanish, unlike English, has only five vowel phonemes. Thus Spanish speakers do not hear or pronounce contrasts such as the following:

bait / bet / bat

cut / cot

cheap / chip

pool / pull

coat / caught

Here are some more examples, this time from Vietnamese (Grognet et al., 1976). Vietnamese speakers learning English do not contrast such pairs of English words as the following:

z / s	flees / fleece
	dyes / dice
ch / sh	much / mush
f / p	laugh / lap
p / b	pin / bin
k / g	Kay / gay
th / t	ether / eater
th / d	weather / wetter / wedder
i / e	pit / Pete
e / a	bet / bat

Nonnative speakers of English (and vernacular dialect speakers) do not hear or pronounce contrasts not made in the native language. Vietnamese phonology does not allow consonant clusters at the ends of words; therefore, in pronouncing English words they may split consonant blends with vowels (*stop* becomes *suhtop*) or delete consonants at the ends of words (*cold* becomes *col*'; *called* becomes *call*). Thus, their auditory discrimination and oral reading may be influenced by the phonological organization of the native language. This is natural and not a sign of linguistic deficiency or disability (Flores, 1984; Goodman & Buck, 1973).

In teaching spelling or word identification, these pairs of words can be treated like any other set of homonyms: teach them in meaningful contexts first. More contextual support reduces potential linguistic interference from phonological diversity.

Therefore, meaning-based, holistic techniques are especially important to successful reading instruction of linguistically diverse learners (see Barnitz, 1985; Carrell, Devine & Eskey, 1988; Rigg & Allen, 1989; Freeman & Freeman, 1992).

Just as phonological systems of native languages influence performance in English, so do the syntactic systems. Davis (1972, pp. 131–132) presented, among other syntactic features, the following sentence structures possibly produced by Spanish speakers learning English (also included in a teachers' guide by the New York City Board of Education, *Teaching English to Puerto Rican Pupils in Grades 1 and 2* (1956, 1963)).

Deletion of subject pronouns and articles	Is green. Is my sister.
Negative morpheme before verb	Jose not (no) is here.
Adjectives after nouns	The dress green.
	The dresses greens.
Deletion of /s/ inflections	He go to church.
	The pencil are here.
Present instead of progressive	He clean now.
Preposition contrasts	In the counter.
	In First St.
Have for be	She have nine years.

Teachers of Vietnamese learners need to be aware of some of the following syntactic characteristics of Vietnamese (Grognet et al., 1976). Vietnamese is a language that does not use suffixes to convey meaning, such as plurals or tense. Meaning is conveyed in other ways, as seen in sentences that translate into English as follows:

I need book.
I need one piece book.
I need three piece book.
I need few piece book.

Plurality is marked by separate morphemes rather than suffixes. Likewise, tense is marked by separate words that are equivalent to the underlined words in the following sentences:

I <u>often</u> drink tea.
I <u>intend to</u> drink tea.
I <u>past tense</u> drink tea.
I <u>about to</u> drink tea.

Because Vietnamese does not use suffixes, native speakers of that language often omit or ignore them in their speaking, writing, and reading of English. Greene (1981) referred to this as the "morpheme conceptualization barrier," but found that Vietnamese speakers who also knew French, a language with suffixes, tended to recognize and produce English suffixes in their writing and reading. Strategies such as sentence expansion, choral reading, language experience approach, creative writing, and, in particular, using children's literature (see listing at the end of Chapter 2) can help students become sensitive to new syntactic structures being learned in English.

Teachers should also know that vocabulary varies across languages. For example, Spanish *penitencia, realizar, libreria,* and *chanza* are not equivalent to *penitentiary, realize, library*, and *chance,* but rather, *penance, accomplish an ambition, bookstore,* and *joke* (Thonis, 1976). French speakers learning English need to learn the meaning contrasts between *cut* and *carve,* for example, because French has one word for both, *couper.* For teaching vocabulary to native and nonnative speakers, strategies such as semantic mapping and semantic feature analysis are recommended.

PRINCIPLES FOR READING AND LANGUAGE DEVELOPMENT

Several principles should guide teachers of nonnative and nonstandard English speaking students. These and related principles were presented in Barnitz (1980, 1982, 1988). The language abilities students bring to school, no matter how variant, can be a rich foundation for learning and developing reading proficiency, if the native and target languages are kept whole in authentic literacy activities (Freeman & Freeman, 1992; Goodman & Goodman, 1978; Rigg & Allen, 1989).

Language–Reading Assessment

Although specific assessment instruments will not be presented here (See Goodman, Goodman, & Hood, 1989, and the rest of this book for a variety of ways to assess learners' abilities), the following discussion will guide teachers' interpretation of test results (Barnitz, 1982).

- In interpreting test results, teachers must be sensitive to cultural and linguistic variation.

Hall and Freedle (1975) cited a study by Williams and Rivers (1972) demonstrating that students' performance on tests is better if the vocabulary matches their cultural backgrounds. For example, in Louisiana the word *parish* is equivalent in meaning to *county* in other parts of the country; the words *carnival, throw,* and *krewe* have particular meanings associated with Mardi Gras; and children play *cabbage ball.* If these items appeared on an IQ test, non-Louisianians would probably be at a cultural disadvantage.

In a similar way, different cultural experiences affect the comprehension of prose. In a study by Reynolds, Taylor, Steffensen, Shirey, and Anderson (1981), urban African-American students comprehended a passage differently than agrarian European-American students. Cultural background knowledge influences the comprehension and recall of information in text (see Au, 1993; Barnitz, 1986; Steffensen, 1987).

Another example of language and cultural influences on tests can be found in auditory discrimination tests (Geissal & Knafle, 1977). Linguistically diverse students may not be able to hear contrasts between word pairs such as thin/tin, sherry/cherry, cot/caught, oil/Earl, and Mary/merry/marry because the linguistic rules and patterns of their dialect or native language do not permit it. Teachers must know dialect or language features in order to attribute an error to the appropriate cause, that is, an auditory problem versus a dialect variation. In fluent reading, these dialect homonym pairs can be interpreted by context just like other homonym pairs, such as knight/night. Hence, caution is needed in interpreting test performance when evaluating students.

- Variations in the situation must be considered in language assessment, as situational variables affect language variation.

Straker (1980) found that bidialectal speakers were able to use their communicative competence to switch between Black English Vernacular and standard English depending on the setting, topic, or audience. Hall, Cole, Reder, and Dowley (1977) also found that lower-income African-American students produce spontaneous language in a supermarket but are less verbal in classroom settings. If their language is evaluated in the classroom only, assessment of their total communicative competence may be incomplete and inaccurate. Similarly, Steffensen and Guthrie (1980) found that variation in the testing situation dramatically influenced the quantity and quality of language produced by urban African-American preschool children.

- Teachers must realize that performance in a vernacular dialect does not imply a deficit in language proficiency.

Linguistic studies on language variation have disproved the **deficit hypothesis**, which states that minority children have underdeveloped, impoverished, and illogical systems of language. (See Labov, 1975, and Burling, 1973, for discussion.) Steffensen (1974, 1978) found that students who speak Black English Vernacular follow the same natural stages of language development as European-American middle class students. Moreover, the *Ann Arbor* case marked a legal end to any claimed validity of the deficit hypothesis (Labov, 1983). This means that teachers must respect the language of ethnic students as different, not deficient. Students should be provided opportunities to acquire oral and written standard English for the situational contexts in which it is expected.

- Literacy assessment must be based on authentic language and literacy tasks and events (Garcia & Pearson, 1991).

Through authentic tasks, students use the entire language system to express themselves in real literacy events. Potentially negative influences of dialect or language diversity are diminished when there is rich situational and textual context. Whatever a student's dialect, functional language use in narrating or retelling a story can be demonstrated. The following is a story retelling by a sixth-grade African-American female student of *Jumanji* (Van Allsburg, 1981), recorded by undergraduate student Kelly Strahan in an urban school. (Some of the dialect is represented by the spelling, but the focus here should be on the fluent cohesiveness of the narrative summary.)

This story is about Judy an Peter. Dey (their) mother an(d) father went to a reception; dey left the(m) home by theyself (theirselves). Judy an(d) Peter say it got a little boring; so, so, dey went outside across the street an dey foun(d) a game. Judys, Judy say, "No, let's wait, let's rea(d) de instruction(s)." Judy read the instructions. Den they start(ed) playin the game. Lots of thangs happen(ed) to a game. Den, Peter roll(ed) de dice; den he stopped on a lion; his sister(r) said, "Peter, look behind you!" on top of the piano, they had a big lion lickin his lips. Den it was Judy turn. Den somethin' happen(ed) to her. An den other thangs . . . Judy and dem, um, when Judy and dem finish(ed) the game, they brought it back across the street. Dey (their) fathe(r) and mothe(r) came home; dey were (a)sleep. Judy shoved at Peter to wake him up an den, his mo(ther), they started to finish the(ir) puzzles. Then this lady came an say, "My two son(s) don't, dey don't read the instructions," and den the, um the two boys went outside; dey went across the street an dey found a puzzle an brought it back.

At first glance, a teacher might misjudge this student's language abilities unless the teacher looks beyond the natural dialect. This short retelling illustrates the student's ability to compose a narrative with an overall gist of the story. (See Irwin and Mitchell, 1983, for a holistic way of assessing retellings; also refer to Figure 6.2 seen earlier in this text.)

Standard English Language Arts Instruction

The language arts consist of communicative competence in language, which is both oral (speaking and listening) and written (writing and reading). You will recall from your language arts methods course that these processes are interrelated in children's development of English. You should also recall from your language arts methods course the basic methods for developing each of these processes of communication. As part of the language arts curriculum, what is the role of standard English as it relates to teaching linguistically diverse students? The following guidelines are relevant (adapted from Barnitz, 1982).

1. Students should be provided opportunities to acquire standard English because with competence in it, they will have economic, political, and social advantages. Standard English is not a prerequisite to learning to read and write (Goodman, 1972; Hudelson, 1989); immersion in authentic standard English materials, such as children's literature, facilitates learning standard patterns (Tompkins & McGee, 1983). However, Shuy (1981b) pointed out that learners usually do not acquire standard features unless they are motivated and see its function in their real lives. Language, and ultimately literacy, is easier to learn when language (as outlined by Goodman, 1986, p. 8) is real and natural, is whole, is sensible, is interesting, is relevant, belongs to the learner, is part of a real event, has social utility, has purpose for the learner, is accessible to the learner, and is chosen by the learner for use.

2. To facilitate learning of standard English, three principles must become part of the philosophy of instruction (Marcus, 1977): (1) students must recognize the ways in which their home language (dialect) varies systematically with the school language; (2) they must be motivated to acquire standard English and to use language and; (3) they must practice language in real life situations. For learning any language, the language–literacy activities must be authentic (Goodman, 1986). Young children learn language through interaction and using language to get things done. Current research on learning standard English implies that vernacular English speakers learn English features when there is substantial meaningful interaction with standard English speakers. Verbal interaction effects a gradual change in the home linguistic system of the learner (Labov & Harris, 1983; Farr & Daniels, 1986; Enright & McCloskey, 1988).

3. A language arts-based reading program must first emphasize sociolinguistic competence, whereby students develop language to inform, entertain, persuade, inquire, nar-

rate, encourage, and so on. Similarly, instruction must be placed within a wider communicative setting of authentic reading for information, entertainment, exposure to persuasion, and so on. Classroom strategies, such as role playing, listening to good models of children's literature, choral speaking, oral presentations, readers theater, and group discussions, can all be related to the passages being read and authentic passages being written.

In teaching reading to vernacular dialect and nonnative speakers of English, teachers must respect the language and culture of their students as the first step toward supporting their literacy development. The teacher's attitude and professional knowledge about language are important to the success of linguistically diverse students. Often, teachers are unknowingly among the causes of delayed reading and language development. Over twenty years ago, Goodman and Buck (1973, p. 6) stated this point more directly:

> The only special disadvantage which speakers of low status dialects suffer in learning to read is one imposed by teachers and schools. Rejection of their dialects and educators' confusion of linguistic difference with linguistic deficiency interferes with the natural process by which reading is acquired and undermines the linguistic self-confidence of divergent speakers. . . . Instruction based on rejection of linguistic difference is the core of the problem.

Teacher attitude and lack of knowledge about linguistic and cultural diversity have been found to be factors in students' delays in learning to read standard English; many teachers fail to take into account language characteristics of the students they teach (Smitherman, 1985). Language or dialect diversity, although it influences performance in English, is not a deficit and therefore need not interfere with learning to read (Wolfram & Christian, 1989; Flores, 1984).

Reading Instruction

The social use of language to get things done is the driving force of language. Young children develop language to play, to explore, to acquire information, and so forth. Reading activities must be purposeful, and instruction of basic reading skills must be placed within this context. For example, students can develop their reading skills within a unit on tourism, reading travel brochures. The reading activity may be placed within the wider social language context of planning a trip to Disney World, including role-playing an afternoon at the travel agency. The students must interact, use their developing language ability and read to plan a vacation. The teacher, within this context, can embed specific teachable units (e.g., sequencing, content vocabulary, word analysis) and language competencies (pronunciation, syntax) appropriate to the situation. Reading instruction then, should be embedded within a functional reading activity that, in turn, is part of a wider social language arts context. Reading instruction for all students, including linguistically diverse students, must be motivated by meaning.

Literature-Based Instruction

Teachers are rediscovering the linguistic, social, and cognitive benefits of literature-based instruction. Research studies document well the positive impact of children's exposure to literature on first and second language acquisition and literacy development and on discourse competence (Allen, 1989; Chomsky, 1972; Eckhoff, 1983; Elley, 1991; Heath, 1982; Morrow, 1992; Phillips, 1989; Pinnell, 1989; Purcell-Gates, 1991; Purcell-Gates &

Dahl, 1988; Wells, 1986). Children's literature allows students to acquire oral and written linguistic knowledge, such as syntax, phonology, vocabulary, text structure; social knowledge, such as ways that characters interact to carry out language functions through discourse, or social values about various cultures; and cognitive knowledge, such as semantic structure of stories, cultural schemata, and so forth. Cohen and Rudolph (1984) argued that the activities conducted with literature are as important as the literature itself. Teachers who use creative dramatics, process writing, readers theater, and other authentic literacy-building events know the linguistic, social, and cognitive benefits for students.

Teachers can assist learners to use children's literature to motivate writing. For example, Cynthia Rylant's (1982) book, *When I Was Young in the Mountains* can be used to help students learn about mountain culture as well as to motivate reflection on students' own lives while writing their own memoirs: *When I was young in* ＿＿＿＿＿＿ . In doing so, the students can make their own individual books or a class book with one page written and illustrated by each student. The students will be integrating their writing with their reading in a social context so that all learners (from various cultures and neighborhoods) can share themselves and their self-generated language with each other. Moreover, in the context of this activity, the students are developing their awareness of complex sentence structure (e.g., subordinated adverbial clauses) while using the language of the author and themselves for their real audience. Tompkins and McGee (1983) recommend children's books as useful in reinforcing standard English patterns. For example, with Gag's *Millions of Cats* (1928), the students can perform a choral reading of "Hundreds of Cats, Thousands of Cats, Millions and Billions and Trillions of Cats" (practicing plural suffixes) while experiencing an interesting parable that also teaches values. (See Suhor and Suhor, 1992, for a discussion of the debate on teaching values through literature.) Or, students can practice *-ed* suffixes and *-er* suffixes while doing choral readings of parts of *Drummer Hoff* by Emberly (1967). However, teachers should focus on the aesthetic, meaningful experience that literature allows. The acquisition of standard structures is a by-product of an authentic literary experience. Students who use only workbooks are deprived of the richness of language, culture, and thinking that literature provides.

In a multicultural classroom, children's literature based on various ethnic cultures can enhance cross-cultural understanding as well as empower learners to read books that relate to their own cultures (Au, 1993; Harris, 1993; Rasinski & Padek, 1990). (See Appendix F for a list of a variety of books recommended for students from various cultural backgrounds.)

Instructional programs based on children's literature are expected to enhance the language, literacy, and, more important, the lives of all students. Thus at the national level, a variety of literature-based literacy instruction projects have been designed (e.g., Gipe, Richards & Barnitz, 1993/94; Morrow, 1992; Pinnell, 1989).

Language Experience Approach

Inasmuch as children's language development is tied to their social, cognitive, and linguistic development, a logical strategy to use in a corrective reading program is the **language experience approach** (Allen, 1976; Hall, 1982; Rigg, 1989; Stauffer, 1980). With this approach, the teacher takes advantage of students' experiences to motivate oral expression and develop reading skill. Students, either individually or in small groups, are led to dictate a story to a teacher who functions as a scribe, editor, and language expander. The teacher is free to interact with the students to elicit elaborations when appropriate. Once the story is written down, the teacher analyzes it for specific functions and structures. The first draft becomes an invaluable first step in language expansion.

For example, the teacher can expand the syntax of the first draft. Fennimore (1980) suggests that a simple sentence can be expanded through systematic questioning for each potential slot in an expanded sentence pattern. For example, starting with a sentence such as *The boy ran,* students can be led to add words for various slots and yield a sentence such as *The happy boy ran slowly through the yard.* Students can also expand their sentences by adding other clauses. Teachers may also lead the students in sentence-combining activities to learn processes of sentence formation (O'Hare, 1973). (See Chapter 7 for other activities.)

Wangberg (1982) suggests making pattern books with beginning readers, and this is also useful for corrective readers. Employing the language experience approach, Wangberg suggests that students make a simple book with a particular pattern, such as *This is a _____* , in order to learn the syntactic pattern and the sight vocabulary for words that match pictures pasted on each page. Students thus learn language patterns along with developing reading vocabulary. Syntactic awareness, the ability to predict meaning from the arrangement of meanings in a sentence, is crucial to reading and can be incorporated into reading comprehension instruction (Barnitz, 1979).

Teachers can ask questions with the language experience approach that elicit more descriptive words or phrases or alternative ways of expressing thoughts, including standard English equivalents to vernacular dialects. Teachers can also teach vocabulary and comprehension through the use of semantic maps (Johnson & Pearson, 1984).

The language experience approach is invaluable in teaching reading to linguistically diverse students. After discussion, these students can dictate a story in their vernacular that is written down in the native dialect with standard spellings. For example, notice the following hypothetical sample:

> My friend, he went to the parade. He don't like the crowd. He climb a tree and he saw the band. And he saw the float.

With any valid reading experience, teachers ask facilitating questions to lead students to generate thinking and language in social settings. Students should be encouraged to express themselves in their natural language or dialect to generate language for a first draft of an experience story. Then, the teacher and students together revise the language by rephrasing or expanding on it. This leads the students to learn editing skills as well as develop an awareness for edited standard English. The teacher leads the students to produce a revised draft of their emerging text through discussion of their experiences with an event, such as a parade. The teacher could ask questions such as "Who went to the parade?" "What did he see or hear?" "Could we add some words, or take some out?"

> My friend went to the parade. He doesn't like crowds. He climbed a tree. He saw the bands. He saw the floats.

The teacher continues to ask questions to elicit responses for further revision and elaboration. For example, "Who is your friend?" *(Nathan)* "What kind of parade?" *(Mardi Gras parade)* "What kinds of bands and floats?" "Can we say/write some of these ideas in one combined sentence?" This will yield an elaborated text with more description and connective words:

> My friend Nathan went to the Mardi Gras parade. Since he doesn't like large crowds, he climbed an oak tree on the street corner. Then he saw the marching bands and the decorated floats.

Rigg (1989) recommends that the language experience approach be used with the following five steps: discussing, dictating, accepting without correcting, revising, and follow-up. Within each of these steps, the teacher engages the students through questioning and dialogue. The teacher may also use various aids, such as webs and maps for helping students organize their thoughts. Students learn their language skills in the context of learning the writing-reading process in a social context of a classroom community.

Experience–Text–Relationship Method

Because reading integrates information in the text with the student's previous experience, teachers must expand the background knowledge of the student; cultural variations in background knowledge affect comprehension (see Andersson & Barnitz, 1984; Au, 1993; Barnitz, 1986; Steffensen, 1987).

The **experience–text–relationship method** (Au, 1979) allows the teacher to motivate the students to talk about their experiences relevant to the central focus of a story or

---

FIGURE

13.1

Transcript of an experience–text–relationship lesson.

Experience Step

Teacher:	. . . Okay, let's think if we could do anything else with a frog. What would you do, Shirley?
Ann:	I wouldn't touch the legs. Yuck.
Shirley:	I would put it in a bucket.
Teacher:	You would put it in a bucket. Okay, that's something different. What would you do with it?
Shirley:	*(Inaudible)*
Ann:	Yeah, you eat the legs?
Teacher:	Okay, Shirley might even eat it. Good, you can eat frog, can't you?

Text Step

Teacher:	. . . Shirley, why did you say Freddy laughed? Okay, read the part that you said—when Freddy laughed.
Shirley:	*(Reading)* "I would take it fishing. Freddy laughed."
Teacher:	Okay, who says, "I would take it fishing"?
Nathan:	Mr. Mays.
Teacher:	Mr. Mays. And why did Freddy laugh?
Ann:	Because maybe he didn't—maybe he didn't know that he was going to use the frog.
Teacher:	No, he laughed for another reason. Ellie? Who can read that?
Ellie:	Because—'cause Mr. Mays didn't know what to do with the frog. That's all he could think was—he didn't know that he could use frogs was—was a bait. That's why Freddy laughed.
Teacher:	Okay, wait a minute. That's not the reason Freddy laughed.
Nathan:	Frogs can't fish.
Teacher:	Right. Okay, Mr. Mays says, "I don't have a frog, but if I did, I'd take it fishing," and Freddy thinks, hah, going fishing with the frog sitting down with the fishing pole?

Relationship Step

Teacher:	. . . Did you know before this that fish like to eat frogs?
Group:	Nooo.
Teacher:	I didn't—I never heard of using frogs for bait. Do you think they really do?
Nathan:	Yeah.
Teacher:	You think so.
Ann:	My daddy—my daddy—use bread.
Teacher:	Yeah, some people use bread. What else do you use for bait?
Shirley:	Fish.
Teacher:	Sometimes you use smaller fishes.

From "Using the Experience–Text–Relationship Method with Minority Children," by Kathryn Hu-Pei Au, *Reading Teacher*, March 1979. Reprinted with permission of the author and the International Reading Association.

content chapter (the experience step); read natural segments of text (the text step); and relate the content of a story with the prior experiences discussed in the story (the relationship step). A sample lesson transcript from Au (1979) illustrates the teacher–student interaction in developing reading of culturally diverse students (Figure 13.1). Techniques like this one allow the teacher and students to bridge the knowledge gap between learners' experiences and the text. Likewise, the experience–text–relationship method allows students to become actively involved with the text and permits culturally compatible styles of interaction between teacher and students. Au and Kawakami (1985) found that a focus on comprehension, rather than on word identification, and a culturally compatible style of interaction greatly improve the quality of reading by sociolinguistically diverse students. Teachers need to recognize that students from various cultures possess culturally unique communication routines that often contrast with the verbal discourse routines of the school (Au, 1993; Cazden, John, & Hymes, 1972; Heath, 1983; Hiebert, 1991; Tharp & Gallimore, 1988). Verbal and cultural diversity need not become barriers to literacy learning if teachers design authentic classroom activities compatible with culturally diverse learners, and if they view teaching as assisting student performance rather than as repetitive recitation (Tharp & Gallimore, 1988).

SUMMARY

This chapter presented an introductory survey of aspects of language and dialect variation that are found in linguistically diverse classrooms. Because diversity is natural, linguistic variations should not be considered deficiencies relative to learners' development of literacy. Linguistically diverse students bring to your classroom a rich foundation for further growth in language, literacy, and culture.

You now know the importance of understanding reading in terms of a wider holistic framework of communicative competence, which consists primarily of using authentic language for getting things done in social contexts, and secondarily of using a set of standard English structures. You also understand the interrelationship of language to reading development. Separating the two will often contribute to the failure that many students face in learning to read and add to the difficulties of corrective readers. In fact, many students, regardless of language background, would less likely need corrective reading instruction if their earlier experiences in school involved more natural, authentic literacy experiences and enriched texts. Use of children's literature, combined with procedures such as the language experience approach or the experience–text–relationship method, and supported by additional techniques focusing on specific language elements, can provide these kinds of literacy experiences. With appropriate professional knowledge about language and reading instruction and the proper respect for linguistically diverse students, teachers will find success in facilitating literacy learning.

SUGGESTED READINGS

Au, K. H. (1993). *Literacy instruction in multicultural settings.* Fort Worth, TX: Harcourt Brace Jovanovich.

> *The author provides teachers with an understanding of cultural and linguistic considerations for teaching reading and writing. Taking a constructivist approach to literacy instruction, the author also emphasizes the roles of cultural discourse interaction and multicultural literature for teaching writing and reading.*

Freeman, Y.S., & Freeman, D.E. (1992). *Whole language for second language learners.* Portsmouth, NH: Heinemann.

> *The authors present theory and practice for teaching second language learners in whole-language classrooms. Lessons for ESL students should be holistic, learner centered, meaningful, and purposeful. Lessons should involve social interaction, interrelate the language arts, and occur in the learner's native language—all for the purpose of building the student's potential.*

Rigg, P., & Allen, V.G. (Eds.). (1989). *When they don't all speak English: Integrating the ESL student into the regular classroom.* Urbana, IL: National Council of Teachers of English.

> *This collection of readings provides a forum for ideas on teaching the language arts in classrooms in which not everyone is a native speaker of English. Authors of various chapters provide practical advice for whole-language literacy instruction for all students. The book provides instructional techniques that are successful for both native and nonnative speakers of English.*

Wolfram, W., & Christian, D. (1989). *Dialects and education: Issues and answers.* Englewood Cliffs, NJ: Prentice Hall Regents.

> *The authors address linguistic aspects of regional and social dialects that may occur in school communities. The authors directly answer questions asked by education professionals about teaching students who speak various dialects.*

TEXT READABILITY

Readability refers to the difficulty level of printed material. Low readability means the material is difficult to read; however, an index for such material will be a high number often given in terms of grade level. Likewise, material with high readability (easy to read) will be reflected by a low index.

Several factors affect the readability of material: the number of difficult or new words, the length and complexity of sentences, the number of new or unfamiliar concepts, the organization and cohesion of the material, the reader's background knowledge for reading the material, and even the material's appearance.

Thus, the use of any readability index as the sole determinant of a book's appropriateness is not advised. (See IRA, NCTE statement on the use of readability formulae in *Reading Today,* 1985, p. 1.) However, if the teacher uses the index in conjunction with other factors affecting readability, determining the readability index of a material can be a valuable and valid exercise (Fry, 1989).

Several methods can be used to determine readability. You will be provided with directions for using three methods: Fry's Graph for Estimating Readability (Fig. A.1), the Raygor Readability Estimate (Fig. A.2), and the cloze procedure (Fig. A.3).

FRY'S GRAPH

When using Fry's graph, be aware that grade-level scores are most valid near the center line on the graph. Scores falling in the gray areas are invalid, and additional samples may be needed. Fry's estimates are considered accurate to within plus or minus one year of the true estimate of readability.

For material that is shorter than 100 words, Forgan and Mangrum (1985, pp. 31–32) provide the following directions for making use of the Fry graph.

1. Count the total number of words in the selection and round down to the nearest ten. For example, if there are forty-four words in your selection, use only the first forty to count the number of syllables and sentences.
2. Count the number of syllables and sentences in the selected words.
3. Multiply the total number of sentences and syllables by the number in the Conversion Chart that corresponds with the number of words in your selection.
4. Refer to Fry's graph, as shown on page 366, to find the grade-level band that indicates the readability level.

F I G U R E

A.I

Fry's readability graph.

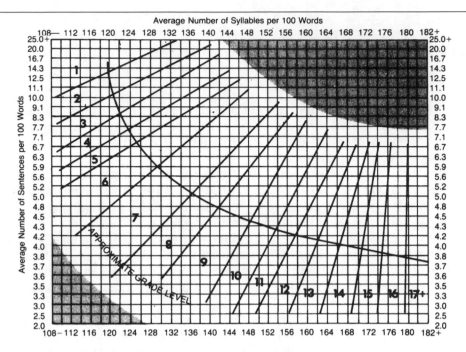

Expanded Directions for Working Readability Graph

1. Randomly select three (3) sample passages and count out exactly 100 words each, beginning with the beginning of a sentence. *Do* count proper nouns, initializations, and numerals.

2. Count the number of sentences in the hundred words, estimating length of the fraction of the last sentence to the nearest one-tenth.

3. Count the total number of syllables in the 100-word passage. If you don't have a hand counter available, an easy way is to simply put a mark above every syllable over one in each word; then when you get to the end of the passage, count the number of marks and add 100. Small calculators can also be used as counters by pushing numeral 1, then pushing the + sign for each word or syllable when counting.

4. Enter graph with *average* sentence length and *average* number of syllables: plot dot where the two lines intersect. Area where dot is plotted will give you the approximate grade level.

5. If a great deal of variability is found in syllable count or sentence count, putting more samples into the average is desirable.

6. A word is defined as a group of symbols with a space on either side: thus, *Joe, IRA, 1945,* and *&* are each one word.

7. A syllable is defined as a phonetic syllable. Generally, there are as many syllables as vowel sounds. For example, *stopped* is one syllable and *wanted* is two syllables. When counting syllables for numerals and initializations, count one syllable for each symbol. For example, *1945* is four syllables, *IRA* is three syllables, and *&* is one syllable.

Note: This "extended graph" does not outmode or render the earlier (1968) version inoperative or inaccurate; it is an extension.

Conversion Chart for Fry's Graph for Selections of Fewer than 100 Words

If the number of words in the selection is:	Multiply the number of syllables and sentences by:
30	3.3
40	2.5
50	2.0
60	1.67
70	1.43
80	1.25
90	1.1

RAYGOR READABILITY ESTIMATE

For those who have a difficult time counting syllables, the Raygor graph is often preferred. With this graph, words of six or more letters are counted as long words. The other procedures used are identical to those of Fry, except numerals are *not* counted when using Raygor.

The Raygor graph.

F I G U R E

A.2

These are the directions for using the Raygor graph:

1. Count out three 100-word passages at the beginning, middle, and end of a book. Be sure to include proper nouns in your word count, but *do not* count numerals.

2. Count the number of sentences in each passage, estimating to the nearest tenth.

3. Circle and count the words having six or more letters. Words having six or more letters are defined as *long* (hard) words.

4. Average the sentence length and the number of long (hard) words over the three samples, and plot the average on the graph.

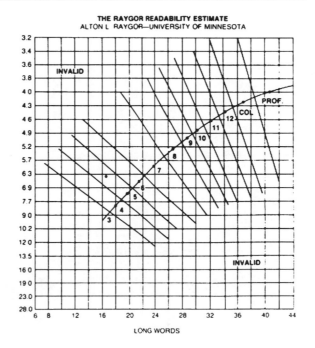

THE RAYGOR READABILITY ESTIMATE
ALTON L RAYGOR—UNIVERSITY OF MINNESOTA

CLOZE PROCEDURE FOR READABILITY/SUITABILITY

The difficulty or ease with which material can be read can also be determined by means of the cloze procedure (Bormuth, 1968; Taylor, 1953). Use of the cloze procedure doesn't yield a readability estimate for the material; rather, it indicates the suitability of material for the student completing the cloze passage. Following the same guidelines for construction and scoring presented in Chapter 6, the example seen in Figure A.3 reveals a score of 70 percent accuracy. This material then would be suitable for this student even if teacher guidance is not available (i.e., a score above 50 percent indicates suitability at an independent level). A score of 30–50 percent indicates an instructional level that requires teacher guidance, and a score of less than 30 percent indicates that the material is unsuitable.

Example of a completed cloze passage for readability.

Directions: Skim through the entire passage *before* you begin to fill in the missing words. Then go back and fill in as many words as you can.

According to Raths, one responsibility of a good teacher is preparing materials. All teachers recognize the _importance_ of available materials for _meeting_ individual needs of each _student_, so they prepare supplemental _materials_ —handouts, review sheets, test _papers_, directions for assignments and _projects_, and summaries from magazines and _newspaper_ articles. Since students must _be_ able to read these _materials_, it is imperative that _teachers_ be able to write _them_ at appropriate reading levels.

Teachers often cannot understand why _their_ students fail an examination _after_ hours of teaching and reviewing. _These_ teachers claim the students _knew_ the answers the day _before_ the test, but on _the_ day of the test _they_ do not seem to _remember_ a thing! When one _examines_ the test items, it _is_ relatively easy to understand _why_ students failed.

The same _problem_ arises if assignment sheets, _study_ outlines, summaries, or other _materials_ are too difficult for _students_. Both teachers and students _are_ frustrated because they are _not_ communicating. Teachers are often _confused_ about talking above the _heads_ of their students, and _must_ take equal caution with _written_ communication.

We are not _suggesting_ that content teachers should _lower_ their course standards; rather, _they_ should do a more _careful_ job of communicating so _their_ students can achieve high _grades_. Just as students do _not_ like teachers to talk _down_ to them, neither do _they_ enjoy materials that insult _their_ reading capabilities, nor do _they_ want to be confused // _by_ materials that are too _difficult_ to understand. Somewhere between these two extremes clear communication is possible (52 total deletions. // indicates the point at which 50 deletions have occurred.)

Actual words for items missed (in order of occurrence from left to right):
inadequacies   items   activities   some   knew   know
course   handouts   become   warned   levels
should   effective   the   standards

Source: Forgan, H. W., & Mangrum, C. T. (1985). *Teaching Content Area Reading Skills*. (3rd ed.) (p. 46). Columbus, OH: Merrill.

INSTRUCTIONAL ENVIRONMENT SURVEY

The following checklist is a compilation of several others previously developed for helping teachers critically examine their classroom environment (Glazer, 1992; Glazer & Brown, 1993; Vacca, Vacca & Gove, 1991).

Directions: Check *yes* if the item is currently true; check *maybe* if you are interested in pursuing this item further; check *no* if the item is not true. Reflect upon the results of the survey after it is completed.

	YES	MAYBE	NO
1. I know my students' interests.	_____	_____	_____
2. I know my students' attitudes and perceptions about reading and writing.	_____	_____	_____
3. My classroom has its own library including:			
a. trade books	_____	_____	_____
b. reference books	_____	_____	_____
c. student-authored books	_____	_____	_____
d. alternate text books	_____	_____	_____
4. I encourage my students to read and write recreationally by providing time for them to do so.	_____	_____	_____
5. There are places for small groups to work on reading and writing activities.	_____	_____	_____
6. There are places for individuals to work quietly.	_____	_____	_____
7. I share what I am reading and writing with my students.	_____	_____	_____
8. I encourage students to share their reading through:			
a. art	_____	_____	_____
b. drama	_____	_____	_____
c. speaking	_____	_____	_____
d. writing	_____	_____	_____
9. I tell students what I like about their work.	_____	_____	_____
10. I do not use reading as a punishment.	_____	_____	_____
11. I do not use writing as a punishment.	_____	_____	_____
12. I know some ways to integrate literature with reading and writing.	_____	_____	_____
13. I know some ways to use trade books with pupils who have special needs or are from a culture diverse from my own.	_____	_____	_____

	YES	MAYBE	NO
14. My classroom contains:			
a. typewriters and/or computers	_____	_____	_____
b. chalkboard space for group writing	_____	_____	_____
c. large sheets of paper on wall for composing	_____	_____	_____
d. transparencies/overhead projector	_____	_____	_____
e. videotaping equipment	_____	_____	_____
15. My classroom has a listening center with tape recorders and headsets.	_____	_____	_____
16. A variety of writing instruments are available to students including:			
a. pencils/pens	_____	_____	_____
b. crayons/colored markers	_____	_____	_____
c. chalk/erasers	_____	_____	_____
17. A variety of supplies are available to students including:			
a. lined paper	_____	_____	_____
b. construction paper	_____	_____	_____
c. tissue paper	_____	_____	_____
d. crepe paper	_____	_____	_____
e. yarn/fabric	_____	_____	_____
f. scissors	_____	_____	_____
g. glue/paste	_____	_____	_____
h. tape, all types	_____	_____	_____
i. stapler/hole punch	_____	_____	_____
j. needle/thread	_____	_____	_____

———— **|** ————

GATHERING AFFECTIVE INFORMATION

The corrective reading program must develop learners who read and who feel good about themselves and their reading ability. To promote positive reading attitudes, a teacher gathers information about students' attitudes and self-concepts. Efforts to change negative attitudes or reinforce positive attitudes proceed once a student's attitudes toward reading are known. A teacher gleans some of this information from observing students for such behaviors as (1) choosing to read a book during free time (2) requesting that a book be read aloud (3) checking out books from the library (4) finishing books started and (5) talking about books read. In addition, paper-and-pencil techniques provide more detailed information as well as a record of this information for interpretation.

The Incomplete Sentence Projective Test (Boning & Boning, 1957) presented here allows each student to write (or provide orally) information regarding how they feel about the item in question (Fig. C.1.). Responses may be more honest if the teacher tells students the information will be used to provide materials they will enjoy. Any interpretation should be modified and verified by observations over time.

Before administering the incomplete sentences, decide whether oral or written responses are most appropriate. Directions for an oral administration might be: "I will begin a sentence with a few words and then stop. When I stop, you tell me the very first thing that you think of to finish the sentence. I will write down just what you say. Let's do a practice sentence. I think pizza tastes _____ . Are you ready to begin?" Directions for a written administration might be: "Finish each sentence with the first idea that comes to your mind. Let's try the first one together."

In order to interpret the results, the following areas have been identified by item number.

Overall attitudes and self-concept: 1, 3, 4, 5, 8, 9, 14, 16, 19, 20, 22, 25, 27, 29, 30, 33, 35, 36, 38, 42

Family relations: 6, 11, 26, 31

School attitudes: 7, 10, 12, 18, 21, 24

Reading process: 2, 28, 32, 34, 37, 40, 41 (Boning and Boning [1957] found that the most revealing responses were to item 40.)

Reading interest: 13, 15, 17, 23 (Use item 17 to get clues for helping direct children toward increased recreational reading.)

Responses to the overall attitudes and self-concept area are very important to evaluate. They often provide insight into a student's academic problems. Some supplementary questions for the reading process and reading interest areas follow.

1. *Supplementary reading process questions:*
   a. Reading is . . .
   b. I cannot read when . . .

FIGURE
C.1

Incomplete sentence projective test.

1. Today I feel ....
2. When I have to read, I ....
3. I get angry when ....
4. To be grown up ....
5. My idea of a good time is ....
6. I wish my parents knew ....
7. School is ....
8. I can't understand why ....
9. I feel bad when ....
10. I wish teachers ....
11. I wish my mother ....
12. Going to college ....
13. To me, books ....
14. People think I ....
15. I like to read about ....
16. On weekends I ....
17. I'd rather read than ....
18. To me, homework ....
19. I hope I'll never ....
20. I wish people wouldn't ....
21. When I finish high school ....
22. I'm afraid ....
23. Comic books ....
24. When I take my report card home ....
25. I am at my best when ....
26. Most brothers and sisters ....
27. I don't know how ....
28. When I read math ....
29. I feel proud when ....
30. The future looks ....
31. I wish my father ....
32. I like to read when ....
33. I would like to be ....
34. For me, studying ....
35. I often worry about ....
36. I wish I could ....
37. Reading science ....
38. I look forward to ....
39. I wish ....
40. I'd read more if ....
41. When I read out loud ....
42. My only regret ....

From Boning, T., and Boning, R. "I'd Rather Read Than . . ." *Reading Teacher*, April 1957, p. 196. Reprinted with permission of the International Reading Association, Newark, DE.

   c. When reading new words I . . .
   d. Reading out loud . . .
   e. I read better when . . .
2. *Supplementary reading interest questions:*
   a. I like reading about . . .
   b. I don't want to read about . . .
   c. The best thing about reading . . .
   d. I laugh when I read about . . .
   e. The best book I know about . . .

STAGES IN SPELLING DEVELOPMENT

The stages represented here should be viewed from a developmental perspective; that is, a student's spelling is likely to change over time so that it resembles the examples seen at each stage. The following stages are more fully discussed in *The Beginnings of Writing*, pp. 100–104 by C. Temple, R. Nathan, N. Burris, and F. Temple.[1]

STAGE 1: PREPHONEMIC SPELLING

The student forms letters accurately but there is no match between letters and phonemes in words. Letter strings *look* like writing, but are not meaningful. The student recognizes that, in some way, letters represent language.

Examples: candy   SCOZ]

went   ƎNᵒC

(strings of letters)   crtogDok

STAGE 2: EARLY PHONEMIC SPELLING

The phonetic principle has been discovered; however, letters for only one or two sounds in a word are generally written down. One or two phonemes in a word are represented, with the rest perhaps omitted altogether or a random string of letters supplied.

Examples: My brother was crying all night.

MBRW KLN+

I like to go to the zoo.

I LK +o G++z

---

[1]The majority of material in this appendix was taken from C. Temple, R. Nathan, N Burris, and F. Temple, *The Beginnings of Writing*, pp. 100–107. Copyright © 1988 by Allyn and Bacon, Boston. Reprinted with permission.

STAGE 3: LETTER–NAME SPELLING

Once the concept of *word* has become stabilized, the student moves quickly to letter–name spelling. The phonemes of a word are represented by letters of the alphabet. The letters used show a relationship to the sound heard in the word. This is an important stage for reading; soon after students produce letter–name spelling, they begin to read.

Examples:

Jackie
I had a apel For lungsh
(I had an apple for lunch.)

bob —
a boy so The man run Awa
(A boy saw the man run away.)

STAGE 4: TRANSITIONAL SPELLING

Once a student begins reading, spelling begins to change as the student notices differences between letter–name spelling and the spelling of the words found in texts. Transitional spelling looks more like standard spelling (e.g., silent letters, unusual letter combinations), but the student is uncertain about when to use some of the standard spelling features. Transitional spellers have not yet integrated all the features of standard spelling. With more exposure to print and more opportunities to write, transitional spellers will become correct spellers.

Examples:

Can I go see a movee wif
My fren Susi sed her mom
sed Oka win we go
(Can I go see a movie with my friend Susie? She said her Mom said ok. When can we go?)

Goin To The zoo is fun I
lik The linz and The big
burdz wit blue feters
(Going to the zoo is fun. I like the lions and the big birds with blue feathers.)

ASSESSING SPELLING DEVELOPMENT

In order to accurately assess spelling development, students must write words they have *not* been taught or memorized. If a student is willing to write freely, then those words can be assessed for spelling development. However, some students are unwilling to write freely because they are not confident of their spelling ability. For these students a more structured approach is needed. Following are recommended word lists for spelling assessment. Direction, scoring, and a scored example for the K–2 list are provided.

Directions

1. Explain to students they are not expected to know how to spell all of these words. You want to know how they *think* the words should be spelled. They should do their best, but this exercise will not be graded.
2. If they are stumped by a word, they should first try the beginning of the word, then the middle, then the end.
3. The teacher will read the word, then the sentence, then read the word again, twice. (Do not exaggerate any of the parts—just say the word normally.)

Spelling List (Grades K–2)

1.	late	Kathy was *late* to school again today.
2.	wind	The *wind* was loud last night.
3.	shed	The wind blew down our *shed*.
4.	geese	The *geese* fly over Texas every fall.
5.	jumped	The frog *jumped* into the river.
6.	yell	We can *yell* as we want on the playground.
7.	chirped	The bird *chirped* when it saw a worm.
8.	once	Jim rode his bike into a creek *once*.
9.	learned	I *learned* to count in school.
10.	shove	Don't *shove* your neighbor when you line up.
11.	trained	I *trained* my dog to lie down and roll over.
12.	year	Next *year* you'll have a new teacher.
13.	shock	Electricity can *shock* you if you aren't careful.
14.	stained	The ice cream spilled and *stained* my shirt.
15.	chick	The egg cracked open and a baby *chick* climbed out.
16.	drive	Bob's sister is learning how to *drive*.

Spelling List (Grades 3 and Up)

1.	setter	Her dog is an Irish *setter*.
2.	shove	Don't *shove* when you line up.
3.	grocery	I'm going to the *grocery* store.
4.	button	Did you lose a *button* from your shirt?

5.	sailor	My cousin is a good *sailor.*
6.	prison	The robber will go to *prison.*
7.	nature	We walked on the *nature* trail.
8.	peeked	He *peeked* at the answers to the test.
9.	special	Tomorrow is a *special* day.
10.	preacher	The *preacher* talked for over an hour.
11.	slowed	We *slowed* down on the bumpy road.
12.	sail	The boat had a torn *sail.*
13.	feature	We saw a double *feature* at the movies.
14.	batter	The first *batter* struck out.

Scoring

The words are scored according to the stage of spelling they reflect. The word is scored:

0 if it is *prephonemic.*
1 if it is *early phonemic.*
2 if it is *letter–name.*
3 if it is *transitional.*
4 if it is *correct.*

For example:

1. Lat   2
2. wnd   2
3. sead   3
4. Gees   3
5. Bout   2
6. uL   2
7. cutp   2
8. L os   2
9. Zud   2
10. suf   2
11. trad   2
12. t er   2
13. s ock   3
14. sad   2
15. cek   2
16. drif   2

The mode should be determined. The mode is the single score that occurred most often. (The average can be distorted by the possibility that the student had memorized some of the spellings.) In the example above, the mode is 2, meaning that most of the student's spellings were in the letter–name stage.

SCORING SYSTEMS FOR WRITING

Regardless of how writing instruction is provided, there comes a time when student writing must be evaluated. Traditionally, all samples of student writing were graded intensively and negatively with every error being marked. This procedure of correcting, tallying errors, and assigning grades, however, did not produce a noticeable improvement in subsequent writing. It drained time and energies without contributing to improved writing or to accurate assessment. It also was threatening to students, and it caused many of them to write only because they feared failure.

Ideally, writing would not be graded; unfortunately, most school systems still require that teachers assign grades or scores. Fortunately, teachers and school districts no longer believe that *all* writing must be scored. When students are writing exploratively, there is no need to formally mark or score their work. However, when the decision is made to score students' writing (e.g., end of a marking period; portfolio assessment; student-selected best work; draft stages), the criteria used to score the writing should get to the heart of writing and should not focus just on mechanical errors.

No one scoring system or approach is ideal. By far the best scoring guides are those that the teacher and students construct together. These guides can be content-specific, focusing the evaluation on those aspects that the teacher and students together have identified as important. If this procedure is not feasible, the teacher should explore other scoring systems and combine the most desirable qualities of each major approach of evaluating and grading students' written products to devise an approach based on students' needs and the instructional writing program. Regardless of the scoring system used, however, the goal of assessment and evaluation should be to help students improve as writers and feel successful (Tompkins, 1990).

HOLISTIC SCORING

Holistic scoring initially labeled a variety of approaches to rank-ordering pieces of writing. It involves judging a piece of writing in terms of the whole instead of its individual parts. Rather than evaluating a piece of writing word for word, marking all errors, pointing out weaknesses, and suggesting changes, the teacher reads the piece as a whole, considers certain features, and immediately assigns a score or grade. The grade may be a single rating for the entire piece of writing, or a set of ratings for different features being considered (Cooper & Odell, 1977). While every aspect of the student writing—content and mechanics—affects the teacher's response, none of them are specifically identified. This system, which is similar to methods used by the National

---

*This appendix was prepared by Ramona C. Moore, doctoral student and long-time writing teacher.

Assessment of Education Progress and the Educational Testing Service, is often used in conjunction with student conferences or peer response groups.

Using holistic scoring, teachers are able to evaluate quickly because they do not circle errors or make comments in the margins. They are also able to evaluate more consistently because the same carefully developed criteria are used for all pieces of writing. This approach, however, is not an appropriate choice for a teacher who wants to assess how well students have used a particular writing form or applied specific writing skills. According to Tompkins (1990), research studies have indicated that the major drawback to this approach in elementary schools is that teachers may bias their assessments by unknowingly placing too much emphasis on mechanics, especially spelling, grammar/usage, and handwriting (Rafoth & Rubin, 1984; Searle & Dillon, 1980). In recent years, holistic scoring has been interpreted more narrowly and includes both impressionistic and focused approaches.

Impressionistic Holistic Scoring

As the name implies, the impressionistic holistic approach involves reading a student's paper quickly and marking it (e.g., 1, 2, 3, or 4; A, B, C, or D) based on some general feeling or impression of the overall quality of the paper. The teacher/reader must read quickly and carefully to arrive at a "feel" for the piece and a score. The paper is then placed in one of three or four piles without any marking. When all of the papers have been read, the teacher goes back to the piles to verify the relative value of the papers, and assigns scores. This approach is efficient and reliable, particularly if the criteria have been shared and illustrated with the writers as well as the readers (raters). This approach has its limitations. Students only know that, when compared to other students' papers, their paper received a 1, a 2, a 3, or a 4. While this overall rating does not give students advice on how to revise the writing, these limitations can be addressed by focusing on developing fluency in first drafting and fine tuning during revision stages.

Focused Holistic Scoring

In focused holistic scoring, the teacher decides upon a number of specific features of the writing to attend to while reading students' papers. The next step is developing a scoring guide with a list of the specific features and distributing it to students before they begin writing. This step ensures that the students know the criteria the teacher will use to assess their writing. An example of a focused holistic approach to scoring students' stories might include *story features* (e.g., setting, characters, problem, and resolution), as a criterion. The teacher would develop a guide listing these features The reading of the paper would then be focused on how these features contribute to the quality of the whole piece of writing. After this focused reading of the students' papers, the teacher would again place a 1, a 2, a 3, or a 4 on the piece, and would end up with three or four stacks of papers ranked as to worth according to the selected criteria.

Roundtable Holistic Scoring

Roundtable holistic scoring is a way of getting students involved in the evaluation process. Students read papers, establish criteria, and evaluate the papers. This process helps students become better judges of their own work and get a clearer idea of their own performance on a particular paper. Then, based on the teacher's input and markings by peers, the student assigns a grade. Since the students established the criteria for evaluation (rubric), they have a clearer idea of what they can or should do to improve their own writing. Kirby, Liner, and Vinz (1988) recommend that this peer scoring system, which was adapted from the one used by Educational Testing Services to rate student writing samples, be "thoroughly structured and patiently implemented" (p. 222).

A Holistic Guide for Evaluating Student Writings

There are many holistic guides available for evaluating student writings. The following guide is recommended by Kirby, Liner, and Vinz (1988) as a reminder of important characteristics of good writing and not as a scale of criteria:

1. Impact: The paper engages the reader; the writer has something to say and is imaginatively involved; the idea is conveyed with fluency or intensity; the writing is convincing.
2. Inventiveness: The paper surprises the reader; new and unexpected elements, such as a clever title, expressive language, unusual ending, are introduced.
3. Individuality: The paper has a voice or a flavor of its own.

OTHER APPROACHES TO SCORING

Anthony, Johnson, Mickelson, and Preece (1991, p. 141) developed the following procedure from a suggestion by Williams (1989). The teacher should respond to the content and not the form. The teacher should also find something honestly complimentary to say and should indicate how the piece might be further developed. If a formal score or mark must be given, the teacher should ensure that all students are doing the same task and that all students are aware of the criteria that will be used in judging/evaluating their work. If students are all working on different tasks, uniform criteria for marking are impossible. Given this situation, the teacher might choose to use the following method:

- Read through all of the papers quickly without a pencil in hand. Place each paper into one of three stacks: above expectation, at expectation, below expectation.
- Reread each paper more carefully. Use the negotiated criteria to determine compliments and criticisms to write in marginal notes. Be sure that the comments indicate how the paper might be improved.
- Add a positive summary comment. Briefly explain how the grade was earned.
- Return the papers to the students and ask them to check your comments and the grade against the negotiated criteria. Schedule individual conferences to deal with students' concerns.

Analytic Scoring

Another approach to scoring student writing is analytic scoring. Whereas holistic scoring focused on an overall assessment of the worth of an entire piece of student writing,

FIGURE
E.I

An analytic scoring system.

	STRONG	AVERAGE	WEAK
Ideas			
1. Ideas are creative.	_____	_____	_____
2. Ideas are well developed.	_____	_____	_____
3. Audience and purpose are considered.	_____	_____	_____
Organization			
1. An organizational pattern is used.	_____	_____	_____
2. Ideas are presented in logical order.	_____	_____	_____
3. Topic sentences are clear.	_____	_____	_____
Style			
1. A good choice of words is displayed.	_____	_____	_____
2. Figurative language is used.	_____	_____	_____
3. A variety of sentence patterns is used.	_____	_____	_____
Mechanics			
1. Most words are spelled correctly.	_____	_____	_____
2. Punctuation and capitalization are used correctly.	_____	_____	_____
3. Standard language is used.	_____	_____	_____

Comments:

analytic scoring focuses on assessing the writing in terms of its individual parts. Tompkins (1990, p. 391) includes an analytic scoring system adapted from Paul Diederich's (1974) scale for high school and college students. This adapted system, (Fig. E-1), which can be used to assess the quality of elementary students' writing, divides the traits of good writing into four categories: ideas, organization, style, and mechanics. This approach places less emphasis on mechanics than do other analytic scoring systems, such as Diederich's.

Evaluation/scoring should be integrated with the other elements of the writing program and not considered as separate from it. It should be a positive learning experience, not a threatening one. One way to ensure that it is as open as possible and not done "over the heads or behind the backs" of students is to involve the students during instruction in negotiating or jointly developing the criteria for assessment and evaluation (Anthony et al., 1991, p. 90) and to stop looking for errors.

EXAMPLES OF SCORING USING TWO DIFFERENT APPROACHES

Focused Holistic Scoring Using Story Features

Prior to having her students write, a teacher identified the features that she would attend to while reading the papers (i.e., setting, characters, problem, resolution). Along with her students, she developed the following list as a guide:

Setting: Does the paper include an appropriate setting?

Characters: Are the characters listed and developed?

Problem: Is the problem obvious?

Resolution: Does the story end with the problem being resolved convincingly and appropriately?

She told her students that while reading each paper, she would focus on the following question: How do these features contribute to the quality of the whole piece of writing? She explained to her students that since she had been trained to use holistic scoring and since she had scored many papers, she did not need a numbered scale. Her purpose in developing the example, however, was to give them a better understanding of how their papers were scored. She also wanted to help them learn how to evaluate and score one another's papers and eventually to evaluate their own writing. Her example was as follows:

4 – All of the story features are included; they contribute to the development of an interesting and original story.

3 – All of the story features are included, but they are not appropriately developed. There is some evidence of originality/believability/imagination.

2 – At least three of the story features are included; the story lacks structure/believability/originality/imagination.

1 – There is little evidence of how story features contribute to the development of a story; there appears to be no story line; the paper lacks structure/believability/originality/imagination.

Using the following student-written edited version placed on the overhead, the teacher talked through her focused scoring procedure.

The People in the Sea*

   One day Eric saw Ariel swimming. He wanted to swim with her so he did. Then they saw a big whale. Then they started to swim fais (fast) and they went to Ariels (Ariel's) father to speack (speak) to him. They said that a whale was chaising (chasing) them all the way her (here). Then Ariel and Eric went swimming again. They saw the whale again and the whale had take (to take) a reast (rest) and forgeat (forget) about them. And they all lived hapily (happily) ever after.

I'm going to read this paper quickly, but I have to tell myself to think of my focus. For this paper I want to know how the story features that we have identified contribute to the quality of the whole piece of writing. (She reads orally.) I notice the setting is in the sea; the characters are Eric, Ariel, the whale, and Ariel's father; the problem is that the whale is chasing them; and the resolution is that the whale forgets about them dur-

*The sample was written by a student who had completed the third grade prior to her participation in a corrective reading program during the summer of 1993. The first draft was collected as part of an extension activity after the student and her teacher had completed a *Find the Features and Connect Them* map (Richards & Gipe, 1993). This edited version, completed after the student and her teacher had conferenced about the story features, end punctuation, and capitalization, was selected by the student as one of her best pieces of writing. The words in parentheses are the words as read to the teacher by the student.

ing his rest so they all lived happily ever after. Now that I have finished reading, I think that this is a pretty good story. All of the features contributed to its development. But I don't think the whale would have to rest, and I don't think he would forget about them. Let's see. I think I will place this paper in this stack because it is similar to the other papers. (She stops her thinking aloud.) My next steps would be to read and sort all of the papers, and then to decide if the papers are in the right stack. This might mean that I have to quickly look over some of the papers again. Once I feel sure that all of the papers in each stack have similar overall qualities, I decide on scores or grades. Going back to "The People in the Sea," I would give this paper (and the other similar ones) a score of 2.

Anthony, Johnson, Mickelson, and Preece's Approach to Scoring

Using the procedure developed by Anthony et al. (1991), the teacher placed "The People in the Sea" in the stack identified as *below expectation*. Using the same negotiated criteria as in the focused scoring, she wrote the following comments on the student's paper:

I like how you have included all of the story features. It also seemed like the wise thing to do to go to Ariel's father for help. I think you could improve your paper by answering some of these questions: What did Eric and Ariel tell her father? What did he tell them? Why would they go back into the water? What could have happened to the whale that would make him take a rest and forget about the swimmers? Do you think they ever thought about the whale again? Your score was a C– because you still need to place yourself as a writer in your reader's mind as well as in your characters' shoes (or should I say flippers?). The ideas in your paper appear to be flowing in with the tide—keep them coming!

—————I—————

BOOKS TO BUILD THE SELF-ESTEEM
OF STUDENTS
IN MULTIETHNIC SETTINGS

There is a disproportionate number of ethnic students, a large number of whom are African-Americans, who do not learn to read and write successfully (Ogbu, 1987). The reasons that this is so are complex. But part of the reason may involve an historical lack of role models within the cultural group who have improved their lot in life as a result of academic success (Ogbu, 1987). Literacy instruction for African-American and other [ethnic groups] needs to [assist] them in meeting both personal and societal goals (Parks, 1987). Schools can change this condition; "multiethnic literature can be used in [classrooms] to affirm the cultural identity of students of diverse backgrounds, and to develop all students' understanding and appreciation of other cultures" (Au, 1993, p. 176). Au (1993) summarizes the benefits of using multiethnic literature:

- Students of diverse backgrounds feel pride in their own identity and heritage.

- Both mainstream students and students of diverse background learn about diversity and the complexity of American society.

- All students gain more complete and balanced views of the historical forces that shaped American society.

- All students can explore issues of social justice. (p. 178)

Teachers and school librarians must seek out "literature that accurately reflects a group's culture, language, history, and values" (Au, 1993, p. 176). The following bibliography is intended to help teachers of all grade levels in their search for quality children's literature. The books mentioned can either be read *by* students or read *to* students.

While less than 2% of all children's books in 1990 were written and/or illustrated by African-Americans (to include Caribbean-Americans), this number is still far in excess of books about Asian Pacific-Americans (includes Chinese, Japanese, Vietnamese, Thai, Filipino, and Hmong), Native Americans, and Latin Americans (includes Mexican, Hispanic, Puerto Rican, Cuban, Central American, and other Latino groups) (Harris, 1993). Thus the bibliography for African-Americans that follows is lengthier and divided into different genres. Although there are notable exceptions (e.g., Virginia Hamilton's *Zeely,* 1967), works prior to 1980 were not included for several reasons: 1) space constraints; 2) more risk of stereotypes in earlier books; and 3) many new and excellent books of which teachers may be unaware. Those authors who have an asterisk by their name have many other works that may be of interest to the reader.

AFRICAN-AMERICAN LITERATURE

Coleen C. Salley

Picture Books

Adoff, Arnold. (1991). *Hard to be six*. NY: Lothrop.

Agard, John. (1989). *The calypso alphabet*. NY: Holt.

Allen, Judy. (1993). *Elephant*. Cambridge, MA: Candlewick.

Allison, Diane. (1992). *This is the key to the kingdom*. Boston: Little Brown.

Appiah, Sonia. (1988). *Amoko and Efua bear*. NY: Macmillan.

Barrett, Joyce Durham. (1989). *Willie's not the hugging kind*. NY: Harper.

Bozylinsky, Hannah. (1993). *Lala salama: An African lullaby*. NY: Philomel.

Buffett, Jimmy. (1988). *Jolly mon*. San Diego, CA: Harcourt.

Bunting, Eve. (1988). *How many days to America?* NY: Clarion.

*Caines, Jeanette. (1980). *Window wishing*. NY: Harper. (Also: *Just us women,* 1982)

*Clifton, Lucille. (1980). *My friend Jacob*. NY: Dutton.

Cowen-Fletcher, Jane. (1993). *It takes a village*. NY: Scholastic.

Craft, Ruth. (1989). *The day of the rainbow*. NY: Viking.

Crews, Donald. (1992). *Shortcut*. NY: Greenwillow. (Also: *Parade*, 1983; *Carousel*, 1982; *School bus,* 1984; *Bicycle race,* 1985; *Big mama's,* 1991)

Cummings, Pat. (1986). *C.L.O.U.D.S*. NY: Lothrop. (Also: *Jimmy Lee did it,* 1985)

Cummings, Pat. (1991). *Clean up your room, Harvey Moon*. NY: Bradbury.

Dale, Penny. (1987). *Bet you can't*. NY: Lippincott.

Daly, Niki. (1992). *Papa's lucky shadow*. NY: Macmillan.

DePaolo, Paula. (1992). *Rosie and the yellow ribbon*. Boston: Little Brown.

Dragonwagon, Crescent. (1990). *Home place*. NY: Macmillan. (Also: *Half a moon and one whole star,* 1986)

Eisenberg, Phyllis Rose. (1992). *You're my Nikki*. NY: Dial.

Falwell, Cathryn. (1993). *Feast for 10*. NY: Clarion.

Flournoy, Valerie. (1980). *The twins strike back*. NY: Dial. (Also: *The patchwork quilt,* 1985)

Goldberg, Whoopi. (1992). *Alice*. NY: Bantam.

Graham, Lorenz. (1993). *Every man heart lay down*. Honesdale, PA: Boyds Mill.

Gray, Libba Moore. (1993). *Miss Tizzy*. NY: Simon & Schuster.

*Greenfield, Eloise. (1980). *Grandmama's joy*. NY: Collins.

*Greenfield, Eloise. (1988). *Grandpa's face*. NY: Philomel.

Grifalconi, Ann. (1993) *Kinda blue*. Boston: Little Brown. (Also: *Darkness and the butterfly,* 1987; *Osa's pride,* 1990; *Flyaway girl,* 1992)

Guy, Rosa. (1992). *Billy the great*. NY: Delacorte.

This bibliography of African-American literature was prepared by Coleen C. Salley, a colleague of the author at the University of New Orleans, and respected children's literature expert.

Hartmann, Wendy. (1993). *All the magic in the world.* NY: Dutton.

Hasely, Dennis. (1988). *My father doesn't know about the woods and me.* NY: Atheneum.

Havill, Juanita. (1993). *Jamaica and Brianna.* Boston: Houghton. (Also: *Jamaica tag-along,* 1989; *Jamaica's find,* 1986)

Hill, Elizabeth Starr. (1991). *Evan's corner.* NY: Viking.

Hoffman, Mary. (1991). *Amazing Grace.* NY: Dial.

Hopkinson, Deborah. (1993). *Sweet Clara and the freedom quilt.* NY: Knopf.

Hort, Lenny. (1991). *How many stars in the sky.* NY: Tambourine.

*Howard, Elizabeth F. (1989). *The train to Lulu's.* NY: Bradbury. (Also: *Chita's Christmas tree,* 1989)

*Howard, Elizabeth F. (1991). *Aunt Flossie's hat (and crab cakes later).* NY: Clarion.

*Howard, Elizabeth F. (1993). *Mac and Marie and the train toss surprise.* NY: Four Winds.

Hru, Dakasi. (1993). *Joshua's Masai mask.* NY: Lee and Lou.

Isadora, Rachel. (1991). *At the crossroads.* NY: Greenwillow.

*Johnson, Angela. (1992). *When I am old with you.* NY: Orchard. (Also: *The leaving morning,* 1992; *One of three,* 1991; *Do like Kyla,* 1990; *Tell me a story, Mama,* 1989)

Johnson, Dolores. (1993). *Your dad was just like you.* NY: Macmillan. (Also: *Now let me fly,* 1993; *What kind of baby-sitter is this?* 1991)

Johnson, Herschel. (1989). *A visit to the country.* NY: Harper.

Jones, Rebecca C. (1991). *Matthew and Tilly.* NY: Dutton.

Kroll, Virginia. (1992). *Masai and I.* NY: Four Winds.

Lauture, Denize. (1992). *Father and son.* NY: Philomel.

Lewin, Hugh. (1984). *Jafta—The journey.* Minneapolis, MN: Carolrhoda. (Also: *The wedding,* 1983; *Jafta's father,* 1983; *Jafta's mother,* 1983; *The journey,* 1984)

Lotz, Karen. (1993). *Can't sit still.* NY: Dutton.

Lyon, George Ella. (1989). *Together.* NY: Orchard.

Martin, Ann. (1992). *Rachel Parker, kindergarten show-off.* NY: Holiday House.

*McKissack, Patricia C. (1992). *A million fish . . . more or less.* NY: Knopf. (Also: *Mirandy and brother wind,* 1988; *Flossie and the fox,* 1987; *Nettie Jo's friends,* 1989)

Mendez, Phil. (1989). *The black snowman.* NY: Scholastic.

Miles, Calvin. (1993). *Calvin's Christmas.* NY: Viking.

Mitchell, Margaree. (1993). *Uncle Jed's barbershop.* NY: Simon & Schuster.

Moss, Marissa. (1990). *Regina's big mistake.* Boston: Houghton.

*Myers, Walter Dean. (1984). *Mr. Monkey and the gotcha bird.* NY: Delacorte.

Otey, Mimi. (1990). *Daddy has a pair of striped shorts.* NY: Farrar.

Patrick, Denise. (1993). *The car washing street.* NY: Tambourine.

Patrick, Denise. (1993). *Red dancing shoes.* NY: Morrow.

Pinkney, Gloria Jean. (1992). *Back home.* NY: Dial.

Polacco, Patricia. (1992). *Chicken Sunday.* NY: Philomel.

Pomerantz, Charlotte. (1989). *The chalk doll.* NY: Lippincott.

Raschka, Chris. (1993). *Yo! Yes!* NY: Orchard. (Also: *Charlie Parker played be bop,* 1992)

Ringgold, Faith. (1992). *Aunt Harriet's underground railroad in the sky.* NY: Crown. (Also: *Tar beach,* 1991)

Ringgold, Faith. (1993). *Dinner at Aunt Connie's house.* NY: Hyperion.

Rosen, Michael J., & Robinson, L. (1992). *Elijah's angel.* San Diego: Harcourt.

Samuels, Vyanne. (1988). *Carry go bring come.* NY: Four Winds.

Schroeder, Alan. (1989). *Ragtime Tumpie.* Boston: Little Brown.

Seed, Jenny. (1989). *Ntombi's song.* NY: Harper.

Shelby, Anne. (1992). *We keep a store.* NY: Orchard.

Spohn, David. (1993). *Home field.* NY: Lothrop.

Stewart, Dianne. (1993). *The dove.* NY: Greenwillow.

Stolz, Mary. (1988). *Storm in the night.* NY: Harper.

Temple, Charles. (1993). *On the river bank.* Boston: Candlewick.

Tusa, Tricia. (1987). *Maebelle's suitcase.* NY: Macmillan.

Walter, Mildred Pitts. (1980). *Ty's one-man-band.* NY: Four Winds.

Walter, Mildred Pitts. (1983). *My mama needs me.* NY: Lothrop. (Also: *Brother to the wind,* 1985)

Whiteside, Karen. (1980). *Brother Mouky and the falling sun.* NY: Harper.

Williams, Vera B. (1986). *Cherries and cherry pits.* NY: Greenwillow. (Also: *More, more, more,* 1990)

Winter, Jeanette. (1988). *Follow the drinking gourd.* NY: Knopf.

Easy Fiction

Anderson, Joan. (1988). *A Williamsburg household.* NY: Clarion.

Blackman, Malorie. (1993). *Girl wonder and the terrific twins.* NY: Dutton.

Bunting, Eve. (1992). *Summer wheels.* San Diego: Harcourt.

*Caines, Jeanette. (1988). *I need a lunch box.* NY: Harper.

Cameron, Ann. (1981). *The stories Julian tells.* NY: Knopf. (Also: *More stories Julian tells,* 1986)

Claverie, Jean. (1990). *Little Lou.* NY: Stewart Talbori.

Cohen, Barbara. (1991). *213 valentines.* NY: Holt.

*Greenfield, Eloise. (1993). *Talk about a family.* NY: Harper.

*Hamilton, Virginia. (1991). *The all-Jahdu story book.* NY: Harcourt.

Jacobs, Shannon. (1991). *Song of the giraffe.* Boston: Little Brown.

Monjo, F. N. (1993). *Drinking gourd.* NY: Harper.

Nelson, Vaunda Micheaux. (1993). *Mayfield crossing.* NY: Putnam.

Sacks, Margaret. (1992). *Themba.* NY: Dutton.

Shearer, John. (1981). *Billy Jo Jive and the walkie-talkie caper.* NY: Delacorte.

Stolz, Mary. (1991). *Go fish.* NY: HarperCollins.

*Taylor, Mildred D. (1990). *Mississippi bridge*. NY: Dial. (Also: *The friendship,* 1987; *The gold Cadillac,* 1987)

Turner, Ann. (1987). *Nettie's trip south*. NY: Macmillan.

Walker, Alice. (1988). *To hell with dying*. San Diego: Harcourt.

Fiction, Middle School

Berry, James. (1991). *Ajeemah and his son*. NY: HarperCollins.

Berry, James. (1993). *The future-telling lady*. NY: Harper.

Case, Dianne. (1991). *Love, David*. NY: Dutton.

Davis, Ossie. (1992). *Just like Martin*. NY: Simon & Schuster.

Edwards, Pat. (1988). *Little John and Plutie*. Boston: Houghton.

Farmer, Nancy. (1992). *Do you know me?* NY: Orchard.

Greene, Bette. (1981). *Get on out of here, Philip Hall*. NY: Dial.

*Greenfield, Eloise. (1992). *Koya Delaney and the good girl blues*. NY: Scholastic.

*Hamilton, Virginia. (1983). *Willie Bea and the time the Martians landed*. NY: Greenwillow.

*Hamilton, Virginia. (1989). *The bells of Christmas*. Boston: Harcourt.

*Hamilton, Virginia. (1990). *Cousins*. NY: Putnam.

*Hamilton, Virginia. (1993). *Plain city*. NY: Scholastic.

Hansen, Joyce. (1993). *The captive*. NY: Scholastic.

Hentoff, Nat. (1981). *Does this school have capital punishment?* NY: Delacorte.

Hodge, Merle. (1993). *For the life of Laetitia*. NY: Farrar.

Hopkins, Lila. (1989). *Talking turkey*. NY: Watts. (Also: *Eating crow,* 1988)

Hunter, Latoya. (1992). *Diary of Latoya Hunter*. NY: Crown.

*Johnson, Angela. (1993). *Toning the sweep*. NY: Orchard.

*Moore, Emily. (1988). *Whose side are you on?* NY: Farrar.

Moore, Yvette. (1991). *Freedom sings*. NY: Orchard.

*Myers, Walter Dean. (1980). *The black pearl and the ghost*. NY: Viking. (Also: *The golden serpent,* 1980)

*Myers, Walter Dean. (1983). *Tales of a dead king*. NY: Morrow.

*Myers, Walter Dean. (1985). *Adventures in Grenada*. NY: Penguin. (Also: *Hidden shrine,* 1985; *Ambush in the Amazon,* 1986; *Duel in the desert,* 1986)

*Myers, Walter Dean. (1992). *The righteous revenge of Artemis Bonner*. NY: HarperCollins.

O'Dell, Scott. (1989). *My name is not Angelica*. Boston: Houghton.

Powell, Pamela. (1992). *The turtle watchers*. NY: Viking.

Prather, Ray. (1992). *Fish and bones*. NY: HarperCollins.

Robinet, Harriette. (1993). *Children of the fire*. NY: Atheneum.

Smith, K. (1989). *Skeeter*. Boston: Houghton.

Smothers, Ethel Footman. (1992). *Down in the piney woods*. NY: Knopf.

Springer, Nancy. (1989). *They're all named wildfire*. NY: Atheneum.

Stolz, Mary. (1992). *Stealing home*. NY: HarperCollins.

Tate, Eleanora. (1980). *Just overnight guest*. NY: Dial.

*Taylor, Mildred. (1981). *Let the circle be unbroken*. NY: Dial.

Thomas, Joyce Carol. (1992). *When the nightingale sings*. NY: HarperCollins.

Walter, Mildred Pitts. (1989). *Have a happy. . . .* NY: Lothrop. (Also: *Trouble's child,* 1985)

Wilson, Johnniece Marshall. (1988). *Oh, brother*. NY: Scholastic.

Yarbrough, Camille. (1989). *The shimmershine queens*. NY: Putnam.

Folktales

*Aardema, Verna. (1989). *Rabbit make a monkey of lion*. NY: Dial. (Also: *Bringing the rain to Kapiti Plain,* 1981; *What's so funny, Ketu?* 1982; *Oh, Kojo! How could you?* 1984; *Princess Gorilla and a new kind of water,* 1988)

*Aardema, Verna. (1991). *Traveling to Tondo*. NY: Knopf.

Abrahams, Roger. (1985). *Afro-American folktales*. NY: Pantheon.

Berry, James. (1989). *Spiderman Anancy*. NY: Holt.

*Bryan, Ashley. (1989). *Turtle knows your name*. NY: Atheneum. (Also: *The cat's purr,* 1985; *Lion and the ostrich chicks, and other African tales,* 1986; *The dancing granny,* 1987; *Sh-Ko and his eight wicked brothers,* 1988)

Dee, Ruby. (1988). *Two ways to count to ten*. NY: Holt.

Diop, Birago. (1981). *Mother crocodile*. NY: Delacorte.

Fairman, Tony. (1991). *Bury my bones but keep my words*. NY: Holt.

Gerson, Mary Joan. (1992). *Why the sky is far away*. Boston: Little Brown.

Grifalconi, Ann. (1986). *The village of round and square houses*. Boston: Little Brown.

*Hamilton, Virginia. (1985). *The people could fly*. NY: Knopf.

*Hamilton, Virginia. (1990). *The dark way*. San Diego: Harcourt. (Also: *In the beginning,* 1988)

Harris, Joel Chandler. (1986). *The adventures of Brer Rabbit*. (Adapted by Van Dyke Parks). San Diego: Harcourt. (Also: *Jump again!* 1987)

Jaquith, Priscilla. (1981). *Bo Rabbit smart for true*. NY: Philomel.

Joseph, Lynn. (1991). *Wave in her pocket: Stories from Trinidad*. NY: Clarion.

Kimmel, Eric. (1992). *Anansi goes fishing*. NY: Holiday House. (Also: *Anansi and the moss covered rock,* 1991)

Lester, Julius. (1988). *More tales of Uncle Remus*. NY: Dial. (Also: *The tales of Uncle Remus,* 1987)

Lester, Julius. (1989). *How many spots does a leopard have?* NY: Scholastic.

Madden, Eric. (1993). *The fire children*. NY: Dial.

Martin, Francesca. (1992). *The honey hunters*. Boston: Candlewick.

McDermott, Gerald. (1992). *Zomo, the rabbit*. San Diego: Harcourt.

*McKissack, Patricia. (1992). *The warb-thirty*. NY: Rendoon.

Mollel, Tololwa M. (1993). *The king and the tortoise*. NY: Clarion. (Also: *Orphan boy,* 1991; *Rhinos for lunch and elephants for supper,* 1991)

San Souci, Robert. (1989). *The talking eggs*. NY: Dial.

San Souci, Robert. (1992). *Sukey and the mermaid*. NY: Four Winds. (Also: *The boy and the ghost,* 1989)

Seeger, Pete. (1986). *Abiyoyo*. NY: Macmillan.

*Steptoe, John. (1987). *Mufaro's beautiful daughters*. NY: Lothrop.

Tadjo, Veronique. (1989). *Lord of the dance*. NY: Lippincott.

Walker, Barbara. (1990). *The dancing palm tree: And other Nigerian folktales*. Lubbock, TX: Texas Tech University.

Poetry

Adoff, Arnold. (1982). *All the colors of the race*. (Ill. John Steptoe). NY: Lothrop.

Adoff, Arnold. (1991). *In for winter, out for spring*. (Ill. Jerry Pinkney). San Diego: Harcourt.

Agard, John. (1989). *The Calypso alphabet*. NY: Holt.

*Bryan, Ashley. (1991). *All night, all day: A child's first book of African-American spirituals*. NY: Atheneum.

*Bryan, Ashley. (1992). *Sing to the sun*. NY: HarperCollins.

Burgie, Irving. (1992). *Caribbean carnival*. NY: Tambourine.

*Clifton, Lucille. (1983). *Everett Anderson's good-bye*. NY: Holt.

Feelings, Tom. (1981). *Daydreamers*. NY: Dial.

Fields, Julia. (1988). *The green lion of Zion Street*. NY: Macmillan.

*Greenfield, Eloise. (1988). *Under the Sunday tree*. (Ill. Amos Ferguson). NY: Harper.

*Greenfield, Eloise. (1989). *Nathaniel talking*. NY: Black Butterfly.

Gunning, Monica. (1993). *Not a copper penny in me house*. Dunmore, PA: Boyds Mills.

Hudson, Wade. (1993). *Pass it on: African-American poetry for children*. NY: Scholastic.

Johnson, James Weldon. (1993). *Lift every voice and sing*. NY: Walker.

Joseph, Lynn. (1991). *Coconut kind of day*. NY: Lothrop.

Langstaff, John. (1991). *Climbing Jacob's ladder*. NY: Macmillan.

Lessac, Frane. (1989). *Caribbean canvas*. NY: Lippincott.

Little, Lessie Jones. (1988). *Children of long ago*. NY: Philomel.

Livingston, Myra Cohn. (1992). *Let freedom ring: A ballad of Martin Luther King, Jr.* NY: Holiday House.

Moss, Thylias. (1993). *I want to be*. NY: Dial.

Ross, Charlemae. (1993). *Christmas Gif'*. NY: Morrow.

Singer, Marilyn. (1989). *Turtle in July*. NY: Macmillan.

Tadjo, Veronique. (1989). *Lord of the dance*. NY: Lippincott.

Thomas, Joyce Carol. (1993). *Brown honey in broomwheet tea: Poems*. NY: HarperCollins.

Nonfiction

Adler, David. A. (1989). *A picture book of Martin Luther King, Jr.* NY: Holiday House. (Also: *Jackie Robinson,* 1989)

Archer, Jules. (1993). *They had a dream*. NY: Viking.

Burchard, S. H. (1980). *Earl Campbell*. San Diego: Harcourt.

Chiasson, John. (1987). *African journey*. NY: Bradbury.

Cox, Clinton. (1993). *The forgotten heroes*. NY: Scholastic.

Davidson, Margaret. (1986). *I have a dream: The story of Martin Luther King*. NY: Scholastic.

Everett, Gwen. (1993). *John Brown*. NY: Rizzoli. (Also: *Lil sis and Uncle Willie . . . William H. Johnson,* 1991)

*Hamilton, Virginia. (1993). *Many thousand gone: African-Americans from slavery to freedom*. NY: Knopf.

Haskins, James. (1993). *Get on board: Story of the underground railroad*. NY: Scholastic.

Haskins, James. (1993). *The march on Washington*. NY: Harper.

Kroll, Virginia. (1993). *African brothers and sisters*. NY: Four Winds.

Levine, Ellen. (1993). *Freedom's children*. NY: Putnam.

Marzollo, Jean. (1993). *Happy birthday Martin Luther King*. NY: Scholastic.

*McKissack, Patricia C. (1984). *Martin Luther King, Jr.: A man to remember*. Chicago: Children's Press. (Also: *Michael Jackson: Superstar,* 1984)

*McKissack, Patricia C. (1992). *Sojourner Truth: Ain't I a woman?* NY: Scholastic. (Also: *Mary McLeod Bethune: A great American educator,* 1987; *Jesse Jackson,* 1989)

*McKissack, Patricia C., & McKissack, Frederick. (1989). *A long hard journey*. NY: Walker.

*McKissack, Patricia C., & McKissack, Frederick. (1991). *Louis Armstrong*. Hillside, NJ: Enslow.

Medearis, Angela. (1993). *Come this far to freedom*. NY: Atheneum.

*Myers, Walter Dean. (1991). *Now is your time!: The African-American struggle for freedom*. NY: HarperCollins.

*Myers, Walter Dean. (1993). *Malcolm X*. NY: Scholastic.

Pinkney, Andrea Davis. (1993). *Alvin Ailey*. NY: Hyperion.

Pinkney, Andrea Davis. (1993). *Seven candles for Kwanzaa*. NY: Dial.

Rochelle, Belinda. (1993). *Witness to freedom: Young people who fought for civil rights*. NY: Dutton.

Scioscia, Mary. (1993). *Bicycle rider*. NY: Harper.

Stanley, Diane. (1988). *Shaka: King of the Zulus*. NY: Morrow.

Towle, Wendy. (1993). *The real McCoy: The life of an African-American inventor*. NY: Scholastic.

ASIAN PACIFIC-AMERICAN LITERATURE

Anno, Mitsumasa. (1983). *Anno's USA*. NY: Philomel.

Bang, Molly. (1985). *The paper crane*. NY: Greenwillow.

Breckler, Rosemary K. (1992). *Hoang breaks the lucky teapot.* Boston: Houghton.

Brown, Tricia. (1991). *Lee Ann: The story of a Vietnamese-American girl.* NY: Putnam.

Garland, Sherry. (1993). *The lotus seed.* San Diego: Harcourt.

Hoyt-Goldsmith, Diane. (1992). *Hoang Anh: A Vietnamese-American boy.* NY: Holiday.

Lord, Bette Bao. (1984). *In the year of the boar and Jackie Robinson.* NY: Harper & Row.

Morey, Janet Nomura, and Dunn, Wendy. (1992). *Famous Asian Americans.* NY: Dutton.

Namioka, Lensey. (1992). *Yang the youngest and his terrible ear.* Boston: Little Brown.

*Say, Allen. (1990). *El Chino.* Boston: Houghton. (Also: *A river dream,* 1988; *The lost lake,* 1989)

Surat, Michele Maria. (1983). *Angel child, dragon child.* Milwaukee, WI: Raintree.

Suzuki, David. (1987). *Looking at the body.* Canada: Stoddart.

*Uchida, Yoshiko. (1985). *The happiest ending.* NY: Atheneum. (Also: *A jar of dreams,* 1981; *The best bad thing,* 1983)

*Uchida, Yoshiko. (1991). *The invisible thread.* Englewood Cliffs, NJ: Julian Messner.

Yee, Paul. (1991). *Roses sing on new snow: A delicious tale.* NY: Macmillan.

*Yep, Laurence. (1991). *The lost garden.* Englewood Cliffs, NJ: Julian Messner.

*Yep, Laurence. (1991). *The star fisher.* NY: Harper. (Also: *The rainbow people,* 1989)

LATIN-AMERICAN/MEXICAN-AMERICAN LITERATURE

Adoff, Arnold. (1988). *Flamboyan.* NY: Harcourt.

Anaya, Rudolfo A. (1987). *The farolitos of Christmas: A New Mexico Christmas story.* Sante Fe: New Mexico Magazine.

Anderson, Joan. (1989). *Spanish pioneers of the Southwest.* NY: Lodestar/Dutton.

Brown, Tricia. (1986). *Hello amigos!* NY: Holt.

Carlson, Lori M., & Ventura, C. L. (1990). *Where angels glide at dawn: New stories from Latin America.* NY: Lippincott.

Codye, Corinn. (1990). *Vilma Martinez.* Milwaukee, WI: Raintree.

Delacre, Lulu. (1989). *Arroz con leche: Popular songs and rhymes from Latin America.* NY: Scholastic.

Garcia, Richard. (1987). *My Aunt Otilia's spirits.* San Francisco: Children's.

Gillies, Jerry. (1988). *Senor alcalde: A biography of Henry Cisneros.* Minneapolis, MN: Dillon Press.

Hewett, Joan. (1989). *Getting elected: The diary of a campaign.* NY: Lodestar/Dutton.

Hewett, Joan. (1990). *Hector lives in the United States now: The story of a Mexican-American child.* NY: Lippincott.

Holman, Felice. (1990). *Secret city, U.S.A.* NY: Scribner's.

Hurwitz, Johanna. (1990). *Class president.* NY: Morrow.

Lomas, Garza C. (1990). *Family pictures/Cuadros de familia.* San Francisco: Children's.

Macmillan, Dianne, & Freeman, Dorothy. (1986). *My best friend, Martha Rodriguez: Meeting a Mexican-American family.* Canada: Messner.

Mango, Karin N. (1987). *Somewhere green.* NY: Four Winds.

Marzollo, Jean. (1987). *Soccer Sam.* NY: Random House.

Meltzer, Milton. (1982). *The Hispanic Americans.* NY: Crowell.

*Mohr, Nicholasa. (1986). *Going home.* NY: Dial. (Sequel to *Felita,* 1979)

*Mohr, Nicholasa. (1988). *In Nueva York.* Houston: Arte Publico. (Also: *Nilda,* 1986; *El Bronx remembered,* 1986)

Morey, Janet, & Dunn, William. (1989). *Famous Mexican Americans.* NY: Cobblehill /Dutton.

*Myers, Walter Dean. (1988). *Scorpions.* NY: Harper.

Ortiz, Cofer Judith. (1990). *Silent dancing: A partial remembrance of a Puerto Rican childhood.* Houston: Arte Publico.

Pena, Sylvia Cavazos. (1987). *Kirikiri: Stories and poems in English and Spanish for children.* Houston: Arte Publico. (Also: *Tun-ta-ca-tun: More stories and poems in English and Spanish for children,* 1986)

Pinchot, Jane. (1989). *The Mexicans in America.* Minneapolis: Lerner.

Rohmer, Harriet, & Rea, Jesus Guerrero. (1988). *Atariba y Niguayona.* San Francisco: Children's.

Soto, Gary. (1987). *The cat's meow.* San Francisco: Strawberry Hill.

Soto, Gary. (1990). *Baseball in April.* San Diego: Harcourt.

Stanek, Muriel. (1989). *I speak English for my mom.* Niles, IL: Whitman.

Taha, Karen T. (1986). *A gift for Tia Rosa.* NY: Bantam.

Taylor, Theodore. (1986). *The Maldonado miracle.* NY: Avon.

Tompert, Ann. (1988). *The silver whistle.* NY: Macmillan.

NATIVE AMERICAN LITERATURE

Amon, Aline. (1981). *The earth is sore: Native Americans on nature.* NY: Atheneum.

*Baylor, Byrd. (1976). *Hawk, I'm your brother.* NY: Scribner's.

Broker, Ignatia. (1983). *Night flying woman: An Ojibway narrative.* St. Paul, MN: Historical Society.

Bruchac, Joseph. (1985). *Iroquois stories: Heroes and heroines, monsters and magic.* Freedom, CA: The Crossing. (Also: cassette tape, 1988)

Cannon, Ann Edwards. (1990). *The shadow brothers.* NY: Delacorte.

Connolly, James Edward. (1985). *Why the possum's tail is bare and other North American Indian nature tales.* Owings Mills, MD: Stemmer.

DePaola, Tomie. (1983). *The legend of the bluebonnet: An old tale of Texas.* NY: Putnam.

Freedman, Russell. (1987). *Indian chiefs.* NY: Holiday.

*Goble, Paul. (1984). *Buffalo woman.* NY: Bradbury. (Also: *Star boy,* 1983)

*Goble, Paul. (1992). *Crow chief.* NY: Orchard. (Also: *Iktomi and the berries,* 1989; *Iktomi and the ducks,* 1990; *Iktomi and the buffalo skull,* 1991)

Hirschfelder, Arlene B. (1986). *Happily may I walk: American Indians and Alaska natives today.* NY: Scribner's.

Ortiz, Simon. (1988). *The people shall continue.* San Francisco: Children's.

Sneve, Virginia Driving Hawk. (1989). *Dancing teepees: Poems of American Indian youth.* NY: Holiday.

Steptoe, John. (1984). *The story of Jumping Mouse: A Native American legend.* NY: Lothrop.

*Strete, Craig K. (1990). *Big thunder magic.* NY: Greenwillow.

FRY'S FIRST THREE HUNDRED INSTANT WORDS

THE INSTANT WORDS* FIRST HUNDRED

Words 1–25	Words 26–50	Words 51–75	Words 76–100
the	or	will	number
of	one	up	no
and	had	other	way
a	by	about	could
to	word	out	people
in	but	many	my
is	not	then	than
you	what	them	first
that	all	these	water
it	were	so	been
he	we	some	call
was	when	her	who
for	your	would	oil
on	can	make	its
are	said	like	now
as	there	him	find
with	use	into	long
his	an	time	down
they	each	has	day
I	which	look	did
at	she	two	get
be	do	more	come
this	how	write	made
have	their	go	may
from	if	see	part

Common suffixes: -s, -ing, -ed, -er, -ly, -est

SECOND HUNDRED

Words 101–125	Words 126–150	Words 151–175	Words 176–200
over	say	set	try
new	great	put	kind
sound	where	end	hand
take	help	does	picture
only	through	another	again
little	much	well	change
work	before	large	off
know	line	must	play
place	right	big	spell
year	too	even	air
live	mean	such	away
me	old	because	animal
back	any	turn	house
give	same	here	point
most	tell	why	page
very	boy	ask	letter
after	follow	went	mother
thing	came	men	answer
our	want	read	found
just	show	need	study
name	also	land	still
good	around	different	learn
sentence	form	home	should
man	three	us	America
think	small	move	world

Common suffixes: -s, -ing, -ed. -er, -ly, -est

THIRD HUNDRED

Words 201–225	Words 226–250	Words 251–275	Words 276–300
high	saw	important	miss
every	left	until	idea
near	don't	children	enough
add	few	side	eat
food	while	feet	face
between	along	car	watch
own	might	mile	far
below	close	night	Indian
country	something	walk	really
plant	seem	white	almost
last	next	sea	let
school	hard	began	above
father	open	grow	girl
keep	example	took	sometimes
tree	begin	river	mountain
never	life	four	cut
start	always	carry	young
city	those	state	talk
earth	both	once	soon
eye	paper	book	list
light	together	hear	song
thought	got	stop	being
head	group	without	leave
under	often	second	family
story	run	later	it's

Common suffixes: -s, -ing, -ed, -er, -ly, -est

From the book: *The Reading Teacher's Book of Lists*, 3/e, by Edward Bernard Fry, Jacqueline E. Kress, Dona Lee Fountoukidis. © 1993. Used by permission of the publisher/Prentice Hall/A Division of Simon & Schuster, Englewood, Cliffs, NJ.

*For additional instant words, see *Spelling Book* by Edward Fry, Laguna Beach Educational Books, 245 Grandview, Laguna Beach, CA 92651.

USEFUL PHONICS GENERALIZATIONS

1. The *c rule*. When *c* comes just before *a, o,* or *u,* it usually has the *hard* sound heard in cat, cot, and cut. Otherwise, it usually has the *soft* sound heard in cent, city, and bicycle.

2. The *g rule*. When *g* comes at the end of words or just before *a, o,* or *u,* it usually has the *hard* sound heard in tag, game, go, and gush. Otherwise, it usually has the *soft* sound heard in gem, giant, and gym.

3. The VC pattern. This pattern is seen in words such as *an, can, candy,* and *dinner.* As a verbal generalization it might be stated as follows: In either a word or syllable, a single vowel letter followed by a consonant letter, digraph, or blend usually represents a short vowel sound. (Note that *C* stands for either a letter, digraph, or blend, e.g., bat, bath, bask.)

4. The VV pattern. This pattern is seen in words such as *eat, beater, peach, see, bait, float,* and *play.* As a verbal generalization it might be stated like this: In a word or syllable containing a vowel digraph, the first letter in the digraph usually represents the long vowel sound and the second letter is usually silent. According to Clymer (1963), this generalization is quite reliable for *ee, oa,* and *ay* (fee, coat, tray) and works about two-thirds of the time for *ea* and *ai* (seat, bait), but is not reliable for other vowel digraphs such as *ei, ie,* or *oo,* or diphthongs, *oi, oy, ou,* and *ow.*

5. The VCE (final e) pattern. This pattern is seen in words such as *ice, nice, ate, plate, paste, flute, vote,* and *clothe.* As a generalization it might be stated this way: In one-syllable words containing two vowel letters, one of which is a final *e,* the first vowel letter usually represents a long vowel sound, and the *e* is silent. If the vowel is not long, try the short sound.

6. The CV pattern. This pattern is seen in one-syllable words such as *he, she, go, my, cry, hotel, going,* and *flying.* As a generalization, it might be stated this way: When there is only one vowel letter in a word or syllable and it comes at the end of the word or syllable, it usually represents the long vowel sound.

7. The *r rule*. This rule applies to words like *far, fare, fair, girl, fur, her,* and *here.* As a generalization it might be stated as follows: The letter r usually modifies the short or long sound of the preceding vowel letter. (See May and Eliot's *To Help Children Read,* 1978, p. 38.)

8. There are basically three syllabication rules worth knowing. These are represented by the *VCCV, VCV,* and the *Cle* patterns. For the VCCV pattern, the rule is to divide between the two consonants. This pattern is represented in words such as *blanket, happy,* and *represent.* For the VCV pattern, the rule is to divide before or after the consonant. Words representing this pattern are *robot, robin, divide,* and *before.* For the last pattern, Cle, the rule is to divide before the consonant. Words representing this pattern are *Bible, uncle, table,* and *example.*

(*Note:* Phonics generalizations should be taught inductively. Known words in a meaningful context should be used to illustrate a letter-sound relationship. When teaching something new, use words familiar to children. To learn whether children can apply what has been taught, use words they cannot read. Practice phonics in context whenever possible. Once a generalization has been taught inductively, concentrate on unknown words in the context of a sentence or brief passage.)

REFERENCES

Aardema, V. (1981). *Bringing the rain to Kapiti Plain*. New York: Dial.

Aaron, I. E., Chall, J. S., Durkin, D., Goodman, K., & Strickland, D. S. (1990a). The past, present, and future of literacy education: Comments from a panel of distinguished educators, Part I. *The Reading Teacher, 43,* 302–311.

Aaron, I. E., Chall, J. S., Durkin, D., Goodman, K., & Strickland, D. S . (1990b). The past, present, and future of literacy education: Comments from a panel of distinguished educators, Part II. *The Reading Teacher, 43,* 370–380.

Adams, M. J. (1990). *Beginning to read: Thinking and learning about print*. In S. Stahl, J. Osborn, & F. Lehr (Eds.), *A summary*. Urbana, IL: Center for the Study of Reading/Reading Research and Education Center.

Alexander, F. (1993). National standards: A new conventional wisdom. *Educational Leadership, 50,* 9–10.

Alexander, J. E., & Cobb, J. (1992). Assessing attitudes in middle and secondary schools and community colleges. *Journal of Reading, 36,* 146–149.

Allen, R. (1976). *Language experiences in communication*. Boston: Houghton Mifflin.

Allen, R., & Allen, C. (1976). *Language experience activities* (2nd ed.). Boston: Houghton Mifflin.

Allen, R., Brown, K., & Yatvin, J. (1986). *Learning language through communication: A functional perspective*. Belmont, CA: Wadsworth.

Allen, V. G. (1989). Literature as support to language acquisition. In P. Rigg & V. G. Allen (Eds.). *When they don't all speak English: Integrating the ESL student into the regular classroom* (pp. 55–64). Urbana, IL: National Council of Teachers of English.

Anderson, L., Raphael, T., Englert, C., & Stevens, D. (1992). *Teaching writing with a new instructional model: Variations in teachers' beliefs, instructional practices, and their students' performance*. National Center for Research on Teacher Learning, Michigan State University, East Lansing, MI.

Anderson, R. C., & Freebody, P. (1981). Vocabulary knowledge. In J. Guthrie (Ed.), *Comprehension and teaching: Research reviews* (pp. 77–117). Newark, DE: International Reading Association.

Anderson, T. H. (1980). Study strategies and adjunct aids. In R. J. Spiro, B. C. Bruce, & W. F. Brewer (Eds.), *Theoretical issues in reading comprehension*. Hillsdale, NJ: Erlbaum.

Andersson, B. V., & Barnitz, J. G. (1984). Cross-cultural schemata and reading comprehension instruction. *Journal of Reading, 28,* 102–108.

Andre, M. E. D. A., & Anderson, T. H. (1978/1979). The development and evaluation of a self-questioning study technique. *Reading Research Quarterly, 14,* 605–623.

Anthony, R., Johnson, T., Mickelson, N., & Preece, A. (1991). *Evaluating literacy: A perspective for change*. Portsmouth, NH: Heinemann.

Arnold, R. D., & Miller, J. (1980). Word recognition skills. In P. Lamb & R. D. Arnold (Eds.), *Teaching reading: Foundations and strategies* (2nd ed.). Belmont, CA: Wadsworth.

Arnold, R. D., & Sherry, N. (1975). A comparison of reading levels of disabled readers with assigned textbooks. *Reading Improvement, 12,* 207–211.

Associated Press, The. (1993, June 23). Conditions worsening for poor children, panel says. *The Times Picayune,* A–9.

Atwell, M. (1980). *The evolution of text: The interrelationship of reading and writing in the composing process*. Doctoral dissertation, Indiana University.

Au, K. (1993a). *Literacy instruction in multicultural settings*. New York: Harcourt Brace Jovanovich.

Au, K. (1993b, April). *New perspectives on assessment: Portfolios and ownership*. Featured speaker for the Organization of Teacher Educators in Reading at the annual meeting of the International Reading Association, San Antonio, TX.

Au, K. H. (1979). Using the experience-text-relationship method with minority children. *The Reading Teacher, 32,* 677–679.

Au, K. H., & Kawakami, A. J. (1985). Research currents: Talk story and learning to read. *Language Arts, 62,* 406–411.

Aulls, M. W. (1978). *Developmental and remedial reading in the middle grades,* Abridged edition. Boston: Allyn and Bacon.

Babbs, P. J. (1984). Monitoring cards help improve comprehension. *The Reading Teacher, 38,* 200–204.

Bailey, M. H. (1967). The utility of phonic generalizations in grades one through six. *The Reading Teacher, 20,* 413–418.

Baker, L. (1979). *Comprehension monitoring: Identifying and coping with text confusions* (Tech. Rep. No. 145). Champaign, IL: University of Illinois, Center for the Study of Reading.

Baker, L., & Brown, A. L. (1984). Meta-cognitive skills and reading. In P. D. Pearson (Ed.), *Handbook of reading research.* New York: Longman.

Barnitz, J. G. (1979). Developing sentence comprehension in reading. *Language Arts, 56,* 902–908, 958.

Barnitz, J. G. (1980). Black English and other dialects: Sociolinguistic implications for reading instruction. *The Reading Teacher, 33,* 779–786.

Barnitz, J. G. (1982). Standard and nonstandard dialects: Principles for language and reading instruction. *Reading: Exploration and Discovery, 5,* 21–32.

Barnitz, J. G. (1985). *Reading development of nonnative speakers of English: Research and instruction* (Monograph No. 63). Language in Education: Theory and Practice series (ERIC Clearinghouse on Languages and Linguistics). Washington, DC: Center for Applied Linguistics, and Orlando, FL: Harcourt Brace Jovanovich. Also available on microfiche, ED 256 182.

Barnitz, J. G. (1986). Toward understanding the effects of cross-cultural schemata and discourse structure on second language reading comprehension. *Journal of Reading Behavior, 18,* 95–116.

Barnitz, J. G. (1988). Sociolinguistic and cultural foundations. In P. M. Lamb & R. D. Arnold (Eds.), *Teaching reading: Foundations and strategies* (3rd ed.). R. C. Katonah, NY: Owen.

Barnitz, J. G. (1994). Discourse diversity: Principles for authentic talk and literacy instruction. *Journal of Reading, 37,* 586–591.

Barr, R. (1984). Beginning reading instruction: From debate to reformation. In P. D. Pearson (Ed.), *Handbook of reading research.* New York: Longman.

Barron, R. F. (1969). The use of vocabulary as an advance organizer. In H. Herber and P. Sanders (Eds.), *Research in reading in the content areas: First year report.* Syracuse, NY: Syracuse University Press.

Bartch, J. (1992). An alternative to spelling: An integrated approach. *Language Arts, 69,* 404–408.

Bartlett, F. C. (1932). *Remembering: A study in experimental and social psychology.* New York: Cambridge University Press.

Bartolome, P. I. (1969). Teachers' objectives and questions in primary reading. *The Reading Teacher, 23,* 27–33.

Base, G. (1986). *Animalia.* New York: Abrams.

Bean, T. W., & Pardi, R. (1979). A field test of a guided reading strategy. *Journal of Reading, 23,* 144–147.

Bear, T., Schenk, S., & Buckner, L. (1992/1993). Supporting victims of child abuse. *Educational Leadership, 50,* 42–47.

Bechtel, J., & Franzblau, B. (1980). *Reading in the science classroom.* Washington, DC: National Education Association.

Beck, I. L. (1981). Reading problems and instructional practices. In G. E. Mackinnon & T. G. Waller (Eds.), *Reading research: Advances in theory and practice* (Vol. 2) (pp. 53–95). New York: Academic Press.

Beck, I. L., & McKeown, M. B. (1981). Developing questions that promote comprehension of the story map. *Language Arts, 58,* 913–917.

Bedsworth, B. (1991). The Neurological Impress Method with middle school poor readers. *Journal of Reading, 34,* 564–565.

Berglund, R. L. (1987). Reading assessment: An interactive process. *Reading Today, 5,* 3, 21.

Berliner, D. C. (1981). Academic learning time and reading achievement. In J. T. Guthrie (Ed.), *Comprehension and teaching: Research reviews.* Newark, DE: International Reading Association.

Betts, E. (1946). *Foundations of reading instruction.* New York: American Book.

Bidwell, S. M. (1990). Using drama to increase motivation, comprehension, and fluency. *Journal of Reading, 34,* 38–41.

Biemiller, A. (1993, December). Students differ: So address differences effectively. *Educational Researcher, 22*(9), 14–15.

Blachowicz, C. L. Z., & Zabroske, B. (1990). Context instruction: A metacognitive approach for at-risk readers. *Journal of Reading, 33,* 504–508.

Bloome, D., & Egan-Robertson, A. (1993). The social construction of intertextuality in classroom reading and writing lessons. *Reading Research Quarterly, 25,* 305–333.

Blume, E. (1990). *Secret survivors.* New York: The Free Press.

Bobrow, D. G., & Norman, P. A. (1975). Some principles of memory schemata. In D. G. Bobrow & A. M. Collins (Eds.), *Representation and understanding: Studies in cognitive science.* New York: Academic Press.

Bond, G. L., & Tinker, M. A. (1967). *Reading difficulties: Their diagnosis and correction.* New York: Appleton-Century-Crofts.

Bond, G. L., Balow, B., & Hoyt, C. (1976). *Silent reading diagnostic test.* Chicago: Rand McNally.

Boning, R. (1985). Getting the main idea. *Specific skills series.* Baldwin, NY: Barnell Loft.

Boning, T., & Boning, R. (1957, April). I'd rather read than. . . . *The Reading Teacher,* 196–200.

Book Links: Connecting books, libraries, and classrooms. Published bimonthly by American Library Association.

Borkowski, J. G., Wehing, R. S., & Turner, L. A. (1986). Attributional retraining and the teaching of strategies. *Exceptional Children, 53,* 130–137.

Bormuth, J. R. (1967). Comparable cloze and multiple-choice comprehension test score. *Journal of Reading, 10,* 291–299.

Bormuth, J. R. (1968). The cloze readability procedure. *Elementary English, 45,* 429–436.

Bormuth, J. R. (1968). Cloze test readability: Criterion reference scores. *Journal of Educational Measurement, 5,* 189–196.

Bormuth, J. R. (1975). The cloze procedure: Literacy in the classroom. In W. D. Page (Ed.), *Help for the reading teacher: New directions in research (pp. 60–90).* Urbana, IL: ERIC Clearinghouse on Reading and Communication Skills.

Bowerman, M. (1976). Semantic factors in the acquisition of rules for word use and sentence construction. In D. Morehead and A. Morehead (Eds.), *Normal and deficient child language.* Baltimore: University Park Press.

Britton, J., Burgess, T., Martin, N., McLeod, A., & Rosen, H. (1975). *The development of writing abilities* (pp. 11–18). Schools Council Research Studies, London: Macmillan.

Bromley, K. (1989). Buddy journals make the reading–writing connection. *The Reading Teacher, 43,* 122–129.

Brown, A. L. (1980). Metacognitive development and reading. In R. J. Spiro, B. C. Bruce, & W. F. Brewer (Eds.), *Theoretical issues in reading comprehension* (pp. 453–481). Hillsdale, NJ: Erlbaum.

Brown, A. L., & DeLoache, J. (1978). Skills, plans, and self-regulation. In R. Siegler (Ed.), *Children's thinking: What develops?* Hillsdale, NJ: Erlbaum.

Brown, C. S. (1985). *Assessing perceptions of language and learning: Alternative diagnostic approaches.* Paper presented at the International Reading Association Convention, New Orleans.

Brown, D. A. (1982). *Reading diagnosis and remediation.* Englewood Cliffs, NJ: Prentice-Hall.

Brozo, W. G. (1990). Learning how at-risk readers learn best: A case for interactive assessment. *Journal of Reading, 33,* 522–527.

Bruer, J. T. (1993). *Schools for thought: A science of learning in the classroom.* Cambridge, MA: The MIT Press: A Bradford Book.

Bryson, M., & Scardamalia, M. (1991). Teaching writing to students at risk for academic failure. In B. Means, C. Chelmer, & M. Knapp (Eds.), *Teaching advanced skills to at-risk students: Views from research and practice* (pp. 141–167). San Francisco: Jossey-Bass.

Buikema, J. L., & Graves, M. F. (1993). Teaching students to use context to infer word meanings. *Journal of Reading, 36,* 450–457.

Bullock, T. L., & Hesse, K. D. (1981). *Reading in the social studies classroom.* Washington, DC: National Education Association.

Burling, R. (1973). *English in black and white.* New York: Holt, Rinehart and Winston.

Burmeister, L. E. (1968). Usefulness of phonic generalizations. *The Reading Teacher, 21,* 349–356.

Burmeister, L. E. (1978). *Reading strategies for middle and secondary school teachers.* Reading, MA: Addison-Wesley.

Burns, P. C. (1980). *Assessment and correction of language arts difficulties.* Columbus, OH: Merrill.

Buros, O. K. (1978). *The eighth mental measurements yearbook*. Highland Park, NJ: Gryphon Press.

Byars, B. (1975). *The lace snail*. New York: Viking.

Call, P. E. (1991). SQ3R + What I Know Sheet = one strong strategy. *Journal of Reading, 35*, 50–52.

Carbo, M., Dunn, R., & Dunn, K. (1986). *Teaching students to read through their individual learning styles*. Reston, VA: Prentice-Hall.

Cardarelli, A. F. (1988). The influence of reinspection on students' IRI results. *The Reading Teacher, 41*, 664–667.

Carle, E. (1987). *The very hungry caterpillar*. New York: Scholastic.

Carr, E., & Ogle, D. (1987). K–W–L plus: A strategy for comprehension and summarization. *Journal of Reading, 30*, 626–631.

Carr, E., & Wixson, K. K. (1986). Guidelines for evaluating vocabulary instruction. *Journal of Reading, 29*, 588–595.

Carr, E., Dewitz, P., & Patberg, J. (1989). Using cloze for inference training with expository text. *The Reading Teacher, 42*, 380–385.

Carrell, P. L., Devine, J., & Eskey, D. E. (Eds.). (1988). *Interactive approaches to second language reading*. Cambridge: Cambridge University Press.

Carver, R. P. (1977). Toward a theory of reading comprehension and rauding. *Reading Research Quarterly, 13*, 6–63.

Carver, R. P. (1990). *Reading rate: A review of research and theory*. New York: Academic Press.

Carver, R. P. (1992). Commentary: Effect of prediction activities, prior knowledge, and text type upon amount comprehended: Using rauding theory to critique schema theory research. *Reading Research Quarterly, 27*, 164–174.

Caskey, H. J. (1970). Guidelines for teaching comprehension. *The Reading Teacher, 23*, 649–654, 669.

Cazden, C. B., John, V. P., & Hymes, D. (Eds.). (1972). *Functions of language in the classroom*. New York: Teachers College Press.

Chaffin, J., Maxwell, B., & Thompson, B. (1983). *Word radar*. Allen, TX: Developmental Learning Materials.

Chant, S. A., & Pelow, R. A. (1979). *Activities for functional reading and language: Preschool through middle school*. Paper presented at the annual meeting of the International Reading Association, Atlanta.

Chase, A. C., & Duffelmeyer, F. A. (1990). VOCAB-LIT: Integrating vocabulary study and literature study. *Journal of Reading, 34*, 188–193.

Ching, D. C. (1976). *Reading and the bilingual child*. Newark, DE: International Reading Association.

Chomsky, C. (1972). Stages in language development and reading exposure. *Harvard Educational Review, 42*, 5–32.

Clark-Johnson, G. (1988). Black children. *Teaching Exceptional Children, 20*, 46–47.

Clay, M. M. (1967). The reading behavior of five-year-old children: A research report. *New Zealand Journal of Educational Studies, 2*, 11–31.

Clay, M. M. (1985). *The early detection of reading difficulties*, (3rd ed.). Portsmouth, NH: Heinemann.

Cleland, C. J. (1981). Highlighting issues in children's literature through semantic webbing. *The Reading Teacher, 34*, 642–646.

Clymer, T. L. (1963). The utility of phonic generalizations in the primary grades. *The Reading Teacher, 16*, 252–258.

Cohen, D., & Rudolph, M. (1984). *Kindergarten and early schooling*. Englewood Cliffs, NJ: Prentice Hall.

Cohn, M. L. (1969). Structured comprehension. *The Reading Teacher, 22*, 440–444, 489.

Coley, J., & Hoffman, D. (1990). Overcoming learned helplessness in at-risk readers. *Journal of Reading, 33*, 497–502.

Collins, A., & Smith, E. E. (1980). *Teaching the process of reading comprehension* (Tech. Rep. No. 182). Champaign, IL: University of Illinois, Center for the Study of Reading.

Cook-Gumperz, J. (Ed.). (1986). *The social construction of literacy*. Cambridge: Cambridge University Press.

Cooper, C., & Odell, L. (Eds.). (1977). *Evaluating writing: Describing, measuring, judging*. Urbana, IL: National Council of Teachers of English.

Cooper, J. D. (1986). *Improving reading comprehension*. Boston: Houghton Mifflin.

Cooper, J. D., Warncke, E. W., Ramstad, P., & Shipman, D. A. (1979). *The what and how of reading instruction*. Columbus, OH: Merrill.

Cooper, L. J. (1952). *The effect of adjustment of basal reading materials on achievement*. Unpublished doctoral dissertation, Boston

University.

Cooter, R. B., & Chilcoat, G. W. (1990). Content-focused melodrama: Dramatic renderings of historical text. *Journal of Reading, 34,* 274–277.

Copeland, E. D., & Love, V. L. (1990). *Attention without tension: A teacher's handbook on attention disorders.* Atlanta: 3 Cs of Childhood, Inc.

Cowan, J. R. (1976). Reading, perceptual strategies and contrastive analysis. *Language Learning, 26,* 95–109.

Cudd, E. T., & Roberts, L. L. (1987). Using story frames to develop reading comprehension in a first grade classroom. *The Reading Teacher, 41,* 74–79.

Cudd, E. T., & Roberts, L. L. (1989). Using writing to enhance content area learning in the primary grades. *The Reading Teacher, 42,* 392–404.

Cullinan, B., & Fitzgerald, S. (1984, December/1985, January). Background information bulletin on the use of readability formulae. *Reading Today, 2*(3), 1.

Cunningham, P. (1982). *Every-pupil response techniques. Effective use of learning time: Research, tips, and materials.* Microworkshop 13 presented at the Annual Meeting of the International Reading Association, Chicago, May.

Curtis, M. E., & McCart, L. (1992). Fun ways to promote poor readers' word recognition. *Journal of Reading, 35,* 398–399.

Dale, E., O'Rourke, J., & Bamman, H. A. (1971). *Techniques of teaching vocabulary.* Palo Alto, CA: Field Educational Publications.

Dale, E., O'Rourke, J., & Barbe, W. (1986). *Vocabulary building: A process approach.* Columbus, OH: Zaner-Bloser.

D'Alessandro, M. (1990). Accommodating emotionally handicapped children through a literature-based reading program. *The Reading Teacher, 44,* 288–293.

Daniels, H. (1991). Commentary on chapter 5 (Teaching writing to students at-risk for academic failure). In B. Means, C. Chalmers, & M. Knapp (Eds.), *Teaching advanced skills to at-risk students: Views from research and practice* (pp. 168–175). San Francisco: Jossey-Bass.

Danielson, K. E. (1992). Picture books to use with older students. *Journal of Reading, 35,* 652–654.

Davey, B. (1983). Think aloud—Modeling the cognitive processes of reading comprehension. *The Reading Teacher, 27,* 44–47.

Davidson, J. L. (1982). The group mapping activity for instruction in reading and thinking. *Journal of Reading, 26,* 52–56.

Davis, A. L. (1972). English problems of Spanish speakers. In D. L. Shores (Ed.), *Contemporary English: Change and variation.* (pp. 123–133), New York: J. B. Lippincott Company.

Davis, C. (1978). The effectiveness of informal assessment questions constructed by secondary teachers. In P. D. Pearson & J. Hansen (Eds.), *Reading: Disciplined inquiry in process and practice* (pp. 13–15). Twenty-seventh Yearbook of the National Reading Conference, Clemson, SC.

Davis, F. B. (1944). Fundamental factors of comprehension in reading. *Psychometrika, 9,* 185–197.

Day, J. D. (1980). *Training summarization skills: A comparison of teaching methods.* Unpublished doctoral dissertation, University of Illinois, Urbana.

DeFina, A. A. (1992). *Portfolio assessment: Getting started.* New York: Scholastic.

Degen, B. (1983). *Jamberry.* New York: Harper & Row.

Denckla, M. B. (1972). Clinical syndromes in learning disabilities: The case for "splitting" vs. "lumping." *Journal of Learning Disabilities, 5,* 401–406.

DeStefano, J. S. (1978). *Language, the learner and the school.* New York: Wiley.

Devine, T. G. (1981). *Teaching study skills: A guide for teachers.* Boston: Allyn and Bacon.

Dewey, J. (1933). *How we think: A restatement of the relation of reflective thinking to the educational process.* Boston: D. C. Heath.

Diederich, P. B. (1974). *Measuring growth in English.* Urbana, IL: National Council of Teachers of English.

Dimino, J., Gersten, R., Carnine, D., & Blake, G. (1990). Story grammar: An approach for promoting at-risk secondary students' comprehension of literature. *Elementary School Journal, 91,* 19–32.

Dionisio, M. (1989). Write? Isn't this reading class? *The Reading Teacher, 36,* 746–749.

Doake, D. B. (1988). *Reading begins at birth.* New York: Scholastic.

Dolch, E. (1953). *Dolch basic sight vocabulary.* Champaign, IL: Garrard.

Dowhower, S. L. (1989). Repeated reading: Research into practice. *The Reading Teacher, 42,* 502–507.

Dreyer, S. (1987). *The bookfinder: Guide to children's literature about the needs and problems of youth aged 2–15*. Circle Pines, MN: American Guidance Services.

Duffelmeyer, F. A., & Duffelmeyer, B. B. (1989). Are IRI passages suitable for assessing main idea comprehension? *The Reading Teacher, 42*, 358–363.

Duffelmeyer, F. A., & Baum, D. D. (1992). The extended anticipation guide revisited. *Journal of Reading, 35*, 654–656.

Duffelmeyer, F. S., Robinson, S. S., & Squier, S. E. (1989). Vocabulary questions on informal reading inventories. *The Reading Teacher, 43*, 142–148.

Duffy, G. G. (1978). Maintaining a balance in objective-based reading instruction. *The Reading Teacher, 31*, 519–523.

Duffy, G. G., Roehler, L. R., & Herrmann, B. A. (1988). Modeling mental processes helps poor readers become strategic readers. *The Reading Teacher, 41*, 762–767.

Dunkeld, C. (1978). Students' notetaking and teachers' expectations. *Journal of Reading, 21*, 542–546.

Durkin, D. (1978). *Teaching them to read* (3rd ed.). Boston: Allyn and Bacon.

Durkin, D. (1978/1979). What classroom observations reveal about reading comprehension instruction. *Reading Research Quarterly, 14*, 481–533.

Durkin, D. (1981). Reading comprehension instruction in five basal reading series. *Reading Research Quarterly, 14*, 515–544.

Durrell, D. D. (1963). *Phonograms in primary grade words*. Boston: Boston University.

Durrell, D. D. (1980). *Durrell analysis of reading difficulty*. New York: Psychological Corporation.

Dyer, H. S. (1968). Research issues on equality of educational opportunity: School factors. *Harvard Educational Review, 38*, 38–56.

Eanet, M. G., & Manzo, A. V. (1976). REAP—a strategy for improving reading/writing study skills. *Journal of Reading, 19*, 647–652.

Earle, R. A. (1976). *Teaching reading and mathematics*. Newark, DE: International Reading Association.

Eckhoff, B. (1983). How reading affects children's writing. *Language Arts, 60*, 607–616.

Edelsky, C. (1986). *Writing in a bilingual program: Habia una vez*. Norwood, NJ: Ablex.

Ekwall, E. E., & Shanker, J. L. (1988). *Diagnosis and remediation of the disabled reader* (3rd ed.). Boston: Allyn and Bacon.

Ekwall, E. E., & Shanker, J. L. (1993). *Ekwall/Shanker reading inventory,* (3rd ed.). Boston: Allyn and Bacon.

Elley, W. (1991). Acquiring literacy in a second language: The effect of book-based programs. *Language Learning, 41*, 375–411.

Ellwood, D. (1988). *Poor support: Poverty in the American family*. New York: Basic Books.

Emans, R. (1967). The usefulness of phonic generalizations above the primary grades. *The Reading Teacher, 20*, 419–425.

Emberly, B. (Adapted by). (1967). *Drummer Hoff*. New York: Prentice-Hall.

Engelmann, S. (1969). *Preventing failure in the primary grades*. Chicago: Science Research Associates.

Englert, C. S., & Thomas, C. C. (1987). Sensitivity to text structure in reading and writing: A comparison between learning disabled and non-learning disabled students. *Learning Disabilities Quarterly, 10*, 93–105.

Enright, D. S., & McCloskey, M. L. (1988). *Integrating English: Developing English language and literacy in the multilingual classroom*. Reading, MA: Addison-Wesley.

ESA Word List. (1977). In E. C. Kennedy, *Classroom approaches to remedial reading*. Itasca, IL: F. E. Peacock.

Estes, T. H., Estes, J. J., Richards, H. C., & Roettger, D. (1981). *Estes attitude scales: Measures of attitude toward school subjects*. Austin, TX: Pro-Ed.

Farr, M., & Daniels, H. (1986). *Language diversity and writing instruction*. New York: ERIC Clearinghouse on Urban Education and Urbana, IL: ERIC Clearinghouse on Reading and Communication Skills.

Farr, R. (1992). Putting it all together: Solving the reading assessment puzzle. *The Reading Teacher, 46*, 26–37.

Farr, R., & Carey, R. F. (1986). *Reading: What can be measured?* (2nd ed.). Newark, DE: International Reading Association.

Fay, L. (1965). Reading study skills: Math and science. In J. A. Figurel (Ed.), *Reading and *inquiry.* Newark, DE: International Reading Association.

Fennimore, F. (1980). Attaining sentence verve with sentence extension. In G. Stanford (Ed.), *Dealing with differences,* Urbana, IL: National Council of Teachers of English.

Fernald, G. M. (1943). *Remedial techniques in basic school subjects.* New York: McGraw-Hill.

Field, M., & Aebersold, J. (1990). Cultural attitudes toward reading: Implications for teachers of ESL/bilingual readers. *Journal of Reading, 33,* 406–414.

Fillmore, C. J. (1968). The case for case. In E. Bach and R. T. Harms (Eds.), *Universals in linguistic theory.* New York: Holt, Rinehart and Winston.

Fitzgerald, J., & Spiegel, D. L. (1983). Enhancing children's reading comprehension through instruction in narrative structure. *Journal of Reading Behavior, 15,* 1–17.

Flavell, J. H. (1976). Metacognitive aspects of problem solving. In L. B. Resnick (Ed.), *The nature of intelligence.* Hillsdale, NJ: Erlbaum.

Flores, B. M. (1984). *Language interference or influence: Toward a theory for Hispanic bilingualism.* Doctoral dissertation, University of Arizona, Tucson.

Flynt, E. S., & Cooter, R. B. (1993). *Flynt-Cooter reading inventory for the classroom.* Scottsdale, AZ: Gorsuch Scarisbrick.

Forgan, H. W., & Mangrum, C. T. (1985). *Teaching content area reading skills* (3rd ed.). Columbus, OH: Merrill.

Fountain Valley Teacher Support System in Reading. (1980). Irvine, CA: Zweig.

Fowler, G. L. (1982). Developing comprehension skills in primary students through the use of story frames. *The Reading Teacher, 37,* 176–179.

Fox, S. E., & Allen, V. G. (1983). *The language arts: An integrated approach.* New York: Holt, Rinehart and Winston.

Frase, L. T., & Schwartz, B. J. (1975). Effect of question production on prose recall. *Journal of Educational Psychology, 67,* 628–635.

Frayer, D. A., Frederick, W. C., & Klausmeier, H. J. (1969). *A schema for testing the level of concept mastery.* (Tech. Rep. No. 16). Madison: University of Wisconsin, R & D Center for Cognitive Learning.

Frazee, B. (1993). Core knowledge: How to get started. *Educational Leadership, 50,* 28–29.

Freedman, G., & Reynolds, E. G. (1980). Enriching basal reader lessons with semantic webbing. *The Reading Teacher, 33,* 677–684.

Freeman, Y. S., & Freeman, D. E. (1992). *Whole language for second language learners.* Portsmouth, NH: Heinemann.

Fry, E. B. (1980). Test review: Metropolitan Achievement Tests. *The Reading Teacher, 34,* 196–201.

Fry, E. B. (1989). Reading formulas—Maligned but valid. *Journal of Reading, 32,* 292–297.

Fry, E. B., Kress, J., & Fountoukidis, D. (1993). *The reading teacher's book of lists.* Englewood Cliffs, NJ: Prentice-Hall.

Furness, E. L. (1971). Proportion, purpose, and process in listening. In S. Duker (Ed.), *Teaching listening in the elementary school* (pp. 53–57). Metuchen, NJ: Scarecrow Press.

Gag, W. (1928). *Millions of cats.* New York: Coward, McCann and Geoghegan.

Gallant, R. (1964). *An investigation of the use of cloze tests as a measure of readability of materials for the primary grades.* Unpublished doctoral dissertation, Indiana University, Bloomington.

Gambrell, L. B., & Bales, R. (1986). Mental imagery and the comprehension monitoring performance of fourth- and fifth-grade poor readers. *Reading Research Quarterly, 11,* 454–464.

Gambrell, L. B., & Jawitz, P. B. (1993). Mental imagery, text illustrations, and children's story comprehension and recall. *Reading Research Quarterly, 28,* 264–276.

Gambrell, L. B., Wilson, R. M., & Gantt, W. N. (1981). Classroom observations of task-attending behaviors of good and poor readers. *Journal of Educational Research, 24,* 400–404.

Garcia, G., & Pearson, P. D. (1991). *Literacy assessment in a diverse society.* (Tech. Rep. No. 525). Champaign, IL: University of Illinois at Urbana-Champaign, Center for the Study of Reading. Also in E. H. Hiebert (Ed.), *Literacy for a diverse society* (pp. 253–278). New York: Teachers College Press.

Garner, R. (1980). Monitoring of understanding: An investigation of good and poor readers' awareness of induced miscomprehension of text. *Journal of Reading Behavior, 12,* 55–64.

Garner, R. (1987). *Metacognition and reading comprehension.* Norwood, NJ: Ablex.

Gates, A. I., & MacGinitie, W. H. (1989). *Gates-MacGinitie reading tests, Level A.* Boston: Riverside.

Geissal, M. A., & Knafle, J. D. (1977). A linguistic view of auditory discrimination tests and exercises. *The Reading Teacher, 31,* 624–644.

Gillespie, C. (1990/1991). Questions about student-generated questions. *Journal of Reading, 34,* 250–257.

Gillet, J. W., & Temple, C. (1994). *Understanding reading problems: Assessment and instruction.* (4th ed.). New York: HarperCollins.

Gipe, J. P. (1977). *An investigation of the effectiveness of four techniques for teaching word meanings with third and fifth grade students.* Unpublished doctoral dissertation, Purdue University, West Lafayette, IN.

Gipe, J. P. (1978/1979). Investigating techniques for teaching word meanings. *Reading Research Quarterly, 14,* 624–644.

Gipe, J. P. (1980). Use of a relevant context helps kids learn new word meanings. *The Reading Teacher, 33,* 398–402.

Gipe, J. P., Richards, J. C., & Barnitz, J. G. (1993–94). Literacy development of urban children through literature-based reading/language arts instruction. *Louisiana Education Research Journal, 19*(1), 27–39.

Glasser, W. (1969). *Schools without failure.* New York: Harper and Row.

Glazer, S. M. (1992). *Reading comprehension: Self-monitoring strategies to develop independent readers.* New York: Scholastic.

Glazer, S. M. (1993). Children and self-assessment: A "risky" experience. *Teaching PreK–8, 23*(8), 106–108.

Glazer, S. M., & Brown, C. S. (1993). *Portfolios and beyond: Collaborative assessment in reading and writing.* Norwood, MA: Christopher-Gordon.

Glazer, S. M., Searfoss, L. W., & Gentile, L. M. (1988). *Reexamining reading diagnosis: New trends and procedures.* Newark, DE: International Reading Association.

Goldenberg, C. (1992/1993). Instructional conversations: Promoting comprehension through discussion. *The Reading Teacher, 46,* 316–326.

Golinkoff, R. M. (1975/1976). A comparison of reading comprehension processes in good and poor comprehenders. *Reading Research Quarterly, 11,* 623–659.

Goodman, K. S. (1968). The psycholinguistic nature of the reading process. In K. S. Goodman (Ed.), *The psycholinguistic nature of the reading process.* Detroit: Wayne State Press.

Goodman, K. S. (1972). Dialect barriers to reading comprehension. In D. L. Shores (Ed.), *Contemporary English: Change and variation.* Philadelphia: Lippincott.

Goodman, K. S. (1973). *Theoretically based studies of patterns of miscues in oral reading performance.* Washington, DC: U.S. Department of Health, Education and Welfare, Office of Education, Bureau of Research.

Goodman, K. S. (1982). Revaluing readers and reading. *Topics in Learning and Learning Disabilities, 1,* 87–93.

Goodman, K. S. (1986). *What's whole in whole language?* Portsmouth, NH: Heinemann.

Goodman, K. S. (1994). Reading, writing, and written texts: A transactional sociopsycholinguistic view. In R. B. Ruddell, M. R. Ruddell, & H. Singer (Eds.), *Theoretical models and processes of reading* (4th ed.) (pp. 1093–1130). Newark, DE: International Reading Association.

Goodman, K. S., & Buck, S. (1973). Dialect barriers to reading comprehension revisited. *The Reading Teacher, 27,* 6–12.

Goodman, K. S., & Goodman, Y. (1978). *Reading of American children whose language is a stable rural dialect of English or a language other than English.* University of Arizona, Final Report, Project NIE-C-00-3-0087. (ERIC Document Reproduction Service No. ED 173754.)

Goodman, K. S., Goodman, Y. M., & Hood, W. J. (1989). *The whole language evaluation book.* Portsmouth, NH: Heinemann.

Goodman, Y., & Burke, C. (1972). *Reading miscue inventory manual: Procedure for diagnosis and evaluation.* New York: Macmillan.

Goodman, Y. M., & Burke, C. (1980). *Reading strategies: Focus on comprehension.*

New York: Holt, Rinehart and Winston.

Goodman, Y. M., Watson, D. J., & Burke, C. L. (1987). *Reading miscue inventory: Alternative procedures.* New York: Richard C. Owen.

Goswami, U., & Mead, F. (1992). Onset and rime awareness and analogies in reading. *Reading Research Quarterly, 27,* 152–162.

Gough, P. B. (1984). Word recognition. In P. D. Pearson (Ed.), *Handbook of reading research* (pp. 225–253). New York: Longman.

Gough, P. B. (1985). One second of reading. In H. Singer & R. B. Ruddell (Eds.), *Theoretical models and processes of reading* (3rd ed.) (pp. 661–686.). Newark, DE: International Reading Association.

Gould, M. (1982). *Golden daffodils.* Reading, MA: Addison-Wesley.

Graves, D. (1988). *Writing: Teachers and children at work.* Portsmouth, NH: Heinemann.

Graves, D. (1992). Help students learn to read their portfolios. In D. Graves & B. Sunstein (Eds.), *Portfolio portraits* (pp. 85–95). Portsmouth, NH: Heinemann.

Graves, D., & Murray, D. (1980). Revision in the writer's workshop and in the classroom. *Journal of Education, 162,* 38–56.

Great Atlantic and Pacific Word List. (1972). From W. Otto & R. Chester, Sight words for beginning readers. *Journal of Educational Research, 65,* 436–443.

Greene, P. J. (1981). *The morpheme conceptualization barrier: Adult non-inflected language speakers' acquisition of English morpheme structures.* Unpublished doctoral dissertation, University of New Orleans.

Greenlaw, M. J. (1992). Using informational books to develop reference skills. In E. B. Freeman & D. G. Person (Eds.), *Using nonfiction trade books in the elementary classroom* (pp. 131–145). Urbana, IL: National Council of Teachers of English.

Griffith, P. L., & Olson, M. W. (1992). Phonemic awareness helps beginning readers break the code. *The Reading Teacher, 45,* 516–523.

Grognet, A. G., Pfannkuche, A., Quang, N. H., Robson, B., Convery, A., Holdzkom, D., Quynh-Hao, H. T., & Vu, T. N. (1976). *A manual for Indochinese refugee education.* Arlington, VA: The National Indochinese Clearinghouse (Center for Applied Linguistics).

Grossman, P. (1992). Why models matter: An alternate view on professional growth in teaching. *Review of Educational Research, 62,* 171–179.

Guszak, F. J. (1967). Teachers' questions and levels of reading comprehension. In T. C. Barrett (Ed.), *The evaluation of children's reading achievement.* Newark, DE: International Reading Association.

Guthrie, J. T., Seifert, M., Burnham, N. A., & Caplan, R. I. (1974). The maze technique to assess, monitor reading comprehension. *The Reading Teacher, 28,* 161–168.

Haggard, M. (1986). The vocabulary self-collection strategy: Using student interest and world knowledge to enhance vocabulary growth. *Journal of Reading, 29,* 634–642.

Hall, M. A. (1982). *Teaching reading as a language experience* (3rd ed.). Columbus, OH: Merrill.

Hall, W. S., Cole, M., Reder, S., & Dowley, J. (1977). Variations in young children's use of language: Some effects of setting and dialect. In R. O. Freedle (Ed.), *Discourse production and comprehension.* Hillsdale, NJ: Ablex.

Hall, W. S., & Freedle, R. (1975). *Culture and language.* New York: Halstead Press.

Hall, W. S., & Guthrie, L. F. (1980). On the dialect question and reading. In R. Spiro, B. Bruce, & W. Brewer (Eds.), *Theoretical issues in reading comprehension.* Hillsdale, NJ: Erlbaum.

Haller, E. J., & Waterman, M. (1985). The criteria of reading group assignments. *The Reading Teacher, 38,* 772–781.

Halliday, M. A. K. (1978). *Language as a social semiotic.* Baltimore: University Park Press.

Hanf, M. B. (1971). Mapping: A technique for translating reading into thinking. *Journal of Reading, 14,* 225–230, 270.

Hanna, G., Schell, L. M., & Schreiner, R. (1977). *The Nelson reading skills test.* Boston: Houghton Mifflin.

Hansell, T. S. (1978). Stepping up to outlining. *Journal of Reading, 22,* 248–252.

Hansen, J. (1987). *When writers read.* Portsmouth, NH: Heinemann.

Harris, A. J., & Jacobson, M. D. (1972). *Basic elementary reading vocabularies.* New York: Macmillan.

Harris, A. J., & Sipay, E. R. (1990). *How to increase reading ability* (9th ed.). New York: Longman.

Harris, V. J. (Ed.). (1993). *Teaching multicultural literature in grades K–8*. Norwood, MA: Christopher-Gordon.

Harste, J., Woodward, V., & Burke, C. (1984). *Language stories and literacy lessons*. Portsmouth, NH: Heinemann.

Harste, J. C., Short, K. G., & Burke, C. (Eds.). (1988). *Creating classrooms for authors*. Portsmouth, NH: Heinemann.

Haskin, I. (1982). A writing program for poor readers and writers and the rest of the class too. *Language Arts, 59,* 854–861.

Hayes, D. A. (1989). Helping students GRASP the knack of writing summaries. *Journal of Reading, 33,* 96–101.

Heath, S. (1982). What no bedtime story means: Narrative skills at home and school. *Language in Society, 11,* 49–76.

Heath, S. (1986). Critical factors in literacy development. In S. deCastell, A. Luke, & K. Egan (Eds.), *Literacy, society and schooling: A reader* (pp. 209–229). New York: Cambridge University Press.

Heath, S. B. (1983). *Ways with words: Language, life and work in communities and classrooms*. Cambridge: Cambridge University Press.

Heckelman, R. G. (1969). A neurological-impress method of remedial reading instruction. *Academic Therapy, 4,* 277–282.

Heilman, A. W. (1976). *Principles and practices of teaching reading* (4th ed.). Columbus, OH: Merrill.

Heilman, A. W., & Holmes, E. A. (1978). *Smuggling language into the teaching of reading*. Columbus, OH: Merrill.

Heimlich, J. E., & Pittelman, S. D. (1986). *Semantic mapping: Classroom applications*. Newark, DE: International Reading Association.

Helfeldt, J. P., & Henk, W. A. (1990). Reciprocal question-answer relationships: An instructional technique for at-risk readers. *Journal of Reading, 33,* 509–515.

Henderson, E. H. (1990). *Teaching spelling* (2nd ed.). Boston, MA: Houghton Mifflin.

Henderson, E. H., & Beers, J. (Eds.). (1980). *Developmental and cognitive aspects of learning to spell*. Newark, DE: International Reading Association.

Henk, W. A., & Selders, M. L. (1984). A test of synonymic scoring of cloze passages. *The Reading Teacher, 38,* 282–287.

Hennings, D. G. (1991). Essential reading: Targeting, tracking, and thinking about main ideas. *Journal of Reading, 34,* 346–353.

Herber, H. L. (1970). *Teaching reading in content areas*. Englewood Cliffs, NJ: Prentice-Hall.

Herrmann, B. A. (1988). Two approaches for helping poor readers become more strategic. *The Reading Teacher, 42,* 24–28.

Hiebert, E. F. (1991). *Literacy for a diverse society: Perspectives, practices and policies*. New York: Teachers College Press.

Hill, M. (1991). Writing summaries promotes thinking and learning across the curriculum—but why are they so difficult to write? *Journal of Reading, 34,* 536–539.

Hillocks, G. (1986). *Research on written composition: New directions for teaching*. Urbana IL: National Conference on Research in English.

Hittleman, D. R. (1983). *Developmental reading, K–8: Teaching from a psycholinguistic perspective*. Boston: Houghton Mifflin.

Hoffman, S. M. (1978). *The effect of a listening skills program on the reading comprehension of fourth grade students*. Unpublished doctoral dissertation, Walden University, Naples, FL.

Hoge, R. D., & Coladarci, T. (1989). Teacher-based judgments of academic achievement: A review of literature. *Review of Educational Research, 59,* 297–313.

Hopkins, C. J. (1979). Using every-pupil response techniques in reading instruction. *The Reading Teacher, 33,* 173–175.

Hopkins, L. B. (1987). *Click, rumble, roar: Poems about machines*. New York: Crowell.

Hudelson, S. (1989). *Write on: Children writing in ESL*. (Language in Education: Theory and Practice series, Monograph No. 72) ERIC Clearinghouse on Languages and Linguistics, Center for Applied Linguistics. Englewood Cliffs, NJ: Prentice-Hall Regents.

Huey, E. B. (1977). *The psychology and pedagogy of reading*. Cambridge, MA: MIT Press. (First published in 1908 by Macmillan).

Hughes, T. O. (1975). *Sentence combining: A means of increasing reading comprehension*. Bloomington, IN: ERIC Clearinghouse on Reading, ED 11 2421.

Hunt, J. (1989). *Illuminations*. New York: Bradbury Press.

Hutchins, P. (1976). *Don't forget the bacon!*

New York: Morrow.

Hymes, D. (1974). *Foundations in sociolinguistics: An ethnographic approach.* Philadelphia: University of Pennsylvania Press.

Illinois State Board of Education. (1988). *Assessing reading in Illinois.* Springfield: Illinois State Board of Education.

International Reading Association. (1988). *New directions in reading instruction.* Newark, DE.

Irwin, J. W. (1991). *Teaching reading comprehension processes,* (2nd ed.). Englewood Cliffs, NJ: Prentice-Hall.

Irwin, J. W., & Baker, I. (1989). *Promoting active reading comprehension strategies.* Englewood Cliffs, NJ: Prentice-Hall.

Irwin, P. A., & Mitchell, J. N. (1983). A procedure for assessing the richness of retellings. *Journal of Reading, 26,* 391–396.

Jackson, L. A. (1981). Whose skills system? Mine or Penny's? *The Reading Teacher, 35,* 260–262.

Jacobowitz, T. (1990). AIM: A metacognitive strategy for constructing the main idea of text. *Journal of Reading, 33,* 620–624.

Jacobson, J. M. (1990). Group vs. individual completion of a cloze passage. *Journal of Reading, 33,* 244–251.

Jensen, J. M., & Roser, N. L. (Eds.). (1993). *Adventuring with books: A booklist for pre-K–grade 6,* (10th ed.). Urbana, IL: National Council of Teachers of English.

Jewell, M. G., & Zintz, M. V. (1986). *Learning to read naturally.* Dubuque, IA: Kendall/Hunt.

Johns, J. L. (1990). *Secondary and college reading inventory.* Dubuque, IA: Kendall/Hunt.

Johns, J. L. (1991). *Basic reading inventory.* Dubuque, IA: Kendall/Hunt.

Johnson, D. D. (1976). *Johnson basic sight vocabulary test manual.* Lexington, MA: Ginn.

Johnson, D. D., & Pearson, P. D. (1984). *Teaching reading vocabulary.* New York: Holt, Rinehart and Winston.

Johnson, M. S., & Kress, R. A. (1965). *Informal reading inventories.* Newark, DE: International Reading Association.

Johnson-Weber, M. (1989). Picture books for junior high. *Journal of Reading, 33,* 219–220.

Johnston, P. (1984). Prior knowledge and reading comprehension test bias. *Reading Research Quarterly, 19,* 219–239.

Johnston, P. (1992). Nontechnical assessment. *The Reading Teacher, 46,* 60–62.

Johnston, P., & Winograd, P. (1985). Passive failure in reading. *Journal of Reading Behavior, 17,* 279–301.

Jongsma, E., & Farr, R. (1993). A themed issue on literacy assessment. *Journal of Reading, 36,* 516–517.

Jorgenson, G. W. (1977). Relationship of classroom behavior to the accuracy of the match between material difficulty and student ability. *Journal of Educational Psychology, 69,* 24–32.

Jorm, A. (1977). Effect of word imagery on reading performance as a function of reader ability. *Journal of Educational Psychology, 69,* 46–54.

Joyce, B., & Weil, M. (1986). *Models of teaching* (3rd ed.). Englewood Cliffs, NJ: Prentice-Hall.

Juel, C. (1991). Cross-age tutoring between student athletes and at-risk children. *The Reading Teacher, 45,* 178–186.

Juliebö, M., & Edwards, J. (1989). Encouraging meaning-making in young writers. *Young Children, 44*(2), 22–25.

Kamm, K. (1979). Focusing reading comprehension instruction: Sentence meaning skills. In C. Pennock (Ed.), *Reading comprehension at four linguistic levels.* Newark, DE: International Reading Association.

Kant, E. (1963). *Critique of pure reason* (2nd ed.). (N. Kemp Smith, Trans.). London: Macmillan. (Originally published 1787).

Karlin, R. (1975). *Teaching elementary reading: Principles and strategies* (2nd ed.). New York: Harcourt Brace Jovanovich.

Karlsen, B., & Gardner, E. F. (1986). *Stanford diagnostic reading tests.* New York: Harcourt Brace Jovanovich. (Order through The Psychological Corporation.)

Karnowski, L. (1989). Using LEA with process writing. *The Reading Teacher, 42,* 462–465.

Kastler, L. A., Roser, N. L., & Hoffman, J. V. (1987). Understanding of the forms and functions of written language: Insights from children and parents. In J. E. Readance & R. S. Baldwin (Eds.), *Research in literacy: Merging perspectives* (pp. 85–92). Rochester, NY: National Reading Conference.

Kavalc, K. (1979). Selecting and evaluating reading tests. In R. Schreiner (Ed.), *Reading tests and teachers: A practical guide* (pp. 9–34). Newark, DE: International Reading Association.

Kavale, K., & Schreiner, R. (1979). The reading processes of above average readers: A comparison of the use of reasoning strategies in responding to standardized comprehension measures. *Reading Research Quarterly, 15,* 102–128.

Kavale, K. A., & Forness, S. R. (1985). *The science of learning disabilities.* San Diego, CA: College-Hill Press.

Kean, J., & Personke, C. (1976). *The language arts, teaching and learning in the elementary school.* New York: St. Martin's Press.

Kelty, A. P. (1955). *An experimental study to determine the effect of listening for certain purposes upon achievement in reading for those purposes.* Abstracts of Field Studies for the Degree of Doctor of Education, 15, 82–95. Greeley: Colorado State College of Education.

Kennedy, E. C. (1977). *Classroom approaches to remedial reading* (2nd ed.). Itasca, IL: F. E. Peacock.

Kirby, D., Liner, T., & Vinz, R. (1988). *Inside out: Developmental strategies for teaching writing.* Portsmouth, NH: Boynton/Cook Publishers.

Kletzien, S. B. (1991). Strategy use by good and poor comprehenders reading expository text of differing levels. *Reading Research Quarterly, 26,* 67–86.

Kletzien, S. B., & Bednar, M. R. (1990). Dynamic assessment for at-risk readers. *Journal of Reading, 33,* 528–533.

Kochman, T. (Ed.). (1972). *Rappin' and stylin': Communication in urban black America.* Chicago: University of Illinois Press.

Kochman, T. (1981). *Black and white styles in conflict.* Chicago: University of Chicago Press.

Kolers, P. A. (1975). Pattern-analyzing disability in poor readers. *Developmental Psychology, 11,* 282–290.

Koskinen, P. A., & Blum, I. H. (1986). Paired repeated reading: A classroom strategy for developing fluent reading. *The Reading Teacher, 40,* 70–75.

Kozol, J. (1991). *Savage inequalities: Children in America's schools.* New York: Crown.

Kramer, J. J., & Conoley, J. C. (Eds.). (1992). *The eleventh mental measurements yearbook.* Lincoln, NE: The University of Nebraska Press.

Labbo, L. D., & Teale, W. H. (1990). Cross-age reading: A strategy for helping poor readers. *The Reading Teacher, 43,* 362–369.

LaBerge, D., & Samuels, S. J. (1974). Toward a theory of automatic information processing in reading. *Cognitive Psychology, 6,* 293–323.

Labov, W. (1975). *The study of nonstandard English.* Urbana, IL: National Council of Teachers of English.

Labov, W. (1983). Recognizing black English in the classsroom. In J. Chambers (Ed.), *Black English: Educational equity and the law.* Ann Arbor, MI: Karoma.

Labov, W. (1988). *Lexical competition in the short order cuisine.* Paper presented at the American Dialect Society meeting, held in conjunction with the Linguistic Society of America annual meeting, New Orleans.

Labov, W., & Harris, W. (1983). *De facto segregation of black and white vernaculars.* Paper presented to the Annual Conference of New Ways of Analyzing Variation in English, Montreal.

Leslie, L., & Caldwell, J. (1990). *Qualitative reading inventory.* Glenview, IL: Scott, Foresman/Little Brown.

Lindfors, J. W. (1989). The classroom: A good environment for language learning. In P. Rigg & V. G. Allen (Eds.). *When they don't all speak English: Integrating the ESL student into the regular classroom* (pp. 39–54). Urbana, IL: National Council of Teachers of English.

Lipson, M., & Wixson, K. (1991). *Assessment and instruction of reading disability: An interactive approach.* New York: HarperCollins.

Loban, W. (1976). *Language development: Kindergarten through grade twelve.* Urbana, IL: National Council of Teachers of English.

Lowenfeld, V. (1970). *Creative and mental growth* (5th ed.). New York: Macmillan.

Lundsteen, S. (1979). *Listening: Its impact on reading and other language arts* (rev. ed.). Urbana, IL: National Council of Teachers of English.

Mandler, J. M., & Johnson, N. S. (1977). Remembrance of things parsed: Story structure and recall. *Cognitive Psychology, 9,* 111–151.

Manzo, A. V. (1969). The ReQuest procedure. *Journal of Reading, 13,* 123–126.

Manzo, A. V. (1975). Guided reading procedure. *Journal of Reading, 18,* 287–291.

Manzo, A. V. (1985). Expansion modules for the ReQuest, CAT, GRP, and REAP reading/study procedures. *Journal of Reading, 28,* 498–502.

Marcus, M. (1977). *Diagnostic teaching of the language arts.* New York: Wiley.

Markman, E. M. (1979). Realizing that you don't understand: Elementary school children's awareness of inconsistencies. *Child Development, 50,* 643–655.

Markman, E. M. (1981). Comprehension monitoring. In W. P. Dickson (Ed.), *Children's oral communication skills.* New York: Academic Press.

Marshmallow. (1971). *Childcraft: The how and why library* (Vol. 6, How things change). Chicago: Field Enterprises Educational Corporation.

Martin, B. (1983). *Brown bear, brown bear, what do you see?* New York: Holt.

Marzano, R. J., & Marzano, J. S. (1988). *A cluster approach to elementary vocabulary instruction.* Newark, DE: International Reading Association.

Mason, J. M. (Ed.). (1989). *Reading and writing connections.* Boston: Allyn and Bacon.

Mathewson, G. C. (1994). Model of attitude influence upon reading and learning to read. In R. B. Ruddell, M. R. Ruddell, & H. Singer (Eds.), *Theoretical models and processes of reading* (4th ed.) (pp. 1131–1161). Newark, DE: International Reading Association.

McAuliffe, S. (1993). A study of the differences between instructional practice and test preparation. *Journal of Reading, 36,* 524–530.

McCormick, S., & Cooper, J. O. (1991). Can SQ3R facilitate secondary learning disabled students' literal comprehension of expository text? *Reading Psychology, 12,* 239–271.

McDermott, G. (1972). *Anansi the spider.* New York: Holt.

McKenna, M. C. (1976). Synonymic versus verbatim scoring of the cloze procedure. *Journal of Reading, 20,* 141–143.

McKeown, M. (1985). The acquisition of word meaning from context by children of high and low ability. *Reading Research Quarterly, 20,* 482–496.

McNeil, J. D. (1974). False prerequisites in the teaching of reading. *Journal of Reading Behavior, 6,* 421–427.

McNeil, J. D. (1992). *Reading comprehension: New directions for classroom practice* (3rd ed.). New York: HarperCollins.

McNinch, G. H. (1981). A method for teaching sight words to disabled readers. *The Reading Teacher, 35,* 269–272.

Memory, D. M. (1990). Teaching technical vocabulary: Before, during, or after the reading assignment? *Journal of Reading Behavior, 22,* 39–53.

Merwin, J. C. (1973). Educational measurement of what characteristic, of whom (or what), by whom, and why. *Journal of Educational Measurement, 10,* 1–6.

Meyer, B. F. (1984). Organizational aspects of text: Effects on reading comprehension and applications for the classroom. In J. Flood (Ed.), *Promoting reading comprehension* (pp. 113–138). Newark, DE: International Reading Association.

Michigan Educational Assessment Program. (1987). *Blueprint for new MEAP reading test.* Lansing: Michigan State Department of Education.

Miller, G. R., & Coleman, E. B. (1967). A set of 36 prose passages calibrated for complexity. *Journal of Verbal Learning and Verbal Behavior, 6,* 851–854.

Mills, H., O'Keefe, T., & Stephens, D. (1992). *Looking closely.* Urbana, IL: National Council of Teachers of English.

Mitchell, J. V. (Ed.). (1985). *The ninth mental measurements yearbook.* Lincoln, NE: The University of Nebraska Press.

Moe, A. J. (1972a). *High frequency words.* St. Paul, MN: Ambassador.

Moe, A. J. (1972b). *High frequency nouns.* St. Paul, MN: Ambassador.

Moe, A. J., & Manning, J. C. (1984). Developing intensive word practice exercises. In J. F. Baumann & D. D. Johnson (Eds.), *Reading instruction for the beginning teacher: A practical guide* (pp. 16–27). Minneapolis, MN: Burgess.

Monroe, M. (1932). *Children who cannot read.* Chicago: University of Chicago Press.

Morrice, C., & Simmons, M. (1991). Beyond reading buddies: A whole language cross-age program. *The Reading Teacher, 44,*

572–577.

Morrow, L. M. (1985a). Reading and retelling stories: Strategies for emergent readers. *The Reading Teacher, 38,* 870–875.

Morrow, L. M. (1985b). *Story retelling: A diagnostic approach for evaluating story structure, language and comprehension.* Paper presented at the International Reading Association Convention, New Orleans.

Morrow, L. M. (1992). The impact of a litera-ture-based program on literacy achieve-ment, use of literature, and attitudes of children from minority backgrounds. *Reading Research Quarterly, 27,* 251–275.

Morrow, L. M., & Smith, J. (1990). The effects of group size on interactive story-book reading. *Reading Research Quar-terly, 25,* 213–231.

Mosenthal, P. B. (1989). The whole language approach: Teachers between a rock and a hard place. *The Reading Teacher, 42,* 628–629.

Murray, D. (1973). Why creative writing isn't—or is. *Elementary English, 50,* 523–25, 556.

Nagy, W. E. (1988). *Teaching vocabulary to improve reading comprehension.* Newark, DE: International Reading Association.

Nagy, W. E., Anderson, R. C., & Herman, P. (1987). Learning word meanings from con-text during normal reading. *American Educational Research Journal, 24,* 237–270.

Nathan, R., Temple, C., Juntunen, K., & Temple, F. (1989). *Classroom strategies that work: An elementary teacher's guide to process writing.* Portsmouth, NH: Heinemann.

Neal, J. C., & Moore, K. (1991/1992). The very hungry caterpillar meets Beowulf in secondary classrooms. *Journal of Reading, 35,* 290–296.

Nelson, K. (1977). *Nelson reading skills tests.* Boston: Riverside.

Neville, D. D., & Searls, E. F. (1991). A meta-analytic review of the effect of sentence-combining on reading comprehension. *Reading Research and Instruction, 31,* 63–76.

The New Advocate. Published quarterly by Christopher-Gordon Publishers.

Newkirk, T. (1982). Young writers as critical readers. *Language Arts, 59,* 451–457.

Newman, J. (1985). *Whole language theory and use.* Portsmouth, NH: Heinemann.

Newmann, F. M., & Wehlage, G. G. (1993). Five standards of authentic instruction. *Educational Leadership, 50,* 8–12.

Nicholson, T., Lillas, C., & Rzoska, M. A. (1988). Have we been misled by miscues? *The Reading Teacher, 42,* 6–10.

Nist, S. L., & Simpson, M. L. (1989). PLAE, a validated study strategy. *Journal of Reading, 33,* 182–186.

Nist, S. L., & Simpson, M. L. (1990). The effects of PLAE upon students' test perfor-mance and metacognitive awareness. In J. Zutell & S. McCormick (Eds.), *Literacy theory and research: Analyses from multi-ple paradigms* (pp. 321–327). Chicago, IL: National Reading Conference.

Nist, S. L., Simpson, M. L., Olejnik, S., & Mealey, D. L. (1989). *The relation between self-selected text learning variables and test performance.* Unpublished manuscript.

Nolan, T. E. (1991). Self-questioning and pre-diction: Combining metacognitive strate-gies. *Journal of Reading, 35,* 132–138.

Norton, D. (1992). Assessing the processes students use as writers. *Journal of Reading, 36,* 244–246.

Norton, D. (1993). *The effective teaching of language arts* (4th ed.). New York: Merrill.

Noyce, R. M., & Christie, J. F. (1989). *Inte-grating reading and writing instruction in grades K–8.* Boston: Allyn and Bacon.

Nutter, N., & Safran, J. (1984). Improving writing with sentence combining exercises. *Academic Therapy, 19,* 449–455.

O'Flahavan, J., & Blassberg, R. (1992). Toward an embedded model of spelling instruction for emergent literates. *Lan-guage Arts, 69,* 409–417.

Ogbu, J. U. (1987). Opportunity structure, cultural boundaries, and literacy. In J. A. Langer (Ed.), *Language, literacy, and cul-ture: Issues of society and schooling* (pp. 149–177). Norwood, NJ: Ablex.

Ogle, D. M. (1986). K–W–L: A teaching model that develops active reading of expository text. *The Reading Teacher, 39,* 564–570.

O'Hare, F. (1973). *Sentence combining: Improving student writing without formal grammar instruction.* Urbana, IL: National Council of Teachers of English.

Olivares, R. A. (1993). *Using the newspaper to teach ESL learners.* Newark, DE: Inter-national Reading Association.

Olshavsky, J. E. (1976/1977). Reading as problem solving: An investigation of strategies. *Reading Research Quarterly, 12,* 654–674.

Orange County Public Schools. (1985). *Reading resource specialist handbook.* Orlando, FL.

Orange County Public Schools. (1986). *Middle school curriculum planning guide for reading.* Orlando, FL.

Otto, W., & Askov, E. N. (1972). *The Wisconsin design for reading skill development.* Minneapolis: National Computer Systems.

Otto, W., & Smith, R. J. (1980). *Corrective and remedial teaching* (3rd ed.). Boston: Houghton Mifflin.

Palincsar, A. S., & Brown, A. L. (1984). Reciprocal teaching of comprehension-fostering and comprehension-monitoring activities. *Cognition and Instruction, 1,* 117–175.

Palincsar, A. S., & Brown, A. L. (1986). Interactive teaching to promote independent learning from text. *The Reading Teacher, 39,* 771–777.

Pallas, A., Natriello, G., & McDill, E. (1989). Changing nature of the disadvantaged population: Current dimensions and future trends. *Educational Researcher, 18,* 16–22.

Paris, S., & Myers, M. (1981). Comprehension monitoring, memory, and study strategies of good and poor readers. *Journal of Reading Behavior, 13,* 7–22.

Paris, S. G., & Lipson, M. Y. (1982). *Metacognition and reading comprehension.* Research colloquium presented at the annual meeting of the International Reading Association, Chicago, IL.

Parks, R. J. (1987). Three approaches to improving literacy levels. *Educational Horizons, 66*(1), 38–41.

Pearson, P. D. (1985). Changing the face of reading comprehension instruction. *The Reading Teacher, 38,* 724–738.

Pearson, P. D., & Johnson, D. D. (1978). *Teaching reading comprehension.* New York: Holt, Rinehart and Winston.

Pennock, C. (Ed.). (1979). *Reading comprehension at four linguistic levels.* Newark, DE: International Reading Association.

Phillips, L. (1989). *Using children's literature to foster written language development* (Report No. 446). University of Illinois at Urbana-Champaign: Center for the Study of Reading.

Pickert, S. M., & Chase, M. L. (1978). Story retelling: An informal technique for evaluating children's language. *The Reading Teacher, 31,* 528–531.

Piercey, D. (1982). *Reading activities in content areas.* Boston: Allyn and Bacon.

Piers, E. V., & Harris, D. B. (1969). *The Piers-Harris children's self concept scale.* Los Angeles: Western Psychological Services.

Pikulski, J. J., & Tobin, A. W. (1982). The cloze procedure as an informal assessment technique. In J. J. Pikulski & T. Shanahan (Eds.), *Approaches to the informal evaluation of reading* (pp. 42–62). Newark, DE: International Reading Association.

Pinnell, G. S. (1989). Success of at-risk children in a program that combines writing and reading. In J. M. Mason (Ed.), *Reading and writing connections* (pp. 237–259). Boston: Allyn and Bacon.

Polette, K. (1989). Using ABC books for vocabulary development in the secondary school. *English Journal, 78,* 78–80.

Powell, W., & Dunkeld, C. (1971). Validity of the IRI reading levels. *Elementary English, 48,* 637–642.

Powell, W. R. (1970). Reappraising the criteria for interpreting informal inventories. In D. DeBoer (Ed.), *Reading diagnosis and evaluation.* Newark, DE: International Reading Association.

Prescourt, W. (1982). Ethnohistorical analysis of an Appalachian settlement school. In G. Spindler (Ed.), *Doing the ethnography of schooling* (pp. 441–453). New York: Holt, Rinehart and Winston.

Prescriptive reading inventory (PRI) reading system. (1980). Monterey, CA: CTB/ McGraw-Hill.

Purcell-Gates, V. (1988). Lexical and syntactic knowledge of written narrative held by well-read-to kindergartners and second graders. *Research in the Teaching of English, 22,* 128–160.

Purcell-Gates, V., & Dahl, K. L. (1991). Low-SES children's success and failure at early literacy learning in skills-based classrooms. *Journal of Reading Behavior, 23,* 1–34.

Rae, G., & Potter, T. C. (1981). *Informal reading diagnosis: A practical guide for the classroom teacher* (2nd ed.). Englewood Cliffs, NJ: Prentice-Hall.

Rafoth, B. A., & Rubin, D. L. (1984). The impact of content and mechanics on judgments of writing quality. *Written Communication, 1,* 446–458.

Rankin, E. F., & Culhane, J. W. (1969). Comparable cloze and multiple-choice comprehension scores. *Journal of Reading, 13,* 193–198.

Raphael, T. E. (1982). Question-answering strategies for children. *The Reading Teacher, 36,* 186–190.

Raphael, T. E. (1986). Teaching question–answer relationships, revisited. *The Reading Teacher, 39,* 516–522.

Raphael, T. E., & Pearson, P. D. (1985). Increasing students' awareness of sources of information for answering questions. *American Educational Research Journal, 22,* 217–235.

Rasinski, T. V., & Padak, N. D. (1990). Multicultural learning through children's literature. *Language Arts, 67*(6), 576–580.

Reutzel, D. R. (1985). Story maps improve comprehension. *The Reading Teacher, 38,* 400–404.

Reutzel, D. R. (1986). Clozing in on comprehension: The cloze story map. *The Reading Teacher, 39,* 524–528.

Revel-Wood, M. (1988). Invitations to read, to write, to learn. In J. C. Harste, K. G. Short, & C. Burke (Eds.), *Creating classrooms for authors* (pp. 169–179). Portsmouth, NH: Heinemann.

Reynolds, R. E., Taylor, M. A., Steffensen, M. S., Shirey, L. L., & Anderson, R. C. (1981). *Cultural schemata and reading comprehension* (Tech. Rep. No. 201). Champaign, IL: University of Illinois, Center for the Study of Reading.

Rhodes, L. K., & Dudley-Marling, C. (1988). *Readers and writers with a difference: A holistic approach to teaching learning disabled and remedial students.* Portsmouth, NH: Heinemann.

Richards, J. C. (1985). *Theoretical orientation and first and third grade teachers' reading instruction.* Unpublished doctoral dissertation, University of New Orleans.

Richards, J. C. (1988). *Personal communication.*

Richards, J. C. (1990). Ideas for helping insecure, cautious writers learn to enjoy writing. *Reading: Exploration and Discovery, 12,* 58–61.

Richards, J. C., & Gipe, J. P. (1992). Activating background knowledge: Strategies for beginning and poor readers. *The Reading Teacher, 45,* 474–476.

Richards, J. C., & Gipe, J. P. (1993). Recognizing information about story characters: A strategy for young and at-risk readers. *The Reading Teacher, 47,* 78–79.

Richards, J. C., Gipe, J. P., & Necaise, M. A. (1993). A game to help young and at-risk readers recognize basic story features and their connections. Manuscript accepted for publication by *The Reading Teacher.*

Richek, M. A. (1987). DRTA: 5 variations that facilitate independence in reading narratives. *Journal of Reading, 30,* 632–636.

Rigg, P. (1989). Language Experience Approach: Reading naturally. In P. Rigg & V. G. Allen (Eds.), *When they don't all speak English: Integrating the ESL student into the regular classroom* (pp. 65–76). Urbana, IL: National Council of Teachers of English.

Rigg, P., & Allen, V. G. (Eds.). (1989). *When they don't all speak English: Integrating the ESL student into the regular classroom.* Urbana, IL: National Council of Teachers of English.

Rinsky, L. A. (1993). *Teaching word recognition skills* (5th ed.). Scottsdale, AZ: Gorsuch Scarisbrick.

Ritts, V., Patterson, M. L., & Tubbs, M. E. (1992). Expectations, impressions, and judgments of physically attractive students: A review. *Review of Educational Research, 62,* 413–426.

Robbins, E. L. (1981). Prescriptive reading inventory: Levels A and B. In L. M. Schell (Ed.), *Diagnostic and criterion-referenced reading tests: Review and evaluation.* (pp. 70–76). Newark, DE: International Reading Association.

Roberts, T. (1976). 'Frustration level' reading in the infant school. *Educational Research, 19,* 41–44.

Robinson, F. P. (1961). *Effective study* (rev. ed.). New York: Harper & Brothers.

Robinson, H. A. (1983). *Teaching reading, writing and study strategies: The content areas.* Boston: Allyn and Bacon.

Robinson, H. M. (1946). *Why pupils fail in reading.* Chicago: University of Chicago Press.

Roe, B., Stoodt, B., & Burns, P. (1991). *Secondary school reading instruction: The content areas* (4th ed.). Dallas, TX: Houghton Mifflin.

Rosenblatt, L. M. (1994). The transactional theory of reading and writing. In R. B. Ruddell, M. R. Ruddell, & H. Singer (Eds.),

Theoretical models and processes of reading (4th ed.) (pp. 1057–1092). Newark, DE: International Reading Association.

Rosenshine, B. V. (1980). Skill hierarchies in reading comprehension. In R. J. Spiro, B. C. Bruce, & W. F. Brewer (Eds.), *Theoretical issues in reading comprehension.* Hillsdale, NJ: Erlbaum.

Ross, E., & Roe, B. (1990). *An introduction to teaching the language arts.* Chicago: Holt, Rinehart and Winston.

Roswell, F., & Chall, J. (1963). *Roswell-Chall auditory blending test.* La Jolla, CA: Essay Press.

Rotter, J. (1966). Generalized expectancies for internal versus external control of reinforcement. *Psychological Monographs, 80,* 1–28.

Routman, R. (1991). *Invitations: Changing as teachers and learners K–12.* Portsmouth, NH: Heinemann.

Rubin, D. (1982). *Diagnosis and correction in reading instruction.* New York: Holt, Rinehart and Winston.

Ruddell, R. B. (1964). A study of the cloze comprehension technique in relation to structurally controlled reading material. In J. A. Figurel (Ed.), *Improvement of reading through classroom practice* (pp. 298–303). Newark, DE: International Reading Association.

Ruddell, R. B. (1965). The effects of oral and written patterns of language structure on reading comprehension. *The Reading Teacher, 18,* 270–275.

Ruddell, R. B., & Ruddell, M. R. (1994). Models of reading and literacy processes: Introduction. In R. B. Ruddell, M. R. Ruddell, & H. Singer (Eds.), *Theoretical models and processes of reading* (4th ed.) (pp. 811–815). Newark, DE: International Reading Association.

Ruddell, R. B., & Unrau, N. J. (1994). Reading as a meaning-construction process: The reader, the text, and the teacher. In R. B. Ruddell, M. R. Ruddell, & H. Singer (Eds.), *Theoretical models and processes of reading* (4th ed.) (pp. 996–1056). Newark, DE: International Reading Association.

Rumelhart, D. E. (1975). Notes on a schema for stories. In D. G. Bobrow & A. M. Collins (Eds.), *Representation and understanding: Studies in cognitive science.* New York: Academic Press.

Rumelhart, D. E. (1980). Schemata: The building blocks of cognition. In R. J. Spiro, B. C. Bruce, & W. F. Brewer (Eds.), *Theoretical issues in reading comprehension* (pp. 33–58). Hillsdale, NJ: Erlbaum.

Rumelhart, D. E. (1994). Toward an interactive model of reading. In R. B. Ruddell, M. R. Ruddell, & H. Singer (Eds.), *Theoretical models and processes of reading* (pp. 864–894). Newark, DE: International Reading Association.

Russell, D. H., & Russell, E. (1979). *Listening aids through the grades* (2nd ed.). New York: Teachers College Press.

Rutland, A. D. (1987). Using wordless picture books in social studies. *History and Social Science Teacher, 22,* 193–196.

Rylant, C. (1982). *When I was young in the mountains.* New York: Dutton.

Sadow, M. W. (1982). The use of story grammar in the design of questions. *The Reading Teacher, 35,* 518–522.

Samuels, S. J. (1979). The method of repeated readings. *The Reading Teacher, 32,* 403–408.

Samuels, S. J. (1988). Decoding and automaticity: Helping poor readers become automatic at word recognition. *The Reading Teacher, 41,* 756–761.

Samuels, S. J. (1994). Toward a theory of automatic information processing in reading, revisited. In R. B. Ruddell, M. R. Ruddell, & H. Singer (Eds.), *Theoretical models and processes of reading* (4th ed.) (pp. 816–837). Newark, DE: International Reading Association.

Sax, G. (1980). *Principles of educational and psychological measurement and evaluation* (2nd ed.). Belmont, CA: Wadsworth.

Schachter, S. W. (1978). Developing flexible reading habits. *Journal of Reading, 22,* 149–152.

Schallert, D., Kleiman, G. M., & Rubin, A. D. (1977). *Analysis of differences between written and oral language* (Tech. Rep. No. 29). Urbana: University of Illinois, Center for the Study of Reading.

Schell, L. M. (Ed.). (1981). *Diagnostic and criterion-referenced reading tests: Review and evaluation.* Newark, DE: International Reading Association.

Schell, L. M., & Hanna, G. S. (1981). Can informal reading inventories reveal strengths and weaknesses in comprehension subskills? *The Reading Teacher, 35,* 263–268.

Schmelzer, R. V. (1975). *The effect of college*

student constructed questions on the comprehension of a passage of expository prose. Doctoral dissertation, University of Minnesota. Dissertation Abstracts International, 36, 2162A.

Schön, D. A. (1987). *Educating the reflective practitioner.* San Francisco, CA: Jossey-Bass.

Schumm, J. S., & Mangrum, C. T. (1991). FLIP: A framework for content area reading. *Journal of Reading, 35,* 120–124.

Schwartz, E., & Sheff, A. (1975). Student involvement in questioning for comprehension. *The Reading Teacher, 29,* 150–154.

Schwartz, R. M. (1988). Learning to learn: Vocabulary in content area textbooks. *Journal of Reading, 32,* 108–117.

Searfoss, L. (1993). Assessing classroom environments. In S. Glazer & C. Brown (Eds.), *Portfolios and beyond: Collaborative assessment in reading and writing* (pp. 11–26). Norwood, MA: Christopher-Gordon.

Searle, D., & Dillon, D. (1980). Responding to student writing: What is said or how it is said. *Language Arts, 57,* 773–781.

Shafer, R. E., Staab, C., & Smith, K. (1983). *Language functions and school success.* Glenview, IL: Scott, Foresman.

Shanahan, T. (1980). The impact of writing instruction on learning to read. *Reading World, 19,* 357–368.

Shannon, P. (1989). *Broken promises: Reading instruction in twentieth-century America.* Granby, MA: Bergin & Garvey.

Shannon, P. (1990). *The struggle to continue: Progressive reading instruction in the United States.* Portsmouth, NH: Heinemann.

Shaw, N. (1989). *Sheep on a ship.* Boston, MA: Houghton Mifflin.

Shertzer, B., & Linden, J. (1979). *Fundamentals of individual appraisal.* Boston: Houghton Mifflin.

Shnayer, S. W. (1969). Relationships between reading interest and comprehension. In J. A. Figurel (Ed.), *Reading and realism.* Newark, DE: International Reading Association.

Short, K. (1993). Teacher research for teacher educators. In L. Patterson, C. Santa, K. Short, & K. Smith (Eds.), *Teachers are researchers: Reflection and action* (pp. 155–159). Newark, DE: International Reading Association.

Shuy, R. W. (1967). *Discovering American dialects.* Urbana, IL: National Council of Teachers of English.

Shuy, R. W. (1981a). A holistic view of language. *Research in the Teaching of English, 15,* 101–111.

Shuy, R. W. (1981b). Learning to talk like teachers. *Language Arts, 58,* 168–174.

Shuy, R. W. (1988). Sentence level language functions. In J. R. Staton, R. W. Shuy, J. K. Peyton, & L. Reed (Eds.), *Dialogue journal communication.* Norwood, NJ: Ablex.

Silva, C., & Yarborough, B. (1990). Help for young writers with spelling difficulties. *Journal of Reading, 34,* 48–53.

Simpson, M. L. (1986). PORPE: A writing strategy for studying and learning in the content areas. *Journal of Reading, 29,* 407–414.

Simpson, M. L. (1987). Alternative formats for evaluating content area vocabulary understanding. *Journal of Reading, 31,* 20–27.

Simpson, M. L., & Nist, S. L. (1984). PLAE: A model for planning successful independent learning. *Journal of Reading, 29,* 218–223.

Simpson, M. L., & Nist, S. L. (1990). Textbook annotation: An effective and efficient study strategy for college students. *Journal of Reading, 34,* 122–129.

Simpson, M. L., Stahl, N. A., & Hayes, C. G. (1989). PORPE: A research validation. *Journal of Reading, 33,* 22–28.

Sinatra, R. (1991). Integrating whole language with the learning of text structure. *Journal of Reading, 34,* 424–433.

Sinatra, R. C., Stahl-Gemake, J., & Berg, D. N. (1984). Improving reading comprehension of disabled readers through semantic mapping. *The Reading Teacher, 38,* 22–29.

Singer, H. (1978). Active comprehension: From answering to asking questions. *The Reading Teacher, 31,* 901–908.

Sipay, E. R. (1990). *Diagnostic decoding tests.* Cambridge, MA: Educators Publishing Service.

Slaughter, H. B. (1988). Indirect and direct teaching in a whole language program. *The Reading Teacher, 42,* 30–34.

Sloyer, S. (1982). *Readers theatre: Story dramatization in the classroom.* Urbana, IL: National Council of Teachers of English.

Smith, C. F., & Kepner, H. S. (1981). *Reading in the mathematics classroom.* Washington, DC: National Education Association.

Smith, F. (1973). *Psycholinguistics and reading.* New York: Holt, Rinehart and Winston.

Smith, F. (1981). Demonstrations, engagement, and sensitivity: The choice between people and programs. *Language Arts, 58,* 634–642.

Smith, F. (1988). *Understanding reading* (4th ed.). Hillsdale, NJ: Erlbaum.

Smith, R. J., & Johnson, D. D. (1980). *Teaching children to read.* Reading, MA: Addison-Wesley.

Smith, R. J., Otto, W., & Hansen, L. (1978). *The school reading program.* Boston: Houghton Mifflin.

Smith, S. P., & Jackson, F. H. (1985). Assessing reading/learning skills with written retellings. *Journal of Reading, 28,* 622–630.

Smitherman, G. (1985). "What go round come round: King in perspective." In C. K. Brooks (Ed.), *Tapping potential: English and language arts for the black learner.* Urbana, IL: National Council of Teachers of English.

Snider, M., Lima, S., & DeVito, P. (1994). Rhode Island's literacy portfolio assessment project. In S. Valencia, E. Hiebert, & P. Afflerbach (Eds.), *Authentic reading assessment: Practices and possibilities* (pp. 71–88). Newark, DE: International Reading Association.

Spache, G. (1963). *Toward better reading.* Champaign, IL: Garrard.

Spache, G. (1976a). *Diagnosing and correcting reading disabilities.* Boston: Allyn and Bacon.

Spache, G. (1976b). *Investigating the issues of reading disabilities.* Boston: Allyn and Bacon.

Spaulding, R. (1983). A systematic approach to classroom discipline, part I. *Phi Delta Kappan, 65,* 48–51.

Speaker, R., & Speaker, P. (1991). Sentence collecting: Authentic literacy events in the classroom. *Journal of Reading, 35,* 92–95.

Stahl, N. A., King, J. R., & Henk, W. A. (1991). Enhancing students' notetaking through training and evaluation. *Journal of Reading, 34,* 614–622.

Stanovich, K. E. (1980). Toward an interactive-compensatory model of individual differences in the development of reading fluency. *Reading Research Quarterly, 16,* 32–71.

Staton, J. (1987). The power of responding in journals. In T. Fulwiler (Ed.), *The journal book* (pp. 47–63). Portsmouth, NH: Heinemann.

Staton, J. (1988). Discussing problems. In J. Staton, R. W. Shuy, J. K. Peyton, & L. Reed (Eds.), *Dialogue journal communication: Classroom, linguistic, social and cognitive views* (pp. 202–244). Norwood, NJ: Ablex.

Stauffer, R. G. (1975). *Directing the reading-thinking process.* New York: Harper & Row.

Stauffer, R. G. (1980). *The language experience approach to the teaching of reading.* New York: Harper & Row.

Stauffer, R. G. (1981). Strategies for reading instruction. In M. Douglas (Ed.), *45th Yearbook of the Claremont Reading Conference,* Claremont, CA.

Steffensen, M. S. (1974). *The acquisition of black English.* Unpublished doctoral dissertation, University of Illinois at Urbana-Champaign.

Steffensen, M. S. (1978). *Bereiter and Engelman reconsidered: The evidence from children acquiring Black English Vernacular* (Tech. Rep. No. 82). Champaign, IL: University of Illinois, Center for the Study of Reading.

Steffensen, M. S. (1987). The effect of context and culture on children's L2 reading: A review. In J. Devine, P. L. Carrell, & D. E. Eskey (Eds.), *Research in reading in English as a second language* (pp. 41–54). Washington: Teachers of English to Speakers of Other Languages.

Steffensen, M. S., & Guthrie, L. F. (1980). *Effect of situation on the verbalization of black inner-city children* (Tech. Rep. No. 180). Champaign, IL: University of Illinois, Center for the Study of Reading.

Stein, N., & Glenn, C. (1979). An analysis of story comprehension in elementary school children. In R. Freedle (Ed.), *New directions in discourse processing.* Norwood, NJ: Ablex.

Sternberg, R. J. (1991). Are we reading too much into reading comprehension tests? *Journal of Reading, 34,* 540–545.

Stevenson, J., & Baumann, J. (1979). *Vocabulary development: Semantic feature analysis and semantic mapping.* Microworkshop presented at the Twenty-fourth

Annual Convention of the International Reading Association, Atlanta.

Sticht, T. G., & Beck, L. J. (1976, August). *Experimental literacy assessment battery (LAB)* (Final Rep. No. AFHRL-TR-76-51). Lowry Air Force Base, CO: Air Force Human Resources Laboratory, Technical Training Division.

Sticht, T. G., & James, J. H. (1984). Listening and reading. In P. D. Pearson (Ed.), *Handbook of reading research* (pp. 293–317). New York: Longman.

Straker, D. Y. (1980). *Situational variables in language use* (Tech. Rep. No. 167). Champaign: University of Illinois, Center for the Study of Reading.

Strickland, E. (1975, October). Assignment mastery. *Reading World,* 25–31.

Strickland, R. G. (1962). The language of elementary school children: Its relationship to the language of reading textbooks and the quality of reading of selected children. Indiana University, Bloomington, *Bulletin of The School of Education, 38,* 1–131.

Strode, S. L. (1993). An adaptation of REAP for the developmental reader. *Journal of Reading, 36,* 568–569.

Suhor, C., & Suhor, B. (1992). *Teaching values in the literature classroom: A debate in print.* Bloomington, IN: ERIC Clearinghouse on Reading and Communication Skills and Urbana, IL: National Council of Teachers of English.

Sulzby, E. (1985). Kindergartners as writers and readers. In M. Farr (Ed.), *Advances in writing research: vol. 1. Children's early writing development* (pp. 127–199). Norwood, NJ: Ablex.

Sulzby, E., & Teale, W. H. (1991). Emergent literacy. In R. Barr, M. L. Kamil, P. Mosenthal, & P. D. Pearson (Eds.), *Handbook of reading research, volume II* (pp. 727–758). White Plains, NY: Longman Publishing Group.

Tadlock, D. F. (1978). SQ3R—why it works, based on an information processing theory of learning. *Journal of Reading, 22,* 110–112.

Tatham, S. M. (1970). Reading comprehension of materials written with select oral language patterns: A study at grades two and four. *Reading Research Quarterly, 5,* 402–426.

Taylor, B. H. (1979). *Good and poor readers, recall of familiar and unfamiliar text.* Paper presented at the 24th Annual Meeting of the International Reading Association, Atlanta.

Taylor, B. H., Harris, L. A., & Pearson, P. D. (1988). *Reading difficulties: Instruction and assessment.* New York: Random House.

Taylor, D., & Dorsey-Gaines, C. (1988). *Growing up literate: Learning from innercity families.* Portsmouth, NH: Heinemann.

Taylor, W. L. (1953). Cloze procedure: A new tool for measuring readability. *Journalism Quarterly, 30,* 415–433.

Teale, W. H., & Sulzby, E. (1986). (Eds.). Emergent literacy: Writing and reading. Norwood, NJ: Ablex.

Teale, W. H., & Sulzby, E. (1989). Emergent literacy: New perspectives. In D. S. Strickland & L. M. Morrow (Eds.), *Emerging literacy: Young children learn to read and write* (pp. 1–15). Newark, DE: International Reading Association.

Temple, C., Nathan, R., Burris, N., & Temple, F. (1988). *The beginning of writing* (2nd ed.) (pp. 105–107). Boston: Allyn and Bacon.

Templeton, S. (1991). *Teaching the integrated language arts.* Boston: Houghton Mifflin.

Tharp, R., & Gallimore, R. (1988). *Rousing minds to life: Teaching, learning, and schooling in social context.* New York: Cambridge University Press.

Thau, A. P. (1991). Vision and literacy. *Journal of Reading, 35,* 196–199.

Thelan, J. (1976). *Improving reading in science.* Newark, DE: International Reading Association.

Thibault, J., & McKee, J. (1982). Practical parenting with Piaget. *Young Children, 38*(1), 133–140.

Thonis, E. W. (1976). *Literacy for America's Spanish speaking children.* Newark, DE: International Reading Association.

Thorndike, E. L. (1917). Reading as reasoning: A study of mistakes in paragraph meaning. *Journal of Educational Psychology, 8,* 323–332. Reprinted in (1971), *Reading Research Quarterly, 6,* 425–434.

Thorndyke, P. (1977). Cognitive structures in comprehension and memory of narrative discourse. *Cognitive Psychology, 9,* 77–110.

Tierney, R. J., Carter, M. A., & Desai, L. E. (1991). *Portfolio assessment in the reading-writing classroom.* Norwood, MA: Christopher-Gordon.

Tierney, R. J., & Pearson, P. D. (1994). Learning to learn from text: A framework for improving classroom practice. In R. B. Ruddell, M. R. Ruddell, & H. Singer (Eds.), *Theoretical models and processes of reading* (4th ed.) (pp. 496–513). Newark, DE: International Reading Association.

Tierney, R. J., Readence, J. E., & Dishner, E. K. (1990). *Reading strategies and practices: A compendium* (3rd ed.). Boston: Allyn and Bacon.

Tompkins, G. (1990). *Teaching writing: Balancing process and product.* New York: Macmillan.

Tompkins, G. (1994). *Teaching writing: balancing process and product* (2nd ed.). New York: Merrill/Macmillan.

Tompkins, G., & Hoskisson, K. (1991). *The language arts curriculum: Content and teaching strategies.* New York: Merrill.

Tompkins, G. E., & McGee, L. M. (1983). Launching nonstandard speakers into standard English. *Language Arts, 60,* 463–469.

Torgeson, J. (1982). The learning disabled child as an active learner. *Topics in Learning and Learning Disabilities, 2,* 45–52.

Trachtenburg, P. (1990). Using children's literature to enhance phonics instruction. *The Reading Teacher, 43,* 648–654.

Troike, R. C. (1972). English and the bilingual child. In D. L. Shores (Ed.), *Contemporary English: Change and variation.* Philadelphia: J. B. Lippincott.

Vacca, J. L., Vacca, R. T., & Gove, M. K. (1991). *Reading and learning to read* (2nd ed.). New York: HarperCollins.

Valmont, W. (1972). Creating questions for informal reading inventories. *The Reading Teacher, 25,* 509–512.

Valmont, W. J. (1983). Cloze and maze instructional techniques: Differences and definitions. *Reading Psychology, 4,* 163–167.

Van Allsburg, C. (1981). *Jumanji.* New York: Houghton Mifflin.

Vygotsky, L. (1986). Problems of general psychology (N. Minick, Trans.). In R. Reiber & A. Carton (Eds.), *The collected works of L. S. Vygotsky* (Vol. 1). New York: Plenum.

Vygotsky, L. S. (1978). *Mind in society: The development of higher psychological processes.* Cambridge, MA: Harvard University Press.

Wadsworth, B. (1989). *Piaget's theory of cognitive and affective development* (4th ed.). New York: Longman.

Wagoner, S. A. (1983). Comprehension monitoring: What it is and what we know about it. *Reading Research Quarterly, 17,* 328–346.

Walker, B. J. (1992). Diagnostic teaching of reading: *Techniques for instruction and assessment.* New York: Macmillan.

Waller, M. B. (1992/1993). Helping crack-affected children succeed. *Educational Leadership, 50,* 57–60.

Wangberg, E. (1982). Pattern books: An activity for beginning reading instruction. *Reading Horizons, 23,* 22–24.

Weaver, C. (1991, Winter). Whole language: What it is and isn't. *Michigan Journal of Reading, 24,* 2–9.

Weaver, C. (1994). *Reading process and practice: From socio-psycholinguistics to whole language.* Portsmouth, NH: Heinemann.

Weaver, P. A. (1979). Improving reading comprehension: Effects of sentence organization instruction. *Reading Research Quarterly, 15,* 129–146.

Webb, C. A. (Ed.). (1993). *Your reading: A booklist for junior high and middle school* (9th ed.). Urbana, IL: National Council of Teachers of English.

Wells, G. (1986). *The meaning makers: Children learning language and using language to learn.* Portsmouth, NH: Heinemann.

Wiesendanger, K. D., & Bader, L. (1992). SCAIT: A study technique to develop students' higher comprehension skills when reading content area material. *Journal of Reading, 35,* 399–400.

Willford, R. (1968). Comprehension: What reading's all about. *Grade Teacher, 85,* 99–103.

Williams, J. D. (1989). *Preparing to teach writing.* Belmont, CA: Wadsworth.

Willig, A., Harnisch, D., Hill, K., & Maehr, M. (1983). Sociocultural and educational correlates of success-failure attributions and evaluation anxiety in the school setting for Black, Hispanic and Anglo children. *American Educational Research Journal, 20,* 385–410.

Wilson, R. M. (1981). *Diagnostic and remedial reading for classroom and clinic* (4th ed.). Columbus, OH: Merrill.

Wilson, R. M., & Cleland, C. J. (1989). *Diagnostic and remedial reading for classroom and clinic* (6th ed.). Columbus, OH:

Merrill.

Wilt, M. (1958). A study of teacher awareness of listening as a factor in elementary education. *Journal of Educational Research, 43,* 626–636.

Winograd, P., & Johnston, P. (1980). *Comprehension monitoring and the error detection paradigm* (Tech. Rep. No. 153). Champaign: University of Illinois, Center for the Study of Reading.

Wiseman, D. (1992). *Learning to read with literature.* Boston: Allyn and Bacon.

Wixson, K. K. (1984). *Vocabulary instruction and children's comprehension of basal stories.* Paper presented at the National Reading Conference, St. Petersburg, FL.

Wolf, K. P. (1993). From informal to informed assessment: Recognizing the role of the classroom teacher. *Journal of Reading, 36,* 518–523.

Wolfe, R., & Lopez, A. (1992/1993). Structured overviews for teaching science concepts and terms. *Journal of Reading, 36,* 315–317.

Wolfram, W. (1991). *Dialects and American English.* Englewood Cliffs, NJ: Prentice-Hall, Inc. and Center for Applied Linguistics.

Wolfram, W., & Christian, D. (1989). *Dialects and education: Issues and answers.* Englewood Cliffs, NJ: Prentice-Hall.

Wong Fillmore, W. L. (1986). Research currents: Equity or excellence? *Language Arts, 63,* 474–481.

Woods, M. L., & Moe, A. J. (1989). *Analytical reading inventory* (4th ed.). Columbus, OH: Merrill.

Word Blaster. (1981). New York: Random House.

Wurth, S. (Ed.). (1992). *Books for you: A booklist for senior high students* (11th ed.). Urbana, IL: National Council of Teachers of English.

Wylie, R. C. (1974). *The self-concept.* Lincoln: University of Nebraska Press.

Wylie, R. E., & Durrell, D. D. (1970). Teaching vowels through phonograms. *Elementary English, 47,* 787–791.

Young, T., & Crow, M. (1992, May-June). Using dialogue journals to help students deal with their problems. *The Clearing House, 65,* 307–310.